METAPHYSICS: THE BIG QUESTIONS

Philosophy: The Big Questions

Series Editor: James P. Sterba, University of Notre Dame, Indiana

Designed to elicit a philosophical response in the mind of the student, this distinctive series of anthologies provides essential classical and contemporary readings that serve to bring the central questions of philosophy alive for today's students. It presents complete coverage of both the Anglo-American tradition of philosophy, as well as the kinds of questions and challenges that it confronts today.

Aesthetics: The Big Questions
Edited by Carolyn Korsmeyer

Epistemology: The Big Questions
Edited by Linda Martín Alcoff

Ethics: The Big Questions
Edited by James P. Sterba

Metaphysics: The Big Questions, Second Edition
Edited by Peter van Inwagen and Dean W. Zimmerman

Philosophy of Language: The Big Questions
Edited by Andrea Nye

Philosophy of Religion: The Big Questions
Edited by Eleonore Stump and Michael J. Murray

Race, Class, Gender, and Sexuality: The Big Questions
Edited by Naomi Zack, Laurie Shrage, and Crispin Sartwell

Philosophy: The Big Questions
Edited by Ruth J. Sample, Charles W. Mills, and James P. Sterba

Forthcoming:

Environmental Philosophy: The Big Questions
Edited by David Richard Keller

METAPHYSICS:

THE BIG QUESTIONS

*EDITED BY PETER VAN INWAGEN AND
DEAN W. ZIMMERMAN*

Blackwell
Publishing

Editorial material and organization © 2008 by Blackwell Publishing

BLACKWELL PUBLISHING
350 Main Street, Malden, MA 02148-5020, USA
9600 Garsington Road, Oxford OX4 2DQ, UK
550 Swanston Street, Carlton, Victoria 3053, Australia

The right of Peter van Inwagen and Dean W. Zimmerman to be identified as the Authors of the
Editorial Material in this Work has been asserted in accordance with the UK Copyright, Designs, and
Patents Act 1988.

First edition published 1998 by Blackwell Publishing
Second edition published 2008 by Blackwell Publishing

9   2016

Library of Congress Cataloging-in-Publication Data

Metaphysics : the big questions/edited by Peter van Inwagen and Dean W.
Zimmerman. — 2nd, rev. & expanded ed.
    p. cm. — (Philosophy, the big questions)
    Includes bibliographical references and index.
    ISBN 978-1-4051-2585-7 (hardcover : alk. paper) — ISBN 978-1-4051-2586-4
(pbk. : alk. paper)   1. Metaphysics.   I. Van Inwagen, Peter.   II. Zimmerman,
Dean W.

    BD111.M575 2008
    110—dc22

                                  2007023099

A catalogue record for this title is available from the British Library.

Set in 10.5 on 12.5 pt Galliard
by SNP Best-set Typesetter Ltd., Hong Kong

For further information on
Blackwell Publishing, visit our website:
www.blackwellpublishing.com

For Roderick M. Chisholm and David Lewis

In Memoriam

CONTENTS

x CONTENTS

PREFACE TO SECOND EDITION

Some metaphysical questions arise upon the least reflection about the world and our place in it. Others are less obvious, presenting themselves only to those willing to think very hard about highly abstract questions. The reader of this anthology will find philosophers grappling with metaphysical questions of both sorts – although we have deliberately decided to favor the less abstract, more immediately accessible ones, since this anthology is intended as an introduction to the subject. The essays and excerpts are largely free of unexplicated technical terminology and symbolism (the only major exception is the chapters by David Lewis and Saul Kripke in Part III, section A). And the topics covered complement those of a number of popular single-author introductions to metaphysics.

Twenty-three of the readings are new to this much-expanded second edition. There are two new sections: "What is Existence?" (essays about ontological commitment and Meinongianism, including Quine's classic "On What There Is"); and "Are There Worlds Other than the Actual World?" (extensive chapters by David Lewis and Saul Kripke on the metaphysics of necessity and possibility). Classic readings by Bertrand Russell and Max Black have been added to the section on universals and individuals, along with David Armstrong's more recent defense of an Aristotelian theory of universals. The section on the mind–body problem has two additional chapters, providing examples of the "identity theory" (David Armstrong) and "neutral monism" (Bertrand Russell). The section on free will is over twice as long. Its new contents include an example of a "hard determinist" (Baron d'Holbach); a paper by Peter van Inwagen, written for this volume, in which he gives his well-known "consequence argument"; two classic papers by Harry Frankfurt; and a charming, little-known argument of John Wisdom's for our having existed since the beginning of time, on the assumption that we are free and that determinism is true. There is now an essay by Eric Olson representing the metaphysics of personal identity sometimes called "animalism" – a view associated with Peter van Inwagen, Olson, Trenton Merricks, and others. There are also new chapters on space, time, persistence through time, causation, the question "why is there a world?," and the cosmological argument.

All the readings are made to fall under a series of questions about "the world." By the expression "the world," we shall usually mean absolutely *everything there is*, not just everything there is within the universe of space and time we inhabit. So, the question whether there is a God – outside or inside space and time – is also a question about the world, in our sense.

The first and largest section, "What Are the Most General Features of the World?," includes readings on existence, universals, individuals, time, space (including, in this edition, C. D. Broad on the structure of space, and whether it contains point-sized regions), causation, and a budget of paradoxes: McTaggart's paradox, paradoxes of motion, of the infinite, of time travel, and of intrinsic change.

The second, and second largest, part asks, "What is Our Place in the World?" Are human beings material objects? Three different forms of materialism are considered, alongside two negative answers to this question: a version of Cartesian dualism, and Derek Parfit's "Buddhist" metaphysics. A slightly different aspect of the mind–body problem is the relationship between the thoughts and sensations we experience, on the one hand, and the physical events going on within our brains and bodies, on the other. Is thinking a kind of brain process, and the mental simply an aspect of the physical? Or are mental states something "extra"? Another pressing question is whether the nature of our world precludes human freedom. We inhabit a universe in which similar causes tend to produce similar effects, allowing for the statement of very precise laws of nature. The seeming inviolability of natural law raises the possibility that the way things will go in the future is an inexorable consequence of the way things were in the distant past. Would that rob us of our freedom, if it were true?

Part III, "Are There Many Worlds?," asks two questions. One is about the nature of necessity and possibility – are there "possible worlds," and if so, what role do they play in the metaphysics of modality? The other is the question of "anti-realism": Is there just one world, one complete inventory of what there is? Or does what there is vary from community to community or person to person?

The fourth part begins with reflection on whether there could be an answer to the question, "Why is There a World?" – that is, Why is there something, rather than nothing? (Derek Parfit's essay is longer and of more recent vintage than the chapter he contributed to this section in the first edition.) The volume ends with two attempts to answer the question by appeal to a necessary being (the Deity of the cosmological and ontological arguments).

The brief introductions to the sections serve three purposes: (i) to indicate how the readings in the section are related to one another; (ii) to point out connections between these selections and readings in other parts of the anthology; and (iii) to suggest supplementary readings – books, articles, and (in a few cases) stories that could be used to introduce the metaphysical problems in each section.

An undergraduate course in metaphysics could profitably use this text alongside a wide variety of books, including classics like Descartes's *Meditations on*

First Philosophy, Berkeley's *Three Dialogues Between Hylas and Philonous*, and Bertrand Russell's *The Problems of Philosophy*. Here are some more recent introductory books that take up many of the questions addressed in this anthology and are appropriate for an undergraduate audience:

William R. Carter, *The Elements of Metaphysics* (Philadelphia, Pennsylvania: Temple University Press, 1990).

Martin Gardner, *The Whys of a Philosophical Scrivener* (New York: St. Martin's, 1999) (Although not strictly an introduction to philosophy or metaphysics, Gardner's "confessional" can be a useful text in introductory philosophy courses.)

D. W. Hamlyn, *Metaphysics* (Cambridge, England: Cambridge University Press, 1984).

William Hasker, *Metaphysics: Constructing a World View* (Downers Grove, Illinois and Leicester, England: Intervarsity Press, 1983).

John F. Post, *Metaphysics: A Contemporary Introduction* (New York: Paragon House, 1991).

Quentin Smith and L. Nathan Oaklander, *Time, Change and Freedom: an Introduction to Metaphysics* (London: Routledge, 1995).

Richard Taylor, *Metaphysics*, 4th edn (Englewood Cliffs, New Jersey: Prentice-Hall, 1992).

Peter van Inwagen, *Metaphysics*, 2nd edn (Cambridge, Mass.: Westview Press, 2002).

The following anthologies and single-author texts may serve as companions to the volume for more advanced students (e.g., upper-level philosophy majors, or beginning graduate students):

D. M. Armstrong, *Universals: An Opinionated Introduction* (Boulder, Col.: Westview Press, 1989).

Bruce Aune, *Metaphysics: The Elements* (Minneapolis: University of Minnesota, 1985).

Steven D. Hales (ed.), *Metaphysics: Contemporary Readings* (Belmont, Cal.: Wadsworth, 1998).

Michael Jubien, *Contemporary Metaphysics* (Oxford: Basil Blackwell, 1997).

Stephen Laurence and Cynthia Macdonald (eds.), *Contemporary Readings in the Foundations of Metaphysics* (Oxford: Basil Blackwell, 1998).

Michael Loux, *Metaphysics: A Contemporary Introduction*, 2nd edn (London: Routledge, 2002).

Theodore Sider, John Hawthorne, and Dean Zimmerman (eds.), *Contemporary Debates in Metaphysics* (Malden, Mass.: Blackwell, 2007).

Our lists of supplementary readings include suggestions for matching up chapters from all of these books with our selections.

Although most of the readings have appeared elsewhere, a few have been written especially for this anthology: Timothy O'Connor, "The Agent as Cause";

Ernest Sosa, "Addendum to 'Nonabsolute Existence and Conceptual Relativity': Objections and Replies"; Richard Swinburne, "Reply to Parfit"; James Van Cleve, "Incongruent Counterparts and Higher Dimensions"; Peter van Inwagen, "The Consequence Argument" and "The Mystery of Metaphysical Freedom"; and Dean Zimmerman, "Temporary Intrinsics and Presentism." José Benardete's contribution, "Grasping the Infinite," includes a parable taken from his book, *Infinity* (Oxford: Clarendon Press, 1964), but is otherwise new. And Zimmerman's "Distinct Indiscernibles and the Bundle Theory" is a considerably expanded version of a dialogue which originally appeared in *Mind*. The general introduction, "What Is Metaphysics?," is a substantive essay based largely on van Inwagen's contribution to *Contemporary Readings in the Foundations of Metaphysics*, edited by Stephen Laurence and Cynthia Macdonald.

PETER VAN INWAGEN
DEAN ZIMMERMAN

SOURCES

The editors and publisher gratefully acknowledge the permission granted to reproduce the copyright material in this book:

1 Lewis, David, and Lewis, Stephanie, "Holes," *Australasian Journal of Philosophy*, 48 (1970) pp. 206–12. Reprinted by permission of Taylor & Francis UK.

2 Quine, W. V. O., "On What There Is," *Review of Metaphysics*, 2 (1948/1949) pp. 21–38. Reprinted by permission of the *Review of Metaphysics*.

3 Chisholm, Roderick M., "Beyond Being and NonBeing," in Rudolf Haller (ed.), *Jenseits von Sein und Nichtsein* (Graz: Akademische Druck- und Verlagsanstalt, 1972) pp. 53–67. Reprinted by permission of Akademische Druck- und Verlagsanstalt, Austria.

4 Russell, Bertrand, "Universals," in *The Problems of Philosophy* (Oxford: Oxford University Press, 1912) pp. 88–100. Reprinted by permission of Oxford University Press.

5 Armstrong, David Malet, "Universals as Attributes," in *Universals: An Opinionated Introduction* (Boulder, Col: Westview Press, 1989). © 1989 by Westview Press. Reprinted by permission of Perseus Books Group.

6 Price, H. H., "Universals and Resemblances," in *Thinking and Experience* (London: Hutchinson's University Library, 1953).

7 Williams, D. C., "The Elements of Being," in "On the Elements of Being," *Review of Metaphysics*, 7 (1953) pp. 3–18, 171–92. Reprinted by permission of the *Review of Metaphysics*.

8 Black, Max, "The Identity of Indiscernibles," *Mind*, 61 (1962) pp. 153–64. Reprinted by permission of Oxford University Press Journals.

9 Zimmerman, Dean W., "Distinct Indiscernibles and the Bundle Theory." Portions of this paper originally appeared under the same title, *Mind*, 106 (1997) pp. 305–9.

10 McTaggart, J. McT. E., "Time," in *The Nature of Existence II* (Cambridge: Cambridge University Press, 1927). Reprinted by permission of Cambridge University Press.

11 Broad, C. D., "McTaggart's Arguments against the Reality of Time," in *Examination of McTaggart's Philosophy, Vol. II, Part I* (Cambridge: Cambridge University Press, 1938). Reprinted by permission.

12 Prior, A. N., "The Notion of the Present," in *Studium Generale, 23* (New York: Springer-Verlag, Inc., 1970) pp. 245–8. Reprinted by kind permission of Springer Science and Business Media.

13 Prior, A. N., "Changes in Events and Changes in Things," Lindley Lecture by the University of Kansas, 1962. Reprinted by kind permission of the Philosophy Department at the University of Kansas.

14 Broad, C. D., "The General Problem of Time and Change," in *Scientific Thought* (London: Routledge and Kegan Paul, 1923). Reprinted by permission.

15 Williams, D. C., "The Myth of Passage," *Journal of Philosophy, 48* (1951) pp. 457–72. Reprinted by permission.

16 Prior, A. N., "Some Free Thinking about Time," in B. J. Copeland (ed.), *Logic and Reality: Essays on the Legacy of Arthur Prior* (Oxford: Oxford University Press, 1996) pp. 47–51. Reprinted by permission of Oxford University Press.

17 Gardner, Martin, "The Fourth Dimension," in *The Ambidextrous Universe* (New York: Basic Books, 1964). Reprinted by kind permission of the author.

18 Van Cleve, James, "Incongruent Counterparts and Absolute Space," in Peter van Inwagen and Dean W. Zimmerman (eds.), *Metaphysics: The Big Questions* (Oxford: Blackwell Publishing, 1998) pp. 111–20. Reprinted by kind permission of the author.

19 Broad, C. D., "The Traditional Conception of Space and the Principle of Extensive Abstraction," in *Scientific Thought* (London: Routledge & Kegan Paul, 1923) pp. 30–51. Reprinted by permission.

20 Black, Max, "Achilles and the Tortoise," *Analysis, 11* (1951) pp. 91–101.

21 Salmon, Wesley C., "A Contemporary Look at Zeno's Paradoxes," in *Space, Time and Motion* (Minneapolis: University of Minnesota Press, 1980). Reprinted by kind permission of Merrilee Salmon.

22 Benardete, José A., "Grasping the Infinite." Portions of this paper originally appeared in *Infinity: an Essay in Metaphysics* (Oxford: Clarendon Press, 1964). Reprinted by kind permission of the author.

23 Lewis, David, "The Paradoxes of Time Travel," *American Philosophical Quarterly, 13* (1976) pp. 145–52. Reprinted by permission of Stephanie Lewis and *American Philosophical Quarterly*.

24 Arnauld, Antoine, and Nicole, Pierre, "Of Confused Subjects which are Equivalent to Two Subjects," in *The Port-Royal Logic*, trans. Thomas S. Baynes, LL.D. (Edinburgh: William Blackwood and Sons, 1851).

25 Olson, Eric, "The Paradox of Increase," *The Monist, 89* July (2006). Reprinted by permission of *The Monist*.

26 Quine, W. V. O., "Identity, Ostension, and Hypostasis," *Journal of Philosophy XLVII, 22* (1950) pp. 621–33. Reprinted by permission.

42 Russell, Bertrand, "Neutral Monism," in *Philosophy*. Reprinted by permission of Taylor & Francis UK.

43 Baron d'Holbach, Paul-Henri Dietrich, "We Are Never Free," in *The System of Nature, or, Laws of the Moral and Physical World, Vol. 1*, trans. H. D. Robinson (Boston: 1868) ch. 11.

44 Hobart, R. E., "Free Will as Involving Determination and Inconceivable Without It," *Mind*, 63 (1934) pp. 1–27. Reprinted by permission of Oxford University Press Journals.

45 Wisdom, John, "Freedom, Causation, and Preexistence," in *Problems of Mind and Matter* (Cambridge: Cambridge University Press, 1963). Reprinted by permission of Cambridge University Press.

46 Chisholm, Roderick M., "Human Freedom and the Self," from the Lindley Lecture, 1964. © 1964 by the Department of Philosophy, University of Kansas. Reprinted by kind permission of Department of Philosophy, University of Kansas.

47 van Inwagen, Peter, "The Consequence Argument."

48 van Inwagen, Peter, "The Mystery of Metaphysical Freedom," in Peter van Inwagen and Dean W. Zimmerman (eds.), *Metaphysics: The Big Questions* (Oxford: Blackwell Publishing, 1998) pp. 365–74. New in first edition.

49 O'Connor, Timothy, "The Agent as Cause," in Peter van Inwagen and Dean W. Zimmerman (eds.), *Metaphysics: The Big Questions* (Oxford: Blackwell Publishing, 1998) pp. 374–80. Reprinted by kind permission of the author.

50 Frankfurt, Harry G., "Alternate Possibilities and Moral Responsibility," *The Journal of Philosophy*, 66 (1969) pp. 829–39. Reprinted by permission.

51 Frankfurt, Harry G., "Freedom of the Will and the Concept of a Person," *The Journal of Philosophy*, 68 (1971) pp. 5–20. Reprinted by permission.

52 Lewis, David K., "Modal Realism at Work," in *On the Plurality of Worlds* (Oxford: Blackwell Publishing, 1986). Reprinted by kind permission of Stephanie Lewis and Blackwell Publishing.

53 Lewis, David K., "Counterparts of Persons and Their Bodies," *The Journal of Philosophy*, 68 (1971) pp. 203–11. Reprinted by permission.

54 Kripke, Saul, "Identity and Necessity," in Milton K. Munitz (ed.), *Identity and Individuation* (New York: New York University Press, 1971) pp. 135–64.

55 Putnam, Hilary, "After Metaphysics, What?" in Kieter Henrich and Rolf-Peter Horstmann (eds.), *Metaphysik nach Kant?* (Stuttgart: Hegel-Kongress, 1987; published in 1988). Reprinted by kind permission of the author and Klett-Cotta.

56 Putnam, Hilary, "Truth and Convention," from Hilary Putnam, "Truth and Convention: On Davidson's Refutation of Conceptual Relativism," *Dialectica*, 41 (1987) pp. 69–77. Reprinted by permission of Blackwell Publishing.

57 Sosa, Ernest, "Nonabsolute Existence and Conceptual Relativity," from Ernest Sosa, "Putnam's Pragmatic Realism," *Journal of Philosophy*, 90 (1990) pp. 605–26. Reprinted by permission.

58 Sosa, Ernest, "Addendum to 'Nonabsolute Existence and Conceptual Relativity': Objections and Replies," in Peter van Inwagen and Dean W. Zimmerman (eds.), *Metaphysics: The Big Questions* (Oxford: Blackwell Publishing, 1998) pp. 407–10. © Ernest Sosa. Reprinted by kind permission of the author.

59 James, William, "The Problem of Being: Chapter 3 of *Some Problems of Philosophy*," in *Some Problems of Philosophy* (New York: Longmans, Green, 1911).

60 Parfit, Derek. "Why Anything? Why This?" Originally published in *London Review of Books*, 22 January and 5 February 1998. © Derek Parfit. Reprinted by kind permission of the author.

61 Swinburne, Richard, "Response to Derek Parfit," in Peter van Inwagen and Dean W. Zimmerman (eds.), *Metaphysics: The Big Questions* (Oxford: Blackwell Publishing, 1998) pp. 427–9. Reprinted by kind permission of the author.

62 Clarke, Samuel, "The Cosmological Argument: An Excerpt from *A Demonstration of the Being and Attributes of God*," in *The Works of Samuel Clarke* (London: John and Paul Knopton, 1738) pp. 8–14.

63 Rowe, William L., "The Cosmological Argument and the Principle of Sufficient Reason," *Man and World, 1* (1968) pp. 278–92. Reprinted by permission of Springer Verlag.

64 St Anselm, "The Ontological Argument: Chapters II–IV of the *Proslogion*," in S. N. Deane (trans.), *St Anselm: Basic Writings, 2nd edition* (LaSalle, Ill.: Open Court Publishing, 1968). Reprinted by permission of Open Court Publishing, a division of Carus Publishing, Peru Ill.

65 Malcolm, Norman, "Anselm's Ontological Arguments," *Philosophical Review, 69* (1960) pp. 41–62. Reprinted by kind permission of Duke University Press.

Every effort has been made to trace copyright holders and to obtain their permission for the use of copyright material. The publisher apologizes for any errors or omissions in the above list and would be grateful if notified of any corrections that should be incorporated in future reprints or editions of this book.

Introduction: What Is Metaphysics?*

What is the Subject Matter of Metaphysics?

It is notoriously hard to provide a satisfactory account of what metaphysics is. Certain twentieth-century coinages like "metaphilosophy" and "metapsychology" encourage the impression that metaphysics is a study that somehow "goes beyond" physics. In reality, however, the Greek phrase "*ta meta ta phusica*," from which our word "metaphysics" is derived, is the term that the early editors of Aristotle's corpus used to refer to his book (from their point of view, his "books") on what he called first philosophy. And this phrase means only "the ones [*sc.* books] that come after the ones about nature." As is often the case, etymology is no guide to meaning.

The best approach to an understanding of what is meant by "metaphysics" is by way of the concepts of appearance and reality. It is a commonplace that the way things seem to be is often not the way they are, that the way things *apparently* are is often not the way they *really* are. The sun apparently moves across the sky – but not *really*. The moon seems larger when it is near the horizon – but its size never *really* changes. We might say that one is engaged in "metaphysics" if one is attempting to get behind all appearances and to describe things as they really are.

An example may be helpful. There are available two "interpretations" of quantum mechanics. One, the standard "Copenhagen" interpretation, implies that particles like electrons in passing from an emitter to a target do not in general follow "trajectories," continuous paths through space. The other interpretation, the work of David Bohm, implies that particles do follow trajectories. It can be shown that these two interpretations are empirically equivalent: they make the same predictions about the outcomes of all possible experiments. This fact has led many physicists and philosophers to say that the question as to which interpretation (if either) describes the way particles *really* behave is a metaphysical question. The two theories both "save the appearances" – or at least, if either fails to save the appearances the other will fail as well, and in the same way – but they are obviously not "the same." Assuming that the concept "following a continuous path through space" is a coherent concept, particles must, as a matter of logic, either follow continuous paths through space – or not. Therefore, both interpretations cannot be correct descriptions of the real behavior of particles – although they could both be incorrect. It would be possible to argue that the question as to which (if either) is correct is impossible to answer and therefore idle. But that is not the same as saying it hasn't got an answer. If it is a meaningful question it has an answer, and if "follows a continuous path through space" is a meaningful phrase, the question is meaningful. The anti-metaphysical attitude is typified by the scientist who is willing to make use of each of two logically inconsistent theories that make the same predictions about possible observations, and who deprecates as idle or meaningless the question of whether either theory describes things as they really are.

Let us try to describe the metaphysical impulse in a little more detail. If one is attempting to "get behind all appearances and describe things as they really are," if one is "engaging in metaphysics," then one is attempting to determine certain things with respect to certain statements (or assertions or propositions or theses), those statements that, if true, would be descriptions of the reality that lies behind all appearances, descriptions of things as they really are. (Primarily to determine which of them are true and which of them are false; but also, perhaps, to determine various other things about them, such as which ones it is reasonable to believe, and which ones are logically consistent with one another.)

Let us call this "reality that lies behind all appearances" simply Reality (with a capital). And let us call statements that, if true, would be descriptions of this Reality *metaphysical statements*. Which statements are, if true, descriptions of Reality? This is a difficult question, because simply from examining a speaker's words it cannot be determined whether the speaker has made a metaphysical statement: one must also examine the context in which those words were spoken. It is necessary to do this because different "restrictions of intended reference" may be in force in different contexts, and this has the consequence that the same words can express different things in different contexts. If, for example, you look into your refrigerator and say sadly "There's no beer," you are not asserting that the existence of that beverage is a myth or an illusion. And this is because, in the context in which you are speaking, you and your audience know that your statement is intended to describe only the state of things inside your refrigerator.

Let us see how this point might apply in a case in which we want to know whether a speaker has made a metaphysical statement. The late Carl Sagan, in his television series *Cosmos*, made the following much-quoted statement: "The cosmos [i.e., the physical universe] is all there is or was or ever will be." Was this a metaphysical statement? Well, that depends. In the context in which Sagan made his statement, were there any restrictions of intended reference in force? Did Sagan, perhaps, intend his statement to apply only to physical things? Was he perhaps saying only that the cosmos was the totality of physical things, past, present, and future? In that case, his statement was not a metaphysical statement, but simply an explanation of the meaning of the word "cosmos." Or did Sagan perhaps make his statement in a context in which there were *no* restrictions of intended reference in force? Did he mean to say that *everything* – everything without qualification – was a part of the cosmos? (Notice that, on the "unrestricted" interpretation of his statement, the statement implies that there is no God – or anything else that is not physical; on the "restricted" interpretation, the statement has no such implication.) In that case, his statement can plausibly be described as a metaphysical statement – for if we learned that there was no God or anything else non-physical, would we not learn something about the reality that lay behind all appearances?

One requirement on a metaphysical statement, then, is that it be made with no restrictions of intended reference in force. A second, and closely related requirement is that the statement represent a serious attempt by the speaker to state the strict and literal truth. We often express ourselves carelessly or loosely or metaphorically. (Restriction of intended reference might be seen as a special case of not speaking "strictly.") We say things like "The sun is trying to come out," "The car doesn't want to start," "Time passes slowly when one is bored," and "Dark, angry clouds filled the sky." Since metaphysics is an attempt to get at how things really are, this requirement is not hard to understand. Those who say things like these do not mean to assert that the sun, the car, or the clouds are conscious beings, or that time can pass at different rates; and, therefore, at least some of the features of these statements do not represent an attempt to say how things really are. When doing metaphysics, such loose talk has to go: one must be willing to take responsibility for the strict and literal consequences of the words one has used to make a statement.

The metaphysician's aim, then, is to make assertions that strictly and literally describe reality and which can, with sufficient effort, be understood by anyone whose intellect is equal to the task. Metaphor may play a heuristic role in metaphysics – as in physics or economics or comparative linguistics – but metaphor must be banished from the metaphysician's "finished product." (The metaphysician may begin by calling space a receptacle or time the moving image of eternity, but at some point in the metaphysician's investigations these metaphors must be replaced with language that is meant to be taken literally. Or, at any rate, if a metaphysical work depends essentially on metaphor, it must be regarded as inherently incomplete, a sort of work in progress.) To say these things is not to say that the metaphysician (necessarily) regards the metaphorical as inferior to the literal; it is merely to demarcate what belongs properly to metaphysics.

May we then understand a metaphysical statement as one that (i) is made in a context in which no restrictions of intended reference are in force and (ii) is such that the speaker who makes it has made a serious effort to speak the strict and literal truth? This would not be satisfactory, for to call a statement "metaphysical" is to imply that it is a very general statement, and these two conditions include nothing that implies generality. An example may help us to understand the kind of generality that a statement must have, to be a metaphysical statement. Suppose Alice says, "All Greeks are mortal." Let us assume that when she makes this statement, no restrictions of intended reference are in force: she means her statement to apply to *all* Greeks, and not only to the members of some "understood" special class of Greeks. And let us assume that this statement represents a serious effort on her part to speak the strict and literal truth. (Since the statement contains no figurative language and no "well, I hope you see what I mean" linguistic shortcuts, this assumption is reasonable enough.) Perhaps these two assumptions imply that her statement, if true, describes Reality, but it certainly does not describe very *much* of Reality. After all, it tells us only about Greeks; it tells us nothing about elephants or neutron stars or even non-Greek human beings. It is therefore not sufficiently general to count as a metaphysical statement.

What sort of statement would be "sufficiently general"? Might we say that to be sufficiently general to be a metaphysical statement, a statement must be about *everything*? This will not do, and for two reasons. First, *any* "all" statement is in one sense "about everything." For example, the statement "All Greeks are mortal" is logically equivalent to "Everything is mortal if it is a Greek," (Every elephant and every neutron star and every non-Greek immortal is mortal if it is Greek.) It is therefore not easy to say in any precise and useful way what it is for a statement to be "about everything." Secondly, even if we ignore this difficulty and decide to rely on our intuitive sense of which statements are "about everything," we shall run up against the fact that most philosophers would want to classify as "metaphysical" many statements that we would, speaking intuitively, say were not "about everything." For example: Every event has a cause (this statement is, intuitively, not about everything, but only about events); Every physical thing is such that it might not have existed (. . . only about physical things); Any two objects that occupy space are spatially related to each other (. . . only about objects that occupy space). And there is a further problem: most philosophers would want to classify as metaphysical certain statements that are not "all" statements, not even ones that pertain to some special class of things like events or physical things: There is a God; Some things have no parts; There could be two things that had all the same properties.

Perhaps in the end, all we can say is this: some "categories" or "concepts" are sufficiently "general" that a statement will count as a "metaphysical statement" if – given that it is made in a context in which no restrictions of intended reference are in force, and given that the person who makes it is making a serious effort to say what is strictly and literally true – it employs only these categories. Among these categories are many that we have already used in our examples: "physical thing," "spatial object," "cause," "event," "part," "property." If we so define "metaphysical statement," then the concept of a metaphysical statement will be open-ended and vague. It will be open-ended in that no final list of the categories that can occur in a "metaphysical statement" will be possible: we could try to make a complete list (we might go through all the historical texts that were uncontroversially "metaphysical" and mark all the categories we came across that seemed to us to be "sufficiently general"), but, even if we had a list that satisfied us for the moment, we should have to admit that we might have to enlarge the list tomorrow. It is vague in that there will be borderline cases of "sufficiently general" categories: words such as "impenetrable," "pain," "straight," and "surface" are possible examples of such borderline cases. But there will also be perfectly clear cases of categories that are not "sufficiently general": "Greek," "chair," "elephant," "neutron star," "diminished-seventh chord," "non-linear partial differential equation," . . . (Words like "chair" and "elephant" can occur in a work on metaphysics, but only in examples meant to illustrate – or in counter examples meant to refute – theses whose statement requires only very general concepts.)

Where does this leave us? Let us suppose that Charles has made a certain statement. Let us suppose that when he made this statement, no restrictions of intended reference were in force. Let us suppose that Charles was willing to take responsibility for the strict and literal consequences of the words he has used to make the statement. And let us suppose that all the concepts or categories that Charles employed in making this statement were "sufficiently general." (And let us suppose that his statement was not some logical truism like "Everything is either material or not material.") Then, or so we would suggest, Charles has made a statement that, if true, describes Reality. That is, he has made a meta-physical statement. And if we try to decide whether his statement is true or false, reasonable or unreasonable, probable or improbable, consistent or inconsistent with various other metaphysical or non-metaphysical statements, then we are engaged in metaphysics.

Is Metaphysics Possible?

Is metaphysics, so conceived, possible? – that is, is it possible to "engage in metaphysics" in the above sense and to reach any interesting or important conclusions? Various philosophers have argued that metaphysics is impossible. The thesis that metaphysics is impossible comes in what might be called strong and weak forms. The strong form of the thesis is this: The goal is not there, since there is no Reality to be described; all the statements we have called metaphysical are false or meaningless. (And it is hard to see how all metaphysical statements could be simply false. If one metaphysician says that everything is material and another says that it is false that everything is material, then, if their statements are meaningful, one or the other of them must be true.) The weak form of the thesis is this: The goal is there, but we human beings are unable to reach it, since the task of describing Reality is beyond our powers; metaphysical statements are meaningful, but we can never discover whether any metaphysical statement is true or false (or dis-cover anything else interesting or important about the class of metaphysical statements).

Let us briefly examine an example of the strong form of the thesis that meta-physics is impossible. In the years between the world wars, the "logical positivists" (including Carnap and other members of the "Vienna Circle") argued that the meaning of a statement consisted entirely in the predictions it made about pos-sible experience. The logical positivists argued that metaphysical statements,

statements that purported to describe Reality, made no predictions about experience. (The metaphysician asks, "Is time real, or are temporal phenomena mere appearances?" But our experiences would be the same – they would be just as they are – whether or not time was real. The metaphysician asks, "Are there universals, or is the appearance of there being attributes and relations a mere appearance, an illusion created by the way we think and speak? "But our experiences would be the same – like *this* – whether or not there were universals. And so, the logical positivists argued, for every metaphysical question. Metaphysical theses, being essentially attempts to *get behind* the way things appear to us, can make no predictions about the way things will appear to us.) Therefore, they argued, metaphysical statements are meaningless. Or, since "meaningless statement" is a contradiction in terms, the "statements" we classify as metaphysical are not really statements at all: they are things that look like statements but aren't, rather as mannequins are things that look like human beings but aren't.

But how does the logical positivist's thesis fare by its own standards? Consider the statement,

> The meaning of a statement consists entirely in the predictions it makes about possible experience.

Does this statement make any predictions about possible experiences? Could some observation show that this statement was true? Could some laboratory experiment show that it was false? It would seem not. It would seem that everything in the world would look the same – like *this* – whether or not this statement was true. And, therefore, if the statement is true it is meaningless; or, what is the same thing, if it is meaningful, it is false. Logical positivism would therefore seem to say of itself that it is false or meaningless; it would seem to be, as some philosophers say, "self-referentially incoherent."

We have not the space to consider all the attempts that have been made to show that the idea of a reality that lies behind all appearances is in some sense defective. (Current exponents of "anti-realism" are only the latest example of such philosophers.) But, for what it is worth, we are convinced that all such attempts are victims of self-referential incoherency. The general case goes like this. Alfred the anti-metaphysician argues that any proposition that does not pass some test he specifies is in some sense defective (it is, say, self-contradictory or meaningless). And he argues that any metaphysical proposition must fail this test. But it invariably turns out that some proposition that is essential to Alfred's anti-metaphysical argument itself fails to pass his test. Or so it seems to us that it invariably turns out. The reader is warned, however, that most anti-metaphysicians will say that we are mistaken, and that their own anti-metaphysical arguments are not self-referentially incoherent. (The remainder will say that everyone who is anyone in philosophy knows that "the self-referential incoherency ploy" is without merit. This response has all the merits of a certain famous, if apocryphal, solicitor's brief: "No case. Abuse plaintiff's counsel.")

What about the "weak form" of the thesis that metaphysics is impossible? Is the search for metaphysical truth a hopeless one, given the limitations of our intellects? Should one simply confess, "Such knowledge is too wonderful for me; it is high, I cannot attain unto it"? In our view, this question can be usefully discussed only in the context of a comprehensive and detailed examination of some actual and serious attempts at metaphysics.[1] But we believe that a close study of the sort of work typified by the contributions to this anthology reveals that a certain modest progress is attainable in metaphysics; those willing to put in some "honest toil" can at least hope to add to what we know about Reality. Progress in metaphysics often comes in disappointingly conditional packages, however; the most a metaphysician can usually be said to have conclusively shown is something of the form: "if such-and-such metaphysical thesis were true, then so-and-so would also have to be the case."

In the remainder of this Introduction, we will attempt to give some content to the very abstract remarks we have made about the nature of metaphysics by examining a particular metaphysical problem.

A Metaphysical Problem: the Existence and Nature of Universals

One very important part of metaphysics has to do with what there is, with what exists. This part of metaphysics is called ontology. Ontology, that is, is that part of metaphysics that deals with metaphysical statements having general forms like "An *X* exists" and "There are *Y*s." (Here, it will be assumed that "there is (are)" and "exist(s)" mean essentially the same thing – that there is no important difference in meaning between "Horses exist" and "There are horses." There are philosophers who deny this thesis: such philosophers exist.) In ontology, the second of our three requirements on a metaphysical statement is especially important – the requirement that the philosopher who makes a metaphysical statement be willing to take responsibility for the strict and literal consequences of the words used to make the statement. This is because we very frequently say things of the forms "An *X* exists" and "There are *Y*s" when we do not think there are *really* any *X*s or *Y*s. An example will help to make what is meant by this clear.

Our friend Jan is an adherent of the metaphysical position known as materialism, the thesis that everything – everything without qualification – is material. We notice, however, that, despite her allegiance to materialism, Jan frequently says things that, when taken strictly and literally, are inconsistent with materialism. For example, just this morning we heard her say, "There's a big hole in my favorite blouse that wasn't there yesterday."[2] But no material object is a hole: material things are made of atoms, and nothing made of atoms is a hole; holes, so to speak, result from the *absence* of atoms. And yet Jan has said that there was one of them in her blouse. We point out to her that she has made a statement that is on the face of it inconsistent with materialism, and she replies:

> It's true that I said there was a hole in my blouse, and that this statement, taken strictly and literally, implies that there is a hole; and it's true that a hole, if there really were such *things* as holes, wouldn't be a material thing. But I was speaking

the language of everyday life; by the standards of metaphysics, I was speaking loosely. What I *could* have said, and what I would have said if I'd known that you were going to hold me responsible for the strict and literal consequences of my words, is that my blouse is *perforate*. The predicate "is perforate," when it is applied to a material object like my blouse, simply says something about the object's *shape*. If you perforate a coin, the resulting object will have a shape different from that of an imperforate, but otherwise identical, coin. When I say that a given material thing is perforate, this obviously does not imply that there is *another* thing, a thing not made of atoms, a thing called a "hole," that is "in" the material thing. The words "there's a hole in this thing" are just an idiomatic way of saying "this thing is perforate."

This speech provides an example of a philosophical tool, extremely important in ontology, called "paraphrase." Various idioms and expressions that are perfectly serviceable for everyday, practical purposes have metaphysically unwanted implications when they are interpreted strictly and literally – which is the way we are supposed to interpret a metaphysician's idioms and expressions. To find a *paraphrase* of a statement involving such "misleading" forms of words is to find a way of conveying what the statement is intended to convey that does not have the unwanted implications. (This is what we imagined Jan doing with the statement "There's a hole in my blouse.")

Metaphysicians have not spent a lot of time disputing about whether there really are holes. But they have spent a lot of time disputing about whether there really are so-called abstract things (such as properties, relations, propositions, and numbers). The medieval dispute about the reality of "universals" is an especially important example of this. This ancient dispute, or something very much like it, goes on today in several different forms. One of these "forms" is due to the work of the American philosopher W.V. Quine.[3] We shall examine it. It will be our example of a way to approach a metaphysical problem.

A universal is, near enough, a property – such as humanity (the property that is "universal" to the members of the class of human beings and to the members of no more inclusive class), wisdom, the color blue, and widowhood. There are *apparently* properties. There is, for example, apparently such a thing as humanity. The members of the class of human beings, as the idiom has it, "have something in common," and what could this "something" be but the property "humanity"? It could certainly not be anything physical, for – Siamese twins excepted – no two human beings have any physical thing in common. And, of course, what goes for the class of human beings goes for the class of birds, the class of white things, and the class of intermediate vector bosons: the members of each of these classes have something in common with one another, and what the members of a class have in common is a property – or so it appears. But there are metaphysicians who contend that this appearance is mere appearance and that *in reality* there are no properties. Other metaphysicians argue that in this case, at least, appearances are not misleading and that there really *are* properties, The metaphysicians who deny the real existence of properties are called nominalists and the metaphysicians who affirm the real existence of properties are called platonists.[4] (Each of these terms could be objected to on historical grounds. But let us pass over these objections.)

How can the dispute between the nominalists and the platonists be resolved? Quine has proposed an answer to this question.[5] Nominalists and platonists have different beliefs about what there is. How should one go about deciding what to believe about what there is? According to Quine, the problem of deciding what to believe about what there is is a very straightforward special case of the problem of deciding what to believe. (The problem of deciding what to believe is no trivial problem, to be sure, but it is a problem everyone is going to have somehow to come to terms with.) Let us look at the problem that is our present concern, the problem of what to believe about the existence of properties. If we want to decide whether to believe that there are properties – Quine tells us – we should examine the beliefs that we already have, and see whether any of them commits us to the existence of properties. If any does, then we have a reason to believe in the existence of properties: it is whatever reason we had for accepting the belief that commits us to the existence of properties – plus the general intellectual requirement that if one becomes aware that one's belief that p commits one to the further belief that q, then one should either believe that q or cease to believe that p.[6] But let us consider an example. Suppose we find the following proposition among our beliefs:

Spiders share some of the anatomical features of insects.

A plausible case can be made for the thesis that this belief commits us to the existence of properties. We may observe, first, that it is very hard to see what an "anatomical feature" (such as "having an exoskeleton") could be if it were not a property: "property," "quality," "characteristic," "attribute," and "feature" are all more or less synonyms. Does our belief that spiders share some of the anatomical features of insects therefore commit us to the existence of "anatomical features"? If we carefully examine the meaning of the sentence "Spiders share some of the anatomical features of insects," we find that what it says is this:

There are anatomical features that insects have and spiders also have.

And it is a straightforward logical consequence of this proposition that there are anatomical features: If there are anatomical features that insects have and spiders also have, then there are anatomical features that insects have; if there are anatomical features that insects have, then there are anatomical features – full stop.

Does this little argument show that anyone who believes that spiders share some of the anatomical features of insects is committed to platonism, to a belief in the existence of properties? How might a nominalist respond? Suppose we present this argument to Ned, a convinced nominalist (who believes, as most people do, that spiders share some of the anatomical features of insects). Assuming that Ned is unwilling simply to have inconsistent beliefs, there would seem to be four possible ways for him to respond to this argument:

(1) He might become a platonist.
(2) He might abandon his belief that spiders share many of the anatomical features of insects.

(3)   He might attempt to show that it does not after all follow from this belief, that there are anatomical features.

(4)   He might admit that his beliefs (his belief in nominalism and his belief that spiders share some of the anatomical features of insects) are apparently inconsistent, affirm his nominalistic faith that this inconsistency is apparent, not real, and confess that, although he is confident that there is some fault in our alleged demonstration that his belief about spiders and insects commits him to the existence of properties, he is at present unable to discover it.

Possibility (2) is not really very attractive. It is unattractive for at least two reasons. First, it seems to be a simple fact of biology that spiders share some of the anatomical features of insects. Secondly, there are many, many "simple facts" that could have been used as the premise of an essentially identical argument for the conclusion that there are properties. (For example: Elements in the same column in the Periodic Table tend to have many of the same chemical properties; Some of the most important characteristics of the nineteenth-century novel are rarely present in the twentieth-century novel.) Possibility (4) is always an option, but no philosopher is likely to embrace it except as a last resort. What Ned is likely to do is to try to avail himself of Possibility (3). He is likely to try to show that his belief about spiders and insects does not in fact commit him to platonism. What he will attempt to do in respect of this belief (and of all the others among his beliefs that apparently commit him to a belief in properties) is just what Jan did in respect of the belief that apparently committed her to a belief in holes: he will try to find a *paraphrase*, a sentence that (i) he could use in place of "Spiders share some of the anatomical features of insects" and (ii) does not even seem to have "There are anatomical features" as one of its logical consequences. If he can do this, then he will be in a position to argue that the commitment to the existence of properties that is apparently "carried by" his belief about spiders and insects is only apparent. And he will be in a position to argue – no doubt further argument would be required to establish this – that the apparent existence of properties is mere appearance (an appearance that is due to the forms of words we use).

Is it possible to find such a paraphrase? (And to find paraphrases of all the other apparently true statements that seem to commit those who make them to the reality of properties?) This is a difficult and technical question. We record our conviction that it is at least very hard to do so.[7] If Quine is right about "ontological commitment," therefore, there is no easy way for anyone to be a consistent nominalist.

It must be emphasized that we have said almost nothing about the *nature* of "properties." If what we have said so far is correct, some of the sentences we use to express certain very ordinary and non-metaphysical beliefs, sentences like "Spiders share some of the anatomical features of insects" and "Elements in the same column in the Periodic Table tend to have many of the same chemical properties," define what we may call the "property role": a property is whatever it is (beyond ordinary things like spiders and chemical elements) that using these sentences to express our beliefs carries prima facie commitment to. And if what we have said so far is correct, it is very hard to avoid the conclusion that objects of *some* sort play the property role. But philosophers who accepted this conclusion could differ fundamentally about the nature of the objects that play this role. Some philosophers think that the property role is played by things that are in some sense constituents of objects, that properties are in some very subtle and abstract sense of the word *parts* of the objects whose properties they are.[8] Other philosophers (including at least one of the editors of this volume) think that this conception of properties is not so much false as meaningless and that the things that play the property role are in no sense parts or constituents of objects, but simply things that can be "said of" objects. According to this view of the nature of properties, the property "being white" is simply something that can be said truly of table salt and the Taj Mahal and cannot be said truly of copper sulfate or the Eiffel Tower. (But what kind of thing would *that* be? You may well ask.) There has perhaps been little progress since the Middle Ages in the attempt to say anything both informative and meaningful about the *nature* of universals, the nature of the things that play the property role. But it can be plausibly argued that even if we do not understand universals much better than the medieval philosophers, we now have a better understanding of the *problem* of universals. We now see that the best way to look at the debate between the nominalist and the platonist is as follows: the task of the nominalist is to establish the conclusion that our beliefs about ordinary things do not commit us to the thesis that anything plays the property role. The task of the platonist is to attempt to establish the conclusion that our beliefs about ordinary things do commit us to the existence of things that play the property role, and to attempt to give a plausible account of the nature of these things.

Notes

*Much of the "Introduction: What is Metaphysics?" originally appeared in Peter van Inwagen, "The Nature of Metaphysics: the State of the Art," in Stephen Laurence and Cynthia Macdonald, eds, *Contemporary Metaphysics: a Reader* (Oxford: Blackwell, 1998). It also contains portions of Peter van Inwagen's entry "Metaphysics," in Adrian Hastings, Alistair Mason, and Hugh Piper, eds., *The Oxford Companion to Christian Thought* (Oxford: Oxford University Press, 2000).

1   For an extremely interesting and sophisticated defense of the weak form of the thesis, see Colin McGinn, *Problems in Philosophy: the Limits of Inquiry* (Oxford: Blackwell, 1993).
2   This example is based on David and Stephanie Lewis, "Holes," *Australasian Journal of Philosophy*, 48 (1970), pp. 206–12, (reprinted as Ch. 1 of this volume).
3   For another, very different form, see David Armstrong, "Universals as Attributes: an Excerpt from *Universals: an Opinionated Introduction*", Ch. 5 of this volume.
4   The philosophers we are calling platonists are often called realists. We will avoid the terms "realist" and "realism," since they have several other meanings in metaphysics.
5   The issues that we are about to discuss are generally said to pertain to "ontological commitment," a term that is due to Quine. For Quine's views on ontological com-

mitment, see his classic essay "On What There Is," reprinted as Ch. 2 in this volume and chapter VII, "Ontic Decision," of his *Word and Object* (Cambridge, Mass.: MIT Press, 1960).

Discussions of ontological commitment are generally rather technical. They are technical because they represent issues of ontological commitment as essentially related to "the existential quantifier," the symbol used in formal logic (it is most often a backwards "E") to express "there is" or "there exists." The tendency of philosophers to connect issues of ontological commitment with the existential quantifier is (in one way) entirely justified, and (in another) somewhat misleading. It is justified because any *technically fully adequate* formulation of Quine's theses on ontological commitment must involve the existential quantifier and the related device of "bound variables." It is misleading because it suggests that it is impossible to present an account of the essential philosophical points contained in these theses without at some point introducing the existential quantifier – and not simply the symbol, but the technical apparatus that governs its use in formal logic and the various philosophical disputes that have arisen concerning its "interpretation." And this is false: it is possible to give a useful introductory account of the philosophical points contained in Quine's various discussions of ontological commitment that contains no "existential apparatus" but the ordinary words and phrases – "there is," "exists" – for which the existential quantifier is the formal replacement. The discussion of "there is" and paraphrase in this introduction is an attempt at such an introductory account of these points.

6 Suppose we were to discover that some belief of ours – that Mars has two moons, let us say – committed us to the existence of properties. Should that discovery move us to question, or perhaps even to abandon, our belief that Mars had two moons? That would depend on whether we had, or thought we had, some reason to believe that there were no properties. If we did think we had some reason to believe that there were no properties, we should have to try to decide whether our reason for thinking that Mars had two moons (presumably we have one) was more or less compelling than our reason for thinking that there were no properties.

7 In one sense, Quine himself believes that the required paraphrase is possible. He believes that statements like our "spider–insect" statement can be understood in such a way that they commit those who make them to nothing other than *sets* – besides, of course, spiders and insects or whatever other "ordinary" objects the statements may mention. But these sets, it must be emphasized, are very far from being ordinary objects. The set of all spiders, for example, is not a spider or any other sort of physical object, and reference to "the set of spiders" cannot be dismissed as a mere linguistic device for referring to all spiders collectively: sets are *objects*. Sets are, in fact, from the point of view of those who call themselves nominalists, hardly more acceptable than properties, and, in present-day discussions of ontology, "nominalism" is generally taken to imply that there are no such objects as sets.

8 Two versions of the view are represented in this anthology: D. C. Williams, "The Elements of Being"; and Zimmerman, "Distinct Indiscernibles and the Bundle Theory" (a dialogue in which the character labeled "A" defends a version of the bundle theory).

Suggestions for further reading

Aune, Bruce, *Metaphysics: the Elements* (Minneapolis: University of Minnesota, 1985), chs 1 and 2: "What is Metaphysics?" and "Existence."

Benardete, José A., *Metaphysics: the Logical Approach* (Oxford: Oxford University Press, 1989), Part 1.

Burke, Michael, "Existence," in Stephen Hales, ed., *Metaphysics: Contemporary Readings* (Belmont, Cal.: Wadsworth, 1998).

Carter, William R., *The Elements of Metaphysics* (Philadelphia, Penn.: Temple University Press, 1990), ch. 1: "Metaphysics."

Gardner, Martin, *The Night is Large* (New York: St Martin's Press, 1996), chs 32 and 43: "The Significance of Nothing" and "The Irrelevance of Everything."

Hamlyn, D. W., *Metaphysics* (Cambridge, UK: Cambridge University Press, 1984), ch. 1: "Introduction."

Hasker, William, *Metaphysics: Constructing a World View* (Downers Grove, Ill., and Leicester, UK: InterVarsity Press, 1983), ch. 1: "Introducing Metaphysics."

Jubien, Michael, *Contemporary Metaphysics* (Oxford: Blackwell, 1997), ch. 1: "Metaphysics."

Laurence, Stephen, and Cynthia Macdonald, *Contemporary Metaphysics: a Reader* (Oxford: Blackwell, 1998), Section 1: "Ontological Commitment and Methodology."

Loux, Michael, *Metaphysics: a Contemporary Introduction* (London: Routledge, 1997), Introduction.

Post, John F., *Metaphysics: a Contemporary Introduction* (New York: Paragon House, 1991), ch. 1: "Is Metaphysics Possible?"

Russell, Bertrand, *The Problems of Philosophy* (New York: H. Holt, 1912), ch. 15: "The Value of Philosophy."

van Inwagen, Peter, *Metaphysics* (Boulder, Col.: Westview Press, 1993), ch. 1: "Introduction."

PART I

WHAT ARE THE MOST GENERAL FEATURES OF THE WORLD?

Introduction

The readings assembled here concern some of the most pervasive and, ultimately, puzzling features of the world. To be "part of the world" is simply *to be*, to exist. So existence, or being, would seem to be the most universal of all features, displayed by the world and everything in it. But what is *existence*, and is it different from *being*? Among the things that exist, is there a deep dichotomy between individual things and the properties they exhibit? Most things – perhaps all things – are in space and time; but what is space and what is time? Is time just another dimension, in many ways like the spatial ones? Time seems quite different from space in some ways, most notably in having a built-in direction. But does the difference between forward and backward directions in time result from the direction of a process of "absolute becoming" – a process producing a distinction between past, present, and future with no spatial analogue? Are finite regions of space infinitely divisible; and if they were, would that render motion impossible? Are things that persist through time spread out in the temporal dimension in the same way they are spread out in the spatial dimensions? Are causal regularities anything more than uniformities that hold everywhere in space-time? Or is there some deeper relation that binds cause to effect?

A What is Existence?

Introduction

Ontology is the part of metaphysics concerned with the question, "What is there?," when that question is taken in the broadest or most unrestricted sense possible. As Peter van Inwagen points out in the introduction to this book ("What is metaphysics?"), sometimes the question "Is there any such-and-such?" means merely, "Restricting our attention for the moment to just things that are so-and-sos, is there a such-and-such among them?" When we ask, for example, "Is there any beer?," we usually mean merely "Restricting our attention to just beverages in the fridge (or in the restaurant, or available for purchase in the county, etc.), is there any beer?" If the last beer has been taken from the fridge at a party, and someone asks, "Is there any beer?," it is a poor joke to say "Yes" and then explain that there is plenty in the grocery store (which is closed, by the way). The metaphysician interested in ontology wants to know what the world is like in its entirety, ignoring nothing. She wants a complete catalogue of "the furniture of the world," but at a very high level of abstraction.

Ontology is one of the oldest parts of philosophy; it has a central place in Plato's philosophy, for instance; and Platonistic ontological views are defended by philosophers even today. Quine, however, says that "Plato's beard" (his catalogue of "what there is") needs shaving – meaning that Plato's ontology is too rich; it is full of entities that Quine finds it hard to accept as real. For instance, Plato says there are universals – features, properties, or attributes that can be attributed to many individuals (whiteness, triangularity, courage, etc.). Quine admits that there are words that can be used to describe many things; but he doubts whether we need to posit some one thing present in all the objects truly described by one such word. For example, on Quine's view, many things can truly be described as red, but there need be no extra thing – "redness" – that somehow unites them or is part of them all.

In van Inwagen's "Introduction: What is metaphysics?," Quine's "On What There Is," and the charming dialogue about "Holes" by David and Stephanie Lewis, we find contemporary philosophers wrestling with the ancient questions of ontology, but using some more recent tools – such as the notions of "existential quantification," and the technique for eliminating "singular terms" known as "Russell's Theory of Definite Descriptions." Phrases of "existential quantification" are simply expressions like "There is a . . . ," "There are some . . . ," "There exists a . . . ," "There exist some . . ." – phrases that can be completed in ever so many ways to affirm the being or existence of different kinds of thing. Statements express "existential commitment" to so-and-sos if they begin with these sorts of phrases and then go on to describe a thing or things that are so-and-so. Van Inwagen, Quine, and the Lewises all share the view that the way to do ontology is to consider all the things one believes to be true, and then to see what statements of existential commitment seem to follow, as a matter of logic, from these beliefs. They all also agree that appearances can be deceiving; that a statement apparently committing someone to the existence of so-and-sos can be regarded as innocent, a mere manner of speaking, if one can readily provide a "paraphrase" of the statement that does not even appear to imply that there are so-and-sos.

Van Inwagen, the Lewises, and Quine do not see an important difference between saying that *there is* a certain kind of thing, and saying that *there exists* a certain kind of thing; both signal existential commitment to things of that kind. But some philosophers – like Quine's fictitious "Wyman," and the Austrian philosopher Alexius Meinong (described by Chisholm in Ch. 3) – think that the difference between "there is . . ." and "there exists . . ." is an important one; that what there is includes more than what exists, and "existence" and "being" come apart. Wyman (and Meinong) say that the things that have being but not existence are ones that merely "subsist" (Meinong using the German word "*bestehen*").

Quine's Wyman takes an extreme view about singular terms – that is, names ("Bill Clinton," "Pegasus") and descriptive phrases that can serve as the subject in a sentence with a singular verb ("Zimmerman's favorite book," "the present king of France"): If a singular term can be meaningfully used in a sentence, then there must be something answering to the term; it must at least subsist. So, Wyman claims not only that there are "ideal entities" such as universals and numbers, but also that there are mythical beasts, such as Pegasus.

Meinong's position (as described by Chisholm) is a little more complicated. Like Wyman, he says that there are "ideal entities" like universals and numbers – they subsist, although they do not exist – and he reserves existence for concrete entities in space and time (in Ch. 4, Russell uses "exist" and "subsist" in the same way). Unlike Wyman, however, Meinong denies that Pegasus, golden mountains, and other merely possible objects either exist *or subsist*. In other words, there are no such things; they have no "*Sein*," no being, whatsoever. So far, then, Meinong agrees with Quine. We can, however, talk meaningfully about these merely possible "objects," ascribing this or that feature. For instance, we can truly say, of Pegasus, that he has wings; and, of the present king of France, that he is French. Meinong used the word "*Sosein*" ("so-being" or "being thus-and-so") to describe the characteristics truly ascribable to an object, whether or not there is such a thing. This led to the principle (first formulated in these terms by his student, Ernst Mally, but propounded by Meinong) of the "independence of the *Sosein* of an object from its *Sein*": an object can be thus-and-so despite the fact that there is no such object. Pegasus can be winged, though there is no Pegasus.

(It should be pointed out that Chisholm does not explicitly *endorse* Meinong's theory; he merely defends it from the charge of absurdity, and makes what he takes to be a strong case for it. Chisholm's own views about the nature of existence, and the way to pursue ontology, were more like those represented here by van Inwagen, the Lewises, and Quine.)

Suggestions for further reading

Alston, William P., "Ontological Commitments," in Laurence and Macdonald (eds.), *Contemporary Readings in the Foundations of Metaphysics* (Oxford: Basil Blackwell, 1998) pp. 46–54.

Aune, Bruce, *Metaphysics: The Elements* (Minneapolis: University of Minnesota, 1985) chs. 1 and 2.

Dorr, Cian, "There are No Abstract Objects," in Hawthorne, Sider, and Zimmerman (eds.), *Contemporary Debates in Metaphysics* (Malden, Mass.: Blackwell, 2007).

Eklund, Matti, "The Picture of Reality as an Amorphous Lump," in Hawthorne, Sider, and Zimmerman (eds.), *Contemporary Debates in Metaphysics* (Malden, Mass.: Blackwell, 2007).

Haack, Susan, "Quantifiers," in Laurence and Macdonald (eds.), *Contemporary Readings in the Foundations of Metaphysics* (Oxford: Basil Blackwell, 1998) pp. 55–68.

Hirsch, Eli, "Ontological Arguments: Interpretive Charity and Quantifier Variance," in Hawthorne, Sider, and Zimmerman (eds.), *Contemporary Debates in Metaphysics* (Malden, Mass.: Blackwell, 2007).

Lambert, Karel, *Meinong and the Principle of Independence: Its Place in Meinong's Theory of Objects, Its Significance in Contemporary Philosophical Logic* (Cambridge: Cambridge University Press, 1983).

Parsons, Terence, *Nonexistent Objects* (New Haven: Yale University Press, 1980), Introduction, and chs. 1 and 2.

Russell, Bertrand, *Introduction to Mathematical Philosophy* (London: George Allen and Unwin, 1919), chs. 15 and 16.

van Inwagen, Peter, "Meta-ontology," *Erkenntnis* 48 (1998), pp. 233–50; reprinted in van Inwagen, *Ontology, Identity, and Modality* (Cambridge: Cambridge University Press, 2001), pp. 13–31.

1 Holes

David Lewis and Stephanie Lewis

Argle: I believe in nothing but concrete material objects.

Bargle: There are many of your opinions I applaud; but one of your less pleasing characteristics is your fondness for the doctrines of nominalism and materialism. Every time you get started on any such topic, I know we are in for a long argument. Where shall we start this time: numbers, colors, lengths, sets, force-fields, sensations, or what?

Argle: Fictions all! I've thought hard about every one of them.

Bargle: A long evening's work. Before we start, let me find you a snack. Will you have some crackers and cheese?

Argle: Thank you. What splendid Gruyère!

Bargle: You know, there are remarkably many holes in this piece.

Argle: There are.

Bargle: Got you!

Bargle: You admit there are many holes in that piece of cheese. Therefore, there are some holes in it. Therefore, there are some holes. In other words, holes exist. But holes are not made of matter; to the contrary, they result from the absence of matter.

Argle: I did say that there are holes in the cheese; but that is not to imply that there are holes.

Bargle: However not? If you say that there are A's that are B's, you are committed logically to the conclusion that there are A's.

Argle: When *I* say that there are holes in something, I mean nothing more nor less than that it is perforated. The synonymous shape-predicates '. . . is perforated' and 'there are holes in . . .' – just like any other shape-predicate, say '. . . is a dodecahedron' – may truly be predicated of pieces of cheese, without any implication that perforation is due to the presence of occult, immaterial entities. I am sorry my innocent predicate confuses you by sounding like an idiom of existential quantification, so that you think that inferences involving it are valid when they are not. But I have my reasons. You, given a perforated piece of cheese and believing as you do that it is perforated because it contains immaterial entities called holes, employ an idiom of existential quantification to say falsely 'There are holes in it.' Agreeable fellow that I am, I wish to have a sentence that sounds like yours and that is true exactly when you falsely suppose your existential quantification over immaterial things to be true. That way we could talk about the cheese without philosophizing, if only you'd let me. You and I would understand our sentences differently, but the difference wouldn't interfere with our conversation until you start drawing conclusions which follow from your false sentence but not from my homonymous true sentence.[1]

Bargle: Oh, very well. But behold: there are as many holes in my piece of cheese as in yours. Do you agree?

Argle: I'll take your word for it without even counting: there are as many holes in mine as in yours. But what I mean by that is that either both pieces are singly-perforated, or both are doubly-perforated, or both are triply-perforated, and so on.

Bargle: What a lot of different shape-predicates you know! How ever did you find time to learn them all? And what does 'and so on' mean?[2]

Argle: Let me just say that the two pieces are equally-perforated. Now I have used only one two-place predicate.

Bargle: Unless I singly-perforate each of these crackers, how will you say that there are as many holes in my cheese as crackers on my plate? Be so kind as not to invent another predicate on the spot. I am quite prepared to go on until you have told me about all the predicates you have up your sleeve. I have a good imagination, and plenty of time.

Argle: Oh, dear . . . (ponders).

Argle: I was wrong. There *are* holes.

Bargle: You recant?

Argle: No. Holes are material objects.

Bargle: I expected that sooner. You are thinking, doubtless, that every hole is filled with matter: silver amalgam, air, interstellar gas, luminiferous ether or whatever it may be.

Argle: No. Perhaps there are no truly empty holes; but I cannot deny that there might be.

Bargle: How can something utterly devoid of matter be made of matter?

Argle: You're looking for the matter in the wrong place. (I mean to say, that's what you would be doing if there were any such things as places, which there aren't.) The matter isn't inside the hole. It would be absurd to say it was: nobody wants to say that holes are inside themselves. The matter surrounds the hole. The lining of a hole, you agree, is a material object. For every hole there is a hole-lining; for every hole-lining there is a hole. I say the hole-lining *is* the hole.

Bargle: Didn't you say that the hole-lining surrounds the hole? Things don't surround themselves.

Argle: Holes do. In my language, 'surrounds' said of a hole (described as such) means 'is identical with.' 'Surrounds' said of other things means just what you think it means.

Bargle: Doesn't it bother you that your dictionary must have two entries under 'surrounds' where mine has only one?

Argle: A little, but not much. I'm used to putting up with such things.

Bargle: Such *whats*?

Argle: Such dictionary entries. They're made of dried ink, you recall.

Bargle: Oh. I suppose you'll also say that '. . . is in . . .' or '. . . is through . . .' said of a hole means '. . . is part of . . .'.

Argle: Exactly so, Bargle.

Bargle: Then do you still say that 'There are holes in the cheese' contains an unanalyzed shape-predicate synonymous with '. . . is perforated'?

Argle: No; it is an existential quantification, as you think it is. It means that there exist material objects such that they are holes and they are parts of the piece of cheese.

Bargle: But we wouldn't say, would we, that a hole is made out of cheese?

Argle: No; but the fact that we wouldn't say it doesn't mean it isn't true. We wouldn't have occasion to say, unless philosophizing, that these walls are perpendicular to the floor; but they are. Anyhow we *do* say that caves are holes in the ground and that some of them are made out of limestone.

Bargle: Take this paper-towel roller. Spin it on a lathe. The hole-lining spins. Surely you'd never say the hole spins?

Argle: Why not?

Bargle: Even though the hole might continue to be entirely filled with a dowel that didn't spin or move at all?

Argle: What difference does that make?

Bargle: None, really. But now I have you: take a toilet-paper roller, put it inside the paper-towel roller, and spin it the other way. The big hole spins clockwise. The little hole spins counter-clockwise. But the little hole is part of the big hole, so it spins clockwise along with the rest of the big hole. So if holes can spin, as you think, the little hole turns out to be spinning in both directions at once, which is absurd.

Argle: I see why you might think that the little hole is part of the big hole, but you can't expect me to agree. The little hole is inside the big hole, but that's all. Hence I have no reason to say that the little hole is spinning clockwise.

Bargle: Consider a thin-walled hole with a gallon of water inside. The volume of the hole is at least a gallon, whereas the volume of the hole-lining is much less. If the hole is the hole-lining, then whatever was true of one would have to be true of the other. They could not differ in volume.

Argle: For 'hole' read 'bottle;' for 'hole-lining' also read 'bottle.' You have the same paradox. Holes, like bottles, have volume – or, as I'd rather say, are voluminous or equi-voluminous with other things – in two different senses. There's the volume of the hole or bottle itself, and there's the volume of the largest chunk of fluid which could be put inside the hole or bottle without compression. For holes, as for bottles, contextual clues permit us to keep track of which we mean.

Bargle: What is the volume of the hole itself? How much of the cheese do you include as part of one of these holes? And how do you decide? Arbitrarily, that's how. Don't try saying you include as little of the cheese as possible, for however much you include, you could have included less.

Argle: What we call a single hole is really many hole-linings. Some include more of the cheese, some include less. Therefore I need not decide, arbitrarily or otherwise, how much cheese is part of the hole. Many different decisions are equally correct.

Bargle: How can a single hole be identical with many hole-linings that are not identical with one another?

Argle: Really there are many different holes, and each is identical with a different hole-lining. But all these different holes are the same hole.

Bargle: You contradict yourself. Don't you mean to say that they all *surround* the same hole – where by 'surround' I mean 'surround,' not 'be identical with'?

Argle: Not at all. I would contradict myself if I said that two different holes were identical. But I didn't; what I said was that they were the same hole. Two holes are the same hole when they have a common part that is itself a hole.

Bargle: You agreed before that there were as many holes in my cheese as crackers on my plate. Are there still?

Argle: Yes; there are two of each left.

Bargle: Two crackers, to be sure, but how can you say there are two holes?

Argle: Thus: there is a hole, and there is another hole that is not the same hole, and every hole in the cheese is the same hole as one or the other.

Bargle: Be so kind as to say 'co-perforated,' not 'same,' and stop pretending to talk about identity when you are not. I understand you now: co-perforation is supposed to be an equivalence relation among hole-linings, and when you say there are two holes you are trying to say that there are two non-identical co-perforation-classes of hole-linings. Really you identify holes not with hole-linings but with *classes* of hole-linings.

Argle: I would if I could, but I can't. No; holes are hole-linings; but when I speak of them as holes, I find it convenient to use 'same' meaning 'co-perforated' wherever a man of your persuasion would use 'same' meaning 'identical.' You know my reason for this trickery: my sentences about sameness of holes will be true just when you wrongly suppose your like-sounding sentences to be. The same goes for sentences about number of holes, since we both analyze these in terms of sameness.[3]

Bargle: You still haven't told me how you say there are as many holes in my cheese as crackers on my plate, without also saying how many there are.

Argle: Here goes. There exist three things X, Y, and Z. X is part of the sum of the crackers, Y is part of the cheese, and Z is part of Y. Every maximal connected part of Y is a hole, and every hole in the cheese is the same hole as some maximal connected part of Y. X overlaps each of the crackers and Z overlaps each maximal connected part of Y. Everything which is either the intersection of X and a cracker or the intersection of Z and some maximal connected part of Y is the same size as any other such thing. X is the same size as Z.[4] [See editors' note, pp. 27–28, for exegesis of Argle's proposal.]

Bargle: Your devices won't work because co-perforation is not an equivalence relation. *Any* two overlapping parts of my cheese have a common part that is a hole-lining, though in most cases the hole-lining is entirely filled with cheese. To be co-perforated is therefore nothing more than to overlap, and overlapping is no equivalence relation. The result is that although, as you say, you can find two hole-linings in this cheese that are not co-perforated, you can find another one that is co-perforated with both of them.

Argle: If you were right that a hole made of cheese could be entirely filled with the same kind of cheese, you could find far more than two non-co-perforated hole-linings; and there would be no such thing as cheese without holes in it. But you are wrong. A hole is a hole not just by virtue of its own shape but also by virtue of the way it contrasts with the matter inside it and around it. The same is true of other shape-predicates; I wouldn't say that any part of the cheese is a dodecahedron, though I admit that there are parts – parts that do not contrast with their surroundings – that are *shaped like* dodecahedra.

Bargle: Consider the paper-towel roller. How many holes?

Argle: One. You know what I mean: many, but they're all the same.

Bargle: I think you must say there are at least two. The left half and the right half are not the same hole. They have no common part, so no common part that is a hole.

Argle: They're not holes, they're two parts of a hole.

Bargle: Why aren't they holes themselves? They are singly-perforated and they are made of matter unlike the matter inside them. If I cut them apart you'd have to say they were holes?

Argle: Yes.

Bargle: You admit that a hole can be a proper part of a bigger – say, thicker-skinned – hole?

Argle: Yes.

Bargle: You admit that they are shaped like holes?

Argle: Yes, but they aren't holes. I can't say why they aren't. I know which things are holes, but I can't give you a definition. But why should I? You already know what hole-linings are. I say the two halves of the roller are only parts of a hole because I – like you – would say they are only parts of a hole-lining. What isn't a hole-lining isn't a hole.

Bargle: In that case, I admit that co-perforation may be an equivalence relation at least among singly-perforated hole-linings.

Argle: All holes are singly-perforated. A doubly-perforated thing has two holes in it that are not the same hole.

Bargle: Are you sure? Take the paper-towel roller and punch a little hole in its side. Now you have a hole in a hole-lining. You'd have to say you have a hole in a hole. You have a little hole which is part of a big hole; the big hole is not singly-perforated; and the little hole and the big hole are the same hole, since the little hole is a common part of each.

Argle: I think not. You speak of *the* big hole; but what we have are two big holes, not the same, laid end to end. There is also the little hole, not the same as either big hole, which overlaps them both. Of course we sometimes call something a hole, in a derivative sense, if it is a connected sum of holes. Any decent cave consists of many holes that are not the same hole, so I must have been speaking in this derivative sense when I said that caves are holes.

Bargle: What peculiar things you are driven to say when philosophy corrupts your mind! Tell me the truth: would you have dreamt for a moment of saying there were two big holes rather than one if you were not suffering under the influence of a philosophical theory?

Argle: No; I fear I would have remained ignorant.

Bargle: I see that I can never hope to refute you, since I no sooner reduce your position to absurdity than you embrace the absurdity.

Argle: Not absurdity; disagreement with common opinion.

Bargle: Very well. But I, for one, have more trust in common opinions than I do in any philosophical reasoning whatever. In so far as you disagree with them, you must pay a great price in the plausibility of your theories.

Argle: Agreed. We have been measuring that price. I have shown that it is not so great as you thought; I am prepared to pay it. My theories can earn credence by their clarity and economy; and if they disagree a little with common opinion, then common opinion may be corrected even by a philosopher.

Bargle: The price is still too high.

Argle: We agree in principle; we're only haggling.

Bargle: We do. And the same is true of our other debates over ontic parsimony. Indeed, this argument has served us as an illustration – novel, simple, and self-contained – of the nature of our customary disputes.

Argle: And yet the illustration has interest in its own right. Your holes, had I been less successful, would have punctured my nominalistic materialism with the greatest of ease.

Bargle: Rehearsed and refreshed, let us return to – say – the question of classes.[5]

Notes

1 *Cf.* W. V. Quine, "On What There Is," *From a Logical Point of View*, 2nd ed. (Cambridge, Mass: Harvard University Press, 1961), p. 13.

2 *Cf.* Donald Davidson, "Theories of Meaning and Learnable Languages," in Y. Bar-Hillel, *Logic, Methodology and Philosophy of Science, Proceedings of the* 1964 *International Congress* (Amsterdam, 1965), pp. 383–94.

3 *Cf.* Quine's maxim of identification of indiscernibles in "Identity, Ostension, and Hypostasis," *From a Logical Point of View*, p. 71; P.T. Geach, "Identity," *Review of Metaphysics* 21 (1967): 3–12.

4 This translation adapts a device from Nelson Goodman and W. V. Quine, "Steps toward a Constructive Nominalism," *Journal of Symbolic Logic* 12 (1947): 109–10.

5 There would be little truth to the guess that Argle is one of the authors and Bargle is the other. We thank Charles Chastain, who also is neither Argle nor Bargle, for many helpful comments.

Editors' Note: To see how Argle's proposed paraphrase will do its job, consider a simple case in which there are two holes in the cheese and two crackers. (See Diagram below.) X is composed of a bit of each cracker. The size of these two bits is not specified precisely; but the second to the last sentence of the paraphrase requires that the bits from each cracker are the same size – in the case of three-dimensional objects, this presumably means "equal in volume." Each bit from a cracker that goes into X can be thought of as the cracker's "representative" – each cracker gets exactly one, equal in size to the other no matter how large or small the individual crackers may be. Y is composed of two hole-linings from the cheese. The description of Y insures that, for each hole in the piece of cheese, there is exactly one hole-lining that goes into Y. (The thicknesses of the hole-linings are not specified; they might have to be larger or smaller depending upon the sizes of the parts of the crackers that go into X.) The final object, Z, is much like X: it is a whole composed of two bits of the cheese, each bit being a representative of one of the hole-linings. Again, the second to the last clause insures that the representatives are equal in size – no matter how large or small the hole-linings might be. The penultimate clause further requires that the representative bits from the hole-linings are also the same size as the representative bits of the crackers in X. Whatever the size of the representatives of the crackers and of the holes, if the whole composed of the cracker representatives is the same size as the whole composed of the hole-representatives, then, and only then, are there the same number of cracker representatives as hole-representatives. In the case of two crackers and two holes, if the representatives are one cubic millimeter in volume, X and Z will both be two cubic millimeters. If the number of cracker- and hole-representatives is the same, then the number of crackers and holes is the same.

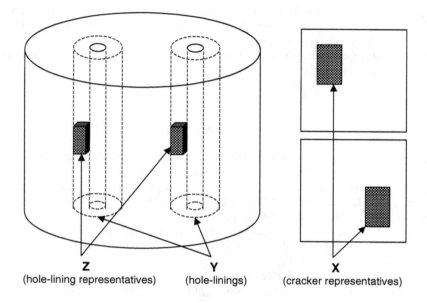

Z	Y	X
(hole-lining representatives)	(hole-linings)	(cracker representatives)

THE CHEESE WITH TWO HOLES AND THE TWO CRACKERS

---

2   On What There Is

W. V. O. Quine

A curious thing about the ontological problem is its simplicity. It can be put in three Anglo-Saxon monosyllables: "What is there?" It can be answered, moreover, in a word – "Everything" – and everyone will accept this answer as true. However, this is merely to say that there is what there is. There remains room for disagreement over cases; and so the issue has stayed alive down the centuries.

Suppose now that two philosophers, McX and I, differ over ontology. Suppose McX maintains there is something which I maintain there is not. McX can, quite consistently with his own point of view, describe our difference of opinion by saying that I refuse to recognize certain entities. I should protest of course that he is wrong in his formulation of our disagreement, for I maintain that there are no entities, of the kind which he alleges, *for* me to recognize; but my finding him wrong in his formulation of our disagreement is unimportant, for I am committed to considering him wrong in his ontology anyway.

When *I* try to formulate our difference of opinion, on the other hand, I seem to be in a predicament. I cannot admit that there are some things which McX countenances and I do not, for in admitting that there are such things I should be contradicting my own rejection of them.

It would appear, if this reasoning were sound, that in any ontological dispute the proponent of the negative side suffers the disadvantage of not being able to admit that his opponent disagrees with him.

This is the old Platonic riddle of non-being. Non-being must in some sense be, otherwise what is it that there is not? This tangled doctrine might be nick-named *Plato's beard*: historically it has proved tough, frequently dulling the edge of Occam's razor.

It is some such line of thought that leads philosophers like McX to impute being where they might otherwise be quite content to recognize that there is nothing. Thus, take Pegasus. If Pegasus *were* not, McX argues, we should not be talking about anything when we use the word; therefore it would be nonsense to say even that Pegasus is not. Thinking to show thus that the denial of Pegasus cannot be coherently maintained, he concludes that Pegasus is.

McX cannot, indeed, quite persuade himself that any region of space-time, near or remote, contains a flying horse of flesh and blood. Pressed for further details on Pegasus, then, he says that Pegasus is an idea in men's minds. Here, however, a confusion begins to be apparent. We may for the sake of argument concede that there is an entity, and even a unique entity (though this is rather implausible), which is the mental Pegasus-idea; but this mental entity is not what people are talking about when they deny Pegasus.

McX never confuses the Parthenon with the Parthenon-idea. The Parthenon is physical; the Parthenon-idea is mental (according any way to McX's version of ideas, and I have no better to offer). The Parthenon is visible; the Parthenon-idea is invisible. We cannot easily imagine two things more unlike, and less liable to confusion, than the Parthenon and the Parthenon-idea. But when we shift from the Parthenon to Pegasus, the confusion sets in – for no other reason than that McX would sooner be deceived by the crudest and most flagrant counterfeit than grant the non-being of Pegasus.

The notion that Pegasus must be, because it would otherwise be nonsense to say even that Pegasus is not, has been seen to lead McX into an elementary con-fusion. Subtler minds, taking the same precept as their starting point, come out with theories of Pegasus which are less patently misguided than McX's, and cor-respondingly more difficult to eradicate. One of these subtler minds is named, let us say, Wyman. Pegasus, Wyman maintains, has his being as an unactualized possible. When we say of Pegasus that there is no such thing, we are saying, more precisely, that Pegasus does not have the special attribute of actuality. Saying that Pegasus is not actual is on a par, logically, with saying that the Parthenon is not red; in either case we are saying something about an entity whose being is unquestioned.

Wyman, by the way, is one of those philosophers who have united in ruining the good old word 'exist'. Despite his espousal of unactualized possibles, he limits the word 'existence' to actuality – thus preserving an illusion of ontological agree-ment between himself and us who repudiate the rest of his bloated universe. We have all been prone to say, in our common-sense usage of 'exist', that Pegasus does not exist, meaning simply that there is no such entity at all. If Pegasus existed he would indeed be in space and time, but only because the word 'Pegasus' has spatio-temporal connotations, and not because 'exists' has spatio-temporal connotations. If spatio-temporal reference is lacking when we affirm the existence of the cube root of 27, this is simply because a cube root is not a spatio-temporal kind of thing, and not because we are being ambiguous in our use of 'exist'. However, Wyman, in an ill-conceived effort to appear agreeable, genially grants us the non-existence of Pegasus and then, contrary to what *we* meant by non-existence of Pegasus, insists that Pegasus *is*. Existence is one thing, he says, and subsistence is another. The only way I know of coping with this obfuscation of issues is to *give* Wyman the word 'exist'. I'll try not to use it again; I still have 'is'. So much for lexicography; let's get back to Wyman's ontology.

Wyman's overpopulated universe is in many ways unlovely. It offends the aesthetic sense of us who have a taste for desert landscapes, but this is not the worst of it. Wyman's slum of possibles is a breeding ground for disorderly elements. Take, for instance, the possible fat man in that doorway; and, again, the possible bald man in that doorway. Are they the same possible man, or two possible men? How do we decide? How many possible men are there in that doorway? Are there more possible thin ones than fat ones? How many of them are alike? Or would their being alike make them one? Are no *two* possible things alike? Is this the same as saying that it is impossible for two things to be alike? Or, finally, is the concept of identity simply inapplicable to unactualized possibles? But what sense can be found in talking of entities which cannot meaningfully be said to be identical with themselves and distinct from one another? These elements are well nigh incorrigible. By a Fregean therapy of individual concepts, some effort might be made at rehabilitation; but I feel we'd do better simply to clear Wyman's slum and be done with it.

Possibility, along with the other modalities of necessity and impossibility and contingency, raises problems upon which I do not mean to imply that we should turn our backs. But we can at least limit modalities to whole statements. We may impose the adverb 'possibly' upon a statement as a whole, and we may well worry about the semantical analysis of such usage; but little real advance in such analysis is to be hoped for in expanding our universe to include so-called *possible entities*. I suspect that the main motive for this expansion is simply the old notion that Pegasus, e.g., must be because it would otherwise be nonsense to say even that he is not.

Still, all the rank luxuriance of Wyman's universe of possibles would seem to come to naught when we make a slight change in the example and speak not of Pegasus but of the round square cupola on Berkeley College. If, unless Pegasus were, it would be nonsense to say that he is not, then by the same token, unless the round square cupola on Berkeley College were, it would be nonsense to say that it is not. But, unlike Pegasus, the round square cupola on Berkeley College cannot be admitted even as an unactualized *possible*. Can we drive Wyman now to admitting also a realm of unactualizable impossibles? If so, a good many embarrassing questions could be asked about them. We might hope even to trap Wyman in contradictions, by getting him to admit that certain of these entities are at once round and square. But the wily Wyman chooses the other horn of the dilemma and concedes that it is nonsense to say that the round square cupola on Berkeley College is not. He says that the phrase 'round square cupola' is meaningless.

Wyman was not the first to embrace this alternative. The doctrine of the meaninglessness of contradictions runs away back. The tradition survives, moreover, in writers such as Wittgenstein who seem to share none of Wyman's motivations. Still I wonder whether the first temptation to such a doctrine may not have been substantially the motivation which we have observed in Wyman. Certainly the doctrine has no intrinsic appeal; and it has led its devotees to such quixotic extremes as that of challenging the method of proof by *reductio ad absurdum* – a challenge in which I seem to detect a quite striking *reductio ad absurdum eius ipsius*.

Moreover, the doctrine of meaninglessness of contradictions has the severe methodological drawback that it makes it impossible, in principle, ever to devise an effective test of what is meaningful and what is not. It would be forever impossible for us to devise systematic ways of deciding whether a string of signs made sense – even to us individually, let alone other people – or not. For, it follows from a discovery in mathematical logic, due to Church, that there can be no generally applicable test of contradictoriness.

I have spoken disparagingly of Plato's beard, and hinted that it is tangled. I have dwelt at length on the inconveniences of putting up with it. It is time to think about taking steps.

Russell, in his theory of so-called singular descriptions, showed clearly how we might meaningfully use seeming names without supposing that the entities allegedly named be. The names to which Russell's theory directly applies are complex descriptive names such as 'the author of *Waverley*', 'the present King of France', 'the round square cupola on Berkeley College'. Russell analyzes such phrases systematically as fragments of the whole sentences in which they occur. The sentence 'The author of *Waverley* was a poet', e.g., is explained as a whole as meaning 'Someone (better: something) wrote *Waverley* and was a poet, and nothing else wrote *Waverley*'. (The point of this added clause is to affirm the uniqueness which is implicit in the word 'the', in '*the* author of *Waverley*'.) The sentence 'The round square cupola on Berkeley College is pink' is explained as 'Something is round and square and is a cupola on Berkeley College and is pink, and nothing else is round and square and a cupola on Berkeley College'.

The virtue of this analysis is that the seeming name, a descriptive phrase, is paraphrased *in context* as a so-called incomplete symbol. No unified expression is offered as an analysis of the descriptive phrase, but the statement as a whole which was the context of that phrase still gets its full quota of meaning – whether true or false.

The unanalyzed statement 'The author of *Waverley* was a poet' contains a part, 'the author of *Waverley*', which is wrongly supposed by McX and Wyman to demand objective reference in order to be meaningful at all. But in Russell's translation, 'Something wrote *Waverley* and was a poet and nothing else wrote *Waverley*', the burden of objective reference which had been put upon the descriptive phrase is now taken over by words of the kind that logicians call bound variables, variables of quantification: namely, words like 'something', 'nothing', 'everything'. These words, far from purporting to be names specifically of the author of *Waverley*, do not purport to be names at all; they refer to entities generally, with a kind of studied ambiguity peculiar to themselves. These quantificational words or bound variables are of course a basic part of language, and their meaningfulness, at least in context, is not to be challenged. But their meaningfulness in no way presupposes there being either the author of *Waverley* or the round square cupola on Berkeley College or any other specifically preassigned objects.

Where descriptions are concerned, there is no longer any difficulty in affirming or denying being. 'There *is* the author of *Waverley*' is explained by Russell as meaning 'Someone (or, more strictly, something) wrote *Waverley* and nothing else wrote *Waverley*'. 'The author of *Waverley* is not' is explained, correspondingly, as the alternation 'Either each thing failed to write *Waverley* or two or more things wrote *Waverley*.' This alternation is false, but meaningful; and it contains no expression purporting to designate the author of *Waverley*. The statement 'The round square cupola on Berkeley College is not' is analyzed in similar fashion. So the old notion that statements of non-being defeat themselves goes by the board. When a statement of being or non-being is analyzed by Russell's theory of descriptions, it ceases to contain any expression which even purports to name the alleged entity whose being is in question, so that the meaningfulness of the statement no longer can be thought to presuppose that there be such an entity.

Now what of 'Pegasus'? This being a word rather than a descriptive phrase, Russell's argument does not immediately apply to it. However, it can easily be made to apply. We have only to rephrase 'Pegasus' as a description, in any way that seems adequately to single out our idea: say 'the winged horse that was captured by Bellerophon'. Substituting such a phrase for 'Pegasus', we can then proceed to analyze the statement 'Pegasus is', or 'Pegasus is not', precisely on the analogy of Russell's analysis of 'The author of *Waverley* is' and 'The author of *Waverley* is not'.

In order thus to subsume a one-word name or alleged name such as 'Pegasus' under Russell's theory of description, we must of course be able first to translate the word into a description. But this is no real restriction. If the notion of Pegasus had been so obscure or so basic a one that no pat translation into a descriptive phrase had offered itself along familiar lines, we could still have availed ourselves of the following artificial and trivial-seeming device: we could have appealed to the *ex hypothesi* unanalyzable, irreducible attribute of *being Pegasus*, adopting, for its expression, the verb 'is-Pegasus', or 'pegasizes'. The noun 'Pegasus' itself could then be treated as derivative, and identified after all with a description: 'the thing that is-Pegasus', 'the thing that pegasizes'.

If the importing of such a predicate as 'pegasizes' seems to commit us to recognizing that there is a corresponding attribute, pegasizing, in Plato's heaven or in the mind of men, well and good. Neither we nor Wyman nor McX have been contending, thus far, about the being or non-being of universals, but rather about that of Pegasus. If in terms of pegasizing we can interpret the noun 'Pegasus' as a description subject to Russell's theory of descriptions, then we have disposed of the old notion that Pegasus cannot be said not to be without presupposing that in some sense Pegasus is.

Our argument is now quite general. McX and Wyman supposed that we could not meaningfully affirm a statement of the form 'So-and-so is not', with a simple or descriptive singular noun in place of 'so-and-so', unless so-and-so be. This supposition is now seen to be quite generally groundless, since the singular noun in question can always be expanded into a singular description, trivially or otherwise, and then analyzed out à la Russell.

We cannot conclude, however, that man is henceforth free of all ontological commitments. We commit ourselves outright to an ontology containing numbers when we say there are prime numbers between 1000 and 1010; we commit ourselves to an ontology containing centaurs when we say there are centaurs; and we commit ourselves to an ontology containing Pegasus when we say Pegasus is. But we do not commit ourselves to an ontology containing Pegasus or the author of *Waverley* or the round square cupola on Berkeley College when we say that Pegasus or the author of *Waverley* or the cupola in question is *not*. We need no longer labor under the delusion that the meaningfulness of a statement containing a singular term presupposes an entity named by the term. A singular term need not name to be significant.

An inkling of this might have dawned on Wyman and McX even without benefit of Russell if they had only noticed – as so few of us do – that there is a gulf between *meaning* and *naming* even in the case of a singular term which *is* genuinely a name of an object. Frege's example will serve: the phrase 'Evening Star' names a certain large physical object of spherical form, which is hurtling through space some scores of millions of miles from here. The phrase 'Morning Star' names the same thing, as was probably first established by some observant Babylonian. But the two phrases cannot be regarded as having the same meaning; otherwise that Babylonian could have dispensed with his observations and contented himself with reflecting on the meanings of his words. The meanings, then, being different from one another, must be other than the named object, which is one and the same in both cases.

Confusion of meaning with naming not only made McX think he could not meaningfully repudiate Pegasus; a continuing confusion of meaning with naming no doubt helped engender his absurd notion that Pegasus is an idea, a mental entity. The structure of his confusion is as follows. He confused the alleged *named object* Pegasus with the *meaning* of the word 'Pegasus', therefore concluding that Pegasus must be in order that the word have meaning. But what sorts of things are meanings? This is a moot point; however, one might quite plausibly explain meanings as ideas in the mind, supposing we can make clear sense in turn of the idea of ideas in the mind. Therefore Pegasus, initially confused with a meaning, ends up as an idea in the mind. It is the more remarkable that Wyman, subject to the same initial motivation as McX, should have avoided this particular blunder and wound up with unactualized possibles instead.

Now let us turn to the ontological problem of universals: the question whether there are such entities as attributes, relations, classes, numbers, functions. McX, characteristically enough, thinks there are. Speaking of attributes, he says: "There are red houses, red roses, red sunsets; this much is pre-philosophical common-sense in which we must all agree. These houses, roses, and sunsets, then, have something in common; and this which they have in common is all I mean by the attribute of redness." For McX, thus, there being attributes is even more obvious and trivial than the obvious and trivial fact of there being red houses, roses, and sunsets. This, I think, is characteristic of metaphysics, or at least of that part of metaphysics called ontology: one who regards a statement on this subject as true at all must regard it as trivially true. One's ontology is basic to the conceptual scheme by which he interprets all experiences, even the most commonplace ones. Judged within some particular conceptual scheme – and how else is judgment possible? – an ontological statement goes without saying, standing in need of no separate justification at all. Ontological statements follow immediately from all manner of casual statements of commonplace fact, just as – from the point of view, anyway, of McX's conceptual scheme – 'There is an attribute' follows from 'There are red houses, red roses, red sunsets.'

Judged in another conceptual scheme, an ontological statement which is axiomatic to McX's mind may, with equal immediacy and triviality, be adjudged false. One may admit that there are red houses, roses, and sunsets, but deny, except as a popular and misleading manner of speaking, that they have anything in common. The words 'houses', 'roses', and 'sunsets' denote each of sundry individual entities which are houses and roses and sunsets, and the word 'red' or 'red object' denotes each of sundry individual entities which are red houses, red roses, red sunsets; but there is not, in addition, any entity whatever, individual or otherwise, which is named by the word 'redness', nor, for that matter, by the word 'househood', 'rosehood', 'sunsethood'. That the houses and roses and sunsets are all of them red may be taken as ultimate and irreducible, and it may be held that McX is no better off, in point of real explanatory power, for all the occult entities which he posits under such names as 'redness'.

One means by which McX might naturally have tried to impose his ontology of universals on us was already removed before we turned to the problem of universals. McX cannot argue that predicates such as 'red' or 'is-red', which we all concur in using, must be regarded as names each of a single universal entity in order that they be meaningful at all. For, we have seen that being a name of something is a much more special feature than being meaningful. He cannot even charge us – at least not by *that* argument – with having posited an attribute of pegasizing by our adoption of the predicate 'pegasizes'.

However, McX hits upon a different stratagem. "Let us grant," he says, "this distinction between meaning and naming of which you make so much. Let us even grant that 'is red', 'pegasizes', etc., are not names of attributes. Still, you admit they have meanings. But these *meanings*, whether they are *named* or not, are still universals, and I venture to say that some of them might even be the very things that I call attributes, or something to much the same purpose in the end."

For McX, this is an unusually penetrating speech; and the only way I know to counter it is by refusing to admit meanings. However, I feel no reluctance toward refusing to admit meanings, for I do not thereby deny that words and statements are meaningful. McX and I may agree to the letter in our classification of linguistic forms into the meaningful and the meaningless, even though McX construes meaningfulness as the *having* (in some sense of 'having') of some abstract entity which he calls a meaning, whereas I do not. I remain free to maintain that the fact that a given linguistic utterance is meaningful (or *significant*, as I prefer to say so as not to invite hypostasis of meanings as entities) is an ultimate and irreducible matter of fact; or, I may undertake to analyze it in terms directly of what people do in the presence of the linguistic utterance in question and other utterances similar to it.

The useful ways in which people ordinarily talk or seem to talk about meanings boil down to two: the *having* of meanings, which is significance, and *sameness* of meaning, or synonymy. What is called *giving* the meaning of an utterance is simply the uttering of a synonym, couched, ordinarily, in clearer language than the original. If we are allergic to meanings as such, we can speak directly of utterances as significant or insignificant, and as synonymous or heteronymous one with another. The problem of explaining these adjectives 'significant' and 'synonymous' with some degree of clarity and rigor – preferably, as I see it, in terms of behavior – is as difficult as it is important. But the explanatory value of special and irreducible intermediary entities called meanings is surely illusory.

Up to now I have argued that we can use singular terms significantly in sentences without presupposing that there be the entities which those terms purport to name. I have argued further that we can use general terms, e.g., predicates, without conceding them to be names of abstract entities. I have argued further that we can view utterances as significant, and as synonymous or heteronymous with one another, without countenancing a realm of entities called meanings. At this point McX begins to wonder whether there is any limit at all to our ontological immunity. Does *nothing* we may say commit us to the assumption of universals or other entities which we may find unwelcome?

I have already suggested a negative answer to this question, in speaking of bound variables, or variables of quantification, in connection with Russell's theory of descriptions. We can very easily involve ourselves in ontological commitments, by saying, e.g., that *there is something* (bound variable) which red houses and sunsets have in common; or that *there is something* which is a prime number between 1000 and 1010. But this is, essentially, the *only* way we can involve ourselves in ontological commitments: by our use of bound variables. The use of alleged names is no criterion, for we can repudiate their namehood at the drop of a hat unless the assumption of a corresponding entity can be spotted in the things we affirm in terms of bound variables. Names are in fact altogether immaterial to the ontological issue, for I have shown, in connection with 'Pegasus' and 'pegasize', that names can be converted to descriptions, and Russell has shown that descriptions can be eliminated. Whatever we say with help of names can be said in a language which shuns names altogether. To be is, purely and simply, to be the value of a variable. In terms of the categories of traditional grammar, this amounts roughly to saying that to be is to be in the range of reference of a pronoun. Pronouns are the basic media of reference; nouns might better have been named pro-pronouns. The variables of quantification, 'something', 'nothing', 'everything', range over our whole ontology, whatever it may be; and we are convicted of a particular ontological presupposition if, and only if, the alleged presuppositum has to be reckoned among the entities over which our variables range in order to render one of our affirmations true.

We may say, e.g., that some dogs are white, and not thereby commit ourselves to recognizing either doghood or whiteness as entities. 'Some dogs are white' says that some things that are dogs are white; and, in order that this statement be true, the things over which the bound variable 'something' ranges must include some white dogs, but need not include doghood or whiteness. On the other hand, when we say that some zoölogical species are cross-fertile, we are committing ourselves to recognizing as entities the several species themselves, abstract though they be. We remain so committed at least until we devise some way of so paraphrasing the statement as to show that the seeming reference to species on the part of our bound variable was an avoidable manner of speaking.

If I have been seeming to minimize the degree to which in our philosophical and unphilosophical discourse we involve ourselves in ontological commitments, let me then emphasize that classical mathematics, as the example of primes between 1000 and 1010 clearly illustrates, is up to its neck in commitments to an ontology of abstract entities. Thus it is that the great mediaeval controversy over universals has flared up anew in the modern philosophy of mathematics. The issue is clearer now than of old, because we now have a more explicit standard whereby to decide what ontology a given theory or form of discourse is committed to: a theory is committed to those and only those entities to which the bound variables of the theory must be capable of referring in order that the affirmations made in the theory be true.

Because this standard of ontological presupposition did not emerge clearly in the philosophical tradition, the modern philosophical mathematicians have not on the whole recognized that they were debating the same old problem of universals in a newly clarified form. But the fundamental cleavages among modern points of view on foundations of mathematics do come down pretty explicitly to disagreements as to the range of entities to which the bound variables should be permitted to refer.

The three main mediaeval points of view regarding universals are designated by historians as *realism*, *conceptualism*, and *nominalism*. Essentially these same three doctrines reappear in twentieth-century surveys of the philosophy of mathematics under the new names *logicism*, *intuitionism*, and *formalism*.

Realism, as the word is used in connection with the mediaeval controversy over universals, is the Platonic doctrine that universals or abstract entities have being independently of the mind; the mind may discover them but cannot create them. *Logicism*, represented by such latter-day Platonists as Frege, Russell, Whitehead, Church, and Carnap, condones the use of bound variables to refer to abstract entities known and unknown, specifiable and unspecifiable, indiscriminately.

Conceptualism holds that there are universals but they are mind-made. *Intuitionism*, espoused in modern times in one form or another by Poincaré, Brouwer, Weyl, and others, countenances the use of bound variables to refer to abstract entities only when those entities are capable of being cooked up individually from ingredients specified in advance. As Fraenkel has put it, logicism holds that classes are discovered while intuitionism holds that they are invented – a fair statement indeed of the old opposition between realism and conceptualism. This opposition is no mere quibble; it makes an essential difference in the amount of classical mathematics to which one is willing to subscribe. Logicists, or realists, are able on their assumptions to get Cantor's ascending orders of infinity; intuitionists are compelled to stop with the lowest order of infinity, and, as an indirect consequence, to abandon even some of the classical laws of real numbers. The modern controversy between logicism and intuitionism arose, in fact, from disagreements over infinity.

Formalism, associated with the name of Hilbert, echoes intuitionism in deploring the logicist's unbridled recourse to universals. But formalism also finds intuitionism unsatisfactory. This could happen for either of two opposite reasons. The formalist might, like the logicist, object to the crippling of classical mathematics; or he might, like the *nominalists* of old, object to admitting abstract entities at all, even in the restrained sense of mind-made entities. The upshot is the same: the formalist keeps classical mathematics as a play of insignificant notations. This play of notations can still be of utility – whatever utility it has already shown itself to have as a crutch for physicists and technologists. But utility need not imply significance, in any literal linguistic sense. Nor need the marked success of mathematicians in spinning out theorems, and in finding objective bases for agreement with one another's results, imply significance. For an adequate basis for agreement among mathematicians can be found simply in the rules which govern the manipulation of the notations – these syntactical rules being, unlike the notations themselves, quite significant and intelligible.*

I have argued that the sort of ontology we adopt can be consequential – notably in connection with mathematics, although this is only an example. Now how are we to adjudicate among rival ontologies? Certainly the answer is not provided by the semantical formula "To be is to be the value of a variable"; this formula serves rather, conversely, in testing the conformity of a given remark or doctrine to a prior ontological standard. We look to bound variables in connection with ontology not in order to know what there is, but in order to know what a given remark or doctrine, ours or someone else's, *says* there is; and this much is quite properly a problem involving language. But what there is is another question.

In debating over what there is, there are still reasons for operating on a semantical plane. One reason is to escape from the predicament noted at the beginning of the paper: the predicament of my not being able to admit that there are things which McX countenances and I do not. So long as I adhere to my ontology, as opposed to McX's, I cannot allow my bound variables to refer to entities which belong to McX's ontology and not to mine. I can, however, consistently describe our disagreement by characterizing the statements which McX affirms. Provided merely that my ontology countenances linguistic forms, or at least concrete inscriptions and utterances, I can talk about McX's sentences.

Another reason for withdrawing to a semantical plane is to find common ground on which to argue. Disagreement in ontology involves basic disagreement in conceptual schemes; yet McX and I, despite these basic disagreements, find that our conceptual schemes converge sufficiently in their intermediate and upper ramifications to enable us to communicate successfully on such topics as politics, weather, and, in particular, language. In so far as our basic controversy over ontology can be translated upward into a semantical controversy about words and what to do with them, the collapse of the controversy into question-begging may be delayed.

It is no wonder, then, that ontological controversy should tend into contro-versy over language. But we must not jump to the conclusion that what there is depends on words. Translatability of a question into semantical terms is no indi-cation that the question is linguistic. To see Naples is to bear a name which, when prefixed to the words 'sees Naples', yields a true sentence; still there is nothing linguistic about seeing Naples.

Our acceptance of an ontology is, I think, similar in principle to our acceptance of a scientific theory, say a system of physics: we adopt, at least insofar as we are reasonable, the simplest conceptual scheme into which the disordered fragments of raw experience can be fitted and arranged. Our ontology is determined once we have fixed upon the over-all conceptual scheme which is to accommodate science in the broadest sense; and the considerations which determine a reason-able construction of any part of that conceptual scheme, e.g. the biological or the physical part, are not different in kind from the considerations which deter-mine a reasonable construction of the whole. To whatever extent the adoption of any system of scientific theory may be said to be a matter of language, the same – but no more – may be said of the adoption of an ontology.

But simplicity, as a guiding principle in constructing conceptual schemes, is not a clear and unambiguous idea; and it is quite capable of presenting a double or multiple standard. Imagine, e.g., that we have devised the most economical set of concepts adequate to the play-by-play reporting of immediate experience. The entities under this scheme – the values of bound variables – are, let us suppose, individual subjective events of sensation or reflection. We should still find, no doubt, that a physicalistic conceptual scheme, purporting to talk about external objects, offers great advantages in simplifying our over-all reports. By bringing together scattered sense events and treating them as perceptions of one object, we reduce the complexity of our stream of experience to a manageable conceptual simplicity. The rule of simplicity is indeed our guiding maxim in assigning sense data to objects: we associate an earlier and a later round sensum with the same so-called penny, or with two different so-called pennies, in obedi-ence to the demands of maximum simplicity in our total world-picture.

Here we have two competing conceptual schemes, a phenomenalistic one and a physicalistic one. Which should prevail? Each has its advantages; each has its special simplicity in its own way. Each, I suggest, deserves to be developed. Each may be said, indeed, to be the more fundamental, though in different senses: the one is epistemologically, the other physically, fundamental.

The physical conceptual scheme simplifies our account of experience because of the way myriad scattered sense events come to be associated with single so-called objects; still there is no likelihood that each sentence about physical objects can actually be translated, however deviously and complexly, into the phenome-nalistic language. Physical objects are postulated entities which round out and simplify our account of the flux of experience, just as the introduction of irrational numbers simplifies laws of arithmetic. From the point of view of the conceptual scheme of the elementary arithmetic of rational numbers alone, the broader arithmetic of rational and irrational numbers would have the status of a convenient myth, simpler than the literal truth (namely the arithmetic of rationals) and yet containing that literal truth as a scattered part. Similarly, from a phenomenalistic point of view, the conceptual scheme of physical objects is a convenient myth, simpler than the literal truth and yet containing that literal truth as a scattered part.

Now what of classes or attributes of physical objects, in turn? A platonistic ontology of this sort is, from the point of view of a strictly physicalistic conceptual scheme, as much of a myth as that physicalistic conceptual scheme itself was for phenomenalism. This higher myth is a good and useful one, in turn, in so far as it simplifies our account of physics. Since mathematics is an integral part of this higher myth, the utility of this myth for physical science is evident enough. In speaking of it nevertheless as a myth, I echo that philosophy of mathematics to which I alluded earlier under the name of formalism. But my present suggestion is that an attitude of formalism may with equal justice be adopted toward the physical conceptual scheme, in turn, by the pure aesthete or phenomenalist.

The analogy between the myth of mathematics and the myth of physics is, in some additional and perhaps fortuitous ways, strikingly close. Consider, for example, the crisis which was precipitated in the foundations of mathematics, at the turn of the century, by the discovery of Russell's paradox and other antinomies of set theory. These contradictions had to be obviated by unintuitive, *ad hoc* devices; our mathematical myth-making became deliberate and evident to all. But what of physics? An antinomy arose between the undular and the corpuscular accounts of light; and if this was not as out-and-out a contradiction as Russell's paradox, I suspect that the reason is merely that physics is not as out-and-out as mathematics. Again, the second great modern crisis in the foundations of mathematics – precipitated in 1931 by Gödel's proof that there are bound to be undecidable statements in arithmetic – has its companion-piece in physics in Heisenberg's indeterminacy principle.

In earlier pages I undertook to show that some common arguments in favor of certain ontologies are fallacious. Further, I advanced an explicit standard whereby to decide what the ontological commitments of a theory are. But the question what ontology actually to adopt still stands open, and the obvious counsel is tolerance and an experimental spirit. Let us by all means see how much of the physicalistic conceptual scheme can be reduced to a phenomenalistic one; still physics also naturally demands pursuing, irreducible *in toto* though it be. Let us see how, or to what degree, natural science may be rendered independent of platonistic mathematics; but let us also pursue mathematics and delve into its platonistic foundations.

From among the various conceptual schemes best suited to these various pursuits, one – the phenomenalistic – claims epistemological priority. Viewed from within the phenomenalistic conceptual scheme, the ontologies of physical objects and mathematical objects are myths. The quality of myth, however, is relative; relative, in this case, to the epistemological point of view. This point of view is one among various, corresponding to one among our various interests and purposes.

Note

*See Goodman and Quine. "Steps toward a constructive nominalism," *Journal of Symbolic Logic*, vol. 12 (1947), pp. 97–122.

3 Beyond Being and Nonbeing

Roderick M. Chisholm

" . . . das Universum in der Gesamtheit des Wirklichen noch lange nicht erschöpft ist."

Meinong

Meinong wrote: "There are objects of which it is true that there are no such objects."[1] But he was well aware that this statement of his doctrine of *Außersein* was needlessly paradoxical. Other statements were: "The non-real" is not "a mere nothing" and "The object as such . . . stands 'beyond being and non-being'."[2] Perhaps the clearest statement was provided by Meinong's follower, Ernst Mally: "*Sosein is independent of Sein*."[3] We could paraphrase Mally's statement by saying: "An object may have a set of characteristics whether or not it exists and whether or not it has any other kind of being."

It is commonly supposed that this doctrine of *Außersein* is absurd and that whatever grounds Meinong may have had for affirming it were demolished by Russell's theory of descriptions. I believe, however, that this supposition is false. I shall attempt here to set forth the doctrine in its most extreme form and I shall then consider what may be said in its favour.

I.

The fundamental theses of Meinong's theory of objects are (1) that there are objects which do not exist and (2) that objects which are such that there are *no* such objects are nonetheless constituted in some way or other and thus may be made the subject of true predication. The second of these two theses is the doctrine of *Außersein*. The first thesis, as Meinong says, is familiar to traditional metaphysics. But traditional metaphysics, he adds, has had "a prejudice in favor of the actual."[4] Though it has had a proper concern for "ideal objects," those things that merely subsist (*bestehen*) and do not exist, it has neglected those things that have no being at all. Hence the need for a more encompassing theory of objects.

Among the characteristic tenets of the theory of objects are the following.

Of objects, some exist and others do not exist. Thus horses are included among objects that exist, and unicorns and golden mountains are included among objects that do not exist.

Of objects that do not exist, some may yet be said to be, or to subsist, and others may not be said to be at all.

Thus if existence is thought of as implying a spatio-temporal locus, then there are certain ideal objects that do not exist. Among these are properties or attributes and the objects of mathematics, as well as states of affairs (what Meinong calls "*Objektive*"). Since there are horses, for example, there is also the being of horses, the being of the being of horses, the nonbeing of the nonbeing of horses, and the being of the nonbeing of the nonbeing of horses. And since there are no unicorns, there is also the nonbeing of unicorns, the being of the nonbeing of unicorns, the nonbeing of the being of unicorns, and the nonbeing of the non- being of unicorns.[5]

But, though every object may correctly be said to be something or other, it is not the case that every object may correctly be said to be.[6] Unicorns, golden mountains, and round squares may not be said to be at all. Everything, however, *is* an object, whether or not it exists or has any other kind of being, and indeed whether or not it is even thinkable. (Whatever is unthinkable, after all, at least has the property of *being* unthinkable.) And every object, clearly, has the charac- teristics it does have whether or not it has any kind of being. This last is the proposition Mally expressed by saying that the *Sosein* of an object is independent of its *Sein*.

The theory of *Außersein* therefore, should be distinguished both from Pla- tonism, as this term is currently interpreted, and from the reism, or concretism, of Brentano and Kotarbinski. Thus the Platonist might be said to reason as follows: "(P) Certain objects that do not exist have certain properties; but (Q) an object has properties if and only if it is real; hence (R) there are real objects that do not exist." The reist, on the other hand, reasons from not-R and Q to not-P; that is to say, he takes as his premises Plato's second premise and the contradictory of Plato's conclusion and then derives the contradictory of Plato's first premise. But Meinong, like Plato and unlike the reist, accepts P as well as R; unlike both Plato and the reist, he rejects Q; and then *he* derives a conclusion that is unacceptable both to the Platonist and to the reist – namely, "(S) The totality of objects extends far beyond the confines of what is merely real."[7]

Once this conclusion is accepted, a number of interesting distinctions may be made. These would seem to be peculiar to Meinong's theory of objects.

Thus objects may be subdivided into those which are possible and those which are impossible. (We should note, incidentally, that to say of an object that it is only a possible object is *not* to say of it that it is only possibly an object. For possible objects, as well as impossible objects, *are* objects.) Possible objects, unlike impossible objects, have noncontradictory *Soseins*. Golden mountains, for example, although they have no kind of being, may be possible objects; for the *Sosein* of a golden mountain need not preclude its *Sein*. But some golden moun- tains are impossible objects – for example, those that are both golden and non-golden, and those that are both round and square. An impossible object is thus an object with a contradictory *Sosein* – a *Sosein* that precludes its object's *Sein*.[8]

Soseins, too, are objects and therefore every *Sosein* has a *Sosein*. An object which is not itself a *Sosein* is an impossible object if it *has* a contradictory *Sosein*. May a *Sosein*, too, be an impossible object? Mally answers this question in a remarkable paragraph which may be paraphrased as follows.

"Like any other object a *Sosein* is an impossible object if *it* has a *Sosein* which precludes its *Sein*; that is to say, a *Sosein* is an impossible object if its own *Sosein* is contradictory. A *Sosein* would have a contradictory *Sosein* if it had the property of being the *Sosein* of an object which does *not* have that *Sosein*. The circularity of a possible square is thus an impossible *Sosein*. For the circularity of a possible square has itself a contradictory *Sosein*: that of being the circularity of something that isn't circular. But an impossible *Sosein* is not the same as a contradictory *Sosein*. The circularity of a possible square must be distinguished from the circularity (and squareness) of a *round* square; the former is an impossible *Sosein*, but the latter is not. The circularity of a round square is a contradictory *Sosein* but *not* an impossible *Sosein*. What is impossible is that there be an object that is both round and square. But it is *not* impossible that a round square be both round and square. Indeed, it is *necessary* that a round square be both round and square."[9]

Objects may also be classified as being either complete or incomplete. Where an impossible object is an object having a *Sosein* that violates the law of contradiction, an *incomplete object* is one having a *Sosein* that violates the law of excluded middle. Of the round squares that were being contemplated just now, it may be neither true nor false to say of the one that was contemplated by you that it is larger than the one that was contemplated by me.[10]

Of all objects, the most poorly endowed would seem to be what Meinong calls *defective objects*. Indeed, they are so poorly endowed that Meinong seems to be uncertain as to whether they are objects at all. If I wish that your wish will come true, then the object of my wish is whatever it is that you happen to wish. And if, unknown to me, *your* wish is that my wish will come true, then the object of your wish is what it is that I happen to wish. But this object, in the circumstances imagined, would seem to have very little *Sosein* beyond that of being our mutual object. Meinong felt, incidentally, that this concept of a defective object might be used to throw light upon the logical paradoxes.[11]

It is a mistake, then, to express the doctrine of *Außersein* by saying that, according to Meinong, such objects as golden mountains and round squares have a kind of being other than existence or subsistence. Meinong's point is that they have no kind of being at all. They are "homeless objects," not even to be found in Plato's heaven.[12]

Why assume, then, that an object may have a *Sosein* and yet no *Sein* – that an object may have a set of characteristics and yet no kind of being at all?

II.

The prima facie case for this doctrine of *Außersein* lies in the fact that there are many truths which *seem*, at least, to pertain to objects which are such that there are no such objects. It is reasonable to assume that this prima facie case would be weakened if we could show, with respect to these truths, that they need not be construed as pertaining to these homeless objects. It is also reasonable to assume, I think, that Meinong's case will be strengthened to the extent that we find ourselves *unable* to show, with respect to any one of these truths, that it need not be construed as pertaining to such objects.

There are at least five groups of such truths that have been singled out in recent literature. (The groups are not mutually exclusive and they may not be exhaustive.) For there would seem to be at least five different sorts of things that we may say of an object that does not exist or have any other kind of being: (1) we may say that the object does not exist; (2) we may say what the object is without implying either that it exists or that it does not exist; (3) we may note what expressions in our language are used to refer to that object; (4) we may say that the object is involved in myth or fiction and that, as so involved, it is richly endowed with attributes; or (5) we may say that someone's intentional attitude is directed upon that object.

Meinong's best case, I think, lies with the final group – with those truths that seem to pertain to the nonexistent objects of our intentional attitudes. But let us consider them all in as favourable a light as we can.

(1) Examples of the first group are "Things that are both round and square do not exist" and "Unicorns do not exist." Can we paraphrase these in such a way that they may be seen to involve no reference to nonexistent objects? The first example presents fewer problems than the second, but it is doubtful that we can paraphrase it in a way that would satisfy Meinong.

The obvious paraphrase of "Things that are both round and square do not exist" would be "Everything that does exist is such that it is not both round and square." But, Meinong would say, where the subject-term of the paraphrase may be taken to refer to any piece of reality one chooses, the subject-term of the original is intended to refer to "what does not exist and is therefore not a piece of reality at all."[13]

The obvious paraphrase of "Unicorns do not exist" would be "Everything that does exist is such that it is not a unicorn." But this, Meinong could say, leaves us with a reference to nonexistent objects. To say of a thing that it is not a unicorn is to say of it that it is not identical with any unicorn; and to say of a thing that it is not identical with any unicorn is to relate it to objects that do not exist.

Hence we may wish to replace "a unicorn," in "Everything that does exist is such that it is not a unicorn," by certain predicates. But what predicates, and how do we decide? Let us suppose (to oversimplify somewhat) that we are satisfied with "single-horned" and "equine." Then we paraphrase "Unicorns do not exist" as "Everything that does exist is such that it is not both single-horned and equine." Meinong may now repeat the objection he had made to our attempted paraphrase of the first example above. And he may add still another.

How did we happen to choose the particular predicates "single-horned" and "equine"? We chose them, Meinong would say, because we know, *a priori*, that all and only unicorns are both single-horned and equine. And this *a priori* statement – "All and only unicorns are both equine and single-horned" – is one in which, once again, we have a subject-term that refers, or purports to refer, to non-existent objects. This statement, however, belongs to the second group and not to the first.

(2) Meinong writes: "If one judges that a perpetual motion machine does not exist, then it is clear that the object whose existence he is denying must have certain properties and indeed certain characteristic properties. Otherwise the judgement that the object does not exist would have neither sense nor justification."[14] Applying a similar observation to our previous example, we may say, of the judgement that unicorns do not exist, that it presupposes that unicorns are both single-horned and equine. "Unicorns are both single-horned and equine" may also be expressed as "Every existing thing is such that if it were a unicorn then it would be both equine and single-horned." But the presence of "a unicorn" in the latter sentence, as we have noted, enables Meinong to say that the sentence does tell us something about unicorns – namely, that if any existing thing were identical with any one of them, then that thing would be both equine and single-horned.[15]

These truths about nonexistent objects which are presupposed, whenever we say of anything that it does not exist, are *a priori*, according to Meinong. Much of what we know about objects, he says, is thus "*daseinsfrei*."[16]

There are some *a priori* statements, according to Meinong, in which non-existent objects are singled out by means of definite descriptions. "Not only is the much heralded gold mountain made of gold, but the round square is as surely round as it is square."[17] What are we to say of "The golden mountain is golden"? According to Russell's theory of descriptions, some sentences of the form "The thing which is F is G" may be paraphrased into sentences of the following form: "There exists an x such that x is F and x is G, and for every (existing) y, if y is F then y is identical with x." Hence if we paraphrase "The golden mountain is golden" in this way, we will have: "There exists an x such that x is both golden and a mountain, and x is golden, and, for every (existing) y, if y is both golden and a mountain then y is identical with x." The resulting sentence would seem to refer only to objects that do exist. But is it an adequate paraphrase?

"The golden mountain is golden," according to Meinong, is *true*. But Russell's paraphrase implies "There exists an x such that x is both golden and a mountain" and is therefore *false*. How can a false statement be an adequate paraphrase of a true one?

Russell, of course, would say that Meinong is mistaken in insisting that "The golden mountain is golden" is true. But how are we to decide who is right, without begging the basic question that is involved?

(3) Semantical statements may seem to provide another type of reference to objects that do not exist or to objects such that there are no such objects. For example, "The word '*Einhorn*' in German designates unicorns"; or "The word '*Einhorn*' in German purports to designate unicorns"; or "The word '*Einhorn*' is used in German ostensibly to designate unicorns". And analogously for the word "unicorn" and its use in English. But Meinong would say – quite correctly, it seems to me – that semantical statements are really a subclass of intentional statements, statements about psychological attitudes and their objects, and hence that they belong to our fifth group below. To say that "*Einhorn*" is used to des-

ignate unicorns, according to Meinong, is to say that "*Einhorn*" is used to express those thoughts and other intentional attitudes that take unicorns as their object.[18]

(4) Statements about objects of fiction and mythology are sometimes taken as paradigm cases of statements about nonexistent objects. Examples are "Sam Weller was Mr. Pickwick's servant" and "Sam Weller was a fictitious character who didn't really exist." But if I am not mistaken, these belong with our intentional statements, below. Thus the first example, as it would ordinarily be intended, pertains to one of the objects of a certain story (if we take "story" in the widest sense of the word). But to say of a thing that it is an object of a certain story is to say either that someone has told a story about that thing or that someone has thought of a story about that thing. And to say that someone has told a story, or that someone has thought of a story, is to make an intentional statement. When we say "Sam Weller was a fictitious character who didn't really exist," we are not only making an intentional statement, about an object of someone's story, but we are also making a statement that belongs to our first group above – a statement saying that the object does not exist. Statements about the object of mythology are analogous, except that it may be necessary to add, again intentionally, that the story in question is one that someone believes.

(5) Meinong's best case, then, would seem to lie with those true *intentional* statements that seem to pertain to objects that do not exist. I shall distinguish four types of such statements.

The first type is exemplified by

(a)   John fears a ghost.

Here we seem to have a straightforward affirmation of a relation between John and a nonexistent object. It is of the essence of an intentional attitude, according to Meinong, that it may thus "have" an object "even though the object does not exist."[19] Can we paraphrase our statement (a) in such a way that the result can be seen to involve no such apparent reference to a nonexistent object? So far as I have been able to see, we cannot. (It is true, of course, that philosophers often invent new terms and then profess to be able to express what is intended by such statements as "John fears a ghost" in their own technical vocabularies. But when they try to convey to us what their technical terms are supposed to mean, then they, too, refer to nonexistent objects such as unicorns.)

It is sometimes said that Meinong did not properly understand the use of words in intentional contexts – or, in the terms of our example, that he did not properly understand the use of the expression "a ghost" in such a sentence as "John fears a ghost." He mistakenly supposed, it is suggested, that the word "ghost" has a *referential* use in "John fears a ghost." But just what was the mistake that Meinong made? He did not make the mistake of supposing that the word "ghost" in "John fears a ghost" is used to refer to something that exists or to something that is real. Is it that the word has a certain nonreferential use in such sentences and that Meinong was not aware of this use? But what *is* that nonreferential use – other than that of being used to tell us that John fears a ghost? I know of four positive suggestions, but they all seem to leave Meinong untouched. Thus it has been said (i) that the word "ghost," in "John fears a ghost," is used, not to describe the object of John's fears, but only to contribute to the description of John himself. This was essentially Brentano's suggestion.[20] But just *how* does "ghost" here contribute to the description of John? It isn't being used to tell us that *John* is a ghost, or that John's *thought* is a ghost, for these things are false, but "John fears a ghost," we may suppose, is true. Surely the only way in which the word "ghost" here contributes to the description of John is by telling us *what* the object is that he fears. It has also been suggested (ii) that the word "ghost," in "John fears a ghost," functions only as part of the longer expression "fears a ghost" and that its use in such contexts has no connection at all with the use it has in such sentences as "There is a ghost." (Compare the use of "unicorn" in "The Emperor decorated his tunic ornately.") That this suggestion is false, however, may be seen by noting that "John fears a ghost" and "John's fears are directed only upon things that really exist" together imply "There is a ghost." It has also been suggested (iii) that the word "ghost," in "John fears a ghost," is used to refer to what in other uses would constitute the sense or connotation of "ghost."[21] In this case, "John fears a ghost" would be construed as telling us that there is a certain relation holding between John and a certain set of attributes or properties. But what attributes or properties, and what relation? John himself may remind us at this point that what he fears is a certain *concretum* and not a set of attributes or properties. It has even been suggested (iv) that the word "ghost," in "John fears a ghost," is being used, in "the material mode," to refer to itself.[22] But John, of course, may not fear the *word* "ghost." What, then, would "John fears a ghost" be used to tell us about John and the word "ghost"?

The second type of intentional statement is exemplified by

(b)   The mountain I am thinking of is golden.

To supply a context for such a statement, we imagine a game in which the participants are told to contemplate a mountain, such as might be found in Atlantis, and are then asked to describe the mountain they have contemplated. Meinong's "The golden mountain is golden," of our second group above, may well leave us speechless, but surely "The mountain I am thinking of is golden" may express a proposition that is true.

Russell's theory of descriptions does not provide us with a way of paraphrasing the statement, for, once again, Russell's procedure would provide us with a statement that is *false* ("There exists an x such that x is a mountain I am thinking of and x is golden, and, for every y, if y is a mountain I am thinking of, then y is identical with x").[23]

The participants in the game we have imagined may well compare mountains: "The mountain you are thinking of differs in interesting respects from the mountain I am thinking of." May we also say that the nonexistent object of one man's intentional attitude is *identical with* the nonexistent object of another man's intentional attitude? I think that we may often assume that this is the case. Such an identity statement provides us with our third example of a Meinongian intentional statement. Thus we may be agnostic and yet affirm

(c)   All Muslims worship the same God.

But this example, I think, is more problematic than the others. If the statement in question were true, we could say, of any two Muslims, that the God that is worshipped by the one is identical with the God that is worshipped by the other. But can we really say this if, as we are also inclined to say, "the God that is worshipped by Muslims does not exist?" Shouldn't we say, at most, that for any two Muslims, x and y, the God that x worships is *very much like* the God that y worships.[24] (And instead of saying "The God that is worshipped by Muslims does not exist," we might express ourselves more accurately by saying "Every Muslim is such that the God that he worships does not exist.") But for Meinong's purpose, of course, it is enough to say that one nonexistent object is "very much like" another.

If we can never be sure that the nonexistent object upon which one man's intentional attitude is directed is identical with the nonexistent object upon which another man's intentional attitude is directed, we can be sure, on occasion, that the nonexistent object upon which one of a certain man's intentional attitudes is directed is identical with a nonexistent object upon which another one of that same man's intentional attitudes is directed. Thus we may say of an obsessed believer:

(d)   The thing he fears the most is the same as the thing he loves the most. Any adequate theory of the emotions would seem to imply that a man may have at any particular time a great variety of attitudes and feelings all directed upon a single object – even though that object does not exist.[25]

The latter example reminds us of what Meinong pointed out in a somewhat different connection – "we can also count what does not exist."[26] For a man may be able to say truly "I fear exactly three people" where all three people are objects that do not exist.

Such intentional statements, then, are what provide the best possible case for Meinong's doctrine of *Außersein*. I think it must be conceded to Meinong that there is no way of paraphrasing any of them which is such that we know both (i) that it is adequate to the sentence it is intended to paraphrase and (ii) that it contains no terms ostensibly referring to objects that do not exist. Doubtless many philosophers are prejudiced against Meinong's doctrine because of the fact that Russell's theory of descriptions, as well as the theory of quantification in the way in which it is interpreted in *Principia Mathematica*, is not adequate to the statements with which Meinong is concerned. But this fact, Meinong could say, does not mean that the statements in question are suspect. It means only that such logic, as it is generally interpreted, is not adequate to intentional phenomena.

Notes

I wish to express my indebtedness to the late Dr. Rudolf Kindinger. Certain portions of this paper are adapted from my "Jenseits von Sein und Nichtsein," in *Dichtung und Deutung: Gedächtnisschrift für Hans M. Wolff*, edited by Karl S. Guthke, Bern-Munich: Francke Verlag 1961.

1   A. Meinong, "Über Gegenstandstheorie," *Gesammelte Abhandlungen*, Leipzig: Johann Ambrosius Barth 1929, *Meinong Gesamtausgabe*, Graz: Akademische Druck-

und Verlagsanstalt 1971, Vol. II, p. 490. This work first appeared in 1904, in the collection *Untersuchungen zur Gegenstandstheorie und Psychologie*, Leipzig: Johann Ambrosius Barth, edited by Meinong. It is translated as "The Theory of Objects," in *Realism and the Background of Phenomenology*, Glencoe, Ill., The Free Press 1960, edited by Roderick M. Chisholm; the quotation above appears on page 83.

2   *Gesammelte Abhandlungen*, Vol. II, pp. 486, 494; English translation in *Realism and the Background of Phenomenology*, pp. 79, 86.

3   "Untersuchungen zur Gegenstandstheorie des Messens," in *Untersuchungen zur Gegenstandstheorie und Psychologie*, pp. 51–120; the quotation may be found on page 127.

4   *Gesammelte Abhandlungen*, Vol. II, p. 485; English translation, p. 78.

5   See *Gesammelte Abhandlungen*, Vol. II, pp. 486–8; English translation, pp. 79–80. The most complete statement of Meinong's theory of states of affairs, or *Objektive*, may be found in Chapter III ("Das Objektiv") of *Über Annahmen*, Second Edition, Leipzig: Johann Ambrosius Barth 1910.

6   "Jeder Gegenstand ist *etwas*, aber nicht jedes Etwas *ist*." Mally, op. cit., p. 126.

7   Compare the quotation at the head of this article; the quotation is from Meinong's posthumous *Zur Grundlegung der allgemeinen Werttheorie*, Graz: Leuschner & Lubensky 1923, edited by Ernst Mally, p. 158; Meinong Gesamtausgabe, Graz: Akademische Druck- u. Verlagsanstalt 1968, Vol. III, p. 638.

8   Once we grasp the nature of an impossible object, according to Meinong, we become aware of "the necessity of its nonbeing." Meinong does not use the expression "necessary object," but he says, with respect to abstract objects, that once we grasp *their* nature, we become aware of "the necessity of their being." See *Über die Stellung der Gegenstandstheorie im System der Wissenschaften*, Leipzig: R. Voitländer Verlag, 1970, p. 76.

9   Paraphrased from Ernst Mally, *op. cit.*, pp. 128–9. I have translated *"Viereck"* as "square", have added italics, and have written "possible square" in two places where Mally wrote only *"Viereck."*

10   On incomplete objects, see Meinong's *Über Möglichkeit und Wahrscheinlichkeit*, Leipzig: Johann Ambrosius Barth 1915, pp. 179–80; also *Über die Stellung der Gegenstandstheorie im System der Wissenschaften*, pp. 118–23.

11   Meinong discusses defective objects, in *Über emotionale Präsentation*, Vienna: Alfred Hölder, 1917, pp. 10–26; *Meinong Gesamtausgabe*, Graz: Akademische Druck- u. Verlagsanstalt 1968, Vol. III, pp. 294–310.

12   See *Über die Stellung der Gegenstandstheorie im System der Wissenschaften*, Section One ("Heimatlose Gegenstände"), p. 8 ff. In the *Introduction to Mathematical Philosophy*, London: George Allen & Unwin, Ltd. 1919, Russell said that, according to Meinong, such objects as the golden mountain and the round square "must have some kind of logical being" (p. 169). But in "On Denoting" and in his earlier writings on Meinong, he does not make this mistake.

13   *Über die Stellung der Gegenstandstheorie im System der Wissenschaften*, p. 38. Meinong's remarks were directed toward the distinction between "Ghosts do not exist (*Gespenster existieren nicht*)" and "No real thing is ghostly (*Kein Wirkliches ist Gespenst*)." Compare Richard L. Cartwright, "Negative Existentials," *Journal of Philosophy*, Vol. LVII (1960), pp. 629–39.

14   *Über Annahmen*, p. 79.

15   By confusing use and mention, one may try to render "Unicorns are both single-horned and equine" into a statement which mentions only words. (Such a statement as "The word 'unicorn' refers to things that are both single-horned and equine" belongs to our third group, below.)

16 A considerable part of Meinong's *Über die Stellung der Gegenstandstheorie im System der Wissenschaften* is devoted to "*Daseinsfreiheit*" and "*Apriorität*."

17 English translation of "The Theory of Objects," page 82; *Gesammelte Abhandlungen*, Vol. II, p. 490. Russell said that if "The round square is round" is true, then "The existent round square is existent" is also true; and the latter statement, he pointed out, implies that there is a round square; see his review of *Untersuchungen zur Gegenstandstheorie und Psychologie*, *Mind*, Vol. XIV (1905), pp. 530–38, esp. p. 533. Meinong replied that "existent" is not a predicate, not a "*Soseinsbestimmung*," and hence he should have said that "The existent round square is existent" is false. Unfortunately, however, he attempted to draw a distinction between "is existent" and "exists" and then said that although the existent round square is existent it does not exist. See *Über die Stellung der Gegenstandstheorie im System der Wissenschaften*, pp. 16–19. Reviewing the latter work, Russell replied: "I must confess that I see no difference between existing and being existent; and beyond this I have no more to say"; *Mind*, Vol. XVI (1907), pp. 436–39, esp. p. 439. Meinong also had difficulties with "The possible round square is possible"; see *Über Möglichkeit und Wahrscheinlichkeit*, pp. 277–89. What he should have said, I think, is that "possible" is not a predicate, not a "*Soseinsbestimmung*," and hence that "The possible round square is possible" is false.

18 See *Über Annahmen*, Second Edition, p. 26.

19 See *Gesammelte Abhandlungen*, Vol. II, p. 383.

20 See Franz Brentano, *The True and the Evident*, London: Routledge Kegan Paul, 1966, English edition edited by Roderick M. Chisholm, pp. 68–9.

21 This interpretation may be suggested by Frege's "Über Sinn und Bedeutung," *Zeitschrift für Philosophie und philosophische Kritik*, Vol. C (1892), pp. 25–50; translated as "On Sense and Nomination," in *Readings in Philosophical Analysis*, New York: Appleton-Century-Crofts, Inc. 1949, edited by Herbert Feigl and Wilfrid Sellars, pp. 85–102.

22 Carnap once suggested that "Charles thinks (asserts, believes, wonders about) A," where "A" is thought of as being the abbreviation of some sentence, may be translated as "Charles thinks 'A'"; *The Logical Syntax of Language*, New York: Harcourt, Brace and Company 1937, p. 248.

23 In "On Denoting" Russell said that "the chief objection" to Meinong's nonexistent objects "is that such objects, admittedly, are apt to infringe the law of contradiction"; see Bertrand Russell, *Logic and Knowledge*, London: George Allen and Unwin 1956, p. 45. Thus the round square that I am thinking of may be an object that is both round and nonround. Meinong's reply was that the law of contradiction (in the form, "For any attribute F, there is nothing that exemplifies F and also does not exemplify F") applies only to what is real or possible; one could hardly expect it to apply to impossible objects such as the round square. See *Über die Stellung der Gegenstandstheorie im System der Wissenschaften*, p. 16. One may also argue that certain possible objects would seem to infringe upon other logical laws. Suppose Jones, who mistakenly believes that F.D.R. was assassinated, tells us that the man he is now thinking about is the assassin of F.D.R.; from Jones' true statement it follows that the man he is thinking about murdered F.D.R.; but for any x and y, if x murdered y, then y was murdered by x; hence F.D.R. *was* murdered – and by a nonexistent object! See James Mish'alani, "Thought and Object," *The Philosophical Review*, Vol. LXXI (1962), pp. 185–201. Meinong's reply could be: The statement "For any x and y, if x murdered y, then y was murdered by x" is true only if our variables range over objects that exist; and, more generally, from the fact that it is a part of the *Sosein* of a nonexistent object x that x stands in a certain relation R to

an existent object y, it does not follow that it is a part of the *Sosein* of y either that y is related by the converse of R to x or that x is related by R to y.

24   P. T. Geach cites this example: "Hob thinks a witch has blighted Bob's mare, and Nob wonders whether she (the same witch) killed Cob's sow"; in "Intentional Identity," *Journal of Philosophy*, Vol. LXIV (1967), pp. 627–32. There is a certain ambiguity in the example, for it may be taken to imply either that the object of Hob's thought, is identical with the object of Nob's wondering or only that Nob *thinks* that it is. Taking it in its first sense, how could we ever find out that it is true? Hob may assure us that he thinks there is one and only one witch who blighted Bob's mare and that he also thinks that that witch is F, G, H, and . . . (where 'F', 'G', and 'H' may be thought of as abbreviating certain predicates); and Nob may assure us that he, too, thinks there is one and only one witch who blighted Bob's mare, that that witch is F, G, H, and . . . , and also, perhaps, that he, Nob, thinks that that witch is the same as the one that Hob believes to have blighted Bob's mare. But our statement of these facts does not entail that the object of Hob's thought is identical with the object of Nob's wondering. And, given that there are no witches, it is difficult to think of anything we could learn from Hob and Nob that would entail it.

25   Thus Meinong's theory of value is based upon this assumption; see *Zur Grundlegung der allgemeinen Werttheorie*, Part II ("*Die Werterlebnisse*").

26   "The Theory of Objects," English translation, p. 79; *Gesammelte Abhandlungen*, Vol. II, p. 487.

B What is the Relationship between an Individual and its Characteristics?

Introduction

The interrelated questions addressed in these readings include: Do the characteristics displayed by individuals have a kind of independent existence? Could two individuals have all the same characteristics? Do individuals consist of nothing but characteristics?

The first question concerns the status of characteristics or properties, attributes that can be shared by any number of individuals. When someone says that two things are exactly similar with respect to shape, this might be taken to imply that there is something – namely, a certain shape – which they have in common. Does this require that we believe in shapes in addition to the things that have shapes? If so, are these extra things in space and time, located right where the objects that have them are located? Or are they, strictly speaking, not themselves in space and time at all? And are they so independent of the things that have them as to be able to exist even though nothing has them – for instance, are there shapes that nothing has?

Bertrand Russell advocates a venerable, Platonistic theory of characteristics (or "universals") according to which they are quite independent of the things that display them. David Armstrong's theory of universals is less profligate than Russell's. He posits far fewer of them, and ties them more closely to their instances by way of a "principle of instantiation": there exists no universal without an instance. H. H. Price considers two alternatives to Russell's Platonistic view of universals. He calls one "the Aristotelian doctrine of *universalia in rebus*," and it corresponds more or less to Armstrong's theory. The other theory rejects universals of either Russell's or Armstrong's sort; Price calls it the "Philosophy of Ultimate Resemblances." According to Price's version of the Aristotelian theory of universals, the characteristics attributed to things are extra entities located in the same place as the objects that are their instances. When two co-existing objects have the same shape, there is something that is present in two places at once. The Philosophy of Resemblances attempts to avoid commitment to such entities by construing talk about common characteristics in terms of similarities among groups of objects. D. C. Williams offers another way to do without universals. Whereas Price construes our statements about "common characteristics" as really about sets of similar objects, Williams makes use of sets of similar "tropes." A trope is supposed to be an *instance* of a property or characteristic, something that can characterize only one individual; unlike the Platonistic or Aristotelian universals, tropes are nonrepeatable things. Williams also claims that objects are composed of tropes, without remainder.

Max Black's dialogue raises the question whether two individuals could have all the same properties. The two characters in Zimmerman's dialogue are pursuing a slightly different question: Do individuals consist of their properties *and nothing more*? (The "properties" in question are universals, not Williams's tropes.)

The problem of universals also receives extensive treatment in the general introduction, "What Is Metaphysics?", above (see section three, "A metaphysical problem: the existence and nature of universals"), and in Ch. 2 (Quine, "On What There Is"). These chapters dovetail nicely with Chs. 4, 5, and 6.

Suggestions for further reading

Aune, Bruce, *Metaphysics: The Elements* (Minneapolis: University of Minnesota, 1985) chs. 3 and 4 ("Universals and Particulars" and "Linguistic Arguments for Abstracta").

Armstrong, D. M., *Universals: An Opinionated Introduction* (Boulder, Col.: Westview Press, 1989).

Carter, William R., *The Elements of Metaphysics* (Philadelphia, Penn.: Temple University Press, 1990) ch. 4 ("Substance").

Dorr, Cian, "There are No Abstract Objects," in Hawthorne, Sider, and Zimmerman (eds.), *Contemporary Debates in Metaphysics* (Malden, Mass.: Blackwell, 2007).

Hamlyn, D. W., *Metaphysics* (Cambridge, UK: Cambridge University Press, 1984) chs. 4 and 5 ("Substance" and "Particular and General").

Jubien, Michael, *Contemporary Metaphysics* (Oxford: Blackwell, 1997) chs. 2, 3, and 8 ("Numbers," "Platonism," and "Modality").

Laurence, Stephen, and Macdonald, Cynthia, *Contemporary Readings in the Foundations of Metaphysics* (Oxford: Basil Blackwell, 1998) Sections 3, 4, and 6 ("Properties and Universals," "Substances," "Tropes").

Loux, Michael, *Metaphysics: A Contemporary Introduction* (London: Routledge, 2002) chs. 1, 2, and 3 ("The Problem of Universals I – Metaphysical Realism," "The Problem of Universals II – Nominalism," and "Concrete Particulars I – Substrata, Bundles, and Substances").

Swoyer, Chris, "Abstract Entities," in Sider, Hawthorne, and Zimmerman (eds.), *Contemporary Debates in Metaphysics* (Malden, Mass.: Blackwell, 2007).

van Inwagen, Peter, *Metaphysics*, 2nd edn (Cambridge, Mass.: Westview Press, 2002) ch. 2 ("Individuality").

---

4   Universals: an Excerpt from *The Problems of Philosophy*

Bertrand Russell

Chapter VIII: How a priori *Knowledge is Possible*

. . . [I]t is very common among philosophers to regard what is *a priori* as in some sense mental, as concerned rather with the way we must think than with any fact of the outer world. We noted in the preceding chapter the three principles commonly called 'laws of thought'. The view which led to their being so named is a natural one, but there are strong reasons for thinking that it is erroneous. Let us take as an illustration the law of contradiction. This is commonly stated in the form 'Nothing can both be and not be', which is intended to express the fact that nothing can at once have and not have a given quality. Thus, for example, if a tree is a beech it cannot also be not a beech; if my table is rectangular it cannot also be not rectangular, and so on.

Now what makes it natural to call this principle a law of *thought* is that it is by thought rather than by outward observation that we persuade ourselves of its necessary truth. When we have seen that a tree is a beech, we do not need to look again in order to ascertain whether it is also not a beech; thought alone makes us know that this is impossible. But the conclusion that the law of contradiction is a law of *thought* is nevertheless erroneous. What we believe, when we believe the law of contradiction, is not that the mind is so made that it must believe the law of contradiction. *This* belief is a subsequent result of psychological reflection, which presupposes the belief in the law of contradiction. The belief in the law of contradiction is a belief about things, not only about thoughts. It is not, e.g., the belief that if we *think* a certain tree is a beech, we cannot at the same time *think* that it is not a beech; it is the belief that if the tree *is* a beech, it cannot at the same time *be* not a beech. Thus the law of contradiction is about things, and not merely about thoughts; and although belief in the law of contradiction is a thought, the law of contradiction itself is not a thought, but a fact concerning the things in the world. If this, which we believe when we believe the law of contradiction, were not true of the things in the world, the fact that we were compelled to *think* it true would not save the law of contradiction from being false; and this shows that the law is not a law of *thought*.

A similar argument applies to any other *a priori* judgement. When we judge that two and two are four, we are not making a judgement about our thoughts, but about all actual or possible couples. The fact that our minds are so constituted as to believe that two and two are four, though it is true, is emphatically not what we assert when we assert that two and two are four. And no fact about the constitution of our minds could make it *true* that two and two are four. Thus our *a priori* knowledge, if it is not erroneous, is not merely knowledge about the constitution of our minds, but is applicable to whatever the world may contain, both what is mental and what is non-mental.

The fact seems to be that all our *a priori* knowledge is concerned with entities which do not, properly speaking, *exist*, either in the mental or in the physical world. These entities are such as can be named by parts of speech which are not substantives; they are such entities as qualities and relations. Suppose, for instance, that I am in my room. I exist, and my room exists; but does 'in' exist? Yet obviously the word 'in' has a meaning; it denotes a relation which holds between me and my room. This relation is something, although we cannot say that it exists *in the same sense* in which I and my room exist. The relation 'in' is something which we can think about and understand, for, if we could not understand it, we could not understand the sentence 'I am in my room'. Many philosophers, following Kant, have maintained that relations are the work of the mind, that things in themselves have no relations, but that the mind brings them together in one act of thought and thus produces the relations which it judges them to have.

This view, however, seems open to objections similar to those which we urged before against Kant. It seems plain that it is not thought which produces the truth of the proposition 'I am in my room'. It may be true that an earwig is in my room, even if neither I nor the earwig nor any one else is aware of this truth; for this truth concerns only the earwig and the room, and does not depend upon anything else. Thus relations, as we shall see more fully in the next chapter, must be placed in a world which is neither mental nor physical. This world is of great importance to philosophy, and in particular to the problems of *a priori* knowledge. In the next chapter we shall proceed to develop its nature and its bearing upon the questions with which we have been dealing.

Chapter IX: The World of Universals

AT the end of the preceding chapter we saw that such entities as relations appear to have a being which is in some way different from that of physical objects, and also different from that of minds and from that of sense-data. In the present chapter we have to consider what is the nature of this kind of being, and also what objects there are that have this kind of being. We will begin with the latter question.

The problem with which we are now concerned is a very old one, since it was brought into philosophy by Plato. Plato's 'theory of ideas' is an attempt to solve this very problem, and in my opinion it is one of the most successful attempts hitherto made. The theory to be advocated in what follows is largely Plato's, with merely such modifications as time has shown to be necessary.

The way the problem arose for Plato was more or less as follows. Let us consider, say, such a notion as *justice*. If we ask ourselves what justice is, it is natural to proceed by considering this, that, and the other just act, with a view to discovering what they have in common. They must all, in some sense, partake of a common nature, which will be found in whatever is just and in nothing else. This common nature, in virtue of which they are all just, will be justice itself, the pure essence the admixture of which with facts of ordinary life produces the multiplicity of just acts. Similarly with any other word which may be applicable to common facts, such as 'whiteness' for example. The word will be applicable to a number of particular things because they all participate in a common nature or essence. This pure essence is what Plato calls an 'idea' or 'form'. (It must not be supposed that 'ideas', in his sense, exist in minds, though they may be apprehended by minds.) The 'idea' *justice* is not identical with anything that is just: it is something other than particular things, which particular things partake of. Not being particular, it cannot itself exist in the world of sense. Moreover it is not fleeting or changeable like the things of sense: it is eternally itself, immutable and indestructible.

Thus Plato is led to a supra-sensible world, more real than the common world of sense, the unchangeable world of ideas, which alone gives to the world of sense whatever pale reflection of reality may belong to it. The truly real world, for Plato, is the world of ideas; for whatever we may attempt to say about things in the world of sense, we can only succeed in saying that they participate in such and such ideas, which, therefore, constitute all their character. Hence it is easy to pass on into a mysticism. We may hope, in a mystic illumination, to *see* the ideas as we see objects of sense; and we may imagine that the ideas exist in heaven. These mystical developments are very natural, but the basis of the theory is in logic, and it is as based in logic that we have to consider it.

The word 'idea' has acquired, in the course of time, many associations which are quite misleading when applied to Plato's 'ideas'. We shall therefore use the word 'universal' instead of the word 'idea', to describe what Plato meant. The essence of the sort of entity that Plato meant is that it is opposed to the particular things that are given in sensation. We speak of whatever is given in sensation, or is of the same nature as things given in sensation, as a *particular*; by opposition to this, a *universal* will be anything which may be shared by many particulars, and has those characteristics which, as we saw, distinguish justice and whiteness from just acts and white things.

When we examine common words, we find that, broadly speaking, proper names stand for particulars, while other substantives, adjectives, prepositions, and verbs stand for universals. Pronouns stand for particulars, but are ambiguous: it is only by the context or the circumstances that we know what particulars they stand for. The word 'now' stands for a particular, namely the present moment; but like pronouns, it stands for an ambiguous particular, because the present is always changing.

It will be seen that no sentence can be made up without at least one word which denotes a universal. The nearest approach would be some such statement as 'I like this'. But even here the word 'like' denotes a universal, for I may like other things, and other people may like things. Thus all truths involve universals, and all knowledge of truths involves acquaintance with universals.

Seeing that nearly all the words to be found in the dictionary stand for universals, it is strange that hardly anybody except students of philosophy ever realizes that there are such entities as universals. We do not naturally dwell upon those words in a sentence which do not stand for particulars; and if we are forced to dwell upon a word which stands for a universal, we naturally think of it as standing for some one of the particulars that come under the universal. When, for example, we hear the sentence, 'Charles I's head was cut off', we may naturally enough think of Charles I, of Charles I's head, and of the operation of cutting off *his* head, which are all particulars; but we do not naturally dwell upon what is meant by the word 'head' or the word 'cut', which is a universal. We feel such words to be incomplete and insubstantial; they seem to demand a context before anything can be done with them. Hence we succeed in avoiding all notice of universals as such, until the study of philosophy forces them upon our attention.

Even among philosophers, we may say, broadly, that only those universals which are named by adjectives or substantives have been much or often recognized, while those named by verbs and prepositions have been usually overlooked. This omission has had a very great effect upon philosophy; it is hardly too much to say that most metaphysics, since Spinoza, has been largely determined by it. The way this has occurred is, in outline, as follows: Speaking generally, adjectives and common nouns express qualities or properties of single things, whereas prepositions and verbs tend to express relations between two or more things. Thus the neglect of prepositions and verbs led to the belief that every proposition can be regarded as attributing a property to a single thing, rather than as expressing a relation between two or more things. Hence it was supposed that, ultimately, there can be no such entities as relations between things. Hence either there can be only one thing in the universe, or, if there are many things, they cannot possibly interact in any way, since any interaction would be a relation, and relations are impossible.

The first of these views, advocated by Spinoza and held in our own day by Bradley and many other philosophers, is called *monism*; the second, advocated by Leibniz but not very common nowadays, is called *monadism,* because each of the isolated things is called a *monad*. Both these opposing philosophies, interesting as they are, result, in my opinion, from an undue attention to one sort of universals, namely the sort represented by adjectives and substantives rather than by verbs and prepositions.

As a matter of fact, if any one were anxious to deny altogether that there are such things as universals, we should find that we cannot strictly prove that there are such entities as *qualities,* i.e. the universals represented by adjectives and substantives, whereas we can prove that there must be *relations,* i.e. the sort of universals generally represented by verbs and prepositions. Let us take in illustration the universal *whiteness.* If we believe that there is such a universal, we shall say that things are white because they have the quality of whiteness. This view, however, was strenuously denied by Berkeley and Hume, who have been followed in this by later empiricists. The form which their denial took was to deny that there are such things as 'abstract ideas'. When we want to think of whiteness, they said, we form an image of some particular white thing, and reason concerning this particular, taking care not to deduce anything concerning it which we cannot see to be equally true of any other white thing. As an account of our actual mental processes, this is no doubt largely true. In geometry, for example, when we wish to prove something about all triangles, we draw a particular triangle and reason about it, taking care not to use any characteristic which it does not share with other triangles. The beginner, in order to avoid error, often finds it useful to draw several triangles, as unlike each other as possible, in order to make sure that his reasoning is equally applicable to all of them. But a difficulty emerges as soon as we ask ourselves how we know that a thing is white or a triangle. If we wish to avoid the universals *whiteness* and *triangularity,* we shall choose some particular patch of white or some particular triangle, and say that anything is white or a triangle if it has the right sort of resemblance to our chosen particular. But then the resemblance required will have to be a universal. Since there are many white things, the resemblance must hold between many pairs of particular white things; and this is the characteristic of a universal. It will be useless to say that there is a different resemblance for each pair, for then we shall have to say that these resemblances resemble each other, and thus at last we shall be forced to admit resemblance as a universal. The relation of resemblance, therefore, must be a true universal. And having been forced to admit this universal, we find that it is no longer worth while to invent difficult and unplausible theories to avoid the admission of such universals as whiteness and triangularity.

Berkeley and Hume failed to perceive this refutation of their rejection of 'abstract ideas', because, like their adversaries, they only thought of *qualities,* and altogether ignored *relations* as universals. We have therefore here another respect in which the rationalists appear to have been in the right as against the empiricists, although, owing to the neglect or denial of relations, the deductions made by rationalists were, if anything, more apt to be mistaken than those made by empiricists.

Having now seen that there must be such entities as universals, the next point to be proved is that their being is not merely mental. By this is meant that whatever being belongs to them is independent of their being thought of or in any way apprehended by minds. We have already touched on this subject at the end of the preceding chapter, but we must now consider more fully what sort of being it is that belongs to universals.

Consider such a proposition as 'Edinburgh is north of London'. Here we have a relation between two places, and it seems plain that the relation subsists independently of our knowledge of it. When we come to know that Edinburgh is north of London, we come to know something which has to do only with Edinburgh and London: we do not cause the truth of the proposition by coming to know it, on the contrary we merely apprehend a fact which was there before we knew it. The part of the earth's surface where Edinburgh stands would be north of the part where London stands, even if there were no human being to know about north and south, and even if there were no minds at all in the universe. This is, of course, denied by many philosophers, either for Berkeley's reasons or for Kant's. But we have already considered these reasons, and decided that they are inadequate. We may therefore now assume it to be true that nothing mental is presupposed in the fact that Edinburgh is north of London. But this fact involves the relation 'north of', which is a universal; and it would be impossible for the whole fact to involve nothing mental if the relation 'north of', which is a constituent part of the fact, did involve anything mental. Hence we must admit that the relation, like the terms it relates, is not dependent upon thought, but belongs to the independent world which thought apprehends but does not create.

This conclusion, however, is met by the difficulty that the relation 'north of' does not seem to *exist* in the same sense in which Edinburgh and London exist. If we ask 'Where and when does this relation exist?' the answer must be 'Nowhere and nowhen'. There is no place or time where we can find the relation 'north of'. It does not exist in Edinburgh any more than in London, for it relates the two and is neutral as between them. Nor can we say that it exists at any particular time. Now everything that can be apprehended by the senses or by introspection exists at some particular time. Hence the relation 'north of' is radically different from such things. It is neither in space nor in time, neither material nor mental; yet it is something.

It is largely the very peculiar kind of being that belongs to universals which has led many people to suppose that they are really mental. We can think *of* a universal, and our thinking then exists in a perfectly ordinary sense, like any other mental act. Suppose, for example, that we are thinking of whiteness. Then *in one sense* it may be said that whiteness is 'in our mind'. We have here the same ambiguity as we noted in discussing Berkeley in Chapter IV. In the strict sense, it is not whiteness that is in our mind, but the act of thinking of whiteness. The connected ambiguity in the word 'idea', which we noted at the same time, also causes confusion here. In one sense of this word, namely the sense in which it denotes the *object* of an act of thought, whiteness is an 'idea'. Hence, if the ambiguity is not guarded against, we may come to think that whiteness is an 'idea' in the other sense, i.e. an act of thought; and thus we come to think that whiteness is mental. But in so thinking, we rob it of its essential quality of universality. One man's act of thought is necessarily a different thing from another man's; one man's act of thought at one time is necessarily a different thing from the same man's act of thought at another time. Hence, if whiteness were the thought as opposed to its object, no two different men could think of it, and no one man could think of it twice. That which many different thoughts of whiteness have in common is their *object*, and this object is different from all of them. Thus universals are not thoughts, though when known they are the objects of thoughts.

We shall find it convenient only to speak of things *existing* when they are in time, that is to say, when we can point to some time *at* which they exist (not excluding the possibility of their existing at all times). Thus thoughts and feelings, minds and physical objects *exist*. But universals do not exist in this sense; we shall say that they *subsist* or *have being*, where 'being' is opposed to 'existence' as being timeless. The world of universals, therefore, may also be described as the world of being. The world of being is unchangeable, rigid, exact, delightful to the mathematician, the logician, the builder of metaphysical systems, and all who love perfection more than life. The world of existence is fleeting, vague, without sharp boundaries, without any clear plan or arrangement, but it contains all thoughts and feelings, all the data of sense, and all physical objects, everything that can do either good or harm, everything that makes any difference to the value of life and the world. According to our temperaments, we shall prefer the contemplation of the one or of the other. The one we do not prefer will probably seem to us a pale shadow of the one we prefer, and hardly worthy to be regarded as in any sense real. But the truth is that both have the same claim on our impartial attention, both are real, and both are important to the metaphysician. Indeed no sooner have we distinguished the two worlds than it becomes necessary to consider their relations.

---

5   Universals as Attributes: an Excerpt from *Universals: an Opinionated Introduction*

David M. Armstrong

I.   Uninstantiated Universals?

If we abandon the idea that particulars are nothing but bundles of universals but still want to recognize universals, then we must return to the traditional view that particulars, tokens, *instantiate* universals: having properties and standing to each other in relations. If we do this, then there are a number of controversial questions that have to be settled. One key question is this. Should we, or should we not, accept a **Principle of Instantiation** for universals? That is, should we, or should we not, demand that every universal be instantiated? That is, for each property universal must it be the case that it is a property of some particular? For each relation universal must it be the case that there are particulars between which the relation holds?

We certainly should not demand that every universal should be instantiated *now*. It would be enough if a particular universal was not instantiated now, but was instantiated in the past, or would be instantiated in the future. The Principle of Instantiation should be interpreted as ranging over all time: past, present, and future. But should we uphold the principle even in this relatively liberal form?

This is a big parting of the ways. We can call the view that there are uninstantiated universals the Platonist view. It appears to have been the view held by Plato, who was also, apparently, the first philosopher to introduce universals. (He spoke of Forms or Ideas – but there was nothing psychological about the Ideas.)

Once you have uninstantiated universals you need somewhere special to put them, a "Platonic heaven," as philosophers often say. They are not to be found in the ordinary world of space and time. And since it seems that any instantiated universal might have been uninstantiated – for example, there might have been nothing past, present, or future that had that property – then if uninstantiated universals are in a Platonic heaven, it will be natural to place all universals in that heaven. The result is that we get two realms: the realm of universals and the realm of particulars, the latter being ordinary things in space and time. Such universals are often spoken of as *transcendent*. (A view of this sort was explicitly held by Russell in his earlier days before he adopted a bundle-of-universals view. See his introductory book *The Problems of Philosophy*, 1912, Chs. 9 and 10.) **Instantiation** then becomes a very big deal: a relation between universals and particulars that crosses realms. The Latin tag used by the Scholastics for a theory of this sort is *universalia ante res*, "universals before things." Such a view is unacceptable to Naturalists, that is, to those who think that the space-time world is all the world that there is. This helps to explain why Empiricists, who tend to be sympathetic to Naturalism, often reject universals.

. . .

If, however, we reject uninstantiated universals, then we are at least in a position, if we want to do it, to bring the universals down to earth. We can adopt the view whose Latin tag is *universalia in rebus*, "universals in things." We can think of a thing's properties as constituents of the thing and think of the properties as universals. This may have been the position of Aristotle. (The scholars differ. Some make him a Nominalist. Some think he believed in this-worldly universals. Certainly, he criticized Plato's otherworldly universals.) *Universalia in rebus* is, of course, a layer-cake view, with properties as universals as part of the internal structure of things. (Relations will be *universalia inter res*, "universals between things" [F.E. Abbott, *Scientific Theism*, 1886].)

There are difficulties in this position, of course, objections that can be brought, as with every other solution to the Problem of Universals. One thing that has worried many philosophers, including perhaps Plato, is that on this view we appear to have multiple locations of the same thing. Suppose *a* is F and *b* is also F, with F a property universal. The very same entity has to be part of the structure of two things at two places. How can the universal be in two places at once? I will come back to this question later in this chapter.

. . .

But our present task is to decide whether or not we ought to countenance uninstantiated universals. The first point to be made is that the onus of proof seems to be firmly on the side of the Platonists. It can hardly be doubted that there is a world of space and time. But a separate realm of universals is a mere hypothesis, or postulation. If a postulation has great explanatory value, then it may be a good postulation. But it has to prove itself. Why should we postulate uninstantiated universals?

One thing that has moved many philosophers is what we may call the argument from the meaning of general terms. Plato, in his *Republic*, had Socrates say, "shall we proceed as usual and begin by assuming the existence of a single essential nature or Form for every set of things which we call by the same name?" (595, trans. F. M. Cornford). Socrates may have been thinking along the following lines. Ordinary names, that is, proper names, have a bearer of the name. If we turn to general terms – words like 'horse' and 'triangular' that apply to many different things – then we need something that stands to the word in the same general sort of relation that the bearer of the proper name stands to the proper name. There has to be an object that constitutes or corresponds to the meaning of the general word. So there has to be something called horseness, and triangularity. But now consider a general word that applies to nothing particular at all, a word like 'unicorn' for instance. It is perfectly meaningful. And if it is meaningful, must there not be something in the world that constitutes or corresponds to the word? So there must be uninstantiated universals.

This "argument from meaning" is a very bad argument. (In fairness to Socrates, it is not clear whether he was using it. Other philosophers have, though, often at a rather unselfconscious level.) The argument depends on the assumption that in every case where a general word has meaning, there is something in the world that constitutes or corresponds to that meaning. Gilbert Ryle spoke of this as the 'Fido'–Fido fallacy. Fido corresponds to the word 'Fido', but there does not have to be some single thing corresponding to a general word.

To go along with the argument from meaning is to be led into a very promiscuous theory of universals. If it is correct, then we know a priori that for each general word with a certain meaning, there exists a universal. This lines up predicates and properties in a nice neat way, but it is a way that we ought to be very suspicious of. Is it that easy to discover what universals there are?

Plato had another line of thought that led him toward uninstantiated universals. This is the apparent failure of things in the ordinary world to come up to exact standards. It seems that nothing in the world is perfectly straight or circular, yet in geometry we discuss the properties of perfectly straight lines or perfect circles. Again, no thing is perfectly changeless. Yet again, it may well be that no act is perfectly just. Certainly no person is perfectly virtuous and no state is perfectly just. Yet in ethical and political discussion (e.g., in the *Republic*) we can discuss the nature of virtue and justice. In general, we perceive the world as falling short of certain standards. This can be explained if, whether we know it or not, we are comparing ordinary things to Forms, which the ordinary things can never fully instantiate. (This can lead one, and perhaps led Plato, to the difficult notion of degrees of instantiation, with the highest degree never realized.)

It is interesting to notice that this argument did not quite lead Plato where he wanted to go in every case. Consider geometry. In geometry one might wish to consider the properties of, say, two intersecting circles. These circles will be perfectly circular. But also, of course, there is only *one* Form of the circle. So what are these two perfect circles? Plato, apparently, had to introduce what he called the Mathematicals. Like the mathematical Forms they were perfect and thus were unlike ordinary things. But unlike the Forms, there could be many tokens of the same type, and in this they were like ordinary things. They were particulars, although perfect particulars. But if this is so, though perhaps the falling away from standards gave Plato an argument for the Mathematicals, it is not clear that it is any argument for the Forms.

But in any case, cannot ideal standards simply be things that we merely think of? We can quite knowingly form thoughts of that which does not exist. In the case of ideal standards nothing comes up to the standard, but by extrapolating from ordinary things that approximate to the standard in different degrees, we can form the thought of something that does come up to the standard. It turns out to be useful to do so. Why attribute metaphysical reality to such standards? They could be useful fictions. As a matter of fact, in the geometrical case it appears that such notions as that of a perfectly straight line or a perfectly circular object may be acquired directly in experience. For cannot something look perfectly straight or perfectly circular, even if it is not in fact so?

One should note that one thing that seems to keep a theory of uninstantiated universals going is the widespread idea that it is sufficient for a universal to exist if it is merely possible that it should be instantiated. I have found in discussion that this idea has particular appeal if it is empirically possible (that is, compatible with the laws of nature) that the alleged universal should have actual instances. Suppose, for instance, that somebody describes a very complex pattern of wallpaper but does not ever sketch the pattern or manufacture the wallpaper. Suppose nobody else does either in the whole history of the universe. It is clear that there was nothing in the laws of nature that prevented the pattern's ever having an instance, from ever having a token of the type. But is not that pattern a monadic universal, a complex and structural universal to be sure, but a universal nonetheless?

In this way, apparently, it is natural for philosophers to argue. But for myself I do not see the force of the argument. Philosophers do not reason that way about particulars. They do not argue that it is empirically possible that present-day France should be a monarchy and therefore that the present king of France exists, although, unfortunately for French royalists, he is not instantiated. Why argue in the same way about universals? Is it that philosophers think that universals are so special that they can exist whether or not particular things, which are contingent only, exist? If so, I think that this is no better than a prejudice, perhaps inherited from Plato.

. . .

From this point on, therefore, I am going to assume the truth of the Principle of Instantiation. As already noted, this does not compel one to abandon a two-realm doctrine. It does not compel one to bring the universals down among ordinary things. But it does *permit* one to do this, and to do so seems the natural way to develop the theory once one rejects uninstantiated universals.

II.   Disjunctive, Negative, and Conjunctive Universals

For simplicity, in this section I will consider property universals only. But the points to be made appear to apply to relations also. We have already rejected uninstantiated universals. But it seems that the potential class of universals needs to be cut down a great deal further if we are to get a plausible theory. I will begin by giving reasons for rejecting disjunctive property universals. By a **disjunctive property** I mean a disjunction of (property) universals. Let us assume that particular electric charges and particular masses are universals. Then having charge C or having mass M (with C and M dummies for determinate, that is, definite values) would be an example of a disjunctive property. Why is it not a universal? Consider two objects. One has charge C but lacks mass M. The other lacks charge C but has mass M. So they have the disjunctive property having charge C or having mass M. But surely that does not show that, in any serious sense, they thereby have something identical? The whole point of a universal, however, is that it should be identical in its different instances.

There is another reason to deny that a disjunction of universals is a universal. There is some very close link between universals and causality. The link is of this nature. If a thing instantiates a certain universal, then, in virtue of that, it has the power to act in a certain way. For instance, if a thing has a certain mass, then it has the power to act upon the scalepan of a balance, or upon scales, in a certain way. Furthermore, different universals bestow different powers. Charge and mass, for instance, manifest themselves in different ways. I doubt if the link between universals and powers is a necessary one, but it seems real. Moreover, if, as seems abstractly possible, two different universals bestowed the very same powers, how could one ever know that they were two different universals? If they affect all apparatus, including our brains, in exactly the same way, will we not judge that we are dealing with one universal only?

Now suppose that a thing has charge C but lacks mass M. In virtue of charge C, it has certain powers to act. For instance, it repels things with like charge. Possession of the disjunctive property C or M adds nothing to its power. This suggests that while C may be a genuine universal, C or M is not.

So I think that we should reject disjunctive universals. A similar case seems to hold against negative universals: the lack or absence of a property is not a property. If having charge C is the instantiation of a universal, then not having C is not the instantiating of a universal.

First, we may appeal to identity again. Is there really something in common, something identical, in everything that lacks charge C? Of course, there might be some universal property that just happened to be coextensive with lacking charge C. But the lack itself does not seem to be a factor found in each thing that lacks charge C.

Second, causal considerations seem to point in the same direction. It is a strange idea that lacks or absences do any causing. It is natural to say that a thing acts in virtue of positive factors alone. This also suggests that absences of universals are not universals.

It is true that there is some linguistic evidence that might be thought to point the other way. We do say things like 'lack of water caused his death'. At the surface, the statement says that a lack of water caused an absence of life. But how seriously should we take such ways of expressing ourselves? Michael Tooley has pointed out that we are unhappy to say 'lack of poison causes us to remain alive'. Yet if the surface way of understanding the first statement is correct, then the second statement should be understood in the same way and thought to be true. Certain counterfactual statements are true in both cases: If he had had water, then he would (could) have still been alive; if we had taken poison, we would have been dead now. These are causal truths. But they tell us very little about the actual causal factors operative in the two cases. We believe, I think, that these actual causal factors could be spelled out in purely positive terms.

It is interesting to notice that conjunctions of universals (having both charge C and mass M) escape the two criticisms leveled against disjunctive and negative universals. With conjunctions we do have identity. The very same conjunction of factors is present in each instance. There is no problem about causality. If a thing instantiates the conjunction, then it will have certain powers as a consequence. These powers will be different from those that the thing would have had if it had had just one of the conjuncts. It may even be that the conjunction can do more than the sum of what each property would do if each was instantiated alone. (As scientists say: There could be synergism. The effect could be more than the sum of each cause acting by itself.)

But there is one condition that ought to be put on conjunctive universals. Some thing (past, present, future) must actually have both properties and at the same time. This, of course, is simply the Principle of Instantiation applied to conjunctive universals.

III.   Predicates and Universals

What has been said about uninstantiated universals, and also about disjunctions and negations of universals, has brought out a most important point. It is that there is no automatic passage from predicates (linguistic entities) to universals. For instance, the expression 'either having charge C or having mass M' is a perfectly good predicate. It could apply to, or be true of, innumerable objects. But as we have seen, this does not mean that there is a universal corresponding to this predicate.

Wittgenstein made a famous contribution to the Problem of Universals with his discussion of **family resemblances**. Wittgenstein was an antimetaphysician, and his object was to dissolve rather than to solve the Problem of Universals. He seems to have thought that what he said about family resemblances was (among other things) a step toward getting rid of the problem. But I think that the real moral of what he said is only that predicates and universals do not line up in any simple way.

In his *Philosophical Investigations* (1953, Secs. 66 and 67) he considered the notion of a *game*. He had this to say about it:

66.   Consider for example the proceedings that we call "games". I mean board-games, card-games, ball-games, Olympic games, and so on. What is common to them all? – Don't say: "There *must* be something common, or they would not be called 'games'" – but *look and see* whether there is anything common to all. – For if you look at them you will not see something that is common to *all*, but similarities, relationships, and a whole series of them at that. To repeat: don't think, but look! – Look for example at board-games, with their multifarious relationships. Now pass to card-games; here you find many correspondences with the first group, but many common features drop out, and others appear. When we pass next to ball-games, much that is common is retained, but much is lost. – Are they all 'amusing'? Compare chess with noughts and crosses. Or is there always winning and losing, or competition between players? Think of patience. In ball games there is winning and losing; but when a child throws his ball at the wall and catches it again, this feature has disappeared. Look at the parts played by skill and luck; and at the games like ring-a-ring-a-roses; here is the element of amusement, but how many other characteristic features have disappeared! And we can go through the many, many other groups of games in the same way; we can see how similarities crop up and disappear.

   And the result of this examination is: we see a complicated network of similarities overlapping and criss-crossing: sometimes overall similarities, sometimes similarities of detail.

67.   I can think of no better expression to characterize these similarities than "family resemblances"; for the various resemblances between members of a family: build, features, colour of eyes, gait, temperament, etc. etc. overlap and criss-cross in the same way. – And I shall say: 'games' form a family.

This has been a very influential passage. Wittgenstein and his followers applied the point to all sorts of notions besides those of a game, including many of the central notions discussed by philosophers. But what should a believer in universals think that Wittgenstein has shown about universals?

Let us agree, as we probably should, that there is no universal of gamehood. But now what of this "complicated network of similarities overlapping and criss-crossing" of which Wittgenstein speaks? All the Realist has to do is to analyze each of these similarities in terms of common properties. That analysis of similarity is not a difficult or unfamiliar idea, though it is an analysis that would be contested by a Nominalist. But there will not be any property that runs through the whole class and makes them all games. To give a crude and oversimplified sketch, the situation might be like this:

Particulars: *a*   *b*   *c*   *d*   *e*
Their properties: FGHJ   GHJK   HJKL   JKLM   KLMN

Here F to N are supposed to be genuine property universals, and it is supposed that the predicate "game" applies in virtue of these properties. But the class of particulars {*a* ... *e*}, which is the class of all tokens of games, is a family in Wittgenstein's sense. Here, though, I have sketched an account of such families that is completely compatible with Realism about universals.

However, Wittgenstein's remarks do raise a big question. How does one decide whether one is or is not in the presence of a genuine property or relation? Wittgenstein says of games, "don't think, but look." As a general recipe, at least, that seems far too simple.

I do not think that there is any infallible way of deciding what are the true universals. It seems clear that we must not look to semantic considerations. As I said in Section I of this chapter, those who argue to particular universals from semantic data, from predicates to a universal corresponding to that predicate, argue in a very optimistic and unempirical manner. I call them **a priori realists**. Better, I think, is **a posteriori realism**. The best guide that we have to just what universals there are is total science.

For myself, I believe that this puts physics in a special position. There seem to be reasons, (scientific, empirical, a posteriori reasons) to think that physics is *the* fundamental science. If that is correct, then such properties as mass, charge, extension, duration, space-time interval, and other properties envisaged by physics may be the true monadic universals. (They are mostly ranges of quantities. Quantities raise problems that will need some later discussion.) Spatiotemporal and causal relations will perhaps be the true polyadic universals.

If this is correct, then the ordinary types – the type red, the type horse, in general, the types of the manifest image of the world – will emerge as preliminary, rough-and-ready, classifications of reality. For the most part they are not false, but they are rough-and-ready. Many of them will be family affairs, as games appear to be. To the one type will correspond a whole family of universals and not always a very close family. And even where the ordinary types do carve the beast of reality along its true joints, they may still not expose those joints for the things that they are. But let it be emphasized that any identification of universals remains rather speculative. In what I have just been saying I have been trying to combine a philosophy of universals with Physicalism. Others may have other ideas.

. . .

VIII. Multiple Location

To bring universals from a platonic realm down to earth, down to space-time, seems to involve saying something rather strange. It seems to follow that universals are, or may be, multiply located. For are they not to be found wherever the particulars that instantiate them are found? If two different electrons each have charge *e*, then *e*, one thing, a universal, is to be found in two different places, the places where the two electrons are, yet entirely and completely in each place. This has seemed wildly paradoxical to many philosophers.

Plato appears to be raising this difficulty in the *Philebus*, 15b–c. There he asked about a Form: "Can it be as a whole outside itself, and thus come to be one and identical in one thing and in several at once, – a view which might be thought to be the most impossible of all?" (trans. A. E. Taylor). A theory that kept universals in a separate realm from particulars would at least avoid this difficulty!

You might try just accepting the multiple location of universals. Some philosophers have. But then a difficulty can be raised: What about relations? Perhaps one can give *properties* a multiple location. But just where will you locate the "multiply located" relations? In the related things? That does not sound right. If *a* precedes *b* is the relation in both *a* and *b*? Or in the thing [*a* + *b*]? Neither answer sounds right. But if it is not in the things, where is it?

I am inclined to meet the difficulty by saying that talk of the location of universals, while better than placing them in another realm, is also not quite appropriate. What should be said first, I think, is that the world is a world of states of affairs. These states of affairs involve particulars having properties and standing in relations to each other. The properties and relations are universals, which means both that different particulars can have the very same property and that different pairs, triples, . . . , of particulars can stand in the very same relation to each other. I do not think that all that is too startling a claim.

But if Naturalism is true, then the world is a single spatiotemporal manifold. What does this come to in terms of the states of affairs theory? That is, how do we reconcile Naturalism with the view sketched in the previous paragraph? It would be an enormous undertaking, presumably involving both fundamental science and philosophy, to give an answer involving even the sketchiest detail. All that can be said here is that the space-time world would have to be an enormous plurality or conjunction of states of affairs, with all the particulars that feature in the states of affairs linked up together (in states of affairs) by spatiotemporal relations.

To talk of locating universals in space-time then emerges as a crude way of speaking. Space-time is not a box into which universals are put. Universals are constituents of states of affairs. Space-time is a conjunction of states of affairs. In that sense universals are "in" space-time. But they are in it as helping to constitute it. I think that this is a reasonable understanding of *universalia in rebus*, and I hope that it meets Plato's objection.

6   Universals and Resemblances: Chapter 1 of *Thinking and Experience*

H. H. Price

When we consider the world around us, we cannot help noticing that there is a great deal of recurrence or repetition in it. The same colour recurs over and over again in ever so many things. Shapes repeat themselves likewise. Over and over again we notice oblong-shaped things, hollow things, bulgy things. Hoots, thuds, bangs, rustlings occur again and again.

There is another and very important sort of recurrence which we also notice. The same pattern or mode of arrangement is found over and over again in many *sets* of things, in many different pairs of things, or triads, or quartets, as the case may be. When A is above B, and C is above D, and E is above F, the above-and-below pattern or mode of arrangement recurs in three pairs of things, and in ever so many other pairs of things as well. Likewise we repeatedly notice one thing inside another, one preceding another, one thing between two others.

These recurrent features sometimes recur singly or separately. The same colour recurs in this tomato, that sunset sky, and this blushing face; there are few other features, if any, which repeat themselves in all three. But it is a noteworthy fact about the world that there are *conjoint* recurrences as well as separate ones. A whole group of features recurs again and again as a whole in many objects. Examine twenty dandelions, and you will find that they have many features in common; likewise fifty cats have very many features in common, or two hundred lumps of lead. In such cases as these there is conjoint recurrence of many different features. Again and again they recur together in a clump or block. This is how it comes about that many of the objects in the world group themselves together into Natural Kinds. A Natural Kind is a group of objects which have *many* (perhaps indefinitely many) features in common. From observing that an object has some of these features, we can infer with a good deal of probability that it has the rest.

These constant recurrences or repetitions, whether separate or conjoint ones, are what make the world a dull or stale or boring place. The same old features keep turning up again and again. The best they can do is to present themselves occasionally in new combinations, as in the black swan or the duck-billed platypus. There is a certain *monotony* about the world. The extreme case of it is found where the same old feature repeats itself in all parts of a single object, as when something is red all over, or sticky all through, or a noise is uniformly shrill throughout its entire duration.

Nevertheless, this perpetual repetition, this dullness or staleness, is also immensely important, because it is what makes conceptual cognition possible. In a world of incessant novelty, where there was no recurrence at all and no tedious repetitions, no concepts could ever be acquired; and thinking, even of the crudest and most primitive kind, could never begin. For example, in such a world nothing would ever be recognizable. Or again, *in so far as* there is novelty in the world, non-recurrence, absence of repetition, so far the world cannot be thought about, but only experienced.

Hitherto I have been trying to use entirely untechnical language, so that we may not commit ourselves unawares to any philosophical theory. But it is at any rate not unnatural, it is not a *very* wild piece of theorizing, to introduce the words 'quality' and 'relation' for referring to those facts about the world to which I have been trying to draw the reader's attention. A *quality*, we say, is a recurrent feature of the world which presents itself in individual objects or events taken singly. Redness or bulginess or squeakiness are examples. A *relation*, on the other hand, is a recurrent feature of the world which presents itself in complexes of objects or events, such as this beside that, this preceding that, or B between A and C. It is also convenient sometimes to speak of *relational properties*. If A precedes B, we may say that A has the relational property of preceding B, and B has the converse relational property of succeeding A.

One further remark may be made on the distinction between qualities and relations. I said just now that a quality presents itself in individual objects or events taken singly, and a relation in complexes of objects or events. But it must not be forgotten that an individual object or event usually (perhaps always) has an *internal* complexity. In its history there is a plurality of temporal phases, and often it has a plurality of spatial parts as well. And there are relations between these parts, or these phases, which it has. Such relations *within* an individual object or event are sometimes said to constitute the 'structure' of the object or event. For scientific purposes, and even for purposes of ordinary common sense prediction, what we most need to know about any object or process is its structure. And from this point of view the chief importance of qualities, such as colour or hardness or stickiness, is that they often enable us to infer the presence of a structure more minute than our unaided senses would reveal. It has often been maintained that sensible qualities are 'subjective'. But subjective or not, they have a most important function. They give us a clue to what the minute structure of objects and events is. If a gas smells like rotten eggs, we can infer that it is sulphuretted hydrogen.

The terms 'quality' and 'relation' enable us to give a simple analysis of *change*. The notion of change has puzzled some philosophers greatly, ever since Heracleitus, or some disciple of his, remarked long ago that πὰντα ῥεῖ 'all things flow'. Indeed, it has sometimes led them to suppose that this world *is* a world of perpetual novelty after all, and not the tedious or boring or repetitious world which it has to be, if conceptual cognition is to be possible. They have, therefore, concluded – rightly, from their premises – that all conceptual cognition is radically erroneous or illusory, a kind of systematic distortion of Reality; so that *whatever* we think, however intelligent or however stupid we may be, we are in error. On this view, only non-conceptual cognition – immediate experience or direct intuition – can be free from error.

These conclusions are so queer that we suspect something is wrong with the premises. We can now see what it is. The notion of Change, as Plato pointed out, has itself to be analysed in terms of the notions of Quality and Relation. In qualitative change, as when an apple changes from being green to being red, an object has quality q_1 at one time and a different quality q_2 at a later time. In relational change, an object A has a relation R_1 to another object B at one time, and a different relation R_2 to B at a later time. At 12 o'clock, for example, it is six inches away from B, at 12.5 it is a mile away from B; at one time the relation it has to B is the relation 'hotter than', at another the relation 'as hot as', at another the relation 'cooler than'. . . .

We may now sum up the results of this ontological discussion so far by introducing another technical term, again not so *very* technical, the term 'characteristic'. Characteristics, we say, are of at least two different types, qualities and relations. What has been said so far then comes to this: there are *recurrent characteristics* in the world, which repeat themselves over and over again in many different contexts. Is it not just an obvious fact about the world, something we cannot help noticing whether we like it or not, that there *are* recurrent characteristics? Now these recurrent characteristics have been called by some philosophers *universals*. And the line of thought we have been pursuing leads very naturally to the traditional Aristotelian doctrine of *universalia in rebus*, 'universals in things'. (To provide for universals of relation, 'things' must be understood to cover complexes as well as individuals. The *res* which the universal 'beside' is in is not this, nor that, but this-and-that.)

I do not propose to discuss the Platonic doctrine of *universalia ante rem*, 'universals anterior to (or independent of) things'. This is not because I think it uninteresting or unimportant, but merely because it is more remote from common sense and our ordinary everyday habits of thought than the Aristotelian theory of *universalia in rebus*. It is a sufficiently difficult task in these days to convince people that there is any sense in talking of universals at all, even in the mild and moderate Aristotelian way.

The doctrine of *universalia in rebus* may, of course, be mistaken, or gravely misleading. There certainly are objections to it, as we shall find presently. But I cannot see that it is in the least absurd or silly, as the most approved thinkers nowadays seem to suppose. Nor can I see that it arises entirely from erroneous views about language, as the same thinkers seem to suppose; for example, from the superstition that all words are names, from which it would follow that general or abstract words must be names of general or abstract entities. On the contrary, this philosophy seems to me to be the result, and the very natural result, of certain *ontological* reflections. It seems to me to arise from reflections about the world; from consideration of what things are, and not – or certainly not merely – from consideration of the way we talk about them. On the contrary, it could be argued that we talk in the way we do, using general terms and abstract terms, because of what we find the world to be; because we find or notice *recurrences* in it.

Let us now consider how the doctrine of *universalia in rebus* might mislead us, although it arises in this natural and plausible way from the ontological considerations which we have been discussing. One danger of it obviously is that universals may be regarded as a sort of *things* or entities, over and above the objects or situations in which they recur. We may indeed emphasize the word 'in'. We may insist that universals are *in* things, and not apart from them as the doctrine of *universalia ante rem* maintains. But is the danger of supposing that they are themselves things or quasi-things entirely removed? Does it not arise over again as soon as we reflect upon the implications of the word 'in' itself?

If it is our profession to be misled – as, of course, it *is* the profession of philosophers – we shall be liable to suppose that redness is in the tomato somewhat as juice is in it, or as a weevil is in it. And if so, what can be meant by saying that redness is recurrent? How can it be *in* thousands of other tomatoes as well, or hundreds of post-boxes, or dozens of blushing faces? It does not make sense to say that a weevil is in many places at once. Again, when the tomato begins to decay and turns brown, where has the redness gone to, which used to be in it?

(The weevil has gone somewhere else; you will find him in the potato basket.) Likewise, where has the brownness come from?

If we prefer to say that the tomato *has* redness, rather than 'redness is in it', we shall again mislead these literal-minded persons, and in the same sort of way. Does the tomato *have* redness as Jones *has* a watch? If so, how can millions of other things have it too?

I confess that I do not think much of these difficulties. The meaning of 'in' and 'have' in this context can be quite easily exhibited by examples, just as their literal meaning can, when we say that there is a weevil in the tomato, or I have a watch. Surely we all know quite well what is being referred to when two things are said to *have* the same colour? And is it really so very difficult to recognize what is meant by saying that the same colour is *in* them both? It is true no doubt that the words 'in' and 'have' are here being used in a metaphorical sense, though not, I think, extravagantly metaphorical. But we must use metaphorical words, or else invent new and technical terms (which are themselves usually metaphorical words taken from a dead language, Greek or Latin). Our ordinary language exists for practical ends, and it has to be 'stretched' in one way or other if we are to use it for purposes of philosophical analysis. And if our metaphors can be cashed quite easily by examples, as these can, no harm whatever is done.

It could, however, be argued that the terminology of 'characteristics', which was current in the last philosophical epoch, some twenty years ago, is better than the more ancient terminology of 'universals'. A characteristic is pretty obviously a characteristic *of* something or other, and cannot easily be supposed to be an independent entity, like the weevil. Nor can we be easily misled into supposing that when something 'has' a characteristic, i.e. is characterized by it, this is at all analogous to the having of a watch. . . .

Henceforth, the Aristotelian theory of *universalia in rebus* will be called 'the Philosophy of Universals' for short. If our argument so far has been correct, the Philosophy of Universals is drawing our attention to certain important facts about the world. Yet it is at the same time proposing an analysis of those facts. We cannot dispute the facts, nor can we dispute their fundamental importance. We cannot deny that something which may be called 'the recurrence of characteristics' is genuinely there. We must also admit that if it were not there, conceptual cognition could not exist. If the world were not like this, if there were no recurrence in it, it could be neither thought about nor spoken about. We could never have acquired any concepts; and even if we had them innately (without needing to acquire them) they could never have been applied to anything.

But though we cannot dispute the facts, nor their importance, we may, nevertheless, have doubts about the analysis of them which the Philosophy of Universals proposes. At any rate, another and quite different analysis of them appears to be possible. It is the analysis offered by what one may call the Philosophy of Ultimate Resemblances. (Henceforth I shall call this 'the Philosophy of Resemblances' for short.) This is the analysis which most contemporary philosophers accept, so far as they consider the *ontological* side of the Problem of Universals at all. It is also accepted by Conceptualists, like Locke. The Philosophy of Resemblances is more complicated than the Philosophy of Universals, and more difficult to formulate. It involves one in long and cumbrous circumlocutions. Yet it claims, not unplausibly, that it keeps closer to the facts which have to be analysed. The unkind way of putting this, the one its critics prefer, is to say that it is 'more naturalistic'. Let us now consider the Philosophy of Resemblances in more detail.

When we say that a characteristic, e.g. whiteness, *recurs,* that it presents itself over and over again, that it characterizes ever so many numerically different objects, what we say is admittedly in some sense true. But would it not be clearer, and closer to the facts, if we said that all these objects resemble each other in a certain way? Is not this the rock-bottom fact to which the Philosophy of Universals is drawing our attention, when it uses this rather inflated language of 'recurrent characteristics'? The Philosophy of Universals of course agrees that all the objects characterized by whiteness do resemble one another. But according to it, resemblance is always derivative, and is just a *consequence* of the fact that the very same characteristic – whiteness, in this case – characterizes all these objects. To use more traditional language, it says that when A resembles B, this is *because* they are both instances of the same universal.

Now this is all very well where the resemblance is exact, but what are we to say when it is not? Let us consider the following series of examples: a patch of freshly fallen snow; a bit of chalk; a piece of paper which has been used for wrapping the meat in; the handkerchief with which I have been dusting a rather dirty mantelpiece; a full evening dress bow-tie which has been left lying about for several years on the floor. All these, we say, are white objects. But are they exactly alike in their colour, if white may be counted as a colour for the purpose of this discussion? Clearly they are not. They are, of course, more or less alike. In fact there is a very considerable degree of colour-likeness between them. But certainly they are not exactly alike in colour. And yet if the very same characteristic, whiteness, is present in them all (as the Philosophy of Universals, apparently, says it is) ought it not to follow that they are exactly alike in colour?

To make quite clear what the point at issue is, we shall have to distinguish, rather pedantically perhaps, between *exact* resemblance in this or that respect and *total* or *complete* resemblance. To put it in another way, resemblance has two dimensions of variation. It may vary in intensity; it may also vary in extent. For example, a piece of writing paper and an envelope, before one has written on either of them, may be exactly alike in colour, and perhaps also in texture. These likenesses between them have the maximum degree of intensity. But the two objects are not completely or totally alike. For one thing, they are unlike in shape. Moreover, the envelope is stuck together with gum and has gum on its flap, while the piece of writing paper has no gum on it. It might perhaps be thought that two envelopes from the same batch *are* completely alike; and certainly they come nearer to it than the envelope and the piece of notepaper. All the same, there is unlikeness in respect of place. At any given time, envelope A is in one place and envelope B is in a different place. On the Relational Theory of Space, this is equivalent to saying that at any given time A and B are related in unlike ways to something else, e.g. the North Pole, or Greenwich Observatory.

According to Leibniz's Principle of the Identity of Indiscernibles, complete or total likeness is an ideal limit which can never quite be reached, though some pairs of objects (the two envelopes, for example) come closer to it than others. For if *per impossibile* two objects were completely alike, place and date included, there would no longer be two objects, but only one. Whether Leibniz's Principle is correct, has been much disputed. But we need not concern ourselves with this dispute. It is sufficient to point out that if there were two objects which resembled each other completely, in date and place as well as in all other ways, and this complete resemblance continued throughout the whole of the histories of both, there could not possibly be any evidence for believing there were two of them. So in this discussion we need not concern ourselves any more with complete or total resemblance, though it is of course an important fact about resemblances that they vary in extent, as well as in degree of intensity.

What does concern us is intensity of resemblance. The maximum intensity of it is what I called 'exact resemblance in this or that respect'. Now some people appear to think that even this is an ideal limit. They seem to think that no two objects are ever *exactly* alike even in one way (e.g. colour, or shape) though, of course, many objects are closely alike in one way or in several. I do not see what evidence we could have for believing such a sweeping negative generalization. It is true that sometimes, when we thought at first that there was an exact likeness in one or more respects between two objects, we may find on more careful examination that there was not. We may have thought that two twins were exactly alike in the conformation of their faces. We look more closely, and find that John's nose is a millimetre longer than William's. But still, there are many cases where there is no discoverable inexactness in a resemblance. We often find that two pennies are indistinguishable in shape, or two postage stamps indistinguishable in colour. And we should not confine ourselves to cases where two or more objects are being compared. There is such a thing as monotony or uniformity within a single object. For example, a certain patch of sky is blue, and the same shade of blue, all over. It is monotonously ultramarine. In other words, all its discernible parts are exactly like each other in colour; at any rate, we can discover no unlikeness of colour between them. Again, there is often no discoverable unlikeness of pitch between two successive phases of the same sound. Will it be said that such monotony is only apparent, not real? But what ground could we have for thinking that no entity is ever really 'monotonous' in this sense, not even in the smallest part of its extent, or throughout the smallest phase of its duration? Thus there is no good ground for maintaining that resemblance of maximum intensity never occurs at all, still less for maintaining that it never *could* occur. Nevertheless, it is not so very common for two objects to be exactly alike even in one way, though monotony within a single object or event is more frequent. What we most usually find in two or more objects which are said to be 'alike' is *close* resemblance in one respect or in several.

We can now return to the controversy between the Philosophy of Resemblances and the Philosophy of Universals. It is argued that if the Philosophy of Universals were right, exact resemblance in one or several respects (resemblance of maximum intensity) ought to be much more common than it is; indeed, that *in*exact resemblance in a given respect, say colour or shape, ought not to exist at all. Of course, there could still be incomplete or partial resemblance, resemblance between two objects in one respect or in several, and lack of resemblance in others. But whenever two objects do resemble each other in a certain respect, it would appear that the resemblance ought to be exact (of maximum intensity), if the Philosophy of Universals were right; either it should be exact, or else it should not exist at all. The Philosophy of Universals tells us that resemblance is derivative, not ultimate; that when two objects resemble each other in a given respect, it is because the very same universal is present in them both. This seems to leave no room for inexact resemblance.

Now if we consider the various white objects I mentioned before – the whole series of them, from the freshly fallen snow to the unwashed bow-tie – how can anyone maintain that the very same characteristic, whiteness, recurs in all of them? Clearly it does not. If it did, they must be exactly alike in their colour; and quite certainly they are not. If we are to use the language of universals or characteristics, shall we not have to say that each of the objects in this series, from the snow to the unwashed tie, is characterized by a *different* characteristic, or is an instance of a *different* universal? In this case, then, the resemblance seems to be ultimate and underivative, *not* dependent on the presence of a single universal in all these objects, although they certainly do resemble each other.

Let us consider another example. Two pennies may be exactly alike in their shape. If so, one may plausibly say that the very same characteristic, roundness, is present in both of them, and that their resemblance is dependent on this. But what about a penny and a sixpence? They certainly *are* alike in shape; but not exactly, because the sixpence has a milled edge and the penny a smooth one. So here again, it would seem, there is no *single* characteristic present in them both, upon which the resemblance could be dependent. This resemblance again seems to be ultimate and underivative.

Thus the Philosophy of Universals, when it makes all resemblance derivative, appears to forget that resemblances have degrees of intensity. Resemblance is treated as if it were degreeless, either present in its maximum degree or else not present at all. In practice, the Philosopher of Universals concentrates his attention on *close* resemblances, and averts his attention from the awkward circumstance that few of them are exact; and resemblances of a lower degree than this (small or moderate ones, not intense enough to be called 'close') are just neglected altogether. But is it not a glaringly obvious fact that resemblances do differ in degree or intensity?

That being so, shall we not be inclined to *reverse* this alleged dependence-relation between 'being alike' and 'being characterized by'? Surely we shall be inclined to say that it is resemblance which is more fundamental than characterization, rather than the other way round. We shall, of course, be willing to go on using terms like 'characteristic' and 'characterized by'; they are part of ordinary language, and everyone has a sufficient understanding of them. But we shall define 'characteristic' in terms of resemblance, and not conversely. Where a number of objects do happen to resemble each other exactly in one respect or three or fifteen, there, and in consequence, we shall be quite willing to say that they have one, or three, or fifteen 'characteristics in common'. But in other cases, where the resemblance is less than exact, we shall not be willing to say this. We shall just say that they resemble each other in such and such a degree, and stop there. In a given set of objects there is whatever degree or resemblance there is. Let us be content to take the facts as we find them.

Turning for a moment to the epistemological side of the matter, surely it is obvious that the applicability of concepts does *not* require an exact resemblance in the objects which a concept applies to? Of course there does have to be a considerable degree of resemblance between all the objects which 'satisfy' a given concept. As we say, there has to be a sufficient likeness between them, e.g. between all the objects to which the concept White applies. What degree of likeness is sufficient, and where the borderline comes between something which falls just within the concept's sphere of application and something else which just falls outside it, is often difficult to decide. For instance, one may wonder whether the *very* dirty bow-tie is white at all. Indeed, it is difficult to see how such a question can be definitely answered, at least in the case of whiteness and many other familiar concepts. The right way to tackle it, perhaps, is to refuse to answer it as it stands. Perhaps we should rather say that a concept may be 'satisfied' in many different degrees; or, in more commonsensical language, that there are good instances and bad instances, better and worse ones, and some so bad that it is arbitrary whether one counts them as instances or not. Thus the piece of chalk is a *better* instance of whiteness than the rather dirty handkerchief is. The patch of freshly fallen snow is a better instance still, perhaps a perfect one. We may give it the mark α (+). Then $\alpha\beta$ is about the right mark for the piece of chalk, and we will give the unwashed bow-tie $\gamma =$, to denote that it is just on the borderline between 'pass' and 'failure'.

It is not easy to see how the doctrine of *universalia in rebus* can make any room for this important and familiar notion of degrees of instantiation. But there is plenty of room for it in Conceptualism, which is the epistemological counterpart of the ontological Philosophy of Resemblances. We must add, in fairness, that there is also plenty of room for it in the Platonic doctrine of *universalia ante rem*. Indeed Plato, or perhaps Socrates, was the first philosopher who noticed that there are degrees of instantiation. This is one of the points, and a good point, which Conceptualism and Platonic Realism have in common.[1]

In the last few pages, I have been discussing the difficulties which the Resemblance Philosophers find in the Philosophy of Universals. But the Philosophy of Resemblances has its difficulties too. The most important ones are concerned with resemblance itself. I shall discuss two of them, and the solutions proposed for them. The first arises from the phrase 'resemblance in respect of...'.

It is obvious that we must distinguish between *different* resemblances. Objects resemble each other in different respects, as well as in different degrees. Red objects resemble each other in one respect, round objects in another respect. The members of a natural kind, for instance cats or oak trees, resemble each other in many respects at once. Thus it would be much too vague if we said that red objects, for example, are just a set of objects which resemble one another, or sufficiently resemble each other. That would not distinguish them from blue objects, or round objects, or any other class of objects one cares to name. We must specify what resemblance it is. Red objects are those which resemble each other 'in a certain respect'. But in *what* respect? And now it looks as if we should have to introduce universals again. Our first answer would probably be that they resemble each other in respect of colour; and this looks very like saying that they are all instances of the universal Colouredness. That is bad enough; but we shall be driven to go farther, because we have not yet said enough to distinguish red objects from blue ones or green ones. Can we stop short of saying that red objects are just those objects which resemble each other in respect of *redness*? And here we seem to be admitting the very point which the Philosophy of Universals is so anxious to maintain; namely that the resemblance between these objects is after all derivative, dependent upon the presence of a single universal, Redness, in them all. To generalize the argument: whenever we say that A, B and C resemble each other in a certain respect, we shall be asked 'In *what* respect?' And how can we answer, except by saying 'in respect of being instances of the universal φ' or 'in respect of being characterized by the characteristic φ'? We may try to get round the difficulty by saying that they resemble each other in a certain *way* (avoiding the word 'respect'), or that there is a certain *sort* of resemblance between them. But when we are asked to specify in *what* way they resemble each other, or what sort of resemblance there is between them, surely we shall still have to answer by mentioning such and such a universal or characteristic: 'The way in which red objects resemble each other is that all of them are instances of the universal Redness, or all of them are characterized by the characteristic Redness.'

This is one of the classical objections to the Philosophy of Resemblances. The argument purports to show that resemblance is not after all ultimate or underivative, but is dependent on the presence of a universal or characteristic which is common to the things which resemble each other. There is something about this objection which arouses our suspicions. It comes perilously near to the tautology 'red things are the things which are red'. The Resemblance philosophers were not undertaking to deny this tautology. They do not deny that *x is red* entails *x is red*. They are only concerned to offer an analysis of *x is red* itself.

Let us now consider the answer they might make to this celebrated objection. Roughly, it consists in substituting 'resemblance *towards . . .*' for 'resemblance in respect of . . .'. Resemblance towards what? Towards certain standard objects, or *exemplars* as I shall call them – certain standard red objects, or standard round objects, or whatever it may be.

It is agreed by both parties that there is a *class* of red objects. The question is, what sort of a structure does a class have? That is where the two philosophies differ. According to the Philosophy of Universals, a class is so to speak a promiscuous or equalitarian assemblage. All its members have, as it were, the same status in it. All of them are instances of the same universal, and no more can be said. But in the Philosophy of Resemblances a class has a more complex structure than this; not equalitarian, but aristocratic. Every class has, as it were, a nucleus, an inner ring of key-members, consisting of a small group of standard objects or exemplars. The exemplars for the class of red things might be a certain tomato, a certain brick and a certain British post-box. Let us call them A, B and C for short. Then a red object is any object which resembles A, B and C as closely as they resemble one another. The resemblance between the exemplars need not itself be a very close one, though it is of course pretty close in the example just given. What is required is only that every other member of the class should resemble the class-exemplars *as* closely as they resemble one another. Thus the exemplars for a class might be a summer sky, a lemon, a post-box, and a lawn. These do resemble one another, though not very closely. Accordingly there is a class consisting of everything which resembles these four entities *as* closely as they resemble each other. It is the class of coloured things, whereas the previous one was the class of red things.

It may be thought that there is still a difficulty about the resemblance between the exemplar objects themselves. In *what respect* do the tomato, the brick and the post-box resemble each other? Surely this question still arises, even though it does not arise about the other members of the class? And how can one answer it, except by saying that these three objects resemble each other in respect of being red, or of being characterized by redness?

But this assumes that we know beforehand what 'being red' is, or what 'being characterized by redness' amounts to. And this begs the question against the Resemblance Philosophy. The Resemblance Philosophers maintain that our knowledge of what it is for something to be red just consists in a capacity to compare any particular object X with certain standard objects, and thereby to discover whether X does or does not resemble these standard objects as closely as they resemble each other. It does not make sense to speak of comparing the standard objects *with themselves*, or to ask whether *they* resemble one another as closely as they do resemble one another. Yet that is just what we should be trying to do, if we tried to say 'in what respect' they are alike. To say that *they* are red, or are characterized by redness, would not be an informative statement, but a tautology.

This objection does however draw our attention to an important point. According to the Philosophy of Resemblances, there cannot be a class unless there are exemplar objects to hold the class together. Nevertheless, the same class may have *alternative* sets of exemplars. The class of red things, we said, consists of everything which resembles the post-box, the tomato and the brick as closely as they resemble each other. It could equally be said to consist of everything which resembles a certain bit of sealing wax, a certain blushing face and a certain sunset sky as closely as *they* resemble each other. In that case, it does make sense to ask whether the post-box, the tomato and the brick are red, or are characterized by redness. And the answer 'Yes, they are' is now no longer tautologous. We are no longer trying, absurdly, to compare them with themselves. We are comparing them with three other things, and discovering that they do all have a sufficient degree of resemblance to these other things. But because there are (within limits) alternative sets of standard objects for the same class, we are led to suppose, erroneously, that a class can exist without any standard objects at all. This or that set of standard objects can be deposed from its privileged position without destroying the unity of the class; and we then suppose, by a process of illegitimate generalization, that the class would still remain what it is if privilege were abolished altogether. There must be *a* set of standard objects for each class, though within limits it does not matter which set of objects have this status.

Thus in the Philosophy of Resemblances, as well as the Philosophy of Universals, there does after all have to be something which holds a class together, if one may put it so. Where the two philosophies differ is, in their view of what that something is. In the Philosophy of Universals, what holds a class together is a universal, something of a different ontological type from the members. In the Philosophy of Resemblances there is no question of different ontological types. There are just particular objects, and there is nothing non-particular which is 'in' them, in the way that a universal is supposed to be 'in' the particulars which are its instances. What holds the class together is a set of nuclear or standard members. Anything which has a sufficient degree of resemblance to these is thereby a member of the class; and 'resembling them sufficiently' means 'resembling them as closely as they resemble each other'.

Again, to turn for a moment to epistemological considerations, it is their relationship to the standard objects or exemplars which enables all these objects to satisfy the same concept, e.g. the concept Red, and likewise enables the same word or other symbol, e.g. the word 'red', to apply to them all. But this is to anticipate. The Philosophy of Resemblances is an *ontological* doctrine, though it may be used as the starting point for certain epistemological theories (Conceptualism, Imagism and Nominalism), just as the Philosophy of Universals may be used as the starting point of a Realist epistemology. If the Philosophy of Resemblances is true at all it might still have been true even if there had been no thinkers and no speakers. As it happens, there are thinkers and speakers too. But there may be many classes in the world, which do exist (because the requisite resemblances do happen to be there) although no mind happens to have formed the corresponding class-concepts, and no speaker has acquired the habit of using the corresponding class-symbols. Thus there is nothing subjectivist or anthropocentric about the Philosophy of Resemblances. It denies that there are universals *in rebus*, but it asserts that there are resemblances *inter res*. Certain objects really are as like the objects A, B and C as these are to one another, whether anyone notices the fact or not. Known or not, spoken of or not, the relationship is there; just as in the Philosophy of Universals objects are instances of universals whether they are known to be so or not. In this respect, both these philosophies are equally 'realistic'.

We must now turn to the second of the classical objections against the Philosophy of Resemblances, an objection so familiar that one might almost call it notorious. It is concerned with resemblance itself. Surely resemblance is itself a universal, present in many pairs or groups of resemblant objects? It is of course, a universal of relation. The instances of it are not individual objects taken singly, but complexes, and each of these complexes is composed of two objects or more. In their attempt to 'get rid of universals', the Philosophers of Resemblance seem to concentrate their attention on universals of *quality* (e.g. redness, colour, shape) and say little or nothing about universals of relation. Hence they have failed to notice that resemblance itself is one of them. But if we are obliged to admit that resemblance at any rate is a genuine universal, a relation which does literally recur in many different situations or complexes, what ground have we for denying that there are other *universalia in rebus* as well?

It may seem audacious to question this formidable argument, which has convinced many illustrious men. But is it as strong as it looks? The Resemblance philosophers might very well reply that it begs the question at issue, that it just assumes what it purports to prove. For after all, what reason is given for the crucial assertion that resemblance is a universal? Apparently none. It is not enough just to say 'surely resemblance at any rate is a universal'. Could any reason be given? We might perhaps try to find one by starting from the linguistic side of the matter. The word 'resemblance', we might say, is an *abstract* word, like the words 'redness' and 'proximity'; therefore it must stand for a universal or characteristic (a relational one, of course). But if this is the argument, it seems to beg the question. For if one does start from a linguistic point of view, the very question at issue is whether abstract words and general words do stand for universals. And if the argument is to be cogent, it ought to be an argument about the noun 'resemblance' in particular, or about the verb 'to resemble' in particular. We ought to be shown that it is somehow peculiarly obvious that *this* word at any rate (or this pair of words) stands for a universal, even though it may be less obvious that other general words do.

Perhaps it will be said, the peculiar obviousness consists in this, that even the people who try to get rid of universals have to use *this* general word at least, or equivalent general words such as 'similar', 'like'. True enough, one cannot speak in a language consisting entirely of proper names and demonstratives. One cannot say anything at all without using some general words. As an observation about the nature of language, this is perfectly indisputable. But the question is, what are its implications? Does it follow that because we must use general words, there are, therefore, general somethings *in rerum natura* which they stand for? That is just the point at issue. One cannot just assume that the answer is 'Yes.' Of course the Philosophy of Resemblances admits that we do use general words, and cannot avoid using them if we are to speak at all. It does not at all deny the fact. But it does deny the conclusion which the Philosophy of Universals draws from it – namely that because we use general words, there must be *general somethings* (universals) which they mean. Has anything been done to show that this denial is mistaken? Nothing. The Philosophy of Universals has just repeated over again the principle which has to be proved, the principle that every general word stands for a universal; adding – what is obvious – that *if* this principle is true, the word 'resemblance' is an illustration of it. Of course. But *is* the principle true?

If the Philosopher of Resemblances is asked to explain how the general word 'resemblance' is used, or what kind of meaning it has, he will presumably point out that there are resemblances of *different orders*. Two cats, A and B, resemble each other, and two sounds, C and D, also resemble each other. These are first-order resemblances. But it is also true that the two-cat situation resembles the two-sound situation, and resembles many other situations too. This is a second-order resemblance. The A–B situation and the C–D situation really are alike, though the constituents of the one are unlike the constituents of the other. In virtue of this second-order likeness (a likeness *between* likeness-situations) we may apply the same general word to both of them; and the word we happen to use for this purpose is the word 'resemblance', in a second-order sense. There is nothing wrong or unintelligible in the notion of second-order resemblance. Or if it be said that there is, we can reply with the *tu quoque* argument that universality must itself be a universal. When it is said that 'cathood is a universal' the word 'universal' is itself a general word, just as 'cat' is when we say 'Pussy is a cat.' So according to the Philosophy of Universals, there must be a universal called 'universality'. And if it is a universal, universality must accordingly be an instance of itself. But this is a contradiction. For according to this Philosophy, anything which is an *instance* of a universal is *ipso facto* a particular, and not a universal. To get out of this difficulty, the Philosophy of Universals must introduce the notion of 'different orders' too. The word 'universal', it has to say, stands for a second-order universal, whereas 'green' or 'cat' or 'in' stand for first-order ones. This is equivalent to saying that the expression 'a universal', or the propositional function 'ϕ is a universal', can occur only in a metalanguage.

This suggests another way in which the Philosophy of Resemblances might reply to the objection that 'resemblance is itself a universal'. The objection assumes that resemblance is just one relation among others: a relation of the same type as 'on top of', or 'near to', or 'side by side with'. But according to the Philosophy of Resemblances, resemblance is not just one relation among others. Indeed, according to this philosophy, it would be misleading to call it 'a relation' at all. It is too fundamental to be called so. For what we *ordinarily* call 'relations' (as well as what we call 'qualities') are themselves founded upon or analysable into resemblance. For example, the relation 'being inside of' is founded upon the resemblance between the Jonah–whale complex, the room–house complex, the match–matchbox complex, etc. Moreover, the Philosophy of Universals itself does not really hold that resemblance is just one relation among others, and in pretending that it does, it is abandoning one of its own fundamental principles; indeed it is abandoning the very one which this argument ('resemblance is itself a universal') is ultimately intended to establish, the principle, namely, that all resemblance is derivative. In the Philosophy of Universals itself, resemblance has a status quite different from relations like 'side by side with' or 'on top of'. Resembling is connected with *being an instance of*. . . in a way that ordinary relations are not. When A resembles B and C, this is supposed to be a direct consequence of the fact that A, B and C are all instances of the same universal; and not only when A, B and C are individual objects (in which case the universal is a universal of quality) but also when they are complexes, so that the universal they are instances of is a relational one, such as 'being inside of'. If resemblance, in the Philosophy of Universals, is to be called a relation at all, it is a relation of a very special sort, quite different from anything to which the word 'relation' is *ordinarily* applied. We should have to say that it is a 'formal' or 'metaphysical' relation (as opposed to a 'natural' or empirical one) just as the relation of instantiation is, if that can be called a relation at all.

So much for the reply the Philosophy of Resemblances might make to this celebrated argument that 'resemblance is itself a universal'. First, it might be objected that the argument begs the question, by just assuming (what it ought to prove) that because 'resemblance' is admittedly a general word, it must stand for a universal. Secondly, the argument overlooks the fact that there are resemblances of different orders. Thirdly, it treats resemblance as one relation among others, parallel in principle to 'side by side with' or 'on top of', whereas the Philosophy of Resemblances maintains that it is too fundamental to be called a relation at all, in the ordinary sense of the word 'relation'. Fourthly, the Philosophy of Universals itself admits, in its own way, that resemblance does *not* have the same status as other relations, in spite of maintaining in this argument that it has.

Thus the Philosophy of Resemblances has an answer to these two classical objections, the one about 'resemblance in respect of' and the one we have just discussed 'that resemblance is itself a universal'. But the Philosophy of Universals also has an answer to the objection about inexact resemblances, and to the complaint that it ignores the different degrees of intensity which resemblances may have. We must consider this answer if we are to do justice to both parties.

The first step is to distinguish between *determinable* and *determinate* characteristics. Universals or characteristics, it is said, have different degrees of determinateness. The adjectives 'determinable' and 'determinate' are too fundamental to be defined. But their meaning can be illustrated. Thus the characteristic of being coloured is a determinable, and the characteristic of being red is a determinate of it. Being red is again a sub-determinable, and has under it the determinates being scarlet, being brick-red, being cherry-red, etc. Likewise, being a mammal is a determinable characteristic, a highly complex one this time. There are many different ways of being a mammal. Being a dog, being a whale, being a man are some of the determinates of this determinable.

Now whenever two objects resemble each other with less than the maximum intensity (i.e. whenever they have what was called an 'inexact' resemblance) we can always say that the same *determinable* characteristic characterizes them both, though not the same determinate one. Two objects may each have a different shade of red. A is scarlet, and B is brick-red. They resemble each other fairly closely, but by no means exactly. That is because redness itself is a determinable characteristic, a sub-determinable falling under the higher determinable colouredness. The two objects do have this determinable characteristic in common, though each of them has a different determinate form of it. So we can still maintain that this resemblance, though inexact, is a derivative, dependent on the presence of the same determinable universal in both objects.

Let us apply these considerations to the two examples given earlier: (1) the various white objects; (2) the penny and the sixpence. It may now be maintained that all my different white objects – from the freshly fallen snow at one end of the series to the unwashed bow-tie at the other – do have a *determinable* characteristic in common; though 'whitish', rather than 'white', would be the appropriate word for it. 'White' might be taken to mean pure white. And pure white is only one determinate of the determinable *whitish*. We certainly should not say that all the objects in this series are pure white. At the most, only the freshly fallen snow is pure white, but not the piece of chalk, or the rather messy bit of paper, or the rather dirty handkerchief, or the very dirty unwashed bow-tie. But we should admit that all of them are 'whitish'.

Let us now consider my other example, the penny and the sixpence, which resemble each other in shape, but inexactly. The penny with its smooth edge and the sixpence with its milled (slightly serrated) edge have different determinate shapes. How is it, then, that they do still resemble each other in shape, though inexactly, and both would be called 'round coins' in ordinary speech? Because the same *determinable* shape – we might more appropriately call it 'roundish' – characterizes both of them; and it characterizes many other things as well, e.g. slightly buckled bicycle wheels, cogwheels with not too large teeth, which resemble each other a good deal less closely than the penny and the sixpence do.

By this expedient the Philosophy of Universals is able to maintain its thesis that all resemblances, inexact ones too, are derivative, and not ultimate, as the Philosophy of Resemblances would have them. Inexact resemblance, we are invited to say, depends upon or is derived from the presence of the same *determinable* characteristic in a number of objects; exact resemblance (resemblance of maximum intensity) depends upon their being characterized by the same *determinate* characteristic.

Perhaps this will also enable us to dispense with the notion of 'degrees of instantiation' which was mentioned earlier. It was not easy to see what could be meant in the Philosophy of *universalia in rebus* by saying that one object is a *better* instance of so-and-so than another, though this notion fits well enough into the Platonic theory of *universalia ante rem*, and into Conceptualism too. Perhaps it could now be suggested that the determinates of some determinables, e.g. 'whitish', 'roundish', are serially ordered. Thus the various determinates of whitishness which characterize the patch of snow, the piece of chalk, the paper, etc., may be arranged in a series beginning with 'pure white'. After this comes 'nearly pure white' (the colour the piece of chalk has), then 'farther from pure white' and then 'farther still from pure white', until we come to a characteristic which is as far from pure whiteness as it can be without ceasing to be a determinate of whitishness at all. The system of marking ($\alpha+$, α, $\alpha-$, $\beta+$, etc.) which we suggested for indicating the 'goodness' or 'badness' of instances can still be used: only it is now applied not to the objects themselves, but to the determinate characteristics by which they are respectively characterized.

Thus this objection to the Philosophy of Universals, that it can make no room for inexact resemblances (resemblances of less than the maximum intensity), turns out after all to be indecisive, although it looked so convincing at first sight. The facts to which this argument draws our attention are of course perfectly genuine, and important too. It is, for example, an important fact about language that most of our general words apply to sets of objects which inexactly resemble one another; and it is an important fact about thinking, that the various objects which 'satisfy' a given concept, e.g. the concept of Crow, do not have to be exactly alike. Nevertheless, this argument does not at all refute the Philosophy of Universals, as it is often supposed to do. All it does is to point out what was lacking in our first rough-and-ready formulation of that philosophy. Certainly the Philosophy of Universals would be quite unworkable *without* the distinction between determinable and determinate universals. The doctrine that universals or characteristics have different degrees of determinacy is an indispensable part of it. But the distinction between determinables and determinates is perfectly consistent with the contention that there are recurrent characteristics in the world, and with the accompanying doctrine that resemblances are derivative, not ultimate. Indeed, it could be argued, the fact that recurrent characteristics do differ in their degree of determinateness is just as obvious as the fact of recurrence itself.

Finally, it is worth repeating that the phrases 'inexact resemblance', 'not exactly alike' are sometimes used in another way, to mean *incomplete* or *partial* resemblance. If A and B are closely alike in a large number of respects, but unlike or not closely alike in one or two, we sometimes say that they are very like each other but not exactly like each other. For example, within the same species of bird we often find that there are slight differences of size or colouring between two individual specimens, although they also resemble each other closely in very many ways. It is obvious that if the phrase 'inexact resemblance' is used in *this* sense, the Philosophy of Universals has no difficulty at all about inexact resemblances. We merely have to say that many universals are common to the two birds, or recur in both of them; and consequently the two individuals resemble each other in a great many respects. We then add that bird A is also an instance of a certain universal φ, while bird B is not an instance of this, but of a certain other universal ψ; and consequently there is a respect in which they are *not* alike. (It may be found, of course, and in this example it almost certainly will be, that though φ and ψ are different determinate universals, they are determinates of the same determinable universal, say 'mottled'.) It must not be forgotten that every individual object is an instance of several universals at once, and often of very many at once. When we compare it with another object, we may easily find that some universals are common to both of them, and other universals are not. It would be a strange misunderstanding of the Philosophy of Universals to suppose that in this philosophy every particular is held to be an instance of only *one* universal. When we say that something is a cat, we are saying that it is an instance of many universals conjointly, and not just of one.

Our discussion has been long and complicated. What conclusion shall we draw from it? It would seem that there is nothing to choose between these two philosophies, the Philosophy of Universals or characteristics (*universalia in rebus*)[2] on the one hand, and the Philosophy of Ultimate Resemblances on the other. At any rate, it would seem that there is nothing to choose between them so long as they are considered as purely ontological doctrines, which is the way we have been considering them in this chapter. Both seem to cover the facts, though only when both are stated with sufficient care. Moreover, they both cover the *same* facts. This strongly suggests that they are two different (systematically different) terminologies, two systematically different ways of saying the same thing. It does not follow that both alike are just pieces of solemn and elaborate trifling. On the contrary, the thing which they both say is of the first importance, and we do need a way of saying it. The efforts which each party has made to provide us with a systematic terminology for saying it have not been a waste of time. For if there were no recurrent characteristics, *or* no resemblances between different objects – whichever way you choose to put it – there could be no conceptual cognition, and no use of general symbols either.

Now if there is only a (systematic) difference of terminology between these two philosophies, it is well to be familiar with both. Each of them may have its misleading features; and when we are in danger of being misled by the one, we may save ourselves by changing over to the other. . . .

Notes

1   In Christian Platonism, where Plato's transcendent 'forms' become concepts in the mind of God, the differences between Platonic Realism and Conceptualism are still further diminished, though they do not disappear altogether.
2   It may be worthwhile to remind the reader that the phrase 'the Philosophy of Universals', as it has been used in this chapter, is *not* intended to cover the Platonic doctrine of *universalia ante rem*.

---

7   The Elements of Being

D. C. Williams

First philosophy, according to the traditional schedule, is analytic ontology, examining the traits necessary to whatever is, in this or any other possible world. Its cardinal problem is that of substance and attribute, or at any rate something cognate with this in that family of ideas which contains also subsistence and inherence, subject and predicate, particular and universal, singular and general, individual and class, and matter and form. It is the question how a thing can be an instance of many properties while a property may inhere in many instances, the question how everything is a case of a kind, a this-such, an essence endowed with existence, an existent differentiated by essence, and so forth. Concerned with what it means to be a thing or a kind at all, it is in some wise prior to and independent of the other great branch of metaphysics, speculative cosmology: what kinds of things are there, what stuff are they made of, how are they strung together?

Although "analytic ontology" is not much practiced as a unit under that name today, its problems, and especially the problem of subsistence and inherence, are as much alive in the latest manifestoes of the logical analysts, who pretend to believe neither in substances nor in universals, as they were in the counsels of Athens and of Paris. Nothing is clear until that topic is clear, and in this essay I hope to do something to clarify it in terms of a theory or schema which over a good many years I have found so serviceable that it may well be true.

Metaphysics is the thoroughly empirical science. Every item of experience must be evidence for or against any hypothesis of speculative cosmology, and every experienced object must be an exemplar and test case for the categories of analytic ontology. Technically, therefore, one example ought for our present theme to be as good as another. The more dignified examples, however, are darkened with a patina of tradition and partisanship, while some frivolous ones are peculiarly perspicuous. Let us therefore imagine three lollipops, made by a candy man who buys sticks from a big supplier and molds candy knobs on them. Lollipop No. 1 has a red, round, peppermint head, No. 2 a brown, round, chocolate head, No. 3 a red, square, peppermint head. The circumstance here which mainly provokes theories of subsistence and inherence is similarity with difference: each lollipop is partially similar to each other and partially different from it. If we can give a good account of this circumstance in this affair we shall have the instrument to expose the anatomy of everything, from an electron or an apple to archangels and the World All.

My chief proposal to that end may be put, to begin with, as nothing more tremendous than that we admit literally and seriously that to say that *a* is partially similar to *b* is to say that a part of *a* is wholly or completely similar to a part of *b*. This is a truism when we construe it with respect to ordinary concrete parts, for example, the sticks in the lollipops. On physical grounds, to be sure, it is not likely that any three solid objects, not even three sticks turned out by mass industry, are exactly similar, but they often look as if they were, and we can intelligibly stipulate for our argument that our exemplary sticks do exactly resemble each other through and through. To say then that each of the lollipops is partially similar to each other, that is, with respect to stick, is to say that there is a stick in each which is perfectly similar to the stick in every other, even though each stick remains as particular and distinct an individual as the whole lollipop. We would seldom give a proper name to a lollipop and still more seldom to the stick in one, but we might easily do so – "Heraplem" for lollipop No. 1, for example, "Paraplete" for its stick, "Boanerp" for No. 2, and "Merrinel" for its stick. Heraplem and Boanerp then *are* partially similar because Paraplete and Merrinel are perfectly similar.

What now of the rest of each lollipop and what of their more subtle similarities, of color, shape, and flavor? My proposal is that we treat them in exactly the same way. Since we cannot find more parts of the usual gross sort, like the stick, to be wholly similar from lollipop to lollipop, let us discriminate subtler and thinner or more diffuse parts till we find some of these which *are* wholly similar. This odd-sounding assignment, of course, is no more than we are accustomed to do, easily and without noticing.

Just as we can distinguish in the lollipops, Heraplem and Boanerp, the gross parts called "sticks," namely, Paraplete and Merrinel, so we can distinguish in each lollipop a finer part which we are used to call its "color" and another called its "shape" – not its kind of color or shape, mind you, but these particular cases, this reddening, this occurrence or occasion of roundness, each as uniquely itself as a man, an earthquake, or a yell. With only a little more hardihood than christened the lollipops and sticks, we can christen our finer components "Harlac" and "Bantic" for the respective color components, let us say, and "Hamis" and "Borcas" for the respective shape components.

In these four new names, the first and last letters are initials of "Heraplem" and "Boanerp," and of "color" and "shape," respectively, but this is a mnemonic device for us, irrelevant to their force as names. "Harlac," for example, is not to be taken as an abbreviation for the description, "the color component of Heraplem." In a real situation like the one we are imagining, "Harlac" is defined ostensively, as one baptizes a child or introduces a man, present in the flesh; the descriptive phrase is only a scaffolding, a temporary device to bring attention to bear on the particular entity being denoted, as a mother of twins might admonish the vicar, "Boadicea is the cross-looking one."

Heraplem and Boanerp are partially similar, then, not merely because the respective gross parts Paraplete and Merrinel (their sticks) are wholly similar but also because the respective fine parts, Hamis and Borcas (their "shapes"), are wholly similar – all this without prejudice to the fact that Hamis is numerically as distinct from Borcas, to which it is wholly similar, and from Harlac, with which it is conjoined in Heraplem, as Harlac is from Bantic, to which it is neither similar nor conjoined, and as the stick Paraplete is from the stick Merrinel, and as the whole lollipop, Heraplem, is from the whole Boanerp. The sense in which Heraplem and Boanerp "have the same shape" and in which "the shape of one is identical with the shape of the other" is the sense in which two soldiers "wear the same uniform" or in which a son "has his father's nose" or our candy man might say "I use the same identical stick, Ledbetter's Triple-X, in all my lollipops." They do not have the same shape in the sense in which two children have the same father, or two streets have the same manhole in the middle of their intersection, or two college boys wear the same tuxedo (and so cannot go to dances together). But while similar in the indicated respects, Heraplem and Boanerp are partially dissimilar inasmuch as their knobs or heads are partially dissimilar, and these are partially dissimilar because some of their finer parts, for example, their colors, are dissimilar.

In like manner, to proceed, we note that Harlac, the color component of No. 1 (Heraplem), though numerically distinct from, is wholly similar to, the color component of No. 3. But No. 1 has not only a color component which is perfectly similar to the color component of No. 3; it has also a flavor component perfectly similar to the flavor component of No. 3. (It does not matter whether we think of the flavor as a phenomenal quality or as a molecular structure in the stuff of the candy.) The flavor-plus-color of No. 1 (and likewise of No. 3) is a complex whose own constituents are the flavor and the color, and so on for innumerable selections and combinations of parts, both gross and fine, which are embedded in any one such object or any collection of them.

Crucial here, of course, is the admission of a fine or subtle part, a diffuse or permeating one, such as a resident color or occurrent shape, to at least as good standing among the actual and individual items of the world's furniture as a gross part, such as a stick. The fact that one part is thus finer and more diffuse than another and that it is more susceptible of similarity no more militates against its individual actuality than the fact that mice are smaller and more numerous than elephants makes them any the less real. To borrow now an old but pretty appropriate term, a gross part, like the stick, is "concrete," as the whole lollipop is, while a fine or diffuse part, like the color component or shape component, is "abstract." The color-plus-shape is less abstract or more nearly concrete than the color alone, but it is more abstract or less concrete than color-plus-shape-plus-flavor, and so on up till we get to the total complex, which is wholly concrete.

I propose now that entities like our fine parts or abstract components are the primary constituents of this or any possible world, the very alphabet of being. They not only are actual but are the only actualities, in just this sense, that whereas entities of all other categories are literally composed of them, they are not in general composed of any other sort of entity. That such a crucial category has no regular name is quite characteristic of first principles and is one reason why the latter are worth pursuing. A description of it in good old phraseology has a paradoxical ring: our thin parts are "abstract particulars." We shall have occasion to use "parts" for concrete entities and "components" for abstract ones (and "constituent" for both), as some British philosophers have used "component" for property and "constituent" for concrete part. Recalling, however, that Santayana used "trope" to stand for the essence of an occurrence,[1] I shall divert the word, which is almost useless in either his or its dictionary sense, to stand for the abstract particular which is, so to speak, the occurrence of an essence.

A trope then is a particular entity either abstract or consisting of one or more concrete entities in combination with an abstraction. Thus Napoleon and Napoleon's forelock are not tropes, but Napoleon's posture is a trope, and so is the whole whose constituents are his forelock and his posture, and so is his residing on Elba.

Turning now briefly from the alphabet of being to a glimpse of its syllabary, we observe two fundamental ways in which tropes may be connected with one another: the way of location and the way of similarity. These are categorially different and indeed systematic counterparts of one another – mirror images, as it were. Location is external in the sense that two tropes per se do not entail or necessitate or determine their location with respect to one another, while similarity is internal in the sense that, given any two tropes, there are entailed or necessitated or determined whether and how they are similar. (What further this prima facie difference amounts to we cannot pursue here.) Location is easiest thought of as position in physical space-time, but I intend the notion to include also all the analogous spreads and arrangements which we find in different conscious fields and indeed in any realm of existence which we can conceive – the whole interior stretch and structure of a Leibnizian monad, for example. Both modes of connection are describable in terms of distance and direction.

We are very familiar in a general way with the numberless distances and directions which compose locations in space and time, but not so used to thinking of the limiting value of such location (though very familiar with the phenomenon itself) – namely, being in the same place at the same time, the unique collocation and interpenetration which we call "belonging to or inhering in, or characterizing, the same thing." Russell calls this "compresence"; I shall follow Whitehead, Keynes, and Mill in calling it "concurrence." Plainly, what I called "color-plus-shape," in the second paragraph back, is not just the sum of a color and a shape but their sum in concurrence; we might have said "color-cum-shape." We can now explain furthermore that Harlac and Bantic, our lollipop colors, are really complex, each consisting of a knob-color and a stick-color in a certain relative location, and similarly for the shapes. Since there are no short words (like "red" and "square") which describe such complex colors and shapes, I shall ignore the sticks (supposed to be all alike) and use our trope names just for the qualities in the respective knobs.

It will not matter if the reader regards the use of "distance" and "direction" for resemblance relations as metaphorical so long as he gets the idea. Here we have no trouble with the notion of the limiting value, zero distance or precise similarity, but may need to think a little more about the lesser similarity or greater difference which holds, e.g., between a red and a purple, and still more, unless we are psychologists or phenomenologists, about such elaborate similarity distances and directions as are mapped on the color cone.

Any possible world, and hence, of course, this one, is completely constituted by its tropes and their connections of location and similarity, and any others there may be. (I think there are few others or none, but that is not necessary to the theory of tropes.) Location and similarity (or whatever else there is) provide all the relations, as the tropes provide the terms, but the total of the relations is not something over and above the total of the terms, for a relation R between tropes a and b is a constitutive trope of the complex $r'(a, b)$ (e.g., the concurrence-sum of Harlac and Hamis), while conversely the terms a and b will be in general composed of constituents in relation – though perhaps no more than the spread of a "smooth" quality, a "quale," such as a color.

Any trope belongs to as many sets or sums of tropes as there are ways of combining it with other tropes in the world. Of special interest however are (1) the set or sum of tropes which have to it the relation of concurrence (the limiting value of location), and (2) the set or sum of those which have to it the relation of precise similarity (the limiting value of similarity, sometimes mischievously called "identity"). Speaking roughly now, the set or sum of tropes concurrent with a trope, such as our color component Harlac, is the concrete particular or thing which it may be said to characterize, in our example the lollipop Heraplem, or, to simplify the affair, the knob of the lollipop at a moment. By parallel, speaking roughly again, the set or sum of tropes precisely similar to a given trope, say Harlac again, may be supposed to be, or at least to correspond formally to, the abstract universal or "essence" which it may be said to exemplify, in our illustration a definite shade of redness. (The tropes approximately similar to the given one provide a less definite universal.)

The phrase "set or sum" above is a deliberate hedge. A set is a *class* of which the terms are members; a sum is a whole of which the terms are parts, in the very primitive sense of "part" dealt with by recent calculi of individuals. In the accompanying figure (figure 1), for instance, the class of six squares, the class of three rows, and the class of two columns are different from each other and from the

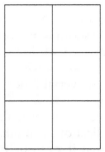

Figure 1

one figure; but the sum of squares, the sum of rows, and the sum of columns are identical with one another and with the whole.

What a difference of logical "type" amounts to, particularly in the philosophy of tropes, is far from clear, but everybody agrees that a sum is of the same type with its terms, as a whole is of the same type with its parts, a man of the same type with his arms and legs. The concept of a class or set, on the other hand, is notably more complex and questionable. A class has not been shown to be in any clear sense an abstract entity, but there is some excuse for considering it of a different type from its members. Convinced that a concrete thing is composed of tropes in a manner logically no different from that in which it is composed of any other exhaustive batch of parts, we have every incentive to say that a concrete thing is not a set but a sum of tropes; and let us so describe it. Whether the counterpart concept of the universal can be defined as the sum of similars – all merely grammatical difficulties aside – is not so clear; there is little doubt that the set or class will do the job.

All the paradoxes which attend the fashionable effort to equate the universal humanity, for example, with the class of concrete men (including such absurdities as that being a featherless biped is then the same as having a sense of humor) disappear when we equate it rather with our new set, the class of abstract particular humanities – the class whose members are not Socrates, Napoleon, and so forth, but the human trope in Socrates, the one in Napoleon, and so forth. Still wilder paradoxes resulted from the more radical nominalistic device of substituting the sum of concrete men for their class, and though most of these also are obviated by taking our sum of similar tropes instead, I am sure that some remain. Because concurrence and similarity are such symmetrical counterparts, I shall not be surprised if it turns out that while the concurrence complex must be a sum, the similarity complex must be a set.

In suggesting how both concrete particulars and abstract universals are composed of or "constructed from" tropes, I aver that those two categories do not divide the world between them. It does not consist of concrete particulars in addition to abstract universals, as the old scheme had it, nor need we admit that it must be constructible either from concrete particulars or from abstract universals, as recent innovators argue. The notions of the abstract and the universal (and hence of the concrete and the particular) are so far independent that their combinations box the logical compass. Socrates is a concrete particular. The component of him which is his wisdom is an abstract particular or "trope." The one general wisdom of which all such wisdoms are members or examples is an abstract universal. The total Socratesity of which all creatures exactly like him are parts or members is a "concrete universal," not in the idealistic but in a strictly accurate sense.

Having thus sorted out the rubrics, we can almost automatically do much to dispel the ancient mystery of predication, so influential in the idea of logical types. The prevalent theory has been that if *y* can be predicated of *x*, or inheres in or characterizes *x*, or if *x* is an instance of *y*, then *x* and *y* must be sundered by a unique logical and ontological abyss. Most of the horror of this, however, which has recently impelled some logicians to graceless contortions of language, is due to taking predication as one indissoluble and inscrutable operation and vanishes when our principles reveal predication to be composed of two distinct but intelligible phases. "Socrates is wise," or generically "*a* is ϕ," means that the concurrence sum (Socrates) includes a trope which is a member of the similarity set (wisdom-in-general). When we contrast a thing with a property or characteristic of it, a substantive with an adjective, we may intend either or both of these connections. . . .

A philosophy of tropes calls for completion in a dozen directions at once. Some of these I must ignore for the present because the questions would take us too far, some because I do not know the answers. . . . What in fact I shall do here is to defend the fundamental notion that there are entities at once abstract, particular, and actual, and this in two ways: the affirmative way of showing how experience and nature evince them over and over, and the negative way of settling accounts with old dialectical objections to them.

I deliberately did not use the word "abstract" to describe our tropes till we had done our best to identify them in other ways, lest the generally derogatory connotation of the word blind us to the reality of objects as plain as the sunlight (for indeed the sunlight is an abstract existent). The many meanings of "abstract" which make it repulsive to the empirical temper of our age suggest that anything abstract must be the product of some magical feat of mind, or the denizen of some remote immaterial eternity. . . .

At its broadest the "true" meaning of "abstract" is *partial, incomplete,* or *fragmentary,* the trait of what is less than its including whole. Since there must be, for everything but the World All, at least something, and indeed many things, of which it is a proper part, everything but the World All is "abstract" in this broad sense. It is thus that the idealist can denounce a cat as "abstract." The more usual practice of philosophers, however, has been to require for "abstractness" the more special sort of incompleteness which pertains to what we have called the "thin" or "fine" or "diffuse" sort of constituent, like the color or shape of our lollipop, in contrast with the "thick," "gross," or chunky sort of constituent, like the stick in it.

If now one looks at things without traditional prepossessions, the existence of abstracta seems as plain as any fact could be. (To call them "abstracta" is bad in so far as the word is artificial, but it helps to avoid the prepossessions, including the implication of transcendent metaphysics, which hang about "abstract entities" and the psychological implication, as if such objects were our own private inventions, of "abstractions.") . . .

I have no doubt that whole things like lollipops, trees, and the moon, do exist in full-blooded concreteness, but it is not they which are present to the senses, and it is not awareness of abstracta which is "difficult, . . . not to be attained without pains and study."[2] To claim primacy for our knowledge of concrete things is "mysticism" in the strict sense, that is, a claim to such acquaintance with a plethoric being as no conceivable stroke of psychophysics could account for. What we primarily see of the moon, for example, is its shape and color and not at all its whole concrete bulk. Generations lived and died without suspecting it had a concrete bulk. If now we impute to it a solidity and an aridity, we do it item by item quite as we impute wheels to a clock or a stomach to a worm. Evaluation is similarly focussed on the abstract. What most men have valued the moon for is its brightness; what a child wants of a lollipop is a certain flavor and endurance. He would much rather have these abstract qualities without the rest of the bulk than the bulk without the qualities. . . .

Though the uses of the trope to account for substances and universals are of special technical interest, the impact of the idea is perhaps greater in those many regions not so staled and obscured by long wont and old opinion and not so well supplied with alternative devices. While substances and universals can be "constructed" out of tropes, or apostrophized in toto for sundry purposes, the trope cannot well be "constructed" out of them and provides the one rubric which is hospitable to a hundred sorts of entity which neither philosophy, science, nor common sense can forgo. This is most obvious in any attempt to treat of the mind, just because the mind's forte is the tuning, focussing, or spotlighting – in brief, the abstraction – which brings abstracta into relief against a void or nondescript background. A pain is a trope par excellence, a mysterious bright pain in the night, for example, without conscious context or classification, yet as absolutely and implacably its particular self as the Great Pyramid. But all other distinguishable contents are of essentially the same order: a love, or a sorrow, or a pleasure.

The notion, however, gets its best use in the theory of knowledge. The "sensible species" of the Scholastics, the "ideas" of Locke and Berkeley, the ideas and impressions of Hume, the sense data of later epistemology – once they are understood as tropes, and as neither things nor essences, a hundred riddles about them dissolve, and philistine attacks on theory of knowledge itself lose most of their point. We need not propose that a red sensum, for example, is perfectly abstract (whatever that might be). But even though it have such distinguishable components as a shape and a size as well as a color, and though the color itself involve the "attributes" of hue, brightness, and saturation, still it is abstract in comparison with a whole colored solid. According to reputable psychologists, furthermore, there can be data much more abstract, professed empiricists to the contrary notwithstanding: data which have color and no other character, or even hue and no other attribute.

. . . A whole soul or mind, if it is not a unique immaterial substance on its own, is a trope. In one manner or another everybody grants that there is a very considerable correlation between the components of conscious experience and the processes of the body. The physical correlates of conscious tropes are then in general physical tropes – the patterns of arrangement and motion which behaviorally or physiologically are beliefs, discriminations, perceptions, desires, and the rest. In our happy-go-lucky way, however, the human functions we generally speak and think about are "mixed tropes," like the "mixed modes" of the Cartesians. A belief, a sensation, an emotion, a purpose – each is partly the conscious item and partly the behavioral one.

On the model of such mixed tropes we must understand a love affair, an act of contrition, or a piece of impudence. A word or a sentence in a particular occurrence is a trope, mental, physical, or mixed. The "same" word in many occurrences is the corresponding universal. This distinction differs from Peirce's between "token" and "type" inasmuch as it avoids the usual identification of the token with the concrete ink splotch, for example, in which our trope inheres – an ill-timed obsession with substance which is out of accord both with ordinary ideas and with the fact that most verbal tropes cannot plausibly be imputed to any special concrete objects anyhow. A word is a product of art, and art is full of analogous tropes. A statue is not a trope, but the connoisseur who gloats over its form, its texture, or its color is gloating over a trope. A musical performance, a song or a symphony, is a trope, and so is a musical theme – not the *kind* of theme, the universal which recurs throughout the same work in all its repetitions, but any single case of it. . . .

If a bit of perceptual behavior is a trope, so is any response to a stimulus, and so is the stimulus, and so therefore, more generally, is every effect and its cause, When we say that the sunlight caused the blackening of the film we assert a connection between two tropes; when we say that sunlight in general causes blackening in general, we assert a corresponding relation between the corresponding universals. Causation is often said to relate events, and generally speaking any event is a trope: a smile, a sneeze, a scream, an election, a cold snap, a storm, a lightning flash, a conspiracy, perhaps a wave, and so on up to such big and important events that they have proper names, like Lulu, the H-bomb explosion. We have called a trope a "case" of its universal, while the universal is the "kind" of the trope, and so it is no surprise that a medical "case" is a trope – in the sense, at any rate, in which a person is said to *have* a case of typhoid fever rather than to *be* a case of it (for the latter "case" stands for the whole concrete individual). A high-school boy, uncoached, has assured me, "Of course there's such a thing as redness – this pencil *has a case of it*."

When a scientist reports a temperature or a velocity or a viscosity, he is reporting a trope – not a universal, because it is a once-for-all occurrence, but not a concrete thing either, though doubtless a component of one. He is likely to call it an "aspect" of the thing or preferably a "state," and generally speaking, a "state" of a thing or a nation is a trope (though "state" too may mean a *kind* of state, the universal). Recent developments in subatomic physics, a none too reliable oracle, suggest that an electron, e.g., just is an existent state and that the common-sense philosophy of the concrete here abdicates altogether in favor of the trope.

Since events and processes are tropes, and also *cases* and *states*, one wonders about "facts," "*states* of affairs," and "what is the *case*." Mary's beauty is a trope; Mary-being-beautiful, the "fact" which makes "Mary is beautiful" true, seems a similar but queerer business. C. I. Lewis is surely right that a state of affairs is "abstract and adjectival" rather than a "chunk,"[3] and it would be delightful to say that a state of affairs stands to its proposition as an ordinary trope does to its property (universal). But I shrink from endowing the theory of tropes with either the assets or the deficits of a theory of facts, of states of affairs, or of propositions.

A variety of trope which has been much entertained by the philosopher unawares is that of geometrical figures, circles, triangles, and so forth. These have been alternately treated as if they were Platonic universals and as if they were concrete particulars, whereas in fact they are neither. Triangularity, to be sure, is an abstract universal, and a triangular object is a concrete particular, but a triangle is an abstract particular. Since a triangle, a circle, or any of the rest, while being particular, is an abstractum exhausted in one thin but salient character, the propensity of many generations of writers for taking them as typical "things" was perhaps largely responsible for that catastrophic doctrine of real essences by which truly concrete things like men or trees are supposed to be similarly dominated by a single essential character in each.

If a geometrical figure is a trope, so is a woman's figure, and so is her complexion or her digestion – in that sense in which she is more concerned to take care of "her figure," "her complexion," "her digestion," than those of anybody else, however similar. Thus too when someone tells her, "I love the sweetness of your voice and the serenity of your brow," he does not mean, if he is wise or faithful, that *kind* of voice and brow, wherever they occur in the world manifold, but these particular cases. But while the complexion of a face, a smile on it, the whole expression of it, and every component of the expression, and the shape of the whole face or of any part of it, all are tropes, the face itself is a *surface*, and some logical philosophers who shy at "abstract entities" think that a surface escapes that epithet. Well, a surface does seem to occupy a sort of borderline status, but this is no more than our doctrine entails, for we have expressly denied that "between the abstract and the concrete there can be no intervening stages."[4]

As the shape is to the surface, perhaps, so the surface is to the solid. The bigger difference is that a surface is "concrete" in two dimensions as a triangle on it is not concrete at all. This sort of quasiconcreteness, we note, belongs also to an instantaneous three-dimensional solid in comparison with one which is appreciably extended in time. Only an old familiarity with the terms of geometry, I think, makes anyone suppose that a surface or an instantaneous solid has in any fundamental way a more robust being than a four-dimensional shape or temperature. Similar questions and answers may be expected to attend such entities as the equator or a hole.

. . . The arguments which I wish especially to weigh now . . . are those which assert that the status of abstractness itself is incompatible with actual existence.

Because our tropes are advocated not as entities additional to concrete things but as constituents of them, any effective denial or defense of them must be an argument, not for or against a transcendent realm of being, but concerning what sorts of constituents are real and which, if any, are not, and hence the rights and significance of analysis.

When the issue is thus narrowed, the principal dialectical objection may be summed up in the old maxim that a true existent must be such as can exist by and in itself, per se and in se. We have called to witness the idealists that if this is taken without reservation, then ordinary concrete things – men's limbs as well as their temperaments, the men as well as their limbs – cannot be real either, for only the world as an eternal whole exists per se and in se. To preserve the advantage of the concrete over the abstract, we must reinterpret "per se" to accommodate the former but not the latter. If we do not altogether beg the question by defining "per se" to mean concrete, the most we can say is that the concrete is comparatively independent of its context and that it can, within wide limits, be moved around without losing its identity. Whereas we can pull the stick or an atom out of a lollipop and even put it back on demand, we cannot strip off its color and shape or extract the pure flavor of it, and still more obviously we cannot assemble a lollipop from such components.

Even this difference, however, fades out under examination. It is merely an accident of physical fact, after all, that sticks are not dissipated when removed from lollipops, or wheels from watches, as a volume of chlorine is when let out of a flask. Many concrete parts are physically incapable of removal, as the Mississippi River is from the Mississippi Valley, and most of them which are removable, as a whelk is from its shell, are so damaged by the operation that they are, as we say, not the same thing at all. But whether removable or not in the ordinary sense of "removable," they are always irremovable in the one queer respect which is cardinal to our kind of question. For the actual events which compose the existence of the watch wheel now before me on the table are numerically as distinct from those which compose the wheel inside the watch ten minutes ago, or back inside the watch again two hours from now, as any of these is from my fingers or from Jupiter. Their community consists logically of only a continuity of similar events or states strung between.

To bring this out best let us use the word "constituents" (what "stand together") for parts or components as they exist within a complex object as we describe it, and the word "ingredients" (what "go into" the object) for those entities with which we operate when we start generating it or when we are through disintegrating it. The wheels of a watch or the stick of a lollipop qua "ingredients" happen to be conspicuously affiliated with the wheels and stick qua "constituents." The milk, sugar, eggs, and flour which went to making a cake, however, or the flaccid and ruined organs dissected out of an animal body, are much less fairly described as "the same as" the constituents of the object while it lasted.

The atomic theory was the great triumph of the feeling that things ought to have concrete parts which are at once constituents and ingredients, but with discontinuous and identityless electrons taking the place of atoms, this reassurance, limited to begin with, has become worth next to nothing. If now we turn back to our abstractions, the situation seems much the same with them. They often cannot be "moved" in even the crude sense in which some concrete things can, but in whatever sense "the same" wheel survives when taken from a watch, in that sense, if we can believe our eyes, the color of a blouse, for example, may be transferred to the wash water, or the glare of an electric light survives for a moment in the positive afterimage.

There remains one severe question, whether abstract qualities do not logically or metaphysically *require* their contexts as concrete entities do not. On the idealist logic of internal relations, everything requires or entails its whole cosmic matrix, but it seems at first sight that even those who deny this extravagance of idealism would have to grant it inconceivable that an abstractum should exist by itself, like the grin left behind by the Cheshire cat, and not as a component of something concrete.

This raises first the question how we define "concrete." If it means merely what does exist unconjoined with further components, then it is a verbalism that whatever exists must be concrete or a component of something concrete. The real question then is whether an entity which is "abstract" in the sense that it is conjoined in something concrete with other abstracta, as the shape of a watch is, for example, may be duplicated elsewhere by an entity precisely similar internally but not thus conjoined with anything. Our instincts say "No," that there is a sort of cosmic standard of concreteness, a certain degree of richness or thickness, which perhaps is a general maximum that nothing can exceed, but which at any rate is a general minimum that an entity must attain in order, as the Scholastics say, "to be apt for existence," or that, in Aristotle's phrase, it "can exist apart."[5]

Plausible though it be, however, that a color or a shape cannot exist by itself, I think we have to reject the notion of a standard concreteness. For it means that from the awareness of even the thinnest abstractum – indeed the thinner the better – we could *deduce* the presence of the rest of a concrete thing, if not its specific character then at least that there is something concrete there, as Descartes deduced from a conscious state the existence of a spiritual substance in which it inhered. It seems to me an analytic principle that all deduction must be analytic so that while any proper component is deducible from the composite which contains it, no composite is deducible from any of its proper components, and hence that abstracta must in principle be as independent of their contexts as concrete things are.

Though it has been interesting to observe, for its own sake, that the abstract and the concrete entities are much alike with respect to independence and manipulability, this was nearly superfluous for our main purpose because the actuality of entities does not in any event depend on whether they are independent and manipulable but only on whether they are *there*. This was the import of our differentiation between constituents and ingredients. The constituents of the universe are not the ingredients of which God made it, if He made it of any, nor the fragments which will supervene when it decomposes, but are the stars and atoms and men, the shapes and tastes and numbers, which are present in it now; and in the same way the constituents of a lollipop, for example, are not the stuffs which went into the kettle, nor the shards which would result from running it through a grinder, but the sectors, the facets, the atoms, the structures, and the qualities which are its current parts and components *in situ*. That things consist of tropes does not imply either that they were made by putting tropes together or that they can be dismantled by taking tropes apart. . . .

The most that can be done by a thesis in first philosophy like ours is to prepare the way for more concrete and synoptic inquiry. We are only beginning to philosophize till we turn from the bloodless proposition that things in any possible world must consist of tropes to specific studies of the sorts of tropes of which the things in this world actually consist. It is a virtue of our thesis that it does not strangle or eviscerate the great problems in the philosophical cradle but keeps them alive to face the test of experience and logic. It will be a further virtue if it assists, as I think it will, in their formulation and appraisal. Are there only physical objects and energies, or only minds or spirits, or are there both? How, specifically, is a physical object constituted, and how a mind, and how are they related? These topics of gigantic hypothesis are the last of philosophy for which the first is made.

Notes

1 Santayana, George, *The Realm of Matter*, ch. 6, in *Works* (New York: Scribner's, 1937), vol. 14, pp. 288–304.
2 Berkeley, George, *Principles of Human Knowledge* (Dublin, 1710), Introd., Sec. 10.
3 C. I. Lewis, *An Analysis of Knowledge and Valuation* (La Salle, Ill.: Open Court, 1946), p. 55.
4 Ibid., p. 475. Lewis, who elsewhere suggests there are degrees of abstractness, is here equating abstractness with universality, and concreteness and *universality*, we know, are just incommensurate.
5 Aristotle, *Metaphysics*, 1070b 36.

8 The Identity of Indiscernibles

Max Black

A: The principle of the Identity of Indiscernibles seems to me obviously true. And I don't see how we are going to define identity or establish the connexion between mathematics and logic without using it.

B: It seems to me obviously false. And your troubles as a mathematical logician are beside the point. If the principle is false you have no right to use it.

A: You simply *say* it's false – and even if you said so three times that wouldn't make it so.

B: Well, you haven't done anything more yourself than assert the principle to be true. As Bradley once said, "assertion can demand no more than counter-assertion; and what is affirmed on the one side, we on the other can simply deny".

A: How will this do for an argument? If two things, *a* and *b*, are given, the first has the property of being identical with *a*. Now *b* cannot have this property, for else *b* would be *a*, and we should have only one thing, not two as assumed. Hence *a* has at least one property, which *b* does not have, that is to say the property of being identical with *a*.

B: This is a roundabout way of saying nothing, for "*a* has the property of being identical with *a*" means no more than "*a* is *a*". When you begin to say "*a* is . . ." I am supposed to know what thing you are referring to as '*a*' and I expect to be told something about that thing. But when you end the sentence with the words ". . . is *a*" I am left still waiting. The sentence "*a* is *a*" is a useless tautology.

A: Are you as scornful about difference as about identity? For *a* also has, and *b* does not have, the property of being different from *b*. This is a second property that the one thing has but not the other.

B: All you are saying is that *b* is different from *a*. I think the form of words "*a* is different from *b*" does have the advantage over "*a* is *a*" that it might be used to give information. I might learn from hearing it used that '*a*' and '*b*' were applied to different things. But this is not what you want to say, since you are trying to use the names, not mention them. When I already know what '*a*' and '*b*' stand for, "*a* is different from *b*" tells me nothing. It, too, is a useless tautology.

A: I wouldn't have expected you to treat 'tautology' as a term of abuse. Tautology or not, the sentence has a philosophical use. It expresses the necessary truth that different things have at least one property not in common. Thus different things must be discernible; and hence, by contraposition, indiscernible things must be identical. Q.E.D.

B: Why obscure matters by this old-fashioned language? By "indiscernible" I suppose you mean the same as "having all properties in common". Do you claim to have proved that two things having all their properties in common are identical?

A: Exactly.

B: Then this is a poor way of stating your conclusion. If *a* and *b* are identical, there is just one thing having the two names '*a*' and '*b*'; and in that case it is absurd to say that *a* and *b* are two. Conversely, once you have supposed there are *two* things having all their properties in common, you can't without contradicting yourself say that *they* are "identical".

A: I can't believe you were really misled. I simply meant to say it is logically impossible for two things to have all their properties in common. I showed that *a* must have at least two properties – the property of being identical with *a*, and the property of being different from *b* – neither of which can be a property of *b*. Doesn't this prove the principle of Identity of Indiscernibles?

B: Perhaps you have proved something. If so, the nature of your proof should show us exactly what you have proved. If you want to call "being identical with *a*" a "property" I suppose I can't prevent you. But you must then accept the consequences of this way of talking. All you mean when you say "*a* has the property of being identical with *a*" is that *a* is *a*. And all you mean when you say "*b* does not have the property of being identical with *a*" is that *b* is not *a*. So what you have "proved" is that *a* is *a* and *b* is not *a*, that is to say, *b* and *a* are different. Similarly, when you said that *a*, but not *b*, had the property of being different from *b*, you were simply saying that *a* and *b* were different. In fact you are merely redescribing the hypothesis that *a* and *b* are different by calling it a case of "difference of properties". Drop the misleading description and your famous principle reduces to the truism that different things are different. How true! And how uninteresting!

A: Well, the properties of identity and difference may be uninteresting, but they *are* properties. If I had shown that grass was green, I suppose you would say I hadn't shown that grass was coloured.

B: You certainly would not have shown that grass had any colour *other than* green.

A: What it comes to is that you object to the conclusion of my argument *following* from the premise that *a* and *b* are different.

B: No, I object to the triviality of the conclusion. If you want to have an interesting principle to defend, you must interpret "property" more narrowly – enough so, at any rate, for "identity" and "difference" not to count as properties.

A: Your notion of an interesting principle seems to be one which I shall have difficulty in establishing. Will you at least allow me to include among "properties" what are sometimes called "relational characteristics" – like *being married to Caesar* or *being at a distance from London*?

B: Why not? If you are going to defend the principle, it is for you to decide what version you wish to defend.

A: In that case, I don't need to count identity and difference as properties. Here is a different argument that seems to me quite conclusive. The only way we can discover that two different things exist is by finding out that one has a quality not possessed by the other or else that one has a relational characteristic that the other hasn't.

If *both* are blue and hard and sweet and so on, and have the same shape and dimensions and are in the same relations to everything in the universe, it is logically impossible to tell them apart. The supposition that in such a case there might really be two things would be unverifiable *in principle*. Hence it would be meaningless.

B: You are going too fast for me.

A: Think of it this way. If the principle were false, the fact that I can see only two of your hands would be no proof that you had just two. And even if every conceivable test agreed with the supposition that you had two hands, you might all the time have three, four, or any number. You might have nine hands, different from one another and all indistinguishable from your left hand, and nine more all different from each other but indistinguishable from your right hand. And even if you really did have just two hands, and no more, neither you nor I nor anybody else could ever know that fact. This is too much for me to swallow. This is the kind of absurdity you get into, as soon as you abandon verifiability as a test of meaning.

B: Far be it from me to abandon your sacred cow. Before I give you a direct answer, let me try to describe a counter-example.

Isn't it logically possible that the universe should have contained nothing but two exactly similar spheres? We might suppose that each was made of chemically pure iron, had a diameter of one mile, that they had the same temperature, colour, and so on, and that nothing else existed. Then every quality and relational characteristic of the one would also be a property of the other. Now if what I am describing is logically possible, it is not impossible for two things to have all their properties in common. This seems to me to *refute* the Principle.

A: Your supposition, I repeat, isn't verifiable and therefore can't be regarded as meaningful. But supposing you *have* described a possible world, I still don't see that you have refuted the principle. Consider one of the spheres, *a*, . . .

B: How can I, since there is no way of telling them apart? *Which* one do you want me to consider?

A: This is very foolish. I mean either of the two spheres, leaving you to decide which one you wished to consider. If I were to say to you "Take any book off the shelf" it would be foolish on your part to reply "Which?"

B: It's a poor analogy. I know how to take a book off a shelf, but I don't know how to identify one of two spheres supposed to be alone in space and so symmetrically placed with respect to each other that neither has any quality or character the other does not also have.

A: All of which goes to show as I said before, the unverifiability of your supposition. Can't you imagine that one sphere has been designated as '*a*'?

B: I can imagine only what is logically possible. Now it is logically possible that somebody should enter the universe I have described, see one of the spheres on his left hand and proceed to call it '*a*'. I can imagine that all right, if that's enough to satisfy you.

A: Very well, now let me try to finish what I began to say about *a* . . .

B: I still can't let you, because you, in your present situation, have no right to talk about *a*. All I have conceded is that if something were to happen to introduce a change into my universe, so that an observer entered and could see the two spheres, one of them could then have a name. But this would be a different supposition from the one I wanted to consider. My spheres don't yet have names. If an observer were to enter the scene, he could perhaps put a red mark on one of the spheres. You might just as well say "By '*a*' I mean the sphere which would be the first to be marked by a red mark if anyone were to arrive and were to proceed to make a red mark!" You might just as well ask me to consider the first daisy in my lawn that would be picked by a child, if a child were to come along and do the picking. This doesn't now distinguish any daisy from the others. You are just pretending to use a name.

A: And I think you are just pretending not to understand me. All I am asking you to do is to think of one of your spheres, no matter which, so that I may go on to say something about it when you give me a chance.

B: You talk as if naming an object and then thinking about it were the easiest thing in the world. But it isn't so easy. Suppose I tell you to name any spider in my garden: if you can catch one first or describe one uniquely you can name it easily enough. But you can't pick one out, let alone "name" it, by just thinking. You remind me of the mathematicians who thought that talking about an Axiom of Choice would really allow them to choose a single member of a collection when they had no criterion of choice.

A: At this rate you will never give me a chance to say anything. Let me try to make my point without using names. Each of the spheres will surely differ from the other in being at some distance from that other one, but at no distance from itself – that is to say, it will bear at least one relation to itself – *being at no distance from*, or *being in the same place as* – that it does not bear to the other. And this will serve to distinguish it from the other.

B: Not at all. *Each* will have the relational characteristic *being at a distance of two miles*, say, *from the centre of a sphere one mile in diameter*, etc. And each will have the relational characteristic (if you want to call it that) of *being in the same place as itself*. The two are alike in this respect as in all others.

A: But look here. Each sphere occupies a different place; and this at least will distinguish them from one another.

B: This sounds as if you thought the places had some independent existence, though I don't suppose you really think so.

To say the spheres are in "different places" is just to say that there is a distance between the two spheres; and we have already seen that will not serve to distinguish them. Each is at a distance – indeed the same distance – from the other.

A: When I said they were at different places I didn't mean simply that they were at a distance from one another. That one sphere is in a certain place does not entail the existence of any *other* sphere. So to say that one sphere is in its place, and the other in its place, and then to add that these places are different seems to me different from saying the spheres are at a distance from one another.

B: What does it mean to say "a sphere is in its place"? Nothing at all, so far as I can see. Where else could it be? *All* you are saying is that the spheres are in different places.

A: Then my retort is, What does it mean to say "Two spheres are in different places"? Or, as you so neatly put it, "Where else could they be?"

B: You have a point. What I should have said was that your assertion that the spheres occupied different places said nothing at all, unless you were drawing attention to the necessary truth that different physical objects must be in different places. Now if two spheres must be in different places, as indeed they must, to say that the spheres occupy different places is to say no more than they are two spheres.

A: This is like a point you made before. You won't allow me to deduce anything from the supposition that there are two spheres.

B: Let me put it another way. In the two-sphere universe, the only reason for saying that the places occupied were different would be that different things occupied them. So in order to show the places were different you would first have to show, in some other way, that the spheres were different. You will never be able to distinguish the spheres by means of the places they occupy.

A: A minute ago, you were willing to allow that somebody might give your spheres different names. Will you let me suppose that some traveller has visited your monotonous "universe" and has named one sphere "Castor" and the other "Pollux"?

B: All right – provided you don't try to use those names yourself.

A: Wouldn't the traveller, at least, have to recognise that *being at a distance of two miles from Castor* was not the same property as being at a distance of two miles *from Pollux*?

B: I don't see why. If he were to see that Castor and Pollux had exactly the same properties, he would see that "being at a distance of two miles from Castor" meant exactly the same as "being at a distance of two miles from Pollux".

A: They couldn't mean the same. If they did, *"being at a distance of two miles from Castor and at the same time not being at a distance of two miles from Pollux"* would be a self-contradictory description. But plenty of bodies could answer to this description. Again if the two expressions meant the same, anything which was two miles from Castor would have to be two miles from Pollux – which is clearly false. So the two expressions don't mean the same and the two spheres have at least two properties not in common.

B: Which?

A: *Being at a distance of two miles from Castor* and *being at a distance of two miles from Pollux.*

B: But now you are *using* the words "Castor" and "Pollux" as if they really stood for something. They are just our old friends '*a*' and '*b*' in disguise.

A: You surely don't want to say that the arrival of the name-giving traveller creates spatial properties? Perhaps we can't name your spheres and therefore can't name the corresponding properties; but the properties must be there.

B: What can this mean? The traveller has not visited the spheres, and the spheres have no names – neither 'Castor', nor 'Pollux', nor '*a*', nor '*b*', nor any others. Yet you still want to say they have certain properties which cannot be referred to without using names for the spheres. You want to say "the property of being at a distance from Castor" though it is logically impossible for you to talk in this way. You can't speak, but you won't be silent.

A: How eloquent, and how unconvincing! But since you seem to have convinced yourself, at least, perhaps you can explain another thing that bothers me: I don't see that you have a right to talk as you do about places or spatial relations in connexion with your so-called "universe". So long as we are talking about our own universe – *the* universe – I know what you mean by "distance", "diameter", "place" and so on. But in what you want to call a universe, even though it contains only two objects, I don't see what such words could mean. So far as I can see, you are applying these spatial terms in their present usage to a hypothetical situation which contradicts the presuppositions of that usage.

B: What do you mean by "presupposition"?

A: Well, you spoke of measured distances, for one thing. Now this presupposes some means of measurement. Hence your "universe" must contain at least a third thing – a ruler or some other measuring device.

B: Are you claiming that a universe must have at least three things in it? What is the least number of things required to make a world?

A: No, all I am saying is that you cannot describe a configuration as *spatial* unless it includes at least three objects. This is part of the meaning of "spatial" – and it is no more mysterious than saying you can't have a game of chess without there existing at least thirty-five things (thirty-two pieces, a chessboard, and two players).

B: If this is all that bothers you, I can easily provide for three or any number of things without changing the force of my counter-example. The important thing, for my purpose, was that the configuration of two spheres was symmetrical. So long as we preserve this feature of the imaginary universe, we can now allow any number of objects to be found in it.

A: You mean any *even* number of objects.

B: Quite right. Why not imagine a plane running clear through space, with everything that happens on one side of it always exactly duplicated at an equal distance in the other side.

A: A kind of cosmic mirror producing real images.

B: Yes, except that there wouldn't be any mirror! The point is that in *this* world we can imagine any degree of complexity and change to occur. No reason to exclude rulers, compasses, and weighing machines. No reason, for that matter, why the Battle of Waterloo shouldn't happen.

A: Twice over, you mean – with Napoleon surrendering later in two different places simultaneously!

B: Provided you wanted to call both of them "Napoleon".

A: So your point is that everything could be duplicated on the other side of the non-existent Looking Glass. I suppose whenever a man got married, his identical twin would be marrying the identical twin of the first man's fiancée?

B: Exactly.

A: Except that "identical twins" wouldn't be *numerically* identical?

B: You seem to be agreeing with me.

A: Far from it. This is just a piece of gratuitous metaphysics. If the inhabitants of your world had enough sense to know what was sense and what wasn't, they would never suppose all the events in their world were duplicated. It would be much more sensible for them to regard the "second" Napoleon as a mere mirror image – and similarly for all the other supposed "duplicates".

B: But they could walk through the "mirror" and find water just as wet, sugar just as sweet, and grass just as green on the other side.

A: You don't understand me. They would not postulate "another side". A man looking at the "mirror" would be seeing *himself*, not a duplicate. If he walked in a straight line toward the "mirror" he would eventually find himself back at his starting point, not at a duplicate of his starting point. This would involve their having a different geometry from ours – but that would be preferable to the logician's nightmare of the reduplicated universe.

B: They might think so – until the twins really began to behave differently for the first time!

A: Now it's you who are tinkering with your supposition. You can't have your universe and change it too.

B: All right, I retract.

A: The more I think about your "universe" the queerer it seems. What would happen when a man crossed your invisible "mirror"? While he was actually crossing, his body would have to change shape, in order to preserve the symmetry. Would it gradually shrink to nothing and then expand again?

B: I confess I hadn't thought of that.

A: And here is something that explodes the whole notion. Would you say that one of the two Napoleons in your universe had his heart in the right place – literally, I mean?

B: Why, of course.

A: In that case his "mirror-image" twin would have the heart on the opposite side of the body. One Napoleon would have his heart on the left of his body, and the other would have it on the right of his body.

B: It's a good point, though it would still make objects like spheres indistinguishable. But let me try again. Let me abandon the original idea of a *plane* of symmetry and suppose instead that we have only a *centre* of symmetry. I mean that everything that happened at any place would be exactly duplicated at a place an equal distance on the opposite side of the centre of symmetry. In short, the universe would be what the mathematicians call "radially symmetrical". And to avoid complications we could suppose that the centre of symmetry itself was physically inaccessible, so that it would be impossible for any material body to pass through it. Now in *this* universe, identical twins would have to be either both right-handed or both left-handed.

A: Your universes are beginning to be as plentiful as blackberries. You are too ingenious to see the force of my argument about verifiability. Can't you see that your supposed description of a universe in which everything has its "identical twin" doesn't describe anything verifiably different from a corresponding universe without such duplication? This must be so, no matter what kind of symmetry your universe manifested.

B: You are assuming that in order to verify that there are two things of a certain kind, it must be possible to show that one has a property not possessed by the other. But this is not so. A pair of very close but similar magnetic poles produce a characteristic field of force which assures me that there are two poles, even if I have no way of examining them separately. The presence of two exactly similar stars at a great distance might be detected by some resultant gravitational effect or by optical interference – or in some such similar way – even though we had no way of inspecting one in isolation from the other. Don't physicists say something like this about the electrons inside an atom? We can verify *that* there are two, that is to say a certain property of the whole configuration, even though there is no way of detecting any character that uniquely characterises any element of the configuration.

A: But if you were to approach your two stars one would have to be on your left and one on the right. And this would distinguish them.

B: I agree. Why shouldn't we say that the two stars are distinguishable – meaning that it would be possible for an observer to see one on his left and the other on his right, or more generally, that it would be *possible* for one star to come to have a relation to a third object that the second star would not have to that third object.

A: So you agree with me after all.

B: Not if you mean that the two stars do not have all their properties in common. All I said was that it was logically possible for them to enter into different relationships with a third object. But this would be a change in the universe.

A: If you are right, nothing unobserved would be observable. For the presence of an observer would always change it, and the observation would always be an observation of something else.

B: I don't say that every observation changes what is observed. My point is that there isn't any *being to the right* or *being to the left* in the two-sphere universe until an observer is introduced, that is to say until a real change is made.

A: But the spheres themselves wouldn't have changed.

B: Indeed they would: they would have acquired new relational characteristics. In the absence of any asymmetric observer, I repeat, the spheres would have all their properties in common (including, if you like, the power to enter into different relations with other objects). Hence the principle of Identity of Indiscernibles is false.

A: So perhaps you really do have twenty hands after all?

B: Not a bit of it. Nothing that I have said prevents me from holding that we can verify *that* there are exactly two. But we could know *that* two things existed without there being any way to distinguish one from the other. The Principle is false.

A: I am not surprised that you ended in this way, since you assumed it in the description of your fantastic "universe". Of course, if you began by assuming that the spheres were numerically different though qualitatively alike, you could end by "proving" what you first assumed.

B: But I wasn't "proving" anything. I tried to support my contention that it is logically possible for two things to have all their properties in common by giving an illustrative description. (Similarly, if I had to show it is logically possible for nothing at all to be seen I would ask you to imagine a universe in which everybody was blind.) It was for you to show that my description concealed some hidden contradiction. And you haven't done so.

A: All the same I am not convinced.

B: Well, then, you ought to be.[1]

Notes

1   The following notes and references might be helpful to anybody wishing to make up his own mind on the questions raised:

The Definition of Identity: See *Principia Mathematica*, vol. i, definition 13.01. The theory of types required Whitehead and Russell to say *x* and *y* are identical if and only if the same predicative functions are satisfied by both. For a similar definition see W. V. Quine, *Mathematical Logic* (1940), definition D 10 (p. 136). See also G. Frege, *The Foundations of Arithmetic* (Oxford, 1940, p. 76).

Self-evidence of the Principle: "I think it is obvious that the principle of Identity of Indiscernibles is not true" (G. E. Moore, *Philosophical Studies*, 1922, p. 307). "Leibniz's 'principles of indiscernibles' is all nonsense. No doubt, all things differ; but there is no logical necessity for it" (C. S. Peirce, *Collected Papers*, 4.311). "Russell's definition of '=' 'won't do; because according to it one cannot say that two objects have all their properties in common (even if this proposition is never true, it is nevertheless *significant*)." (L. Wittgenstein, *Tractatus Logico-Philosophicus*, 5.5302). See also C. H. Langford, "Otherness and dissimilarity" in MIND, vol. xxxix (1930), pp. 454–461.

Bradley's remark: Not made in connexion with *this* topic. See *Ethical Studies*, 2nd edn., 1927, p. 165. Bradley affirmed what he called "the Axiom of the Identity of Indiscernibles" (*The Principles of Logic*, 2nd ed., 1928, p. 288).

Identity as a relational property: ". . . numerical identity, which is a dyadic relation of a subject to itself of which nothing but an existent individual is capable" (C. S. Peirce, *Collected Papers*, 1.461).

The proof of the principle by treating identity as a property: "It should be observed that by 'indiscernibles' he [Leibniz] cannot have meant two objects which agree as to *all* their properties, for one of the properties of *x* is to be identical with *x*, and therefore this property would necessarily belong to *y* if *x* and *y* agreed in *all* their properties. Some limitation of the common properties necessary to make things indiscernible is therefore implied by the necessity of an axiom" (*Principia Mathematica*, vol. i, p. 51). *Cf.* K. Grelling, "Identitas indiscernibilium" in *Erkenntnis*, vol. vi (1936), pp. 252–259.

Counter-examples: C. D. Broad tries to refute McTaggart's form of the principle ("The dissimilarity of the diverse") by the example of a universe consisting of two minds, without bodies, that are exactly alike in all respects. *(Examination of*

McTaggart's Philosophy, vol. i, p. 176). Broad holds however, that "either spatial or temporal separation involves dissimilarity" *(op. cit.*, p. 173).

The argument from verifiability: "To say that B and C are 'really' two, although they seem one, is to say something which, if B and C are totally indistinguishable, seems wholly devoid of meaning" (B. Russell, *An Inquiry into Meaning and Truth*, 1940, p. 127).

The distinguishability of asymmetric bodies and their mirror images: There is a famous discussion of this in Kant's *Critique of Pure Reason*. See, for instance, H. Vaihinger, *Kommentar zur Kant's Kritik der reinen Vernunft*, 1922, vol. ii, pp. 518–532 ("Anhang – Das Paradoxon der symmetrischen Gegenstände").

---

9   Distinct Indiscernibles and the Bundle Theory*

Dean W. Zimmerman

A: Like Locke, you think an object must be something more than its properties. So you posit a mysterious "substratum," an unreachable "kernel" that bears properties but is not itself a property. This is metaphysics at its most gratuitous and pernicious. All we observe or detect are the properties of things, and a particular substance is nothing more than a bundle of properties.

B: So you say. But remember the puzzle I put to you many years ago:

> Isn't it logically possible that the universe should have contained nothing but two exactly similar spheres? We might suppose that each was made of chemically pure iron, had a diameter of one mile, that they had the same temperature, color, and so on, and that nothing else existed. Then every quality and relational characteristic of the one would also be a property of the other. Now if what I am describing is logically possible, it is not impossible for two things to have all their properties in common.[1]

You have yet to satisfy me that your bundle theory of substance is compatible with the possibility of such a world.

A: I must admit, your two-sphere world had me worried for a time. But it now seems clear to me that the possibility you described poses no real threat to the bundle theory.

B: How so? The spheres have to be bundles of the very same universals; and they can't be distinguished by their relations to one another, either. Throwing in relations to different *places* won't help, since the places in question are indiscernible, too. If you posit distinct but indiscernible places, doesn't this amount to the recognition of things that are something more than mere bundles of universals? The only way out is to deny that the two-sphere world is really possible. But I know you too well to think that you'll take that route; you're not one of these "modally-challenged"[2] philosophers, unable to recognize a possibility when they see one.

A: Ah, but there *is* another way out.[3] In order to see it, you must first recall that the universals I'm bundling into substances are not, of course, Platonic entities existing outside of space and time somewhere. They're "immanent universals," located right where and when their instances are.

B: Oh, you're bundling *tropes,* particular *instances* of universals, which can differ *solo numero.* That will solve the problem – but it's cheating, from the point of view of the traditional bundle theory. You've brought brute particularity back into your metaphysical picture; you're not bundling real *universals* any longer.

A: No, immanent universals aren't tropes; they're real universals, wholly present in each instance. They differ from Platonic universals only in being spatiotemporally located.

B: So the blueness on the surface of one sphere, say, is numerically identical with the blueness on the surface of another sphere of exactly the same hue?

A: Right. And you're probably beginning to see how I'll answer the two-sphere challenge. It's quite simple really: the situation you describe is surely possible; but it is a world in which a *single* bundle of universals – the universals of solidity, mass, shape, color, etc. collocated in one of the spheres – is *at some distance from itself.*

B: "At some distance from itself"! Surely that's a contradiction.

A: If so, then the very idea of an immanent universal is contradictory. An immanent universal will routinely be "at some distance from itself," in the sense that it is wholly present in more than one place. If you grant me immanent universals, then you must allow that my redescription of the sphere-world is consistent.

B: But it is a *redescription,* is it not? The world I described contains *two* spheres. But your bi-located bundle is just *one* thing that shows up in two places.

A: Granted, you *say* the world has two distinct spheres in it; but to insist on including this as part of the description of the world is to beg the question against the bundle theorist. I submit that the possibility your story illustrates is simply this: *a symmetrical universe,* a world in which the pattern of properties exemplified on one side of a certain plane is precisely mirrored on the opposite side. You want to insist that, in addition, the objects on the one side of the plane of symmetry are *numerically distinct* from those on the other. But it is not at all clear to me that *that* is possible.

B: Let me see if I understand how your immanent universals fit together to constitute an object. Take one of the homogeneous spheres. Suppose it's uniformly blue all over. You want to say that the blueness on the one side is identical with the blueness on the other, the blueness on the top half is identical with the blueness on the bottom half, and so on?

A: Exactly; although the example presents certain difficulties – no one seems to agree about what blueness is, or about whether it's an intrinsic property on the surfaces of objects. But we can just let blueness stand for some real intrinsic property present all over the surface of the homogeneous sphere.

B: Fine. Now you would agree, I imagine, that the sphere possesses certain causal capabilities in virtue of the universals involved in it.

A: I suppose so; although I have no settled views about the metaphysics of causation.

B: Nor have I. But one thing that does seem clear to me is that, for example, a sphere translates motion to another ball when it strikes it in virtue of its mass and speed, but not in virtue of its color; and it causes a blue image to appear on a Polaroid in virtue of its color but not its mass; and so on. And generally, when the sphere causes something to happen, it will usually be only some of its properties that are causally significant. Furthermore, it is often only the properties possessed by a *part* of an object that are relevant to its producing a given effect. For instance, a Polaroid of one of our blue spheres has a blue image because of the blueness on only one side. Its backside could have been red or green for all it matters to this particular causal transaction.

A: I think I'm beginning to see where you're headed. You want to say that the blueness on the side of the sphere facing the camera has to be distinct from the blueness on the back of the sphere, since only the former figures among the causes of the blue image.

B: Yes, that's more or less what I'm working up to.

A: I answer that causal relations among universals, like so many other relations among them, must be relativized in various ways. Take distance, for example. If the spheres are five feet in diameter, and one diameter apart, then blueness will be five feet from itself, and ten feet from itself, and fifteen feet from itself, and so on. There is no contradiction here, since distance relations are relativized: blueness is five feet from itself relative to the surfaces that are closest; ten feet from itself relative to the inner surface of one and the far side of the other. Similarly, blueness causes the blue image on the film relative to one side of the sphere, but not relative to the other side.

B: You want to say, then, that blueness "causes-from-*here*" the image, where "here" is the location of the surface facing the camera; but it doesn't "cause-from-*there*" the image, if "there" is the location of the surface on the other side?

A: Yes, something like that. However, talk about relativizing to *locations* may not be the best way to put it.

B: Right. For I'll ask what these locations are like. If they're literal parts of some kind of substantival space, then I'll ask if they are or are not identical with bundles of universals. If they're not, then you've brought in brute particularity again. If they are bundles of universals, I'll want to know what distinguishes the one from the other.

A: But in the case you've described, there *is* a difference between the region of space occupied by the surface facing the camera and the region occupied by the surface facing away from it. The former is *closer to a camera* than the latter. So it is relative-to-the-space-that-is-closer-to-a-camera that blueness causes the image; and this space can be identified with a bundle of space-properties (pointhood or regionhood, say) plus the relational property of *being such-and-such a distance from a camera*.

And now that I put it this way, I see that I needn't even go along with your initial suggestion that causing must be relativized to locations in space. I can just as easily say that it is blueness relative to the surface of one half of the sphere that causes the image; and the causally relevant half can be identified with a bundle of universals that includes the relational property *being such-and-such a distance from a camera*. This property isn't part of the otherwise indiscernible bundle making up the sphere's other half. So I can distinguish between the causing that blueness does from *here*, and the causing it does (or doesn't do) from *there*, by reference not to different parts of space but to the different objects that are here and there – objects that are different because they are identical with bundles that include different properties.

B: Suppose there is an exactly similar camera on the opposite side as well. Then each half of the sphere will be made of precisely the same bundle of universals, even if you include these funny relational properties like "being a certain distance from a camera." Doesn't this force you to admit that the causal contribution made by blueness must be relativized to a *place*, and not to a part of the object?

A: No; for now there is no need to distinguish between the causal role played by blueness relative to the front half of the sphere and the causal role it plays relative to the back of the sphere. If this is a perfectly symmetrical world, the cameras, like the spheres in the original two-sphere world, are really one and the same bundle at some distance from itself; and the causal relation holding between blueness and camera on one side is identical with the causal relation holding between blueness and camera on the other.

B: This is making me dizzy. Crossing the axis of symmetry in the camera–sphere–camera world is like passing through the looking glass: the camera you leave behind is identical with the one in front of you!

But now suppose there is something indeterministic about these cameras; whether or not the blueness causes a blue image depends upon some quantum-mechanical fluctuation, say. Up to a given time *t,* the causal relations between blueness and camera are the same on either side; and at *t* an image forms on the film of both cameras. The image is caused by the way the sphere looked right up to *t,* but not because of the way it looked at *t* – in other words, it's not a case of simultaneous causation. Now, given that the process is indeterministic, and that the cameras are independent, there was some chance that only one camera would work, that only one blue image would be formed. But how can you make sense of this possibility? One wants to say: if the shutter of the camera on *this* side had failed to open, as it could well have done, then the blueness on this side would have failed to cause a blue image while the blueness on the other side would have succeeded. You can't say that, though; for the blueness on this side is identical with the blueness on the other side, and the camera on this side is identical with the camera on that side – in fact this side of the sphere is identical with that side! So it is impossible that the one do something that the other does not do.

A: There are a couple of ways I can try to allow for the possibilities you describe, depending on the theory of time I hold. Suppose that I'm a "presentist" – in other words, that I think the only things that exist are those that exist *now*. Someone who holds this view cannot, I expect, hold that two bundles of universals differ now in virtue only of their relations to future things. But the presentist bundler can admit that there is a possible world just like the one you describe up to *t,* but diverging thereafter in virtue of the fact that one camera works and the other doesn't. This is a world in which a single camera-ish bundle of universals is located at some distance from itself for a while, and then is located at some distance from a *distinct* camera-ish bundle of universals – a non-functioning camera-ish bundle of universals, as it happens.

B: But, since the before-*t* cameras and blueness were really one camera and one blueness, the presentist won't be able to say that there is a world in which *this* camera works and *that* one doesn't, and another world in which *that* camera works and *this* one doesn't.

A: True enough; although the possibility that *can* be allowed for is still fairly close to the one you're after.

B: Not by my lights. But in any case, I know you're not a presentist; you're a "four-dimensionalist." You think everything "co-exists" in a big space–time block. So what would you say?

A: What I would say about your two cameras is this: a world in which one camera fails to function is a world in which the camera-ish bundles were distinguished *from the start* in virtue of their differing spatiotemporal relations to later camera-ish bundles. But you are right that I cannot allow that it's possible, in the world where "both" cameras work, to pick out one side of the sphere and one camera and assert that they could have failed to produce a picture while the other side and the other camera succeeded. For, on my view, "they" are not two but one.

B: It seems to me that the possibility you are able to recognize is not even close to the one I pointed out. I said that blueness could have failed to bring about its result relative to *this* side and *this* camera, while succeeding relative to the *other* side and the *other* camera. All you can admit is that blueness could have succeeded relative to this side and this camera while also being a part of a hemisphere distinct from any camera or hemisphere in the original world. The whole sphere in this other possible world has a *different* side relative to which blueness fails to cause an image in a *different* camera.

A: I grant you that. But doesn't your description of the case just presuppose the falsity of my bundle-theoretic approach, which says that a "pair" of complete indiscernibles is really one and the same bundle at some distance from itself? You ask: Couldn't the pair of this side and this camera have been differently causally related than the pair of that side and that camera? But, in the situation you've described, I say the "two" pairs are really one pair in close proximity to itself. So of course I can't allow that "one" of the pairs can do something which the "other" pair doesn't do.

B: I don't think *I'm* the one begging the question here. Let's simplify the example a bit. Suppose that nothing exists save two electrons – or, if you like, that the same bundle of electron-ish properties appears on opposite sides of a symmetrical universe. Suppose further that electrons obey indeterministic laws. In that case, even though the electron on the one side is now indiscernible from the one on the other, it remains possible that differences will emerge later on – in other words, it is possible that *this* one have a future differing from *that* one. And even in the case of an eternally symmetrical, two-electron universe in which differences never emerge, such differences were nonetheless possible – both logically or metaphysically possible, and physically or causally possible, too. But you cannot recognize this possibility: on your view the "electrons" must *really* be a single bundle, and so nothing could be true of the one but false of the other.

A: I fear we may have reached an impasse; for this objection of yours depends upon the resolution of another long-standing quarrel between us: namely, how best to analyze statements involving necessity and possibility.

B: You're still peddling your "counterpart theory," I imagine?

A: Naturally. And your argument tacitly assumes the falsity of a counterpart-theoretic analysis of what it means to say that something is necessarily so-and-so, or possibly such-and-such.[4] On my view, the possibilities open to a given object are not determined by what *it* does in other possible worlds, but rather by what its *counterparts* do in other possible worlds – and a counterpart is similar to, but not identical with, the original object. Take the fact that I could have been a doctor. Being a doctor represents a real possibility for me just because there is a doctor in some merely possible world who is more like me than anyone else there – he is my "counterpart" in that world. A world with twins who tie in resembling me more than any others in their world is one in which I have two counterparts; there are two possibilities open for me in such a world – each of the twins is a "possible me."[5] I can say something similar about the statement "The (so-called) 'two' electrons could have diverged": this statement is true just in case the single bi-located electron-bundle in the symmetrical world has *two* counterparts inhabiting some other world, and the two counterparts differ there in the required ways.

B: Well, you know what I think of your counterpart semantics for modal ascriptions. But even if I grant you that, I don't see how it helps. Suppose I let you say that the one bi-located electron could have been either of its two counterpart electrons in the divergent world. Still, something more is possible in the symmetrical world: the electron on the one side could have developed differently while the one on the other side did not. But if "they" are identical, "they" must have the same counterparts in every possible situation – and so there's no possible world in which the one *but not the other* has a counterpart with a particular future.

A: I'm not so sure about that. But the more I think about this alleged possibility, the less troubled I am by it. Who says it has to be possible for the "one" electron to change its state without "the other" doing so as well? I say they're the same bundle; so when I think about it, I have a hard time even imagining what you're talking about.

B: Just another case of philosophical theory corrupting modal judgment. Let me try one last time to help you grasp the eminently possible situation I'm thinking about: there are just two electrons, they are and remain exactly alike, and the behavior of each one evolves independently of the other. Think of them as being far apart, and moving away from each other at a constant rate. Now, given that each behaves in accordance with slightly indeterministic laws, there are ways in which each one *could* come to differ from the other in the future, although in fact they remain in synch. But there is no way you can allow for the *possibility* of the one doing something that the other does not.

A: I'll admit that there is something a little bit odd about ruling out the alleged possibilities you describe. But why can't I just hold a bundle theory for the objects in the *actual* world? After all, it is only in these bizarrely symmetrical universes that problems arise.

B: So you want to restrict your thesis to just those worlds that lack distinct indiscernibles?

A: Something like that, yes.

B: Doesn't the *ad hoc* nature of the restriction bother you? Pick a couple of almost indiscernible particles in the actual world. Couldn't they (or at least a pair just like them) exist in a world by themselves, where they remain distinct because of some small change which the one undergoes but the other does not?

A: As long as they remain distinct bundles of universals, I can't see that your earlier objections have any foothold.

B: Not in that world. But we are only a small step from *another* world where the one fails to undergo this little change. Suddenly, you have to give up your metaphysics of pure bundles, and posit underlying substrata or some such things. Surely it is implausible to suppose that a tiny change in the global distribution of intrinsic properties would require a radical change in ontology![6]

A: That does sound a bit unsatisfactory. But your objections have begun to seem less and less pressing to me. Perhaps there is really no need to retreat to a contingent version of the bundle theory. Call me "modally challenged" if you like, but I'm no longer at all sure that the two independently evolving but indiscernible electrons you describe really are possible; it's not obvious to me that, given that the "two" really are indiscernible, one of them *could* behave in a certain way while the other does not.

B: Well, it would be obvious to you, if you weren't such a devotee of the bundle theory.

Notes

*   Although the character called "*B*" in this dialogue claims to be the same as the "*B*" of Max Black's dialogue (Ch. 8), it is not so clear whether this dialogue's A is the same as Black's A. Both As are committed to the identity of indiscernibles; however, Black's may or may not have been a "bundle theorist."

1   Max Black, "The Identity of Indiscernibles," in his *Problems of Analysis* (Ithaca, N. Y.: Cornell University Press, 1954), p. 83; and reprinted as Ch. 8 in this volume.

2   Compare Richard Gale's epithet, "modally other-abled" in Gale, "Some Difficulties in Theistic Treatments of Evil," in *The Evidential Argument from Evil,* ed. Daniel Howard-Snyder (Bloomington and Indianapolis: Indiana University Press, 1996), p. 213.

3   This response to Black's spheres is given by John O'Leary-Hawthorne, "The Bundle Theory of Substance and the Identity of Indiscernibles," *Analysis,* 55 (1995), pp. 191–6.

4   David Lewis defends counterpart theory in "Counterpart Theory and Quantified Modal Logic," reprinted in his *Philosophical Papers,* vol. 1 (Oxford: Oxford University Press, 1983) and as Ch. 53 in this volume. I hasten to add that A is not intended to resemble Lewis in any other respect.

5   Compare David Lewis's strategy for introducing haecceitistic modal differences for joint possibilities in his *On the Plurality of Worlds* (Oxford: Blackwell, 1986), pp. 230–3.

6   This argument comes from Robert M. Adams, "Primitive Thisness and Primitive Identity," *Journal of Philosophy,* 76 (1979), pp. 5–26; cf. also D. M. Armstrong, *Universals: an Opinionated Introduction* (Boulder, Col.: Westview Press 1989), pp. 64–70.

C What is Time? What is Space?

Introduction

The readings under this heading fall into four groups. First there is McTaggart's paradox and Broad's criticism of it. One part of McTaggart's argument is supposed to refute the notion that there is an objective fact about what events are present, a fact that is constantly changing. Many contemporary philosophers defend this part of McTaggart's argument (see the works by D. H. Mellor and Paul Horwich listed below); but Broad's refutation of McTaggart still seems to us to be decisive.

The second group represents three different theories about the nature of the distinction between past, present, and future: (i) only what is present is real, (ii) present and past are both real, (iii) present, past, and future are equally real. The first essays in this group are A. N. Prior's "The Notion of the Present" and "Changes in Events and Changes in Things." The first is a brief manifesto for a doctrine often called "presentism": the thesis that what exists is only what exists at present – events and individuals that are wholly past or future are strictly non-existent. The second essay by Prior provides a deeper sense of how he thinks we should make sense of talk about the past and the future, if only the present is real. Broad defends a "growing block" theory of time – both present *and past* events and things are real; the distinction between present and past is just the difference between what has most recently been added to the sum total of reality and what is buried deeper within the four-dimensional block of space-time. D. C. Williams advocates the view of time that is probably most popular with contemporary philosophers: all events and things are equally real, spread out in a four-dimensional space-time block. "There is in fact no more a single rolling Now than there is a single rolling Here along a spatial line." Prior's lecture, "Some Free Thinking about Time," includes an important criticism of Williams's four-dimensionalism (Prior's "thank goodness that's over" argument). Prior also discusses connections between logic and theories of time, and offers a response to the contention that relativity implies a four-dimensional block universe.

The third part of this section consists of several readings on the nature of space. Chs. 17 and 18 ask whether the phenomenon of "enantiomorphism" supports the doctrine of absolute space. A right- and left-hand glove are a pair of enantiomorphs – objects alike in all geometrical properties, but differing in "shape" nonetheless. Martin Gardner explains how Kant came to the view that the difference between two such objects must be due to differences in their relations to a Newtonian absolute space in which they are embedded. Gardner criticizes Kant's argument; part of his criticism depends upon the fact that, in a four-dimensional space, the left-hand glove could be "flipped over" and turned into a right-hand glove. James Van Cleve, in a paper written for this anthology, considers the implications of Kant's argument in more detail. The second half of his paper (the "Dialogue on Higher Dimensions") raises objections to the possibility of spaces with more than three dimensions. The chapter from C. D. Broad's *Scientific Thought* asks whether space contains point-sized parts, or only regions of finite size.

The final four papers concern familiar paradoxes of space and time – the first three, paradoxes of the actually infinite; the last, paradoxes of time travel. Only one comment seems necessary here, and that concerns the role of José Benardete's essay. The question he considers is whether we can claim to have any notion of an infinitely large collection other than something like "a collection with more members than any human being could count." In order to adopt Wesley Salmon's response to Zeno's paradoxes, we must obviously have a grasp of mathematical infinities that is more robust than this; but, as Benardete's parable of the "Gumquats" makes evident, there are reasons to think such notions must remain forever beyond our ken. Benardete offers a "dispositionalist" response to Kripke's Wittgensteinian skepticism about meaning, and concludes with a brief statement of the implications of his position for the infinite task paradoxes.

There are quite a few connections between these readings and others in this anthology. Zimmerman's "Temporary Intrinsics and Presentism" (Ch. 29) includes defense of Prior's theory of time. Near the end of "Changes in Events and Changes in Things," Prior tries to explain how talk about past and future things can be meaningful without implying that past or future things exist; near the end of "The General Problem of Time and Change," Broad attempts the same with respect to just future things; and in Ch. 19, Broad shows us how to describe space in terms of "points" without committing ourselves to literal point-sized regions. Each of these three passages illustrates the use of paraphrase to avoid unwanted ontological commitments, a strategy discussed in van Inwagen's introductory essay, and central to Chs. 1 and 2. In Chs. 26–8, below, Quine and Lewis defend a four-dimensionalist metaphysics of "temporal parts," much like that of Williams's Ch. 15. Lewis's essay on time travel (Ch. 23), besides advocating temporal parts, offers a compatibilist theory of freedom of action that can be set alongside the arguments for and against compatibilism in Part Two, section B.

Suggestions for further reading

Abbott, E. A., *Flatland: A Romance of Many Dimensions* (New York: Dover, 1952).

Aune, Bruce, *Metaphysics: The Elements* (Minneapolis: University of Minnesota, 1985) ch. 6 ("Worlds, Objects, and Structure").

Banchoff, Thomas S., *Beyond the Third Dimension: Geometry, Computer Graphics, and Higher Dimensions* (New York: Scientific American Library, 1990).

Benardete, José A., *Infinity* (Oxford: Clarendon Press, 1964).

Borges, Jorge Luis, "Avatars of the Tortoise," included in *Labyrinths, Selected Stories and Other Writings* (New York: New Directions, 1964).

Gardner, Martin, *The Night Is Large* (New York: St. Martin's Press, 1996), ch. 7 ("Can Time Stop? The Past Change?").

—, *Time Travel and Other Mathematical Bewilderments* (New York: W. H. Freeman, 1988), ch. 1 ("Time Travel").

—, *The Unexpected Hanging and Other Mathematical Diversions* (New York: Simon and Schuster, 1969), ch. 6 ("The Church of the Fourth Dimension").

Hamlyn, D. W., *Metaphysics* (Cambridge, UK: Cambridge University Press, 1984) ch. 7 ("Space and Time").

Horwich, Paul, *Asymmetries in Time* (Cambridge, Mass.: MIT, 1987), ch. 2.

Lovecraft, H. P., *At the Mountains of Madness and Other Novels* (Sauk City, Wisc.: Arkham House, 1964). Includes the story "The Dreams in the Witch-House" – witches, demons, and aliens in the fourth dimension!

Mellor, D. H., *Real Time* (Cambridge: Cambridge University Press, 1981). See ch. 6, "The Unreality of Tense," for Mellor's defense of McTaggart.

Moore, A. W., *The Infinite* (London: Routledge, 1990).

Quinton, Anthony, "Spaces and Times," *Philosophy* 37 (1962), pp. 130–47.

Ray, Christopher, *Time, Space and Philosophy* (London: Routledge, 1991).

Rucker, Rudy, *Geometry, Relativity and the Fourth Dimension* (New York: Dover, 1977).

—, *The Fourth Dimension: A Guided Tour of the Higher Universes* (Boston: Houghton Mifflin, 1984).

—, *Infinity and the Mind* (Boston: Birkhauser, 1982).

—, (ed.) *Mathenauts: Tales of Mathematical Wonder* (New York: Arbor House, 1987). Includes the following stories involving the fourth dimension: Greg Bear, "Tangents"; Martin Gardner, "Left or Right?"; and Rudy Rucker, "Message Found in a Copy of Flatland".

Shoemaker, Sydney, "Time Without Change," *The Journal of Philosophy* 66 (1969), pp. 363–81; reprinted in his *Identity, Cause, and Mind* (Cambridge: Cambridge University Press, 1984).

Smart, J. J. C., "The Tenseless Theory of Time," in Sider, Hawthorne, and Zimmerman (eds.), *Contemporary Debates in Metaphysics* (Malden, Mass.: Blackwell, 2007).

Smith, Quentin, and Oaklander, L. Nathan, *Time, Change and Freedom: an Introduction to Metaphysics* (London: Routledge, 1995) Dialogues 3 and 6 ("The Relational and Substantival Theories of Time" and "The Passage of Time"), and Appendix A ("Physical Time in Einstein's Special Theory of Relativity").

Taylor, Richard, *Metaphysics*, 4th edn (Englewood Cliffs, N.J.: Prentice-Hall, 1992) chs. 7, 8, 9 ("Space and Time," "The Relativity of Time and Space," "Temporal Passage").

Zimmerman, Dean, "The Privileged Present: Defending an 'A-Theory' of Time," in Sider, Hawthorne, and Zimmerman (eds.), *Contemporary Debates in Metaphysics* (Malden, Mass.: Blackwell, 2007).

---

10   Time: an Excerpt from *The Nature of Existence*

J. McT. E. McTaggart

303.   It will be convenient to begin our enquiry by asking whether anything existent can possess the characteristic of being in time. I shall endeavour to prove that it cannot.

It seems highly paradoxical to assert that time is unreal, and that all statements which involve its reality are erroneous. Such an assertion involves a departure from the natural position of mankind which is far greater than that involved in the assertion of the unreality of space or the unreality of matter. For in each man's experience there is a part – his own states as known to him by introspection – which does not even appear to be spatial or material. But we have no experience which does not appear to be temporal. Even our judgments that time is unreal appear to be themselves in time.

304. Yet in all ages and in all parts of the world the belief in the unreality of time has shown itself to be singularly persistent . . .

305. Positions in time, as time appears to us *prima facie*, are distinguished in two ways. Each position is Earlier than some and Later than some of the other positions. To constitute such a series there is required a transitive asymmetrical relation, and a collection of terms such that, of any two of them, either the first is in this relation to the second, or the second is in this relation to the first. We may take here either the relation of 'earlier than' or the relation of 'later than', both of which, of course, are transitive and asymmetrical. If we take the first, then the terms have to be such that, of any two of them, either the first is earlier than the second, or the second is earlier than the first.

In the second place, each position is either Past, Present, or Future. The distinctions of the former class are permanent, while those of the latter are not. If M is ever earlier than N, it is always earlier. But an event, which is now present, was future, and will be past.

306. Since distinctions of the first class are permanent, it might be thought that they were more objective, and more essential to the nature of time, than those of the second class. I believe, however, that this would be a mistake, and that the distinction of past, present, and future is as *essential* to time as the distinction of earlier and later, while in a certain sense it may . . . be regarded as more *fundamental* than the distinction of earlier and later. And it is because the distinctions of past, present, and future seem to me to be essential for time, that I regard time as unreal.

For the sake of brevity I shall give the name of the *A* series to that series of positions which runs from the far past through the near past to the present, and then from the present through the near future to the far future, or conversely. The series of positions which runs from earlier to later, or conversely, I shall call the *B* series. The contents of any position in time form an event. The varied simultaneous contents of a single position are, of course, a plurality of events. But, like any other substance, they form a group, and this group is a compound substance. And a compound substance consisting of simultaneous events may properly be spoken of as itself an event.[1]

307. The first question which we must consider is whether it is essential to the reality of time that its events should form an *A* series as well as a *B* series. It is clear, to begin with, that, in present experience, we never *observe* events in time except as forming both these series. We perceive events in time as being present, and those are the only events which we actually perceive. And all other events which, by memory or by inference, we believe to be real, we regard as present, past, or future. Thus the events of time as observed by us form an *A* series.

308.   It might be said, however, that this is merely subjective. It might be the case that the distinction of positions in time into past, present, and future, is only a constant illusion of our minds, and that the real nature of time contains only the distinctions of the *B* series – the distinctions of earlier and later. In that case we should not perceive time as it really is, though we might be able to *think* of it as it really is.

This is not a very common view, but it requires careful consideration. I believe it to be untenable, because, as I said above, it seems to me that the *A* series is essential to the nature of time, and that any difficulty in the way of regarding the *A* series as real is equally a difficulty in the way of regarding time as real.

309.   It would, I suppose, be universally admitted that time involves change. In ordinary language, indeed, we say that something can remain unchanged through time. But there could be no time if nothing changed. And if anything changes, then all other things change with it. For its change must change some of their relations to it, and so their relational qualities. The fall of a sand-castle on the English coast changes the nature of the Great Pyramid.

If, then, a *B* series without an *A* series can constitute time, change must be possible without an *A* series. Let us suppose that the distinctions of past, present, and future do not apply to reality. In that case, can change apply to reality?

310.   What, on this supposition, could it be that changes? Can we say that, in a time which formed a *B* series but not an *A* series, the change consisted in the fact that the event ceased to be an event, while another event began to be an event? If this were the case, we should certainly have got a change.

But this is impossible. If *N* is ever earlier than *O* and later than *M*, it will always be, and has always been, earlier than *O* and later than *M*, since the relations of earlier and later are permanent. *N* will thus always be in a *B* series. And as, by our present hypothesis, a *B* series by itself constitutes time, *N* will always have a position in a time-series, and always has had one. That is, it always has been an event, and always will be one, and cannot begin or cease to be an event.

Or shall we say that one event *M* merges itself into another event *N*, while still preserving a certain identity by means of an unchanged element, so that it can be said, not merely that *M* has ceased and *N* begun, but that it is *M* which has become *N*? Still the same difficulty recurs. *M* and *N* may have a common element, but they are not the same event, or there would be no change. If, therefore, *M* changed into *N* at a certain moment, then at that moment, *M* would have ceased to be *M*, and *N* would have begun to be *N*. This involves that, at that moment, *M* would have ceased to be an event, and *N* would have begun to be an event. And we saw, in the last paragraph, that, on our present hypothesis, this is impossible.

Nor can such change be looked for in the different moments of absolute time, even if such moments should exist. For the same argument will apply here. Each such moment will have its own place in the *B* series, since each would be earlier or later than each of the others. And, as the *B* series depends on permanent relations, no moment could ever cease to be, nor could it become another moment.

311.   Change, then, cannot arise from an event ceasing to be an event, nor from one event changing into another. In what other way can it arise? If the characteristics of an event change, then there is certainly change. But what characteristics of an event can change? It seems to me that there is only one class of such characteristics. And that class consists of the determinations of the event in question by the terms of the *A* series.

Take any event – the death of Queen Anne, for example – and consider what changes can take place in its characteristics. That it is a death, that it is the death of Anne Stuart, that it has such causes, that it has such effects – every characteristic of this sort never changes. 'Before the stars saw one another plain,' the event in question was the death of a Queen. At the last moment of time – if time has a last moment – it will still be the death of a Queen. And in every respect but one, it is equally devoid of change. But in one respect it does change. It was once an event in the far future. It became every moment an event in the nearer future. At last it was present. Then it became past, and will always remain past, though every moment it becomes further and further past.[2]

Such characteristics as these are the only characteristics which can change. And, therefore, if there is any change, it must be looked for in the *A* series, and in the *A* series alone. If there is no real *A* series, there is no real change. The *B* series, therefore, is not by itself sufficient to constitute time, since time involves change.

312.   The *B* series, however, cannot exist except as temporal, since earlier and later, which are the relations which connect its terms, are clearly time-relations. So it follows that there can be no *B* series when there is no *A* series, since without an *A* series there is no time.

313.   We must now consider three objections which have been made to this position. The first is involved in the view of time which has been taken by Mr Russell, according to which past, present, and future do not belong to time *per se*, but only in relation to a knowing subject. An assertion that *N* is present means that it is simultaneous with that assertion, an assertion that it is past or future means that it is earlier or later than that assertion. Thus it is only past, present, or future, in relation to some assertion. If there were no consciousness, there would be events which were earlier and later than others, but nothing would be in any sense past, present, or future. And if there were events earlier than any consciousness, those events would never be future or present, though they could be past.

If *N* were ever present, past, or future in relation to some assertion *V*, it would always be so, since whatever is ever simultaneous to, earlier than, or later than, *V*, will always be so. What, then, is change? We find Mr Russell's views on this subject in his *Principles of Mathematics*, Section 442. 'Change is the difference, in respect of truth or falsehood, between a proposition concerning an entity and the time T, and a proposition concerning the same entity and the time T', provided that these propositions differ only by the fact that T occurs in the one where T' occurs in the other.' That is to say, there is change, on Mr Russell's view, if the proposition 'at the time T my poker is hot' is true, and the proposition 'at the time T' my poker is hot' is false.

314.   I am unable to agree with Mr Russell. I should, indeed, admit that, when two such propositions were respectively true and false, there would be change. But then I maintain that there can be no time without an A series. If, with Mr Russell, we reject the A series, it seems to me that change is essential, goes with it, and that therefore time, for which change is essential, goes too. In other words, if the A series is rejected, no proposition of the type 'at the time T my poker is hot' can ever be true, because there would be no time.

315.   It will be noticed that Mr Russell looks for change, not in the events in the time-series, but in the entity to which those events happen, or of which they are states. If my poker, for example, is hot on a particular Monday, and never before or since, the event of the poker being hot does not change. But the poker changes, because there is a time when this event is happening to it, and a time when it is not happening to it.

But this makes no change in the qualities of the poker. It is always a quality of that poker that it is one which is hot on that particular Monday. And it is always a quality of that poker that it is one which is not hot at any other time. Both these qualities are true of it at any time – the time when it is hot and the time when it is cold. And therefore it seems to be erroneous to say that there is any change in the poker. The fact that it is hot at one point in a series and cold at other points cannot give change, if neither of these facts changes – and neither of them does. Nor does any other fact about the poker change, unless its presentness, pastness, or futurity change.

316.   Let us consider the case of another sort of series. The meridian of Greenwich passes through a series of degrees of latitude. And we can find two points in this series, S and S', such that the proposition 'at S the meridian of Greenwich is within the United Kingdom' is true, while the proposition 'at S' the meridian of Greenwich is within the United Kingdom' is false. But no one would say that this gave us change. Why should we say so in the case of the other series?

Of course there is a satisfactory answer to this question if we are correct in speaking of the other series as a time-series. For where there is time, there is change. But then the whole question is whether it is a time-series. My contention is that if we remove the A series from the *prima facie* nature of time, we are left with a series which is not temporal, and which allows change no more than the series of latitudes does.

317.   If, as I have maintained, there can be no change unless facts change, then there can be no change without an *A* series. For, as we saw with the death of Queen Anne, and also in the case of the poker, no fact about anything can change, unless it is a fact about its place in the *A* series. Whatever other qualities it has, it has always. But that which is future will not always be future, and that which was past was not always past.

It follows from what we have said that there can be no change unless some propositions are sometimes true and sometimes false. This is the case of propositions which deal with the place of anything in the *A* series – 'the battle of Waterloo is in the past', 'it is now raining'. But it is not the case with any other propositions.

318.   Mr Russell holds that such propositions are ambiguous, and that to make them definite we must substitute propositions which are always true or always false – 'the battle of Waterloo is earlier than this judgment', 'the fall of rain is simultaneous with this judgment'. If he is right, all judgments are either always true, or always false. Then, I maintain, no facts change. And then, I maintain, there is no change at all.

I hold, as Mr Russell does, that there is no *A* series. (My reasons for this will be given below.) And I regard the reality lying behind the appearance of the *A* series in a manner not completely unlike that which Mr Russell has adopted. The difference between us is that he thinks that, when the *A* series is rejected, change, time, and the *B* series can still be kept, while I maintain that its rejection involves the rejection of change, and, consequently, of time, and of the *B* series . . .

324.   We conclude, then, that the distinctions of past, present, and future are essential to time, and that, if the distinctions are never true of reality, then no reality is in time. . . .

325.   I now pass to the second part of my task. Having, as it seems to me, succeeded in proving that there can be no time without an *A* series, it remains to prove that an *A* series cannot exist, and that therefore time cannot exist. This would involve that time is not real at all, since it is admitted that the only way in which time can be real is by existing. . . .

329.   Past, present, and future are incompatible determinations. Every event must be one or the other, but no event can be more than one. If I say that any event is past, that implies that it is neither present nor future, and so with the others. And this exclusiveness is essential to change, and therefore to time. For the only change we can get is from future to present, and from present to past.

The characteristics, therefore, are incompatible. But every event has them all.[3] If *M* is past, it has been present and future. If it is future, it will be present and past. If it is present, it has been future and will be past. Thus all the three characteristics belong to each event. How is this consistent with their being incompatible?

330.   It may seem that this can easily be explained. Indeed, it has been impossible to state the difficulty without almost giving the explanation, since our language has verb-forms for the past, present, and future, but no form that is common to all three. It is never true, the answer will run, that *M is* present, past, and future. It *is* present, *will be* past, and *has been* future. Or it *is* past, and *has been* future and present, or again *is* future, and *will be* present and past. The characteristics are only incompatible when they are simultaneous, and there is no contradiction to this in the fact that each term has all of them successively.

331.   But what is meant by 'has been' and 'will be'? And what is meant by 'is', when, as here, it is used with a temporal meaning, and not simply for predication? When we say that *X* has been *Y*, we are asserting *X* to be *Y* at a moment of past time. When we say that *X* will be *Y*, we are asserting *X* to be *Y* at a moment of future time. When we say that *X* is *Y* (in the temporal sense of 'is'), we are asserting *X* to be *Y* at a moment of present time.

Thus our first statement about *M* – that it is present, will be past, and has been future – means that *M* is present at a moment of present time, past at some moment of future time, and future at some moment of past time. But every moment, like every event, is both past, present, and future. And so a similar difficulty arises. If *M* is present, there is no moment of past time at which it is past. But the moments of future time, in which it is past, are equally moments of past time, in which it cannot be past. Again, that *M* is future and will be present and past means that *M* is future at a moment of present time, and present and past at different moments of future time. In that case it cannot be present or past at any moments of past time. But all the moments of future time, in which *M* will be present or past, are equally moments of past time.

332.   And thus again we get a contradiction, since the moments at which *M* has any one of the three determinations of the *A* series are also moments at which it cannot have that determination. If we try to avoid this by saying of these moments what had been previously said of *M* itself – that some moment, for example, is future, and will be present and past – then 'is' and 'will be' have the same meaning as before. Our statement, then, means that the moment in question is future at a present moment, and will be present and past at different moments of future time. This, of course, is the same difficulty over again. And so on infinitely.

Such an infinity is vicious. The attribution of the characteristics past, present, and future to the terms of any series leads to a contradiction, unless it is specified that they have them successively. This means, as we have seen, that they have them in relation to terms specified as past, present, and future. These again, to avoid a like contradiction, must in turn be specified as past, present, and future. And, since this continues infinitely, the first set of terms never escapes from contradiction at all.[4]

The contradiction, it will be seen, would arise in the same way supposing that pastness, presentness, and futurity were original qualities, and not, as we have decided that they are, relations. For it would still be the case that they were characteristics which were incompatible with one another, and that whichever had one of them would also have the other. And it is from this that the contradiction arises.

333.   The reality of the *A* series, then, leads to a contradiction, and must be rejected. And, since we have seen that change and time require the *A* series, the reality of change and time must be rejected. And so must the reality of the *B* series, since that requires time. Nothing is really present, past, or future. Nothing is really earlier or later than anything else or temporally simultaneous with it. Nothing really changes. And nothing is really in time. Whenever we perceive anything in time – which is the only way in which, in our present experience, we do perceive things – we are perceiving it more or less as it really is not. . . .

Notes

1   It is very usual to contemplate time by the help of a metaphor of spatial movement. But spatial movement in which direction? The movement of time consists in the fact that later and later terms pass into the present, or – which is the same fact expressed in another way – that presentness passes to later and later terms. If we take it the first way, we are taking the *B* series as sliding along a fixed *A* series. If we take it the second way, we are taking the *A* series as sliding along a fixed *B* series. In the first case time presents itself as a movement from future to past. In the second case it presents itself as a movement from earlier to later. And this explains why we say that events come out of the future, while we say that we ourselves move towards the future. For each man identifies himself especially with his present state, as against his future or his past, since it is the only one which he is directly perceiving. And this leads him to say that he is moving with the present towards later events. And as those events are now future, he says that he is moving towards the future.

Thus the question as to the movement of time is ambiguous. But if we ask what is the movement of either series, the question is not ambiguous. The movement of the *A* series along the *B* series is from earlier to later. The movement of the *B* series along the *A* series is from future to past.

2   The past, therefore, is always changing, if the *A* series is real at all, since at each moment a past event is further in the past than it was before. This result follows from the reality of the *A* series, and is independent of the truth of our view that all change depends exclusively on the *A* series. It is worth while to notice this, since most people combine the view that the *A* series is real with the view that the past cannot change – a combination which is inconsistent.

3   If the time-series has a first term, that term will never be future, and if it has a last term, that term will never be past. But the first term, in that case, will be present and past, and the last term will be future and present. And the possession of two incompatible characteristics raises the same difficulty as the possession of three.

4   It may be worth while to point out that the vicious infinite has not arisen from the impossibility of *defining* past, present, and future, without using the terms in their own definitions. On the contrary, we have admitted these terms to be indefinable. It arises from the fact that the nature of the terms involves a contradiction, and that the attempt to remove the contradiction involves the employment of the terms, and the generation of a similar contradiction.

11   McTaggart's Arguments against the Reality of Time: an Excerpt from *Examination of McTaggart's Philosophy*

C. D. Broad

We come at last to McTaggart's destructive arguments. . . .

3.1. *The Main Argument.* We take as an established premise that any series which could count as a temporal series would have to consist of terms which have *A*-characteristics and which individually change in respect of their *A*-characteristics. McTaggart tries to prove that there is a contradiction involved in this condition, and therefore that nothing could be a temporal series. If he is right, then, the characteristic of being a *B*-series, i.e., a series in which the terms are events and the relation is that of 'earlier than', is a delusive characteristic.

The essence of the argument is as follows: (i) The various determinate *A*-characteristics are incompatible with each other, in the usual way in which different determinates under the same determinable are so. McTaggart confines his statement to past, present, and future. But, of course, if it is true at all, it is equally true of any two degrees of pastness or of futurity.

(ii) Every event has all the *A*-characteristics; for every event has all degrees of futurity, has presentness, and has all degrees of pastness. The only possible exceptions would be that last event, if there were one, and the first event, if there were one. But, even so, the last event would have presentness and all degrees of futurity, though it would not have pastness. And the first event would have presentness and all degrees of pastness, though it would not have futurity. Thus every event has a plurality of determinate *A*-characteristics, whilst no two *A*-characteristics are compatible with each other.

(iii) McTaggart admits that, at first sight, this seems to lead to no difficulty. After all, no event has two different *A*-characteristics at any *one* moment; though each event has a different *A*-characteristic at each different moment.

(iv) McTaggart claims to show, however, that this attempted answer is useless, because it leads either to a contradiction or to a vicious infinite regress. His argument is as follows.

Suppose we try to avoid the contradiction of a term *M* being past, present, and future by saying that *M is now* present, *will be* past, and *has been* future; or by saying that *M is now* future, *will be* present, and *will be* past; or by saying that *M is now* past, *has been* present, and *has been* future. We must then raise the question of what we mean by these temporal copulas. According to McTaggart, there is only one possible analysis. To say that *S has been P* means 'There is a moment *t*, such that *S* has *P* at *t* and *t* is past.' To say that *S is now P* means

'There is a moment *t*, such that *S* has *P* at *t* and *t* is present.' To say that *S will be P* means 'There is a moment *t*, such that *S* has *P* at *t* and *t* is future.'

Now substitute *M* for *S*, and substitute the *A*-characteristics for *P*. We get the following results. '*M is now* present' means 'There is a moment *t*, such that *M* has presentness at *t* and *t* is present.' Again, '*M will be* past' means 'There is a moment *t*, such that *M* has pastness at *t* and *t* is future.' Lastly, '*M has been* future' means 'There is a moment *t*, such that *M* has futurity at *t* and *t* is past.'

The next stage of the argument . . . is very difficult to follow, as stated by McTaggart; but I have no doubt as to what is the essential point of it. I shall first quote McTaggart's argument in his own words, and shall then restate in my own way what is substantially the same argument. McTaggart's statement runs as follows: '. . . every moment, like every event, is both past, present, and future. . . . If *M* is present, there is no moment of past time at which it is past. But the moments of future time, in which it is past, are equally moments of past time, in which it cannot be past. Again, that *M* is future and will be present and past means that *M* is future at a moment of present time, and present and past at different moments of future time. In that case it cannot be present or past at any moments of past time. But all the moments of future time, in which *M* will be present or past, are equally moments of past time.'

I will now try to put the essential points of this very obscure argument clearly. The question is whether the three propositions '*M* is now present, *M* has been future, and *M* will be past' are mutually compatible. McTaggart wants to show that they are not. *(a)* Consider the proposition '*M* will be past.' According to McTaggart this means 'There is a moment *t*, such that *M* has pastness at *t* and *t* is future.' But, according to him, any moment that is future is also *present*. Therefore it follows that there is a moment *t*, such that *M* has pastness at *t* and *t* is *present*. But this is equivalent to the proposition '*M* is now past.' This is incompatible with the proposition '*M* is now present.' Thus '*M will be* past' entails '*M is now* past', and the latter is inconsistent with '*M* is now present.' Therefore '*M* will be past' is inconsistent with '*M* is now present.'

(b) Now consider the proposition '*M* has been future.' According to McTaggart, this means 'There is a moment *t*, such that *M* has futurity at *t* and *t* is past.' But, according to him, any moment that is past is also *present*. Therefore it follows that there is a moment *t*, such that *M* has futurity at *t* and *t* is *present*. But this is equivalent to the proposition '*M* is now future.' This is incompatible with the proposition '*M* is now present.' Thus '*M has been* future' entails '*M is now* future', and the latter is inconsistent with '*M* is now present.' Therefore '*M* has been future' is inconsistent with '*M* is now present.'

(c) If the argument in paragraphs *(a)* and *(b)* were valid, it would have proved that both the propositions '*M* will be past' and '*M* has been future' are inconsistent with the proposition '*M* is now present.' It remains to show that these two propositions are inconsistent with *each other*. This is easily done. From the argument in paragraph *(a)* we conclude that '*M* will be past' entails '*M* is now past.' From the argument in paragraph *(b)* we conclude that '*M* has been future' entails '*M* is now future.' But the two propositions '*M* is now past' and '*M* is now future' are incompatible with each other. Therefore the two propositions '*M* will be past'

and 'M has been future' are incompatible with each other. Thus, if the argument is valid, it would prove that *each* of the three propositions 'M is now present', 'M has been future', and 'M will be past' is incompatible with the other two. . . .

If we had started, instead, with the three propositions 'M is now past, M has been present, and M has been future', or 'M is now future, M will be present, and M will later on be past', a similar argument would have led to a similar result. So McTaggart claims to have shown that the original contradiction of M being past, present, and future breaks out again in the amended statement that M *is now* present, *has been* future, and *will be* past; and in the amended statement that M *is now* past and *has been* present, and future; and in the amended statement that M *is now* future and *will be* present and past.

(v) Of course there is *prima facie* a perfectly simple answer to this alleged contradiction. . . . Instead of admitting in paragraph (*a*) above that the future moment at which M has pastness is also present, we ought only to have admitted that it *will be* present. And, instead of admitting in paragraph (*b*) above that the past moment at which M has futurity is also present, we ought only to have admitted that it *has been* present. The argument would then have broken down at the first move.

McTaggart rejects this answer on the following grounds. According to him, we shall have to analyse the statement that a certain *moment* is now present, has been future, and will be past, in a similar way to that in which we analysed the corresponding statements about the *event* M. To say that t *will be* present, e.g., must mean that there is a moment t' such that t has presentness at t' and t' is future. To say that t *has been* present must mean that there is a moment t', such that t has presentness at t' and t' is past. Thus the same contradiction will arise at the second stage about *moments* as arose at the first stage about *events*. Any attempt to remove it in the same way will merely lead to a third stage at which the same contradiction will break out. We start on an infinite regress; which is vicious, because each step is needed in order to remove a contradiction in the previous stage, and at each stage the same contradiction breaks out again.

This is the main argument by which McTaggart persuaded himself that nothing can have *A*-characteristics. If nothing can have them, nothing can change in respect of them. If nothing can change in respect of *A*-characteristics, there can be no processes of qualitative change. And, if there can be no processes of qualitative change, no series can be a *B*-series. And so neither *A*-characteristics nor *B*-relations, nor qualitative change or persistence, can apply to anything. All these ostensible characteristics are delusive.

3.11. *Criticism of the Main Argument.* We must now consider whether this argument of McTaggart's is valid. I should suppose that every reader must have felt about it as any healthy-minded person feels about the Ontological Argument for the existence of God, viz., that it is obviously wrong somewhere, but that it may not be easy to say precisely what is wrong with it.

(i) I cannot myself see that there is any contradiction to be avoided. When it is said that pastness, presentness, and futurity are incompatible predicates, this is true only in the sense that no one term could have two of them *simultaneously* or *timelessly*. Now no term ever appears to have any of them timelessly, and no term ever appears to have any two of them simultaneously. What appears to be the case is that certain terms have them *successively*. Thus there is nothing in the temporal appearances to suggest that there is a contradiction to be avoided.

(ii) What are we to say, then, about McTaggart's alleged vicious infinite regress? In the first place we must say that, since there is no contradiction to be avoided, there is no need to start on any regress in order to avoid a contradiction. Secondly, we may well ask why McTaggart should assume that, e.g., '*M* is now present' *must* be analysed into 'There is a moment *t*, such that *M* has presentness at *t* and *t* is present.' Similarly, we may ask why he should assume that, e.g., 'The moment *t* has been future' *must* be analysed into 'There is a moment *t′*, such that *t* has futurity at *t′* and *t′* is past.'

(*a*) In the first place, we note that McTaggart has suddenly introduced the notion of *moments,* in addition to that of *events.* No justification whatever has been given for this. It would seem to imply that the temporal copulas 'is now', 'has been', and 'will be' presuppose some form of the Absolute Theory of Time. This is surely not obvious.

(*b*) The real motive of this analysis, and the real cause of the subsequent infinite regress, seems to me to be a certain assumption which McTaggart tacitly makes. He assumes that what is meant by a sentence with a *temporal copula* must be completely (and more accurately) expressible by a sentence or combination of sentences in which there is no temporal copula, but only *temporal predicates* and non-temporal copulas. And the regress arises because there remains at every stage a copula which, if taken as non-temporal, involves the *non-temporal* possession by a term of certain temporal predicates which could belong to it only *successively.*

Take, e.g., the general analysis of '*S* is now *P*' into 'There is a moment *t*, such that *S* has *P* at *t* and *t* is present.' The only motive for making this analysis is that it seems at first sight to have got rid of the temporal copula 'is now'. The predicate 'having *P* at *t*' may be said to belong to *S* timelessly or sempiternally if it belongs to *S* at all. And we are tempted to think that the 'is' in '*t* is present' is a timeless copula too. Now the source of McTaggart's regress is that, if you take the 'is' in '*t* is present' to be timeless, you will have to admit that *t* is also past and future in the same timeless sense of 'is'. Now this is impossible, for it is obvious that *t* can have these predicates only in succession. If, to avoid this, you say that the 'is' in '*t* is present' means 'is now', you have not got rid of temporal copulas. Therefore, if you are committed at all costs to getting rid of them, you will not be able to rest at this stage. At every stage of the analysis you will have a copula which, if taken to be *non-temporal,* leads to a contradiction, and, if taken to be *temporal,* needs to be analysed further in terms of temporal predicates and non-temporal copulas.

Now it seems to me that the proper interpretation of the regress is that it disproves the assumption that temporal copulas can be replaced by temporal predicates and non-temporal copulas. Since there is nothing necessary or self-evident about this assumption, the regress raises no objection to the *prima facie* appearance that events become and pass away and that they stand to each other in relations of temporal sequence and simultaneity.

(iii) It may be worth while to go into a little more detail about the question of temporal copulas and temporal predicates before leaving this topic. Let us take the sentences 'It will rain', 'It is now raining', and 'It has rained.' The utmost that can be done with the first is to analyse it into 'There is (in some non-temporal sense of "is") an event characterised non-temporally by raininess, and it is now future.' The corresponding analyses of the second and third would be got by substituting 'it is now present' and 'it is now past', respectively, for 'it is now future' in the analysis of the first. Even if this kind of analysis be accepted as correct, we have not got rid of the temporal copula 'is now'.

Another type of analysis would be to make 'It will rain' equivalent to 'There is (in some non-temporal sense of "is") an event characterised non-temporally by raininess, and it will be present.' The corresponding analyses of the second and third would be got by substituting 'it is now present' and 'it has been present', respectively, for 'it will be present' in the analysis of the first. Here we get rid of two out of the three *A*-characteristics, but have to keep all three temporal copulas. In the previous kind of analysis we got rid of two out of the three temporal copulas, but had to keep all three *A*-characteristics. So, on neither kind of analysis, can we get rid of *all* temporal copulas; and, on both kinds of analysis, we have to introduce at least one temporal predicate in addition to temporal copulas. Now the original sentences 'It will rain', 'It is now raining', and 'It has rained' express the facts in the most natural and simple way without introducing temporal predicates in addition to temporal copulas. So both kinds of analysis seem to be worthless. They complicate instead of simplifying; they make nothing intelligible which was not intelligible before; and they suggest false analogies with non-temporal propositions.

Quite apart from the fact that such 'analyses' serve no useful purpose, it seems to me that they fail to express what we have in mind when we use such sentences as 'It has rained' or 'It will rain.' When I utter the sentence 'It has rained', I do *not* mean that, in some mysterious non-temporal sense of 'is', there *is* a rainy event, which momentarily possessed the quality of presentness and has now lost it and acquired instead some determinate form of the quality of pastness. What I mean is that raininess has been, and no longer is being, manifested in my neighbourhood. When I utter the sentence 'It will rain', I do *not* mean that, in some mysterious non-temporal sense of 'is', there *is* a rainy event, which now possesses some determinate form of the quality of futurity and will in course of time lose futurity and acquire instead the quality of presentness. What I mean is that raininess will be, but is not now being, manifested in my neighbourhood.

The fact is that what are called 'statements about past events' are statements to the effect that certain characteristics, which constitute descriptions of possible events, have been and no longer are being manifested. What are called 'statements about future events' are statements to the effect that certain characteristics, which constitute descriptions of possible events, will be but are not yet being manifested.

To sum up. I believe that McTaggart's main argument against the reality of Time is a philosophical 'howler' of the same kind as the Ontological Argument for the existence of God. The fallacy of the Ontological Argument consists in treating being or existence as if it were a predicate like goodness, and in treating instantial propositions as if they were characterising propositions. The fallacy in McTaggart's argument consists in treating absolute becoming as if it were a species of qualitative change, and in trying to replace temporal copulas by non-temporal copulas and temporal adjectives. Both these 'howlers', like the Fall of Adam, have been over-ruled to good ends. In each case one can see that there is something radically wrong with the argument; and one's desire to put one's finger on the precise point of weakness stimulates one to clear up linguistic confusions which would otherwise have remained unnoticed and unresolved. I suspect that plenty of other philosophers have made the same mistake as St Anselm and the same mistake as McTaggart. But, since they did not draw such startling consequences from their confusions as these eminent men did, these errors have been allowed to rest in decent obscurity.

---

12   The Notion of the Present

A. N. Prior

Before directly discussing the notion of the present, I want to discuss the notion of the real. These two concepts are closely connected; indeed on my view they are one and the same concept, and the present simply *is* the real considered in relation to two particular species of unreality, namely the past and the future. So let's begin with the real in general.

Philosophers often speak as if the real world were just one of a number of different big boxes in which various things go on, the other boxes having such labels as 'the mind' or 'the world of Greek mythology'. For example, centaurs exist in the world of Greek mythology but not in the real world, aeroplanes exist in the real world but not in the world of Greek mythology, and horses and men exist both in the real world and in the world of Greek mythology. Again, Anselm addresses himself to people who held that God does not exist in the real world but only in the mind, and claimed to have a proof that if God exists in the mind he must exist in the real world too. Leibniz contrasted the real or actual world with an infinity of merely possible worlds in which various things happen which do not happen in the actual world. All these ways of talking suggest that the real world or the actual world is just a *region* of some larger universe which contains other regions as well – possible worlds, imaginary worlds, and so on.

I want to suggest – I don't of course claim that there's anything original in this suggestion – that this way of conceiving the relation between the real and the unreal is profoundly mistaken and misleading. The most important way in which it is misleading is that it minimises, or makes a purely arbitrary matter, the vast and stark *difference* that there is between the real and every form of unreality.

For talking of the real as one 'region' among others immediately suggests the question, 'In that case, what is so special about the real world in contrast with all other regions? – is it not a kind of narrow-mindedness and parochialism to think that it has anything special about it that none of the others have?' One philosopher, Meinong, has indeed said precisely that it *is* just narrow-mindedness and parochialism to single out the real world as a region of special interest; the 'prejudice in favour of the actual', he called it. Well, I want to argue that this is *not* just narrow-mindedness and parochialism, and that it becomes obvious enough what is so special about the real world as soon as we drop this metaphor of boxes or regions and become a little more literal.

To say that there are centaurs in the world of Greek mythology is surely *not* to say that there are centaurs in some remote and peculiar region, but just to say that *Greek myth-makers have said that* there are centaurs. Similarly, to say that there are centaurs in some person's mind is to say that *that person thinks or imagines that* there are centaurs. And to say that there are possible worlds in which there are centaurs is just to say that *it could be that* there are centaurs. In general, to say that X is the case in some non-real world is just to say 'X is the case' with some modifying prefix like 'Greek myth-makers have said that', 'Jones imagines that', or 'It could be that'. But to say that X is the case in the real or the actual world, or that it is really or actually or in fact the case, is just to say that it is the case – flat, and without any prefix whatever. To say that there are centaurs in the real world, for example, is not to say that there are centaurs in some region of the universe in which we happen to have more interest than in others; it is simply to say that *there are centaurs*. Talk of the real world, in other words, is not a metaphorical fudging-up of talk in which our sentences have a special kind of prefix, but a fudging-up of talk in which the relevant sentences have no prefixes at all. 'Really', 'actually', 'in fact', 'in the real world' are strictly *redundant* expressions – that, and not any prejudice or provincialism, is their specialness.

So to say that although there are no centaurs in the real world there are some in the world of Greek mythology, is just to say that *although there are no centaurs Greek myth-makers have said that there are;* to say that although God does not exist in reality he exists in the mind, is just to say that *although God does not exist people may imagine that he does*; to say that although Sextus raped Lucretia in the real world there is a possible world in which he didn't, is just to say that *although Sextus raped Lucretia he need not have done so*. There is, if you like, no other place than the real world for God or centaurs to exist in or for Sextus to rape Lucretia in; for God or centaurs to exist in the real world, or for Sextus to rape Lucretia in the real world, is just for God or centaurs to exist, or for Sextus to rape Lucretia. Again, 'Greek myth-makers have said that there are centaurs in the real world' is all one with 'Greek myth-makers have said that there are centaurs', and so is 'Greek myth-makers in the real world have said that there are centaurs.'

And now the present. It is tempting to think of the present as a region of the universe in which certain things happen, such as the war in Vietnam, and the past and the future as other regions in which other things happen, such as the battle of Hastings and men going to Mars. But to this picture there is the same objection as to the picture of the 'real world' as a box or region among other boxes or regions. It doesn't bring out what is so *special* about the present; and to be more specific, it doesn't bring out the way in which the present is *real* and the past and future are not. And I want to suggest that the reality of the present consists in what the reality of anything else consists in, namely the absence of a qualifying prefix. To say that Whitrow's lecture is past is to say that *it has been the case* that Whitrow is lecturing. To say that Scott's lecture is future is to say that *it will be the case* that Scott is lecturing. But to say that my lecture is present is just to say that *I am lecturing* – flat, no prefixes. The pastness of an event, that is to say its having taken place, is not the same thing as the event itself; nor is its futurity; but the presentness of an event *is* just the event. The presentness of my lecturing, for instance, is just my lecturing. Moreover, just as a real thought of a centaur, and a thought of a real centaur, are both of them just a thought of a centaur, so the present pastness of Whitrow's lecture, and its past presentness, are both just its pastness. And conversely, its pastness is its present pastness, so that although Whitrow's lecture isn't now present and so isn't real, isn't a fact, nevertheless its pastness, its *having* taken place, *is* a present fact, *is* a reality, and will be one as long as time shall last.

Notoriously, much of what is present isn't present permanently; the present is a shifting, changing thing. That is only to say that much of what is the case, of what is real and true, is constantly changing. Not everything, of course; some things that are the case also have always been the case and will always be the case. I imagine scientists have a special interest in such things. And among the things that not only are the case but always have been and always will be, are the laws of change themselves, I mean such laws as that if anything *has* occurred then for ever after it *will have* occurred (like Whitrow's lecture). These are the laws of what is now called *tense logic*, and the conception of the present that I have just been suggesting is deeply embedded in the syntax of that discipline. So that conception underlies, or anyhow seems to underlie, what is now a pretty flourishing systematic enterprise. . . .

---

13 Changes in Events and Changes in Things

A. N. Prior

The basic question to which I wish to address myself in this lecture is simply the old one, does time really flow or pass? The problem, of course, is that genuine flowing or passage is something which occurs *in* time, and *takes* time to occur. If time itself flows or passes, must there not be some 'super-time' in which it does so? Again, whatever flows or passes does so at some *rate*, but a rate of flow is just the amount of movement in a given *time*, so how could there be a rate of flow of time itself? And if time does not flow at any rate, how can it flow at all?

A natural first move towards extricating ourselves from these perplexities is to admit that talk of the flow or passage of time is just a metaphor. Time may be, as Isaac Watts says, *like* an ever-rolling stream, but it isn't really and literally an ever-rolling stream. But *how* is it like an ever-rolling stream? What is the literal truth behind this metaphor? The answer to this is not, at first sight, difficult. Generally when we make such remarks as 'Time does fly, doesn't it? – why, it's already the 16th', we mean that some date or moment which we have been looking forward to as future, has ceased to be future and is now present and on its way into the past. Or more fundamentally, perhaps, some future *event* to which we have been looking forward with hope or dread is now at last occurring, and soon will have occurred, and will have occurred a longer and longer time *ago*. We might say, for example, 'Time does fly, I'm already 47', that is, my birth is already that much past, 'and soon I shall be 48', i.e. it will be more past still. Suppose we speak about something 'becoming more past' not only when it moves from the comparatively near past to the comparatively distant past, but also when it moves from the present to the past, from the future to the present, and from the comparatively distant future to the comparatively near future. Then whatever is happening, has happened, or will happen is all the time 'becoming more past' in this extended sense; and just this is what we mean by the flow or passage of time. And if we want to give the *rate* of this flow or passage, it is surely very simple – it takes one exactly a year to get a year older, i.e. events become more past at the rate of a year per year, an hour per hour, a second per second.

Does this remove the difficulty? It is far from obvious that it does. It's not just that an hour per hour is a queer sort of rate – *this* queerness, I think, has been exaggerated, and I shall say more about it in a minute – but the whole idea of events changing is at first sight a little strange, even if we abandon the admittedly figurative description of this change as a *movement*. By and large, to judge by the way that we ordinarily talk, it's *things* that change, and events don't change but *happen*. Chairs, tables, horses, people change – chairs get worn out and then mended, tables get dirty and then clean again, horses get tired and then refreshed, people learn things and forget them, or are happy and then miserable, active and then sleepy, and so on, and all these are changes, and chairs, tables, horses and people are all what I mean by things as opposed to events. An accident, a coronation, a death, a prizegiving, are examples of what we'd call events, and it does seem unnatural to describe these as changing – what these do, one is inclined to say, is not to change but to happen or occur.

One of the things that make us inclined to deny that events undergo changes is that events *are* changes – to say that such and such an event has occurred is generally to say that some thing has, or some things have, changed in some way. To say, for instance, that the retirement of Sir Anthony Eden occurred in such and such a year is just to say that Sir Anthony then retired and so suffered the change or changes that retirement consists in – he had been Prime Minister, and then was not Prime Minister. Sir Anthony's retirement is or was a change concerning Sir Anthony; to say that it itself changes or has changed sounds queer because it sounds queer to talk of a change changing.

This queerness, however, is superficial. When we reflect further we realize that changes do change, especially if they go on for any length of time. (In this case we generally, though not always, call the change a *process* rather than an event, and there are other important differences between events and processes besides the length of time they take, but these differences are not relevant to the present discussion, so I shall ignore them and discuss changes generally, events and processes alike.) Changes do change – a movement, for example, may be slow at first and then rapid, a prizegiving or a lecture may be at first dull and afterwards interesting, or vice versa, and so on. It would hardly be too much to say that modern science began when people became accustomed to the idea of changes changing, e.g. to the idea of acceleration as opposed to simple motion. I've no doubt the ordinary measure of acceleration, so many feet per second per second, sounded queer when it was first used, and I think it still sounds queer to most students when they first encounter it. Ordinary speech is still resistant to it, and indeed to the expression of anything in the nature of a comparison of a comparison. We are taught at school that 'more older', for example, is bad English, but why shouldn't I say that I am more older than my son than he is than my daughter? And if we have learned to talk of an acceleration of a foot per second per second without imagining that the second 'second' must somehow be a different kind of 'second' from the first one – without imagining that if motion takes place in ordinary time, acceleration must take place in some super-time – can we not accustom ourselves equally to a change of 'a second per second' without any such imagining?

Changes do change, then, but this does not leave everything quite simple and solved. For there's still something odd about the change that we describe figuratively as the flow or passage of time – the change from an event's being future to its being present, and from its being present to its being more and more past. For the other changes in events which I have mentioned are ones which go on in the event *while it is occurring*; for example, if a lecture gets duller or a movement faster then this is something it does *as it goes on*; but the change from past to still further past isn't one that occurs while the event is occurring, for all the time that an event is occurring it isn't past but present, in fact the presentness of an event just *is* its happening, its occurring, as opposed to its merely having happened or being merely about to happen. We might put it this way: the things that change are *existing* things, and it's while they exist that they change, e.g. it's existing men, not non-existent men, that get tired and then pick up again; Julius Caesar, for example, isn't now getting tired and picking up again, unless the doctrine of immortality is true and he exists now as much as he ever did. And such changes as the change in the rate of movement are similarly changes that go on in events or processes while they exist, that is, while they exist in the only sense in which events and processes do exist, namely while they are occurring. But getting more and more past seems to be something an event does when it *doesn't* exist, and this seems very queer indeed.

We may retrace our steps to this point by looking at some of the literature of our subject. Professor C.D. Broad, in the second volume of his *Examination of McTaggart's Philosophy*, says that the ordinary view that an event, say the death of Queen Anne, is in the indefinitely distant future and then less and less future and then present and then goes into the more and more distant past – this ordinary story, Broad says, cannot possibly be true because it takes the death of Queen Anne to be at once a mere momentary thing and something with an indefinitely long history. We can make a first answer to this by distinguishing between the history that an event *has*, and the bit of history that it *is*. The bit of history that Queen Anne's death is, or was, is a very very short bit, but that doesn't prevent the history that it has from being indefinitely long. Queen Anne's death is part of the history of Queen Anne, and a very short part of it; what is long is not this part of the history of Queen Anne, but rather the history of this part of her history – the history of this part of her history is that first it was future, then it was present, and so on, and this can be a long history even if the bit of history that it is the history *of* is very short. There is not, therefore, the flat contradiction that Broad suggests here. There is, however, the difficulty that we generally think of the history of a thing as the sum of what it does and what happens to it *while it is there* – when it ceases to be, its history has ended – and this does make it seem odd that there should be an indefinitely long history of something which itself occupies a time which is indefinitely short.

But if there is a genuine puzzle here, it concerns what is actually going on also. For whatever goes on for any length of time – and that means: whatever goes on – will have future and past phases as well as the immediately present one; its going on is in fact a continual passage of one phase after another from being future through being present to being past. Augustine's reflections, in the eleventh chapter of his *Confessions*, on the notion of a 'long time', are relevant here. Just when, he asks, is a long time long? Is it long when it is present, or when it is past or future? We need not, I think, attach much importance to the fact that Augustine concentrates on so abstract a thing as a 'time' or an interval; his problems can be quite easily re-stated in terms of *what goes on* over the interval; in fact he himself slips into this, and talks about his childhood, a future sunrise and so on. When, we may ask, does a process go on for a long time – while it is going on, or when it lies ahead of us, or is all over?

Augustine is at first driven to the view that it is when it is present that a time is long, for only what *is* can be long or short (paragraph 18). We can give the same answer with processes – it is when they are going on that they go on for a long time. But then, as Augustine points out, there are these phases. A hundred years is a long time, but it's not really present all at once, and even if we try to boil down the present to an hour, 'that one hour passes away in flying particles'. 'The present hath no space' (20). Augustine had apparently not heard of the 'specious present', but even if he had it would not have helped him much – most of the happenings we are interested in take longer than that. He tries out the hypotheses that the past and the future, and past and future events, in some sense after all 'are' – that there is some 'secret place' where they exist all the time, and from which they come and to which they go. If there is no such place, then where do those who foresee the future and recall the past, discern these things? 'For that which is not, cannot be seen' (22).

Well, Augustine says, he doesn't know anything about that, but one thing that he does know is that wherever 'time past and to come' may 'be', 'they are not there as future, or past, but present. For if there also they be future, they are not yet there; if there also they be past, they are no longer there. Wheresoever then is whatsoever is, it is only as present' (23). Of course there are present 'traces' or images of past things in our memories, and present signs and intentions on the basis of which we make our future forecasts (23, 24), and sometimes Augustine seems satisfied with this – past, present, and future, he says, 'do exist in some sort, in the soul, but otherwhere do I not see them' (26). But sometimes he seems far from content with this – *that which* we remember and anticipate, he says, is different from these signs, and is *not* present (23, 24) – and, one must surely add, is *not* 'in the soul'.

It is time now to be constructive, and as a preparation for this I shall indulge in what may seem a digression, on the subject of Grammar. English philosophers who visit the United States are always asked sooner or later whether they are 'analysts'. I'm not at all sure what the answer is in my own case, but there's another word that Professor Passmore once invented to describe some English philosophers who are often called 'analysts', namely the word 'grammaticist', and that's something I wouldn't at all mind calling myself. I don't deny that there are genuine metaphysical problems, but I think you have to talk about grammar at least a little bit in order to solve most of them. And in particular, I would want to maintain that most of the present group of problems about time and change, though not quite all of them, arise from the fact that many expressions which look like nouns, i.e. names of objects, are not really nouns at all but concealed verbs, and many expressions which look like verbs are not really verbs but concealed conjunctions and adverbs. That is a slight over-simplification, but before we can get it stated more accurately we must look more closely at verbs, conjunctions, and adverbs.

I shall assume that we are sufficiently clear for our present purposes as to what a noun or name is, and what a sentence is, and given these notions, we can define a verb or verb-phrase as an expression that constructs a sentence out of a name or names. For instance, if you tack the verb 'died' on the name 'Queen Anne' you get the sentence 'Queen Anne died', and if you tack the phrase 'is an undertaker' on the name 'James Bowels' you get the sentence 'James Bowels is an undertaker', so that this is a verb-phrase. I say 'out of a name *or names*' because some verbs have to have an object as well as a subject. Thus if you put the verb 'loves' between the names 'Richard' and 'Joan' you get the sentence 'Richard loves Joan'; this verb constructs this sentence out of these two names; and the phrase 'is taller than' would function similarly. Logicians call verbs and verb-phrases 'predicates'; 'died' and 'is an undertaker' would be 'one-place' predicates, and 'loves' and 'is taller than' are 'two-place' predicates. There are also expressions which construct sentences, not out of names, but out of sentences. If an expression constructs a sentence out of two or more other sentences it is a conjunction, or a phrase equivalent to a conjunction. For example 'Either – or –' functions in this way in 'Either it will rain or it will snow'. If the expression constructs a sentence out of one other sentence it is an adverb or adverbial phrase, like 'not' or 'It is not the case that' or 'allegedly' or 'It is alleged that', or 'possibly' or 'It is possible that'. Thus by attaching these expressions to 'It is raining' we obtain the sentences

It is not raining;
It is not the case that it is raining;
It is allegedly raining;
It is alleged that it is raining;
It is possibly raining;
It is possible that it is raining.

One very important difference between conjunctions and adverbs, on the one hand, and verbs, on the other, is that because the former construct sentences out of sentences, i.e. the same sort of thing as they end up with, they can be applied again and again to build up more and more complicated sentences, like 'It is allegedly possible that he will not come', which could be spread out as

It is said that (it is possible that (it is not the case that (he will come))).

You can also use the same adverb twice and obtain such things as double negation, alleged allegations and so on. Verbs, because they do not end up with the same sort of expression as what they start with, cannot be piled up in this way. Having constructed 'Queen Anne died' by the verb 'died' out of the name 'Queen Anne', you cannot do it again – 'Queen Anne died died' is not a sentence.

Turning now to our main subject, I want to suggest that putting a verb into the past or future tense is exactly the same sort of thing as adding an adverb to the sentence. 'I *was* having my breakfast' is related to 'I am having my breakfast' in exactly the same way as 'I am *allegedly* having my breakfast' is related to it, and it is only an historical accident that we generally form the past tense by modifying the present tense, e.g. by changing 'am' to 'was', rather than by tacking on an adverb. In a rationalized language with uniform constructions for similar functions we could form the past tense by prefixing to a given sentence the phrase 'It was the case that', or 'It has been the case that' (depending on what sort of past we meant), and the future tense by prefixing 'It will be the case that'. For example, instead of 'I will be eating my breakfast' we could say

'It will be the case that I am eating my breakfast',

and instead of 'I was eating my breakfast' we could say

'It was the case that I am eating my breakfast'.

The nearest we get to the latter in ordinary English is 'It was the case that I *was* eating my breakfast', but this is one of those anomalies like emphatic double negation. The construction I am sketching embodies the truth behind Augustine's suggestion of the 'secret place' where past and future times 'are', and his insistence that wherever they are, they are not there as past or future but as present. The past is not the present but it *is* the past present, and the future is not the present but it *is* the future present.

There is also, of course, the past future and the future past. For these adverbial phrases, like other adverbial phrases, can be applied repeatedly – the sentences to which they are attached do not have to be simple ones; it is enough that they be sentences, and they can be sentences which already have tense-adverbs, as we might call them, within them. Hence we can have such a construction as

'It will be that case that (it has been the case that (I am taking off my coat))',

or in plain English, 'I will have taken off my coat'. We can similarly apply repeatedly such *specific* tense-adverbs as 'It was the case forty-eight years ago that'. For example, we could have

'It will be the case seven months hence that (it was the case forty-eight years ago that (I am being born))',

that is, it will be my forty-eighth birthday in seven months' time.

To say that a change has occurred is to say at least this much: that something which was the case formerly is not the case now. That is, it is at least to say that for some sentence *p* we have

It was the case that *p*, and it is not the case that *p*.

This sentence *p* can be as complicated as you like, and can itself contain tense-adverbs, so that one example of our formula would be

It was the case 5 months ago that (it was the case only 47 years ago that (I am being born)), and it is not now the case that (it was the case only 47 years ago that (I am being born)),

that is, I am not as young as I used to be. This last change, of course, is a case of precisely that recession of events into the past that we are really talking about when we say that time flows or passes, and the piling of time-references on top of one another, with no suggestion that the time-words must be used in a different sense at each level, simply reflects the fact that tense-adverbs *are* adverbs, not verbs.

An important point to notice now is that while *I* have been talking about words – for example about verbs and adverbs – for quite a long time, the sentences that I have been using as examples have *not* been about words but about real things. When a sentence is formed out of another sentence or other sentences by means of an adverb or conjunction, it is not *about* those other sentences, but about whatever they are themselves about. For example, the compound sentence

'Either I will wear my cap or I will wear my beret' is not about the sentences 'I will wear my cap' and 'I will wear my beret'; like them, it is about me and my headgear, though the information it conveys about these is a little less definite than what either of them would convey separately. Similarly, the sentence 'It will be the case that I am having my tooth out' is not about the sentence 'I am having my tooth out'; it is about me. A genuine sentence about the sentence 'I am having my tooth out' would be one stating that it contained six words and nineteen letters, but 'It will be the case that I am having my tooth out', i.e. 'I will be having my tooth out', is quite obviously not a sentence of this sort at all.

Nor is it about some abstract entity named by the clause 'that I am having my tooth out'. It is about me and my tooth, and about nothing else whatever. The fact is that it is difficult for the human mind to get beyond the simple subject-predicate or noun-verb structure, and when a sentence or thought hasn't that structure but a more complex one we try in various ways to force it into the subject-predicate pattern. We thus invent new modes of speech in which the subordinate sentences are replaced by noun-phrases and the conjunctions or adverbs by verbs or verb-phrases. For example, instead of saying

(1)   *If* you have oranges in your larder you have been to the greengrocer's,

we may say

(2)   Your having oranges in your larder *implies* your having been to the greengrocer's,

which looks as if it has the same form as 'Richard loves Joan' except that 'Your having oranges in your larder' and 'Your having been to the grocer' seem to name more abstract objects than Richard and Joan, and implying seems a more abstract activity than loving. We can rid ourselves of this suggestion if we reflect that (2) is nothing more than a paraphrase of (1). Similarly

(3)   It is now six years since it was the case that I am falling out of a punt,

could be re-written as

(4)   My falling out of a punt has receded six years into the past.

This suggests that something called an event, my falling out of a punt, has gone through a performance called receding into the past, and moreover has been going through this performance even after it has ceased to exist, i.e. after it has stopped happening. But of course (4) is just a paraphrase of (3), and like (3) is not about any objects except me and that punt – there is no real reason to believe in the existence either now or six years ago of a further object called 'my falling out of a punt'.

What I am suggesting is that what looks like talk about events is really at bottom talk about things, and that what looks like talk about changes in events is really just slightly more complicated talk about changes in things. This applies *both* to the changes that we say occur in events when they are going on, like the change in speed of a movement ('movement' is a *façon de parler*; there is just the moving car, which moves more quickly than it did), *and* the changes that we say occur in events when they are not going on any longer, or not yet, e.g. my birth's receding into the past ('birth' is a *façon de parler* – there's just me being born, and then getting older),

It's not all quite as simple as this, however. This story works very well for me and my birth and my fall out of the punt, but what about Queen Anne? Does Queen Anne's death getting more past mean that *Queen Anne* has changed from having died 250 years ago to having died 251 years ago, or whatever the period is? – that *she* is still 'getting older', though in a slightly extended sense? The trouble with this, of course, is just that Queen Anne doesn't exist now any more than her death does. There are at least two different ways in which we might deal with this one. We might, in the first place, say that our statement really is about Queen Anne (despite the fact that she 'is no more'), and really is, or at least entails, a statement of the form

It was the case that *p*, and is not now the case that *p*,

namely

It was the case that it was the case only 250 years ago that Queen Anne is dying, and is not now the case that it was the case only 250 years ago that Queen Anne is dying,

but we may add that this statement does not record a 'change' in any natural sense of that word, and certainly not a change in Queen Anne. A genuine record of change, we could say, must not only be of the form above indicated but must meet certain further conditions which we might specify in various ways. And we could say that although what is here recorded *isn't* a change in the proper sense, it is *like* a change in fitting the above formula. The flow of time, we would then say, is merely metaphorical, not only because what is meant by it isn't a genuine change; but the force of the metaphor can still be explained – we use the metaphor because what we call the flow of time does fit the above formula. On this view it might be that not only the recession of Queen Anne's death but my own growing older will not count as a change in the strict sense, though growing older is normally *accompanied* by genuine changes, and the phrase is commonly extended to cover these – increasing wisdom, bald patches, and so on.

But can a statement really be *about* Queen Anne after she has ceased to be? I do not wish to dogmatize about this, but an alternative solution is worth mentioning. We might paraphrase 'Queen Anne has died' as 'Once there was a person named "Anne", who reigned over England, etc., but there is not now any such person'. This solution exploits a distinction which we may describe as one between *general facts* and *individual facts*. That someone has stolen my pencil is a general fact; that John Jones has stolen my pencil, if it is a fact at all, is an individual fact. It has often been said – for example, it was said by the Stoic logicians – that there are no general facts without there being the corresponding individual facts. It cannot, for example, be the case that 'someone' has stolen my pencil, unless it is the case that some specific individual – if not John Jones, then somebody else – has stolen it. And in cases of this sort the principle is very plausible, indeed it is obviously true. I have read that some of the schoolmen described the subject of sentences like 'someone has stolen my pencil' as an *individuum vagum*, but of course this is a makeshift – forcing things into a pattern again. There are no 'vague individuals', and if a pencil has been stolen at all it has been stolen not by a vague individual but by some quite definite one, or else by a number of such. There are vague statements, however, and vague thoughts, and the existence of such statements and thoughts is as much a fact about the real world as any other; and when we describe the making of such statements and the entertaining of such thoughts, we do encounter at least partly general facts to which no wholly individual facts correspond. If I allege or believe that someone has stolen my pencil, there may be *no* specific individual with respect to whom I allege or believe that *he* stole my pencil. There is *alleged or believed to be* an individual who stole it, but there is *no individual who is alleged or believed* to have stolen it (not even a vague one). So while it is a fact that I allege or believe that someone stole it, there is no fact of the form 'I allege (or believe) that X stole it'. The one fact that there is, is no doubt an individual fact in so far as it concerns me, but is irreducibly general as far as the thief is concerned. (There may indeed be *no* thief – I am perhaps mistaken about the whole thing – but this is another question; our present point is that there may be no one who is even said or thought to be a thief, though it is said or thought *that there is* a thief.)

Returning now to Queen Anne, what I am suggesting is that the sort of thing that we unquestionably do have with 'It is said that' and 'It is thought that', we also have with 'It will be the case that' and 'It was the case that'. It *was the case that someone* was called 'Anne', reigned over England, etc., even though *there is not now anyone* of whom it was the case that *she* was called 'Anne', reigned over England, etc. What we must be careful about here is simply getting our prefixes in the right order. Just as

(1)   I think that (for some specific X (X stole my pencil))

does not imply

(2)   For some specific X (I think that (X stole my pencil)),

so

(3)   It was the case that (for some specific X (X is called 'Anne', reigns over England, etc.))

does not imply

(4)   For some specific X (it was the case that (X is called 'Anne', reigns over England, etc.)).

On this view, the fact that Queen Anne has been dead for some years is not, in the strict sense of 'about', a fact about Queen Anne; it is not a fact about anyone or anything – it is a *general* fact. Or if it is about anything, what it is about is not Queen Anne – it is about the earth, maybe, which has rolled around the sun so many times since there was a person who was called 'Anne', reigned over England, etc. (It would then be a *partly* general fact – individual in so far as it concerns the earth, but irreducibly general as far as the dead queen is concerned. But if there are – as there undoubtedly are – irreducibly partly general facts, could there not be irreducibly wholly general ones?) Note, too, that the fact that this fact is not about Queen Anne, cannot itself be a fact about Queen Anne – its statement needs rephrasing in some such way as 'There is no person who was called "Anne", etc., and about whom it is a fact that, etc.'

On this view, the recession of Queen Anne's death into the further past is quite decidedly not a change in Queen Anne, not because we are using 'change' in so tight a sense that it is not a change at all, but because Queen Anne doesn't herself enter into this recession, or indeed, now, into any fact whatever. But the recession *is* still a change or quasi-change in the sense that it fits the formula 'It was the case that p, but is not now the case that p' – this formula continues to express what is common to the flow of a literal river on the one hand (where it was the case that such-and-such drops were at a certain place, and this is the case no longer) and the flow of time on the other.

---

14   The General Problem of Time and Change: an Excerpt from *Scientific Thought*

C. D. Broad

· · · We are naturally tempted to regard the history of the world as existing eternally in a certain order of events. Along this, and in a fixed direction, we imagine the characteristic of presentness as moving, somewhat like the spot of light from a policeman's bull's-eye traversing the fronts of the houses in a street. What is illuminated is the present, what has been illuminated is the past, and what has not yet been illuminated is the future. The fact that the spot is of finite area expresses the fact that the Specious Present is not a mere point but is of finite, though short, duration. Such analogies may be useful for some purposes, but it is clear that they explain nothing.

· · ·

. . . We say: 'Of course the event E has futurity for a certain stretch of time, then it has presentness for a short subsequent stretch, and it has pastness at all other moments.' Now the question at once arises: 'Can we treat the change of an *event* in respect to its *temporal* qualities as just like the change of a *thing* with respect to qualities like red and green?'

To answer this question we must try to see what we mean when we say that a certain thing T changes from red to green. So far as I can see, our meaning is somewhat as follows: There is a certain long-lasting event in the history of the world. This stands out in a noticeable way from other events which overlap it wholly or partly. If successive short sections in time be taken of this long event, adjacent sections have spatial continuity with each other, and predominant qualitative resemblance to each other. On these grounds the whole long event is treated as the history of a single thing T. But, although adjacent short sections are *predominantly* alike in their qualities, there may be adjacent sections which differ very markedly in *some* quality, such as colour. If you can cut the history of the thing in a certain moment, such that a slice of its history before that is red and a slice after that is green, we say that the thing T has changed from red to green at that moment. To say that a thing changes, thus simply means that its history can be cut up into a series of adjacent short slices, and that two adjacent slices may have qualitative differences.

. . .

If we reflect, we shall notice that there are two quite different senses in which an entity can be said to change its relational properties. An example of the first is where Tom Smith, the son of John Smith, becomes taller than his father. An example of the second is where Tom Smith ceases to be the youngest son of John Smith, and becomes the last son but one. What is the difference between these two cases? In the first we have two partially overlapping life-histories, T and J. If we cut up both into successive short sections we find that the earlier sections of T have the relation of 'shorter than' to the contemporary sections of J, whilst the later sections of T have the relation of 'taller than' to the contemporary sections of J. In the second we have quite a different state of affairs. When we say that T is the youngest son of J we mean that there is no entity in the universe of which it is true to say both that it is a son of J and that it is younger than T. When we say that T has ceased to be the youngest son of J we mean that the universe does contain an entity of which it is true to say both that it is a son of J and that it is younger than T. In the first case then, we simply have a difference of relation between different corresponding sections of two existing long events. In the latter, the difference is that a certain entity has changed its relational properties because a second entity, which did not formerly exist (and therefore could stand in *no* relation whatever to T), has begun to exist, and consequently to stand in certain relations to T, who is a member of the same universe as it.

Now it is obvious that the change that happens to an event when it ceases to be present and becomes past is like the change of Tom Smith when he ceases to be the youngest son of John Smith; and the continuous retreat of an event into the more and more remote past is like the successive departure of Tom from being the 'baby' of the family, as John Smith (moved by the earnest exhortations of the Bishop of London) produces more and more children. A Specious Present of mine is just the last thin slice that has joined up to my life-history. When it ceases to be present and becomes past this does not mean that it has changed its relations to anything to which it was related when it was present. It will simply mean that other slices have been tacked on to my life-history, and, with their existence, relations have begun to hold, which could not hold before these slices existed to be terms to these relations. To put the matter in another way: When an event, which was present, becomes past, it does not change or lose any of the relations which it had before; it simply acquires in addition new relations which it *could* not have before, because the terms to which it now has these relations were then simply non-entities.

It will be observed that such a theory as this accepts the reality of the present and the past, but holds that the future is simply nothing at all. Nothing has happened to the present by becoming past except that fresh slices of existence have been added to the total history of the world. The past is thus as real as the present. On the other hand, the essence of a present event is, not that it precedes future events, but that there is quite literally *nothing* to which it has the relation of precedence. The sum total of existence is always increasing, and it is this which gives the time-series a sense as well as an order. A moment t is later than a moment t' if the sum total of existence at t includes the sum total of existence at t' together with something more.

We are too liable to treat change from future to present as if it were analogous to change from present to past or from the less to the more remote past. This is, I believe, a profound mistake. I think that we must recognise that the word 'change' is used in three distinct senses, of which the third is the most fundamental. These are (i) Change in the attributes of things, as where the signal lamp changes from red to green; (ii) Change in events with respect to pastness, as where a certain event ceases to be present and moves into the more and more remote past; and (iii) Change from future to present. . . .

Let us call the third kind of change *Becoming*. . . . [W]e can see by direct inspection that becoming is of so peculiar a character that it is misleading to call it change. When we say that a thing changes in quality, or that an event changes in pastness, we are talking of entities that exist both before and after the moment at which change takes place. But, when an event becomes, it *comes into existence*; and it was not anything at all until it had become. You cannot say that a future event is one that succeeds the present; for a present event is defined as one that is succeeded by nothing. We can put the matter, at choice, in one of two ways. We can either say that, since future events are non-entities, they cannot stand in any relations to anything, and therefore cannot stand in the relation of succession to present events. Or, conversely, we can say that, if future events succeeded present events, they would have the contradictory property of succeeding something that has no successor, and therefore they cannot be real.

It has long been recognised that there are two unique and irreducible, though intimately connected types of judgment. The first asserts that S is or exists; and is called an *existential* judgment. The second asserts that S is so and so, or has such and such a characteristic. This may be called a *characterising* judgment. The connexion between the two is that a thing cannot be so and so without *being*, and that it cannot be without being *so and so*.[1] Meinong, with the resources of the German tongue at his disposal, coins the convenient words *Sein* and *Sosein*. Now it seems to me that we have got to recognise a third equally fundamental and irreducible type of judgment, viz., one of the form: S becomes or comes into existence. Let us call these *genetic* judgments. I think that much of the trouble about Time and Change comes from our obstinate attempts to reduce such judgments to the characterising form. Any judgment can be *verbally* reduced to this form. We can reduce 'S is' to 'S is existent.' But the reduction is purely verbal, and those who take it seriously land in the sloughs of the Ontological Argument. Similarly 'S is future' is verbally a judgment that ascribes a characteristic to an event S. But, if we are right, this must be a mistake; since to have a characteristic implies to exist (at any rate in the case of particulars, like events), and the future does not exist so long as it is future.

Before passing on there is one more verbal ambiguity to be noted. The same word *is* is used absolutely in the existential judgment 'S is', and as a connective tie in the characterising judgment 'S is P.' Much the same is true of the word *becomes*. We say 'S becomes', and we say 'S becomes P.' The latter type of judgment expresses qualitative change, the former expresses coming into existence.

The relation between existence and becoming (and consequently between characterisation and becoming) is very intimate. Whatever is has become, and the sum total of the existent is continually augmented by becoming. There is no such thing as *ceasing* to exist; what has become exists henceforth for ever. When we say that something has ceased to *exist* we only mean that it has ceased to be *present*; and this only means that the sum total of existence has increased since any part of the history of the thing became, and that the later additions contain no events sufficiently alike to and sufficiently continuous with the history of the thing in question to count as a continuation of it. For complete accuracy a slight modification ought to be made in the statement that 'whatever is has become'. Long events do not become bodily, only events short enough to fall in Specious Presents become, as wholes. Thus the becoming of a long event is just the successive becoming of its shorter sections. We shall have to go more fully into the question of Specious Presents at a later stage.

. . .

If the future, so long as it is future, be literally nothing at all, what are we to say of judgments which profess to be about the future?

Undoubtedly we do constantly make judgments which profess to be about the future. Weather forecasts, nautical almanacs, and railway time-tables, are full of such judgments. Admittedly no judgment about the future is absolutely certain (with the possible exception of the judgment that there will always be events of some kind or other); but this is irrelevant for our present purpose. No historical judgment about the past is absolutely certain either; and, in any case, our question is not whether we can have *certain* knowledge about the future, but is the prior question: What are we really *talking about* when we profess to make judgments about the future, and what do we *mean* by the truth or falsity of such judgments?

We cannot attempt to answer these questions till we have cleared up certain points about the nature of judgments in general. First, we must notice that the question: 'What is a certain judgment about?' is ambiguous. It may mean: 'What is the subject or subjects of the judgment?' or: 'To what fact does the judgment refer?' The fact to which a judgment refers is the fact that renders it true or false. It is true, if it has the peculiar relation of concordance to the fact to which it refers; and false, if it has the relation of discordance to this fact. Discordance, I think, is a positive relation which is incompatible with concordance; it is not the mere absence of concordance. I see no reason to suppose that the reference of a judgment to a fact is a third independent relation over and above the relations of concordance and discordance. I take it to be just the disjunction 'concordance-or-discordance'; and I suppose that to say that J refers to F simply means that F is the fact which either makes J true by concording with it or false by discording with it.

Now people make many judgments, which have nothing to do with the future, but are nevertheless apparently about objects which do not, in fact, exist. Many English peasants, in the Middle Ages, must have made the judgments 'Puck exists' or 'Puck has turned the milk.' And the latter of these, of course, implies the former. I will assume (in spite of Sir Conan Doyle) that Puck does not in fact exist. What were these men referring to, in our sense of the word? To answer this we have simply to ask: What fact made their judgments false? The answer is that it is the negative fact that no part of the universe was characterised by the set of characteristics by which they described Puck to themselves. Their judgment boils down to the assertion that some part of the existent is characterised by this set of characteristics, and it is false because it discords with the negative fact that the set in question characterises no part of the universe. Naturally they did not know that this was what their judgment referred to, or they would not have made it. But, in our sense of reference, there is no reason why a person who makes a judgment should know what it refers to.

Now it would obviously be absurd to say that what these men were *talking about* was the negative fact that no part of the universe has the characteristics which they ascribe to Puck. Hence we see the need of distinguishing between what a judgment refers to and what the person who makes the judgment is talking about. What they were talking about was a certain set of characteristics, viz., those by which they described Puck to themselves. This may be called the logical subject of their judgment. It is something real and independent of the judging mind; having the kind of reality and independence which is characteristic of universals, and not, of course, that which is characteristic of particular existents. Thus, although there is no such being as Puck, people who profess to be judging about him are not judging about nothing (for they are judging about a set of characteristics which is itself real, though it does not happen to characterise any particular existent). Nor are they referring to nothing (for they are referring – though they do not know it – to an important negative fact about the existent).

Since the non-existence of Puck is compatible with the fact that the judgment 'Puck exists' is an intelligible statement about something real, we may hope that the non-existence of the future may prove to be compatible with the existence and intelligibility of judgments which profess to be about the future. Up to a point the two kinds of judgment can be treated in much the same way. The judgment which is *grammatically* about 'Puck' proves to be *logically* about the set of characteristics by which the assertor describes Puck to himself. Similarly the judgment 'To-morrow will be wet', which is grammatically about 'to-morrow', is logically about the characteristic of wetness. The non-existence of to-morrow is therefore consistent with the fact that the judgment is about something.

Still there is one very important difference between the two kinds of judgment. Judgments like 'Puck exists' are not only *about* something; they also *refer to* some fact which makes them true or false. This fact may be negative, but it is a real fact about the existent world. If we ask what fact judgments ostensibly about the future refer to, we must answer that there is no such fact. If I judge, to-day, that to-morrow will be wet, the only fact which this judgment can refer to, in our sense of the word, is the fact which renders it true or false. Now it is obvious that this fact is the wetness or fineness of to-morrow when to-morrow comes. To-day, when I make the judgment, there is no such fact as the wetness of to-morrow and there is no such fact as the fineness of to-morrow. For these facts can neither of them begin to be till to-morrow begins to be, which does not happen till to-morrow becomes to-day. Thus judgments which profess to be about the future do not refer to any fact, whether positive or negative, at the time when they are made. They are therefore at that time neither true nor false. They will become true or false when there is a fact for them to refer to; and after this they will remain true or false, as the case may be, for ever and ever. If you choose to define the word *judgment* in such a way that nothing is to be called a judgment unless it be either true or false, you must not, of course, count 'judgments' that profess to be about the future as judgments. If you accept the latter, you must say that the Law of Excluded Middle does not apply to all judgments. If you reject them, you may say that the Law of Excluded Middle applies to all genuine judgments; but you must add that 'judgments' which profess to be about the future are not genuine judgments when they are made, but merely enjoy a courtesy title by anticipation, like the eldest sons of the higher nobility during the lifetime of their fathers. For convenience, I shall continue to speak of them as judgments.

So far then, we have determined two facts about judgments which profess to be concerned with the future. (*a*) They are about something, viz., some characteristic or set of characteristics; and (*b*) they do not refer to any fact at the time when they are made. This is clearly not a complete analysis. Two further points need to be cleared up. (*a*) If such judgments when made do not refer to anything, how is it that, if certain events become, the judgment is verified, and, if other events become, it is refuted? (*b*) If such judgments are about characteristics, what precisely is it that they assert about these characteristics?

(*a*) Suppose I judge to-day that to-morrow will be wet. Nothing that may happen to-morrow will be relevant to this judgment except the state of the weather, and nothing will then make it true except the wetness of the weather.

This is true enough, but it does not prove that the judgment refers to any fact, in our sense of reference. With *any* judgment we can tell what *kind* of fact will verify or refute it, as soon as we know what the judgment is about and what kind of assertion it makes. But no amount of inspection of a judgment itself will show us *the particular fact* which makes it true if it is true and false if it is false. There is therefore no inconsistency between the statement that we can know at once what *kind of fact* would verify a judgment about the future, and the statement that such judgments do not refer to any *fact* when made.

(*b*) As regards any judgment we have to consider not only what it is about, but also what it asserts about its subject or subjects. These two questions are not altogether free from ambiguity, and this ambiguity must be cleared up before we consider the special question as to what judgments that profess to be about the future assert. (1) There is the confusion between what a judgment is about and what it refers to. This we have already dealt with. (2) There is the distinction between what a judgment is ostensibly about and what it is really about. If you had asked a peasant, who said that Puck had turned the milk, what he was talking about, he would have said that he was talking about a certain individual fairy. This is what the judgment professes to be about. What it is really about is a certain set of characteristics. Roughly speaking, we may say that what a judgment professes to be about can be determined by a grammatical analysis of the sentence in which the judgment is expressed. Although there is always a connexion between the grammatical structure of a sentence and the logical structure of a judgment, it is highly dangerous to suppose that what the sentence is grammatically about is the name of what the judgment is logically about. (3) When these two confusions have been set aside and we are quite definitely dealing with the *judgment,* and neither with the *fact* to which it refers nor the *sentence* which expresses it, there is still a difficulty as to how much is to be included under the head of what the judgment is about and how much is to be included under the head of what the judgment asserts. Take first a very simple characterising judgment, like '3 is a prime'. What is this about, and what does it assert? We should all agree that it is at any rate about the number 3. But is it about the characteristic of primeness too? If you say Yes, what is there left for it to assert? If you say No, how can you face the obviously equivalent judgment 'Primeness is a characteristic of 3'? Exactly the same kind of difficulty arises over a relational proposition, like '3 is greater than 2'. We should all at this time of day agree that it is at least about the numbers 2 and 3. But is it or is it not about the relation of greater? I think that we must say that the former judgment is about primeness as much as it is about the number 3, and that the latter is about the relation of greater as much as it is about the numbers 2 and 3. Really it is as misleading to say that the first asserts primeness as to say that it asserts 3. The minimum that it asserts is the primeness of 3. Similar remarks apply to the second. If we like to use the useful word *tie,* which Mr W.E. Johnson[2] has lately introduced into logic, we might say that the first judgment is about the number 3 and the characteristic of primeness, and asserts that they are connected by the characterising tie. The second is about the numbers 3 and 2 and the relation greater, and asserts that they are connected by the relational tie in the order 3 to 2. But we might equally well distinguish different kinds of assertion, and say that the first is about the number 3 and the characteristic of primeness, and makes a characterising assertion about them. In the case of the second we should talk of a relating assertion.

So far we have purposely chosen examples which are about timeless objects, like numbers. Let us now take the series of judgments: 'It has rained', 'It is raining', and 'It will rain', which are about events, and contain an essential reference to time. The first may be analysed as follows: 'There is an event which is characterised by raininess, and the sum total of existence when the judgment is made includes all and more than all which it includes when this event becomes'. The second may be analysed as follows: 'There is an event which is characterised by raininess, and the sum total of existence is the same when this event becomes and when the judgment is made.' Thus judgments about the past and the present can be analysed into judgments which involve the four familiar types of assertion – the existential, the characterising, the genetic, and the relational. But the judgment that it will rain cannot be analysed in a similar way. It cannot mean anything that begins with the statement: 'There *is* an event', for the only events that there are are the events that have become up to the time when the assertion is made; the sum total of existence does not contain future events. We can only restate the judgment in the form: 'The sum total of existence will increase beyond what it is when the judgment is made, and some part of what will become will be characterised by raininess'. We cannot then analyse *will* away, as we can *has been* and *is now*. Every judgment that professes to be about the future would seem then to involve two peculiar and not further analysable kinds of assertion. One of these is about becoming; it asserts that further events will become. The other is about some characteristic; it asserts that this will characterise some of the events which will become. If then we ask: What are judgments which profess to be about future events really about? the answer would seem to be that they are about some characteristic and about becoming. And if it be asked: What do such judgments assert? the only answer that I can give is that they assert that the sum total of existence will increase through becoming, and that the characteristic in question will characterise some part of what will become. These answers are compatible with the non-existence of the future. The only 'constituents' of the judgment, when it is made, are the characteristic – which has the kind of reality which universals possess – and the concept of becoming. About these the judgment makes certain assertions of a quite peculiar and not further analysable kind. Something called *to-morrow* is not a constituent of judgments which are grammatically about 'to-morrow', any more than an individual called *Puck* is a constituent of judgments which profess to be about 'Puck'.

I have thus tried to show that there is an extreme difference between judgments which profess to be about future events and those which are about past or present events. The former, when made, do not refer to anything, and therefore are not literally true or false, though it is possible for anyone who understands their meaning to see what kind of fact *will* eventually make them true or false as the case may be. Again, *is now* and *has been* need not be taken as new and ultimate types of assertion, but *will be* apparently must be so taken. Nevertheless, although the future is nothing and although judgments which profess to be about future events refer to nothing, they are not about nothing. They are about some characteristic and about becoming; and, so far as I can see, they make an unique and not further analysable kind of assertion about these terms. . . .

Notes

1   *Über die Stellung der Gegenstandstheorie* (Leipzig: R. Voitlander, 1907), and elsewhere [e.g., Alexius Meinong, 'The Theory of Objects', in R. M. Chisholm (ed.), *Realism and the Background of Phenomenology* (Glencoe, Ill.: The Free Press, 1960)].
2   W. B. Johnson, *Logic* (Cambridge: Cambridge University Press) vol. i.

---

15   The Myth of Passage

D. C. Williams

AT EVERY MOMENT each of us finds himself the apparent center of the world, enjoying a little lit foreground of the here and now, while around him there looms, thing beyond thing, event beyond event, the plethora of a universe. Linking the furniture of the foreground are sets of relations which he supposes also to bind the things beyond and to bind the foreground with the rest. Noteworthy among them are those queerly obvious relations, peculiarly external to their terms, which compose the systems of space and time, modes of connection exhaustively specifiable in a scheme of four dimensions at right angles to one another. Within this manifold, for all that it is so firmly integrated, we are immediately struck by a disparity between the three-dimensional spread of space and the one dimension of time. The spatial dimensions are in a literal and precise sense perpendicular to one another, and the submanifold which they compose is isotropic, the same in all directions. The one dimension of time, on the other hand, although it has the same formal properties as each of the other three, is at least sensuously different from them as they are not from one another, and the total manifold is apparently not isotropic. Whereas an object can preserve the same shape while it is so shifted that its height becomes its breadth, we cannot easily conceive how it could do so while being shifted so that its breadth becomes its duration.

The theory of the manifold, I think, is the one model on which we can describe and explain the foreground of experience, or can intelligibly and credibly construct our account of the rest of the world, and this is so because in fact the universe is spread out in those dimensions. There may be Platonic entities which are foreign to both space and time; there may be Cartesian spirits which are foreign to space; but the homely realm of natural existence, the total of world history, is a spatiotemporal volume of somewhat uncertain magnitude, chockablock with things and events. Logic, with its law of excluded middle and its tenseless operators, and natural science, with its secular world charts, concur inexorably with the vision of metaphysics and high religion that truth and fact are thus eternal.

I believe that the universe consists, without residue, of the spread of events in space-time, and that if we thus accept realistically the four-dimensional fabric of juxtaposed actualities we can dispense with all those dim nonfactual categories which have so bedeviled our race: the potential, the subsistential, and the influential, the noumenal, the numinous, and the nonnatural. But I am arguing here, not that there is nothing outside the natural world of events, but that the theory of the manifold is anyhow literally true and adequate to that world: true, in that the world contains no less than the manifold; adequate, in that it contains no more.

Since I think that this philosophy offers correct and coherent answers to real questions, I must think that metaphysical difficulties raised against it are genuine too. There are facts, logical and empirical, which can be described and explained only by the concept of the manifold; there are facts which some honest men deem irreconcilable with it. Few issues can better deserve adjudication. The difficulties which we need not take seriously are those made by primitive minds, and by new deliberate primitivists, who recommend that we follow out the Augustinian clue, as Augustine did not, that the man who best feels he understands time is he who refuses to think about it.

Among philosophical complainants against the manifold, some few raise difficulties about space – there are subjectivistic epistemologists, for example, who grant more reality to their own past and future than to things spatially beyond themselves. The temporal dimension of the manifold, however, bears the principal brunt. Sir James Jeans regretted that time is mathematically attached to space by so "weird" a function as the square root of minus one,[1] and the very word "weird," being cognate with "*werden*," to become, is a monument to the uncanniness of our fourth dimension. Maintaining that time is in its essence something wholly unique, a flow or passage, the "time snobs" (as Wyndham Lewis called them) either deny that the temporal spread is a reality at all, or think it only a very abstract phase of real time. Far from disparaging time itself, they conceive themselves thus to be "taking time seriously" in a profounder sense than our party who are content with the vast reaches of what is, was, and will be.

The more radical opposition to the manifold takes time with such Spartan seriousness that almost none of it is left – only the pulse of the present, born virginally from nothing and devouring itself as soon as born, so that whatever past and future there be are strictly only the memory and anticipation of them in this Now.[2] One set of motives for this view is in the general romantic polemic against logic and the competence of concepts. The theory of the manifold is the logical account of events par excellence, the teeth by which the jaws of the intellect grip the flesh of occurrence. The Bergsonian, who thinks that concepts cannot convey the reality of time because they are "static," the Marxist who thinks that process defies the cadres of two-valued logic, and the Heideggerian who thinks that temporality, history, and existence are leagued outside the categories of the intellect, thus have incentives for denying, in effect, all the temporal universe beyond what is immanent in the present flare and urge.

To counter their attack, it is a nice and tempting question whether and how concepts are "static," whether and how, in any case, a true concept must be similar to its object, and whether and how history and existence are any more temporal than spatial. But we cannot here undertake the whole defense of the intellect against its most violent critics. We shall rather notice such doubters as trust and use conceptual analysis and still think there are cogent arguments against the manifold. One argument to that effect is an extreme sharpening of the positivistic argument from the egocentric predicament. For if it is impossible for my concepts to transcend experience in general, it may well be impossible for them to transcend the momentary experience in which they are entertained. Conversely, however, anybody who rejects the arguments for instantaneous solipsism, as most people do, must reject this argument for diminishing the manifold. The chief mode of argument is rather the finding of an intolerable anomaly in the statement that what was but has ceased, or what will be but has not begun, nevertheless is. This reflection has been used against the reality of the future, in particular, by philosophers as miscellaneous as Aristotle and neoscholastics, C. D. Broad, Paul Weiss, and Charles Hartshorne. In so far as it is an argument from logic, charging the manifold with self-contradiction, it would be as valid against the past as against the future; but, I have argued, it is by no means valid.[3]

The statement that a sea fight not present in time nevertheless exists is no more contradictory than that one not present in space nevertheless exists. If it seems so, this is only because there happens to be a temporal reference (tense) built into our verbs rather than a spatial reference (as in some languages) or than no locative reference (as in canonical symbolic transcriptions into logic).

I am not to contend now for the reality of the manifold, however, but against the extra *weirdness* alleged for time both by some champions who reject the manifold out of hand and by some who contend anyhow that it is not the whole story, both parties agreeing that the temporal dimension is not "real time," not "the genuine creative flux." If our temporalist means by this that the theory of temporal extension, along with the spatial models provided by calendars, kymographs, and statistical time charts, is in the last analysis fictitious, corresponding to nothing in the facts, he is reverting, under a thin cloak of dissimulation, to the mere rejection which we have agreed to leave aside. If he means, at the other extreme, no more than that the theory and the models themselves are not identical, either numerically or qualitatively, with the actual temporal succession which they represent, he is uttering a triviality which is true of every theory or representation. If he means that the temporal spread, though real and formally similar to a spatial spread, is qualitatively or intuitively very different from it, or lies in a palpably and absolutely unique direction, he says something plausible and important but not at all incompatible with the philosophy of the manifold.

He is most likely to mean, however, another proposition which is never more than vaguely expressed: that over and above the sheer spread of events, with their several qualities, along the time axis, which is analogous enough to the spread of space, there is something extra, something active and dynamic, which is often and perhaps best described as "passage." This something extra, I am going to plead, is a myth: not one of those myths which foreshadow a difficult truth in a metaphorical way, but altogether a false start, deceiving us about the facts, and blocking our understanding of them.

The literature of "passage" is immense, but it is naturally not very exact and lucid, and we cannot be sure of distinguishing in it between mere harmless allegorical phenomenology and the special metaphysical declaration which I criticize. But "passage," it would seem, is a character supposed to inhabit and glorify the present, "the passing present,"[4] "the moving present,"[5] the "travelling *now.*"[6] It is "the passage of time as actual . . . given now with the jerky or whooshy quality of transience."[7] It is James' "passing moment."[8] It is what Broad calls "the transitory aspect" of time, in contrast with the "extensive."[9] It is Bergson's living felt duration. It is Heidegger's *Zeitlichkeit.* It is Tillich's "moment that is creation and fate."[10] It is "the act of becoming," the mode of potency and generation, which Hugh King finds properly appreciated only by Aristotle and Whitehead.[11] It is Eddington's "ongoing" and "the formality of taking place,"[12] and Dennes' "surge of process."[13] It is the dynamic essence which Ushenko believes that Einstein omits from the world.[14] It is the mainspring of McTaggart's "A-series" which puts movement in time,[15] and it is Broad's pure becoming.[16] Withal it is the flow and go of very existence, nearer to us than breathing, closer than hands and feet.

So far as one can interpret these expressions into a theory, they have the same purport as all the immemorial turns of speech by which we describe time as *moving,* with respect to the present or with respect to our minds. Time flows or flies or marches, years roll, hours pass. More explicitly we may speak as if the perceiving mind were stationary while time flows by like a river, with the flotsam of events upon it; or as if presentness were a fixed pointer under which the tape of happenings slides; or as if the time sequence were a moving-picture film, unwinding from the dark reel of the future, projected briefly on the screen of the present, and rewound into the dark can of the past. Sometimes, again, we speak as if the time sequence were a stationary plain or ocean on which we voyage, or a variegated river gorge down which we drift; or, in Broad's analogy, as if it were a row of house fronts along which the spotlight of the present plays. "The essence of nowness," Santayana says, "runs like fire along the fuse of time."[17]

Augustine pictures the present passing into the past, where the modern pictures the present as invading the future,[18] but these do not conflict, for Augustine means that the *events* which were present become past, while the modern means that *presentness* encroaches on what was previously the future. Sometimes the surge of presentness is conceived as a mere moving illumination by consciousness, sometimes as a sort of vivification and heightening, like an ocean wave heaving along beneath a stagnant expanse of floating seaweed, sometimes as no less than the boon of existence itself, reifying minute by minute a limbo of unthings.

Now, the most remarkable feature of all this is that while the modes of speech and thought which enshrine the idea of passage are universal and perhaps ineradicable, the instant one thinks about them one feels uneasy, and the most laborious effort cannot construct an intelligible theory which admits the literal truth of any of them. The obvious and notorious fault of the idea, as we have now localized it, is this. Motion is already defined and explained in the dimensional manifold as consisting of the presence of the same individual in different places at different times. It consists of bends or quirks in the world line, or the space-time worm, which is the four-dimensioned totality of the individual's existence. This is motion in space, if you like; but we can readily define a corresponding "motion in time." It comes out as nothing more dramatic than an exact equivalent: "motion in time" consists of being at different times in different places.

True motion then is motion at once in time and space. Nothing can "move" in time alone any more than in space alone, and time itself cannot "move" any more than space itself. "Does this road go anywhere?" asks the city tourist. "No, it stays right along here," replies the countryman. Time "flows" only in the sense in which a line flows or a landscape "recedes into the west." That is, it is an ordered extension. And each of us proceeds through time only as a fence proceeds across a farm: that is, parts of our being, and the fence's, occupy successive instants and points, respectively. There is passage, but it is nothing extra. It is the mere happening of things, their existence strung along in the manifold. The term "the present" is the conventional way of designating the cross section of events which are simultaneous with the uttering of the phrase, and "the present moves" only in that when similar words occur at successively different moments, they denote, by a twist of language essentially the same as that of all "egocentric particulars," like "here" and "this," different cross sections of the manifold.

Time travel, *prima facie*, then, is analysable either as the banality that at each different moment we occupy a different moment from the one we occupied before, or the contradiction that at each different moment we occupy a different moment from the one which we are then occupying – that five minutes from now, for example, I may be a hundred years from now.[19]

The tragedy then of the extra idea of passage or absolute becoming, as a philosophical principle, is that it incomprehensibly doubles its world by reintroducing terms like "moving" and "becoming" in a sense which both requires and forbids interpretation in the preceding ways. For as soon as we say that time or the present or we move in the odd extra way which the doctrine of passage requires, we have no recourse but to suppose that this movement in turn takes time of a special sort: $time_1$ moves at a certain rate in $time_2$, perhaps one $second_1$ per one $second_2$, perhaps slower, perhaps faster. Or, conversely, the moving present slides over so many seconds of $time_1$ in so many seconds of $time_2$. The history of the new moving present, in $time_2$, then composes a new and higher time dimension again, which cries to be vitalized by a new level of passage, and so on forever.

We hardly needed to point out the unhappy regress to which the idea of time's motion commits us, for any candid philosopher, as soon as he looks hard at the idea, must *see* that it is preposterous. "Taking place" is not a formality to which an event incidentally submits – it is the event's very being. World history consists of actual concrete happenings in a temporal sequence; it is not necessary or possible that happening should happen to them all over again. The system of the manifold is thus "complete" in something like the technical logical sense, and any attempted addition to it is bound to be either contradictory or supererogatory.

Bergson, Broad, and some of the followers of Whitehead[20] have tried to soften the paradoxes of passage by supposing that the present does not move across the total time level, but that it is the very fountain where the river of time gushes out of nothingness (or out of the power of God). The past, then, having swum into being and floated away, is eternally real, but the future has no existence at all. This may be a more appealing figure, but logically it involves the same anomalies of metahappening and metatime which we observed in the other version.

What, then, we must ask, were the motives which drove men to the staggering philosophy of passage? One of them, I believe, we can dispose of at once. It is the innocent vertigo which inevitably besets a creature whose thinking is strung out in time, as soon as he tries to think of the time dimension itself. He finds it easiest to conceive and understand purely geometrical structures. Motion is more difficult, and generally remains vague, while time per se is very difficult indeed, but being now identified as the principle which imports motion into space, it is put down as a kind of quintessential motion itself. The process is helped by the fact that the mere further-along-ness of successive segments, either of a spatial or of a temporal stretch, can quite logically be conceived as a degenerate sort of change, as when we speak of the flow of a line or say that the scenery changes along the Union Pacific.

A rather more serious excuse for the idea of passage is that it is supposed necessary and sufficient for adding to the temporal dimension that intrinsic *sense* from earlier to later in which time is supposed to differ radically from any dimension of space.[21] A meridian of longitude has only a direction, but a river has a "sense," and time is in this like the river. It is, as the saying goes, irreversible and irrevocable. It has a "directed tension."[22] The mere dimension of time, on the other hand, would seem to be symmetrical. The principle of absolute passage is bidden to rectify this symmetry with what Eddington called "time's arrow."

It might be replied that science does not supply an arrow for time because it has no need of it. But I think it plain that time does have a sense, from early to late. I only think that it can be taken care of on much less draconian principles than absolute passage. There is nothing in the dimensional view of time to preclude its being generated by a uniquely asymmetrical relation, and experience suggests powerfully that it is so generated, But the fact is that every real series has a "sense" anyhow. This is provided, if by nothing else, then by the sheer numerical identity and diversity of terms.

In the line of individual things or events, a, b, c, . . . z, whether in space or in time, the "sense" from a to z is *ipso facto* other than the "sense" from z to a. Only because there is a difference between the ordered couple $a;z$ and the couple $z;a$ can we define the difference between a symmetrical and an asymmetrical relation. Only because there are already two distinguishable "ways" on a street, determined by its individual ends, can we decide to permit traffic to move one way and prohibit it the other. But a sufficient difference of sense, finally, would appear to be constituted, if nothing else offered, by the inevitably asymmetrical distribution of properties along the temporal line (or any other). Eddington has been only one of many scientists who think the arrow is provided for the cosmos by the principle of entropy, and entropy has been only one principle thus advocated.[23]

In so far as what men mean by "the irrevocability of the past" is the causal circumstance that we can affect the future in a way we cannot affect the past, it is just a trait of the physicist's arrow. They often mean by it, however, only the inexorability of fact, that what is the case is the case, past, present, or future; or the triviality that the particular events of 1902, let us say, cannot also be the events of 1952. Very similar events might be so, however, and if very few of them are, this is the fault of the concrete nature of things and not of any grudge on the part of time.[24]

The final motive for the attempt to consummate or supplant the fourth dimension of the manifold with the special perfection, the grace and whiz, of passage is the vaguest but the most substantial and incorrigible. It is simply that we *find* passage, that we are immediately and poignantly involved in the whoosh of process, the felt flow of one moment into the next. Here is the focus of being. Here is the shore whence the youngster watches the golden mornings swing toward him like serried bright breakers from the ocean of the future. Here is the flood on which the oldster wakes in the night to shudder at its swollen black torrent cascading him into the abyss.

It would be futile to try to deny these experiences, but their correct description is another matter. If they are in fact consistent with our theory, they are no evidence against it; and if they are entailed by it, they are evidence in its favor. Since the theory was originally constructed to take account of them, it would be odd if they were inconsistent with it or even irrelevant to it. I believe that in fact they are neither, and that the theory of the manifold provides the true and literal description of what the enthusiastic metaphors of passage have deceptively garbled.

The principal reason why we are troubled to accommodate our experience of time to the intellectual theory of time goes very deep in the philosophy of philosophy. It is that we must here scrutinize the undoctored fact of perception, on the one hand, and must imagine our way into a conceptual scheme, and envisage the true intrinsic being of its objects, on the other hand, and then pronounce on the numerical identity of the first with the second. This is a very rare requirement. Even such apt ideas as those of space and of physical objects, as soon as we contemplate them realistically, begin to embarrass us, so that we slip into the assumption that the real objects of the conceptions, if they exist at all, exist on a different plane or in a different realm from the sensuous spread and lumpiness of experience. The ideas of time and of the mind, however, do not permit of such evasion. Those beings are given in their own right and person, filling the foreground. Here for once we must fit the fact directly into the intellectual form, without benefit of precedent or accustomed criteria. First off, then, comparing the calm conceptual scheme with the turbid event itself, we may be repelled by the former, not because it is not true to the latter, but because it *is* not the latter. When we see that this kind of diversity is inevitable to every concept and its object, and hence is irrelevant to the validity of any, we demur because the conceptual scheme is indifferently flat and third-personal, like a map, while the experienced reality is centripetal and perspectival, piled up and palpitating where we are, gray and retiring elsewhere.

But this is only because every occasion on which we compare the world map with experience has itself a single specific location, confronting part of the world, remote from the rest. The perspectivity of the view is exactly predictable from the map. The deception with respect to time is worse than with respect to space because our memories and desires run timewise and not spacewise. The jerk and whoosh of this moment, which are simply the real occurrence of one particular batch of events, are no different from the whoosh and being of any other patch of events up and down the eternal time-stretch. Remembering some of the latter, however, and anticipating more, and bearing in mind that while they happen they are all called "the present," we mistakenly hypostatize *the* Present as a single surge of bigness which rolls along the time axis. There is in fact no more a single rolling Now than there is a single rolling Here along a spatial line – a standing line of soldiers, for example, though each of them has the vivid presentment of his own here.

Let us hug to us as closely as we like that there is real succession, that rivers flow and winds blow, that things burn and burst, that men strive and guess and die. All this is the concrete stuff of the manifold, the reality of serial happening, one event after another, in exactly the time spread which we have been at pains to diagram. What does the theory allege except what we find, and what do we find that is not accepted and asserted by the theory? Suppose a pure intelligence, bred outside of time, instructed in the nature of the manifold and the design of the human spacetime worm, with its mnemic organization, its particular delimited but overlapping conscious fields, and the strands of world history which flank them, and suppose him incarnated among us: what could he have expected the temporal experience to be like except just about what he actually discovers it to be? How, in brief, could processes and experiences which endure and succeed each other along the time line appear as anything other than enduring and successive processes and a stream of consciousness?

The theory of the manifold leaves abundant room for the sensitive observer to record any describable difference he may find, in intrinsic quality, relational texture, or absolute direction, between the temporal dimension and the spatial ones. He is welcome to mark it so on the map. The very singleness of the time dimension, over against the amalgamated three dimensions of space, may be an idiosyncrasy with momentous effects; its *fourthness*, so to speak, so oddly and immensely multiplying the degrees of freedom embodied in the familiar spatial complex, was bound to seem momentous too.

The theory has generally conceded or emphasized that time is unique in these and other respects, and I have been assuming that it was right to do so. In the working out of this thesis, however, and in considering the very lame demurrals which oppose it, I have come a little uneasily to the surmise that the idea of an absolute or intrinsic difference of texture or orientation is superfluous, and that the four dimensions of the manifold compose a perfectly homogeneous scheme of location relations, the same in all directions, and that the oddity of temporal distances is altogether a function of features which occupy them – a function of *de facto* pattern like the shape of an arrow, like the difference between the way in and the way out of a flytrap, and like the terrestrial difference between up and down.

Even a person who believes that temporal distances are a categorially peculiar mode of relation, intrinsically different from spatial distance, regardless of how they are filled, must grant that they nevertheless *are* filled differently: things, persons, and events, as a matter of natural fact, are strung along with respect to the time axis in rhythms and designs notably different from those in which they are deployed spacewise. Entropy and the other scientific criteria for the "sense" from past to future distinguish no less the whole temporal direction from the spatial ones. The very concept of "things" or "individual substances" derives from a peculiar kind of coherence and elongation of clumps of events in the time direction. Living bodies in particular have a special organized trend timewise, a *conatus sese conservandi*, which nothing has in spatial section. Characteristic themes of causation run in the same direction, and paralleling all these, and accounting for their importance and obviousness to us, is the pattern of mental events, the stream of consciousness, with its mnemic cumulation and that sad anxiety to *keep going* futureward which contrasts strangely with our comparative indifference to our spatial girth.

The same fact of the grain and configuration of events which, if it does not constitute, certainly accompanies and underlines the "senses" of space and time, has other virtues which help to naturalize experience in the manifold. It accounts for the apparent *rate* of happening, for example; for the span of the specious present; and for the way in which the future is comparatively malleable to our present efforts and correspondingly dark to our present knowledge. An easy interpretation would be that the world content is uniquely organized in the time direction because the time direction itself is aboriginally unique. Modern philosophical wisdom, however, consists mostly of trying the cart before the horse, and I find myself more than half convinced by the oddly repellent hypothesis that the peculiarity of the time dimension is not thus primitive but is wholly a resultant of those differences in the mere *de facto* run and order of the world's filling.

It is conceivable, then, though perhaps physically impossible, that one four-dimensional part of the manifold of events be slued around at right angles to the rest, so that the time order of that area, as composed by its interior lines of strain and structure, runs parallel with a spatial order in its environment. It is conceivable, indeed, that a single whole human life should lie thwartwise of the manifold, with its belly plump in time, its birth at the east and its death in the west, and its conscious stream perhaps running alongside somebody's garden path.[25]

It is conceivable too then that a human life be twisted, not 90° but 180°, from the normal temporal grain of the world. F. Scott Fitzgerald tells the story of Benjamin Button who was born in the last stages of senility and got younger all his life till he died a dwindling embryo.[26] Fitzgerald imagined the reversal to be so imperfect that Benjamin's stream of consciousness ran, not backward with his body's gross development, but in the common clockwise manner. We might better conceive a reversal of every cell twitch and electron whirl, and hence suppose that he experienced his own life stages in the same order as we do ours, but that he observed everyone around him moving backward from the grave to the cradle. True time travel, then, is conceivable after all, though we cannot imagine how it could be caused by beings whose lives are extended in the normal way: it would consist of a man's life-pattern, and the pattern of any appliances he employed, running at an abnormal rate or on an abnormal heading across the manifold.

As the dimensional theory accommodates what is true in the notion of passage, that is, the occurrence of events, in contrast with a mythical rearing and charging of time itself, so it accounts for what is true in the notions of "flux," "emergence," "creative advance," and the rest. Having learned the trick of mutual translation between theory and experience, we see where the utter misrepresentation lies in the accusation that the dimensional theory denies that time is "real," or that it substitutes a safe and static world, a block universe, a petrified *fait accompli*, a *totum simul*, for the actuality of risk and change.

Taking time with the truest seriousness, on the contrary, it calmly diagnoses "novelty" or "becoming," for example, as the existence of an entity, or kind of entity, at one time in the world continuum which does not exist at any previous time. No other sort of novelty than this, I earnestly submit, is discoverable or conceivable – or desirable. In practice, the modern sciences of the manifold have depicted it as a veritable caldron of force and action. Although the theory entails that it is true at every time that events occur at other times, it emphatically does not entail that all events happen at the same time or at every time, or at no time, It does not assert, therefore, that future things "already" exist or exist "forever." Emphatically also it does not, as is frequently charged, "make time a dimension of space,"[27] any more than it makes space a dimension of time.

The theory of the manifold, which is thus neutral with respect to the amount of change and permanence in the world, is surprisingly neutral also toward many other topics often broached as though they could be crucial between it and the extra idea of passage. It is neutral, so far, toward whether space and time are absolute and substantival in the Democritean and Newtonian way, or relative and adjectival in Spencer's and Whitehead's way, or further relativistic in Einstein's way. The theory of space does not, as Bergson pretended, have any preference for discontinuity over continuity, and while a time order in which nothing exists but the present would be fatal to any real continuity, the philosophy of the manifold is quite prepared to accept any verdict on whether space or time or both are continuous or discrete, as it is also on whether they are finite or infinite. Instead of "denying history," it preserves it, and is equally hospitable to all philosophies of history except such as themselves deny history by disputing the objectivity and irrevocability of historical truth. It does not care whether events eternally recur, or run along forever on the dead level as Aristotle thought, or enact the ringing brief drama of the Christian episode, or strive into the Faustian boundless. It is similarly neutral toward theories of causation and of knowledge.

The world manifold of occurrences, each eternally deter*minate* at its own place and date, may and may not be so deter*mined* in its texture that what occurs at one juncture has its sufficient reason at others. If it does evince such causal connections, these may be either efficient (as apparently they are) or final (as apparently they are not). The core of the causal nexus itself may be, so far as the manifold is concerned, either a real connection of Spinoza's sort, or Whitehead's, or the scholastics', or the mere regular succession admitted by Hume and Russell. It was a mistake for Spinoza to infer, if he did, that the eternal manifold and strict causation entail one another, as it is a worse mistake for the scholastics, Whitehead, Ushenko, and Weiss to infer the opposite (as they seem to), that "real time" and "real causation" entail one another.[28] The theory is similarly noncommittal toward metaphysical accounts of individual substances, which it can allow to be compounds of form and matter or mere sheaves of properties.

The theory of the manifold makes a man at home in the world to the extent that it guarantees that intelligence is not affronted at its first step into reality. Beyond that, the cosmos is as it is. If there is moral responsibility, if the will is free, if there is reasonableness in regret and hope in decision, these must be ascertained by more particular observations and hypotheses than the doctrine of the manifold. It makes no difference to our theory whether we are locked in an ice pack of fate, or whirled in a tornado of chance, or are firm-footed makers of destiny. It will accept benignly either the Christian Creator, or the organic and perfect Absolute, or Hume's sand pile of sensation, or the fluid melee of contextualism, or the structured world process of materialism.

The service which the theory performs with respect to all these problems is other than dictating solutions of them. It is the provision of a lucent frame or arena where they and their solutions can be laid out and clearheadedly appraised in view of their special classes of evidence. Once under this kind of observation, for example, the theories of change which describe becoming as a marriage of being and not-being, or an interpenetration of the present with the future and the past, become repulsive, not because they conflict especially with the philosophy of the manifold, but because if they are not mere incantations they contradict themselves. When we see that the problem how Achilles can overtake the tortoise is essentially the same as the problem how two lines can intersect one another obliquely, we are likely to be content with the simple mathematical intelligibility of both. When we see that the "change" of a leaf's color from day to day is of the same denomination as its "change" from inch to inch of its surface, we are less likely to hope that mysterious formulas about the actualization of the potential and the perdurance of a substratum are of any use in accounting for either of them.

If then there is some appearance of didactic self-righteousness in my effort here to save the pure theory of the manifold from being either displaced or amended by what I think is the disastrous myth of passage, this is because I believe that the theory of the manifold is the very paradigm of philosophic understanding. It grasps with a firm logic, so far as I can see, the most intimate and pervasive of facts; it clarifies the obscure and assimilates the apparently diverse.

Most of the effect of the prophets of passage, on the other hand, is to melt back into the primitive magma of confusion and plurality the best and sharpest instruments which the mind has forged. Some of those who do this have a deliberate preference for the melting pot of mystery as an end in itself. Others, I suppose, hope eventually to cast from it a finer metal and to forge a sharper point. No hope of that sort is altogether chimerical. But I suggest that if a tithe of the animus and industry invested in that ill-omened enterprise were spent on the refinement and imaginative use of the instrument we have, whatever difficulties still attend it would soon be dissipated.

Notes

1   *The Mysterious Universe.* New York, Macmillan, 1930, p. 118.
2   This I think is a fair description of G. H. Mead's doctrine in *The Philosophy of the Present.* See also, e.g., Schopenhauer: *The World as Will and Idea*, Bk. 4, Sec. 54.
3   "The Sea Fight Tomorrow," above.
4   Dennes, W. R., in California, University, Philosophical Union, *The Problem of Time.* Berkeley, Univer. of Calif., 1935, p. 103.
5   Stearns, I., in *Rev. Met.*, 4:198, 1950.
6   Santayana: *Realms of Being*, in *Works*, Vol. 14, p. 254.
7   Lewis: *An Analysis of Knowledge and Valuation*, p. 19. This is pretty surely phenomenology, not metaphysics, but it is too good to omit.
8   James: *A Pluralistic Universe*, p. 254.
9   Broad: *An Examination of McTaggart's Philosophy*, Vol. 2, Pt. 1, p. 271.
10 Tillich, Paul: *The Interpretation of History.* New York, Scribner's, 1936, p. 129.
11 King, H. R., in *J. Phil.*, 46:657–670, 1949. This is an exceptionally ingenious, serious, and explicit statement of the philosophy which I am opposing.
12 Eddington, Arthur S.: *Space, Time, and Gravitation*, New York, Macmillan, 1920, p. 51; *The Nature of the Physical World*, New York, Macmillan, 1928, p. 68.
13 Dennes: *loc. cit.*, pp. 91, 93.
14 Ushenko, Andrew P.: *Power and Events.* Princeton, Princeton Univer., 1946, p. 146.
15 McTaggart, John M. E.: *The Nature of Existence.* Cambridge, Cambridge Univer., 1927, Vol. 2, Bk. 5, Chap. 33.
16 Broad: *Scientific Thought*, p. 67; *Examination of McTaggart's Philosophy*, Vol. 2., p. 277.
17 *Realms of Being*, in *Works*, Vol. 15, p. 90.
18 *Confessions*, Bk. 11, Chap. 14; cf. E. B. McGilvary, in *Phil. Rev.*, 23:121–145, 1914.
19 "He may even now – if I may use the phrase – be wandering on some plesiosaurus-haunted oolitic coral reef, or beside the lonely saline seas of the Triassic Age" – H. G. Wells, *The Time Machine*, epilogue. This book, perhaps the best yarn ever written, contains such early and excellent accounts of the theory of the manifold that it has been quoted and requoted by scientific writers. Though it makes slips, its logic is better than that of later such stories.
20 Bergson's theory of the snowball of time may be thus understood; the past abides in the center while ever new presents accrete around it. For Broad, see *Scientific Thought*, p. 66, and on Whitehead, see King, *loc. cit.*, esp. p. 663.
21 See, for example, Broad: *Scientific Thought*, p. 57.
22 Tillich, *op. cit.*, p. 245.
23 *The Nature of the Physical World*, Chap. 3. For the present scientific state of the question, see Adolf Grünbaum: *Philosophical Problems of Space and Time*, New York, Knopf, 1963.
24 Dennes argues thus, *loc. cit.*

25   I should expect the impact of the environment on such a being to be so wildly queer and out of step with the way he is put together, that his mental life must be a dragged-out monstrous delirium. Professor George Burch has suggested to me that it might be the mystic's timeless illumination. Whether these diagnoses are different I shall not attempt to say.

26   "The Curious Case of Benjamin Button," in *Tales of the Jazz Age*. New York, Scribner's, 1922.

27   See Charles Hartshorne: *Man's Vision of God, and the Logic of Theism*, Chicago, Willett, Clark, 1941, p. 140, and Tillich, *op. cit.*, pp. 132, 248; and remember Bergson's allegation that the principle of the manifold "spatializes" time.

28   See, for example, Whitehead: *Process and Reality*, p. 363; Weiss, Paul: *Nature and Man*, New York, Holt, 1947.

---

16   Some Free Thinking about Time

A. N. Prior

There's a dispute among philosophers – indeed there has always been this dispute among philosophers – as to whether time is real. Some say yes, and some say no, and some say it isn't a proper question; I happen to be one of the philosophers who say yes. All attempts to deny the reality of time founder, so far as I can see, on the problem of explaining the *appearance* of time's passage: for appearing is itself something that occurs in time. Eddington once said that events don't happen, we merely come across them; but what is *coming across* an event but a happening?

So far, then, as I have anything that you could call a philosophical creed, its first article is this: I believe in the reality of the distinction between past, present, and future. I believe that what we see as a progress of events *is* a progress of events, a *coming to pass* of one thing after another, and not just a timeless tapestry with everything stuck there for good and all.

To bring out the difference of viewpoint I have in mind, let me mention a small logical point. Logic deals, at bottom, with statements. It enquires into what statements follow from what – but logicians aren't entirely agreed as to what a statement *is*. Ancient and medieval logicians thought of a statement as something that can be true at one time and false at another. For example, the statement 'Socrates is sitting down' is true so long as he *is* sitting down, but becomes false when he gets up. Most modern logicians, however, say that if a statement is true at any time, it's true all the time – once true, always true. Confronted with the example 'Socrates is sitting down', they would say that this isn't really a statement, but only a piece of a statement. It needs to be completed by some unambiguous specification of the time at which he is sitting down, for example, at exactly 3 p.m. (Greenwich mean time) on June 15th, 326 BC. And when we say that he *is* sitting down at this time and date, we don't need to change this 'is' to 'was', because in this sort of statement 'is' hasn't any tense at all – the complete statement tells us a timeless property of a date or moment; that date or moment just *is*, eternally, a Socrates-sitting-downy date or moment.

Such a notion of what a statement is seems clearly to reflect what I have called the tapestry view of time, and I believe accordingly that this is a point at which logicians ought to retrace their steps. I think the logically primary sense of the word 'statement' is the old sense, the sense in which a statement which is true at one time may be false at another time, and in which the *tense* of statements must be taken seriously. I don't think these are just fragments of 'statements' in some more fundamental sense of the word; on the contrary, the allegedly tense-less statements of modern logic are just a special case of statements in the old sense – they are statements which happen to be either always false or always true, and the 'is' that occurs in them is not really a tenseless 'is' but is just short for 'is, always has been, and always will be'.

This belief, or prejudice, of mine is bound up with a belief in real freedom. One of the big differences between the past and the future is that once something has become past, it is, as it were, out of our reach – once a thing has happened, nothing we can do can make it not to have happened. But the future is to some extent, even though it is only to a very small extent, something we can make for ourselves. And this is a distinction which tenseless logic is unable to express. In my own logic with tenses I would express it this way: We can lay it down as a law that whatever *now is* the case *will always have been* the case; but we can't interchange past and future here and lay it down that whatever *now is* the case *has always been going to be* the case – I don't think that's a logical law at all; for if something is the work of a free agent, then it wasn't going to be the case until that agent decided that it was. But if happenings are just properties timelessly attached to dates, I don't see how you can make this distinction.

This general position that I want to uphold has come under fire from different quarters at different times. In the Middle Ages it was menaced by the theologians, many of whom, like Thomas Aquinas, taught that God doesn't experience time as passing, but has it present all at once. In other words, God sees time as a tapestry. Other medieval theologians such as Duns Scotus argued, I think very sensibly, that since time *isn't* a tapestry, either God *doesn't* see it that way or He has an illusion about it, and since He hasn't any illusions He doesn't see it that way but sees it as it is, as passing. I would go further than Duns Scotus and say that there are things about the future that God doesn't yet know because they're not yet there to be known, and to talk about knowing them is like saying that we can know falsehoods. God cannot know that 2 and 2 are 5, because 2 and 2 *aren't* 5, and if He's left some matter to someone's free choice, He cannot know the answer to the question 'How will that person choose?' because there isn't any answer to it until he has chosen.

Nowadays it's not so much the theologians we have to contend with as the scientists, and the philosophical interpreters of the scientists. Many philosophical upholders of what I've called the tapestry view of time claim that they have on their side a very august scientific theory, the theory of relativity, and of course it wouldn't do for mere philosophers to question august scientific theories. Well, I've tried to find out recently exactly what is the strength of this argument, and I'll discuss it with you now as simply as I can, though I'll have to warn you that it's not *very* simple. The physical facts seem to be more or less like this: *My* experience has a quite definite time-order, of which I am immediately aware; and *your* experience has a definite time-order, of which *you* are immediately aware; and similarly for any observer, no matter where he is, or how he is moving. Moreover, if you were to calculate the time-order of my experiences, I would agree with your result, and similarly, if I were to calculate yours. The trouble arises when we come to *compare* one another's experiences – when, for example, I want to know whether I saw a certain flash of light before you did, or you saw it before I did. Even about points like this there is often agreement all round, but we can't depend on it. It could happen that if I assumed myself to be stationary and you moving, I'd get one result – say that I saw the flash first – and if you assumed that you were stationary and I moving, you'd get a different result. I could explain your result by saying that the speed of your movement had made your measuring instruments go haywire; but you could explain my results in the same way. And it appears to be established that in such a case there would be no physical way of deciding which of us is right; that is, there is no way of determining whether the light-signal first crossed my path or yours. And the conclusion drawn in the theory of relativity is that this question – the question as to which of us is right, which of us really saw it first – is a meaningless question; outside our private paths, the time-direction and space-direction just aren't as distinct as that.

Now I don't want to be disrespectful to people whose researches lie in other fields than my own, but I feel compelled to say that this just won't do. I think we have excellent grounds for insisting that the question in question is *not a* meaningless one, and I'll try and explain what its meaning is. People who are doing relativity physics are concerned with the relations of before and after and simultaneity, but these aren't the first things as far as the real passage of time is concerned – the first thing is the sequence of past, present, and future, and this is not just a private or local matter, different for each one of us; on the contrary, pastness, presentness, and futurity are properties of events that are independent of the observer; and under favourable conditions they are *perceived* properties of events. We all know what it is to wait for something – an examination, for example; or coming home from the war; or Christmas. What we're waiting for begins by being future; it *hasn't yet* come to pass. Then a time comes when it does come to pass – when it's *present*, and we're aware of its presentness, and there's no mistaking it. And then it's past, and we say, perhaps, 'Thank goodness all that's over'; and we all know quite well what this 'being over' is, and couldn't mistake it for anything else. I have a very good friend and colleague in Australia, Professor Smart of Adelaide, with whom I often have arguments about this. He's an advocate of the tapestry view of time, and says that when we say '*X* is now past' we just mean 'The latest part of *X* is earlier than this utterance.' But, when at the end of some ordeal I say 'Thank goodness that's over', do I mean 'Thank goodness the latest part of that is earlier than this utterance'? I certainly do not; I'm not thinking about the utterance at all, it's the *overness*, the *now-endedness*, the *pastness* of the thing that I'm thankful for, and nothing else. Past and future are in fact not to be defined in terms of earlier or later, but the other way round – '*X* is earlier than *Y*' means 'At some time *X* was past and *Y* was present', and '*X* is later than *Y*' means the opposite of this.

Coming back to this allegedly meaningless question as to whether you or I saw the light-flash first, surely what it means is just this: When I was seeing the flash, *had* you already seen it, or had you not? In other words, when my seeing it was a *present* fact, had your seeing it become a *past* fact, or had it not? And I just cannot be persuaded that such a question is meaningless – its meaning seems to me perfectly obvious. When an event *X* is happening, another event *Y* either *has* happened or *has not* happened – 'having happened' is not the kind of property that can attach to an event from one point of view but not from another. On the contrary, it's something like *existing*; in fact to ask what has happened *is* a way of asking what exists, and you can't have a thing existing from one point of view but not existing from another, although of course its existence may be *known* to one person or in one region, without being known to or in another.

So it seems to me that there's a strong case for just digging our heels in here and saying that, relativity or no relativity, if I say I saw a certain flash before you, and you say you saw it first, one of us is just wrong – or misled it may be, by the effect of speed on his instruments – even if there is just no physical means whatever of deciding which of us it is. To put the same point another way, we may say that the theory of relativity isn't about *real* space and time, in which the earlier–later relation is defined in terms of pastness, presentness, and futurity; the 'time' which enters into the so-called space–time of relativity theory isn't this, but is just part of an artificial framework which the scientists have constructed to link together observed facts in the simplest way possible, and from which those things which are systematically concealed from us are quite reasonably left out.

This sort of thing has happened before, you know. When that formidable mathematical engine the differential calculus was first invented, its practitioners used to talk a mixture of excellent mathematics and philosophical nonsense, and at the time the nonsense was exposed for what it was by the philosopher Berkeley, in a pamphlet entitled 'A Defence of Free Thinking in Mathematics'. And the mathematicians saw in the end that Berkeley was right, though it took them about a century and a half to come round to it. They came round to it when they became occupied with problems which they could solve only by being accurate on the points where Berkeley had shown them to be loose; then they stopped thinking of the things he had to say as just a reactionary bishop's niggling, and began to say them themselves. Well, it may be that some day the mathematical physicists will want a sound logic of time and tenses; and meanwhile the logician had best go ahead and construct it, and abide his time.

17 The Fourth Dimension: an Excerpt from *The Ambidextrous Universe*

Martin Gardner

Immanuel Kant, the great German philosopher of the eighteenth century, was the first eminent thinker to find a deep philosophical significance in mirror imagery. That an asymmetric object could exist in either of two mirror-image forms seemed to Kant both puzzling and mysterious. Before discussing some of the implications Kant drew from left–right asymmetry, let us first see if we can recapture something of the mood in which he approached this topic.

Imagine that you have before you, on a table, solid models of the enantiomorphic polyhedrons shown in figure 2. The two models are *exactly alike* in all geometrical properties. Every edge of one figure has a corresponding edge of the same length on the other figure. Every angle of one figure is matched by a duplicate angle on the other. No amount of measurement or inspection of either figure will disclose a single geometrical feature not possessed by the other. They are, in a sense, identical, congruent figures. Yet clearly they are *not* identical!

This is how Kant expressed it, in Section 13 of his famous *Prolegomena to All Future Metaphysics*: "What can more resemble my hand or my ear, and be in all points more like, than its image in the looking-glass? And yet I cannot put such a hand as I see in the glass in the place of its original. . . ."

That two objects can be exactly alike in all properties, yet unmistakably different, is certainly one reason why the looking-glass world has such an eerie quality for children and for primitive people when they encounter it for the first time. Of course the major source of spookiness is simply the appearance behind the glass of a world that looks as real as the world in front, yet is completely illusory. If you want to puzzle and fascinate a small child, stand him in front of a large

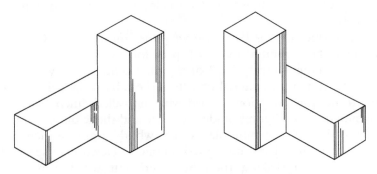

Figure 2 Enantiomorphic polyhedrons

wall mirror at night, in a dark room, and hand him a flashlight. When he shines the flashlight into the mirror the beam goes straight into the room behind the glass and illuminates any object toward which he aims it! This strong illusion of a duplicate room is spooky enough, but it grows even spookier when one becomes aware of the fact that everything in the duplicate room "goes the other way." It is the *same* room, yet it isn't.

Exactly what Kant made of all this is a tangled, technical, controversial story. . . .

Kant's first published paper, *Thoughts on the True Estimation of Living Forces* (1747), contains a remarkable anticipation of *n*-dimensional geometry. Why, he asks, is our space three-dimensional? He concludes that somehow this is bound up with the fact that forces such as gravity move through space, from a point of origin, like expanding spheres. Their strength varies inversely with the square of the distance. Had God chosen to create a world in which forces varied inversely with the *cube* of the distance, a space of four dimensions would have been required. (Similarly, though Kant did not mention it, forces in 2-space, moving out from a point source in expanding circles, would vary only inversely with the distance.) Kant here adopted a view of space which had been put forth a century earlier by Gottfried Wilhelm von Leibniz, the great German philosopher and mathematician. Space has no reality apart from material things; it is nothing more than an abstract, mathematical description of relations that hold between objects. Although the notion of a fourth dimension had occurred to mathematicians, it had been quickly dropped as a fanciful speculation of no possible value. No one had hit on the fact that an asymmetric solid object could (in theory) be reversed by rotating it through a higher space; it was not until 1827, eighty years after Kant's paper, that this was first pointed out by August Ferdinand Moebius, the German astronomer for whom the Moebius strip is named. It is surprising, therefore, to find Kant writing as early as 1747: "A science of all these possible kinds of space [spaces of more than three dimensions] would undoubtedly be the highest enterprise which a finite understanding could undertake in the field of geometry." . . . "If it is possible," he adds, "that there are extensions with other dimensions, it is also very probable that God has somewhere brought them into being; for His works have all the magnitude and manifoldness of which they are capable." Such higher spaces would, however, "not belong to our world, but must form separate worlds."

In 1768, in a paper *On the First Ground of the Distinction of Regions in Space*, Kant abandoned the Leibnitzian view of space for the Newtonian view. Space is a fixed, absolute thing – the "ether" of the nineteenth century – with a reality of its own, independent of material objects. To establish the existence of such a space, Kant turned his attention toward what he called "incongruent counterparts" – asymmetric solid figures of identical size and shape but opposite handedness, such as snail shells, twining plants, hair whorls, right and left hands. The existence of such twin objects, he argued, implies a Newtonian space. To prove it, he made use of a striking thought experiment which can be stated as follows.

Imagine that the cosmos is completely empty save for one single human hand. Is it a left or right hand? Since there are no intrinsic, measurable differences between enantiomorphic objects, we have no basis for calling the hand left or right. Of course if you imagine yourself looking at the hand, naturally you will see it as either left or right, but that is equivalent to putting yourself (with your sense of handedness) into 3-space. You must imagine the hand in space to be completely removed from all relationships with other geometrical structures. Clearly it would be as meaningless to say that the hand is left or right as it would be to say it is large or small, or oriented with its fingers pointing up or down.

Suppose now that a human body materializes in space near the hand. The body is complete except for both hands; they have been severed at the wrist and are missing. It is evident that the hand will not fit both wrists. It will fit only one – say the left wrist. Therefore it is a left hand. Do you see the paradox confronting us? If it proves to be a left hand, by virtue of fitting the left wrist, it must have been a left hand *before* the body appeared. There must be some basis, some ground, for calling it "left" even when it is the sole object in the universe! Kant could see no way of providing such a ground except by assuming that space itself possessed some sort of absolute, objective structure – a kind of three-dimensional lattice that could furnish a means of defining the handedness of a solitary, asymmetric object.

A modern reader, familiar with n-dimensional geometry, should have little trouble seeing through the verbal confusion of Kant's thought experiment. In fact, while I was writing this chapter, Kant's error was effectively exposed by an episode in Johnny Hart's syndicated comic strip called *B.C.*, in newspapers of July 26, 1963. One of Hart's cavemen has just invented the drum. He strikes a log with a stick held in one hand and says, "That's a left flam." Then he hits the log with a stick in his other hand and says, "That's a right flam."

"How do you know which is which?" asks a spectator.

The drummer points to the back of one hand and replies, "I have a mole on my left hand."

Let us see how this relates to Kant's error. Imagine that Flatland contains nothing but a single, flat hand. It is true that it is asymmetrical, but it is meaningless to speak of it as left or right if there is no other asymmetric structure on the plane. This is evident from the fact that we in 3-space can view the hand from either side of the plane and see it in either of its two mirror-image forms. The situation changes if we introduce a handless Flatlander and *define* "left" as, say, the side on which his heart is located. This by no means entails that the hand was "left" or "right" before introducing the Flatlander, because *we can introduce him in either of two enantiomorphic ways.* Place him in the plane one way, the hand becomes a left hand. Turn him over, place him the other way, and the hand becomes a right hand – "right" because it will fit the wrist on the side opposite the heart.

Does this mean that the hand alters its handedness, or that the Flatlander's heart magically hops from one side of his body to the other? Not at all. Neither the hand nor the Flatlander changes in any respect. It is simply that their relations to each other in 2-space are changed. It is all a matter of words.

18 Incongruent Counterparts and Higher Dimensions

James Van Cleve

Incongruent Counterparts and Absolute Space

Incongruent counterparts are asymmetrical objects that come in mirror-image forms, such as left and right human hands. In a paper published in 1768, Kant argued that the existence of such objects is relevant to the debate between Newton and Leibniz on the ontological status of space.[1] Newton regarded space as a thing in its own right – a vast aetherial container without walls, in which everything else that exists lives and moves and has its being. Leibniz believed that the existence of such an entity would generate various absurd pseudopossibilities, such as the possibility that the entire material cosmos might have been shifted three miles to the east or four miles to the west. How could God have had any reason to actualize one rather than another of these possibilities? Accordingly, Leibniz proposed that space is not a genuine entity, but simply a *façon de parler*; all talk of space may be replaced by talk of the spatial relations among material things. Kant agreed with Leibniz early in his career, but reflection on incongruent counterparts led him to believe that Newton was right after all – space is an absolute being, not just a system of relations.

The argument of Kant's 1768 paper may be assembled and set forth as follows:

(1) A hand is left or right (as the case may be) either (a) solely in virtue of the *internal* relations among the parts of the hand or (b) at least partly in virtue of the *external* relations of the hand to something outside it – if not other material objects, then space itself.

(2) But a hand is not left or right solely in virtue of its internal relations, since these are the *same* for right and left. ("The right hand is similar and equal to the left hand. And if one looks at one of them on its own, examining the proportion and the position of its parts to each other, and scrutinising the magnitude of the whole, then a complete description of the one must apply in all respects to the other, as well.")[2]

(3) Nor is a hand right or left even partly in virtue of its relations to other material objects, since a hand that was all alone in the universe would still be right or left. ("Imagine that the first created thing was a human hand. That hand would have to be either a right hand or a left hand.")[3]

(4) Therefore, a hand is left or right (as the case may be) at least partly in virtue of its relation to absolute space. ("Our considerations, therefore, make it clear that differences, and true differences at that, can be found in the constitution of bodies . . . [which] relate exclusively to *absolute* and *original* space . . .")[4]

Since the argument is plainly valid, there are four possible responses to it. (i) One may reject the first premise, maintaining that left and right do not consist in relations of any sort, but are irreducible intrinsic properties. This view is not very plausible, and I do not know of anyone who has advocated it. (ii) One may reject the second premise, maintaining that right and left, though intrinsic properties of hands as wholes, consist in relations among a hand's own parts. Call this view *internalism*. (iii) One may reject the third premise, maintaining that right and left consist in relations to material objects outside the hand. Call this view *externalism*. (iv) One may accept the conclusion, and with it the existence of absolute space. Call this view *absolutism*. In recent critical commentary on Kant's argument, internalism has been advocated by Earman, externalism by Gardner, and absolutism by Nerlich.[5]

Kant rejected internalism because he thought the relevant internal relations were limited to distances between points and angles between lines; these relations are indeed the same in a left hand as in a right. Defenders of internalism may protest that Kant has overlooked a key internal relation, namely, the *direction* in which some points lie from others. May we not say that as you look at the palms of your hands, the direction from thumb to fingertips to wrist is clockwise in the left hand and counterclockwise in the right? But advocates of the other two positions we have distinguished would question whether direction is really an internal relation. Externalists would say that direction can be defined only by reference to an outside material thing (e.g., a clock), and Kant himself maintained that it can be defined only by reference to space as an entity. ("The direction, however, in which this order of parts is orientated, refers to the space outside the thing.")[6]

One phenomenon relevant to the evaluation of Kant's argument is *the fourth dimension*. For Kant, that space has three dimensions is the very paradigm of a synthetic but necessary proposition. But for many thinkers since Kant, propositions about the topological structure of space, such as this one, are contingent, and dimensions beyond the familiar three are perfectly possible. How would the possibility of a fourth spatial dimension bear on Kant's argument?

As the reader will know from the preceding selection by Gardner, in a space of four dimensions an object like a hand could be flipped over so as to become its own incongruent counterpart. The point is readily grasped with the help of lower-dimensional analogs. If tokens of the letters "p" and "q" are confined to a two-dimensional sheet of newsprint, neither can be twisted or turned so as to make it occupy the space of the other; but if we are permitted to lift one of the letters out of the plane of the page and turn it over, the feat can be accomplished. Just so in a four-dimensional space: a left hand could be turned around so as to fit in the space now occupied by a right. Glovemakers would no longer have to manufacture separate left and right models!

These facts about what is possible given an extra dimension are relevant to Kant's argument in two ways. First, they furnish a new argument against internalism. For internalism, the rightness of a hand is an intrinsic property of it. (Even though it consists in relations among the parts, it is intrinsic to the hand as a whole, as in our unnamed alternative (i) above.) Intrinsic properties are those that are shared between an object and any duplicate of it, and whether two objects are duplicates is not affected simply by moving one of them about. (The hardware store clerk has complied with my request to make a duplicate of my key even if the original I handed to her was pointing toward the ceiling and the one she returns to me is pointing toward the floor.) Since in four-dimensional space you could convert a right hand into a left simply by moving it about, it follows that rightness and leftness are not intrinsic properties. So internalism is refuted.

Secondly, the possibility of a fourth dimension undercuts the thought-experiment of the solitary hand that Kant used against externalism. Kant maintained that a hand all alone in the universe would necessarily be left or right, in which case its rightness or leftness could not consist in its relations to any other material thing. Gardner and others have denied this, maintaining that the first created hand would be neither right nor left; it would become one or the other only upon the introduction of a second hand (or a human body for the hand to attach to). Though perhaps implausible at first blush, Gardner's position gains enormously in force once we accept the possibility of a fourth dimension. If four-dimensional spaces are possible (even if not actual), then the difference between a right and a left hand comes to no more than the difference between a "p" and a "q," or between an arrow pointing up and an arrow pointing down. That is to say, it is merely a matter of orientation, and orientation seems inherently to involve a relation to something else. Two objects can be alike or different in their orientation, but an object considered by itself has no orientation at all. So externalism appears to be vindicated.

Another phenomenon relevant to the evaluation of Kant's argument is *the fall of parity*. This refers to the finding, first made in the 1950s, that some laws of nature are sensitive to the distinction between right and left. For example, some particles more often decay into a left-handed configuration than a right, and the outcome of some physical processes can depend on whether the initial conditions assume a right- or a left-handed form. It would not be more suprising in principle if we were to discover that a left glove, when tossed into the air, generally lands palm up, whereas a right lands palm down.

The fall of parity has been adduced as showing that Kant was wrong to maintain that the difference between right and left can only be grasped ostensively, in which case it presumably could not be communicated in binary code to a distant galaxy. We *could* communicate the difference (according to Kant's critics) simply by sending the directions for one of the parity-violating experiments: "Let a bunch of X-particles decay; the decay configuration you will get most often is the one we call left."[7]

However that may be, it seems to me that the fall of parity shows that Kant was correct about something else: namely, that externalism is false. If being right or left is only a matter of being the same or different in orientation as some other object, how can it be a law of nature that certain processes always (or even just usually) have left-handed outcomes? That would be like a law of nature that instructs a seed to grow, not into a watermelon vine or something of a certain intrinsic description, but into the same type of plant that a neighboring seed will grow into.[8]

If the points briefly developed above are correct, a significant conclusion emerges. I have suggested (1) that in response to Kant's argument we must be either internalists, externalists, or absolutists; (2) that externalism is refuted by the fall of parity; and (3) that internalism would be refuted if four-dimensional spaces were possible. It follows either that absolutism is correct (as Kant maintained) or that four-dimensional spaces are impossible (as he also maintained). So Kant was right about at least one thing.

Dialogue on Higher Dimensions

Treios: Let me tell you my latest argument against the fourth dimension. It occurred to me as I was reading what Martin Gardner has to say about the fourth dimension in connection with Kant's puzzle about incongruent counterparts – things like left and right hands. He points out that in a four-dimensional space, you could turn a right hand over so as to make it a left.

Philomath: Yes, mathematicians have known that ever since Moebius. So what's your argument?

Treios: It follows that in four-dimensional space, right and left hands would not be incongruent after all. They would be intrinsically alike, just differently oriented, like arrows pointing in opposite directions. But the difference between right and left is obviously more profound than that. The rightness or leftness of a hand is an intrinsic, recognizable property of it; you can tell that a hand is right or left just by looking at it alone.

Philomath: I disagree. You can't tell that a single hand is right because a single hand can't *be* right. It makes sense to call a hand right or left only in relation to another hand.

Treios: I don't see how you can say that. If I toss you a glove, you can tell me instantly whether it's right or left without comparing it with another glove.

Philomath: Let me qualify my position. You can judge a hand or glove to be right or left without reference to another hand or glove, but you still have to refer to *some* other asymmetrical object, if only your own body.

Treios: I don't see the need for a body, either. A disembodied observer could still tell whether a hand was left or right.

Philomath: I'll grant you that for the sake of argument. I still maintain that your observer would need a vantage point, and could judge a hand to be right or left only in relation to his vantage point.

Treios: I'll grant the need for a vantage point, but I don't see why the observer's judgments of left or right would have to be relative to it. A right hand presents the same recognizable *Gestalt* to *all* vantage points.

Philomath: Not at all. To an observer capable of moving about in four-dimensional space, a hand would appear sometimes as right, sometimes as left.

Treios: But the fourth dimension is just what I am arguing against.

Philomath: Precisely – so your argument begs the question. Don't you see that a Flatlander could use the same argument against the possibility of *three-*

dimensional space? "There is an intrinsic difference between a p and a q," he might claim, "and you can tell which sort of letter you are dealing with by looking at it alone." But viewers outside the plane of Flatland could see the same letter now as a p, now as a q, just as easily as we can go around to the other side of a shop window.

Treios: I see you are going to keep bringing in the Flatlanders. I'll read *Flatland* before we meet again.

* * *

Treios: I have now read *Flatland*.[9] It's a marvelous little book, but it hasn't convinced me. Do you want to hear my main objection to it?

Philomath: Shoot.

Treios: I think we should distinguish between not seeing the possibility of something and seeing the impossibility of it. I think the condition of the Flatlanders is simply inability to see the possibility of three-dimensional space, which I admit does not give them good reason to disbelieve in it. But I think what we possess in regard to the fourth dimension is something more than that – not just inability to visualize it, but positive insight into its impossibility.

Philomath: A dubious distinction, if you ask me.

Treios: Let me illustrate it for you. Do you see that it is possible for there to be a closed curve no four points of which are the vertices of a square?

Philomath: No; it is an unsolved problem whether that is possible.

Treios: Do you see it to be *im*possible, then?

Philomath: Of course not. I just said that it is an unsolved problem.

Treios: Very well; now let's change the example. Do you see that it is possible for there to be a cube with 13 edges?

Philomath: That's absurd.

Treios: Just as I expected. In the first case, you don't see the possibility of a thing, but you don't see its impossibility, either. In the second case, you positively see that it is impossible for a cube to have 13 edges.

Philomath: Seeing has nothing to do with it; it's just that if something had 13 edges we wouldn't call it a cube. But let's get back to the fourth dimension. How do you claim to see that it's impossible?

Treios: Try to visualize more than three perpendicular lines meeting at the corner of this desk – one more line coming in at right angles to each of the other three edges. I bet you can't do it.

Philomath: (*Shrugs.*) Agreed.

Treios: Now is it just that you can't see how to fit a fourth line in? Or is it something positive – you see that there is no place for it to go?

Philomath: Whichever it is, I don't set any store by it. Mathematicians can prove all kinds of interesting properties of four-dimensional figures, and the resulting geometry is perfectly consistent. You are trying to set limits on possibility that are narrower than those of logical consistency, but consistency is the only game in town.

* * *

Treios: Let me ask you this. Are you as willing to believe in negative dimensions as you are in higher positive dimensions? Two-dimensional planes are bounded by lines of dimension one and lines are bounded by points of dimension zero; might points be bounded by items of dimension minus-one?

Philomath: I have no use for negative dimensions.

Treios: My question is whether you think them possible.

Philomath: No, but it is not for any reason you can use against the fourth dimension. Points are not bounded by anything at all. As Euclid says, "a point is that which hath no parts."

Treios: That only raises the question whether the zero-dimensional entities we normally call points really are points in Euclid's sense. Maybe items of dimension zero are bounded by items of dimension minus-one, which are in turn bounded by items of dimension minus-two, and so on.

Philomath: I can't make any sense of that.

Treios: But I'm only extending in the downward direction the analogies you are so happy with going up.

Philomath: OK, I take back my opposition to negative dimensions. Though at present I have no conception of them, I don't say they are impossible. Maybe some day the mathematics of negative dimensions will be worked out.

Treios: It is hard to make headway against someone with so open a mind.

Philomath: It is harder against a closed mind, I assure you.

*   *   *

Treios: Let me try one more time to see if I can't get you to agree that you positively see one of the implications of higher dimensions to be impossible. In three-dimensional space, a one-dimensional loop or an infinite line does not suffice to separate one part of space from the rest, but a two-dimensional surface, such as an infinite plane or the surface of a sphere, *does* separate one part of space from the rest. You can't get from the inside of the sphere to the outside without going through the surface.

Philomath: Yes; Poincaré used the generalization of that fact to define what it is for a space to have dimension *n*.

Treios: That's just what my argument is going to rely on. In four-dimensional space, a two-dimensional surface would not separate space into two parts. A box or a sphere (*cupping his hands*) would no longer completely enclose a region of space, just as a circle (*making a circle with his thumb and forefinger*) does not completely enclose any region of three-dimensional space. So in four-dimensional space, there would be a path by which a beetle could get out of a closed box without going through a wall. And *that*, I hope you will admit, is impossible.

Philomath: If there were a fourth dimension, there would be such a path.

Treios: Yes, that is one of my premises. To which I add, there can be no such a path, so there is no fourth dimension.

Philomath: I wasn't just repeating your premise. My point was that for all we know there could be a fourth dimension, so for all we know there could be such a path.

Treios: Well, I don't know what to say. That the beetle is completely surrounded by the box, so that there's no way out without going through a wall, is as obvious to me as anything ever gets.

Philomath: It's not obvious to everybody. Some people *do* succeed in visualizing the fourth dimension.

Treios: I have my doubts about that. From what I've read, I have the impression that their supposed "seeing" of the fourth dimension is really just a matter of interpreting certain figures or dances of lines on a computer screen as manifestations of something four-dimensional. If we saw a point expand to a sphere and contract again to a point, we could say "This is how a hypersphere would look as it passed through three-dimensional space." But it is also how a point would look as it grew to a sphere and shrank again to a point.

Philomath: It is not always just a matter of what you call interpretation. Sometimes something clicks and one sees a configuration as four-dimensional, just as when you see a Necker cube drawn on paper as three-dimensional.

Treios: I'll believe that when it happens to me. In the meantime, I hope you'll forgive me for doubting that it happens to others. When I find something inconceivable myself, I am bound to find it inconceivable that others find it conceivable.

Philomath: You just don't get it. The lesson of Flatland is completely lost on you. There is not one of your arguments that a Flatlander could not use against the third dimension. "There is an intrinsic difference between a p and a q. There cannot be more than two lines meeting at right angles. A dot cannot escape from a square without passing through a side. Therefore, there can be no third dimension – and no one who visualizes it, either." Every one of your arguments could be used by a Flatlander, and every one of them would be wrong.

Treios: You're taking for granted just what I questioned, that the Flatlanders' state of mind in regard to the third dimension could be something positive like ours in regard to the fourth. In that case, isn't what you are presenting me with a completely generalizable skeptical argument? Isn't it possible to challenge *any* claim to knowledge, however firm and convincing its grounds, by dreaming up beings who would have similar grounds and be mistaken? As easily as we can imagine Flatlanders who are deluded about the structure of space, can we not imagine beings who are deluded about the basic laws of logic? Who think they see that it is impossible for something to have both color and shape – to be both red and square, for example? And could we not then challenge our own belief in the impossibility of contradictions by saying that for all we know our situation may be like theirs? If this is your position, I have no answer to it. I can only point out that it leaves us knowing practically nothing but the Cartesian *cogito.* If it is *not* your position, I wonder why you are so selective about which of our intuitions you will let us rely upon.

Philomath: I must get to class. I'll think about that and see you again tomorrow.

Notes

1 Immanuel Kant, "Concerning the Ultimate Ground of the Differentiation of Directions in Space," in *Theoretical Philosophy, 1755–1770,* vol. I in *The Cambridge Edition*

of the Works of Immanuel Kant, translated and edited by David Walford in collaboration with Ralf Meerbote (Cambridge: Cambridge University Press, 1992), pp. 365–72.

2   Ibid. p. 370.

3   Ibid., p. 371, correcting one error.

4   Ibid., p. 371.

5   John Earman, "Kant, Incongruous Counterparts, and the Nature of Space and Space–Time," *Ratio*, 13 (1971), pp. 1–18; Martin Gardner, this volume; Graham Nerlich, "Hands, Knees, and Absolute Space," ch. 2 of *The Shape of Space* (Cambridge: Cambridge University Press, 1976). Relevant work by these authors and others is reprinted in *The Philosophy of Right and Left*, edited by James Van Cleve and Robert E. Frederick (Dordrecht: Kluwer Academic Publishers, 1991). Nerlich actually subscribes to externalism as regards the properties of leftness and rightness, but he holds that this is an argument analogous to Kant's works for a different pair of properties, being enantiomorphic and being homomorphic. Roughly, an object is enantiomorphic if it could have an incongruent counterpart and homomorphic otherwise.

6   Walford, *Theoretical Philosophy*, p. 365. In many earlier translations, the German word *Gegend* is misleadingly rendered as "region" rather than "direction." On the reasons for preferring "direction" to "region," see Walford, pp. 456–7.

7   See Martin Gardner, "The Ozma Problem and the Fall of Parity," in Van Cleve and Frederick, *Philosophy of Right and Left*, pp. 75–95, or Gardner's *The New Ambidextrous Universe*, 3rd edn (New York: W. H. Freeman, 1990).

8   For further development of this point, see my "Introduction to the Arguments of 1770 and 1783," in Van Cleve and Frederick, *Philosophy of Right and Left*, pp. 15–26, especially pp. 20–22.

9   Edward A. Abbott, *Flatland* (New York: Dover Books, 1952), first published in 1884.

19   The Traditional Conception of Space, and the Principle of Extensive Abstraction: an Excerpt from *Scientific Thought*

C. D. Broad

Let us now ask ourselves: What is the irreducible minimum of properties that the ordinary scientist ascribes to the Space of nature? (i) He holds that it is in some sense continuous, and that it has three dimensions. We need not go into the accurate mathematical definitions of continuity and dimensions. Roughly we mean by the former that any two spaces that do not overlap are at once separated and joined by another space, and that all these spaces are parts of the one big Space of nature. By saying that Space has three dimensions we roughly mean that three independent bits of information are needed to fix the position of a point.

(ii) Again, the scientist and the ordinary layman draw a sharp distinction between Space and the things in Space. They hold that Space, as such, never causes anything. *Mere* position has no effect on any property of matter. If we move a bit of matter about, it may of course change in shape or size. The mercury column of a thermometer will do this if we move it from outside the window to a place near the fire. But the traditional view is that the *mere* change in position is not enough to account for this. The length has changed because the mercury has altered its position with respect to certain *matter* in Space. The complete inactivity of Space is, I think, for the plain man *the* mark that distinguishes it from matter in Space. Whenever it seems to break down we feel perplexed and uncomfortable. I can illustrate this in two ways. (*a*) On the older theories of physics there was supposed to be a peculiar kind of matter, called Ether, that filled all Space. On these theories the Ether was supposed to produce all kinds of effects on ordinary matter, and it became almost a family pet with certain physicists. As physics has advanced, less and less has been found for the Ether to do. In proportion as this has happened physicists have begun to ask: "Do we mean by the Ether anything more than empty Space?" On Lorentz's theory of electro-dynamics, it is difficult to see that the Ether is anything but the concept of absolute Space; and that eminent scientist's attitude towards it recalls Mrs Micawber's statement that she "will never desert Mr Micawber."

(*b*) Conversely, many mathematicians have conceived Spaces in which difference of position does make a difference to the shapes and sizes of bodies, and have successfully explained physical phenomena thereby. Prof. Clifford is one example, and Einstein, in his theory of gravitation, is another. But we do not as yet feel comfortable with the theories of this type, however well they may explain the facts, because they seem to involve the action of Space on matter, and this seems to upset all means of distinguishing between the two. The average intelligent physicist will accept from the mathematician any kind of Space that fits the observable facts, so long as it does not act on matter. But the wilder kind of Spaces that the pure mathematician can offer him he refuses to accept as Spaces at all, because it is part of what he means by Space that it shall be indifferent to, and thus distinguishable from, its content. It may be that we ought not to accept this objection as ultimate, because the sharp separation between the three concepts of Space, Time, and Matter has all the appearance of being artificial; but in the present chapter we are confining ourselves to the traditional view.

Space then, at present, is to be thought of as a single infinite, three-dimensional receptacle, in which all the events of nature have their being, but which is indifferent to them. If we reflect, we shall see that the evidence for the existence of such an object is by no means obvious. We can neither see nor touch empty spaces; what we see and touch are bits of matter. Now of course most things in which scientists believe cannot be perceived by the senses; no one can see or touch a hydrogen atom or a light-wave. Such objects are inferred by the scientist from the perceptible effects which they are supposed to produce. But Space is not even in this position. For, as we saw, the essence of Space on the traditional view, is that it does not produce any effects. Obviously then the existence of Space cannot be inferred from its supposed perceptible effects, since it is not supposed to have any. If then Space is neither perceived nor inferred, whence do we get the concept of it?

In dealing with both Space and Time there are two distinct sets of concepts used, which we might call *distributive* and *collective*. The collective properties of Space and Time are those that belong to them as individual wholes. Thus the questions of how we come to believe that there is one Space, that it is Euclidean, that it can be distinguished from the matter in it, and so on, are questions concerning collective properties of space. On the other hand, there are certain concepts that apply, not so much to Space as an individual whole, as to every bit of space. These are distributive properties, such as divisibility, order of points on lines, and so on. In this and the next chapter we shall confine ourselves to distributive properties of Space and Time respectively; it is only at a much later stage that the question of one Space or Time, and its distinction from things or events in it can be faced.

Now all the distributive properties that we ascribe to Space have their root in certain facts that we can directly observe in our fields of view, and to a lesser extent, in our fields of touch. Whenever I open my eyes I am aware of a variously coloured field. This is extended, or spread out, and this extendedness is the root of my notion of surfaces and volumes. Again, within the total field certain specially coloured patches will stand out against a background; *e.g.*, there might be two green patches, which are in fact the visual appearances of a pair of trees. Such patches have shapes and sizes; and here we have the sensible basis of the concepts of definite figures. Then, between any two such outstanding patches there will always be an extended background with a different colour, which at once joins and separates the patches. If, *e.g.*, we are in fact looking at two trees, standing up against a cloudless sky, our field of view will consist of two characteristically shaped green patches separated and surrounded by a blue extension. In the visual field there is nothing to correspond to the notion of empty space, for the whole field is occupied by some colour or other. Still, the visual experience that we have been describing does suffice to give us, in a rough form, the distributive concepts of extension, shape, size, between-ness, and continuity. And it suggests, though it does not by itself actually give us, another concept. A field of view does not come sharply to an end at its edges. It fades gradually away, and the details become less and less definite the further they are from the centre. Thus there is nothing in the experience to suggest that the field of view is an independent complete whole; it rather presents itself as a fragment of something bigger. This suggestion is strengthened by the fact that when we move our heads slightly the new field of view is only slightly different from the old one. Some details that were distinct have become less so, others that were indistinct have become clearer; a little that was present has vanished and a little that was not present has been added at the extreme edges; but the bulk of the field has scarcely altered. This confirms the feeling that any field of view is only a fragment of a larger whole, and I believe that it is one of the roots of the limitless character which we ascribe to Space.

Much the same concepts are crudely presented to us in our tactual fields. When I grasp anything it feels extended, and some things feel bigger than others. Again, if the thing has projections, I can feel them as standing out from a background of "feeling" in the same kind of way in which the green patches stand out from the blue background in the visual field. . . . [A]ll the information gained in this way is extremely crude, as compared with the concepts that we use in geometry and apply in physics. We see and feel finite surfaces and lumps of complicated shapes, not the unextended points and the lines without breadth of the geometers. And the spatial relations that we can immediately recognise between outstanding patches in our fields of view are equally crude. They are not relations between points and straight lines, but between rough surfaces and volumes. All that I am maintaining is that these crude objects of sense-awareness do have properties that are evidently spatial, and that we can see in them the germs of the refined notions of points, straight lines, etc. The question is: "How are the refined terms and their accurately definable relations, which we use in our mathematics and physics, but cannot perceive with our senses, connected with the crude lumps or surfaces and their rough relations, which we actually do sense?

. . . What we perceive is always objects with some magnitude and duration, and the relations that our perception tells us about are always between such objects. Have we any right to believe that finite objects consist of parts of *no* magnitude, or that such parts, if they exist at all, will have relations in the least like those which hold between finite areas and volumes? A point is something different in kind from a volume or area, however small. We know what we mean when we say that a big area can be cut up into smaller ones; but it is not at all clear what we mean when we say that it can be cut up into points. The one thing that is certain is that the sense in which points are parts of volumes must be different from the sense in which little volumes are parts of bigger ones. The latter sense of part and whole is one that we find exemplified among perceived objects. The former is not, and we are bound to define it before we can feel comfortable in using points and instants.

We commonly slur over this difficulty by entertaining two incompatible notions of points, and using them alternately as convenience requires. This expedient is not unfamiliar to theologians, and to business men returning their incomes for purposes of taxation. When we want to talk of an area as analysable into points we think of points as little volumes. If we feel qualms about this we usually suppress them with the excuse which Midshipman Easy's nurse gave for her baby, that "after all, it was a very little one." When we want to think of points as having exactly definite distances we take them to have "position but no magnitude," as Euclid put it. Now nothing will make these two conceptions of points consistent with each other. Either points are extended or they are not. If they are not, how can they fit together along their sides and edges (which they will not possess) to make a finite volume or area? If they are, in what sense can you talk of *the* distance between them, or of *the* direction determined by a pair of them? To call them infinitesimal volumes or areas only darkens counsel; for the word *infinitesimal* here only serves to cover the attempt to combine these two incompatible qualities.

The method by which such difficulties as these have been overcome is due to Whitehead, who has lately worked it out in full detail in his *Principles of Natural*

Knowledge, and his *Concept of Nature*, two epoch-making works. To explain it in full would take us into regions of mathematical logic which I do not propose to penetrate in the present book. But the problem is so important, and the method is of such general application in bridging the gaps between the crude facts of sense and the refined concepts of mathematical physics that I shall give a sketch of it.

The first thing to notice is that it does not in the least matter to science what is the *inner nature* of a term, provided it will do the work that is required of it. If we can give a definition of points which will make them fulfil a certain pair of conditions, it will not matter though points in themselves should turn out to be entities of a very different kind from what we had supposed them to be. The two conditions are (i) that points must have to each other the kind of relations which geometry demands; and (ii) that points must have to finite areas and volumes such a relation that a reasonable sense can be given to the statement that such areas and volumes can be exhaustively analysed into sets of points. *Any* entity that answers these conditions will do the work of a point, and may fairly be called a *point*, no matter what its other properties may be. This important fact, that what really matters to science is not the inner nature of objects but their mutual relations, and that any set of terms with the right mutual relations will answer all scientific purposes as well as any other set with the same sort of relations, was first recognised in pure mathematics. Whitehead's great merit is to have applied it to physics.

I will first illustrate it from pure mathematics, and then consider its application to our present problem. Consider such irrational numbers as $\sqrt{2}$ and $\sqrt{3}$. Why do we call them *numbers*? Simply because they obey the formal laws of addition and multiplication which integers, like 2 and 3, obey; *i.e.*, because they have to each relations with the same formal properties as the relations that hold between integers. Now numbers like $\sqrt{2}$ and $\sqrt{3}$ were at first defined as the limits of certain series of rational numbers. Thus $\sqrt{2}$ was defined as the limit of the series of rational fractions whose squares are less than 2. Similarly $\sqrt{3}$ was defined as the limit of the series of rational fractions whose squares are less than 3. Then you can define what you are going to mean by the *addition* and *multiplication* of such limits. These will be new senses of addition and multiplication. The sign + does not stand for the same relation when we talk of $\sqrt{3} + \sqrt{2}$, as when we talk of 2 + 3. But addition and multiplication, in the new senses, have the same formal properties as they have when used in the old sense. Thus, *e.g.*, $\sqrt{2} + \sqrt{3} = \sqrt{3} + \sqrt{2}$ just as 2 + 3 = 3 + 2. We have extended the meaning of *addition* and *multiplication*; but, as they have precisely the same logical properties in both senses, no harm is done by using the same name for both, and talking of the addition and multiplication of irrationals. Consequently there is no harm in calling $\sqrt{2}$ and $\sqrt{3}$ *numbers*; for we agreed that any set of entities were to count as numbers, provided they had to each other relations with the same logical properties as the relations between familiar numbers, like 2 and 3, possess. Now all reasoning depends entirely on the logical or formal properties of the objects reasoned about, and therefore we can henceforth reason about irrationals as if they were ordinary numbers.

In exactly the same way, if we can define objects which have to each other relations with the same formal properties as the relations between geometrical points, these objects will do all the work of points, and can be called points, whatever their internal structure may be. Once this is grasped an initial difficulty can be removed. We are apt to think of points as internally simple, because they are said to have no parts and no magnitude. But none of the uses to which we put points in geometry or physics depend on this supposed internal simplicity. The usefulness of points depends entirely on the fact that any pair of them define a unique relation with very simple logical properties, viz., the straight line joining them. Now we see that *any* terms whatever that are related to each other by a relation with these properties will do this part of the work of points. Hence we must not be surprised if we should find that points are not really simple, but have a complex internal logical structure. This is what we *shall* find. But we shall also find that, in spite of the logical complexity of points, a clear sense can be given to the statement that they have no parts and no magnitude.

We can now go a step further. I said that irrationals *used* to be defined as the limits of certain series of rationals. They are not so defined nowadays. Why is this? The answer is that, if we define them in this way, it is not certain that there is anything answering to the definition. $\sqrt{2}$ is said to be the limit of the series of rationals whose squares are less than 2. But how do you know that this series has a limit at all; *i.e.*, roughly speaking, how do you know that there exists a number which the series continually approaches, but never reaches? The fact is that we do not know it and cannot prove it. It follows that, if we define irrationals in this way, it is not certain that there are any irrationals; $\sqrt{2}$ might be a symbol which stands for nothing at all, like the phrase "The present King of France," which has a meaning but no application. We want therefore to get a definition that shall amount to much the same thing as the definition by limits, but shall not leave us in any doubt as to the existence of something answering to it.

Now very much the same difficulty arises over points. I will put it in this way. We are naturally tempted to define points as the limits of certain series of areas or volumes, just as we defined irrationals as the limits of certain series of rationals. And these attempted definitions *are* steps in the right direction. But they are not ultimately satisfactory, because they leave the existence of points, as of irrationals, doubtful. Let me illustrate this with regard to points. We saw that, as we take smaller and smaller areas or volumes, the spatial relations between them become simpler and more definite. Now we can imagine a series of areas or volumes, one inside the other, like a nest of Chinese boxes. Suppose, *e.g.*, that it was a set of concentric spheres. As you pass to smaller and smaller spheres in the series you get to things that have more and more approximately the relations which points have in geometry. You might therefore be tempted to define a point, such as the common centre of the spheres, as the limit of this series of spheres one inside the other. But at once the old difficulty would arise: "Is there any reason to suppose that this series has a limit?" Admittedly it has no last term; you can go on finding spheres within spheres indefinitely. But the mere fact that it does not have a last term is no proof that it does have a limit. The limit of an endless series might be described as the first term that comes after all the terms of the endless series. But this implies that the series in question forms part of some bigger series; otherwise there is no beyond. Now it is not at all obvious that our endless series of concentric spheres does form part of any bigger series, or that there is any term that comes after every sphere in it. Hence there is no certainty that points, defined as the limits of such series, exist.

How is such a difficulty to be overcome? It was first overcome for irrational numbers, and Whitehead then showed that it might be dealt with in the same way for points. The solution will at first sight strike those who are unfamiliar with it as a mere *tour de force*; nevertheless it is perfectly valid, and really does the trick. Instead of defining $\sqrt{2}$ as the *limit* of the series of rational numbers whose squares are less than 2, it is defined as *this series itself*. That is $\sqrt{2}$ is defined as the series of all rational numbers whose squares are less than 2. There is no doubt that there is such a thing as $\sqrt{2}$, so defined. For there certainly are rational numbers, like 1 and 1.2 and 2.5, and so on. And it is certain that the squares of some of them are less than 2, that the squares of others of them are greater than 2, and that the squares of none of them are equal to 2. It is therefore certain that there is a definite class of rationals whose squares are less than 2, and that it has an infinite number of members. It is equally certain that the numbers in this class form a series, when arranged in order of magnitude. Thus there is no doubt of the existence of the series which is said to be the meaning of $\sqrt{2}$.

But the difficulty that will be felt at first will be a different one. The reader will be inclined to say: "I don't doubt that $\sqrt{2}$, as defined by you, exists; what I very gravely doubt is whether, as defined by you, it is what I or anyone else mean by $\sqrt{2}$. By $\sqrt{2}$ I understand a certain number of a peculiar kind; I do not mean a series of numbers or of anything else." The answer to that difficulty is that series of this kind will serve every purpose for which irrationals, like $\sqrt{2}$ and $\sqrt{3}$, are used in mathematics. You can define addition and multiplication for such series, and they have exactly the same logical properties as the addition and multiplication of integers or of rational fractions. Lastly, taking this definition of $\sqrt{2}$, you can give a perfectly definite meaning to the statement that the length of the diagonal of a square, whose side is of unit length, is represented by $\sqrt{2}$. The position is therefore this. The definition of irrationals defines something that certainly exists. And this something has all the formal properties and will do all the work of irrationals. The sole objection to it is that it is paradoxical, in so far as it assigns a complex internal structure to irrationals which we did not suspect them of having. But that objection is really unimportant, because of the general principle that in science it is only the logical properties of the relations between our terms that matter, and not their internal logical structure. The objection is just a prejudice to be got over, like our feeling that the inhabitants of Australia must be precariously hanging on to the earth by suction, like flies on a ceiling.

Now we deal with the difficulty about points in an exactly similar way. We should like to say that points are the limits of series of smaller and smaller volumes, one inside the other, like Chinese boxes. But we cannot feel any confidence that such series have limits and therefore that points, so defined, exist. Now there is no doubt that such series themselves exist; ordinary perception makes us acquainted with their earlier and bigger terms, and the assumption that

Space is continuous guarantees the later ones. We see, on reflection, that it is of the very nature of any area or volume to have parts that are themselves areas or volumes. We, therefore, boldly define points, not as the limits of such series, but as such series themselves. This is exactly like the procedure adopted in defining irrationals.

There are certain additional difficulties of detail in defining points, which do not arise in defining irrationals. I will just indicate them and refer the reader to

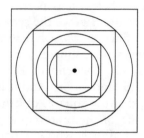

Whitehead for the complete solution of them. (i) There may be a great many different series of converging volumes which would all commonly be said to converge to the same point. This is illustrated for areas in the figure above, where the series of circles and the series of squares might equally be taken to define the point which is their common centre. Now, of course, the point cannot reasonably be identified with one of these series rather than with another. We, therefore, define the point, not as any one of these series of converging volumes, but as the class of all the volumes in any of the series that would commonly be said to converge to the point. (ii) Not all series of converging volumes converge to points; some converge to lines, and others to areas. An example of a series of areas converging to a straight line is illustrated below. (It should be noticed that, although for simplicity of drawing I have always taken series of *areas* in my diagrams, the fundamental fact is series of *volumes*, and areas need definition, like points and lines.)

The general principle is however, always the same. Points, straight lines and areas are all defined as series of converging volumes. But the series that define points differ in certain assignable ways from those that define straight lines, and

these in turn differ in certain assignable ways from those which define areas. Ordinary perception gives us examples of each kind of series, and the only difficulty is to state in formal logical terms these differences which we can all vaguely see and feel. To do this properly is, of course, a very hard job, but it can be and has been done. Many of these additional complications arise because Space has three dimensions, whilst the series of real numbers has only one. Consequently, as a matter of history, moments of Time were defined in this way before points of Space. Time forms a one-dimensional series, like the real numbers, and, therefore presents an easier problem than Space for this method.

Before going further I want to remove a legitimate ground of doubt which will probably be in the minds of most careful readers to whom the subject is new. Many will say: "This is no doubt highly ingenious, but are we not merely moving in a circle? May not the theory be summed up by saying that points are those series of volumes that converge to points? If so, are we not plainly using the notion of point in order to define it?" This would of course be a fatal objection if it were well founded, but it is not. The theory may roughly be summed up in the statement that a point is a series of volumes that would *commonly be said to converge* to that point. The whole question is whether the common phrase "converging to the point p" really involves a reference to points. If it does the definition of points is circular and useless; if it does not there is no vicious circle in the theory. Now the essence of the theory is that it can state the meaning of such phrases as "converging to a point" in terms which involve nothing but volumes and their relations to each other. We see certain series of volumes which we say "converge to a point," *e.g.*, series of concentric spheres. We see other series of volumes of which we do not say this. Here is a perceptible difference in perceptible objects. This difference, which can be seen and felt, must be expressible in terms of volumes and their relations to each other. It cannot really involve a relation to something that can neither be seen nor felt, such as a point. Thus a series of volumes is said to converge to a point simply and solely because of certain relations which hold between the volumes of the series. Another series of volumes is said not to converge to a point simply and solely because certain other relations exist between the volumes of this series. These relations, as well as their terms, are perceptible, and this is how we come to distinguish two such series. It only remains to state the differences of relation, which can thus be seen and felt, in definite terms that can be grasped by the intellect. This the present theory does. For example, a series of confocal conicoids could be defined as one whose members cut each other at right angles; a definition which makes no mention of their common focus, but simply mentions a relation which the members of the series have to each other. There is thus no circularity in the definition of points by this method.

The method which we have been sketching, by which the accurate concepts of science are defined in terms of perceptible objects and their perceptible relations, is called by Whitehead the *Principle of Extensive Abstraction*. Our next question is: Do points, lines, etc., as defined by Extensive Abstraction, fulfil the conditions that we laid down for them at the beginning? The first was that they must have to each other the sort of relations that points, etc., are said to have to each other in geometry. For instance, two points must define a unique relation with certain logical properties, viz., the straight line that joins them. Intersecting straight lines must define planes, and so on. Points, straight lines, and planes, defined as above, do in fact have relations of this kind to each other. The detailed

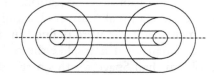

proof of this must here be taken on trust, but I shall take one example to indicate roughly the way in which these results come about. Take two different series of concentric spheres, one in one place and the other in another. Choose any sphere out of one set and any sphere out of another. There will be a certain crude perceptible relation between them. For instance, as shown in the diagram above, there will be a volume which connects and contains both of them, which does not wholly contain any pair of larger spheres in the two series, but more than contains any pair of smaller spheres in the two series.

Let us call this the *containing volume* of the selected pair. As we take smaller and smaller pairs of spheres from the two series it is easy to see that the corresponding containing volumes form a series of Chinese boxes of the usual kind. Now this series of containing volumes is obviously of the sort that defines a straight line. Our two series of spheres are of the sort that define points; the points that they define are what we commonly call the centres of the two systems. And it is easy to see roughly that the line defined by the series of containing volumes is what we call the line joining the two centres. Of course, for accurate mathematical treatment, many more refinements are needed; but I hope that the example will suffice to show in a rough way how points, as defined by us, determine straight lines, as defined by us.

The second condition which points had to fulfil was that it must be possible to give a clear meaning to the statement that finite volumes and areas can be completely analysed into sets of points. Now we can see at once that, *whatever* a point may be, it is certain that it cannot be part of a volume in the sense in which a little volume can be part of a bigger one. The latter is the fundamental relation; it holds only between finite volumes, and it is perceptible. In this sense points, however defined, could not be parts of volumes. Divide a volume as long as you like and you will get nothing but smaller volumes. Put points together as much as you like (if this permission conveys anything to you) and you will not get any volume, however small. In fact the whole notion of "putting together" points is absurd, for it tries to apply to points a relation which can only hold between volumes or areas. To put together means to place so that the edges touch; and a point, having no area or volume, has no edges. We see then that, whatever definition we give of points, we must not expect them to be parts of volumes in the plain straightforward sense in which the Great Court is part of the college buildings of Trinity. It is therefore no special objection to our definition of points that points, as defined by us, could not be parts of volumes in the plain straightforward sense.

The sense in which a point p is contained in a volume v is roughly the following. We say that p is contained in v if, after a certain volume has been reached

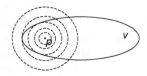

in the series that defines p, all subsequent volumes in this series are parts, in the plain straightforward sense, of the volume v. The diagram illustrates this definition.

The sense in which any volume can be exhaustively analysed into points is roughly the following: Any pair of volumes of which both are contained in v, but of which neither is wholly contained in the other, belong to series which define different points, both of which are contained in v in the sense just defined. Of course both these definitions need further refinements to cover all cases that can arise.

Now what precisely has been accomplished by all this? We have shown the exact connexion between what we can and do perceive, but cannot deal with mathematically, and what we can and do deal with mathematically, but cannot perceive. We perceive volumes and surfaces, and we perceive certain relations between them, viz., that they intersect, or that one is contained in the other, or that they are separated and both contained in some third volume or surface. We do not perceive the points without volume and the lines without breadth, in terms of which geometry and physics are stated and worked out. On the one hand, we cannot make geometry into a deductive science at all except in terms of points, etc. On the other hand, we want to be able to apply geometry to the actual world, and not to treat it as a mere mathematical fairy tale. It is essential therefore that the connexion between what we perceive, but cannot directly treat mathematically, and what we cannot perceive, but can treat mathematically, should be made clear. This is what we have tried to do, following the method of Extensive Abstraction laid down and worked out by Whitehead.

It seems to me that the more we reflect the more clearly we see that something like the course that we have followed is necessary if the application of geometry (and also of rational mechanics) to the real world is to be justified. The world of pure mathematics with its points, straight lines, and planes, its particles, instants, and momentary configurations, has an appearance of unnatural smoothness and tidiness, as compared with the rough complexity of the perceptible world. Yet the laws of geometry and mechanics came out of the study of that world, and return to it in the form of applied mathematics. What I have tried to do is to show in rough outline how the two are connected, in the hope that the reader may be encouraged to consult the original authorities to learn how the same method establishes the connexion in the minutest details.

I think that possibly two difficulties may still remain in the reader's mind, (i) He may say: "Men used geometry for thousands of years, and applied it, and yet they knew nothing of these definitions of points, straight lines, and planes." I answer that this is perfectly true, and that it perfectly illustrates the difference between the special sciences and Critical Philosophy. Certainly people used the concepts of point and straight line, and used them correctly as the results show. But equally certainly they had the most confused ideas as to what they meant by points and straight lines, and could not have explained why a geometry stated in terms of these and their relations should apply so accurately to a world in which nothing of the kind was perceptible. It is the business of Critical Philosophy not to rest content with the successful use of such concepts, but to disentangle their meaning and thus determine the limits within which they can safely be employed.

(ii) The second question that may be asked is: "Do points, straight lines, etc., really exist in the same sense as volumes, or are they merely convenient and perhaps indispensable fiction?" This seems to me to be an important point, on which even authorities like Mr Russell often speak with a strangely uncertain voice. . . .

The right answer to the question appears to me to be the following: Points, etc., as defined by us, are not fictions; they are not made by our minds, but discovered by them, just as America was discovered, and not created, by Columbus's voyage. On the other hand, they do not exist in precisely the same sense in which finite volumes exist. They are real in their own kind, but it is a different kind from that of volumes. It is through no mere accidental limitation of our senses that we cannot perceive the points and straight lines of the geometers, whilst we can see and feel volumes. Only particulars can be perceived by the senses; and point are not particulars. They are classes of series of volumes, or, to be more accurate, are the logical sums of such classes. The volumes and the series of volumes that define points exist quite literally, and the earlier and bigger terms of these series can be perceived. The points themselves are rather complicated logical functions of these. They exist in the sense that they are determinate functions of real series of actually existing particulars.

---

20   Achilles and the Tortoise

Max Black

1.   Suppose Achilles runs ten times as fast as the tortoise and gives him a hundred yards' start. In order to win the race Achilles must first make up for his initial handicap by running a hundred yards; but when he has done this and has reached the point where the tortoise started, the animal has had time to advance ten yards. While Achilles runs these ten yards, the tortoise gets one yard ahead; when Achilles has run this yard, the tortoise is a tenth of a yard ahead; and so on, without end. Achilles never catches the tortoise, because the tortoise always holds a lead, however small.

This is approximately the form in which the so-called "Achilles" paradox has come down to us. Aristotle, who is our primary source for this and the other paradoxes attributed to Zeno, summarizes the argument as follows: "In a race the quickest runner can never overtake the slowest, since the pursuer must first reach the point whence the pursued started, so that the slower must always hold a lead" (*Physics*, 239b).

2.   It would be a waste of time to prove, by independent argument, that Achilles *will* pass the tortoise. Everybody knows this already, and the puzzle arises because the conclusion of Zeno's argument is known to be absurd. We must try to find out, if we can, exactly what mistake is committed in this argument.

3.   A plausible answer that has been repeatedly offered takes the line that "this paradox of Zeno is based upon a mathematical fallacy" (A.N. Whitehead, *Process and Reality* [New York, 1929], p. 107).

Consider the lengths that Achilles has to cover, according to our version of the paradox. They are, successively, a hundred yards, ten yards, one yard, a tenth of a yard, and so on. So the total number of yards he must travel in order to catch the tortoise is

$$100 + 10 + 1 + \frac{1}{10} + \ldots$$

This is a convergent geometrical series whose sum can be expressed in decimal notation as 11.1̄, that is to say exactly 11⅑. When Achilles has run this number of yards, he will be dead level with his competitor; and at any time thereafter he will be actually ahead.

A similar argument applies to the time needed for Achilles to catch the tortoise. If we suppose that Achilles can run a hundred yards in ten seconds, the number of seconds he needs in order to draw level is

$$10 + 1 + \frac{1}{10} + \frac{1}{100} + \ldots$$

This, too, is a convergent geometrical series, whose sum is expressed in decimal notation as 11.1̄, that is to say exactly 11⅑. This, as we should expect, is one tenth of the number we previously obtained for the length of the race. (For Achilles was running at ten yards per second.)

We can check the calculation without using infinite series at all. The relative velocity with which Achilles overtakes the tortoise is nine yards per second. Now the number of seconds needed to cancel the initial gap of a hundred yards at a relative velocity of pursuit of nine yards per second is 100 divided by 9, i.e., 11⅑. This is exactly the number we previously obtained by summing the geometrical series representing the times needed by Achilles. Achilles is actually running at ten yards per second, so the actual distance he travels is $10 \times 11\frac{1}{9}$, or 111⅑, as before. Thus we have confirmed our first calculations by an argument not involving the summation of infinite series.

4. According to this type of solution, the fallacy in Zeno's argument is due to the use of the words "never" and "always." Given the premise that "the pursuer must first reach the point whence the pursued started," it does *not* follow, as alleged, that the quickest runner "never" overtakes the slower: Achilles does catch the tortoise at some time – that is to say at a time exactly 11⅑ seconds from the start. It is wrong to say that the tortoise is "always" in front: there is a place – a place exactly 111⅑ yards from Achilles' starting point – where the two are dead level. Our calculations have shown this, and Zeno failed to see that only a finite time and finite space are needed for the infinite series of steps that Achilles is called upon to make.

5. This kind of mathematical solution has behind it the authority of Descartes and Peirce and Whitehead – to mention no lesser names – yet I cannot see that it goes to the heart of the matter. It tells us, correctly, when and where Achilles and the tortoise will meet, *if* they meet; but it fails to show that Zeno was wrong in claiming they *could not* meet.

Let us be clear about what is meant by the assertion that the sum of the infinite series

$$100 + 10 + 1 + \frac{1}{10} + \frac{1}{100} + \ldots$$

is 111⅑. It does not mean, as the naïve might suppose, that mathematicians have succeeded in adding together an infinite number of terms. As Frege pointed out in a similar connection,[1] this remarkable feat would require an infinite supply of paper, an infinite quantity of ink, and an infinite amount of time. If we had to add all the terms together, we could never prove that the series had a finite sum. To say that the sum of the series is 111⅑ is to say that if enough terms of the series are taken, the difference between the sum of that *finite number* of terms and the number 111⅑ becomes, and stays, as small as we please. (Or to put it another way: Let *n* be any number less than 111⅑. We can always find a finite number of terms of the series whose sum will be less than 111⅑ but greater than *n*.)

Since this is all that is meant by saying that the infinite series has a sum, it follows that the "summation" of all the terms of an infinite series is not the same thing as the summation of a finite set of numbers. In one case we can get the answers by working out a finite number of additions; in the other case we *must* "perform a limit operation," that is to say, we must prove that there is a number whose difference from the sum of the initial members of the series can be made to remain as small as we please.

6. Now let us apply this to the race. The series of distances traversed by Achilles is convergent. This means that if Achilles takes enough steps whose sizes are given by the series one hundred yards, ten yards, one yard, one-tenth yard, etc., the distance *still to go* to the meeting point eventually becomes, and stays, as small as we please. After the first step he still has 11⅑ yards to go; after the second, only 1⅑ yard; after the third, no more than ⅑ yard; and so on. The distance still to go is reduced by nine-tenths at each move.

But the distance, however much reduced, still remains to be covered; and after each step there are infinitely many steps still to be taken. The logical difficulty is that Achilles seems called upon to perform *an infinite series of tasks*, and it does not help to be told that the tasks become easier and easier, or need progressively less and less time in the doing. Achilles may get nearer to the place and time of his rendezvous, but his task remains just as hard, for he still has to perform what seems to be logically impossible. It is just as hard to draw a very small square circle as it is to draw an enormous one: we might say both tasks are infinitely hard. The logical difficulty is not in the extent of the distance Achilles has to cover but in the apparent impossibility of his traveling any distance whatsoever. I think Zeno had enough mathematical knowledge to understand that if Achilles could run 111⅑ yards – that is to say, keep going for 11⅑ seconds – he would indeed have caught the tortoise. The difficulty is to understand how Achilles could arrive anywhere at all without first having performed an infinite series of acts.

7.   The nature of the difficulty is made plainer by a second argument of Zeno, known as the "Dichotomy" which, according to Aristotle, is "the same in principle" (*Physics*, 239b). In order to get from one point to another, Achilles must first reach a third point midway between the two; similarly, in order to reach this third point he must first reach a fourth point; to reach this point he must first reach another point; and so on, without end. To reach *any* point, he must first reach a nearer one. So, in order to be moving at all, Achilles must already have performed an infinite series of acts – must, as it were, have traveled along the series of points from the infinitely distant and *open* "end." This is an even more astounding feat than the one he accomplishes in winning the race against the tortoise.

The two arguments are complementary: the "Achilles" shows that the runner cannot reach any place, even if he gets started; while the "Dichotomy" shows that he cannot get started, i.e., cannot leave any place he has reached.

8.   Mathematicians have sometimes said that the difficulty of conceiving the performance of an infinite series of tasks is factitious. All it shows, they say, is the weakness of human imagination and the folly of the attempt to make a mental image of mathematical relationships. The line really does have infinitely many points, and there is no logical impediment to Achilles' making an infinite number of steps in a finite time. I shall try to show that this way of thinking about the race is untenable.

9.   I am going to argue that the expression, "infinite series of acts," is self-contradictory, and that failure to see this arises from confusing a series of acts with a series of numbers generated by some mathematical law. (By an "act" I mean something marked off from its surroundings by having a definite beginning and end.)

In order to establish this by means of an illustration I shall try to make plain some of the absurd consequences of talking about "counting an infinite number of marbles." And in order to do this I shall find it convenient to talk about counting an infinite number of marbles as if I supposed it was sensible to talk in this way. But I want it to be understood all the time that I do not think it sensible to talk in this way, and that my aim in so talking is to show how absurd this way of talking is. Counting may seem a very special kind of "act" to choose, but I hope to be able to show that the same considerations apply to an infinite series of any kind of acts.

10.   Suppose we want to find out the number of things in a given collection,[2] presumably identified by some description. Unless the things are mathematical or logical entities it will be impossible to deduce the size of the collection from the description alone; and somebody will have to do the work of taking a census. Of course he can do this without having any idea of how large the collection will turn out to be: his instructions may simply take the form, "Start counting and keep on until there is nothing left in the collection to count." This implies that there will be a point at which there will be "nothing left to count," so that the census-taker will then know his task to have been completed.

   Now suppose we can know that the collection is infinite. If, knowing this, we were to say, "Start counting, and continue until there is nothing left to count" we should be practicing a deception. For our census-taker would be led to suppose that sooner or later there would be nothing left to count, while all the time we would know this supposition to be false. An old recipe for catching guinea pigs is to put salt on their tails. Since they have no tails, this is no recipe at all. To avoid deception we should have said, in the case of the infinite collection, "Start counting and *never* stop." This should be enough to tell an intelligent census-taker that the collection is infinite, so that there is no sense in trying to count it.

   If somebody says to me, "Count all the blades of grass in Hyde Park," I might retort, "It's too difficult; I haven't enough time." But if some cosmic bully were to say, "Here is an infinite collection; go ahead and count it," only logical confusion could lead me to mutter, "Too difficult; not enough time." The trouble is that, no matter what I do, the result of all my work will not and cannot count as compliance with the instructions. If somebody commands me to obey a certain "instruction," and is then obliging enough to add that nothing that I can do will count as compliance with that instruction, only confusion could lead me to suppose that any genuine task had been set.

11.   However, some writers have said that the difficulty of counting an infinite collection is just a matter of *lack of time*. If only we could count faster and faster, the whole job could be done in a finite time; there would still never be a time at which we were ending, but there would be a time at which we already would have ended the count. It is not necessary to finish counting; it is sufficient that the counting shall have been finished.

   Very well. Since the task is too much for human capacity, let us imagine a machine that can do it. Let us suppose that upon our left a narrow tray stretches into the distance as far as the most powerful telescope can follow; and that this tray or slot is full of marbles. Here, at the middle, where the line of marbles begins, there stands a kind of mechanical scoop; and to the right, a second, but empty tray, stretching away into the distance beyond the farthest reach of vision. Now the machine is started. During the first minute of its operation, it seizes a marble from the left and transfers it to the empty tray on the right; then it rests a minute. In the next half-minute the machine seizes a second marble on the left, transfers it, and rests half-a-minute. The third marble is moved in a quarter of a minute, with a corresponding pause; the next in one-eighth of a minute; and so on until the movements are so fast that all we can see is a gray blur. But at the end of exactly four minutes the machine comes to a halt, and now the left-hand tray that was full seems to be empty, while the right-hand tray that was empty seems full of marbles.

Let us call this an *infinity machine*. And since it is the first of several to be described let us give it the name "Alpha."

12. I hope nobody will object that the wear and tear on such a machine would be too severe; or that it would be too hard to construct. We are dealing with the logical coherence of ideas, not with the practicability of mechanical devices. If we can conceive of such a machine without contradiction, that will be enough; and believers in the "actual infinite" will have been vindicated.

13. An obvious difficulty in conceiving of an infinity machine is this. How are we supposed to know that there are infinitely many marbles in the left-hand tray at the outset? Or, for that matter, that there are infinitely many on the right when the machine has stopped? Everything we can observe of Alpha's operations (and no matter how much we slow it down) is consistent with there having been involved only a very large, though still finite, number of marbles.

14. Now there is a simple and instructive way of making certain that the machine shall have infinitely many marbles to count. Imagine the arrangements modified as follows. Let there be only *one* marble in the left-hand tray to begin with, and let some device always return *that same marble* during the time at which the machine is resting. Let us give the name "Beta" to a machine that works in this way. From the standpoint of the machine, as it were, the task has not changed. The difficulty of performance remains exactly the same whether the task, as in Alpha's case, is to transfer an infinite series of qualitatively similar but different marbles; or whether the task, as in Beta's case, is constantly to transfer the *same* marble – a marble that is immediately returned to its original position. Imagine Alpha and Beta set to work side by side on their respective tasks: every time the one moves, so does the other; if one succeeds in its task, so must the other; and if it is impossible for either to succeed, it is impossible for *each*.

15. The introduction of our second machine, Beta, shows clearly that the infinite count really is impossible. For the single marble is always returned, and each move of the machine accomplishes nothing. A man given the task of filling three holes by means of two pegs can always fill the third hole by transferring one of the pegs; but this automatically creates another empty place, and it won't help

in the least to "keep on trying" or to run through this futile series of operations faster and faster. (We don't get any nearer to the end of the rainbow by running faster.) Now our machine, Beta, is in just this predicament: the very act of transferring the marble from left to right immediately causes it to be returned again; the operation is self-defeating and it is logically impossible for its end to be achieved. Now if this is true for Beta, it must be true also for Alpha, as we have already seen.

16.   When Hercules tried to cut off the heads of Hydra, two heads immediately grew where one had been removed. It is rumored that the affair has been incorrectly reported: Zeus, the all powerful, took pity on Hercules and eased his labor. It was decreed that only *one* head should replace the head that had been cut off and that Hercules should have the magical power to slash faster and faster in geometrical progression. If this is what really happened, had Hercules any cause to be grateful? Not a bit. Since the head that was sliced off immediately grew back again, Hercules was getting nowhere, and might just as well have kept his sword in its scabbard.

17.   Somebody may still be inclined to say that nevertheless when the machine Beta finally comes to rest (at the end of the four minutes of its operation) the single marble might after all be found in the right-hand tray, and this, if it happened, would *prove* that the machine's task had been accomplished. However, it is easy to show that this suggestion will not work.

I said, before, that "some device" always restored the marble to its original position in the left-hand tray. Now the most natural device to use for this purpose is another machine – Gamma, say – working like Beta but *from right to left*. Let it be arranged that no sooner does Beta move the marble from left to right than Gamma moves it back again. The successive working periods and pauses of Gamma are then equal in length to those of Beta, except that Gamma is working while Beta is resting, and vice versa. The task of Gamma, moreover, is exactly parallel to that of Beta, that is, to transfer the marble an infinite number of times from one side to the other. If the result of the whole four minutes' operation by the first machine is to transfer the marble from left to right, the result of the whole four minutes' operation by the second machine must be to transfer the marble from right to left. But there is only one marble and it must end somewhere. If it ought to be found on the right, then by the same reasoning it ought to be found on the left. But it cannot be both on the right and on the left. Hence neither machine can accomplish its task, and our description of the infinity machines involves a contradiction.

18.   These considerations show, if I am not mistaken, that the outcome of the infinity machine's work is independent of what the machine is supposed to have done antecedently. The marble might end up on the right, on the left, or nowhere. When Hercules ended his slashing, Zeus had to decide whether the head should still be in position or whether, after all, Hercules' strenuous efforts to do the impossible should be rewarded.

Hercules might have argued that every time a head appeared, he had cut it off, so no head ought to remain; but the Hydra could have retorted, with equal force, that after a head had been removed another had always appeared in its place, so a head ought to remain in position. The two contentions cancel one another and neither would provide a ground for Zeus' decision.

Even Zeus, however, could not abrogate the continuity of space and motion; and this, if I am not mistaken, is the source of the contradiction in our description of the machine Beta. The motion of the marble is represented, graphically, by a curve with an infinite number of oscillations, the rapidity of the oscillations increasing constantly as approach is made to the time at which the machine comes to rest. Now to say that motion is continuous is to deny that any real motion can be represented by a curve of this character. Yet every machine that performed an infinite series of acts in a finite time would have to include a part that oscillated "infinitely fast," as it were, in this impossible fashion. For the beginning of every spatio-temporal act is marked by a change in the velocity or in some other magnitude characterizing the agent.

19.   It might be thought that the waiting intervals in the operations of the three infinity machines so far described have been essential to the argument. And it might be objected that the steps Achilles takes are performed consecutively and without intervening pauses. I will now show that the pauses or "resting periods" are not essential to the argument.

Consider for this purpose two machines, Delta and Epsilon, say, that begin to work with a single marble each, but in opposite directions. Let Delta start with the marble a and Epsilon with the marble b. Now suppose the following sequence of operations: while Delta transfers marble a from left to right in one minute, Epsilon transfers marble b from right to left; then Delta moves b from left to right in half a minute while Epsilon returns a from right to left during the same time; and so on, indefinitely, with each operation taking half the time of its predecessor. During the time that either machine is transporting a marble, its partner is placing the other marble in position for the next move.[3] Once again, the total tasks of Delta and Epsilon are exactly parallel: if the first is to succeed, both marbles must end on the right, but if the second is to succeed, both must end on the left. Hence neither can succeed, and there is a contradiction in our description of the machines.

20.   Nor will it help to have a machine – Phi, say – transferring marbles that become progressively smaller in geometrical progression.[4] For, by an argument already used, we can suppose that while Phi is performing its operations, one of the machines already described is going through its paces at the same rates and at the same times. If Phi could complete its task, Alpha, Beta, Gamma, Delta and Epsilon would have to be able to complete their respective tasks. And we have already seen that this is not possible. The sizes of the successive tasks have nothing to do with the logical impossibility of completing an infinite series of operations. Indeed it should be clear by this time that the logical possibility of the existence of any one of the machines depends upon the logical

possibility of the existence of all of them or, indeed, of any machine that could count an infinite number of objects. If the idea of the existence of any one of them is self-contradictory, the same must be true for each of them. The various descriptions of these different hypothetical devices simply make it easier for us to see that one and all are logically impossible. And though a good deal more might be said about this, I hope I have said enough to show why I think this notion of counting an infinite collection is self-contradictory.

21.   If we now reconsider for a moment the arguments that have been used in connection with our six infinity machines, we can easily see that no use was made of the respects in which counting differs from any other series of acts. Counting differs from other series of acts by the conventional assignment of numerals to each stage of the count, and in other respects, too. But every series of acts is like counting in requiring the successive doing of things, each having a beginning and end in space or time. And this is all that was used or needed in our arguments. Since our arguments in no way depended upon the specific peculiarities of counting they would apply, as I said at the outset, to any infinite series of acts.

22.   And now let us return to Achilles. If it really were necessary for him to perform an infinite number of *acts* or, as Aristotle says "to pass over or severally to come in contact with infinite things" (*Physics*, 233a), it would indeed be logically impossible for him to pass the tortoise. But all the things he really does are finite in number; a finite number of steps, heart beats, deep breaths, cries of defiance, and so on. The track on which he runs has a finite number of pebbles, grains of earth, and blades of grass,[5] each of which in turn has a finite, though enormous, number of atoms. For all of these are things that have a beginning and end in space or time. But if anybody says we must imagine that the atoms themselves occupy space and so are divisible "in thought," he is no longer talking about spatio-temporal things. To divide a thing "in thought" is merely to halve the numerical interval which we have assigned to it. Or else it is to suppose – what is in fact physically impossible beyond a certain point – the actual separation of the physical thing into discrete parts. We can of course choose to say that we shall represent a distance by a numerical interval, and that every part of that numerical interval shall also count as representing a distance; then it will be true a priori that there are infinitely many "distances." But the class of what will then be called "distances" will be a series of pairs of numbers, not an infinite series of spatio-temporal things. The infinity of this series is then a feature of one way in which we find it useful to *represent* the physical reality; to suppose that therefore Achilles has to *do* an infinite number of things would be as absurd as to suppose that because I can attach two numbers to an egg I must make some special effort to hold its halves together.

23.   To summarize: I have tried to show that the popular mathematical refutation of Zeno's paradoxes will not do, because it simply assumes that Achilles can perform an infinite series of acts. By using the illustration of what would be

involved in counting an infinite number of marbles, I have tried to show that the notion of an infinite series of acts is self-contradictory. For any material thing, whether machine or person, that set out to do an infinite number of acts would be committed to performing a motion that was discontinuous and therefore impossible. But Achilles is not called upon to do the logically impossible; the illusion that he must do so is created by our failure to hold separate the finite number of real things that the runner has to accomplish and the infinite series of numbers by which we describe what he actually does. We create the illusion of the infinite tasks by the kind of mathematics that we use to describe space, time, and motion.

Notes

1 *Grundgesetze der Arithmetik*, 2 (1903), §124. Or see my translation in *Translations from the Philosophical Writings of Gottlob Frege* (Oxford, 1952), p. 219.
2 Or class or set or aggregate, etc.
3 An alternative arrangement would be to have three similar machines constantly circulating three marbles.
4 Somebody might say that if the marble moved by Beta eventually shrank to nothing there would be no problem about its final location.
5 Cf. Peirce: "I do not think that if each pebble were broken into a million pieces the difficulty of getting over the road would necessarily have been increased; and I don't see why it should if one of these millions – or all of them – had been multiplied into an infinity" (*Collected Papers* [Cambridge, Mass., 1931], 6.182).

---

21   A Contemporary Look at Zeno's Paradoxes: an Excerpt from *Space, Time, and Motion*

Wesley C. Salmon

The Paradoxes of Motion

Our knowledge of the paradoxes of motion comes from Aristotle who, in the course of his discussions, offers a paraphrase of each. Zeno's original formulations have not survived.[1]

(1)   *Achilles and the Tortoise.*   Imagine that Achilles, the fleetest of Greek warriors, is to run a footrace against a tortoise. It is only fair to give the tortoise a head start. Under these circumstances, Zeno argues, Achilles can never

catch up with the tortoise, no matter how fast he runs. In order to overtake the tortoise, Achilles must run from his starting point A to the tortoise's original starting point T_0 (see figure 3). While he is doing that, the tortoise will have moved ahead to T_1. Now Achilles must reach the point T_1. While Achilles is covering this new distance, the tortoise moves still farther to T_2.

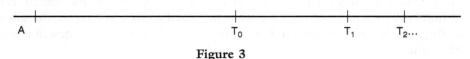

Figure 3

Again, Achilles must reach this new position of the tortoise. And so it continues; whenever Achilles arrives at a point where the tortoise *was*, the tortoise has already moved a bit ahead. Achilles can narrow the gap, but he can never actually catch up with him. This is the most famous of all of Zeno's paradoxes. It is sometimes known simply as "The Achilles."

(2)   *The Dichotomy.*   This paradox comes in two forms, progressive and regressive. According to the first, Achilles cannot get to the end of any racecourse, tortoise or no tortoise; indeed, he cannot even reach the original starting point T_0 of the tortoise in the previous paradox. Zeno argues as follows. Before the runner can cover the whole distance he must cover the first half of it (see figure 4).

Figure 4

Then he must cover the first half of the remaining distance, and so on. In other words, he must first run one-half, then an additional one-fourth, then an additional one-eighth, etc., always remaining somewhere short of his goal. Hence, Zeno concludes, he can never reach it. This is the progressive form of the paradox, and it has very nearly the same force as Achilles and the Tortoise, the only difference being that in the Dichotomy the goal is stationary, while in Achilles and the Tortoise it moves, but at a speed much less than that of Achilles.

The regressive form of the Dichotomy attempts to show, worse yet, that the runner cannot even get started. Before he can complete the full distance, he must run half of it (see figure 5). But before he can complete the first half, he must run half of that, namely, the first quarter. Before he can complete the first quarter, he must run the first eighth. And so on. In order to

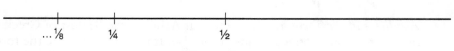

Figure 5

cover any distance no matter how short, Zeno concludes, the runner must already have completed an infinite number of runs. Since the sequence of runs he must already have completed has the form of a regression,

$$\dots \tfrac{1}{16}, \tfrac{1}{8}, \tfrac{1}{4}, \tfrac{1}{2},$$

it has no first member, and hence, the runner cannot even get started.

(3) *The Arrow.* In this paradox, Zeno argues that an arrow in flight is always at rest. At any given instant, he claims, the arrow is where it is, occupying a portion of space equal to itself. During the instant it cannot move, for that would require the instant to have parts, and an instant is by definition a minimal and indivisible-element of time. If the arrow did move during the instant it would have to be in one place at one part of the instant, and in a different place at another part of the instant. Moreover, for the arrow to move during the instant would require that during the instant it must occupy a space larger than itself, for otherwise it has no room to move. As Russell says, "It is never moving, but in some miraculous way the change of position has to occur *between* the instants, that is to say, not at any time whatever."[2] This paradox is more difficult to understand than Achilles and the Tortoise or either form of the Dichotomy, but another remark by Russell is apt: "The more the difficulty is meditated, the more real it becomes."

(4) *The Stadium.* Consider three rows of objects A, B, and C, arranged as in the first position of figure 6. Then, while row A remains at rest, imagine rows B and C moving in opposite directions until all three rows are lined up as shown in the second position. In the process, C_1 passes twice as many B's as A's; it lines up with the first A to its left, but with the second B to its left. According to Aristotle, Zeno concluded that "double the time is equal to half."

First Position					Second Position		
	A_1	A_2	A_3		A_1	A_2	A_3
B_1	B_2	B_3			B_1	B_2	B_3
		C_1	C_2	C_3	C_1	C_2	C_3

Figure 6

Some such conclusion would be warranted if we assume that the time it takes for a C to pass to the next B is the same as the time it takes to pass to the next A, but this assumption seems patently false. It appears that Zeno had no appreciation of relative speed, assuming that the speed of C relative to B is the same as the speed of C relative to A. If that were the only foundation for the paradox we would have no reason to be interested in it, except perhaps as a historical curiosity. It turns out, however, that there is an interpretation of this paradox which gives it serious import.

Suppose, as people occasionally do, that space and time are atomistic in character, being composed of space-atoms and time-atoms of non-zero size, rather than being composed of points and instants whose size is zero.[3] Under these circumstances, motion would consist in taking up different discrete locations at different discrete instants. Now, if we suppose that the As are not moving, but the Bs move to the right at the rate of one place per instant while the Cs move to the left at the same speed, some of the Cs get past some of the Bs without ever passing them. C_1 begins at the right of B_2 and it ends up at the left of B_2, but there is no instance at which it lines up with B_2; consequently, there is no time at which they pass each other – it never happens.

It has been suggested that Zeno's arguments fit into an overall pattern.[4] Achilles and the Tortoise and the Dichotomy are designed to refute the doctrine that space and time are continuous, while the Arrow and the Stadium are intended to refute the view that space and time have an atomic structure. The paradox of plurality [not discussed here], also fits into the total schema. Thus, it has been argued, Zeno tries to cut off all possible avenues to escape from the conclusion that space, time, and motion are not real but illusory.

It is extremely tempting to suppose, at first glance, that the first three of these paradoxes at least arise from understandable confusions on Zeno's part about concepts of the infinitesimal calculus. It was in this spirit that the American philosopher C. S. Peirce, writing early in the twentieth century, said of Achilles that "this ridiculous little catch presents no difficulty at all to a mind adequately trained in mathematics and logic."[5] There is no reason to think he regarded any of Zeno's other paradoxes more highly.

We should begin by noting that, although the calculus was developed in the seventeenth century, its foundations were beset with very serious logical difficulties until the nineteenth century – when Cauchy clarified such fundamental concepts as functions, limits, convergence of sequences and series, the derivative, and the integral; and when his successors Dedekind, Weierstrass, et al., provided a satisfactory analysis of the real number system and its connections with the calculus. I am firmly convinced that Zeno's various paradoxes constituted insuperable difficulties for the calculus in its pre-nineteenth-century form, but that the nineteenth-century achievements regarding the foundations of the calculus provide means which go far toward the resolution of Zeno's paradoxes. Let us see what light these purified concepts can throw on the paradoxes of motion.[6]

The sum of an infinite series

It is hard to guess how deep or subtle Zeno's actual reasoning was; experts differ on the point.[7] It may have been that Zeno's original version of Achilles and the Tortoise involved the following sort of argument: since Achilles must traverse an infinite number of distances, each greater than zero, in order to catch up with the tortoise, he can never do so, for such a process would take an infinite amount of time. Against this form of the argument Aristotle quite appropriately pointed out that the time span during which Achilles chases after the tortoise can likewise be subdivided into infinitely many non-zero intervals, so Achilles has infinitely many non-zero time intervals in which to traverse the infinitely many non-zero space intervals. But this response can hardly be adequate, for the question still remains: how can infinitely many positive intervals of time OR space add up to anything less than infinity? The answer to this question was not provided until Cauchy offered a satisfactory treatment of convergent series in the first half of the nineteenth century.

The first concept we need is the *limit* of an infinite sequence. An infinite sequence is simply an ordered set of terms $\{S_n\}$ which correspond in a one-to-one fashion with the positive integers – each term of the sequence being coordinated by the subscript n to a positive integer. The sequence is said to be *convergent* if it has a limit. To say that such a sequence has a limit means that there is some number L (the limit) such that the terms of the sequence become and remain arbitrarily close to that value as we run through the successive terms. More precisely, for any number ϵ greater than 0, there is some positive integer N such that for every term S_n with $n > N$, the difference between S_n and L is less than ϵ. In the sequence

½, ¼, ⅛, . . . , ½n, . . .

the limit is 0, since the difference between the terms of the sequence and 0 is arbitrarily small for sufficiently large values of n. If, for example, we choose ϵ = ⅒, by the time we reach the fourth term S_4 = ¹⁄₁₆, the difference between that term and L (= 0) is less than ⅒, and the difference remains less than ⅒ for every subsequent member of the sequence. For ϵ = ¹⁄₁₀₀, $|S_n - 0|$ is less than ϵ for n = 7, and the difference remains less than ¹⁄₁₀₀ for every subsequent term. Similarly, ϵ may be chosen as small as we like, say ¹⁄₁,₀₀₀,₀₀₀ or ¹⁄₁,₀₀₀,₀₀₀,₀₀₀, provided it is greater than zero, and there is some point in this sequence beyond which all remaining terms differ from L by less than ϵ. It is easy to show, by completely parallel reasoning, that the sequence

½, ¾, ⅞, . . . , 1 − ½n, . . .

converges to the limiting value of 1.

After the concept of the limit of a sequence has been defined, it can be used to define the sum of an infinite *series*. An infinite series is simply an infinite sequence of terms which are related to one another by addition; for example,

½ + ¼ + ⅛ + . . . + ½n, + . . .

Such a sum is not defined in elementary arithmetic, for ordinary addition is restricted to sums of finite numbers of terms, but this operation can be extended very naturally to an infinite series. In order to define the sum of an infinite *series*

$$s_1 + s_2 + s_3 + \ldots$$

we form the *sequence* of partial sums,

$S_1 = s_1$
$S_2 = s_1 + s_2$
$S_3 = s_1 + s_2 + s_3$
etc.

Each of these partial sums is a sum with a finite number of terms, and it involves only the familiar operation of addition from elementary arithmetic. We have already defined the limit of an infinite sequence. If the *sequence* of partial sums,

$$S_1, S_2, S_3, \ldots$$

has a limit, we say that the infinite *series*

$$s_1 + s_2 + s_3 + \ldots$$

is convergent, and we define its sum as the limit of the sequence of partial sums. This amounts to saying, intuitively, that the sum of a convergent infinite series is a number that can be approximated arbitrarily closely by adding up a sufficient (finite!) number of terms. Given this definition of the sum of an infinite series, it becomes perfectly meaningful to say that the infinitely many terms of a convergent series have a finite sum.

Both the first form of the Dichotomy and the Achilles paradoxes present us with infinite series to be summed. In the Dichotomy, for instance, it is shown that the runner, to cover a racecourse that is one mile in length, must cover the following series of non-overlapping distances:

$$\tfrac{1}{2} + \tfrac{1}{4} + \tfrac{1}{8} + \ldots$$

Each term of this series is greater than zero. We form the sequence of partial sums

$S_1 = \tfrac{1}{2}$
$S_2 = \tfrac{1}{2} + \tfrac{1}{4} = \tfrac{3}{4}$
$S_3 = \tfrac{1}{2} + \tfrac{1}{4} + \tfrac{1}{8} = \tfrac{7}{8}$
etc.

As we noted above, this sequence converges to the limit 1; that is the sum of this convergent infinite series. Achilles and the Tortoise is quite analogous. If Achilles can run twice as fast as the tortoise, and the tortoise has a head start of one-half of the course, the infinite series generated by Achilles running to each subsequent starting point of the tortoise is precisely the one we have just summed. To whatever extent these paradoxes raised problems about the intelligibility of adding up infinitely many positive terms, the nineteenth-century theory of convergent sequences and series resolved the problem.

Instantaneous velocity

An initial reaction to the paradox of the Arrow might be the suspicion that it hinges on a confusion between the concepts of instantaneous motion and instantaneous rest. Perhaps Zeno did feel that the only way for an arrow to be at a particular place was to be at rest – that the notion of instantaneous non-zero velocity was illegitimate. If Zeno argued – we have no way of knowing whether he did or not – that at every moment of its flight the arrow is at some place in its trajectory, and hence at every moment of its flight it has velocity zero, then he would have been correct in concluding that its velocity during the whole course of its flight would be zero, rendering the arrow motionless. Nineteenth-century mathematics showed, however, that one of these assumptions is incorrect. It is entirely intelligible to attribute non-zero instantaneous velocities to moving objects when an instantaneous velocity is understood as a derivative – namely, the rate of change of position with respect to time. This derivative is defined as the limit of the average velocity during decreasing non-zero intervals of time. Suppose, for example, that the arrow flies at a uniform speed. We find that in one second it covers ten feet, in one-tenth of a second it covers one foot, in one-hundredth of a second it covers one-tenth of a foot, and so on. As we take these *average* velocities over decreasing finite time intervals which converge to an instant t_1, the average velocities approach a limit of ten feet per second, and this is, by definition, the instantaneous velocity of the arrow at t_1. The same can be said for every moment during its flight; it travels its whole course at ten feet per second, and its velocity at each moment is ten feet per second. If Zeno felt that the only intelligible instantaneous velocity is zero, nineteenth-century mathematics proved him wrong.

The infinitesimal calculus was, of course, developed in the seventeenth century, and it made use of instantaneous velocities. These were, unfortunately, considered to be infinitesimal distances covered in infinitesimal times. It was against such notions that Berkeley leveled his broadside in *The Analyst*,[8] characterizing infinitesimals as "ghosts of recently departed quantities." It is possible that Zeno's Arrow paradox was also directed against just such a conception. If we try to conceive of finite motion over a finite distance during a finite time as being composed of a large number of motions over infinitesimal distances during infinitesimal times, enormous confusion is likely to ensue. How much space does an arrow occupy during an infinitesimal time? Is it just as large as the arrow, or is it a wee bit larger? If it is larger, then how does the arrow get from one part of that space to another? And if not, then how can the arrow be moving at all? And how long is an infinitesimal time span? Does it have parts or not? If so, how can we characterize motion during its parts? If not, how can motion occur during this infinitesimal time? These are questions that Zeno and his fellow Greeks could not answer, and to which modern calculus prior to Cauchy had no satisfactory answer either. This is why I remarked earlier that nineteenth-century – not seventeenth-century – mathematics held an important key, in the concept of the derivative, to the resolution of Zeno's Arrow paradox.

Mathematical functions

There is, however, still an underlying problem about instantaneous velocity. We have seen how such a concept can be defined intelligibly, but this definition makes essential reference to what is happening at neighboring instants. Instantaneous velocity is defined as a limit of a sequence of average velocities over finite time intervals; without some information about what happens in these intervals we can say nothing about the instantaneous velocity. If we know simply that the center of the arrow was at the point s_1 at time t_1 we can draw no conclusion whatever about its velocity at that instant. Unless we know what the arrow was doing at other times close to t_1 we *cannot* distinguish instantaneous motion from instantaneous rest. It was just this consideration, I believe, which led the philosopher Henri Bergson to say that Zeno's Arrow paradox calls attention to the absurd proposition ". . . that movement is made of immobilities."[9] Bergson concluded that the Arrow paradox proves that the standard mathematical characterization of motion must be wrong. We must look at this argument a little more closely.

In modern physics, motion is treated as a functional relationship between points of space and instants of time. The formula for the motion of a freely falling body, for example, is

$$x = f(t) = \tfrac{1}{2}gt^2.$$

Such formulas make it possible, by employing the function f, to compute the position x given a value of time t. But to understand this treatment of motion fully, it is necessary to have a clear conception of mathematical functions. Before the nineteenth century there was no satisfactory treatment of functions; functions were widely regarded as things which moved or flowed. Such a conception is of no help in attempting to resolve Zeno's paradoxes; on the contrary, Zeno's paradoxes of motion constitute severe difficulties for any such notion of mathematical functions. The situation was dramatically improved when Cauchy defined a function as simply a pairing of numbers from one set with numbers from another set. The numbers of the first set are the *values of the argument*, sometimes called the *independent variable*; the numbers of the second set (which need not be a different set) are the *values of the function*, sometimes called the *dependent variable*. For example, the function $F(x) = y = x^2$ pairs real numbers with non-negative real numbers. With the number 2 it associates the number 4, with the number -1 it associates the number 1, with the number $\tfrac{1}{2}$ it associates the number $\tfrac{1}{4}$, and so forth. Now according to Cauchy, the mathematical function F simply *is* the set of all such pairs of numbers [namely, that shown in Table 1].

Table 1

x	$F(x) = x^2$
1	1
2	4
3	9
$\frac{1}{2}$	$\frac{1}{4}$
$\frac{1}{3}$	$\frac{1}{9}$
-2	4
-1	1
etc.	etc.

Similarly, the function f used to describe the motion of a falling body is nothing more or less than a pairing of the values of the position variable x with values of the time variable t. At $t = 0$, $x = 0$; at $t = 1$, $x = 16$; at $t = 2$, $x = 64$. This is how we say, in mathematical language, that a body starting from rest in the vicinity of the surface of the earth and falling freely travels 16 feet in the first second, 48 feet in the next second, and so on.

Let us now apply this conception of a mathematical function to the motion of an arrow; to keep the arithmetic simple, let it travel at the uniform speed of ten feet per second in a straight line, starting from $x = 0$ at $t = 0$. At any subsequent time t, its position $x = 10t$. Accordingly, part of what we mean by saying that the arrow moved from point A ($x = 10$) to point B ($x = 30$) is simply that it was *at* A when $t = 1$, and it was *at* B when $t = 3$. When we ask how it got from A to B, the answer is that it occupied each of the intervening points x ($10 < x < 30$) at suitable times t ($1 < t < 3$) – that is, satisfying the equation $x = 10t$. For example, when $t = 2$, the arrow was at the point C ($x = 20$). When we ask how it got from A to C, the answer is again: by occupying the intervening positions at suitable times. Notice that this answer is *not*: by zipping through the intervening points at ten feet per second. The requirement is that the arrow be *at* the appropriate point *at* the appropriate time – nothing is said about the instantaneous velocity of the arrow as it occupies each of these points. This approach has been appropriately dubbed "the at-at theory of motion." Once the motion has been described by a mathematical function that associates positions with times, it is then possible to differentiate the function and find its derivative, which in turn provides the instantaneous velocities for each moment of travel. But the motion itself is described by the pairing of positions with times alone. Thus, Russell was led to remark, "Weierstrass, by strictly banishing all infinitesimals, has at last shown that we live in an unchanging world, and that the arrow, at every moment of its flight, is truly at rest. The only point where Zeno probably erred was in inferring (if he did infer) that, because there is no change, therefore the world must be in the same state at one time as at another. This consequence by no means follows. . . ."[10]

What Russell is saying is basically sound, although he does perhaps phrase it overdramatically. It is not that the arrow is "truly at rest" during its flight; rather, the motion consists in being *at* a particular point *at* a particular time, and regarding each individual position at each particular moment, there is no distinction between being at rest at the point and being in motion at the point. The distinction between rest and motion arises only when we consider the position of the body at a number of different moments. This means that, aside from *being at* the appropriate places at the appropriate times, there is no *additional* process of *moving* from one to another. In this sense, there is no absurdity at all in supposing motion to be composed of immobilities.[11]

Although this way of viewing motion is, I believe, logically impeccable, it may be psychologically difficult to accept. Perhaps the problem can best be seen in connection with the regressive form of the Dichotomy paradox. Here we have Achilles at the starting point at the very moment at which the race begins. What, we ask, must he do first? Well, someone might say, first he has to run to the starting point of the tortoise. But that answer cannot be correct, for before he can do that, he must run to a point halfway between his and the tortoise's respective starting points. Before he can do that, however, he must get to a point halfway to the halfway point. And so on. We are off on the infinite regress. It seems that there is no first thing for him to do; whatever we suppose his first task to be, there is another that must be completed before he can finish it. There is, in other words, no first interval for him to cross. This conclusion is true. But it does *not* follow that Achilles cannot get started.

Consider the arrow once more. Suppose it is at point C midway in its flight path. When we ask how it gets from C to B we may be wondering, consciously or unconsciously, where it goes next – how it gets to the next point. But this question is surely illegitimate, for we are thinking of the arrow's path as a continuous one. Since the points in a continuum are densely ordered, there is no next point. Between any two distinct points there is another (and, hence, infinitely many). The question about Achilles, which we just considered in connection with the regressive Dichotomy, may arise from the same psychological source. We may feel that his first act must be to get to the point next to his starting point, but no such point exists. According to the at-at theory of motion, this fact is no obstacle to motion. Both space and time are regarded as continuous, and hence, densely ordered. True, there is no next point of space for Achilles to occupy, but also there is no next moment of time in which he must do so. For each moment of time there is a corresponding point, and for each spatial point there is a corresponding moment; nothing more is required.

The psychological compulsion to demand a next point or a next moment may arise from the fact that we do not experience time as a continuum of instants without duration, but rather, as a discrete series of specious presents, each of which lasts perhaps a few milliseconds. Aside from anthropomorphism, however, there is no reason to try to impose the discrete structure of psychological time upon the mathematical notion of time as a continuum, since the continuous conception has proved itself such an extremely fruitful tool for the description of physical motion.[12]

Limits of functions

There is one final issue, arising out of the paradoxes of motion, that was significantly clarified by nineteenth-century foundations of mathematics. During the preceding two centuries, while the calculus floated on vague spatial and temporal intuitions, there was considerable controversy about the ability of a function to reach its limit. Some functions seemed to do so; others did not. It was all quite baffling. This puzzle relates directly to Zeno's paradoxes of Achilles and the Tortoise and the progressive form of the Dichotomy. Achilles seems capable of chasing the tortoise right up to the point of overtaking him, but can he reach that limiting point? Likewise, on the track by himself, Achilles seems capable of traversing the various fractional parts of the course right up to the finish line, but can he achieve that limit? Again, the definitions of functions and limits provided in the nineteenth century come nicely to the rescue. A limit is simply a number. A function is simply a pairing of two sets of numbers. If the limit happens to be one of the numbers in the set of values of the function, then the function does assume the limiting value for some value of its argument variable. If not, then the function never assumes the limiting value. No further question about the ability of a function to "reach" its limit can properly arise.

There can be no serious doubt that the aforementioned nineteenth-century mathematical developments went a long way in resolving the problems Zeno raised about space, time, and motion. The only question is whether there are any remaining problems associated with the paradoxes of motion. Beginning about 1950, a number of mathematically sophisticated writers, who were fully aware of the foregoing considerations, felt that an important problem still remained. One of the most articulate was Max Black, who argued that the analysis of Achilles' attempt to catch the tortoise into an infinite sequence of distinct runs introduces a severe logical difficulty.[13] The problem, specifically, is whether it even makes sense to suppose that anyone has completed an infinite sequence of runs. Black puts the matter forcefully and succinctly when he says that the mathematical operation of summing an infinite series will tell us where and when Achilles will catch the tortoise if he can catch the tortoise at all, but that is a big "if." There is, Black argues, a fundamental difficulty in supposing that he can catch the tortoise, for, he maintains, "the expression, 'infinite series of acts,' is self-contradictory."[14]

Black's argument is based upon consideration of a number of imaginary machines that transfer balls from one tray to another.[15] Suppose, for instance, that there are two machines, Hal and Pal, each equipped with a tray in front. When a ball is placed in Hal's tray, he moves it to Pal's tray; when a ball is placed in Pal's tray, he moves it to Hal's tray. They have a sort of friendly rivalry about getting rid of the balls. Suppose, further, that they are programmed in such a way that each successive transfer of the ball takes a shorter time; in particular, when the ball is first put into either tray, the machine takes ½ minute to move it to the other tray, next time it takes ¼ minute, next time it takes ⅛ minute, and so forth. (Actually, it is more like a frantic compulsion to get rid of the ball; they carry the maxim "It is more blessed to give than to receive" to a ridiculous extreme.) We begin by putting a ball in Hal's tray, and he takes ½ minute to move it to Pal's tray. Pal then takes ½ minute to put it back in Hal's tray, during which time Hal is resting. Then Hal takes ¼ minute to transfer it to Pal's tray, while Pal is resting; in the next ¼ minute Pal returns it to Hal's tray while Hal rests. As the process goes on, the pace increases until we see just a blur, but at the end of two minutes it is over, and both machines come to rest. The ball has been transferred infinitely many times; in fact, each machine has made infinitely many transfers (and enjoyed infinitely many rest periods) during the two minutes.

Now, we must ask, where is the ball? Is it in Hal's tray? No, it cannot be in Hal's tray, because every time it was put in, Hal removed it. Is it in Pal's tray? No, because every time it was put there Pal removed it. Black concludes that the supposition that this infinite sequence of tasks has been completed leads to an absurdity.

Another hypothetical infinity machine – perhaps the simplest – is the Thomson lamp.[16] This lamp is of a common variety; it has a single push-button switch on its base. If the lamp is off and you push the switch, the lamp turns on; if the lamp is on and you push the switch, the lamp turns off. Now suppose that someone pushes the switch an infinite number of times; he accomplishes this by completing the first thrust in ½ minute, the second in ¼ minute, the third in ⅛ minute, much as the runner in the Dichotomy is supposed to cover the infinite sequence of distances in decreasing times. Consider the final state of the lamp after the infinite sequence of switchings. Is the lamp on or off? It cannot be on, for each time it was on it was switched off. It cannot be off, for each time it was off it was switched on.

The speed of switching demanded is, of course, beyond human capability, but we are concerned with logical possibilities, not "medical" limitations. Moreover, there are mechanical difficulties inherent in the speed required of Hal and Pal as well as Thomson's lamp, but we are not concerned with problems of engineering. Further, there is no use trying to evade the question by saying that the bulb would burn out or the switch would wear out. Even if we could cover such eventualities by technological advances, there remains a logical problem in supposing that an infinite sequence of switching (or ball transfers) has been achieved. The lamp must be both on and off, and also, neither on nor off. This is a thoroughly unsatisfactory state of affairs.

Black and Thomson are *not* maintaining that Achilles cannot overtake the tortoise and finish the race. We all know that he can, and to argue otherwise would be silly. Black is arguing that it is incorrect to *describe* either feat as "completing an infinite sequence of tasks," and Thomson draws a similar moral. They are suggesting that the paradoxes arise because of a misdescription of the situation.

These authors have focused upon a fundamental point. We must begin by realizing that no definition, by itself, can provide the answer to a *physical* problem. Take the simplest possible case, the familiar definition of arithmetical addition of two terms. We find, *by experience*, that it applies in some situations and not in others. If we have m apples in one basket and n oranges in another, then we will have $m + n$ pieces of fruit if we put them together in the same container. (Popular folklore notwithstanding, we obviously can "add" apples and oranges.) However, as is well known, if we have m quarts of alcohol in one bucket, and n quarts of water in another, we will not have $m + n$ quarts of solution if we put them together in the same container. The situation is simply another instance of the relation between pure and applied mathematics discussed in the preceding chapter [not included here]. We can define various mathematical operations within pure mathematics, but that is no guarantee of their applicability to the physical world. If such operations are to be applied in the description of physical facts we must determine empirically whether a given physical operation is an admissible interpretation of a given mathematical operation. We have just seen that the combining of apples and oranges in fruit baskets is a suitable counterpart of arithmetical addition, while the mixing of alcohol and water is not. A more significant example occurs in Einstein's special theory of relativity, where composition of velocities is seen not to be a physical counterpart of standard vector addition.

The same sort of question arises when we consider applying the (now standard) definition of the sum of an infinite series. Does a given physical situation correspond to a particular mathematical operation, in this case, the operation of summing an infinite series? Black concludes that the running of a race does not correspond to the summing of an infinite series, for the completion of an infinite sequence of tasks is a logical impossibility. Thus, the running of a race cannot correctly be described as completing an infinite sequence of tasks. This conclusion has far-reaching implications for modern science. If it is right, the usual scientific description of the racecourse as an infinitely divisible mathematical continuum is fundamentally incorrect. It may be a useful idealization for some purposes, but Zeno's paradoxes show that the description cannot be literally correct. The inescapable consequence of this view would seem to be that mathematical physics needs a radically different mathematical foundation if it is to deal adequately with physical reality.

Before accepting any such result, we must examine the infinity machines more closely. They do involve difficulties, but Black and Thomson have not identified them accurately. Consider Thomson's lamp. (The same considerations will apply to Black's infinity machines or any of the others.) Thomson has described a physical switching process that occupies one minute. Given that we begin at t_0 with the lamp off, and given that a switching occurs at $t_1 = \frac{1}{2}$, $t_2 = \frac{3}{4}$, and so on, we have a description that tells, for any moment *prior to* the time $T = 1$ (that is, one minute after t_0), whether the lamp is on or off. For $T = 1$, and subsequent times, it tells us nothing. For any time *prior to* T that the lamp is on, there is a subsequent time *prior to* T that the lamp is off, and conversely. But this does not imply that the lamp is both on and off at T; we can make any supposition we like without logical conflict. We have, in effect, a function defined over a half-open interval $0 \le t < 1$, and we are asked to infer its value at $t = 1$. Obviously, there is no definite answer to such a question. If the function approached a limit at $t = 1$, it would be natural to extend the definition of the function by making that limit the value of the function at the end point. But the "switching function" describing Thomson's lamp has no such limit, so any extension we might choose would seem arbitrary.[17] The same goes for the position of the ball Hal and Pal pass back and forth. In the Dichotomy and the Achilles paradoxes, by contrast, the "motion function" of the runner does approach a limit, and this limit provides a suitably appealing answer to the question about the location of the runner at the conclusion of his sequence of runs.[18]

One cannot escape the feeling, however, that there are significant and as yet unmentioned differences between the infinite sequence of runs Achilles must make to catch the tortoise and the infinite sequence of ball transfers executed by Black's machines (or the infinite sequence of switch pushes required by the Thomson lamp). And there is at least one absolutely crucial difference. Consider the motion of the ball as it is passed back and forth between Hal and Pal. Say that the trays are three inches apart. Then the ball is made to traverse this *fixed* positive distance infinitely many times. In order to do so, it must travel an *infinite* distance in a finite length of time. Now, no one is interested in showing that Achilles can run an infinite distance in a finite amount of time – he is fast, but not that fast. The problem is to show how he can run a *finite* distance that can be subdivided into an infinite number of subintervals.

Achilles can make his run if he can achieve a fixed positive velocity; the ball which travels back and forth over the fixed distance between Hal and Pal must achieve velocities that increase without any bound. This difficulty could, of course, be repaired. Suppose we stipulate that the distances covered by the ball, like the distances Achilles must cover, decrease as the time available for each transit decreases. This can be done by making the trays of Hal and Pal move closer and closer during the two-minute interval, so that they coincide in the middle at the end of the infinite sequence of transfers. But now there is no problem at all about the position of the ball at the end – it is right in the middle in both trays! Similar considerations apply to the Thomson lamp. In order to accomplish a switching, the button must be moved a certain finite distance, say $1/8$ inch. If this is done infinitely many times, the finger which pushes the button and the button itself must traverse an infinite total distance. A necessary, though not sufficient, condition for the convergence of an infinite series is that the terms converge to zero. In order to overcome this difficulty, the switch would have to be modified in some suitable way, in which case an answer can be given to the question regarding the final on–off state of the lamp.[19]

In the literature on Zeno's paradoxes of motion, especially that concerned with the infinity machines, a good deal of emphasis has been placed on the question of whether Achilles can be said to perform an infinite series of *distinct* tasks. When we divide up the racecourse into an infinite series of positive subintervals, it is often claimed, we are artificially breaking up what is properly considered one motion into infinitely many parts which – so the allegation goes – cannot be considered as individual tasks. In order to clarify this question, Adolf Grünbaum has given Achilles a fictitious twin – a doppelgänger – who runs a parallel racecourse, starting and finishing at the same time as the original Achilles.[20]

The new Achilles is a jerky runner. He starts out and runs the first half of the course twice as fast as his counterpart, and then stops and waits for him. When the slower one reaches the midpoint, the interloper runs twice as fast to the three-quarter mark, and again waits for the slower to catch up. He repeats the same performance for each of the remaining infinite series of subintervals. Grünbaum calls the original Achilles, who runs smoothly from start to finish, the *legato runner*; his new twin, who starts and stops, is called the *staccato runner*. The important facts about the staccato runner are: (1) He reaches the end of the course at the same time as the legato runner; if the original Achilles can run the course, so can the staccato runner. (2) The staccato runner takes a rest of finite (non-zero) duration between each of his infinite succession of runs; hence, there can be no question that he performs an infinite sequence of *distinct* runs. (3) The staccato runner (while he is running) runs at a fixed velocity which is simply twice that of his legato mate, so he is not involved in the kinds of ever-increasing velocities that were required in the unmodified Black and Thomson devices.

There is just one final feature of the staccato Achilles which might be a source of worry. Although he is not required to achieve indefinitely increasing velocities, he is required to do a lot of sudden stopping and starting, shifting instantaneously from velocity zero to velocity $2v$ (where v is the legato runner's velocity) and back again. This clearly involves infinite accelerations – and infinitely many of them. One could reasonably doubt the possibility of this degree of jerkiness. It turns out, however, that even the discontinuity in velocity is not a necessary feature of the staccato runner. The physicist Richard Friedberg has shown, by means of a complicated mathematical function, how to describe the motion of a more sophisticated (and less jerky!) staccato runner who covers *each* of the infinite sequence of subintervals by starting from rest, accelerating continuously to a maximum finite velocity, decelerating smoothly to rest, and remaining at rest for the required interval between runs. This staccato runner executes a motion conforming to a continuous function; his velocity (first derivative) and acceleration (second derivative) are continuous, as are all of the higher time-derivatives as well. Moreover, the peak velocities that occur in the successively shorter runs also decrease, converging to zero as the length of the run also converges to zero.[21] It is hard to see what kind of logical (or conceptual) objection can be raised against this kind of motion. But if the sophisticated staccato runner's series of tasks is feasible, so would be the motions of any of the appropriately modified infinity machines. The motion of the ball passed between Hal and Pal, for example, could be described by a combination of two such functions – the first would describe a sequence of motions from left to right with interspersed periods of rest; the second would consist of a similar sequence, but with the motions from right to left. The second set of motions would be executed during the periods of rest granted by the first function, and the first set of motions would occur during the rest periods granted by the second function. It therefore appears that a suitably designed Hal–Pal pair of infinity machines are logically possible if the *legato* Achilles – the one we all granted from the beginning – can complete his ordinary garden-variety run.

The Discrete vs the Continuous

The infinitesimal calculus has long been – and still is – the basic mathematical tool in the description of physical reality. It employs variables that range over continuous sets of values, and the functions it deals with are continuous. Although the calculus has been completely "arithmetized," so that its *formal* development does not demand any geometrical concepts, it is still applied to phenomena that occur in physical space. Its applicability to spatial occurrences is achieved through analytic geometry, which begins with a one-to-one correspondence between the points on a line and the set of real numbers. The set of real numbers constitutes a continuum in the strict mathematical sense; consequently, the order-preserving one-to-one correspondence between the real numbers and the points of the geometrical line renders the line a continuum as well. If, moreover, the geometrical line is a correct representation of lines in physical space, then physical space is likewise continuous. Motion is treated, moreover, as a function of a continuous time variable, and the function itself is continuous. The continuity of the motion function is essential, for velocity is regarded as the first derivative of such a function, and acceleration as the second derivative. Functions which are not continuous are not differentiable, and hence they do not even have derivatives. Continuity is buried deep in standard mathematical physics. It is for this reason that we have concerned ourselves at length with the problems continuity gives rise to.[22]

A serious objection might be raised, however, to the view that the mathematical continuum provides a precise and literal representation of physical reality. Since physics customarily uses such idealizations as frictionless planes, point-masses, and ideal gases, the argument could go, it might be reasonable to suppose that the mathematical continuum is another idealization that is convenient for some purposes, but does not provide a *completely* accurate description of space, time, and motion. There is, in addition, ample precedent for treating magnitudes that are known to be discrete as if they were continuous. The law of radioactive decay, for example, employs a continuous exponential function even though it is universally acknowledged that the phenomenon it describes involves discrete disintegrations of individual atoms. Where very large finite numbers of entities are involved, the fiction of an infinite collection is often a convenient one which yields good approximations to what actually happens. In electromagnetic theory, for another example, the infinitesimal calculus is used extensively in dealing with charges, even though all the evidence points to the quantization of charges. It has sometimes been suggested that these considerations hold the solution to Zeno's paradoxes. For instance, the physicist P. W. Bridgman has said, "With regard to the paradoxes of Zeno . . . if I literally thought of a line as consisting of an assemblage of points of zero length and of an interval of time as the sum of moments without duration, paradox would then present itself."[23]

Although I am in complete agreement with the claim that physics uses idealizations to excellent advantage, it does not seem to me that this provides any basis for an answer to Zeno's paradoxes of plurality or motion. The first three paradoxes of motion purport to show a priori that motion, if it occurs, must be discontinuous. Indeed, Zeno's intention, as far as we can tell, seems to have been to prove a priori that motion cannot occur. With the exception of a very few metaphysicians of the stripe of F. H. Bradley, most philosophers would admit that the question of whether anything moves must be answered on the basis of empirical evidence, and that the available evidence seems overwhelmingly to support the affirmative answer. Given that motion is a fact of the physical world, it seems to me a further empirical question whether it is continuous or not. It may be a very difficult and highly theoretical question, but I do not think it can be answered a priori. Other philosophers have disagreed. Alfred North Whitehead believed that Zeno's paradoxes support the view that motion is atomistic in character, while Henri Bergson seemed to hold an a priori commitment to the continuity of motion.[24] It seems to me that considerable importance attaches to the analysis of Zeno's paradoxes for just this reason. Space and time may, as some physicists have suggested, be quantized, just as some other parameters, such as charge, are taken to be.[25] If this is so, it must be a conclusion of sophisticated physical investigation of the spatio-temporal structure of the atomic and sub-atomic domains. A priori arguments, such as Zeno's paradoxes, cannot sustain any such conclusion. The fine structure of space–time is a matter for theoretical physics, not for a priori metaphysics, physicists and philosophers alike notwith-standing. The result of our attempts to resolve Zeno's paradoxes of motion is not a proof that space, time, and motion are continuous; the conclusion is rather that for all we can tell a priori it is an open question whether they are continuous or not.

Before we finally leave Zeno's paradoxes, something should be said about the view of space, time, and motion as discrete quantities. The historical evidence suggests that some of Zeno's arguments were directed against this alternative; that is a plausible interpretation of the Stadium paradox at any rate. Zeno seems to have realized that, if space and time both have discrete structure, there is a standard type of motion that must always occur at a fixed velocity. If, for instance, an arrow is to fly from position A to position B in as nearly continuous a fashion as is possible in discrete space and time, then it must occupy adjacent space atoms at adjoining atoms of time. In other words, the standard velocity would be one atom of space per atom of time. To travel at a lesser speed, the arrow would have to occupy at least some of the space atoms for more than one time atom; to travel at a greater speed, the arrow would have to skip some of the intervening space atoms entirely, never occupying them in the course of the trip. All of this sounds a bit strange, perhaps, but surely not logically contradictory; this is the way the world might be. Moreover, it is possible, as Zeno's original Stadium paradox shows, for two arrows to pass one another traveling in opposite direc-tions without ever being located next to one another. Imagine two paths, located as close together as possible in our discrete space, between A and B. Let one arrow travel one of these paths from A to B, while the other travels the other path from B to A (see figure 7). Suppose that the arrow traveling the upper track leaves A and occupies the first square on the left, while the arrow traveling the lower track leaves B at the same (atomic) moment of time, occupying the first square on the right end of his path. Let each arrow move along its track at the rate of one square for each atom of time. At the fourth moment, the upper arrow is just to the left of the lower arrow; at the next moment, the upper arrow is just to the right of the lower arrow. At no moment are they side-by-side – they get past one another, but there is no event which qualifies as the passing (if we mean being located side-by-side traveling in the opposite directions). This is strange perhaps, but again, it is hardly logically impossible.

A
1	2	3	4	5	6	7	8
8	7	6	5	4	3	2	1
B

Figure 7

The mathematician Hermann Weyl has, however, posed a basic difficulty for those who would like to quantize space.[26] If we think of a two-dimensional space as being made up of a large number of tiles (something like figure 7), we get into immediate trouble over certain geometrical relations. Suppose for example, that we have a right triangle ABC in such a space (see figure 8). Consider, first, the tiles drawn with solid lines. If the positions A, B, and C represent the respective corner tiles, then we see that the side AB is four units long, the side AC is four units long, and the hypotenuse BC is also four units long. The Pythagorean theorem says, however, that the square of the hypotenuse equals the sum of the squares of the other two sides. This means that a right triangle with two legs of four units each should have a hypotenuse about $5\frac{2}{3}$ units long. The Pythagorean theorem is at least approximately true in physical space, as we have found by

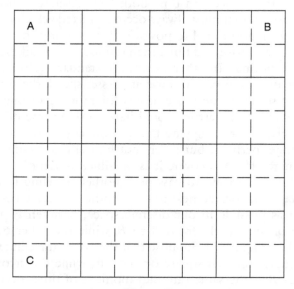

Figure 8

much experience. The result based upon tile-counting does not begin to approximate the correct result.

This example shows something important about approximations. It is easy to see that discontinuous motion in discrete space and time would be difficult to distinguish from continuous motion if our space and time atoms were small enough. It might be tempting to suppose that our geometrical relations would approach the accustomed ones if we make our tiles small enough. This, unfortunately, is not the case, as you can see by taking the finer grid in Figure 8 given by the broken and solid lines together. Instead of 16 tiles, we now have 64 tiles covering the same region of space. But looking at our triangle *ABC* once more, we see that all three sides are now 8 units long. No matter how small we make the squares, the hypotenuse remains equal in length to the other two sides. No wonder this is sometimes called the "Weyl tile" argument![27] This is one case in which transition to very small atoms does not help at all to produce the needed approximation to the obvious features of macroscopic space. It shows the danger of assuming that such approximation will automatically occur as we make the divisions smaller and smaller.

It is important to resist any temptation to account for the difficulty by saying that the diagonal distance across a tile is longer than the breadth or height of a tile, and that we must take that difference into account in ascertaining the length of the hypotenuse of the triangle. Such considerations are certainly appropriate if we are thinking of the tiles as subdivisions of a continuous background space possessing the familiar Euclidean characteristics. But the basic idea behind the tiles in the first place was to do away with continuous space and replace it by discrete space. In discrete space, a space atom constitutes one unit, and that is all there is to it. It cannot be regarded as properly having a shape, for we cannot ascribe sizes to parts of it – it has no parts.

Now, I do not mean to argue that there is no consistent way of describing an atomic space or time. It would be as illegitimate to try to prove the continuity of space and time a priori as it would be to try to prove their discreteness a priori. But, in order to make good on the claim that space and time are genuinely quantized, it would be necessary to provide an adequate geometry based on these concepts. I am not suggesting that this is impossible, but it is no routine mathematical exercise, and I do not know that it has actually been done.[28]

Notes

1 These formulations are taken from Wesley C. Salmon, *Zeno's Paradoxes* (Indianapolis: Bobbs-Merrill 1970), pp. 8–12.

2 Bertrand Russell, *Our Knowledge of the External World* (New York: W. W. Norton, 1929), p. 189.

3 See J. O. Wisdom, "Achilles on a Physical Racecourse," reprinted in Salmon, *Zeno's Paradoxes*.

4 See G. E. L. Owen, "Zeno and the Mathematicians," reprinted in Salmon, *Zeno's Paradoxes*.

5 Charles Hartshorne and Paul Weiss, eds, *The Collected Papers of Charles Sanders Peirce* (Cambridge, Mass.: Harvard University Press, 1935), § 6. 177–184.

6 For an excellent discussion of these developments see Carl B. Boyer, *The History of the Calculus and its Conceptual Development* (New York: Dover Publications, 1959).

7 Zeno's paradoxes pose enormous problems in historical scholarship; for some of the details see Gregory Vlastos, "Zeno of Elea," in the *Encyclopedia of Philosophy*, ed, Paul Edwards (New York: Macmillan and Free Press, 1967).

8 Reprinted in James R. Newman, ed., *The World of Mathematics* (New York: Simon and Schuster, 1956).

9 Henri Bergson, *Creative Evolution*, trans. Arthur Mitchell (New York: Holt, Rinehart and Winston, 1911), relevant passages reprinted in Salmon, *Zeno's Paradoxes*, quotation from p. 63.

10 Bertrand Russell, *The Principles of Mathematics*, 2nd edn (New York: W. W. Norton, 1943), p. 347.

11 The contrary view, that this is indeed an absurdity, is based upon the elementary fallacy of composition. This is the only non-trivial, non-artificial instance of this fallacy I have ever encountered.

12 For detailed and enlightening discussions of the relations between "physical time" and "psychological time," see Adolf Grünbaum, "Relativity and the Atomicity of Becoming," *Review of Metaphysics*, IV (1950–1), pp. 143–86.

13 Max Black, "Achilles and the Tortoise," *Analysis*, XI (1950–1), pp. 91–101; reprinted in Salmon, *Zeno's Paradoxes*.

14 Ibid., p. 72 in Salmon.

15 The idea of an infinity machine was first suggested by Hermann Weyl, *Philosophy of Mathematics and Natural Science* (Princeton, N.J.: Princeton University Press, 1949). See Salmon, *Zeno's Paradoxes*, p. 201, for relevant quotation.

16 James Thomson, "Tasks and Super-Tasks," *Analysis*, XV (1954–5), pp. 1–13; reprinted in Salmon, *Zeno's Paradoxes*.

17 The "switching function" may be defined as follows: let 1 represent the "on-state" of the lamp, and let 0 represent the "off-state." This function has a determinate value for each value of $t < 1$, but it fluctuates infinitely often between 0 and 1 in any neighborhood of $t = 1$; hence, it has no limit at $t = 1$.

18 The arguments of this paragraph were given by Paul Benacerraf, "Tasks, Super-Tasks, and the Modern Eleatics," *Journal of Philosophy*, LIX (1962), pp. 765–84; reprinted in Salmon, *Zeno's Paradoxes*.

19 This analysis of infinity machines and their modifications is due to Adolf Grünbaum, "Modern Science and Zeno's Paradoxes of Motion," Part II, in Salmon, *Zeno's Paradoxes*, pp. 218–44.

20 Ibid., Part I, "The Zenonian Runners," pp. 204–18.

21 See Salmon, *Zeno's Paradoxes*, pp. 215–16, for the details.

22 A continuous function is, intuitively, one that can be plotted by means of a line that has no gaps in it – one that can be drawn without lifting the pencil from the paper on which the function is being plotted. For a respectable mathematical treatment of the concept of continuity, in terms requiring no previous mathematical training beyond high school, see Richard Courant and Herbert Robbins, *What is Mathematics?* (New York: Oxford University Press, 1941), Ch. VI.

23 P. W. Bridgman, "Some Implications of Recent Points of View in Physics," *Revue Internationale de Philosophie*, III (1949), p. 490; quoted by Grünbaum, see Salmon, *Zeno's Paradoxes*, p. 177.

24 See Salmon, *Zeno's Paradoxes*, pp. 16–20, for discussion of metaphysical interpretations of these paradoxes; see pp. 59–66 for a famous passage from Bergson.
25 See Grünbaum, "Modern Science and Zeno's Paradoxes of Motion," Part III, in Salmon, *Zeno's Paradoxes*, pp. 244–60, for an assessment of the extent to which the quantization of space and time has been accomplished.
26 Weyl, *op. cit.*, p. 43. See Salmon, *Zeno's Paradoxes*, p. 175, for the relevant quotation.
27 "Weyl" is pronounced like "vile".
28 See Peter D. Asquith, *Alternative Mathematics and Their Status*, Ph.D. dissertation, Indiana University, 1970.

22   Grasping the Infinite

José A. Benardete

Once upon a time, long ago, a great controversy broke out among the Gumquats, plunging that ancient, benighted people into a state of confusion perilously close to civil war. A young hero had arisen to challenge some of the most deeply cherished beliefs of the tribe. With all the truculence of youth and ambition, he insisted that, contrary to received opinion, it must be admitted that there are a definite number of leaves in the jungle, a definite number of fish in the ocean, a definite number of stones in the valley. It was a profound mistake, he argued, to suppose that the stones in the valley were really innumerable, uncountable, numberless, indeed so plentiful as to be quite *without number*. The Gumquats at this time were fortunate enough to possess a decimal system of counting, but they rarely had any occasion to count beyond 100. Ancient records were on hand to prove that the highest that anyone had ever counted, in all the recorded history of the tribe, was to the number 488. This number was popularly regarded with almost sacred awe, it was chanted during the holy festivals, and it was held highly unlikely that anyone would ever count beyond it. It seemed to represent the very limit of human achievement.

To the horror of the old, to the delight of the young, our hero gathered the whole tribe together and undertook to break the spell of superstition under which they languished. In full view of all, he proceeded to count up to 200, then on to 300, 400, and as he moved on to 486, 487, 488! a great hush fell upon the tribe, 489! – the young burst forth with cheers, the old clapped their hands upon their ears, refusing to listen to this transgression. Our hero was unable to reach 500. Spears and rocks were being hurled in all directions. It was war. Happily enough, a venerable high priest intervened to compose the passions of the contending factions. He was wise and judicious. "I am prepared to overlook this frivolous trespass," he said charitably. "A mere aberration of youth. But I cannot countenance the dangerous heresy which is being urged upon us. I stand by the faith of our fathers that the leaves in the jungle, the fish in the ocean, the stones in the valley are all really innumerable, uncountable, numberless, indeed so plentiful as to be quite without number. If there be a definite number of stones in the valley, then they must be countable. Do you agree?" The high priest addressed his question to our hero, "Yes, they must be countable," answered our hero with mock humility. "Our fathers," continued the priest, "have bequeathed to us the conviction that the stones in the valley are without number, they have taught us that they are uncountable. It is now being urged that they are really countable after all. Very well, young man: prove it! Let us see you count the stones in the valley. I am afraid," added the priest with a supercilious smile, you will find this task somewhat more difficult than merely counting beyond 488." Our hero was not unprepared for this challenge. "I am not able to count the stones in the valley," he said simply. This admission threw his followers into a state of wild dismay. They had been so much awed by his earlier performance that they had come to believe that when he insisted that the stones in the valley were really countable, this could only mean that he possessed the power actually to count them. "I am not able to count the stones in the valley," our hero repeated. "But they are countable nonetheless. God is able to count them. Do you deny that God is able to count the stones in the valley?" All eyes were fixed upon the high priest. How would he answer this damaging question? "God is able to do all things," replied the priest unctuously. "God then is able to count the stones in the valley," our hero pressed on. "But then there must certainly exist a definite number of stones in the valley if God is able to count them!" He paused to let this point sink in. "I do not deny that in a very loose and lax manner of speaking the stones in the valley may perhaps be said to be innumerable. Certainly, they cannot be counted by man. But they can be counted by God, and it is God, not man, who is the measure of all things. From God's point of view, there is a definite number of stones in the valley." So beguilingly persuasive were our hero's words that not only did they succeed in restoring the young to confidence but even the old were visibly shaken in their faith. Murmurs rippled through the crowd. Of course, there is a definite number of stones in the valley! They could almost see them all in their mind's eye, God having attached a number to each stone by a little tag.

Surely the ancestral faith was utterly exploded. What was there left for the old priest to say? "Young man," he spoke with surprising calm. "You are doubtless familiar with the Great Rapids to the north. Are these Rapids navigable or unnavigable?" "Everyone knows that they are savagely unnavigable," replied our hero, puzzled by this odd turn in the controversy. "And what of toadstools?" asked the priest. "Are they edible or inedible?" "They are inedible," replied our hero uneasily. "And what of tigers? Are they ridable or unridable?" "It is impossible to ride a tiger," said the young man testily. "Really?" murmured the priest with evident irony. "God is able to ride the tiger. Tigers must be ridable. God is free to dine on the toadstool. Toadstools must be edible. God is able to navigate the Great Rapids. The Rapids must be navigable." He paused to allow his young adversary an opportunity to speak, but our hero could only stammer in confusion. "I am not surprised by your hesitation," the old man said. "When we say that the Great Rapids are unnavigable, are we so impious as to deny that God is able to navigate them? Certainly not. We mean simply that they cannot be navigated by man. When we say that toadstools are inedible, are we denying that they are edible for God? Certainly not. We mean merely that they are inedible for man. When we say that tigers are unridable . . . But I need scarcely continue. When we say that the stones in the valley are innumerable and uncountable, are we denying that God is able to number them and count them? How absurd! We mean merely that they are innumerable and uncountable – for man! You do not suppose that it is a loose manner of speaking to say that the Great Rapids are unnavigable?" "No," said our hero weakly. "No more is it a loose manner of speaking to say that the stones in the valley, the fish in the ocean, the leaves in the forest are all innumerable, uncountable, numberless, indeed so plentiful as to be quite without number," boomed the old man. "But I have already counted almost to 500," protested our hero desperately. "If I were to continue counting on and on, I would eventually reach a number equal to the number of stones in the valley." "Of course!" replied the priest with disdain. "If! If! If you were to continue counting on and on . . . ! If you were to succeed in navigating the Great Rapids, then you would prove that they are navigable after all. What good is this 'if'? The 'if' doesn't make the Rapids navigable, nor does your 'if' make the stones in the valley numberable and countable."

The old man grew suddenly gentle. "My boy, you have allowed yourself to be transported by a fit of divine enthusiasm unsuitable to a mere mortal. From God's point of view, the stones in the valley are indeed countable, the Great Rapids are indeed navigable, toadstools are indeed edible, tigers are indeed ridable. All things are possible for God. But God's point of view is suitable only for God. Man is truly the measure of all things, not as they are in themselves (Heaven forbid!), but as they are for man. The great numbers that you envisage exist only in the mind of God; they do not exist for man; they are divine and holy; they are not to be profaned by human presumption. My boy, you must rest content with speaking the language of men: the language of God is his alone. You must speak as our fathers have always spoken. You must say that the Great Rapids are unnavigable, that toadstools are inedible, that tigers are unridable; above all, you must say that the stones in the valley are innumerable, that the fish in the ocean are uncountable, that the leaves in the forest are numberless, and that they are all so plentiful as to be quite without number."

The young man bowed his head in a spirit of abject contrition, and the tribe of Gumquats, restored to their ancestral faith, returned to their dogmatic slumbers.

This fable may not be uninstructive; it is designed, above all, to illuminate the Gumquat concept of the infinite. Although we have neglected to mention that concept expressly, it will not be difficult to reconstruct on the basis of the evidence presented. The Gumquats believe not only that the stones in the valley are *literally* uncountable and hence *literally* without number, they also believe that they are infinitely many. They are persuaded that they are so plentiful as to be *literally* infinite. Are they mistaken in their conviction? No. When they insist that there are infinitely many stones in the valley, they mean merely that if one (i.e., a human being) were to be so foolish as to attempt to count all the stones in the valley, he would never reach the *end* of his task; he would die in the process. In that sense the stones are infinite, endless. If the literal meaning of a word is admitted to be the non-metaphorical meaning that it bears in common discourse, then it must be confessed that the stones in the valley are not only infinite but *literally* infinite, and not merely in Gumquat but in vernacular English as well. It will have become only too evident that the Gumquats are no alien tribe of savages living remote in the jungle. They live directly in our midst: we are the Gumquats. Their language is our language. Their concept of number is our concept of number – as it is found in mufti in common discourse. The only difference is that above and beyond this vulgar concept of number we have grown accustomed to another, rather more elevated concept that supplies the underpinning to our very simplest formal arithmetic. We wish to say that the vulgar (or "proto-") concept is scarcely more than a vestigial remnant, quite without ontological import. Surely it is a hard fact that there are a definite number of leaves in the jungle. In a very crude sense, they are doubtless uncountable; but how can it be denied that they are countable *in principle*? And yet we do not wish to say that toadstools are in principle edible or the Great Rapids in principle navigable. The Gumquats fail to note any difference in all these cases. What is our justification for adopting a divine perspective in regard to number and only in regard to number, being quite content to preserve our human perspective in regard to the other concepts? Whatever the reason, it is evident that a divine dignity attaches to our standard concept of number which is altogether absent elsewhere.

One must not suppose that the Gumquats are ignorant of the distinction between what is possible in principle and what is merely feasible in practice. That distinction governs all their thought. The Gumquats are persuaded that there are a definite number of leopards in the forest, but no one supposes that it is at all possible, practically speaking, to count them. Slinking about most elusively, the leopard is believed to be almost extinct in those parts. In the event of famine all of the leopards roaming the vast forest might well be driven by their hunger to descend *en masse* upon the Gumquats and, being but few in number (if popular opinion is to be credited in this matter), they would then be readily available for counting. Never has a Gumquat been heard to say that the leopards in the forest are innumerable. Countable they are believed to be – in principle, though it is obvious enough that no one could be expected to count them in the ordinary course of things. How different the leaves of the jungle and the stones of the valley: these are all accessible and hence uncountable even in principle; and though the fish in the ocean are in large measure unavailable, it is not for *that* reason that they are believed to be innumerable. The distinction between what is possible in principle and what is merely feasible in practice, is but one of many distinctions that effect subtle modulations in the Gumquat language. Sometimes a Gumquat may be heard to say that the wives of the Great King (he has forty-six wives) are innumerable, uncountable, numberless, even infinite. But this is merely hyperbole. What is meant is that it must be difficult for the Great King, as for his subjects, to keep track of them – they are so many. Thus a distinction is drawn between what is infinite in the strict sense, the literally infinite, and what is infinite in a

loose sense, the metaphorically infinite. Whereas the leaves of the jungle are supposed to be infinite in the strict sense, *literally* infinite, it is only in a loose, metaphorical sense that the wives of the Great King are ever said to be infinite. It ought
to come as no surprise that the Gumquats insist that the leaves of the jungle are
literally infinite. If the distinction between finite and infinite, between the countable and the uncountable, is to be recognized in vulgar discourse, if these concepts
are to arise at all in mufti, it is imperative that they have a *use* in the language:
they must be negotiable and cashable in terms of the actual experience of the
Gumquats. What possible use could they have for the distinction between finite
and infinite, between the countable and the uncountable, as that distinction is
enshrined in our standard concept? The standard concept of the infinite simply
has no application in the form of life that constitutes vulgar practice. Not that a
Gumquat may not be moved to remark that the stars in the heavens are infinite,
but he has no occasion to mean anything more by his remark than that they are
infinite in the sense that the leaves of the jungle are known to be infinite.

It would be a great mistake to appeal to *logical* possibility in an effort to prove
that (the Gumquats notwithstanding) it is a hard fact that there are a definite
number of stones in the valley. It may not be humanly possible, but it is surely
logically possible, to count them all. Certainly. It is also logically possible for a
man to navigate the Great Rapids, to dine on the toadstool, to ride the tiger. It
is logically possible for gold to cure measles. But this is to say no more than that
the statement "Gold has the power to cure measles" is free of self-contradiction.
From this mere logical possibility we are not entitled to conclude that gold has
the power to cure measles. So, too, though it is logically possible that the stones
of the valley might all be counted, we have no right to suppose that they are
really countable after all. We might as well say that toadstools are *really* edible.
Logical possibility is no measure of what is really the case.

The vitality of the proto-concept comes through to us most strongly when it
is seen to satisfy all of the Peano postulates.[1] Not certainly in the precise sense
that Peano intended, for the Peano postulates are designed to express our standard concept of number; but at least *nominally*, these postulates are satisfied by
the proto-concept of numbers as well. Consider the five Peano postulates. (1) 0
is a number. (2) The immediate successor of any number is a number. (3) There
are no two numbers with the same successor. (4) 0 is not the successor of any
number. (5) Every property of 0, which belongs to the successor of every number
with this property, belongs to all numbers. All five postulates are accepted by the
Gumquats, but they refuse to admit that these five postulates logically (i.e., in
terms of their proto-logic) entail an infinite progression – infinite being here
understood in the standard sense. That there are infinitely many numbers, they
admit, but only in the proto-sense of infinite: no man can exhaust all the numbers
by counting, just as no man can count all the leaves of the jungle.[2]

Very close to being a Gumquat himself, Wittgenstein could write,

Suppose that children are taught that . . . God created an infinite number of
stars. . . . Queer: when one takes something of this sort as a matter of course, as if
it were in one's stride, it loses its whole paradoxical aspect. It is as if I were to be

told: Don't worry, this series, or movement, goes on without ever stopping. We are as it were excused the labor of thinking of an end. "We won't bother about an end." It might also be said: "for us the series is infinite." "We won't worry about an end to this series; for us it is always beyond our ken."[3]

No wonder that Kripgenstein (Saul Kripke's version of Wittgenstein) insists that what *we* designate by "+" can as readily be taken to be quaddition as addition since the quum of *n* and *m* is the same as the sum of *n* and *m* when the sum of *n* and *m* belongs to the domain of Gumquat numbers; otherwise (bizarrely enough) *n* + *m* (i.e., *n* quus *m*) = 5. So "*n* + *m*" even for us is really only determinate in the Gumquat domain, with "+" being neutral as between plus and quus.[4] Quaddition then is not to be distinguished from addition except when it comes to *large* numbers, though we are encouraged to believe that even the simple sentence "5 quus 7 = 12" fails to mean the same thing as "5 plus 7 = 12", since "quus" and "plus" designate different mathematical functions.

Granted that the substratum of our mathematical practice is supplied by Gumquat arithmetic, what justifies us in supposing that beyond that substratum lies anything other than sheer mythology, as I take Kripke's Wittgensteinian skeptic to be in effect insisting? Kripke's skeptic poses his challenge in terms of both constitution and justification. Kripke writes, "An answer to the skeptic must satisfy two conditions. First, it must give an account of what fact it is (about my mental state) that constitutes my meaning plus, not quus. But further, there is a condition that any putative candidate for such a fact must satisfy. It must, in some sense, show how I am justified in supposing that I am engaged in addition rather than quaddition."[5] Where are we to look for that problematic "fact" of which Kripgenstein despairs?

Because the "quus" paradox is designed by Kripgenstein merely to point up a difficulty about meaning across the board, one paradox may help defuse another. Grass in the past having always been green, philosophers argue as against David Hume that we do have reason to believe that it will be green tomorrow. Not so, says Nelson Goodman's skeptic, who argues that since grass has always been grue in the past we have equal reason to suppose that it will be grue tomorrow, where the word "grue" is defined as applying to something if it is green prior to tomorrow and otherwise blue. So empirical induction from past experience urges us to believe that grass will be grue (i.e., blue) tomorrow. Shifting now to meaning, Kripgenstein argues that the "quus" paradox can be generalized to apply to any predicate, in particular to "green." The word "green" applies to any one of these grue things that we have been observing, right? And never to anything observed by us to be not grue. So grue has no less right to be what the noise "green" expresses in our language.[6]

If I do mean grue by "green" then my evident projection of "green" into the future entails my expecting grass to be blue tomorrow. But surely I know myself to be free of any such expectation . . . unless indeed Kripgenstein is simply playing fast and loose with a skepticism that was selectively designed to apply only to meaning. Actually, there is a deep issue here, arising precisely from Wittgenstein's having convinced philosophers, by means of rich scenarios of almost novelistic detail, that someone's expecting (or not expecting) the telephone to ring in the next hour consists in a battery of multigrade dispositions to behave in various ways. More generally, it is only against the background of a dispositionalist theory of mind, now widely accepted, that Kripgenstein can have any bite at all; in its absence he can only appear dotty. Quite properly then a peculiarly Kripgensteinian skepticism as to my knowing, on a privileged first-person basis, that I do not expect grass to be blue tomorrow, can be seen to be astringently activated. How something (anything, myself included) is disposed to behave in various counterfactual circumstances (e.g., an elastic rubber ball's being prone to bounce on rolling off a table) can only be known – so goes the powerful argument – by means of familiar inductive procedures.

The trick now in rebutting Kripke's skeptic lies in carrying the dispositionalist account one step further. Knowing itself, for Wittgenstein, is also to be construed dispositionally, for example, as regards the belief component in knowledge. So my knowing that in applying "green" to grass I do not expect it to be blue tomorrow consists in one disposition riding piggy-back on another.[7] Therein lies my justification for insisting that I do not mean grue by "green," a move all the more attractive to those already impressed by the recent turn to reliabilist accounts of justification in theory of knowledge. No need then to posit an internal scanning device (e.g., introspection) whereby I monitor my belief and desire states.[8] More important still, no need to posit such a device in regard to what I mean by "green" or "+."

Granted now that much of the sting has been removed from Kripgenstein's *general* challenge, the special one posed by large numbers can only be aggravated by my own heavy-duty dispositionalism. Assume (absurdly) that grasp of the concept of addition consists in the disposition to give the right answer to *any* addition problem ranging over all of the standard numbers. How can that mere disposition, albeit error-free, be justified in any concrete case if one may not even know that one is engaged in addition? The point is well taken. More is required. Grasp of the concept of addition requires an ability (to add numbers) whose exercise (in normal conditions anyway) involves knowing what one is doing – where this piggy-backed knowing may also be taken dispositionally, for example, in a readiness to provide an informal proof of one's answer. This enhanced dispositionality provides justification enough.

The fact that we are prone to make mistakes in adding long strings of numerals provides Kripke with another, independent objection to dispositionalism. This "error" version Christopher Peacocke undertakes to dispel, and in no merely *ad hoc* fashion through a systematic account of what it is to grasp a concept anyway, though he leaves it very much open whether his theory can accommodate large numbers.[9] Error aside, does my ability to add extend to astronomically large numbers? Hardly, any more than my ability to ride a bicycle (on a horizontal surface) extends to steeper inclines. Thus my shift from dispositions to abilities, while welcome in its own right, merely serves to exacerbate large numbers *per se*. Nor can I simply rely on my knowing the truth of the following proposition. The equation "$n + m = r$" is true for arbitrary n, m and r if and only if $n + m = r$.[10] What proposition is that supposed to be? That will depend first on whether

n, m and r are allowed to range beyond the Gumquat domain. Secondly, it will depend on whether the expression "+" means quus or plus or neither (being neutral between them). How then to convince myself that I do grasp the standard proposition to which the science of mathematics is presumed to be committed? For no book has ever explained how to execute the shift from Gumquat to standard arithmetic. It is not as if one can be expected to use the construction of the (positive and negative) integers out of (sets of ordered pairs of) the standard natural numbers as a model for antecedently constructing the standard natural numbers in their turn out of Gumquat numbers.

Seeking reassurance, I propose to design a scientific experiment which will verify, albeit by indirection, my prediction that "5" would certainly not be my answer to any relevant "+ one" query addressed to me on the counterfactual supposition of my counting well beyond the domain of Gumquat numbers. Posing the issue in its sharpest form, I shall even pretend that any such extra-Gumquat counting by me violates the very laws of nature, which laws I further assume to be robust enough to sustain counterfactuals themselves. If I have somewhat pretentiously mentioned conducting a scientific experiment it is largely the literary imagination that will preside, quite in accord with the Gumquat fable itself, by providing such novelistic detail as might ensure psychological and sociological verisimilitude. Genuine enough, however, the experiment is modeled on one drafted by me a few years ago[11] in connection with Glaucon's hypothesis about human nature in the second book of Plato's *Republic*. Formulated expressly as a "subjunctive" counterfactual, Glaucon's hypothesis urges that if any human being could only make himself invisible with the ring of Gyges, thereby becoming free to commit murder with impunity, he would wade through blood in his drive to become tyrant of his country. Assume with me that becoming relevantly "invisible" is also contrary to the laws of nature, thereby converting Glaucon's hypothesis into another contralegal. No matter. To the rescue comes one of Boccaccio's Calandrino stories in which the credulous fellow is duped into believing that invisibility is his to assume at will. In order then to verify how someone *would* behave if – contrary to the laws of nature – he could pass invisibly among people committing murder undetected, it is enough to verify how he *will* behave tomorrow after being hoaxed, with weighty "evidence" that exploits the marvels of recent technology, into believing himself (even rationally) to be so endowed. Enhanced dispositionalism can thus call even upon contralegal dispositions as well as the more familiar sort. With our Calandrino model firmly in hand, it is easy now to verify how anyone (Gumquat or not) would answer the question: "Is the number of leaves in the jungle +1 equal to 5?" simply by verifying how he will in fact answer it after coming to believe, again through weighty "evidence," that someone has succeeded in counting them one by one.

Not that we have any incentive to verify (or falsify) the hypothesis that he would of course answer in the negative. The point is just that thanks to the hypothesis *being* verifiable (or falsifiable) it is not to be doubted that there is a higher-order dispositional fact of the matter as to whether one means by "+" quus rather than plus; assuming indeed that Kripke's second challenge about justification can be met in the present case. For I agree with Kripke that the higher-order dispositional fact specified by me (i.e., being disposed to answer in the negative the question posed) fails all by itself to provide justification for one's answer. Why suppose that one's answer is the right one? Perhaps one has committed a computational error. Put quite so baldly as that, the suggestion is readily seen to be absurd. No long string of numerals here regarding which we are liable, for obvious reasons, to go astray. But perhaps someone believes that the number of leaves in the jungle is just 4. So that sort of case will also have to be banished. Granted now that a combination of such banal facts rules out "quus" as being what one means by "+," we can at least entertain the hope that by continuing in the same vein we might succeed, more positively, in pinning down plus as what "+" means in our language.

Anticipating a favorable outcome, I can even indicate, still more ambitiously, how it can be expected to bear on the infinity machines that Zeno's negative arguments have unexpectedly inspired in our time, by being restyled in an affirmative mode. Along that line we can suppose with Crispin Wright that "in my sleep, say, a genie granted me appropriately boundless computational powers" to test Zenonically every even number (for being the sum of two prime numbers), all to be completed in one minute, thereby inviting Wright to produce an omega proof of Goldbach's Conjecture. Even allowing with Adolf Grünbaum the *kinematic* coherence of the scenario, Wright can "see grounds for nothing but scepticism" when it comes to "explaining" how "it could be clear to me on waking that that was what" the genie "had done," how more particularly one could "discover that one has ceased to have *any* limitations of speed, or accuracy, of computation."[12] Well, let's allow the occasional mistake to be made here also, though double checking and even omega checking can remedy such lapses. More to the point, once it is recalled that being "clear" about something, for example, the non-denumerability of the real numbers, is to be understood in richly dispositional terms, Wright's genie should have no difficulty in endowing him with suitable cognitive capacities to ride piggy-back on his computational powers. As to how one might "discover" in oneself these preternatural capacities and powers, there is no great difficulty in principle. Suppose that on pain of death you are ordered to jump fifty, even a thousand feet. Suppose further that, unbeknownst to you, you have been invested with the strength to fulfill that command. No surprise now, surely, if you succeed in saving your life, though the fashionable view today that insists on explaining behavior as resulting from a combination of belief and desire (forgetting the need for the relevant capacity) may well be perplexed by the outcome. Although the desire is there in full force, the relevant belief is absent. Yet jump you will.

Notes

1   Peano showed that all the mathematics of the natural numbers could be derived from three primitive notions (0, number, successor) and the five postulates discussed in the text. – [Eds]

2   In his 1970 paper 'Wang's Paradox," in his *Truth and other Enigmas* (Cambridge, Mass: Harvard University Press, 1978), Michael Dummett in effect charges the "strict finitism" of Gumquat arithmetic with being infected with a semantic incoher-

ence that is already evident in the vagueness of observational terms like "green" with their liability to the Sorites paradox. Satisfied that such terms are validated by linguistic practice, Crispin Wright in his 1982 "Strict Finitism," in his *Realism, Meaning and Truth*, 2nd edition (Oxford: Blackwell, 1993), argues that "strict finitism remains the natural outcome" of Dummett's own deflationary approach to mathematics, by being "powerfully buttressed by the ideas of the later Wittgenstein" (p. 166).

3 Ludwig Wittgenstein, *Remarks on the Foundations of Mathematics*, ed. G. H. von Wright et al. (Oxford: Blackwell; 1956), part IV, section 14, p. 141.

4 Saul Kripke, *Wittgenstein on Rules and Private Language* (Cambridge, Mass: Harvard University Press, 1982), pp. 7–9. See also p. 27 where quaddition is "redefined."

5 Ibid., p. 11.

6 Kripke links "quus" to grue on pp. 58–9.

7 A refinement on Wittgenstein was supplied by Gilbert Ryle in his classic chapter "Dispositions and Occurrences," *The Concept of Mind* (London: Hutchinson, 1949) when he wrote, "'Know' is a capacity verb . . . signifying that the person described can bring things off, or get things right" (p. 133). Merely "to believe that the ice is dangerously thin is . . . to be prone to skate warily." But "to say that he keeps to the edge because he knows that the ice is thin is to . . . give quite a different sort of 'explanation'" (pp. 134–5).

8 This piggy-back effect will be especially relished when viewed in connection with Sydney Shoemaker's critique of "self-blindness" whereby someone can – absurdly – only learn of his own beliefs and desires by means of the standard third-person gathering of evidence that he exercises in regard to others. See his *The First-Person Perspective and other Essays* (Cambridge, UK: Cambridge University Press, 1996).

9 Christopher Peacocke, *A Study in Concepts* (Cambridge, Mass: MIT Press, 1992), p. 137.

10 Featured by the dominant school in philosophy of language today (associated above all with Donald Davidson), disquotational propositions of this sort cease to be unproblematic when viewed in terms of Kripgenstein. See Kripke's discussion of Davidson on pp. 71–2.

11 See my "The Ring of Gyges: an Aristotelian Approach to Ethics," *Proceedings of the Creighton Club*, April 1992, Meeting of the New York State Philosophical Association.

12 Crispin Wright, *Realism, Meaning and Truth*, 2nd edition (Oxford: Blackwell, 1993), p. 147.

---

23 The Paradoxes of Time Travel

David Lewis

Time travel, I maintain, is possible. The paradoxes of time travel are oddities, not impossibilities. They prove only this much, which few would have doubted: that a possible world where time travel took place would be a most strange world, different in fundamental ways from the world we think is ours.

I shall be concerned here with the sort of time travel that is recounted in science fiction. Not all science fiction writers are clear-headed, to be sure, and inconsistent time travel stories have often been written. But some writers have thought the problems through with great care, and their stories are perfectly consistent.[1]

If I can defend the consistency of some science fiction stories of time travel, then I suppose parallel defenses might be given of some controversial physical hypotheses, such as the hypothesis that time is circular or the hypothesis that there are particles that travel faster than light. But I shall not explore these parallels here.

What is time travel? Inevitably, it involves a discrepancy between time and time. Any traveler departs and then arrives at his destination; the time elapsed from departure to arrival (positive, or perhaps zero) is the duration of the journey. But if he is a time traveler, the separation in time between departure and arrival does not equal the duration of his journey. He departs; he travels for an hour, let us say; then he arrives. The time he reaches is not the time one hour after his departure. It is later, if he has traveled toward the future; earlier, if he has traveled toward the past. If he has traveled far toward the past, it is earlier even than his departure. How can it be that the same two events, his departure and his arrival, are separated by two unequal amounts of time?

It is tempting to reply that there must be two independent time dimensions; that for time travel to be possible, time must be not a line but a plane.[2] Then a pair of events may have two unequal separations if they are separated more in one of the time dimensions than in the other. The lives of common people occupy straight diagonal lines across the plane of time, sloping at a rate of exactly one hour of time$_1$ per hour of time$_2$. The life of the time traveler occupies a bent path, of varying slope.

On closer inspection, however, this account seems not to give us time travel as we know it from the stories. When the traveler revisits the days of his childhood, will his playmates be there to meet him? No; he has not reached the part of the plane of time where they are. He is no longer separated from them along one of the two dimensions of time, but he is still separated from them along the other. I do not say that two-dimensional time is impossible, or that there is no way to square it with the usual conception of what time travel would be like. Nevertheless I shall say no more about two-dimensional time. Let us set it aside, and see how time travel is possible even in one-dimensional time.

The world – the time traveler's world, or ours – is a four-dimensional manifold of events. Time is one dimension of the four, like the spatial dimensions except that the prevailing laws of nature discriminate between time and the others – or rather, perhaps, between various timelike dimensions and various spacelike dimensions. (Time remains one-dimensional, since no two timelike dimensions are orthogonal.) Enduring things are timelike streaks: wholes composed of temporal parts, or *stages*, located at various times and places. Change is qualitative difference between different stages – different temporal parts – of some enduring thing, just as a "change" in scenery from east to west is a qualitative difference between the eastern and western spatial parts of the landscape. If this paper should change your mind about the possibility of time travel, there will be a difference of opinion between two different temporal parts of you, the stage that started reading and the subsequent stage that finishes.

If change is qualitative difference between temporal parts of something, then what doesn't have temporal parts can't change. For instance, numbers can't change; nor can the events of any moment of time, since they cannot be subdivided into dissimilar temporal parts. (We have set aside the case of two-dimensional time, and hence the possibility that an event might be momentary along one time dimension but divisible along the other.) It is essential to distinguish change from "Cambridge change," which can befall anything. Even a number can "change" from being to not being the rate of exchange between pounds and dollars. Even a momentary event can "change" from being a year ago to being a year and a day ago, or from being forgotten to being remembered. But these are not genuine changes. Not just any old reversal in truth value of a time-sensitive sentence about something makes a change in the thing itself.

A time traveler, like anyone else, is a streak through the manifold of space-time, a whole composed of stages located at various times and places. But he is not a streak like other streaks. If he travels toward the past he is a zig-zag streak, doubling back on himself. If he travels toward the future, he is a stretched-out streak. And if he travels either way instantaneously, so that there are no intermediate stages between the stage that departs and the stage that arrives and his journey has zero duration, then he is a broken streak.

I asked how it could be that the same two events were separated by two unequal amounts of time, and I set aside the reply that time might have two independent dimensions. Instead I reply by distinguishing time itself, *external time* as I shall also call it, from the *personal time* of a particular time traveler: roughly, that which is measured by his wristwatch. His journey takes an hour of his personal time, let us say; his wristwatch reads an hour later at arrival than at departure. But the arrival is more than an hour after the departure in external time, if he travels toward the future; or the arrival is before the departure in external time (or less than an hour after), if he travels toward the past.

That is only rough. I do not wish to define personal time operationally, making wristwatches infallible by definition. That which is measured by my own wristwatch often disagrees with external time, yet I am no time traveler; what my misregulated wristwatch measures is neither time itself nor my personal time. Instead of an operational definition, we need a functional definition of personal time: it is that which occupies a certain role in the pattern of events that comprise the time traveler's life. If you take the stages of a common person, they manifest certain regularities with respect to external time. Properties change continuously as you go along, for the most part, and in familiar ways. First come infantile stages. Last come senile ones. Memories accumulate. Food digests. Hair grows. Wristwatch hands move. If you take the stages of a time traveler instead, they do not manifest the common regularities with respect to external time. But there is one way to assign coordinates to the time traveler's stages, and one way only (apart from the arbitrary choice of a zero point), so that the regularities that hold with respect to this assignment match those that commonly hold with respect to external time. With respect to the correct assignment properties change continuously as you go along, for the most part, and in familiar ways. First come infantile stages. Last come senile ones. Memories accumulate. Food digests. Hair grows. Wristwatch hands move. The assignment of coordinates that yields this match is the time traveler's personal time. It isn't really time, but it plays the role in his life that time plays in the life of a common person. It's enough like time so that we can – with due caution – transplant our temporal vocabulary to it in discussing his affairs. We can say without contradiction, as the time traveler prepares to set out, "Soon he will be in the past." We mean that a stage of him is slightly later in his personal time, but much earlier in external time, than the stage of him that is present as we say the sentence.

We may assign locations in the time traveler's personal time not only to his stages themselves but also to the events that go on around him. Soon Caesar will die, long ago; that is, a stage slightly later in the time traveler's personal time than his present stage, but long ago in external time, is simultaneous with Caesar's death. We could even extend the assignment of personal time to events that are not part of the time traveler's life, and not simultaneous with any of his stages. If his funeral in ancient Egypt is separated from his death by three days of external time and his death is separated from his birth by three score years and ten of his personal time, then we may add the two intervals and say that his funeral follows his birth by three score years and ten and three days of *extended personal time*. Likewise a bystander might truly say, three years after the last departure of another famous time traveler, that "he may even now – if I may use the phrase – be wandering on some plesiosaurus-haunted oolitic coral reef, or beside the lonely saline seas of the Triassic Age."[3] If the time traveler does wander on an oolitic coral reef three years after his departure in his personal time, then it is no mistake to say with respect to his extended personal time that the wandering is taking place "even now."

We may liken intervals of external time to distances as the crow flies, and intervals of personal time to distances along a winding path. The time traveler's life is like a mountain railway. The place two miles due east of here may also be nine miles down the line, in the west-bound direction. Clearly we are not dealing here with two independent dimensions. Just as distance along the railway is not a fourth spatial dimension, so a time traveler's personal time is not a second dimension of time. How far down the line some place is depends on its location in three-dimensional space, and likewise the location of events in personal time depends on their locations in one-dimensional external time.

Five miles down the line from here is a place where the line goes under a trestle; two miles further is a place where the line goes over a trestle; these places are one and the same. The trestle by which the line crosses over itself has two different locations along the line, five miles down from here and also seven. In the same way, an event in a time traveler's life may have more than one location in his personal time. If he doubles back toward the past, but not too far, he may be able to talk to himself. The conversation involves two of his stages, separated in his personal time but simultaneous in external time. The location of the conversation in personal time should be the location of the stage involved in it. But there are two such stages; to share the locations of both, the conversation must be assigned two different locations in personal time.

The more we extend the assignment of personal time outwards from the time traveler's stages to the surrounding events, the more will such events acquire multiple locations. It may happen also, as we have already seen, that events that are not simultaneous in external time will be assigned the same location in personal time – or rather, that at least one of the locations of one will be the same as at least one of the locations of the other. So extension must not be carried too far, lest the location of events in extended personal time lose its utility as a means of keeping track of their roles in the time traveler's history.

A time traveler who talks to himself, on the telephone perhaps, looks for all the world like two different people talking to each other. It isn't quite right to say that the whole of him is in two places at once, since neither of the two stages involved in the conversation is the whole of him, or even the whole of the part of him that is located at the (external) time of the conversation. What's true is that he, unlike the rest of us, has two different complete stages located at the same time at different places. What reason have I, then, to regard him as one person and not two? What unites his stages, including the simultaneous ones, into a single person? The problem of personal identity is especially acute if he is the sort of time traveler whose journeys are instantaneous, a broken streak consisting of several unconnected segments. Then the natural way to regard him as more than one person is to take each segment as a different person. No one of them is a time traveler, and the peculiarity of the situation comes to this: all but one of these several people vanish into thin air, all but another one appear out of thin air, and there are remarkable resemblances between one at his appearance and another at his vanishing. Why isn't that at least as good a description as the one I gave, on which the several segments are all parts of one time traveler?

I answer that what unites the stages (or segments) of a time traveler is the same sort of mental, or mostly mental, continuity and connectedness that unites anyone else. The only difference is that whereas a common person is connected and continuous with respect to external time, the time traveler is connected and continuous only with respect to his own personal time. Taking the stages in order, mental (and bodily) change is mostly gradual rather than sudden, and at no point is there sudden change in too many different respects all at once. (We can include position in external time among the respects we keep track of, if we like. It may change discontinuously with respect to personal time if not too much else changes discontinuously along with it.) Moreover, there is not too much change altogether. Plenty of traits and traces last a lifetime. Finally, the connectedness and the continuity are not accidental. They are explicable; and further, they are explained by the fact that the properties of each stage depend causally on those of the stages just before in personal time the dependence being such as tends to keep things the same.[4]

To see the purpose of my final requirement of causal continuity, let us see how it excludes a case of counterfeit time travel. Fred was created out of thin air, as if in the midst of life; he lived a while, then died. He was created by a demon, and the demon had chosen at random what Fred was to be like at the moment of his creation. Much later someone else, Sam, came to resemble Fred as he was when first created. At the very moment when the resemblance became perfect, the demon destroyed Sam. Fred and Sam together are very much like a single person: a time traveler whose personal time starts at Sam's birth, goes on to Sam's destruction and Fred's creation, and goes on from there to Fred's death. Taken in this order, the stages of Fred-*cum*-Sam have the proper connectedness and continuity. But they lack causal continuity, so Fred-*cum*-Sam is not one person and not a time traveler. Perhaps it was pure coincidence that Fred at his creation and Sam at his destruction were exactly alike; then the connectedness and continuity of Fred-*cum*-Sam across the crucial point are accidental. Perhaps instead the demon remembered what Fred was like, guided Sam toward perfect resemblance, watched his progress, and destroyed him at the right moment. Then the connectedness and continuity of Fred-*cum*-Sam has a causal explanation, but of the wrong sort. Either way, Fred's first stages do not depend causally for their properties on Sam's last stages. So the case of Fred and Sam is rightly disqualified as a case of personal identity and as a case of time travel.

We might expect that when a time traveler visits the past there will be reversals of causation. You may punch his face before he leaves, causing his eye to blacken centuries ago. Indeed, travel into the past necessarily involves reversed causation. For time travel requires personal identity – he who arrives must be the same person who departed. That requires causal continuity, in which causation runs from earlier to later stages in the order of personal time. But the orders of personal and external time disagree at some point, and there we have causation that runs from later to earlier stages in the order of external time. Elsewhere I have given an analysis of causation in terms of chains of counterfactual dependence, and I took care that my analysis would not rule out causal reversal *a priori*.[5] I think I can argue (but not here) that under my analysis the direction of counterfactual dependence and causation is governed by the direction of other *de facto* asymmetries of time. If so, then reversed causation and time travel are not excluded altogether, but can occur only where there are local exceptions to these asymmetries. As I said at the outset, the time traveler's world would be a most strange one.

Stranger still, if there are local – but only local – causal reversals, then there may also be causal loops: closed causal chains in which some of the causal links are normal in direction and others are reversed. (Perhaps there must be loops if there is reversal; I am not sure.) Each event on the loop has a causal explanation, being caused by events elsewhere on the loop. That is not to say that the loop as a whole is caused or explicable. It may not be. Its inexplicability is especially remarkable if it is made up of the sort of causal processes that transmit information. Recall the time traveler who talked to himself. He talked to himself about time travel, and in the course of the conversation his older self told his younger self how to build a time machine. That information was available in no other way. His older self knew how because his younger self had been told and the information had been preserved by the causal processes that constitute recording, storage, and retrieval of memory traces. His younger self knew, after the conversation, because his older self had known and the information had been preserved by the causal processes that constitute telling. But where did the information come from in the first place? Why did the whole affair happen? There is simply no answer. The parts of the loop are explicable, the whole of it is not. Strange! But not impossible, and not too different from inexplicabilities we are already inured to. Almost everyone agrees that God, or the Big Bang, or the entire infinite past of the universe, or the decay of a tritium atom, is uncaused and inexplicable. Then if these are possible, why not also the inexplicable causal loops that arise in time travel?

I have committed a circularity in order not to talk about too much at once, and this is a good place to set it right. In explaining personal time, I presupposed that we were entitled to regard certain stages as comprising a single person. Then in explaining what united the stages into a single person, I presupposed that we were given a personal time order for them. The proper way to proceed is to define personhood and personal time simultaneously, as follows. Suppose given a pair of an aggregate of person-stages, regarded as a candidate for personhood, and an assignment of coordinates to those stages, regarded as a candidate for his personal time. Iff [6] the stages satisfy the conditions given in my circular explanation with respect to the assignment of coordinates, then both candidates succeed: the stages do comprise a person and the assignment is his personal time.

I have argued so far that what goes on in a time travel story may be a possible pattern of events in four-dimensional space-time with no extra time dimension; that it may be correct to regard the scattered stages of the alleged time traveler as comprising a single person; and that we may legitimately assign to those stages and their surroundings a personal time order that disagrees sometimes with their order in external time. Some might concede all this, but protest that the impossibility of time travel is revealed after all when we ask not what the time traveler *does*, but what he *could do*. Could a time traveler change the past? It seems not: the events of a past moment could no more change than numbers could. Yet it seems that he would be as able as anyone to do things that would change the past if he did them. If a time traveler visiting the past both could and couldn't do something that would change it, then there cannot possibly be such a time traveler.

Consider Tim. He detests his grandfather, whose success in the munitions trade built the family fortune that paid for Tim's time machine. Tim would like nothing so much as to kill Grandfather, but alas he is too late. Grandfather died in his bed in 1957, while Tim was a young boy. But when Tim has built his time machine and traveled to 1920, suddenly he realizes that he is not too late after all. He buys a rifle; he spends long hours in target practice; he shadows Grandfather to learn the route of his daily walk to the munitions works; he rents a room along the route; and there he lurks, one winter day in 1921, rifle loaded, hate in his heart, as Grandfather walks closer, closer, . . .

Tim can kill Grandfather. He has what it takes. Conditions are perfect in every way: the best rifle money could buy, Grandfather an easy target only twenty yards away, not a breeze, door securely locked against intruders, Tim a good shot to begin with and now at the peak of training, and so on. What's to stop him? The forces of logic will not stay his hand! No powerful chaperone stands by to defend the past from interference. (To imagine such a chaperone, as some authors do, is a boring evasion, not needed to make Tim's story consistent.) In short, Tim is as much able to kill Grandfather as anyone ever is to kill anyone. Suppose that down the street another sniper, Tom, lurks waiting for another victim, Grandfather's partner. Tom is not a time traveler, but otherwise he is just like Tim: same make of rifle, same murderous intent, same everything. We can even suppose that Tom, like Tim, believes himself to be a time traveler. Someone has gone to a lot of trouble to deceive Tom into thinking so. There's no doubt that Tom can kill his victim; and Tim has everything going for him that Tom does. By any ordinary standards of ability, Tim can kill Grandfather.

Tim cannot kill grandfather. Grandfather lived, so to kill him would be to change the past. But the events of a past moment are not subdivisible into temporal parts and therefore cannot change. Either the events of 1921 timelessly do include Tim's killing of Grandfather, or else they timelessly don't. We may be tempted to speak of the "original" 1921 that lies in Tim's personal past, many years before his birth, in which Grandfather lived; and of the "new" 1921 in which Tim now finds himself waiting in ambush to kill Grandfather. But if we do speak so, we merely confer two names on one thing. The events of 1921 are doubly located in Tim's (extended) personal time, like the trestle on the railway, but the "original" 1921 and the "new" 1921 are one and the same. If Tim did not kill Grandfather in the "original" 1921, then if he does kill Grandfather in the "new" 1921, he must both kill and not kill Grandfather in 1921 – in the one and only 1921, which is both the "new" and the "original" 1921. It is logically impossible that Tim should change the past by killing Grandfather in 1921. So Tim cannot kill Grandfather.

Not that past moments are special; no more can anyone change the present or the future. Present and future momentary events no more have temporal parts than past ones do. You cannot change a present or future event from what it was originally to what it is after you change it. What you *can* do is to change the present or the future from the unactualized way they would have been without some action of yours to the way they actually are. But that is not an actual change: not a difference between two successive actualities. And Tim can certainly do as much; he changes the past from the unactualized way it would have been without him to the one and only way it actually is. To "change" the past in this way, Tim need not do anything momentous; it is enough just to be there, however unobtrusively.

You know, of course, roughly how the story of Tim must go on if it is to be consistent: he somehow fails. Since Tim didn't kill Grandfather in the "original" 1921, consistency demands that neither does he kill Grandfather in the "new" 1921. Why not? For some commonplace reason. Perhaps some noise distracts him at the last moment, perhaps he misses despite all his target practice, perhaps his nerve fails, perhaps he even feels a pang of unaccustomed mercy. His failure by no means proves that he was not really able to kill Grandfather. We often try and fail to do what we are able to do. Success at some tasks requires not only ability but also luck, and lack of luck is not a temporary lack of ability. Suppose our other sniper, Tom, fails to kill Grandfather's partner for the same reason, whatever it is, that Tim fails to kill Grandfather. It does not follow that Tom was unable to. No more does it follow in Tim's case that he was unable to do what he did not succeed in doing.

We have this seeming contradiction: "*Tim doesn't, but can, because he has what it takes*" versus "*Tim doesn't, and can't, because it's logically impossible to change the past.*" I reply that there is no contradiction. Both conclusions are true, and for the reasons given. They are compatible because "can" is equivocal.

To say that something can happen means that its happening is compossible with certain facts. *Which* facts? That is determined, but sometimes not determined well enough, by context. An ape can't speak a human language – say, Finnish – but I can. Facts about the anatomy and operation of the ape's larynx and nervous system are not compossible with his speaking Finnish. The corresponding facts about my larynx and nervous system are compossible with my speaking Finnish. But don't take me along to Helsinki as your interpreter: I can't speak Finnish. My speaking Finnish is compossible with the facts considered so far, but not with further facts about my lack of training. What I can do, relative to one set of facts, I cannot do, relative to another, more inclusive, set. Whenever the context leaves it open which facts are to count as relevant, it is possible to equivocate about whether I can speak Finnish. It is likewise possible to equivocate about whether it is possible for me to speak Finnish, or whether I am able to, or whether I have the ability or capacity or power or potentiality to. Our many words for much the same thing are little help since they do not seem to correspond to different fixed delineations of the relevant facts.

Tim's killing Grandfather that day in 1921 is compossible with a fairly rich set of facts: the facts about his rifle, his skill and training, the unobstructed line of fire, the locked door and the absence of any chaperone to defend the past, and so on. Indeed it is compossible with all the facts of the sorts we would ordinarily count as relevant in saying what someone can do. It is compossible with all the facts corresponding to those we deem relevant in Tom's case. Relative to these facts, Tim can kill Grandfather. But his killing Grandfather is not compossible with another, more inclusive set of facts. There is the simple fact that Grandfather was not killed. Also there are various other facts about Grandfather's doings after 1921 and their effects: Grandfather begat Father in 1922 and Father begat Tim in 1949. Relative to these facts, Tim cannot kill Grandfather. He can and he can't, but under different delineations of the relevant facts. You can reasonably choose the narrower delineation, and say that he can; or the wider delineation, and say that he can't. But choose. What you mustn't do is waver, say in the same breath that he both can and can't, and then claim that this contradiction proves that time travel is impossible.

Exactly the same goes for Tom's parallel failure. For Tom to kill Grandfather's partner also is compossible with all facts of the sorts we ordinarily count as relevant, but not compossible with a larger set including, for instance, the fact that the intended victim lived until 1934. In Tom's case we are not puzzled. We say without hesitation that he can do it, because we see at once that the facts that are not compossible with his success are facts about the future of the time in question and therefore not the sort of facts we count as relevant in saying what Tom can do.

In Tim's case it is harder to keep track of which facts are relevant. We are accustomed to exclude facts about the future of the time in question, but to include some facts about its past. Our standards do not apply unequivocally to the crucial facts in this special case: Tim's failure, Grandfather's survival, and his subsequent doings. If we have foremost in mind that they lie in the external future of that moment in 1921 when Tim is almost ready to shoot, then we exclude them just as we exclude the parallel facts in Tom's case. But if we have foremost in mind that they precede that moment in Tim's extended personal time, then we tend to include them. To make the latter be foremost in your mind, I chose to tell Tim's story in the order of his personal time, rather than in the order of external time. The fact of Grandfather's survival until 1957 had already been told before I got to the part of the story about Tim lurking in ambush to kill him in 1921. We must decide, if we can, whether to treat these personally past and externally future facts as if they were straightforwardly past or as if they were straightforwardly future.

Fatalists – the best of them – are philosophers who take facts we count as irrelevant in saying what someone can do, disguise them somehow as facts of a different sort that we count as relevant, and thereby argue that we can do less than we think – indeed, that there is nothing at all that we don't do but can. I am not going to vote Republican next fall. The fatalist argues that, strange to say, I not only won't but can't; for my voting Republican is not compossible with the fact that it was true already in the year 1548 that I was not going to vote Republican 428 years later. My rejoinder is that this is a fact, sure enough; however, it is an irrelevant fact about the future masquerading as a relevant fact about the past, and so should be left out of account in saying what, in any ordinary sense, I can do. We are unlikely to be fooled by the fatalist's methods of disguise in this case, or other ordinary cases. But in cases of time travel, precognition, or the like, we're on less familiar ground, so it may take less of a disguise to fool us. Also, new methods of disguise are available, thanks to the device of personal time.

Here's another bit of fatalist trickery. Tim, as he lurks, already knows that he will fail. At least he has the wherewithal to know it if he thinks, he knows it implicitly. For he remembers that Grandfather was alive when he was a boy, he knows that those who are killed are thereafter not alive, he knows (let us suppose) that he is a time traveler who has reached the same 1921 that lies in his personal past, and he ought to understand – as we do – why a time traveler cannot change the past. What is known cannot be false. So his success is not only not compossible with facts that belong to the external future and his personal past, but also is not compossible with the present fact of his knowledge that he will fail. I reply that the fact of his foreknowledge, at the moment while he waits to shoot, is not a fact entirely about that moment. It may be divided into two parts. There is the fact that he then believes (perhaps only implicitly) that he will fail; and there is the further fact that his belief is correct, and correct not at all by accident, and hence qualifies as an item of knowledge. It is only the latter fact that is not compossible with his success, but it is only the former that is entirely about the moment in question. In calling Tim's state at that moment knowledge, not just belief, facts about personally earlier but externally later moments were smuggled into consideration.

I have argued that Tim's case and Tom's are alike, except that in Tim's case we are more tempted than usual – and with reason – to opt for a semi-fatalist mode of speech. But perhaps they differ in another way. In Tom's case, we can expect a perfectly consistent answer to the counterfactual question: what if Tom had killed Grandfather's partner? Tim's case is more difficult. If Tim had killed Grandfather, it seems offhand that contradictions would have been true. The killing both would and wouldn't have occurred. No Grandfather, no Father; no Father, no Tim; no Tim, no killing. And for good measure: no Grandfather, no family fortune; no fortune, no time machine; no time machine, no killing. So the supposition that Tim killed Grandfather seems impossible in more than the semi-fatalistic sense already granted.

If you suppose Tim to kill Grandfather and hold all the rest of his story fixed, of course you get a contradiction. But likewise if you suppose Tom to kill Grandfather's partner and hold the rest of his story fixed – including the part that told of his failure – you get a contradiction. If you make *any* counterfactual supposition and hold all else fixed you get a contradiction. The thing to do is rather to make the counterfactual supposition and hold all else as close to fixed as you consistently can. That procedure will yield perfectly consistent answers to the question: what if Tim had not killed Grandfather? In that case, some of the story I told would not have been true. Perhaps Tim might have been the time-traveling grandson of someone else. Perhaps he might have been the grandson of a man killed in 1921 and miraculously resurrected. Perhaps he might have been not a time traveler at all, but rather someone created out of nothing in 1920 equipped with false memories of a personal past that never was. It is hard to say what is the least revision of Tim's story to make it true that Tim kills Grandfather, but certainly the contradictory story in which the killing both does and doesn't occur is not the least revision. Hence it is false (according to the unrevised story) that if Tim had killed Grandfather then contradictions would have been true.

What difference would it make if Tim travels in branching time? Suppose that at the possible world of Tim's story the space-time manifold branches; the branches are separated not in time, and not in space, but in some other way. Tim travels not only in time but also from one branch to another. In one branch Tim is absent from the events of 1921; Grandfather lives. Tim is born, grows up, and vanishes in his time machine. The other branch diverges from the first when Tim turns up in 1921; there Tim kills Grandfather and Grandfather leaves no descendants and no fortune; the events of the two branches differ more and more from that time on. Certainly this is a consistent story; it is a story in which Grandfather both is and isn't killed in 1921 (in the different branches); and it is a story in which Tim, by killing Grandfather, succeeds in preventing his own birth (in one of the branches). But it is not a story in which Tim's killing of Grandfather both does occur and doesn't: it simply does, though it is located in one branch and not in the other. And it is not a story in which Tim changes the past. 1921 and later years contain the events of both branches, coexisting somehow without interaction. It remains true at all the personal times of Tim's life, even after the killing, that Grandfather lives in one branch and dies in the other.[7]

Notes

1   I have particularly in mind two of the time travel stories of Robert A. Heinlein: "By His Bootstraps," in R. A. Heinlein, *The Menace from Earth* (Hicksville, N.Y., 1959), and "– All You Zombies –," in R. A. Heinlein, *The Unpleasant Profession of Jonathan Hoag* (Hicksville, N.Y., 1959).

2   Accounts of time travel in two-dimensional time are found in Jack W. Meiland, "A Two-Dimensional Passage Model of Time for Time Travel," *Philosophical Studies,* vol. 26 (1974), pp. 153–73; and in the initial chapters of Isaac Asimov, *The End of Eternity* (Garden City, N.Y., 1955). Asimov's denouement, however, seems to require some different conception of time travel.

3   H. G. Wells, *The Time Machine, An Invention* (London 1895), epilogue. The passage is criticized as contradictory in Donald C. Williams, "The Myth of Passage," *The Journal of Philosophy,* vol. 48 (1951), p. 463.

4   I discuss the relation between personal identity and mental connectedness and continuity at greater length in "Survival and Identity," in *The Identities of Persons,* ed. Amélie Rorty (Berkeley and Los Angeles, 1976).

5   "Causation," *The Journal of Philosophy,* vol. 70 (1973), pp. 556–67; the analysis relies on the analysis of counterfactuals given in my *Counterfactuals* (Oxford, 1973).

6   "Iff" is short for "if and only if". – [Eds]

7   The present paper summarizes a series of lectures of the same title, given as the Gavin David Young Lectures in Philosophy at the University of Adelaide in July, 1971. I thank the Australian–American Educational Foundation and the American Council of Learned Societies for research support. I am grateful to many friends for comments on earlier versions of this paper; especially Philip Kitcher, William Newton-Smith, J. J. C. Smart, and Donald Williams.

Notes

D How do Things Persist through Changes of Parts and Properties?

Introduction

To the question, How do things persist through changes of parts?, the authors of the Port-Royal Logic answer: They don't! They defend "mereological essentialism": the thesis that nothing can survive the gain or loss of any parts. Eric Olson explains how an ancient puzzle, "The Paradox of Increase," could well drive one to adopt this extreme view; and he considers the range of alternative metaphysical theories about persistence through time that are generated by attempts to solve the paradox. One such theory is a doctrine known as "the metaphysics of temporal parts." It is advocated in the excerpts from W. V. O. Quine and David Lewis. Their position, unlike mereological essentialism, can easily allow for change of parts over time. But many philosophers, including Olson, find the view hard to swallow (Olson raises a battery of objections to temporal parts in section 11 of Ch. 25). In "The Problem of Temporary

Intrinsics," Lewis argues that only the metaphysics of temporal parts is compatible with the fact that things change in their intrinsic properties. Zimmerman, on the other hand, points out that a presentist (like Prior; see Chs. 12, 13, and 16) has no problem of temporary intrinsics; and he argues that Lewis is wrong to say presentism "goes against what we all believe."

The essays of this section are closely related to Chs. 35–9 in Part II, section A. In Ch. 25, Olson shows why philosophers might well be driven to extreme views like those of Chisholm (Ch. 35) and Swinburne (Ch. 39).

Suggestions for further reading

Armstrong, D. M., *Universals: An Opinionated Introduction* (Boulder, Col.: Westview Press, 1989) pp. 2–4.

Aune, Bruce, *Metaphysics: The Elements* (Minneapolis: University of Minnesota, 1985) ch. 5 ("Changing Things").

Carter, William R., *The Elements of Metaphysics* (Philadelphia, Penn.: Temple University Press, 1990) chs. 5 and 6 ("Parts and Wholes" and "Change").

Hales, Stephen, *Metaphysics: Contemporary Readings* (Belmont, Cal.: Wadsworth, 1998) Section 10 ("Mereology").

Hawthorne, John, "Three-Dimensionalism vs. Four-Dimensionalism," in Sider, Hawthorne, and Zimmerman (eds.), *Contemporary Debates in Metaphysics* (Malden, Mass.: Blackwell, 2007).

Jubien, Michael, *Contemporary Metaphysics* (Oxford: Blackwell, 1997) chs. 4 and 9 ("Identity" and "Things and Their Parts").

Loux, Michael, *Metaphysics: A Contemporary Introduction*, 2nd edn (London: Routledge, 2002) ch. 6 ("Concrete Particulars II – Persistence Through Time").

Markosian, Ned, "Restricted Composition," in Sider, Hawthorne, and Zimmerman (eds.), *Contemporary Debates in Metaphysics* (Malden, Mass.: Blackwell, 2007).

Sider, Theodore, "Temporal Parts," in Sider, Hawthorne, and Zimmerman (eds.), *Contemporary Debates in Metaphysics* (Malden, Mass.: Blackwell, 2007).

Smith, Quentin, and Oaklander, L. Nathan, *Time, Change and Freedom: an Introduction to Metaphysics* (London: Routledge, 1995) Dialogue 5 ("The Problem of Change").

Taylor, Richard, *Metaphysics*, 4th edn (Englewood Cliffs, N.J.: Prentice-Hall, 1992) ch. 7 ("Space and Time").

Van Cleve, James, "The Moon and Sixpence: A Defense of Mereological Universalism," in Sider, Hawthorne, and Zimmerman (eds.), *Contemporary Debates in Metaphysics* (Malden, Mass.: Blackwell, 2007).

van Inwagen, Peter, *Metaphysics*, 2nd edn (Cambridge, Mass.: Westview Press, 2002) pp. 169–71.

24 Of Confused Subjects Which Are Equivalent to Two Subjects: an Excerpt from *The Port-Royal Logic*

Antoine Arnauld and Pierre Nicole

It is important, in order to understand better the nature of what is called the subject in propositions, to add here a remark which has been made in more important works than this, but which, since it belongs to logic, may find a place here.

It is, that when two or more things which have some resemblance succeed each other in the same place, and, principally, when there does not appear any obtrusive difference between them, although men may distinguish them in speaking metaphysically, they nevertheless do not distinguish them in their ordinary speech; but, embracing them under a common idea, which does not exhibit the difference, and denotes only what they have in common, they speak of them as if they were the same thing.

Thus, though we change the air every moment, nevertheless we consider the air which surrounds us as being always the same; and we say that from being cold it has become warm, as if it were the same, whereas, often that air which we feel cold is not the same as that which we find warm.

This water, we also say, in speaking of a river, was turbid two days ago, and, behold, now it is clear as crystal; while it is impossible it could be the same water. *In idem flumen* (says Seneca), *bis non descendimus, manet idem fluminis nomen, aqua transmissa est.*[1] [*Epistolæ*, lviii.]

We consider the bodies of animals, and speak of them, as being always the same, though we are assured, that at the end of a few years there remains no part of the matter which at first composed them; and not only do we speak of them as the same body, without considering what we say, but we do so also when we reflect expressly on the subject. For common language allows us to say, – *The body of this animal was composed ten years ago of certain parts of matter, and now it is composed of parts altogether different.* There appears to be some contradiction in speaking thus; for if the parts were altogether different, then is it not the same body. This is true; but we speak of it, nevertheless, as the same body. And what renders these propositions true is, that the same term is taken for different subjects in this different application.

Augustus said that he had found the city of Rome of brick, and had left it of marble. In the same way we say of a town, of a mansion, of a church, that it was destroyed at such a time, and rebuilt at such another time. What then is this *Rome*, which was at one time of brick, and at another time of marble? What are these towns, these mansions, and churches, which are destroyed at one time, and rebuilt at another? Is the *Rome* of brick the same as the *Rome* of marble? No;

but the mind, nevertheless, forms to itself a certain confused idea of *Rome*, to which it attributes these two qualities – being of brick at one time, and of marble at another. And when it afterwards forms propositions about it, and says, for example, that *Rome*, which was brick before the time of Augustus, was marble when he died, – the word Rome, which appears to be only one subject, denotes, nevertheless, two, which are really distinct, but united under the confused idea of Rome, which prevents the mind from perceiving the distinction of these subjects.

It is in this way that we have cleared up, in the work[2] whence we have borrowed this remark, the affected perplexity which the (Calvinist) ministers delight to find in that proposition – *This is my body*, which no one would ever find, following the light of common sense. For, as we should never say that it was a proposition very perplexed, and very difficult to be understood, if we said of a church which had been burned and rebuilt – *This church was built ten years ago, and has been rebuilt in a twelvemonth*; in the same way, we could not reasonably say there was any difficulty in understanding this proposition, – *That which is bread at this moment is my body at this other moment.* It is true that it is not the same *this* in these different moments, as the burned church and the rebuilt church are not really the same church; but the mind conceiving the bread and the body of Jesus Christ under the common idea of a present object, which it expresses by *this*, attributes to that object, which is really twofold, and only a unity of confusion, the being bread at one moment, and the body of Jesus Christ at another, just as, having formed of that church burned and rebuilt, the common idea of a church, it gives to that confused idea two attributes, which cannot belong to the same subject.

Hence it follows that, taken in the sense of the Catholics, there is no difficulty in the proposition, *This is my body*, since it is only an abridgment of this other proposition, which is perfectly clear, – *That which is bread at this moment is my body at this other moment* – and since the mind supplies all that is not expressed. For as we have remarked at the end of the First Part, when we use the demonstrative pronoun *hoc* to denote something which is presented to our senses, the precise idea formed by the pronoun remaining confused, the mind adds thereto the clear and distinct ideas obtained from the senses, in the form of an incidental proposition. Thus, when Jesus Christ pronounced the word *this*, the minds of the apostles added to it, *which is bread*, and as they conceived that it was bread at that moment, they made also the addition of time, and thus the word *this* formed also this idea, – *This which is bread at this moment.* In the same way, when Christ said *that it was his body*, they conceived that *this was his body at that moment.* Thus the expression, *This is my body*, formed in them that total proposition, *This which is bread at this moment is my body at this other moment*, and the expression being clear, an abridgment of the proposition which diminishes nothing of the idea, is so also.

And as to the difficulty proposed by the ministers, that the same thing cannot be bread and the body of Jesus Christ, since it belongs equally to the extended proposition – *This which is bread at this moment is my body at this other moment* – and to the abridged proposition – *This is my body*; it is clear that this is no better than a frivolous wrangling, which might be alleged equally against these propositions – *This church was burned at such a time, and rebuilt at such another time*. They must all be disintricated, through this way of conceiving many separate subjects under a single idea, which occasions the same term to be taken sometimes for one subject and sometimes for another, while the mind does not perceive this transition from one subject to another.

After all, we do not here profess to decide the important question touching the way in which we ought to understand these words – *This is my body* – whether in a figurative or in a literal sense; for it is not enough to show that a proposition *may* be taken in a certain sense, it ought to be further proved that it *must* be so taken. But as there are some ministers who, on the principles of a false logic, obstinately maintain that the words of Jesus Christ cannot bear the catholic sense, it is not out of place to show here, briefly, that the catholic sense has in it nothing but what is clear, reasonable, and conformed to the common language of all mankind.

Notes

1 "We do not go into the same river twice; the name of the river remains the same, but the water has passed by."
2 *Traité de la Perpétuité de la Foi*, by Arnauld and Nicole (Paris, 1672).

---

25 The Paradox of Increase

Eric T. Olson

1.

It seems evident that things sometimes get bigger by acquiring new parts. But there is an ancient argument purporting to show that this is impossible: the paradox of increase or growing argument.[1]

Here is a sketch of the paradox. Suppose we have an object A, and we want to make it bigger by adding a part, B. That is, we want to bring it about that A first lacks and then has B as a part. Imagine, then, that we conjoin B to A in some appropriate way. Never mind what A and B are, or what this conjoining amounts to: let A be anything that can gain a part if anything *can* gain a part, and let B be the sort of thing that can become a part of A, and suppose we do whatever it would take to make B come to be a part of A if this is possible at all. Have we thereby made B a part of A?

It seems not. We seem only to have brought it about that B is attached to A, like this:

before: [A] [B]   after: [A | B]

Figure 1

We have rearranged A's surroundings by giving it a new neighbor, but we haven't given it a new part. If A has come to be a part of anything, it is the thing made up of A and B after our conjoining. But that thing didn't gain any new parts either. It didn't exist at all when we started: our conjoining B to A brought it into existence. Or if it did exist at the outset, it already had B as a part then and we merely changed it from a disconnected or "scattered" object (like an archipelago) to a connected one.

So we have failed to give A a new part. And since this reasoning makes no assumptions about the nature of A or B or the manner in which we conjoined them, it seems to follow that nothing could ever increase in size by gaining a new part. The very idea of growth by addition of parts is incoherent.

Now I believe that some things can grow by acquiring parts; but it takes a good deal of controversial metaphysics to show how they can. The paradox of increase really is a paradox: its conclusion is more or less incredible, yet we cannot resist it without accepting something that looks nearly as bad. I begin by discussing some of the paradox's implications (§§2–5). I then state it in a more careful way that makes its premises explicit (§6). The remainder of the paper asks what it would take to solve it (§§7–12).

2.

If the paradox of increase prevents anything from growing by gaining parts, a similar argument – running the paradox of increase in reverse – is likely to rule out a thing's shrinking by losing parts. Suppose we want to make an object X – anything at all – smaller by removing a part, Y. That is, we want to bring it about that X first has and then lacks Y as a part. Imagine, then, that we detach Y from X in some appropriate way: let us do whatever would bring it about that Y ceases to be a part of X if X can ever lose a part and carry on without it. Have we thereby made it the case that X no longer has Y as a part? Have we made X smaller? It seems not. X starts out made up of Y and something else – "the rest of X", which I shall call Z – like this:

before: [Z | Y]   after: [Z]   [Y]
              X   X?

Figure 2

Afterwards Y is no longer attached to Z. But what has happened to X? It doesn't seem to exist any longer; or if it does still exist, it still has Y as a part, and we have merely changed it from a connected object to a scattered one. Either way, it doesn't get any smaller by losing a part. And of course Y and Z don't lose any parts either. It seems that nothing we can do would ever make anything smaller than it was before by virtue of having lost a part.

This is the amputation paradox or shrinking argument.[2] Like the growing argument, it assumes nothing about the nature of X or Y or the manner in which Y is detached. So it threatens to show that nothing could ever lose a part: the very idea of shrinking by losing parts is incoherent.

These arguments purport to rule out a thing's growing by gaining a part or shrinking by losing one. If they are sound, it is hard to see how anything could exchange an old part for a new one without shrinking or growing either. So they suggest the general conclusion that nothing can have different parts at different times: it is absolutely impossible for anything to have a certain part at one time and exist without having that thing as a part at another time. Nothing can change any of its parts. If a thing has such and such parts, this must be a permanent and unchangeable feature of it. Call this the *doctrine of mereological constancy*:

> Necessarily, if x is a part of y at some time, then x is part of y at every time when y exists.

Let us not confuse mereological constancy with the better-known doctrine of *mereological essentialism*, that things have their parts essentially. We might state it like this:

> If x is a part of y at some time, then necessarily x is a part of y at every time when y exists.

Mereological essentialism entails mereological constancy but not vice versa. Suppose P is now a part of me. Mereological essentialism says that it is necessary that I have P as a part at every time when I exist. That of course rules out my having P as a part at one time and lacking it at another time. But the impossibility of my having P as a part at one time and lacking it at another would not rule out my existing without ever having P as a part. It might be possible for me to have had different parts all along, even I cannot *change* my parts. My having a certain part might be an unchangeable but contingent feature of me. Having a certain part might be like having a certain birthplace. I can't change my birthplace: it couldn't be the case that my birthplace was Aberdeen during my first twenty years and Karachi afterwards. But I could have had a different birthplace from the start: I might have been born in Karachi.

That said, those who hold mereological constancy are likely to hold mereological essentialism as well. It is easy enough to construct modal versions of the growing and shrinking arguments: just replace the words 'before' and 'after' in the diagrams with 'actual' and 'possible'. We might think that X could have been smaller at some time by lacking a part, Y. But if we try to imagine X without Y as a part, we only get a scenario in which Z – the rest of X – is not attached to Y. X itself doesn't exist in this possible situation; or if it does, it still has Y as a part and is merely a scattered object instead of a connected one. So we haven't imagined anything as being smaller than it actually is. The very idea that a thing might have lacked a part that it actually has (or have had a part that it actually lacks) is incoherent. Or at least this seems to be so if growing and shrinking are impossible.

We will revisit the modal argument in §11. Let us return now to mereological constancy.

3.

What would it mean if mereological constancy were true? Its consequences appear to be shattering. Change a spoke on your bicycle and the result is a numerically different bike from the one you began with. For that matter, you get a new bike whenever so much as a single atom falls off. Given the rate at which bicycles shed atoms, this would mean that you can't ride the same bicycle twice.

We may not lose sleep over the identity of bicycles. Some things, though, mean more to us. Consider your mother. She is made up at least partly of atoms: many atoms are parts of her. (Or maybe she is made up of perceptions – mental states and events – as Hume suggested. It makes no difference for our purposes. Suppose she is made of atoms.) Owing to metabolic turnover, those atoms are constantly coming and going. If mereological constancy is true, the being we now call "your mother" is not the being we called your mother a moment ago, or the being who will answer to that description a moment hence. The being we now call your mother cannot be the being we called your mother a moment ago because she has parts now that were not parts, a moment ago, of the being we called your mother then. Thus, according to mereological constancy, what appears to be a persisting human being is in reality a series of numerically different beings, succeeding one another at a rate of trillions per second.

What happens to your mother, then, when her metabolic processes assimilate or expel an atom? Mereological constancy does not answer this question – or it gives at best a partial answer, namely that she doesn't gain or lose any parts. That doesn't tell us what happens to your mother because it doesn't tell us whether the atoms she assimilates were parts of her before she assimilated them as well as afterwards; nor does it tell us whether the atoms she sheds thereby cease to be parts of her.

Suppose your mother's atoms don't remain parts of her when they are expelled, and likewise that no atom is a part of her before her metabolism assimilates it. Then according to mereological constancy your mother – or the being we now call your mother – exists for only as long as all her current atoms remain caught up in her metabolism: not long at all. As soon as she sheds an atom, she perishes and is instantly replaced by someone else: a being very like the woman who existed a moment earlier – so much like her that no one could ever tell the difference – but numerically different because she has different parts.

What if your mother's atoms do remain parts of her when her metabolism expels them, and were already parts of her before she took them in? In that case she presumably continues to exist for as long as her atoms exist, no matter how those atoms come to be arranged. (If your mother's atoms remain parts of her even when they are scattered to the four winds, it is hard to see what *could* cause them to cease to be parts of her, short of annihilating them.) So the being we now call your mother survives the expulsion of an atom, and merely charges thereby from a connected object to a scattered one. She begins to disperse. In a few years' time, when all her current atoms have been expelled, she will be scattered thinly across the biosphere. She was similarly scattered in the past. She has existed for billions of years. She has spent most of her career as a nondescript and highly rarefied cloud of interstellar dust. Much later she became confined to the earth, and at one point she coalesced into human form – but not for long, for she will begin almost instantly to disperse once more. She will then immediately be replaced by a numerically different maternal being, just as she is according to the first story (where she perishes when she expels an atom). The difference is that on the second story the beings that successively bear your mother's name exist before and after they take on human form, whereas on the first story they exist only for the brief moment when they are human.

Either way, nothing persists as a human being for more than a moment. You can't shake hands with the same person twice. The same goes for all ordinary objects. They come and go in a flash. Ours is a Heraclitean world of constant flux, where nothing persists, save perhaps tiny particles and "masses of matter" which never change their parts.

This seems incredible. A great many of our beliefs imply that people and bicycles not only persist but remain people or bicycles for many years. I believe, for instance, that I was once smaller than I am now, and that I have a mother, and that I am married. For that matter, I believe that I am the person who began writing this sentence a moment ago. None of these things could be true if I existed as a human being for only a moment.

Nor are beliefs of this sort mere intellectual speculations. They are some of our deepest convictions. Important practical attitudes and social institutions depend on them. Take moral responsibility: you can be responsible for an action only if you did it (or you at least had some hand in its doing). If we don't persist as human agents, then no one is ever responsible for anything, for by the time any action is done those who did it no longer exist, or at any rate are no longer the sort of beings that can be responsible for anything. Or promising: why keep a promise when both the promiser and the promisee have long since passed away? Or prudence: why save for my retirement if I am never going to retire, and the old men who benefit will all be someone else? Come to that, why do anything? Nothing I do is ever going to benefit *me*. The only possible reason for acting would seem to be the altruistic wish to benefit future generations.

4.

The doctrine of mereological constancy looks hard to live with. Most of us will reject it out of hand, and assume that the reasoning leading to it is therefore mistaken. We will see the paradox of increase in the way that we see Zeno's paradoxes: we know that things can change their parts, just as we know that things can move; the only question is how. But not all philosophers find mereological constancy troubling. Some argue that it is not as bad as it seems. We know how good philosophers can be at making seemingly absurd claims appear respectable. Let us see how they might defend mereological constancy.

Some philosophers say that despite appearances none of the things we say and do when engaged in the ordinary business of life assert or imply or presuppose that anything persists through time. Everything we ordinarily say and do is therefore entirely compatible with mereological constancy. That doctrine may conflict with things we say in philosophy seminars, but it doesn't conflict with the ordinary beliefs that really matter. Call this the *revisionary proposal*.[3] (It is an interesting fact that no one ever responds to Zeno's paradoxes in this way. No one says, "Yes, motion is impossible, but that's nothing to worry about. Despite appearances, none of the things we say and do when engaged in the ordinary business of life assert or imply or presuppose that anything moves.")

How could the things we say and do in ordinary life be compatible with mereological constancy? Suppose we say,

Judy was a schoolteacher in 1980 and is now retired.

This appears to assert that some one thing is both a schoolteacher in 1980 and retired now, which according to the doctrine of mereological constancy is false, given that no retiree now has all and only the parts that any schoolteacher had in 1980. But maybe it doesn't really assert this. Maybe it doesn't assert that anything persists at all. Perhaps when we say such things we are only speaking *as if* something persisted because that is a convenient way to talk. (You can imagine how inconvenient it would be if we had to call every new momentary object by a different name.) Maybe we are only doing what Hume called "feigning a continu'd being" (1978: 208).

How could this be? Well, consider this sentence:

The Prime Minister was a woman in 1980 and is now a man.

We wouldn't ordinarily use this to assert that some one thing is both a woman in 1980 and a man now. If we are using the language of identity over time when we say this, we are using it loosely: all we *mean* is that a woman who existed in 1980 and a man who exists now relate to one another in some way other than identity – that they both hold the office of Prime Minister, to be precise, one in 1980 and one now. According to the revisionary proposal, in saying that Judy was a teacher in 1980 and is now retired, we are likewise saying only that a teacher of 1980 and a retiree who exists now relate to one another in some way other than identity.

This other relation might be something physical: some sort of spatiotemporal continuity, perhaps. Or it might be a kind of psychological continuity. Or maybe something else. The nature of this other relation, according to the revisionary proposal, is one of the subjects of the philosophy of personal identity. (The revisionary proposal suggests that what we call personal identity is not about the numerical identity of people at all, for the numerical identity of people is no different from the numerical identity of other composite objects, which given mereological constancy is a dull and dreary affair.) So the revisionary proposal has it that our claim about Judy is equivalent to something like this:

Judy is retired, and she is psychologically continuous with someone who was a schoolteacher in 1980,

which looks compatible with mereological constancy.

Of course, even if this right, it is only one example of an ordinary claim that appears to conflict with mereological constancy. It also seems to be true that there are people I have met twice. It won't be as easy to give an account of what this claim means that is compatible with mereological constancy as it is for the retired-schoolteacher case. But revisionists are resourceful people.

What about the practical attitudes and social institutions that seem to require people to persist through time – responsibility, promising, and so on? The revisionary proposal says that they are not based on numerical identity at all, but on some other relation. It might be some sort of psychological continuity: perhaps you are now responsible for the past actions of anyone who is then psychologically continuous with you as you are now, even if that person is not you but someone else. If anyone psychologically continuous with you once made a promise to someone, perhaps you are obliged to keep that promise to anyone who is now psychologically continuous with the promisee. Perhaps we couldn't care less what happens to *ourselves* tomorrow, or even whether we shall exist tomorrow at all; we care only about those who will be psychologically continuous with us tomorrow. Maybe your desire to live to see your great-grandchildren is in no way frustrated by the fact that by the time your great-grandchildren exist you will no longer be in a position to see or be aware of anything. According to the revisionary proposal it makes no practical difference at all if mereological constancy is true and we are all momentary beings.

5.

A second way of trying to make the doctrine of mereological constancy more attractive is to say that whatever dire implications it may have for composite objects, we ourselves are immune to them because we are not composite. We have no proper parts (no parts other than ourselves). We are mereologically simple. Thus, although material things may be fleeting, *we* still persist as we always thought. Call this the *reactionary proposal*.[4]

We could even use the paradox of increase to argue against materialism – the view that we are material things. The paradox implies that we could only be things that don't change their parts, since nothing can change its parts. But what *material* things that don't change their parts could we be? We might be momentary beings that exist only as long as their atoms remain in human form. Or we might be long-lived beings that are human for only a moment and spend most of their careers as rarefied clouds. Or maybe each of us might be a tiny physical particle (a view that Chisholm (1989) once defended). But despite what the revisionists may say, we cannot take these claims seriously. No *sensible* view about our nature is compatible with materialism. And if we are not material (even partly material), then we are immaterial. To put it another way: If we were anything other than immaterial things, we should have different parts at different times, which according to the paradox is impossible; so we are immaterial. The only account of our nature that is compatible with our having the careers we think we have is that we are immaterial.

I like this better than any of the traditional arguments against materialism. If there is a weakness in the inference from mereological constancy to our being immaterial, it is this. Consider those material things that, according to mereological constancy, take on human form for a moment before either passing away or gradually dispersing. Each of those beings has, for a moment at least, a working human brain and nervous system (perhaps longer than a moment if the atoms a thing sheds remain parts of it). It is surrounded by a community of thinkers and speakers. It has the same evolutionary history as we have. That sounds like it ought to suffice for these beings to have mental properties. They ought to be conscious and intelligent, just as we are, for as long as they remain in human form. The material object that is now human and sitting in your chair ought to be a subject of your current thoughts and sensations: it ought to think what you now think and feel what you now feel.

But if there are material beings thinking our thoughts, even if each one thinks for only a moment, there are unlikely to be *im*material beings thinking our thoughts as well. No one ever supposed that for each human person there is, at any moment, both an entirely material thing and an entirely immaterial thing, each bearing all the mental properties that the person has then. And if there is no immaterial thing thinking your thoughts, you cannot be an immaterial thing. (Surely we are not *un*thinking immaterial things.)

Those who say that you and I are immaterial will want to deny that any material things think our thoughts. But the argument from mereological constancy, by itself anyway, gives no grounds for such a denial. The fact that material things have careers very different from the ones we thought they have doesn't obviously rule out their being able to think while they are human. The argument implies that we are either immaterial things or material things with alien careers; but it doesn't say why we must choose the first alternative over the second. For that we should need a reason to suppose that the material things we should be if we are material things at all would lack the mental properties that we have.

Is there such a reason? It might seem impossible for a thing to think for only a billionth of a second. That just isn't long enough. (At any rate it isn't long enough for anything human to think given the laws of nature. Fast-paced beings for whom a second felt like a century feels to us might be able to think for a billionth of a second; but that is irrelevant to our situation.) Since no material thing would have more than a billionth of a second to think, given mereological constancy, it would follow that no material thing could think.

If this is true, the argument from mereological constancy to the falsity of materialism is on strong ground. As you might expect, however, it is disputed. Some say that even if no *isolated* being that existed for only a billionth of a second could think, a thing can think for any length of time – even for an instant – if it has the right causal antecedents (Sider 2001: 197f.). What something does for a moment might count as thinking in part because of what other beings do at earlier (and perhaps later) times, in something like the way that a tiny splotch of paint represents a window in part because of its position relative to other splotches of paint. What it is right to say here seems to me to be anyone's guess.[5]

6.

But do we really have to choose between the revisionary and reactionary proposals – between Heraclitus and Descartes? Must we accept that nothing can have different parts at different times?

The argument for this, or more precisely for the claim that nothing can grow by gaining a part, was that if we try to give A a new part, B, we shall only succeed in attaching something to A and changing its surroundings. Let us set out this reasoning in more detail. (I leave it as an exercise for the reader to do the same for the amputation paradox.)

Suppose for the sake of argument that conjoining B to A in some appropriate way *does* make it a part of A: A lacks B as a part before we attach it, and has it as a part afterwards. Suppose, that is, that A and B don't come to make up some new thing, as Figure 1 invites us to think, but rather that A comes to be made up of B and something else. Of course, that something else *appears* to be A: it is made of the same matter as A was a moment earlier (supposing that A is a material thing), and that matter is arranged in the same way. It differs from A as it was before only in its surroundings.[6] The fact that the thing B ends up attached to what appears to be A is what supports the claim that B never comes to be a part of A. But let us see if we can resist this conclusion. To avoid assuming the point at issue, call the thing that looks like A and ends up attached to B, C. Suppose, then, that when we coinjoin B to A we make it a part of A, so that A comes to be made up of B and C, like this:

Figure 3

Is this picture coherent? Well, let us ask where C came from. Where was it before we attached B? Presumably it existed then: conjoining B to A didn't bring C into being. If conjoining two objects adds anything to the furniture of the earth, it ought to be something made up of those two objects. We don't expect it to create a new object that is just like one of the original objects was before the attachment. We can make this more vivid by imagining the process in reverse: suppose A is made up of C and B and we want to make it smaller by removing B as a part. If attaching B to A brings C into being, then detaching B again ought to destroy C. But surely we can't destroy an object merely by detaching from it a thing that was never a part of it.

Suppose, then, that C existed before B was attached. Now C was the same size as A was then: attaching B didn't make C any larger or smaller. A and C must have occupied exactly the same place before B was attached: Figure 3 ought to show A and C superimposed on the left-hand side. But their relationship then was more intimate than mere co-location: as we have noted, they were made of the same matter then (if they are material things). A's gaining a part could hardly require it, before it got the new part, to share its location with something made of *different* matter. More generally, A and C share all their proper parts then. Or at least there are things that *compose* A, and also compose C before B is attached– where some things, the *xs*, compose something *y* if and only if each of the *xs* is a part of *y*, no two of the *xs* share a part, and every part of *y* shares a part with one or more of the *xs*. Let us abbreviate the claim that there are things that compose A and also compose C by saying that A and C *coincide mereologically*.

But *can* two different things coincide mereologically? Can two material things be made of the same matter at the same time? Can the same parts make up two different wholes at once? Do your own atoms, for instance, now make up two different beings, you and something else – a sort of internal *doppelgänger* of you? It seems not. If that is right, then A and C really were the same thing before we attached B, just as it appeared.

But now our story has fallen apart. C didn't acquire B as a part: that was the whole point of introducing C. But if C is really just A, and C didn't acquire B as a part, then A didn't acquire B as a part either, contradicting our original assumption. The supposition that A gains a part has therefore been reduced to absurdity.

What assumptions did we make in this reasoning? Well, we began by supposing, for *reductio*, that B comes to be a part of A:

1. A acquires B as a part.

In that case, we reasoned, A comes to be composed of B and a third thing, "the rest of A apart from B", which we called C:

2. When A acquires B as a part, A comes to be composed of B and C.

This is an important premise. Now it follows from 2 and the definition of 'compose' that B doesn't come to be a part of C when we attach it:

3. C does not acquire B as a part.

Next we assumed that making B a part of A doesn't bring C into being; rather, C exists before we attach B to it:

4. C exists before B is attached.

This is another crucial premise. Now it is part of the story that C doesn't get any bigger or smaller when we attach B: it has the same boundaries, before B is attached, as A has then. What's more, there are things that compose A and also compose C then:

5. C coincides mereologically with A before B is attached.

This follows from 2, 3, and 4, given that C doesn't grow or shrink when B is attached. Our next premise was that

6. No two things can coincide mereologically at the same time.

And 5 and 6 imply that

7. C = A.

But if C *is* A, and C doesn't acquire B as a part (3), then neither does A:

8. A does not acquire B as a part,

contrary to our original assumption, 1. Supposing that A gets bigger by gaining a part has led to a contradiction.

There is no easy way of resisting this argument. As far as I can see, we can avoid its conclusion only by taking on one of five serious metaphysical commitments. Each of these commitments strikes me as highly implausible. In any case they are all very interesting and completely different from one another. The paradox of increase is a sort of metaphysical crossroads, offering a number of paths, each leading off into its own peculiar landscape. Which of the paths one finds attractive or repugnant reveals a good deal about one's cast of mind.

In the remainder of this essay I will sketch these five proposals for solving the paradox. Since each is a large topic in itself, I shall have to be brief.

7.

One way of resisting the argument is to challenge its logic.[7] Someone might say that C and A are one thing before we attach B and two things afterwards. What started out as a thing and itself have come to be a thing and another thing. Identity is time-relative: things might be identical at one time and distinct at another, just as you and I might be neighbors at one time and not neighbors at another time. So all that follows from 5 and 6 is that C is identical with A before B is attached, not that C is identical with A *simpliciter*. If C is not A after B is attached, then the fact that C doesn't gain B as a part does not imply that A doesn't gain B as a part, and the argument fails. We might call this proposed solution the *way of funny logic* – though it is no mere logical hypothesis, but has important metaphysical implications for the nature of identity.

Beguiling though the way of funny logic may appear, it is hard to take seriously. Suppose that C and A are one thing now but two things tomorrow. The suggestion is that tomorrow B will be a part of A and not a part of C. A is about to grow. C isn't. That means that A now has a property that C now lacks, namely being such that it will have B as a part tomorrow. At any rate there is something now true of A that is not now true of C. But C and A are supposed to be the very same thing now. How can a thing now have a property that that very thing now lacks? How can a thing be about to grow when that very thing is *not* about to grow? (Funny logicians have an answer to this question. But to my mind their answer does little to blunt the force of the objection.)

8.

If the growing argument is logically impeccable, those who reject its conclusion will have to deny one of its premises. The first substantial premise is 2, that if A acquires B as a part, it comes to be composed of B and "the rest of A", C. This assumption makes trouble because C appears to be identical with A; and since C doesn't acquire B as a part, it follows that A doesn't either. So we might solve the paradox by denying that there is ever such a thing as C. Of course, there has to be *something* in the box labelled 'C' in Figure 3. B is never A's only part; there is another part of A that B ends up attached to. But there is no *one* such thing as "all of A apart from B". There is no thing whose boundary the box represents. There are only a lot of smaller things – D, E, and F, say – each of which partly fills that space. We can illustrate this by re-drawing the picture so:

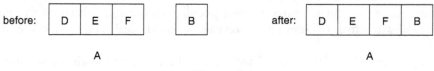

Figure 4

A starts out composed of D, E, and F, and when it gains B as a part it comes to be composed of D, E, F, and B. But D, E, and F don't themselves compose anything after B is attached: there is nothing that has D, E, and F as parts then, and every part of which then shares a part with D, E, or F. The view is not merely that D, E, and F don't then compose anything interesting, or don't compose a "genuine object" or the like. The claim has to be that they don't then make up anything at all. Suppose that D, E, F, and G each have a mass of 1 kg. Then there is nothing on the right-hand side of the diagram that has a mass of 3 kg and does not overlap B.

Call this the *way of sparse ontology.*[8] It contradicts the widely held view that composition is universal: that any things whatever always compose something bigger. Not everyone finds universal composition attractive – it implies the existence of all sorts of things that most of us would rather do without, such as a thing composed of your left ear, the biggest fish in the sea, and the color blue. In fact it implies that almost all objects are mere ontological junk. But the way of sparse ontology implies that there are fewer things than almost anyone would have thought.

If it is to provide a general solution to the paradox of increase, the way of sparse ontology must imply that nothing ever has a proper part that it once coincided with. This is surprising. Suppose we make a house bigger by adding an extension, in a way that doesn't disturb any of the house's original parts. (Think of a house made of Lego bricks.) Most of us probably thought that after the building work there remains such a thing as "the original part of the house", made up of those bricks that composed the house before the building work began. The way of sparse ontology denies this: it says that if it was possible for the house to get bigger in this way, that is because there is no such thing, afterwards, as the original part of the house. The bricks that compose the house beforehand cease to compose anything the moment the house begins to grow. (Sparse ontologists may want to say that there are no houses either: though there are bricks "arranged domestically", they never compose anything. But to deny that any objects ever compose anything capable of growing would be to accept the doctrine of mereological constancy. So the way of sparse ontology implies that *some* things behave, or could behave, in this way.)

The corresponding solution to the amputation paradox is to deny that anything ever has a proper part that it could be pared down to. Assuming that you could survive the loss of your left hand, this implies that there is now no such thing as your left-hand complement – "all of you but your left hand". Maybe no one cares about left-hand complements. But the way of sparse ontology implies that there is no such thing as your *head* either – assuming that it is possible for you to survive, at least briefly, being pared down to a head. Our nursery-school ontology of parts of the body is shot through with error.

Of course, sparse ontologists can argue that despite appearances their view is compatible with everything we say and do in the ordinary business of life (van Inwagen 1990: 98–114): when we say that someone has a large head, for instance, we are not implying the existence of a head, but at most the existence of things – atoms, say – "arranged capitally". Still, it isn't very nice.

9.

A third way of resisting the argument is to accept that C exists after B is attached, but deny that it exists beforehand (step 4). We could say, rather, that attaching B to A brings C into being. If C doesn't exist before B is attached, then there is no reason to suppose that C is A, thus blocking the argument. The general principle behind this thinking is that whenever any object gains a part, a new thing, composed of the object's original parts, is thereby created. Because it implies that things come into being and pass away in a surprising way, we might call this the *way of funny persistence conditions.*[9]

This is hardly a nice solution to the paradox, however. Suppose we have a house made entirely of red Lego bricks, and we make it bigger by adding an extension made entirely of blue bricks. The way of funny persistence conditions implies that when the original red house expands by acquiring blue parts, a *new* red house, composed of the original house's original bricks, immediately comes into being to take its place. Or perhaps we shouldn't call the new object a *house*: maybe no proper part of a house can be a house itself. In any case, the building work creates a new material object very like a house. Now when we lay bricks, we may expect to create a new object made up of those bricks. But laying only blue bricks is a strange way of creating an object made up entirely of red bricks.

If we apply the way of funny persistence conditions to the amputation paradox, we get the claim that whenever anything loses a part, the complement of that part – the thing composed of all the object's parts save those that overlap the lost part – ceases to exist. So there *is* now such a thing as your head, but cutting away the rest of you would necessarily destroy it (supposing you survive the adventure, anyway): the head you would be in this badly maimed condition would not be the head you once had. No undetached head could ever come to be a live, detached head. In general, it is possible to destroy an object merely by moving things that were never parts of it.

To be fair, there are important considerations in support of the way of funny persistence conditions – as there are for the way of sparse ontology. But we must press on.

10.

The next important claim we made in stating the paradox was 6, that no two things can coincide mereologically at the same time. Given that A and C coincide mereologically before we attached B, it follows from this claim that they are identical. But many philosophers say that different things *can* coincide mereologically at once. Why can't C exist before B is attached without being identical with A? In that case A would begin by coinciding mereologically with C and end up with C and B as parts. The corresponding solution to the amputation paradox would say that when an object shrinks by losing a part, it comes to coincide mereologically with the complement of that part – the largest part of the object that didn't share a part, before the loss, with the lost part. Call this the *way of coincidence* (Wiggins 1968, Thomson 1983, Baker 2000: ch. 2).

Some will find this a neat solution to the paradox: simply drop the dogmatic assumption that no two things can be in the same place and made of the same matter at once. Others will be uneasy. There is something at least a little bit odd in saying that what enables a thing to gain parts is the fact that it coincides with something that *can't* gain parts.

In any case, the way of coincidence raises a pointed question (Burke 1992, Olson 2001): If A gets bigger, why doesn't C get bigger too? If conjoining B to A makes it a part of A, why doesn't conjoining it in the same way to C make it a part of C? It is no accident, according to the way of coincidence, that A acquires B as a part and C doesn't: if we conjoined B a thousand times, it would come to be a part of A each time and would never become a part of C. A, but not C, has the *capacity* to grow by gaining B as a part. Presumably C cannot gain any parts at all. This is surprising. Aren't A and C exactly alike before the attachment? They have the same parts then, arranged in the same way. They are physically identical. They have the same surroundings. They may even have the same past history. There appears to be no difference between A and C that could account for their differing capacities to acquire parts.

We might try to explain it in terms of a difference in kind: A can acquire new parts because it is an organism or a person or a thing of some other "mereologically inconstant" kind; C cannot change its parts because it is a "mass of matter" or a "mereological sum" or the like. But this is little help. Suppose we ask what it is about A that *makes* it an organism rather than a mass of matter, and what it is about C that makes it a mass of matter and not an organism. Ordinarily we expect there to be physical differences between organisms and non-organisms. We think we can tell whether something is an organism by observing it. But there is no such difference between A and C. (They will of course have different histories. But they needn't: an organism newly created *ex nihilo* would surely be able to grow if anything can.) It looks as if what makes A an organism rather than a mass of matter is nothing more than the sort of thing it can survive: it is an organism because, in addition to having all the right physical properties (which C shares), it can also gain new parts. C is not an organism merely because it cannot gain parts. But if we say that A is able to gain parts because it is an organism, we cannot also say that it is an organism because it can gain parts.

Coincidentalists will apparently have to say that there is no explanation of why A but not C can gain parts. Nothing *makes* them able or unable to gain parts. They just are. A's capacity and C's incapacity to gain new parts are *basic* properties of them: we cannot explain their having these properties in terms of their having any other properties, in the way that we can explain why an object is fragile in terms of the way its particles are bonded together. And surely things have to have *some* basic properties: not all properties can be such that a thing's having them is explainable in terms of its having some other properties. Still, this proposal conflicts with our expectation that physically identical material objects tend to behave identically in physically identical situations.

Most coincidentalists will want to say that coinciding objects differ in other ways too, besides the capacity to change their parts. They will want to say, for instance, that you and I are conscious and intelligent, whereas the masses of matter (or whatever) coinciding with us that make it possible for us to gain parts are not conscious or intelligent. Otherwise there would be *two* conscious, intelligent beings thinking your thoughts, and it is hard to see how you could ever know which one you are – the conscious human being that can gain parts or the conscious mass of matter that can't. (If it seems obvious that you are the human being, it ought to seem equally obvious to the mass of matter that *it* is a human being, even though it isn't. How do you know that *you*'re not making this mistake?) Coincidentalists will be no better able to explain why these things differ mentally from us than they can explain why they differ from us in their ability to gain parts. Most of us probably thought that our mental abilities are explained by our physical structure. (Perhaps our surroundings are also relevant.) But if, as the coincidentalists say, there are beings with the same physical structure and surroundings as we have but no mental properties (or mental properties very different from ours), this cannot be the case. At any rate a thing's having the right structure and surroundings will not by itself explain why it has mental properties. Coincidentalists may have to say that things' mental properties are basic in the same way as their capacity to gain parts is – not an appealing thought.[10]

11.

Here is one final proposal. A, B, and C are extended in time, much as a sausage is extended in space. And they are composed of temporal parts. A temporal part of something is a part of it that takes up "all of that object" that is located between two times, a bit like a section of a sausage. (An uncut section, that is. Imagine a butcher eyeing up a sausage and contemplating which of the infinitely many sections she should cut away from the rest of it.) We commonly speak of *events* as having temporal parts: the first half of a football game would be a temporal part of the game. The idea is that all things capable of changing their parts have temporal parts.

How does this solve the paradox? Suppose, to make things simple, that A's acquiring B is the only change of parts in its career and that B comes to an end when A does. Then A is composed of C and the temporal part of B located after it is attached, or more precisely the largest such part. The best way to illustrate this is to replace our "before" and "after" pictures with a spacetime diagram, where the vertical axis represents space and the horizontal axis time:

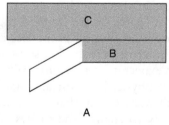

A

Figure 5

Here A is the shaded object. Because the later temporal parts of A but not the earlier ones include temporal parts of B, A gains B as a part.

Call this the *way of temporal parts* (Heller 1984, Sider 2001: ch. 5). Most of those who accept it hold the more general view that all persisting things are made up of temporal parts, sometimes called "four-dimensionalism" because it implies that persisting things are extended in one dimension of time as well as the three dimensions of space.

The way of temporal parts is hard to compare with the alternatives because it holds that things have their parts without temporal qualification. Up to now we have spoken of the parts a thing has *at some time*, much as we speak of how tall something is at some time. But according to the way of temporal parts, things have their parts timelessly. Thus, A is timelessly composed of C and the largest post-attachment temporal part of B. Saying that A has certain parts, on this view, is like saying that 4 is less than 7: it isn't the case at some time, or for that matter at every time; it is the case without any temporal qualification at all. A thing may have parts that are located at different times, just as it may have parts located in different places, but they are parts of it *simpliciter*. So it is perhaps a bit misleading to say that things *change* their parts: the truth of the matter is simply that A's later temporal parts overlap B and its earlier temporal parts don't.

Like the way of coincidence, the way of temporal parts rejects 6, the claim that no two things can coincide mereologically at a time. But because four-dimensionalists take parthood to be timeless, they understand 6 differently from coincidentalists. On their view, for things to coincide at a time is simply for them to share those of their temporal parts that are located then. So as they see it, A coincides with C before B is attached only in something like the way in which two roads might coincide for part of their length.

Four-dimensionalists accept the atemporal analog of 6: that no two things can coincide mereologically *simpliciter*. A differs mereologically from C, on their view, in that A but not C has the later temporal parts of B as parts. This gives the way of temporal parts an advantage over the way of coincidence: it is not committed to the mysterious view that things can differ qualitatively – in their kind, their capacity to gain parts, and their mental capacities, for instance – without differing in their internal structure or surroundings.

Four-dimensionalism is a powerful metaphysical theory, offering answers to a wide range of difficult questions. It is also highly controversial. It is to metaphysics rather as act utilitarianism is to ethics. Here are just two controversial implications of the way of temporal parts.

First, if it is to offer a general solution to the paradox, all things capable of changing their parts must be made up of temporal parts. More strongly, they must be made up of *arbitrary* temporal parts: for every moment or stretch of time in a thing's career, there must be a temporal part of that thing located exactly then. If persisting things had temporal parts corresponding to only some stretches of their careers, nothing would guarantee that there is any such thing as the temporal part of B that extends from its attachment to C until its demise, throwing the way of temporal parts into doubt.

So the way of temporal parts implies that every ordinary object is accompanied by an infinite number of beings just like it only shorter-lived. There are as many temporal segments of you located now as there are stretches of your career that include the present moment. During the time it takes you to read this sentence, an infinite number of these beings come into existence, and an infinite number of them pass away. The world is fantastically crowded with objects: just the opposite of the sparse ontology of §8. As if this weren't bad enough already, it raises the problem of how you can know which of these beings you are. You may think you have existed for many years, and that many more years lie in store for you. But your temporal part that extends from midnight last night until midnight tonight would appear to think in the same way as you do. (It would be mysterious if it didn't.) And it presumably has the same reason to believe that *it* is going to enjoy a long future as you have to believe that you are. Yet its belief is sadly mistaken. How do you know that you're not making this mistake? Your belief that you will still exist tomorrow looks entirely unwarranted.[11]

Second, recall the modal paradox from §2. We all think that at least some objects might have been smaller by lacking some of the parts they actually have: your house, for instance, might have had a brick missing. But if we try to imagine an object, X, without one of its parts, Y, we seem to get only a possible situation in which the complement of Y, Z, is not attached to Y:

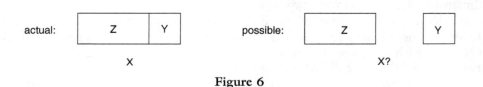

Figure 6

X itself either doesn't exist at all in this possible situation, or it exists and has the very parts it actually has and is merely a scattered object instead of a connected one. How can it be possible, then, for a thing to exist with different parts from the ones it actually has?

The other ways of solving the paradox of increase all suggest ways of solving the modal paradox as well. The way of funny logic suggests that X and Z, though actually distinct, are identical in the merely possible situation: what are in fact a thing and another thing might have been a thing and itself. Friends of sparse ontology will say that there is actually no such thing as Z, but only a lot of smaller things that jointly fill that space. The way of funny persistence conditions suggests that Z doesn't exist in the merely possible situation. Friends of coincidence can say that X simply coincides mereologically with Z on the right-hand side. Each of these proposals would enable X to exist in a possible situation where it lacks Y as a part.

What about the way of temporal parts? It gives an account of how a house can *lose* a brick, but it suggests no account of how the house might have had a brick missing all along. In fact it seems to imply that a house could not have existed with a brick missing.[12] If Y were not a part of X, and neither were any replacement for Y, then X could exist only by coinciding mereologically with Z:

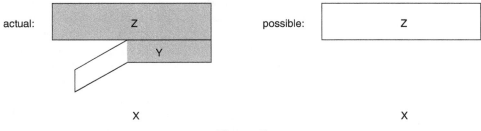

Figure 7

But four-dimensionalism denies that any two things can coincide mereologically. So it looks as if X could not possibly exist without having Y as a part. More generally, nothing could exist without having all the parts it actually has. Similar reasoning – swapping 'actual' and 'possible' in the diagram – suggests that nothing could have had parts it doesn't actually have either. The way of temporal parts appears to imply mereological essentialism.

Now I said in §2 that mereological essentialism entails mereological constancy: if everything has its parts essentially, then nothing can have different parts at different times. How can I now say that the way of temporal parts makes mereological essentialism true and mereological constancy false? Well, what I said in §2 is true if mereological essentialism and mereological constancy are stated as they are there, in terms of things' having parts at times. But as we noted earlier, on the way of temporal parts things have their parts timelessly speaking: for x to be a part of y at a time t is for the temporal part of x located at t to be (timelessly) a part of the temporal part of y located at t (Sider 2001: 57; see also Olson 2006). Applying this to the time-relative doctrine of mereological constancy of §2, we get *timeless mereological constancy*:

> Necessarily, if a temporal part of x located at t is a part of the temporal part of y located at t, then every temporal part of y has a temporal part of x as a part.

The timeless version of mereological essentialism that four-dimensionalism seems to imply is this:

> If x is a part of y, then it is not possible for y to exist without having x as a part.

And timeless mereological essentialism does not entail timeless mereological constancy: even if a house could not have had different parts from those it in fact has, some of its temporal parts may still include temporal parts of a certain brick while others don't.

But a solution to the paradox of increase that lands us with mereological essentialism is hardly a solution at all. Suppose you had eaten less this morning than you actually did – even just a few atoms less. In that case the human being bearing your name would have different parts from you. According to mereological essentialism, it would therefore be someone else: *you* wouldn't exist in that situation at all. Or if you did, you wouldn't be a human being, but rather a scattered object composed of the very atoms – or rather temporal parts of atoms – that in fact compose you. So mereological essentialism implies that it is impossible for you to have eaten less than you actually did this morning and been a human being. But isn't it obvious that this *is* possible?

Some four-dimensionalists try to avoid this consequence by endorsing modal counterpart theory. The story is too complex to summarize here.[13] It is, in any case, highly contentious.

12.

We have considered five accounts of how things might acquire new parts despite appearances to the contrary. None is very nice. At any rate they all have some pretty surprising consequences. We may even doubt whether any is better than the disease it is meant to cure: mereological constancy might not look so bad once we have seen the alternatives.

Someone might try combining some of these proposed solutions. Maybe things don't all gain and lose parts in the same way: perhaps the way of sparse ontology is right for organisms and the way of funny persistence conditions is right for artefacts, say; or perhaps it is the other way round. Or one might say that only some composite objects can change their parts, while mereological constancy is true for others. This sort of "mixed" solution might seem only to add the counterintuitive consequences of one "pure" solution to those of another, rather like explaining some unlikely events by appeal to extra-terrestrial meddling and others by appeal to magic. But some of the pure solutions may look more attractive if we take them to apply only in certain cases rather than across the board: for instance, it may be easier to believe that organisms have no proper parts that they can survive being pared down to than it is to believe this about houses.

Mixed accounts are in danger of being unprincipled. While it may be easy enough to *say* that the way of sparse ontology is right for organisms and the way of funny persistence conditions is right for artefacts, it will be harder to explain why this should be so. Why should organisms have fewer parts than houses have? One would like to think that there was a satisfying answer to such questions. And maybe there is; but it isn't easy to see. Developing a mixed solution would be a large and difficult project.

I am not aware of any other solution to the paradox. I suppose it would be rash to assume that there is none. But no other solution is likely to be any nicer than these.[14]

Notes

1 An elegant modern statement of the paradox (and the inspiration for this paper) is Chisholm 1976: 157f. The ancient sources are obscure. The introduction to Rea 1997 (as well as the rest of the volume) is a useful guide to these regions.

2 The most important discussion of the amputation paradox is probably van Inwagen 1981. See also Heller 1984.

3 Defenses of this claim include Chisholm 1976: 97–104, Sider 1996, 2001: 188–208, and Hawley 2001: ch. 2–3. The claim that our practical attitudes are not based on identity over time is most famously defended by Parfit (1984: ch. 12).

4 The doctrine of mereological constancy was popular among 18th-century advocates of the reactionary proposal: see for instance Leibniz 1982: 238 and the snippets by Butler and Reid in Perry 1975. See also Chisholm 1976: ch. 3 and Zimmerman 2003. A variant of the reactionary proposal is the Aristotelian view that living organisms have no proper parts: they can grow or shrink by assimilating or expelling matter, but neither particles nor internal organs nor hands or feet are parts of them. This view is difficult to reconcile with the fact that matter is made up of particles, however.

5 Shoemaker 1999 gives an ingenious argument that would rule out any material thing's thinking if mereological constancy were true. I suspect that his argument is incompatible with our being partless immaterial substances, though he disagrees: see Olson 2002a, Shoemaker 2004.

6 This is a fib. It probably isn't true that anything ever gains a part without changing internally at least a little bit. It certainly isn't true if a thing comes to be a part of an object by coming to interact causally with that object in some way – by becoming physically bonded to it, say, or by getting caught up in its metabolic processes. Because the relevance of this point to the paradox and its proposed solutions is unclear to me, I will ignore it, though not without some unease.

7 See e.g. Myro 1986 (who attributes the view to Grice), and Gallois 1990 or 1998. Sider 2001: 165–76 is a helpful critical discussion.

8 Van Inwagen 1981, Lowe 2002: 75f. The classic defense of the sparse ontology of material objects is van Inwagen 1990a; see also Merricks 2001. For what it's worth, this is my own favorite solution to the paradox. I argue for this sort of view in a different way in Olson 1995.

9 Burke 1994, 1996; Hoffman and Rosenkrantz 1997: 157; Rea 2000. It seems to have been the view of Chrysippus as well: see Burke 1994: 129f.

10 The only serious attempt I know of to explain why things coinciding with us cannot think is Shoemaker 1999. See note 5 for further references.

11 Olson 2002b discusses a possible solution to this problem. It would also solve the coincidentalist's problem of how you can know you are not the mass that now constitutes you.

12 A similar argument is given in van Inwagen 1990b.

13 For the basics of counterpart theory see Lewis 1971, 1986: 248–263. The world still awaits a good critique of counterpart theory.

14 For perceptive comments on earlier versions of this paper I am grateful to audiences at London, Leeds, Nottingham, Oxford, and Sheffield, and to Bryan Frances, Briggs Wright, and especially David Hershenov.

References

Baker, L. R. 2000. *Persons and Bodies*. Cambridge: Cambridge University Press.

Burke, M. 1992. Copper statues and pieces of copper. *Analysis* 52: 12–17.

—. 1994. Dion and Theon: An essentialist solution to an ancient puzzle. *Journal of Philosophy* 91: 129–139.

—. 1996. Tibbles the cat: A modern sophisma. *Philosophical Studies* 84: 63–73.

Chisholm, R. 1976. *Person and Object*. La Salle, IL: Open Court. Partly reprinted in Rea 1997.

—. 1989. Is there a mind-body problem? In *On Metaphysics*. Minneapolis: University of Minnesota Press. Partly reprinted in P. van Inwagen and D. Zimmerman, ed., *Metaphysics: The Big Questions*. Malden, MA: Blackwell 1998. (Original work 1979.)

Gallois, A. 1990. Occasional Identity. *Philosophical Studies* 58: 203–244.

—. 1998. *Occasions of Identity*. Oxford: Oxford University Press.

Hawley, K. 2001. *How Things Persist*. Oxford: Oxford University Press.

Heller, M. 1984. Temporal parts of four-dimensional objects. *Philosophical Studies* 46: 323–334. Reprinted in Rea 1997.

Hoffman, J. and G. Rosenkrantz. 1997. *Substance: Its Nature and Existence*. London: Routledge.

Hume, D. 1978. *A Treatise of Human Nature*. Oxford: Oxford University Press. (Original work 1739.)

Leibniz, G. W. 1982. *New Essays on Human Understanding*. Cambridge: Cambridge University Press. (Original work published posthumously in 1765.)

Lewis, D. 1971. Counterparts of persons and their bodies. *Journal of Philosophy* 68: 203–211. Reprinted in his *Philosophical Papers* vol. I, New York: Oxford University Press, 1983.

—. 1986. *On the Plurality of Worlds*. Oxford: Blackwell.

Lowe, E. J. 2002. *A Survey of Metaphysics*. Oxford: Oxford University Press.

Merricks, T. 2001. *Objects and Persons*. Oxford: Oxford University Press.

Myro, G. 1986. Identity and time. In R. Grandy and R. Warner, eds., *The Philosophical Grounds of Rationality*. New York: Oxford University Press. Reprinted in Rea 1997.

Olson, E. 1995. Why I have no hands. *Theoria* 61: 182–197.

—. 2001. Material coincidence and the indiscernibility problem. *Philosophical Quarterly* 51: 337–355.

—. 2002a. What does functionalism tell us about personal identity? *Noûs* 36: 682–698.

—. 2002b. Thinking animals and the reference of 'I'. *Philosophical Topics* 30: 189–208.

—. 2006. Temporal parts and timeless parthood. *Noûs* 40: 738–52.

Parfit, D. 1984. *Reasons and Persons*. Oxford: Oxford University Press.

Perry, J. (ed.). 1975. *Personal Identity*. Berkeley: University of California Press.

Rea, M. (ed.). 1997. *Material Constitution*. Lanham: Rowman & Littlefield.

—. 2000. Constitution and kind membership. *Philosophical Studies* 97: 169–193.

Shoemaker, S. 1999. Self, body, and coincidence. *Proceedings of the Aristotelian Society, Supplementary Volume* 73: 287–306.

—. 2004. Functionalism and personal identity – A reply. *Noûs* 38: 525–533.

Sider, T. 1996. All the world's a stage. *Australasian Journal of Philosophy* 74: 433–53.

—. 2001. *Four-Dimensionalism*. Oxford: Oxford University Press.

Thomson, J. J. 1983. Parthood and identity across time. *Journal of Philosophy* 80: 201–220. Reprinted in Rea 1997.

van Inwagen, P. 1981. The doctrine of arbitrary undetached parts. *Pacific Philosophical Quarterly* 62: 123–137. Reprinted in Rea 1997.

—. 1990a. *Material Beings*. Ithaca: Cornell University Press.

—. 1990b. Four-dimensional objects. *Noûs* 24: 245–255.

Wiggins, D. 1968. On being in the same place at the same time. *Philosophical Review* 77: 90–95. Reprinted in Rea 1997.

Zimmerman, D. 2003. Material people. In M. Loux and D. Zimmerman, eds., *The Oxford Handbook of Metaphysics*. Oxford: Oxford University Press.

26   Identity, Ostension, and Hypostasis

W. V. O. Quine

Identity is a popular source of philosophical perplexity. Undergoing change as I do, how can I be said to continue to be myself? Considering that a complete replacement of my material substance takes place every few years, how can I be said to continue to be I for more than such a period at best?

It would be agreeable to be driven, by these or other considerations, to belief in a changeless and therefore immortal soul as the vehicle of my persisting self-identity. But we should be less eager to embrace a parallel solution of Heracleitus's parallel problem regarding a river: "You cannot bathe in the same river twice, for new waters are ever flowing in upon you."

The solution of Heracleitus's problem, though familiar, will afford a convenient approach to some less familiar matters. The truth is that you *can* bathe in the same *river* twice, but not in the same river stage. You can bathe in two river stages which are stages of the same river, and this is what constitutes bathing in the same river twice. A river is a process through time, and the river stages are its momentary parts. Identification of the river bathed in once with the river bathed in again is just what determines our subject matter to be a river process as opposed to a river stage.

Let me speak of any multiplicity of water molecules as a *water*. Now a river stage is at the same time a water stage, but two stages of the same river are not in general stages of the same water. River stages are water stages, but rivers are not waters. You may bathe in the same river twice without bathing in the same water twice, and you may, in these days of fast transportation, bathe in the same water twice while bathing in two different rivers.

We begin, let us imagine, with momentary things and their interrelations. One of these momentary things, called *a*, is a momentary stage of the river Caÿster, in Lydia, around 400 BC. Another, called *b*, is a momentary stage of the Caÿster two days later. A third, *c*, is a momentary stage, at this same latter date, of the same multiplicity of water molecules which were in the river at the time of *a*. Half of *c* is in the lower Caÿster valley, and the other half is to be found at diffuse points in the Aegean Sea. Thus *a*, *b*, and *c* are three objects, variously related. We may say that *a* and *b* stand in the relation of river kinship, and that *a* and *c* stand in the relation of water kinship.

Now the introduction of rivers as single entities, namely, processes or time-consuming objects, consists substantially in reading identity in place of river kinship. It would be wrong, indeed, to say that *a* and *b* are identical; they are merely river-kindred. But if we were to point to *a*, and then wait the required two days and point to *b*, and affirm identity of the objects pointed to, we should thereby show that our pointing was intended not as a pointing to two kindred river stages but as a pointing to a single river which included them both. The imputation of identity is essential, here, to fixing the reference of the ostension.

These reflections are reminiscent of Hume's account of our idea of external objects. Hume's theory was that the idea of external objects arises from an error of identification. Various similar impressions separated in time are mistakenly treated as identical; and then, as a means of resolving this contradiction of identifying momentary events which are separated in time, we invent a new nonmomentary object to serve as subject matter of our statement of identity. Hume's charge of erroneous identification here is interesting as a psychological conjecture on origins, but there is no need for us to share that conjecture. The important point to observe is merely the direct connection between identity and the positing of processes, or time-extended objects. To impute identity rather than river kinship is to talk of the river Caÿster rather than of *a* and *b*.

Pointing is of itself ambiguous as to the temporal spread of the indicated object. Even given that the indicated object is to be a process with considerable temporal spread, and hence a summation of momentary objects, still pointing does not tell us *which* summation of momentary objects is intended, beyond the fact that the momentary object at hand is to be in the desired summation. Pointing to *a*, if construed as referring to a time-extended process and not merely to the momentary object *a*, could be interpreted either as referring to the river Caÿster of which *a* and *b* are stages, or as referring to the water of which *a* and *c* are stages, or as referring to any one of an unlimited number of further less natural summations to which *a* also belongs.

Such ambiguity is commonly resolved by accompanying the pointing with such words as "this river," thus appealing to a prior concept of a river as one distinctive type of time-consuming process, one distinctive form of summation of momentary objects. Pointing to *a* and saying "this river" – or ὅδε ὅ ποταμός, since we are in 400 BC – leaves no ambiguity as to the object of reference if the word "river" itself is already intelligible. "This river" means "the riverish summation of momentary objects which contains this momentary object."

But here we have moved beyond pure ostension and have assumed conceptualization. Now suppose instead that the general term "river" is not yet understood, so that we cannot specify the Caÿster by pointing and saying "This river is the Caÿster." Suppose also that we are deprived of other descriptive devices. What we may do then is point to *a* and two days later to *b* and say each time, "This is the Caÿster." The word "this" so used must have referred not to *a* nor to *b*, but beyond to something more inclusive, identical in the two cases. Our specification of the Caÿster is not yet unique, however, for we might still mean any of a vast variety of other collections of momentary objects, related in other modes than that of river kinship; all we know is that *a* and *b* are among its constituents. By pointing to more and more stages additional to *a* and *b*, however, we eliminate more and more alternatives, until our listener, aided by his own tendency to favor the most natural groupings, has grasped the idea of the Caÿster. His learning of this idea is an induction: from our grouping the sample momentary objects *a*, *b*, *d*, *g*, and others under the head of Caÿster, he projects a correct general hypothesis as to what further momentary objects we would also be content to include.

Actually there is in the case of the Caÿster the question of its extent in space as well as in time. Our sample pointings need to be made not only on a variety of dates, but at various points up and down stream, if our listener is to have a representative basis for his inductive generalization as to the intended spatiotemporal spread of the four-dimensional object Caÿster.

In ostension, spatial spread is not wholly separable from temporal spread, for the successive ostensions which provide samples over the spatial spread are bound to consume time. The inseparability of space and time characteristic of relativity theory is foreshadowed, if only superficially, in this simple situation of ostension.

The concept of identity, then, is seen to perform a central function in the specifying of spatio-temporally broad objects by ostension. Without identity, *n* acts of ostension merely specify up to *n* objects, each of indeterminate spatio-temporal spread. But when we affirm identity of object from ostension to ostension, we cause our *n* ostensions to refer to the same large object, and so afford our listener an inductive ground from which to guess the intended reach of that object. Pure ostension plus identification conveys, with the help of some induction, spatiotemporal spread. . . .

---

27   In Defense of Stages[1]: Postscript B to "Survival and Identity"

David Lewis

Some would protest that they do not know what I mean by "more or less momentary person-stages, or time-slices of continuant persons, or persons-at-times." Others do know what I mean, but don't believe there are any such things.

The first objection is easy to answer, especially in the case where the stages are less momentary rather than more. Let me consider that case only; though I think that instantaneous stages also are unproblematic, I do not really need them. A person-stage is a physical object, just as a person is. (If persons had a ghostly part as well, so would person-stages.) It does many of the same things that a person does: it talks and walks and thinks, it has beliefs and desires, it has a size and shape and location. It even has a temporal duration. But only a brief one, for it does not last long. (We can pass over the question how long it can last before it is a segment rather than a stage, for that question raises no objection of principle.) It begins to exist abruptly, and it abruptly ceases to exist soon after. Hence a stage cannot do everything that a person can do, for it cannot do those things that a person does over a longish interval.

That is what I mean by a person-stage. Now to argue for my claim that they exist, and that they are related to persons as part to whole. I do not suppose the doubters will accept my premises, but it will be instructive to find out which they choose to deny.

First: it is possible that a person-stage might exist. Suppose it to appear out of thin air, then vanish again. Never mind whether it is a stage *of* any person (though in fact I think it is). My point is that it is the right sort of thing.

Second: it is possible that two person-stages might exist in succession, one right after the other but without overlap. Further, the qualities and location of the second at its appearance might exactly match those of the first at its disappearance. Here I rely on a *patchwork principle* for possibility: if it is possible that X happen intrinsically in a spatiotemporal region, and if it is likewise possible that Y happen in a region, then also it is possible that both X and Y happen in two distinct but adjacent regions. There are no necessary incompatibilities between distinct existences. Anything can follow anything.

Third: extending the previous point, it is possible that there might be a world of stages that is exactly like our own world in its point-by-point distribution of intrinsic local qualities over space and time.

Fourth: further, such a world of stages might also be exactly like our own in its causal relations between local matters of particular fact. For nothing but the distribution of local qualities constrains the pattern of causal relations. (It would be simpler to say that the causal relations supervene on the distribution of local qualities, but I am not as confident of that as I am of the weaker premise.)

Fifth: then such a world of stages would be exactly like our own simpliciter. There are no features of our world except those that supervene on the distribution of local qualities and their causal relations.

Sixth: then our own world is a world of stages. In particular, person-stages exist.

Seventh: but persons exist too, and persons (in most cases) are not person-stages. They last too long. Yet persons and person-stages, like tables and table-legs, do not occupy spatiotemporal regions twice over. That can only be because they are not distinct. They are part-identical; in other words, the person-stages are parts of the persons.

Let me try to forestall two misunderstandings. (1) When I say that persons are maximal R-interrelated[2] aggregates of person-stages, I do *not* claim to be reducing "constructs" to "more basic entities." (Since I do not intend a reduction to the basic, I am free to say without circularity that person-stages are R-interrelated aggregates of shorter person-stages.) Similarly, I think it is an informative necessary truth that trains are maximal aggregates of cars interrelated by the ancestral of the relation of being coupled together (count the locomotive as a special kind of car). But I do not think of this as a reduction to the basic. Whatever "more basic" is supposed to mean, I don't think it means "smaller." (2) By a part, I just mean a subdivision. I do not mean a well-demarcated subdivision that figures as a unit in causal explanation. Those who give "part" a rich meaning along these lines[3] should take me to mean less by it than they do.

Notes

1 On this topic I am much indebted to discussions with Saul Kripke and with Denis Robinson. Kripke's views on related matters were presented in his lectures on "Identity through Time," given at Princeton in 1978 (and elsewhere); Robinson's in "Re-Identifying Matter," *Philosophical Review*, 91 (1982), pp. 317–41.
2 The "R-relation" is that "relation of mental continuity and connectedness that matters in survival." – [Eds].
3 Such as D.H. Mellor, in his *Real Time* (Cambridge: Cambridge University Press, 1981), Ch. 8.

---

28   The Problem of Temporary Intrinsics: an Excerpt from *On the Plurality of Worlds*

David Lewis

Let us say that something persists iff,[1] somehow or other, it exists at various times; this is the neutral word.[2] Something perdures iff it persists by having different temporal parts, or stages, at different times, though no one part of it is wholly present at more than one time; whereas it endures iff it persists by being wholly present at more than one time. Perdurance corresponds to the way a road persists through space; part of it is here and part of it is there, and no part is wholly present at two different places. Endurance corresponds to the way a universal, if there are such things, would be wholly present wherever and whenever it is instantiated. Endurance involves overlap: the content of two different times has the enduring thing as a common part. Perdurance does not.

(There might be mixed cases: entities that persist by having an enduring part and a perduring part. An example might be a person who consisted of an enduring entelechy ruling a perduring body; or an electron that had a universal of unit negative charge as a permanent part, but did not consist entirely of universals.

But here I ignore the mixed cases. And when I speak of ordinary things as perduring, I shall ignore their enduring universals, if such there be.)

Discussions of endurance versus perdurance tend to be endarkened by people who say such things as this: 'Of course you are wholly present at every moment of your life, except in case of amputation. For at every moment all your parts are there: your legs, your lips, your liver. . . .' These endarkeners may think themselves partisans of endurance, but they are not. They are perforce neutral because they lack the conceptual resources to understand what is at issue. Their speech betrays – and they may acknowledge it willingly – that they have no concept of a temporal part. (Or at any rate none that applies to a person, say, as opposed to a process or a stretch of time.) Therefore they are on neither side of a dispute about whether or not persisting things are divisible into temporal parts. They understand neither the affirmation nor the denial. They are like the people – fictional, I hope – who say that the whole of the long road is in their little village, for not one single lane of it is missing. Meaning less than others do by 'part', since they omit parts cut crosswise, they also mean less than others do by 'whole'. They say the 'whole' road is in the village; by which they mean that every 'part' is; but by that, they only mean that every part cut lengthwise is. Divide the road into its least lengthwise parts; they cannot even raise the question whether those are in the village wholly or only partly. For that is a question about crosswise parts, and the concept of a crosswise part is what they lack. Perhaps 'crosswise part' really does sound to them like a blatant contradiction. Or perhaps it seems to them that they understand it, but the village philosophers have persuaded them that really they couldn't, so their impression to the contrary must be an illusion. At any rate, I have the concept of a temporal part; and for some while I shall be addressing only those of you who share it.[3]

. . . The principal and decisive objection against endurance, as an account of the persistence of ordinary things such as people or puddles, is the problem of temporary intrinsics. Persisting things change their intrinsic properties. For instance shape: when I sit, I have a bent shape; when I stand, I have a straightened shape. Both shapes are temporary intrinsic properties; I have them only some of the time. How is such change possible? I know of only three solutions.

(It is not a solution just to say how very commonplace and indubitable it is that we have different shapes at different times. To say that is only to insist – rightly – that it must be possible somehow. Still less is it a solution to say it in jargon – as it might be, that bent-on-Monday and straight-on-Tuesday are compatible because they are 'time-indexed properties' – if that just means that, somehow, you can be bent on Monday and straight on Tuesday.)

First solution: contrary to what we might think, shapes are not genuine intrinsic properties. They are disguised relations, which an enduring thing may bear to times. One and the same enduring thing may bear the bent-shape relation to some times, and the straight-shape relation to others. In itself, considered apart from its relations to other things, it has no shape at all. And likewise for all other seeming temporary intrinsics; all of them must be reinterpreted as relations that something with an absolutely unchanging intrinsic nature bears to different times. The solution to the problem of temporary intrinsics is that there aren't any temporary intrinsics. This is simply incredible, if we are speaking of the persistence of ordinary things. (It might do for the endurance of entelechies or universals.) If we know what shape is, we know that it is a property, not a relation.

Second solution: the only intrinsic properties of a thing are those it has at the present moment. Other times are like false stories; they are abstract representations, composed out of the materials of the present, which represent or misrepresent the way things are. When something has different intrinsic properties according to one of these ersatz other times, that does not mean that it, or any part of it, or anything else, just has them – no more so than when a man is crooked according to the Times, or honest according to the News. This is a solution that rejects endurance; because it rejects persistence altogether. And it is even less credible than the first solution. In saying that there are no other times, as opposed to false representations thereof, it goes against what we all believe. No man, unless it be at the moment of his execution, believes that he has no future; still less does anyone believe that he has no past.

Third solution: the different shapes, and the different temporary intrinsics generally, belong to different things. Endurance is to be rejected in favour of perdurance. We perdure; we are made up of temporal parts, and our temporary intrinsics are properties of these parts, wherein they differ one from another. There is no problem at all about how different things can differ in their intrinsic properties.

Notes

1 'Iff' is short for 'if and only if'. – [Eds]
2 My discussion of this problem is much indebted to David M. Armstrong, 'Identity Through Time', in *Time and Cause: Essays Presented to Richard Taylor*, ed. by Peter van Inwagen (Dordrecht: D. Reidel, 1980); and to Mark Johnston. I follow Johnston in terminology.
3 I attempt to explain it to others in *Philosophical Papers*, vol. 1 (Oxford: Oxford University Press, 1983), pp. 76–7; reprinted in this volume as 'In Defense of Stages: Postscript B to "Survival and Identity"'. But I have no great hopes, since any competent philosopher who does not understand something will take care not to understand anything else whereby it might be explained.

---

29 Temporary Intrinsics and Presentism*

Dean W. Zimmerman

David Lewis develops something like an antinomy concerning change which he calls "the problem of temporary intrinsics." The resolution of this puzzle provides his primary motivation for the acceptance of a metaphysics of temporal parts.[1]

Lewis's own discussion is extremely compressed, showing up as a digression in a book about modality. So I shall set forth in some detail what I take to be his line of reasoning before suggesting that, at least for those philosophers who take seriously the distinction between past, present, and future, the argument poses no special threat.

The Structure of Lewis's Argument

Lewis's argument for temporal parts has the following structure. He offers reasons to deny that "the only intrinsic properties of a thing are those it has at the present moment"[2] – reasons, that is, for rejecting the "second solution" he considers. But if, in addition to the intrinsic properties I have now, I also have the intrinsic properties I have at other times, then I will end up having pairs like *being bent* and *being straight* – pairs that are, in some sense, incompatible. The challenge is then to answer the question: How can I have a pair of incompatible properties?[3] Lewis thinks there are only two possible ways to answer this question. The first is unacceptable, and the second leads to the doctrine of temporal parts:

(1)   My being both bent and straight is like my son's being both tall and short – tall for a two-year-old, say, but short by comparison with most people. This strategy for dealing with apparent contradiction construes the seemingly incompatible properties as really relations to other things (in the case of tall and short, relations to different comparison classes). The version of this strategy that Lewis considers for temporary intrinsics is his "first solution": that shapes and other seemingly intrinsic properties "are disguised relations, which an enduring thing may bear to times."[4] There is no more difficulty in standing in the *bent-at* relation to one time and the *straight-at* relation to another than there is in bearing the *tall-for-a* relation to two-year-olds and the *short-for-a* relation to the citizens of the United States as a whole. But Lewis doesn't like this solution; he thinks it is tantamount to the rejection of intrinsic properties altogether.

(2)   There's only one way left, says Lewis, to make the apparent contradiction go away while retaining the incompatibility of *being bent* and *being straight*; and that is to treat it as we do the case of the road that is both bumpy and smooth. How can a road be both? Easily: by having one part that is bumpy and another that is smooth. So, analogously, the only way for me to be both bent and straight is for me to have a part that is bent and a part that is straight. But these cannot be ordinary spatial parts of me, like an arm or a hand. The bent "part" of me is exactly my size and shape, with arms, legs, torso, and head; and likewise for the straight "part" of me. And, like the different spatial parts of the road, these different parts of me must be distinct one from another. So I emerge as a whole spread out along the temporal dimension with different (temporal) parts for the different times I occupy, much as the road is a whole spread out along the spatial dimension with different (spatial) parts for the different places it occupies.

I am willing to grant Lewis's assertion that, once someone admits that I have more properties than just those I have now, she must choose between alternatives (1) and (2). And perhaps it is true that (1) eliminates temporary intrinsics altogether. At the very least, it eliminates temporary *monadic* properties ("one-place" properties, properties that are not relations); and it's easy to see why someone might think that *really* intrinsic properties should be monadic.[5] What I want to question instead is the very first move: Why suppose that I must have more than just the properties I have now?

Serious Tensers and Presentists

Before looking at Lewis's answer, I want to make clear what view Lewis is targeting: namely, "presentism." A closely related position is that of one who "takes tense seriously." As shall appear, one can't very well be a presentist without taking tense seriously, although it is possible to do the reverse.

When a philosopher says, "The only properties I have are those I have now," it is tempting to respond by saying: This thesis is either an uninteresting, tautologous truth; or an obvious falsehood. If the first occurrence of "have" is in the present tense, then the assertion is equivalent to "The only properties I have now are those I have now." Who could disagree? But how dull! On the other hand, suppose this "have" is an instance of what philosophers sometimes call a "tenseless" verb. To say that I (tenselessly) have some property, for instance that I (tenselessly) am straight, is to say something more or less equivalent to this: "Either I was straight, or I am straight, or I will be straight." But "The only properties I (tenselessly) have are those I have now" is true only if either I never change or I exist for but an instant. Taken, then, in the only way in which it can be true (i.e., with the first "have" in the present tense), the claim seems too trivial to be the focus of a substantive philosophical debate.

I am convinced that there *is* an important disagreement between those who take tense seriously and those who don't. Precisely what the disagreement boils down to will depend to some extent upon metaphysical theses about what kinds of things are, in the first instance, true and false. Here is one example; but I believe that nothing much hinges on accepting just this view about the most fundamental bearers of truth. Suppose you think that the sentences we write down and utter are true or false in virtue of their expressing *propositions* that are true or false in some more basic sense. A proposition is something that can be expressed in many different ways; it can be believed by one person and disbelieved by another; and, at least in the case of a proposition that isn't about a particular sentence or thought, it would have existed and been either true or false even in the absence of all sentences or thoughts. This familiar conception of the ultimate bearers of truth and falsehood[6] can be conjoined with a tensed or a tenseless theory about the nature of the proposition. On a tensed construal, a proposition's being true is not typically a once-and-for-all thing. The sentence "I am bent" could now be used by me to express a true proposition; but the proposition in question hasn't always been true, and it won't continue to be true for very long.

A tenseless account of propositions, on the other hand, takes them to be like statements made using tenseless verbs: each is either always true, or never true.

The competition between the tensed and tenseless approaches to the fundamental bearers of truth gives rise to a familiar dispute over the importance of "tense logic." Logic is all about describing the most general patterns of truth-preserving inference. If the things that are true and false can be true but *have been false*, or *be about to become false*, then some of the patterns of inference logicians should be interested in will involve temporal notions. On the tensed conception of truths, it is a question of logic whether, for example, the proposition: It will be the case that I am bent, implies the proposition: It was the case that it will be the case that I am bent. Thus relations like being true simultaneously, and being true earlier or later than, will turn out to be, at least in part, logical notions.[7] On the other hand, those who take truth-bearers to correspond to tenseless statements will regard this as a blunder: temporal relations are for science and (perhaps) metaphysics to explore; but they are not part of the subject matter of logic.[8]

The philosopher who takes a tensed approach to the bearers of truth regards each of them as making a claim about what is the case *now*. Of course some propositions are eternally true: in other words, there are propositions which, either necessarily, or as a matter of contingent fact, have always been true and will always be true. That two and two make four is an example of the first sort. And historical propositions expressed by tenseless statements, such as my utterance in a lecture of "Plato believes in universals," are examples of the latter sort. But the proponent of tensed truth-bearers will insist that the true proposition expressed is composed of tensed propositions; it's a disjunction of three propositions: Either Plato (now) believes in universals, or he did, or he will.[9] This is a truth, but it is made out of three other propositions, only one of which is true, and each of which concerns what is now the case.

I shall call a philosopher who takes this sort of position a "serious tenser." Those who do not take tense seriously include D. H. Mellor, J. J. C. Smart, and others who defend what is sometimes called the "new tenseless theory of time": the thesis that the meaning of every tensed utterance can be captured by stating, in a tenseless language of eternal truths, the conditions in which the utterance would be true.[10] It should be evident that there can be a real dispute between the serious tenser and someone who rejects this view.[11]

Many serious tensers are also *presentists*. The presentist says: "The only things that exist are those that exist at present." The "once was" no longer exists and the "will be" doesn't exist yet. But the proponents of presentism are also confronted with a skeptical challenge to the significance of their thesis. Is the first occurrence of "exist" in the presentist's assertion a tensed one? Then the presentist is simply making a fuss over a pointless tautology: "The only things that exist now (i.e. at present) are those that exist at present." Who denies this? Or is "exist" here a tenseless verb, equivalent to "existed or exists now or will exist"? But then it's an implausible metaphysical thesis: the claim that everything exists at all times, that nothing can have a less than eternal history. So presentism is either a boring truth or an interesting falsehood.

Presentism is neither; it is a substantive thesis, and one that is not equivalent to the claim that everything exists eternally. Just as the serious tenser thinks there is, at bottom, only one kind of truth, and that is "truth-now"; so the presentist thinks there is only one largest class of all real things, and this class contains nothing that lies wholly in the past or future.[12] Presentism is, in fact, a thesis about the range of things to which one should be "ontologically committed."

Philosophers are always looking out for the ontological commitments of their views – where someone is ontologically committed to a certain kind of thing just in case something she believes implies that something of that kind exists. There are many perfectly sensible truths which, on the surface, seem to require the existence of highly problematic entities – *entia non grata*, as it were. Consider, for example, the following:

(1)   Jeeves was nonplussed by the dearth of champagne in the ice box.
(2)   Moriarty is the most well-known criminal in detective fiction.
(3)   Courage is a virtue displayed by many people.
(4)   There could have been a person who is not one of those who actually exist.

On the face of it, these are statements about such things as dearths, fictional characters, characteristics that may be possessed by many people, and merely possible persons. One might think that it could be inferred from them that: there is at least one dearth, there are some fictional criminals, there is something displayed by every courageous person, there are merely possible people. But each of these statements can seem hard to swallow for one reason or another.

A dearth of champagne isn't a kind of *thing*, a sort of invisible anti-champagne located where the champagne should be. To say that Jeeves was nonplussed by the dearth of champagne is simply to say that there was no champagne in the ice box, and that he was taken aback by the situation.

Nor are there some criminals (among the least dangerous of criminals) who are fictional. Fictional characters are not an odd group of people who, for some reason, we cannot meet in the way we meet other people, but can only get to know through stories. Statements about, say, Moriarty must really be elliptical for claims about the stories Arthur Conan Doyle wrote that had the name "Moriarty" in them.[13]

It might seem less problematic to suppose that there are some things called "virtues," of which courage is one. But if courage is something that can be displayed (or possessed or exemplified) by many different people at once, then some puzzling questions immediately arise. For how could anything be displayed in many different places at once, except by having a part displayed in each of those places and only there? Those philosophers particularly perplexed by this question (called "nominalists") claim that (3) doesn't imply that there is one thing possessed by all the courageous people. Some nominalists would say that each of the courageous people has his or her own particular instance of courageousness (in D. C. Williams's terminology, a courageousness "trope"[14]), and that statements about courage are really about the big group or heap of all these instances.

For present purposes, the final case is the most illuminating. Do we really want to say that there are some merely possible people? That some people are tall, some are short, and some are nonexistent – the limiting case of diminutive stature, as it were? Philosophers who answer, No, are called "modal actualists": they hold that there are no nonactual things. But then how to make sense of (4)? One strategy is to posit individual essences for nonexistent individuals, and then construe talk about nonactuals as really talk about these essences. Then (4) becomes the claim that there is an unexemplified individual essence that would be the essence of a person if it were exemplified.[15] Another is to say that what (4) really comes to is the claim that it is possible that there be something that is a person and is not identical with Jones, Robinson, . . . or any of the other actual people. This is an assertion about the possible truth of a certain proposition (that there be something that is a person and is not identical with . . .); the proposition itself isn't about any particular nonactual thing; and it is not equivalent to the claim that there is something that is a possible person and is not identical with. . . .[16]

These are some typical attempts to avoid ontological commitment to undesirable entities. Statements which, on the surface, seem to imply that there are certain problematic entities, are given philosophical glosses or paraphrases which seem to capture the truth in question while avoiding the implication that the troublesome things exist. The presentist is engaged in precisely the same sort of enterprise. But the truths that bother her are of this sort:

(5)   There was a person who is not one of the people who presently exist.
(6)   There will be a person who is not one of the people who presently exist.

The presentist is a "temporal actualist" – she is troubled by the fact that (5) and (6) seem to imply that there are some people who do not now exist, just as the modal actualist is bothered by the fact that (4) seems to imply that there are some people who do not actually exist. How can there *be* something that no longer exists, or that hasn't existed yet, she wonders? And so the presentist tries to show that the truth of (5) and (6) doesn't really conflict with her thesis that no nonpresent things exist.

One way of trying to show this would be to make use of individual essences again: (5) becomes the proposition that there is an individual essence not now exemplified that was once exemplified, and was then the essence of a person; and analogously for (6). Another is to insist that the truth of (5) implies only that it was the case that there is someone not identical with Jones, Robinson, . . . or any other presently existing person; but not that there is someone who used to exist and is not identical with Jones, Robinson, . . . And likewise for (6).[17]

How is presentism related to taking tense seriously? The presentist must, I think, be a serious tenser. At the very least, tenseless statements that ostensibly require ontological commitment to past and future things must be treated as equivalent to tensed truths that do not. And the presentist could not very well regard all the fundamental truth-bearers as eternally true, corresponding to tenseless statements. For, she says, one of the truths is that wholly future things, like my first grandchild, do not exist – and such truths had better be susceptible to change. On the other hand, the serious tenser need not be a presentist. Quentin Smith, for example, is a non-presentist serious tenser.[18] According to Smith, fundamental truths are all tensed; but past and future individuals and events, although no longer present, nonetheless exist. Ostensible ontological commitment to such things cannot, on Smith's view, be paraphrased away.

But the combination of rejecting presentism while taking tense seriously is an unstable one. For the primary motivation for treating the fundamental truth-bearers as mutable and true *now* is the desire to do justice to the feeling that what's in the past is over and done with, and that what's in the future only matters because it will eventually be present. This is the source of the importance Prior attaches to the exclamation "Thank goodness that's over!"[19] If yesterday's headache still exists, and remains as painful as ever, then why should I be relieved now? Would the mere fact that it's no longer present justify this attitude? Most serious tensers, including Smith himself, will agree that it would not. And so, to render reasonable our special concern for the present, Smith strips past and future events of all their interesting intrinsic properties. For instance, yesterday's headache, although it exists, is no longer painful. It has a past-oriented property, *having been painful* – a sort of backwards-looking relation to the property *being painful*. But it is not painful now, and that's why it no longer concerns us.[20]

Although this view makes sense of our relief when pain is past, I find it unappealing in the extreme. The past and future events and objects it posits are too ghostly to be real. A painful headache cannot exist without being painful; a tanker explosion cannot exist without being violent and loud; Plato cannot exist while having neither body nor soul. What's left of these past and future things and events is too thin: yesterday's headache is still an event, but it isn't painful or throbbing or much of anything else; Plato is still a substance, I suppose, but he doesn't talk or think or walk or sleep or have any spatial location. Neither Plato nor headache has any of the ordinary intrinsic properties it displayed while present. Smith's efforts to preserve the intuition behind "Thank goodness that's over!" while rejecting presentism are, I judge, unsuccessful. Past and future things become nearly-bare particulars, unreal echoes of their once or future selves. The serious tenser is much better off without them.

Why does Lewis Reject Presentism?

The serious tenser says that it is simply not true that I have the property *being straight* if I am bent now. I was straight, and will be again; but I am not now, and so there is no problem of my having incompatible intrinsic properties. Of course philosophers are free to invent a tenseless language in which "I am straight" is true just in case I either am now or was or will be straight. Who can stop philosophers from inventing peculiar ways of speaking? But the bare fact that one can talk this way doesn't create any problem about my having incompatible properties.

What is Lewis's response to this serious-tenser solution of the problem of temporary intrinsics? He seems to suppose (reasonably, I think) that someone who takes this line must be a presentist. But, by Lewis's lights, presentism is too incredible to be believed. Presentism "rejects endurance; because it rejects persistence altogether"; and it "goes against what we all believe" by implying that "there are no other times." "No man, unless it be at the moment of his execution, believes that he has no future; still less does anyone believe that he has no past." And yet, says Lewis, the presentist denies these obvious facts.[21]

This string of claims represents what might be called the "no persistence objection" to presentism. Lewis takes it that the following thesis of "Persistence through Change" is obviously true:

(PC)   There are (at least) two different times; one at which I am bent, another at which I am straight.[22]

Lewis thinks that (PC) is a simple expression of my belief that I persist through changes in my posture: there are times when I'm bent and times when I'm straight. The presentist is committed to the nonexistence of all times but one, the present. (PC) says there is more than one time; so presentism and (PC) are incompatible.

The serious-tenser dissolution of the problem of temporary intrinsics given at the beginning of this section does not require the truth of presentism; a non-presentist serious tenser like Smith has little to fear from Lewis's argument. But Smith's combination of views has turned out to be unacceptable; and so the tensed response to the problem of temporary intrinsics stands or falls with presentism.

In order for Lewis's argument to have any teeth, (PC) must have two features: (i) it must be something we all, on reflection, believe; and (ii) it must require ontological commitment to the existence of more than one time. To be something commonly believed, (PC) must correspond to the humdrum assertion that I am bent at some times and straight at others. The question is whether this belief in my persistence through change – and the similar belief had by anyone who can remember changing posture – implies that there exist more times than the present.

If the statements used to express ordinary beliefs could be counted on to wear their ontological commitments on their sleeves, then an affirmative answer would be justified. But virtually everyone must allow that many statements expressing commonsensical beliefs do *not* wear their ontological commitments on their sleeves. It would be just like Bertie Wooster to respond to Jeeves's report about the dearth of champagne in the ice box by saying: "Well, at least there's *something* in the ice box." The source of the joke here would be that, generally speaking, from the fact that there's a such-and-such in the ice box, it follows that there is something in the ice box. But when the "such-and-such" is a *dearth* of something, it doesn't follow. Why? Because the assertion that there's a dearth of something is just a fancy (and old-fashioned) way of saying that there isn't any of that something – and that's compatible with there being *nothing at all* in the ice box.

Compare (PC) with a precisely parallel case involving ontological commitment to nonactuals. I suppose that most of us believe that we could have been put in situations that would have resulted in our lives going differently than they have in fact gone. There are certain possible experiences and events which, had they happened, would have prevented me from becoming a philosopher. But does this statement commit me to the existence of nonactual experiences and events? I should think not.

A few people have believed in the existence of alternative universes, just as real and concrete as this one, but with things going differently in them – worlds in which, for instance, the Axis powers win World War II, and the US is partitioned between Germany and Japan.[23] David Lewis, in fact, believes in the literal existence of alternative universes, just as concrete as our actual world, in which every possible way things could go actually plays itself out.[24] But Lewis is one of the exceptions that prove the rule. The rest of us cannot bring ourselves to believe that there is such an event as the Axis powers' winning the war, an event with which, fortunately, we are not space–time neighbors. It's not that we ordinarily ignore these nonactual events because they are "far" from us, unreachable from our world. Rather, we think they simply are not.

How do we know that we aren't, implicitly, committed to the existence of such merely possible events? Well, we just ask ourselves whether we think they exist – whether we think that there are such things, whether we think we stand in real relationships with them. The answer comes back a resounding No. And then, if we are philosophers, we go about the business of finding plausible paraphrases for our beliefs ostensibly about nonactual possibilities – paraphrases that seem to us to capture more or less what we believed all along, but which do not even appear to imply that there are situations involving me that don't occur, or whole worlds full of people and events that are not actual. If it were to become clear that there is no way to do this, then perhaps we would feel forced to reconsider our judgment that our beliefs about alternate possibilities do not implicitly commit us to the existence of such things. But that's not usually the way things go in philosophy: there's usually more than one way to skin a philosophical cat; usually several competing approaches to a given philosophical problem emerge as favorites, with much to be said for and against each of them. And so it is here: there are ever so many fairly plausible projects under way for paraphrasing away ostensible commitment to nonactual things and situations, each with its own advantages and disadvantages, and few confront such grave obstacles as to suggest that they are absolute dead-ends.

The presentist believes that the situation is precisely parallel when it comes to my belief that there are times at which I'm bent and times at which I'm straight. Does this commit me to the existence of times other than the present? Well, when I ask myself whether I think that my childhood exists, or the time of my death, the snows of yesteryear, or the light of other days, the answer comes back a resounding No. Is it just that I feel that past and future things and events can be regarded as nonexistent because they are "temporally far" from me? I think not – the past is no more, and the future is not yet, in the strictest sense. And so those who share this judgment begin the work of philosophical paraphrase, trying to find plausible construals of statements like (5), (6), and (PC) that capture what is meant but do not involve direct reference to nonpresent times,

individuals, and events. So, for instance, (PC) can be taken as a tenseless statement expressing a disjunction of tensed propositions: Either I was bent and would
become or had previously been straight, or I was straight and would become or
had previously been bent, or I will be bent and will have been or be about to
become straight, or I will be straight and will have been or be about to become
bent. Surely this tensed disjunction is true if (PC) is true; furthermore, it contains
no mention of anything like a nonpresent time. So, given the presentist's desire
to avoid ontological commitment to nonpresent times, this tensed statement
provides a perfectly sensible paraphrase of my conviction that I can persist
through change of shape.

Furthermore, it is not as if Lewis himself allows (PC) to stand as it is, with no
paraphrastic gloss. After all, he thinks that I am bent at one time and straight at
another only in virtue of the fact that I have temporal parts located at these times,
one of which is bent, the other straight. So "there is a time at which I am bent,"
as it occurs in (PC), receives the paraphrase "there is a time at which I have a
temporal part that is bent." Lewis salvages our common conviction that we persist
through change by introducing the uncommon notion of a temporal part. But
if his temporal-parts reading of (PC) captures enough of our pretheoretical convictions to be acceptable, then surely he must allow the presentist similar leeway
in her attempt to affirm persistence through change while avoiding talk of nonpresent times.[25]

The large-scale project of paraphrasing truths ostensibly about nonpresent
times and things is as complex and difficult as the counterpart project concerning
nonactuals. Ways must be found to capture all truths about past and future things
without the appearance of ontological commitment to such things.[26] Presentists
must, for example, find a way to understand statements ostensibly about relations
that hold between presently existing things and things in the past and future.
Causation is one instance of this problem: the causal relation holds between
events; but no relation can hold between a present event and some future or past
event, since such events do not exist. Must the presentist then conclude that no
event in the present can be caused by anything earlier, or cause anything later?[27]
Such difficulties must be overcome for presentism to remain plausible.

And there are familiar chestnuts bedeviling *anyone* (presentist or not) who
takes tense seriously, such as McTaggart's paradox[28] and the puzzle about the
rate at which the present "moves." Is this rate one minute per minute? It couldn't
very well move any faster! And yet this doesn't sound like a proper rate at all.[29]
Perhaps most worrisome is that positing facts about what is present *absolutely*
(and not merely about what is "present relative to me" or "present relative to
my inertial frame") seems inconsistent with a well-confirmed scientific theory:
special relativity.[30] But, as indicated in the notes to this and the previous paragraph, these are problems which presentists and others who take tense seriously
have tried to address. Have the solutions been satisfactory? Perhaps not in every
case. But rejecting presentism on the basis of such problems would require careful
exploration of these debates – debates which have nothing to do with the
problem of temporary intrinsics *per se*. Furthermore, there is reason to be hopeful
that they will be resolved in the presentist's favor – or at least that they will not
be resolved decisively in favor of her opponents After all, as John Bigelow points

out, presentism was accepted everywhere by nearly everyone until a mere hundred or so years ago.[31] A thesis with a track record like that shouldn't be expected to go down without a fight.

So far as I know, all presentists (and almost all who take tense seriously) reject the doctrine of temporal parts; indeed Prior, Geach, and Chisholm have been among its most vocal opponents.[32] What I have tried to show is that the part of Lewis's argument aimed at these philosophers requires considerable buttressing before it will convince. In particular, we need a reason to think that some truths ostensibly about nonpresent things cannot be given plausible paraphrases that eschew commitment to such things. So far as I can see, there isn't any reason to think this is so. At any rate, Lewis hasn't (yet) given us one.

Notes

* A very distant ancestor of this paper was presented at meetings of the Central States Philosophical Association in 1990. I am grateful to my commentator on that occasion, Mark Heller, for his excellent criticisms and suggestions (which formed the basis of his paper, "Things Change," *Philosophy and Phenomenological Research*, 52 (1992), pp. 695–704); and to Roderick Chisholm, who was also present. Later on, Trenton Merricks (who, for no good reason, was *not* present at the talk) provided useful comments as well. Recent work that should be consulted includes: Merricks, "Endurance and Indiscernibility," *Journal of Philosophy*, 91 (1994), pp. 165–84; Sally Haslanger, "Endurance and Temporary Intrinsics," *Analysis*, 49 (1989), pp. 119–25; Peter M. Simons, "On Being Spread Out in Time: Temporal Parts and the Problem of Change," in *Existence and Explanation*, ed. by Wolfgang Spohn, Bas C. van Fraassen, and Brian Skyrms (Dordrecht: Kluwer, 1991), pp. 131–47; and Mark Hinchliff, "The Puzzle of Change," *Philosophical Perspectives*, vol. 10: *Metaphysics*, ed. by James E. Tomberlin (Oxford: Blackwell, 1996), pp. 119–36. I am extremely grateful to David Lewis, who provided extensive criticism of a late draft, and saved me from a number of serious mistakes. But it should not be assumed that he agrees with anything that I now say about his argument from temporary intrinsics.

1   Cf. David Lewis, *On the Plurality of Worlds* (Oxford: Blackwell, 1986), pp. 202–3; the relevant passage is reprinted in this volume as "The Problem of Temporary Intrinsics: an Excerpt from *On the Plurality of Worlds.*" Page references are to the excerpt in this volume.
2   Cf. Lewis, "The Problem of Temporary Intrinsics," p. 269.
3   It might be replied that there is no problem with having both if the verb "having" is taken *tenselessly* (that is, in such a way that "I have both" is equivalent to something like: "I had, now have, or will have the one; and I had, now have, or will have the other"). But then we should want to know why these properties deserve the label "incompatible." How do they differ from a pair of compatible intrinsics, like *being red* and *being round?*
4   Lewis, "The Problem of Temporary Intrinsics," p. 268.
5   One might, however, allow intrinsic properties to be monadic but treat the *having* of them as a relation between a thing, a property, and a time. See, for example, Peter van Inwagen, "Four-dimensional Objects," *Noûs*, 24, and Sally Haslanger, "Endurance and Temporary Intrinsics."

6   It can be found in Bolzano, Frege, Church, Chisholm, and Plantinga, to name but a few.

7   This point of view is exemplified by A. N. Prior, "The Notion of the Present" and "Some Free Thinking about Time," reprinted in this volume, and Peter Geach, "Some Problems about Time."

8   See Gerald J. Massey, "Tense Logic! Why Bother?," *Noûs*, 3 (1969), pp. 17–32.

9   If the tenseless verb used in my lecture were the ordinary historical present tense, the proposition in question would lack the final conjunct; only the more arcane tenseless verb introduced by philosophers is used to express disjunctive propositions with disjuncts concerning the future.

10   Mellor, *Real Time* (Cambridge: Cambridge University Press, 1981), ch. 5; J. J. C. Smart, "Time and Becoming," reprinted in his *Essays Metaphysical and Moral* (Oxford: Blackwell, 1987). For further defenders of the new tenseless theory, see the contributions of L. Nathan Oaklander, Michelle Beer, and Clifford Williams to Part 1 of *The New Theory of Time*, ed. by Oaklander and Quentin Smith (New Haven, Conn.: Yale University Press, 1994); for criticisms, see Quentin Smith's contributions to Part 1 of the same volume, and his *Language and Time* (Oxford: Oxford University Press, 1993).

11   Some have held that there are both tenselessly true propositions and "tensedly true" propositions, and that the former are not equivalent to disjunctions of the latter. But this is a minority opinion; most who take at least *some* fundamental truth-bearers to be mutable regard all truth as tensed truth. For some reasons to do so, see Roderick M. Chisholm and Dean W. Zimmerman, "Tense and Theology," *Noûs*, 31 (1997), pp. 262–5.

12   For a paradigmatic statement of this position, see Prior, "The Notion of the Present," reprinted in this volume.

13   On some problems for carrying out this project, see Peter van Inwagen, "Creatures of Fiction," *American Philosophical Quarterly*, 14 (1977), pp. 299–308; "Fiction and Metaphysics," *Philosophy and Literature*, 7 (1983), pp. 67–77; and "Pretense and Paraphrase," in Peter J. McCormick, ed., *The Reasons of Art* (Ottawa: University of Ottawa Press, 1985), pp. 414–22.

14   See Williams, "The Elements of Being," reprinted in this volume.

15   Compare Alvin Plantinga, "Actualism and Possible Worlds," *Theoria*, 42 (1976), pp. 139–60; reprinted in *The Possible and the Actual*, ed. by Michael J. Loux (Ithaca, N.Y.: Cornell University Press, 1979).

16   See Prior, *Papers on Time and Tense* (Oxford: Clarendon Press, 1968), pp. 142–3; and Kit Fine's Postscript to Prior and Fine, *Worlds, Times and Selves* (London: Duckworth, 1977).

17   For a general discussion of the treatment of past and future individuals in tense logic, see Prior, *Past, Present and Future* (Oxford: Clarendon Press, 1967), ch. 8. See also Chisholm, "Referring to Things That No Longer Exist," *Philosophical Perspectives*, vol. 4: *Action Theory and Philosophy of Mind* (1990), pp. 545–56.

18   See Quentin Smith, *Language and Time* (New York: Oxford University Press, 1993), see esp. ch. 5.

19   See Prior, "Some Free Thinking about Time," reprinted in this volume; and his "Thank Goodness That's Over," reprinted in Prior, *Papers in Logic and Ethics* (London: Duckworth, 1976).

20   Incidentally, Smith's approach to past and future events and things provides him with the means to define "being present" – something he claims cannot be done. Just take all the kinds of intrinsic properties which a contingent thing cannot have

when it is wholly past or future; and then say a thing is present just in case either it is a necessary thing (and so must always be present), or it is a contingent thing that has properties belonging to this special class.

21   Lewis, "The Problem of Temporary Intrinsics," p. 206.

22   This thesis, and its name, are taken from personal correspondence with Lewis, and used with his permission.

23   Such is the world of the "alternate history" novel, *The Man in the High Castle*, by Philip K. Dick. Dick became convinced that such alternate streams of history are not mere fictions, but that they are real; he claimed to have been able to "recall" events from lives lived in other worlds.

24   For Lewis's reasons for believing in concrete worlds besides this one, see his *On the Plurality of Worlds* (for the senses in which his worlds are *concrete*, see section 1.7 of the book). I should point out that, unlike Dick, Lewis's reasons are purely theoretical and *a priori*, not empirical.

25   I owe this point to Trenton Merricks.

26   For some presentist responses to the problem, cf. Prior, *Past, Present and Future*, ch. 8 ("Time and Existence"); Prior, *Papers on Time and Tense*, ch. 8 ("Time, Existence, and Identity"); R. M. Chisholm, "Referring to Things That No Longer Exist"; and John Bigelow, "Presentism and Properties," in *Philosophical Perspectives*, vol. 10: *Metaphysics*, pp. 35–52.

27   John Bigelow and I have offered, independently, very similar solutions to this problem. Cf. the final section of my "Chisholm and the Essences of Events," in *The Philosophy of Roderick M. Chisholm* (The Library of Living Philosophers), ed. by Lewis Hahn (La Salle, Ill.: Open Court, 1997); and Bigelow's "Presentism and Properties," p. 47.

28   Cf. McTaggart, "Time: An Excerpt from *The Nature of Existence*," this volume; and, for a response which, by my lights, completely dissolves this "paradox," cf. Reading 6: C. D. Broad, "McTaggart's Arguments against the Reality of Time," also in this volume.

29   D. C. Williams raises the puzzle about the rate of passage in "The Myth of passage," this volume. Presentists can hope that Ned Markosian has settled the problem for good and all in his "How Fast Does Time Pass?," *Philosophy and Phenomenological Research*, 53 (1993), pp. 829–44.

30   Prior's description of the problem and his response may be found in "Some Free Thinking about Time," reprinted in this volume. Cf. also Geach, "Some Problems about Time," *Proceedings of the British Academy*, Vol. LI (1966). More recent treatments may be found in Quentin Smith, *Language and Time*, ch. 7. For one scientist who thinks that Prior may have been right about the prematurity of giving up on the notion of absolute simultaneity, cf. J. S. Bell, *Speakable and Unspeakable in Quantum Mechanics* (Cambridge: Cambridge University Press, 1987), p. 77; and Bell's remarks in *The Ghost in the Atom*, ed. by P. C. W. Davies and J. R. Brown (Cambridge: Cambridge University Press, 1986), esp. pp. 48–51.

31   Bigelow, "Presentism and Properties," pp. 35–6.

32   For characteristic rejections of temporal parts, cf. Prior, "Some Free Thinking about Time"; Geach, "Some Problems about Time"; and Chisholm, *Person and Object: A Metaphysical Study* (La Salle, Ill.: Open Court, 1976), Appendix A, pp. 138–44. For a serious tenser who accepts temporal parts, see Quentin Smith, "Personal Identity and Time," *Philosophia*, 22 (1993) pp. 155–67.

E How do Causes Bring about their Effects?

Introduction

David Hume sets the stage for contemporary debates about causation by asking what more there could be to the notion besides spatiotemporal contiguity (causes never operate at a spatial distance, or over a temporal gap), temporal succession (causes precede their effects), and constant conjunction (resembling causes are always and everywhere followed by resembling effects). Thomas Reid rejects Hume's reduction of causation to such relations, and claims to have immediate acquaintance with active causal power to produce effects – but in only one case: that of his own actions.

Bertrand Russell, in the spirit of Hume, argues that there is nothing more to the relation of cause and effect than "nearly invariable antecedence." Near the end of the selection from her *A Modern Introduction to Logic*, Susan Stebbing responds to Russell's attempt to undermine more substantive accounts of the causal relation. But her main goal is to show how common-sense causal notions become refined by scientific knowledge, resulting in an analysis of causation in terms of (what has come to be called) "nomic subsumption": a pair of events falling under a causal law. Elizabeth Anscombe argues (contra Stebbing, Russell, and Hume) that events can be causally related without their subsumption by anything like a causal law.

Reid's views find expression elsewhere, in essays by Chisholm and O'Connor (Chs. 46 and 49). In Ch. 48, van Inwagen questions the explanatory significance of Reid's claim that the causation involved in agency is better understood than causation between events. Stebbing's relation of "immanent causation" is put to use elsewhere in the volume. In Ch. 36, Sydney Shoemaker defends, for the case of persons, a version of what he calls "the causal continuity account" of identity over time. On such a theory, earlier and later stages of a persisting thing must be bound together by relations of immanent causation. (Warning! In Ch. 46, Chisholm uses "immanent causation" to mean something quite different.)

Suggestions for further reading

Armstrong, D. M., *Universals: An Opinionated Introduction* (Boulder, Col.: Westview Press, 1989) pp. 82–4.

Aune, Bruce, *Metaphysics: The Elements* (Minneapolis: University of Minnesota, 1985) ch. 6 ("Worlds, Objects, and Structure").

Carroll, John W., "Nailed to Hume's Cross?," in Sider, Hawthorne, and Zimmerman (eds.), *Contemporary Debates in Metaphysics* (Malden, Mass.: Blackwell, 2007).

Carter, William R., *The Elements of Metaphysics* (Philadelphia, Penn.: Temple University Press, 1990) ch. 9 ("Causal Determinism").

Hales, Stephen, *Metaphysics: Contemporary Readings* (Belmont, Cal.: Wadsworth, 1998) Section 7 ("Concreta: Events," readings by Bennett, Kim, and Lombard).

Laurence, Stephen, and Macdonald, Cynthia, *Contemporary Readings in the Foundations of Metaphysics* (Oxford: Basil Blackwell, 1998) Section 5 ("Events," readings by Lombard and Kim).

Loux, Michael, *Metaphysics: A Contemporary Introduction*, 2nd edn (London: Routledge, 2002) ch. 4 ("Propositions and Their Neighbors").

Schaffer, Jonathan, "Causation and Laws of Nature: Reductionism," in Sider, Hawthorne, and Zimmerman (eds.), *Contemporary Debates in Metaphysics* (Malden, Mass.: Blackwell, 2007).

Taylor, Richard, *Metaphysics*, 4th edn (Englewood Cliffs, N.J.: Prentice-Hall, 1992) ch. 10 ("Causation").

30 Constant Conjunction: an Excerpt from *A Treatise of Human Nature*

David Hume

To begin regularly, we must consider the idea of *causation*, and see from what origin it is deriv'd. 'Tis impossible to reason justly, without understanding perfectly the idea concerning which we reason; and 'tis impossible perfectly to understand any idea, without tracing it up to its origin, and examining that primary impression, from which it arises. The examination of the impression bestows a clearness on the idea; and the examination of the idea bestows a like clearness on all our reasoning.

Let us therefore cast our eye on any two objects, which we call cause and effect, and turn them on all sides, in order to find that impression, which produces an idea of such prodigious consequence. At first sight I perceive, that I must not search for it in any of the particular *qualities* of the objects; since, which-ever of these qualities I pitch on, I find some object, that is not possest of it, and yet falls under the denomination of cause or effect. And indeed there is nothing existent, either externally or internally, which is not to be consider'd either as a cause or an effect; tho' 'tis plain there is no one quality, which universally belongs to all beings, and gives them a title to that denomination.

The idea, then, of causation must be deriv'd from some *relation* among objects; and that relation we must now endeavour to discover. I find in the first place, that what-ever objects are consider'd as causes or effects, are *contiguous*; and that nothing can operate in a time or place, which is ever so little remov'd from those of its existence. Tho' distant objects may sometimes seem productive of each other, they are commonly found upon examination to be link'd by a chain of causes, which are contiguous among themselves, and to the distant objects; and when in any particular instance we cannot discover this connexion, we still presume it to exist. We may therefore consider the relation of CONTIGUITY as essential to that of causation; at least may suppose it such, according to the general opinion, till we can find a more[1] proper occasion to clear up this matter, by examining what objects are or are not susceptible of juxtaposition and conjunction.

The second relation I shall observe as essential to causes and effects, is not so universally acknowledg'd, but is liable to some controversy. That of PRIORITY of time in the cause before the effect. Some pretend that 'tis not absolutely necessary a cause shou'd precede its effect; but that any object or action, in the very first moment of its existence, may exert its productive quality, and give rise to another object or action, perfectly co-temporary with itself. But beside that experience in most instances seems to contradict this opinion, we may establish the relation of priority by a kind of inference or reasoning. 'Tis an establish'd maxim both in natural and moral philosophy, that an object, which exists for any time in its full perfection without producing another, is not its sole cause; but is assisted by some other principle, which pushes it from its state of inactivity, and makes it exert that energy, of which it was secretly possest. Now if any cause may be perfectly co-temporary with its effect, 'tis certain, according to this maxim, that they must all of them be so; since any one of them, which retards its operation for a single moment, exerts not itself at that very individual time, in which it might have operated; and therefore is no proper cause. The consequence of this wou'd be no less than the destruction of that succession of causes, which we observe, in the world; and indeed, the utter annihilation of time. For if one cause were co-temporary with its effect, and this effect with *its* effect, and so on, 'tis plain there wou'd be no such thing as succession, and all objects must be co-existent.

If this argument appear satisfactory, 'tis well. If not, I beg the reader to allow me the same liberty, which I have us'd in the preceding case, of supposing it such. For he shall find, that the affair is of no great importance.

Having thus discover'd or suppos'd the two relations of *contiguity* and *succession* to be essential to causes and effects, I find I am stopt short, and can proceed no farther in considering any single instance of cause and effect. Motion in one body is regarded upon impulse as the cause of motion in another. When we consider these objects with the utmost attention, we find only that the one body approaches the other; and that the motion of it precedes that of the other, but without any sensible interval. 'Tis in vain to rack ourselves with *farther* thought and reflexion upon this subject. We can go no *farther* in considering this particular instance.

Shou'd any one leave this instance, and pretend to define a cause, by saying it is something productive of another, 'tis evident he wou'd say nothing. For what does he mean by *production*? Can he give any definition of it, that will not be the same with that of causation? If he can; I desire it may be produc'd. If he cannot; he here runs in a circle, and gives a synonimous term instead of a definition.

Shall we then rest contented with these two relations of contiguity and succession, as affording a compleat idea of causation? By no means. An object may be contiguous and prior to another, without being consider'd as its cause. There is a NECESSARY CONNEXION to be taken into consideration; and that relation is of much greater importance, than any of the other two above-mention'd.

Here again I turn the object on all sides, in order to discover the nature of this necessary connexion, and find the impression, or impressions, from which its idea may be deriv'd. When I cast my eye on the *known qualities* of objects, I immediately discover that the relation of cause and effect depends not in the least on *them*. When I consider their *relations*, I can find none but those of contiguity and succession; which I have already regarded as imperfect and unsatisfactory. Shall the despair of success make me assert, that I am here possest of an idea, which is not preceded by any similar impression? This wou'd be too strong a proof of levity and inconstancy; since the contrary principle has been already so firmly establish'd, as to admit of no farther doubt; at least, till we have more fully examin'd the present difficulty.

We must, therefore, proceed like those, who being in search of any thing, that lies conceal'd from them, and not finding it in the place they expected, beat about all the neighbouring fields, without any certain view or design, in hopes their good fortune will at last guide them to what they search for. . . .

Suppose two objects to be presented to us, of which the one is the cause and the other the effect; 'tis plain, that from the simple consideration of one, or both these objects we never shall perceive the tie, by which they are united, or be able certainly to pronounce, that there is a connexion betwixt them. 'Tis not, therefore, from any one instance, that we arrive at the idea of cause and effect, of a necessary connexion of power, of force, of energy, and of efficacy. Did we never see any but particular conjunctions of objects, entirely different from each other, we shou'd never be able to form any such ideas.

But again; suppose we observe several instances, in which the same objects are always conjoin'd together, we immediately conceive a connexion betwixt them, and begin to draw an inference from one to another. This multiplicity of resembling instances, therefore, constitutes the very essence of power or connexion, and is the source, from which the idea of it arises. In order, then, to understand the idea of power, we must consider that multiplicity; nor do I ask more to give a solution of that difficulty, which has so long perplex'd us. For thus I reason. The repetition of perfectly similar instances can never *alone* give rise to an original idea, different from what is to be found in any particular instance, as has been observ'd, and as evidently follows from our fundamental principle, *that all ideas are copy'd from impressions.* Since therefore the idea of power is a new original idea, not to be found in any one instance; and which yet arises from the repetition of several instances, it follows, that the repetition *alone* has not that effect, but must either *discover* or *produce* something new, which is the source of that idea. Did the repetition neither discover nor produce any thing new, our ideas might be multiply'd by it, but wou'd not be enlarg'd above what they are upon the observation of one single instance. Every enlargement, therefore, (such as the idea of power or connexion) which arises from the multiplicity of similar instances, is copy'd from some effects of the multiplicity, and will be perfectly understood by understanding these effects. Wherever we find any thing new to be discover'd or produc'd by the repetition, there we must place the power, and must never look for it in any other object.

But 'tis evident, in the first place, that the repetition of like objects in like relations of succession and contiguity *discovers* nothing new in any one of them; since we can draw no inference from it, nor make it a subject either of our demonstrative or probable reasonings,[2] as has been already prov'd. Nay suppose we cou'd draw an inference, 'twou'd be of no consequence in the present case; since no kind of reasoning can give rise to a new idea, such as this of power is; but wherever we reason, we must antecedently be possest of clear ideas, which may be the objects of our reasoning. The conception always precedes the understanding; and where the one is obscure, the other is uncertain; where the one fails, the other must fail also.

Secondly, 'Tis certain that this repetition of similar objects in similar situations *produces* nothing new either in these objects, or in any external body. For 'twill readily be allow'd, that the several instances we have of the conjunction of resembling causes and effects are in themselves entirely independent, and that the communication of motion, which I see result at present from the shock of two billiard-balls, is totally distinct from that which I saw result from such an impulse a twelve-month ago. These impulses have no influence on each other. They are entirely divided by time and place; and the one might have existed and communicated motion, tho' the other never had been in being.

There is, then, nothing new either discover'd or produc'd in any objects by their constant conjunction, and by the uninterrupted resemblance of their relations of succession and contiguity. But 'tis from this resemblance, that the ideas of necessity, of power, and of efficacy, are deriv'd. These ideas, therefore, represent not any thing, that does or can belong to the objects, which are constantly conjoin'd. This is an argument, which, in every view we can examine it, will be found perfectly unanswerable. Similar instances are still the first source of our idea of power or necessity; at the same time that they have no influence by their similarity either on each other, or on any external object. We must therefore, turn ourselves to some other quarter to seek the origin of that idea.

Tho' the several resembling instances, which give rise to the idea of power, have no influence on each other, and can never produce any new quality *in the object*, which can be the model of that idea, yet the *observation* of this resemblance produces a new impression *in the mind*, which is its real model. For after we have observ'd the resemblance in a sufficient number of instances, we immediately feel a determination of the mind to pass from one object to its usual attendant, and to conceive it in a stronger light upon account of that relation. This determination is the only effect of the resemblance; and therefore must be the same with power or efficacy, whose idea is deriv'd from the resemblance. The several instances of resembling conjunctions lead us into the notion of power and necessity. These instances are in themselves totally distinct from each other, and have no union but in the mind, which observes them, and collects their ideas. Necessity, then, is the effect of this observation, and is nothing but an internal impression of the mind, or a determination to carry our thoughts from one object to another. Without considering it in this view, we can never arrive at the most distant notion of it, or be able to attribute it either to external or internal objects, to spirit or body, to causes or effects.

The necessary connexion betwixt causes and effects is the foundation of our inference from one to the other. The foundation of our inference is the transition arising from the accustom'd union. These are, therefore, the same.

The idea of necessity arises from some impression. There is no impression convey'd by our senses, which can give rise to that idea. It must, therefore, be deriv'd from some internal impression, or impression of reflexion. There is no internal impression, which has any relation to the present business, but that propensity, which custom produces, to pass from an object to the idea of its usual attendant. This therefore is the essence of necessity. Upon the whole, necessity is something, that exists in the mind, not in objects; nor is it possible for us ever to form the most distant idea of it, consider'd as a quality in bodies. Either we have no idea of necessity, or necessity is nothing but that determination of the thought to pass from causes to effects and from effects to causes, according to their experienc'd union. . . .

'Tis now time to collect all the different parts of this reasoning, and by joining them together form an exact definition of the relation of cause and effect, which makes the subject of the present enquiry. . . .

There may two definitions be given of this relation, which are only different, by their presenting a different view of the same object, and making us consider it either as a *philosophical* or as a *natural* relation; either as a comparison of two ideas, or as an association betwixt them. We may define a CAUSE to be 'An object precedent and contiguous to another, and where all the objects resembling the former are plac'd in like relations of precedency and contiguity to those objects, that resemble the latter.' If this definition be esteem'd defective, because drawn from objects foreign to the cause, we may substitute this other definition in its place, *viz.* 'A CAUSE is an object precedent and contiguous to another, and so united with it, that the idea of the one determines the mind to form the idea of the other, and the impression of the one to form a more lively idea of the other.' Shou'd this definition also be rejected for the same reason, I know no other remedy, than that the persons, who express this delicacy, should substitute a juster definition in its place. But for my part I must own my incapacity for such an undertaking. When I examine with the utmost accuracy those objects, which are commonly denominated causes and effects, I find, in considering a single instance, that the one object is precedent and contiguous to the other; and in inlarging my view to consider several instances, I find only, that like objects are constantly plac'd in like relations of succession and contiguity. Again, when I consider the influence of this constant conjunction, I perceive, that such a relation can never be an object of reasoning, and can never operate upon the mind, but by means of custom, which determines the imagination to make a transition from the idea of one object to that of its usual attendant, and from the impression of one to a more lively idea of the other. However extraordinary these sentiments may appear, I think it fruitless to trouble myself with any farther enquiry or reasoning upon the subject, but shall repose myself on them as on establish'd maxims.

Notes

1 [Book I,] part IV, sect. 5.
2 [Book I,] part III, sect. 6.

31 Efficient Cause and Active Power: an Excerpt from *Essays on the Active Powers of the Human Mind*

Thomas Reid

That active power is an attribute, which cannot exist but in some being possessed of that power, and the subject of that attribute, I take for granted as a self-evident truth. Whether there can be active power in a subject which has no thought, nor understanding, no will, is not so evident. . . .

When I observe a plant growing from its seed to maturity, I know that there must be a cause that has power to produce this effect. But I see neither the cause nor the manner of its operation.

But in certain motions of my body, and directions of my thought, I know, not only that there must be a cause that has power to produce these effects, but that I am that cause; and I am conscious of what I do in order to the production of them.

From the consciousness of our own activity, seems to be derived, not only the clearest, but the only conception we can form of activity, or the exertion of active power. . . .

If it be so that the conception of an efficient cause enters into the mind, only from the early conviction we have that we are the efficients of our own voluntary actions, which I think is most probable, the notion of efficiency will be reduced to this, that it is a relation between the cause and the effect, similar to that which is between us and our voluntary actions. This is surely the most distinct notion, and, I think, the only notion we can form of real efficiency.

Now it is evident, that, to constitute the relation between me and my action, my conception of the action, and will to do it, are essential. For what I never conceived, nor willed, I never did.

If any man, therefore, affirms, that a being may be the efficient cause of an action, and have power to produce it, which that being can neither conceive nor will, he speaks a language which I do not understand. If he has a meaning, his notion of power and efficiency must be essentially different from mine; and, until he conveys his notion of efficiency to my understanding, I can no more assent to his opinion, than if he should affirm, that a being without life may feel pain.

It seems therefore to me most probable, that such beings only as have some degree of understanding and will, can possess active power; and that inanimate beings must be merely passive, and have no real activity. Nothing we perceive without us affords any good ground for ascribing active power to any inanimate being; and every thing we can discover in our own constitution, leads us to think, that active power cannot be exerted without will and intelligence.

32   Psychological and Physical Causal Laws: an Excerpt from *The Analysis of Mind*

Bertrand Russell

The traditional conception of cause and effect is one which modern science shows to be fundamentally erroneous, and requiring to be replaced by a quite different notion, that of *laws of change*. In the traditional conception, a particular event A caused a particular event B, and by this it was implied that, given any event B, some earlier event A could be discovered which had a relation to it, such that –

(1)   Whenever A occurred, it was followed by B;
(2)   In this sequence, there was something "necessary," not a mere *de facto* occurrence of A first and then B.

The second point is illustrated by the old discussion as to whether it can be said that day causes night, on the ground that day is always followed by night. The orthodox answer was that day could not be called the cause of night, because it would not be followed by night if the earth's rotation were to cease, or rather to grow so slow that one complete rotation would take a year. A cause, it was held, must be such that under no conceivable circumstances could it fail to be followed by its effect.

As a matter of fact, such sequences as were sought by believers in the traditional form of causation have not so far been found in nature. Everything in nature is apparently in a state of continuous change,[1] so that what we call one "event" turns out to be really a process. If this event is to cause another event, the two will have to be contiguous in time; for if there is any interval between them, something may happen during that interval to prevent the expected effect. Cause and effect, therefore, will have to be temporally contiguous processes. It is difficult to believe, at any rate where physical laws are concerned, that the earlier part of the process which is the cause can make any difference to the effect, so long as the later part of the process which is the cause remains unchanged. Suppose, for example, that a man dies of arsenic poisoning, we say that his taking arsenic was the cause of death. But clearly the process by which he acquired the arsenic is irrelevant: everything that happened before he swallowed it may be ignored, since it cannot alter the effect except in so far as it alters his condition at the moment of taking the dose. But we may go further: swallowing arsenic is not really the proximate cause of death, since a man might be shot through the head immediately after taking the dose, and then it would not be of arsenic that he would die. The arsenic produces certain physiological changes, which take a finite time before they end in death. The earlier parts of these changes can be ruled out in the same way as we can rule out the process by which the arsenic was acquired. Proceeding in this way, we can shorten the process which we are calling the cause more and more. Similarly we shall have to shorten the effect. It may happen that immediately after the man's death his body is blown to pieces by a bomb. We cannot say what will happen after the man's death, through merely knowing that he has died as the result of arsenic poisoning. Thus, if we are to take the cause as one event and the effect as another, both must be shortened indefinitely. The result is that we merely have, as the embodiment of our causal law, a certain direction of change at each moment. Hence we are brought to differential equations as embodying causal laws. A physical law does not say "A will be followed by B," but tells us what acceleration a particle will have under given circumstances, i.e. it tells us how the particle's motion is changing at each moment, not where the particle will be at some future moment.

Laws embodied in differential equations may possibly be exact, but cannot be known to be so. All that we can know empirically is approximate and liable to exceptions; the exact laws that are assumed in physics are known to be somewhere near the truth, but are not known to be true just as they stand. The laws that we actually know empirically have the form of the traditional causal laws, except that they are not to be regarded as universal or necessary. "Taking arsenic is followed by death" is a good empirical generalization; it may have exceptions, but they will be rare. As against the professedly exact laws of physics, such empirical generalizations have the advantage that they deal with observable phenomena. We cannot observe infinitesimals, whether in time or space; we do not even know whether time and space are infinitely divisible. Therefore rough empirical generalizations have a definite place in science, in spite of not being exact or universal. They are the data for more exact laws, and the grounds for believing that they are *usually* true are stronger than the grounds for believing that the more exact laws are *always* true.

Science starts, therefore, from generalizations of the form, "A is usually followed by B." This is the nearest approach that can be made to a causal law of the traditional sort. It may happen in any particular instance that A is *always* followed by B, but we cannot know this, since we cannot foresee all the perfectly possible circumstances that might make the sequence fail, or know that none of them will actually occur. If, however, we know of a very large number of cases in which A is followed by B, and few or none in which the sequence fails, we shall in *practice* be justified in saying "A causes B," provided we do not attach to the notion of cause any of the metaphysical superstitions that have gathered about the word.

There is another point, besides lack of universality and necessity, which it is important to realize as regards causes in the above sense, and that is the lack of uniqueness. It is generally assumed that, given any event, there is some one phenomenon which is *the* cause of the event in question. This seems to be a mere mistake. Cause, in the only sense in which it can be practically applied, means "nearly invariable antecedent." We cannot in practice obtain an antecedent which is *quite* invariable, for this would require us to take account of the whole universe, since something not taken account of may prevent the expected effect. We cannot distinguish, among nearly invariable antecedents, one as *the* cause, and the others as merely its concomitants: the attempt to do this depends upon a notion of

cause which is derived from will, and will (as we shall see later) is not a[
sort of thing that it is generally supposed to be, nor is there any reason [
that in the physical world there is anything even remotely analogous to v
is supposed to be. If we could find one antecedent, and only one, that was *quite*
invariable, we could call that one *the* cause without introducing any notion
derived from mistaken ideas about will. But in fact we cannot find any antecedent
that we know to be quite invariable, and we can find many that are nearly so.
For example, men leave a factory for dinner when the hooter sounds at twelve
o'clock. You may say the hooter is *the* cause of their leaving. But innumerable
other hooters in other factories, which also always sound at twelve o'clock, have
just as good a right to be called the cause. Thus every event has many nearly
invariable antecedents, and therefore many antecedents which may be called
its cause. . . .

Note

1   The theory of quanta suggests that the continuity is only apparent. If so, we shall be
    able theoretically to reach events which are not processes. But in what is directly
    observable there is still apparent continuity, which justifies the above remarks for
    the present.

---

33   Causality: an Excerpt from
A Modern Introduction to Logic

L. Susan Stebbing

The Common-sense Notion of Cause

The plain man quite well understands how to use the word 'cause'. Most transitive verbs, except those that express emotional attitudes, express causation, e.g.
make, produce, influence, cure, fell, cook, raise, build, destroy. If the plain man is
asked, 'What do you mean by a cause?' he will probably reply 'What makes a
thing happen.' He knows that he is using the notion of cause when he says, 'The
child died from pneumonia', 'It was a fused wire that set the house on fire', 'The
heat has expanded the railway line', 'She moved the clock so roughly that it has
stopped.' He means something definite when he says, 'You won't find a cure for
cancer until you know its cause.' This correct *use* of the notion of causation is,
however, compatible with an extremely confused conception of what exactly
causation is. The discussions of philosophers have done little, if anything, to clear
up these confusions. There is some justification for Mr Russell's remark that 'the

word "cause" is so inextricably bound up with misleading associations as to make its complete extrusion from the philosophical vocabulary desirable'.[1] But, whatever may be the case with philosophy, it is not possible to expel the word or the conception from science. 'Cause' expresses a concept indispensable to the earlier stages of the attempt to order the facts of experience. It is by reference to this concept that the conception of uniformities may be made determinate. It is from this point of view that we have now to consider what is meant by causal connexion. . . .

Consider the proposition *The rain wets the pavement*. This might be expressed by 'The rain causes the pavement to be wet.' In asserting such a proposition the plain man would mean that on this occasion the pavement would not have been wet unless the rain had fallen on it. He would be ready to admit that on other occasions the wetness might be due to the spraying from a water-cart, or from a burst water-main. Again, 'Charles I died because his head was cut off' would be taken to mean that the beheading of Charles I was that occurrence that ended his life; that had the axe not struck his neck with some degree of force he would not have died as and when he did die. Thus common sense seems to regard the cause as an occurrence *relevant* to the happening of the effect. Given that the cause occurs, then the effect occurs. It seems clear that the conception of causation is confined by common sense to what happens in space and time (or in time only in the case of mental events[2]) and to this only in so far as what happens is regarded as changing, that is, as altering in character. In the example, 'The rain wets the pavement', clearly it is *the falling of the rain* that is the cause, and what it causes is a change *in the character* of the pavement. It does not cause *the pavement* but the *wetness* of the pavement which was previously dry. If the pavement had not been there, there could not be a wet *pavement*; but the pavement may be there without being *wet*. Or, to take an example given in an earlier chapter, 'The air pulse chills the hot wire.' Here the effect is *a change in the temperature* of the wire. Thus the notion of causation seems to be applied to a change in the character of something. We have used 'occurrence' to denote a spatio-temporal happening having determinate characters, or properties. Thus *the cause* is an occurrence related to some other occurrence, *the effect*. 'Occurrence' suggests something changing. But the effect is considered to be a change in something which relative to it continues unchanged.

The notion of cause, then, seems to arise when we observe a change occurring in something. It is obvious that common sense will pay most attention to striking changes. A change is striking when it is sensationally impressive or emotionally affecting. It is for such changes that common sense seeks causes. Further, in determining which of the various occurrences that are present is to be taken as *the* cause common sense again selects what is striking. This selection is due to the practical attitude of the plain man who wants to know not only *what has caused* a given effect but *how to produce* such an effect on another occasion. This practical attitude is reflected in the traditional problems of causation. On the one hand, the occurrence selected as *the cause* has been isolated from other occurrences which are in fact joint-factors with it; on the other hand, the occurrence regarded as *the effect* has been left unanalysed so that different sets of factors have been regarded as the *same* effect. Hence has arisen what is known as the problem of the plurality of causes. The hackneyed illustration 'Many causes may produce death' affords the best example. There are more ways of killing a cat than drowning it in butter. Each of these ways would effectually kill the cat, although its state of mind and body might be very different according to what mode of killing it was actually adopted. The procedure of a coroner's court is based upon the assumption that if the total characters of the effect-occurrence, viz. *the death of the person*, be made determinate, then the precise character of the cause-occurrence can be ascertained. This assumption may be mistaken but it is at least plausible. It suggests a refinement of the common-sense notion of cause, and one, moreover, that would be quite useless to common sense. For practical purposes it is a positive advantage to know various different ways of obtaining a certain result, and it is often irrelevant for the given purpose what *other* results are also brought about. Thus, if a man desires to kill his enemy he can achieve his object by stabbing him through the heart, or by poisoning him, or by drowning him, and so on. One can obtain roast pig by burning down the house that contains the pig. The method may be wasteful, but it does not *therefore* fail of its effect. A desire to roast pigs with less expensive apparatus would suggest the elimination of certain factors from the causal occurrence, and this would involve the elimination of certain factors from the effect-occurrence.

Again, since its standpoint is practical, common sense can afford to ignore those conditions that are usually present and can therefore be taken for granted. For example, the plain man wants to light a match. He rubs it on the side of the match-box and obtains the desired result. He would say that the friction caused the flame. If, however, the operation were performed inside a jar from which the air had been exhausted, it would be found that the match did not light. He would thus find that the presence of oxygen is also necessary for the production of the effect. Since, however, air is always present when the plain man strikes a match, he takes its presence for granted and pays attention to those factors only in the total situation which he is aware of as changing. . . .

Development of the Common-sense Notion of Cause

We have seen that as practical agents we start from a complex situation within which we desire to bring about certain changes. Provided that the desired result is achieved what *else* is achieved can be neglected. Similarly with what is *not* desired. It is what is *always* present when death is present that matters from the practical point of view. Hence, 'death' stands for a set of properties abstracted from a complex set of conditions. Whenever a man is shot through the heart, *he dies*. Whenever *a man is dead*, he ceases to respond to our entreaties. The italicized words stand for complex situations which, in each case, is from the practical point of view a *single* occurrence. Such occurrences, taken as *single*, are of varying degrees of abstractness. Thus *death* is an abstraction requiring analysis. Such analysis takes us away from the standpoint of common sense. It involves looking at the whole situation retrospectively, not prospectively. The former attitude is that of the coroner's court and the scientific investigator, the latter is that of the practical agent; the one is concerned with *knowing*, the other with *doing*. Both are concerned with uniformities, i.e. regular connexions. The practical agent, however, is content with a relation that is determinate only in the direction *from* cause *to* effect: *wherever X occurs, E occurs*. Such a relation may be many–one: given the cause, then the effect is determined, but not conversely. But the scientific investigator wants to find a relation that is equally determinate in either direction, that is, he seeks a one–one relation: *wherever X occurs, E occurs, and E does not occur unless X has occurred*. He has accordingly to analyse the conditions into their constituent factors so that he may ascertain whether any are irrelevant, and whether any, though necessary, are not sufficient to the occurrence of the result. The appearance of a plurality of causes, for example, that death may sometimes be caused by pneumonia, sometimes by drowning, etc., or that thirst may be quenched by water or by cider, arises from the neglect of certain factors in the total situation that constitutes the effect-occurrence. This should be clear from what has preceded. . . .

We pinch a piece of india-rubber and its shape changes. We drop a lump of sugar into hot coffee and it dissolves. Here we have two examples of common-sense things whose characteristics change. The india-rubber left lying on the table does not change in shape. The sugar in the bowl does not dissolve. If the table is pinched, it does not change in shape. This last example suggests that the occurrence of an effect depends upon the nature of both the things that are brought into relation. The same movement of pinching will change the shape of the india-rubber but will not change the shape of the table. Thus the common-sense notion of cause seems to involve three assumptions: (1) that it is things that enter into the causal relation; (2) that the characteristics which belong to the thing, or, as common sense would say, 'the nature of the thing', is relevant to the causal situation; (3) that things left to themselves do not undergo changes. The attempt to see what precisely is involved in these assumptions may enable us to understand more clearly what causation is.

(1)   The conception of what constitutes a *thing* is more or less vague. . . . But common sense distinguishes between a *thing* and *its states*. For example, the paper covering a wall would be regarded as a thing; the changes in colour as the wall-paper fades would be regarded as *states* of the wall-paper. These states also have characteristics. For example, the state of the wall-paper has the characteristic of being a pale grey-blue. The wall-paper is a thing; it has characteristics of a different kind; for example, it has the characteristic of altering in colour under the action of sunlight. Or consider *this piece of india-rubber*. It is a thing; it has the characteristic of altering in shape when pinched. *This lump of sugar* is another thing; it has the characteristic of *dissolving in water*. These characteristics of *fading*, of *elasticity*, of *solubility* belong to the thing not to its states. We shall call such characteristics *causal characteristics*.[3] Each state of the thing has determinate characteristics, a definite shade of colour, a definite shape, and so on. Such characteristics we shall call *primary characteris-*

tics. When a thing changes from one state to another these primary characteristics may be different. Since these states are states *of* the thing we say that *the thing* changes. But we want also to regard the thing as *persisting through* its changes. It is for this reason that we seek for a cause of change but not of persistence. What changes are the states; what does not change is the thing *of* which the states are states. The state of a thing is an occurrence. We easily recognize this in the case of water that has become frozen. We recognize the water *in a frozen state* and we see that this is an occurrence that has happened to the water. We do not so easily recognize *persisting in a state* as an occurrence. For example, if the table is in the state of continuing to be a definite shade of brown, we do not commonly think of this persisting in a definite shade as an occurrence. But if the table is knocked over we think of it as in the state of falling. There is no logical justification for thus distinguishing between these two cases. In both cases the table *has* a certain state, or is *in* a certain state, and each state has determinate, primary characteristics. Common sense usually calls such primary characteristics 'simple qualities'. Although it is *things* that common sense regards as entering into the causal relation, it is not *a thing* that is taken to be the cause but a certain *state* of the thing. For example, a table is not a cause, but a table *in the state of falling* may cause some one's leg to be hurt. It is, however, a state *of the table*, so that the causal relation involves reference to things.

(2) What common sense calls 'the nature of the thing' is the set of characteristics that belong to it. But common sense does not clearly distinguish between the causal characteristics which belong to the thing and the primary characteristics which belong to its states. Nor is common sense at all clear with regard to the distinction between a *state* of a thing and a *characteristic.* . . . The causal characteristics of a thing are what the chemist calls the 'properties' of a chemical substance, such as a fat or a metal. We can now define this notion. *A causal characteristic of a thing is a characteristic mode of behaviour in relation to other things.* Thus *'the nature of a thing'* includes those characteristics that it exhibits in relation to other things. . . .

(3) The assumption that 'things left to themselves' do not undergo change, also fails of precision, since it involves the notion of 'one thing'. The conception of what constitutes *one thing* is vague. Whether X is to be called one thing or an aggregate of things depends, so far as common sense is concerned, mainly upon practical considerations. A lampstand and the electric-light bulb and the shade all constitute *one thing* if the lamp be used to light a room. From the point of view of purchasing the lamp, there are at least three things. . . . Apart from purely practical purposes common sense would probably regard *one thing* as definable by reference to the occupation of a sensibly continuous spatial boundary, either neglecting the time dimension or including it under the notion of persistence of sensibly similar characteristics through a period of time. We have seen that common sense distinguishes between a thing and its states. When there is considerable alteration in the primary characteristics, then common sense would

refuse to admit the persistence of the thing. Thus common sense requires sensible continuity of characteristics, and assumes that there is such sensible continuity even when it has not been continuously perceived. Hence, it is argued, if there is a change in the sensible characteristics manifested by a thing in a certain state, there must be something to *make* it change. In this way arises the assumption that things left to themselves do not change. For example, given that a candle is one thing, then common sense does not expect it to change while the candle is standing unlighted on the table. If the candle which was standing upright in the candlestick is, after a few hours, bending over the candlestick, common sense assumes that something other than the candle has caused the change, e.g. the heat of the room. It is a causal characteristic of the candle to become bent under certain conditions of temperature. These conditions are dependent upon other things, for example, the fire, the relative positions of the fire and the candle, etc. From the causal point of view these conditions constitute one situation, or set of related things, which may be regarded as a *system*. If the candle in its stick were regarded as one system, we should have to distinguish at least three different things, viz. candlestick, tallow, wick. These things are in spatio-temporal relations. If no change were occurring in this system, then it would be assumed that no change would occur *unless* something outside the system, e.g. a fire, or a lighted match, came into spatio-temporal relation with it. If, however, change were occurring in the candle-system independently of anything outside it, then it would be assumed that something was going on all the time *in* the system, whether it were at first perceptible or not.

We see, then, that the attempt to analyse a total causal situation involves the distinction of different factors standing in spatio-temporal relations. *What* occurs will be dependent upon the causal characteristics of the things in that situation. Thus the fire which melts the candle merely warms the brass candlestick. A roaring fire in the kitchen does not melt the candle in the bedroom. The factors in a causal situation must be in spatio-temporal proximity.[4] But not everything in the given situation is relevant to the given causal occurrence. If it were there would be no causal uniformities since some factors in the situation do not recur. No two causal situations are exactly alike. A causal uniformity is a connexion between factors *recognizable as the same* on different occasions of their occurrence, i.e. under varying conditions and at different places and times.

The development of the common-sense notion of cause brings out several points of importance. The consideration of these will enable us to make clear certain distinctions with regard to which common sense is confused.

(1)   A causal uniformity is an abstraction since it connects sets of recurrent characteristics belonging to events which do not recur.

(2)   Neither the distinction between a thing and its states, nor the distinction between the qualities that a thing has and the way in which it behaves in relation to other things is clearly drawn at the level of common sense. . . .

. . . These distinctions throw light upon the distinction, so vaguely conceived by common sense, between *cause* and *condition*. Since the causal characteristics of the thing are its characteristic modes of behaviour in relation to other things, it follows that how a thing behaves depends upon what other things are in relation to it. This may be made clearer by means of an example. Let us consider a simple experiment. A bell so arranged that it can be continuously rung by clockwork is hung by silk threads inside a glass jar. The air in the jar is exhausted by an air-pump. As the air is withdrawn, the sound decreases, and very soon ceases to be heard, although the tongue of the bell still strikes against its sides. Given this arrangement, then, the air is a necessary condition for the propagation of sound. Now, it would commonly be said that the striking of the bell was the sufficient cause of the sound. This experiment shows that a material medium, such as air or water, is also required for the production of the sound. This material medium is then said to be a *condition*. Both the air and the striking of the bell are necessary for the production of the sound; together they are sufficient. Reflection upon this distinction emphasizes the importance of the causal characteristics of things. In the bell experiment the medium has the causal characteristic of being able to propagate sound-waves; the bell has the causal characteristic of vibrating in such a way when struck as to set up sound-waves in a suitable medium in spatio-temporal proximity to it. A condition is, then, whatever must be present in a given situation in order that a causal characteristic of a thing may be manifested in a state of the thing, which state will have certain determinate characteristics. This state is the effect. The cause is that state of some other thing upon which the effect is consequent. In the example of the bell, the cause may be said to be the impact of the tongue upon the sides; the effect is the vibration of the sides which has for *its* effect the communication of sound-waves to the surrounding air. This distinction between cause and condition cannot be made perfectly precise and is misleading if pressed too far. What is important is to distinguish between a *sufficient* condition and a *necessary* condition. A condition X is a *sufficient condition* of an occurrence A provided that whenever X is present A occurs. But if A may occur when X is absent, then X, though a sufficient, is not a *necessary* condition of A. Thus a condition N is a *necessary condition* of A provided that A never occurs in the absence of N. A condition NS is a *necessary and sufficient condition* of an occurrence A provided that (i) whenever NS is present A occurs, and (ii) whenever NS is absent A does not occur. Owing to the failure of common sense to recognize these distinctions X is sometimes said to be 'the cause' of A when it is a necessary but not a sufficient condition, and also when it is a sufficient but not a necessary condition. This ambiguity in the use of the word 'cause' is due to the *practical* interests of common sense, which, as we saw, leads to the selection of a striking, or impressive, factor out of the set of factors that are jointly sufficient and independently necessary to the production of the effect. Hence, common sense fails to recognize that what we have to take into account is a system the parts of which are in mutual dependence. This dependence is causal dependence.

(3)   It follows from what has just been said that the distinction between cause and effect cannot be made as sharply as common sense makes it. The emphasis must be placed upon the relation, *cause* and *effect* being merely the terms in the relation, selected because they are striking, or practically important, or are easily discriminated. This practical emphasis leads, as we saw, to the neglect of other factors that are relevant, and hence to the conception of the causal relation as being not only asymmetrical but also many–one. But it is usually assumed that if the cause and the effect are determined with equal precision, the relation will be one–one, so that given the effect, the cause is thereby determined, given the cause, the effect is thereby determined. . . .

(4)   Common sense assumes that if in a system in which no change has been occurring, a change begins to occur, then that system must be in causal relation to something outside it which causes the change. Such causation is called *transeunt*. Thus we are led to the distinction between a thing left to itself and a thing not so left. We saw that this distinction is vague. It must be replaced by the distinction between an *isolated system* and *a system in causal relations to something outside the system*. Changes occurring in an isolated system are determined by the mutual relations of the parts. Such determination is called *immanent causation*. For example, the works of a watch constitute an isolated system. Once the watch is wound up the changes occurring in it are causally determined by the mutual relations of the parts of the works. Thus the movement of the hands over the dial is immanently caused. If however, the watch is put in very cold or very hot temperatures, the temperature of the surrounding medium will cause a change in the metal case which will cause a change in the working of the watch. This would be an example of transeunt causation. The business of a good watch-maker is to construct a watch as little subject as possible to changes occurring outside the watch-case. His ideal would be the construction of a completely isolated system, save for the fact that the watch must be periodically wound up by external agency. This ideal is unattainable. The distinction between systems that are causally isolated and systems that are not cannot be made absolute. The latter may always be regarded as sub-systems in a wider system. But unless there were systems that are practically isolated with regard to many changes occurring in these systems, the discovery of causal uniformities would be impossible. . . .

Our discussion of causation has shown that there is a close interrelation between causal uniformities, or, as we may call them, causal laws, and things. The attempt to determine more precisely the nature of this interrelation takes us beyond the standpoint of common sense.

Causal Laws and the Behaviour of Things

We have seen that the way in which a thing, for example, a lump of sugar, a candle, a poker, a living being, will behave in a given situation depends both upon the nature of the thing and upon the nature of the situation in which it is placed. This lump of sugar dissolves in water; this piece of gold does not. The poker put into a fire will become red-hot; when it is taken out and put in the fender it will become cold again, and will revert (approximately) to its former condition. The thing has characteristics which distinguish it from other things. Some of its characteristics are causal characteristics, i.e. modes of behaviour in relation to other things, e.g. *solubility in water* which belongs to this lump of sugar. The thing has also non-causal characteristics relating to the kind of primary characteristics exhibited by its states. The states of the thing have determinate characteristics. These determinate characteristics of the states are *caused* by the causal characteristics and the situation in which the thing is placed. For example, the determinate characteristics of the state of the poker when it is red-hot are *being red* and *being hot*. These characteristics are caused by the causal characteristics *altering in colour* and *altering in temperature* (which belong to *the poker*, not to its states) and by the situation, viz. the fire.

So far we have considered definite examples of things, *this poker*, *this lump of sugar*. But each of these is recognized as belonging to a class consisting of *things of a certain sort*, or as we have called them *natural kinds*. Every instance of *a kind of thing* has certain characteristics of a certain sort which makes it the *sort of thing* it is, and is what we mean by a *kind*. The way in which a thing behaves depends upon its kind. These modes of behaviour are causal laws. Wherever there are things of a certain kind in certain situations there will be certain modes of behaviour, that is certain variations in the primary characteristics of the states of the thing. These changes *recur* under suitable conditions at different times and places. Hence, the characteristic modes of behaviour of things are recurrent modes of change. Causal laws are the laws of these recurrent modes of change.

There can be no doubt that we do distinguish kinds of things by observing their modes of behaviour in the presence of other things, that is in different situations. We observe the primary characteristics of the states of a thing, and we know that that kind of thing has states having those characteristics. If the thing fails to exhibit that mode of behaviour which is characteristic of that kind of thing, we know that we were mistaken as to the kind of thing it was. For example, we may see a dish of apples which *look like* Blenheim pippins. We may take up one and bite it, only to find that it tastes of soap. We conclude (rightly) that *this thing* is a piece of soap made to look like a Blenheim pippin. It *isn't* a Blenheim pippin because it doesn't behave like one. Thus we see that the distinguishing characteristics of a kind involve modes of behaviour, i.e. causal laws. The notion of kinds of things, then, leads us to the consideration of causation and conditions. . . .

To say that X is the necessary and sufficient condition of the occurrence of E is, then, to say that X *alone* is relevant to the occurrence of E. It might be objected that, if we can discover what is relevant only by eliminating what is irrelevant, then we could never tell whether permanent factors in the universe, for example, the presence of the fixed stars, are relevant to a given causal situation, for example, *sugar dissolving in water*. This is true, but it is also unimportant since the statement of the given causal law does not require us to take account of the fixed stars, nor should we ever be concerned with causal situations in the absence of the fixed stars. Moreover, although the annihilation of the fixed stars might affect the result, we have not the slightest reason for supposing that this would be the case. On the other hand, we do find that the substitution of gold for sugar in the water does not yield the result *dissolving in water*. It seems, then, that experience does provide us with examples of multiformities, and with examples of causal occurrences that are independent of other causal occurrences happening contemporaneously and in the same neighbourhood. That is to say that there are relatively independent causal series. The difference between the causal set A_1, A_2, A_3 ... and the causal set B_1, B_2, B_3 ... depends upon the different natures of A and B. We have seen what is meant by the phrase 'the nature of' in this context. It is the fact that A has a certain nature, or is a thing of a certain kind, which determines in what situations A is a causal factor.

It is important to distinguish causal laws from the particular causal propositions which exemplify them. It is the causal law that is fundamental. A particular causal proposition asserts a definite causal occurrence happening once, and once only, for example, *This shot through his heart caused this man's death*. In asserting that this man's death was *caused* by his being shot through the heart we are asserting more than the historical fact that two particular occurrences were conjoined. This is clear, since there are many occurrences happening together (simultaneously or successively) which we should not regard as being causally connected. It may be that what *more* we are asserting is simply that this is an instance of a conjunction of two occurrences of a certain sort such that the one is *always* conjoined with the other, or it may be that we are asserting that the two occurrences are related by a unique relation of causation. We shall consider in the next section what can be said in favour of either of these two views. Whatever view we adopt we must admit that there would be no significance in the assertion of causation unless we at least meant to assert that *whenever* a given occurrence happens, then some other given occurrence happens. The causal law which the example given above exemplifies can be stated precisely. Whenever there is an occurrence which is the passage of a bullet through a man's heart, there follows an occurrence which is the cessation of the beating of the heart. Thus the form of such a causal law is: Whenever an occurrence having the property Φ happens at a time t_1 to a thing of the kind K_1, then an occurrence having the property ψ happens at a time t_2 to a thing of the kind K_2. It may be the case that (i) Φ and ψ are properties of the same sort; (ii) K_1 and K_2 are the same thing; (iii) t_1 and t_2 are the same time. When (iii) is the case, there is an instance of simultaneous causality. In the examples we have given the *things* have been of different degrees of complexity, e.g. *gold*, an element, *water*, an inorganic compound, *heart*, *man*, organic compounds. The behaviour of each of these kinds is expressed by causal laws. These causal laws will differ in the degree of their abstractness, and from some points of view and with regard to certain problems the differences between the *kind* of these kinds, or sorts, of things will be very important. But it is sufficient here to notice that the *simplest* causal law is abstract. . . .

Causation and Regular Sequence[5]

The problem we have now to discuss is whether causal laws express *nothing but* regularities of sequence. If so, it would follow that all regular sequences are causal, e.g. the sequence of day and night. If not, the difficulty arises of finding some characteristic distinguishing regular sequences that are causal from those that are not.

There is undoubtedly something to be said in favour of the view that causal regularities are nothing but observed regularities of sequence. Its best-known recent exponent is Mr Bertrand Russell.[6] Unfortunately his argument is so carelessly expressed that it is difficult to extract the main points. Perhaps they may be said to lie in the two following considerations. Starting with the admission that causal laws are of the form 'A causes B', e.g. 'Arsenic causes death', Mr Russell argues that such laws are liable to exception, and that, consequently, they cannot be universal and necessary. Now a 'law' that has exceptions would not generally be regarded as a law. Mr Russell, however, does not take this view, for he seems to wish to maintain that *A causes B*, expresses a law and that it *means* 'A is the nearly invariable antecedent of B'. By 'nearly invariable' Mr Russell seems to mean 'almost *unvarying*'. He argues that we cannot say that arsenic always causes death since a man who has swallowed arsenic 'might be shot through the head immediately after taking the dose, and then it would not be of arsenic that he would die.' Again, it 'may happen that immediately after the man's death his body is blown to pieces by a bomb. We cannot say what will happen after the man's death, through merely knowing that he has died as the result of arsenic poisoning.' Accordingly, he argues that 'if we are to take the cause as one event and the effect as another, both must be shortened indefinitely'.[7] We are thus left with laws expressing the direction of change from moment to moment. The upshot of this argument appears to be that since a change occupies a finite time, and since a change A that is usually followed by a change B may be interrupted before the completion of the process, we cannot assert that 'A is always followed by B', so long as we are concerned with perceptible changes. Thus causal laws are not universal. The second point concerns the difficulty of finding any *one* event which can be regarded as *the* cause of a given event. This difficulty leads Mr Russell to deny the uniqueness of the causal relation. He argues: 'Cause, in the only sense in which it can be practically applied, means "nearly invariable antecedent". We cannot in practice obtain an antecedent which is *quite* invariable, for this would require us to take account of the whole universe, since something not taken account of may prevent the expected effect.' The man who first swallowed arsenic, who was immediately afterwards shot through the head, and whose body was, immediately after death, blown to pieces by a bomb is said to provide an illustration of such 'prevention'. Hence Mr Russell concludes that 'in fact we cannot find any antecedent that we know to be quite invariable', but 'we can find many that are nearly so. For example, men leave a factory for dinner when the hooter sounds at twelve o'clock. You may say the hooter is *the* cause of their leaving. But innumerable other hooters in other factories, which also always sound at twelve o'clock, have just as good a right to be called the cause. Thus every event has many nearly invariable antecedents, and therefore many antecedents which may be called its cause.'

If Mr Russell's view be correct, then *every* regular sequence is causal, since there is nothing more in the notion of cause than regularity of sequence. Thus night will be the cause of day and day will be the cause of night. On this view we should have to admit that the blowing of the hooters was the cause of the position of the hands of the clock when the men began to leave the factory for dinner, and that the blowing of the hooter in a Manchester factory caused both the departure of the men from that factory and also the departure of the men from factories in Liverpool and in London, and conversely. The most surprising point with regard to Mr Russell's argument is his belief that such an account of causation gives the only sense in which the notion can be practically applied. Presumably we apply the notion of cause when we use it for purposes of inference. It is not obvious that the hooter illustration could be used satisfactorily in practice, so that it may be doubted whether this definition of causal connexion could be recommended on the ground of its practical utility. It is unlikely, however, that the reasons Mr Russell gives for his view are in fact the reasons that led him to it. Possibly his main reason for adopting such a paradoxical view is to be found in the extreme difficulty of pointing out *any* characteristic which suffices to distinguish regular sequences that are causal from those that are not. This difficulty may have led to the conclusion that there is no such characteristic. Such an argument is by no means conclusive. Dr Broad has put this point very clearly.[8] He argues that if causation did involve a unique and not further analysable relation it would be 'impossible to define it in any but tautologous terms'. In that case it 'might be that regular sequence was not even *part* of what we mean by causation, but was merely a sign (though by no means an infallible one) by which the presence of this other relation is indicated'. Dr Broad admits that we do not seem to be directly acquainted with any 'extra factor' in causation in the way in which, for instance, we are directly acquainted with the unique and unanalysable relation of inside and outside in space. Thus it remains *possible* that the main reason for rejecting Mr Russell's view may simply be its paradoxical consequences. But, as Dr Broad further argues, 'there are many cases where we should admit regular sequence and *unhesitatingly deny* causation', although, he adds, 'there are perhaps no cases where we can *unhesitatingly assert* causation in addition to regular sequence'. It may certainly be admitted that the working scientist would unhesitatingly deny that the blowing of a hooter in Manchester was the cause of the departure of the London workmen.

If we ask why the hooter illustration is paradoxical we may be able to discover the 'extra factor' that is missing from Mr Russell's account. Dr Broad says, 'the missing factor seems to be a certain spatio-temporal continuity between the sequent events', and he adds, 'I am inclined to think that it is the absence of such continuity between the blowing of the Manchester hooter and the movement of the London workmen which makes me so certain that the former is not a cause of the latter.' This suggestion will meet the difficulty only if 'a *certain* spatio-temporal continuity' be interpreted as involving reference to continuity of change of character of the events happening in Manchester, or in London. It is the absence of continuous change of character that leads to the paradox. If what we have already said about causal laws is correct, then it is a mistake to suppose that one *event* causes another *event*. We have insisted that it is an event's having a certain character that causes another event having a certain character to have some other character. The missing factor must then be found in the character of the event. Causal laws connect changes in the characters of events, and there must be continuity in this change of character. That this reference to character is essential is shown by the fact that we speak of '*regular sequences*'. Events do not recur. As we have seen, we can speak of the *same* cause on different occasions only because the causal connexion is primarily between the characters, and is derivatively between the events to which these characters belong. Mr Russell's view is, then, to be rejected because it takes no account of the continuity of change of *character* that is essential to causation. We conclude that causation cannot be regarded as *equivalent to* regular sequence.

. . . Those who hold the view that science makes no use of the notion of cause have generally been more interested in the physical than in the biological and social sciences. Thus Mr Russell says 'in advanced sciences such as gravitational astronomy, the word "cause" never occurs', and he adds, 'the reason why physics has ceased to look for causes is that, in fact, there are no such things'.[9] It may certainly be admitted that 'in advanced sciences' the notion of cause is replaced by the notion of functional dependence. But it is a mistake to suppose that apart from the 'advanced sciences' there is no scientific method. On the contrary, the development of science from its earliest stages to its most advanced stages has been continuous. It is the merest dogmatism to confine the 'sciences' to physics and to argue that because the physicist does not employ the notion of cause, therefore 'science' has no use for it. The most superficial acquaintance with the earlier stages of a science is enough to reveal that the notion of cause is indispensable. There is no doubt, for instance, that the word 'cause' frequently occurs in the works of biologists.[10] Those sciences that are concerned with the recurrent modes of behaviour of different *kinds* of things undoubtedly use the notion of cause in the form of causal laws. The bio-chemist carries out careful experiments with regard to the action of chemicals upon living organisms in order to discover their modes of behaviour, that is, their causal laws. Thus, for instance, he uses such expressions as 'Nitrites cause a fall in blood-pressure', and he employs the notion of cause when he infers that an injection of amylnitrite will cause such a fall in blood-pressure. He is content to leave to philosophers doubts as to the validity of the concept of cause so long as he is able to continue to use it. Hence, it seems rash to conclude from an examination of the *words* used by physicists that 'there are no such things' as causes.

Notes

1   *Mysticism and Logic* (New York: Longmans, Green, 1918), p. 180. Mr Russell himself has recently based his philosophy of science upon the conception of 'causal

lines', which, however, he does not attempt to analyse, and which perhaps cannot bear the weight of the construction he rests upon it.

2   Common sense certainly regards mental events as non-spatial, and somewhat waveringly applies the conception of causation to such events. It is not necessary for our purpose to discuss this application. Hence, our discussion is limited to non-mental events.

3   The expression 'causal characteristic' is taken from Dr C. D. Broad (see *The Mind and its Place in Nature* (London: Routledge & Kegan Paul), p. 432). In the discussion of this problem I am, as always, much indebted to Dr Broad's writings.

4   In saying that there must be 'spatio-temporal proximity', I mean that the various factors cannot be separated by a spatio-temporal gap.

5   This section should be omitted on a first reading.

6   See *The Analysis of Mind*, chap. V [reprinted, in part, in this volume].

7   See Reading 32, p. 291, in this volume.

8   *The Mind and its Place in Nature*, pp. 453–6.

9   *Mysticism and Logic*, p. 180.

10   We have seen that the physicist also employs the *notion* of cause, although no doubt its analysis would be different in the case of the physical sciences from its analysis in the biological sciences.

---

34   Causality and Determination

G. E. M. Anscombe

I

It is often declared or evidently assumed that causality is some kind of necessary connection, or alternatively, that being caused is – non-trivially – instancing some exceptionless generalization saying that such an event always follows such antecedents. Or the two conceptions are combined.

Obviously there can be, and are, a lot of divergent views covered by this account. Any view that it covers nevertheless manifests one particular doctrine or assumption. Namely:

If an effect occurs in one case and a similar effect does not occur in an apparently similar case, there must be a relevant further difference.

Any radically different account of causation, then, by contrast with which all those diverse views will be as one, will deny this assumption. Such a radically opposing view can grant that often – though it is difficult to say generally when – the assumption of relevant difference is a sound principle of investigation. It may grant that there are necessitating causes, but will refuse to identify causation as such with necessitation. It can grant that there are situations in which, given the initial conditions and no interference, only one result will accord with the laws of nature; but it will not see general reason, in advance of discovery, to suppose that any given course of things has been so determined. So it may grant that in many cases difference of issue can rightly convince us of a relevant difference of circumstances; but it will deny that, quite generally, this *must* be so.

The first view is common to many philosophers of the past. It is also, usually but not always in a neo-Humeian form, the prevailing received opinion throughout the currently busy and productive philosophical schools of the English-speaking world, and also in some of the European and Latin American schools where philosophy is pursued in at all the same sort of way; nor is it confined to these schools. So firmly rooted is it that for many even outside pure philosophy, it routinely determines the meaning of 'cause', when consciously used as a theoretical term: witness the terminology of the contrast between 'causal' and 'statistical' laws, which is drawn by writers on physics – writers, note, who would not conceive themselves to be addicts of any philosophic school when they use this language to express that contrast.

The truth of this conception is hardly debated. It is, indeed, a bit of *Weltanschauung*: it helps to form a cast of mind which is characteristic of our whole culture.

The association between causation and necessity is old; it occurs for example in Aristotle's *Metaphysics*: 'When the agent and patient meet suitably to their powers, the one acts and the other is acted on OF NECESSITY.' Only, with 'rational powers', an extra feature is needed to determine the result: 'What has a rational power [e.g. medical knowledge, which can kill *or* cure] OF NECESSITY does what it has the power to do and as it has the power, when it has the desire' (Book IX, Chapter V).

Overleaping the centuries, we find it an axiom in Spinoza, 'Given a determinate cause, the effect follows OF NECESSITY, and without its cause, no effect follows' (*Ethics*, Book I, Axiom III). And in the English philosopher Hobbes:

> A cause simply, or an entire cause, is the aggregate of all the accidents both of the agents how many soever they be, and of the patients, put together; which when they are supposed to be present, IT CANNOT BE UNDERSTOOD BUT THAT THE EFFECT IS PRODUCED at the same instant; and if any of them be wanting, IT CANNOT BE UNDERSTOOD BUT THAT THE EFFECT IS NOT PRODUCED. (*Elements of Philosophy Concerning Body*, Chapter IX)

It was this last view, where the connection between cause and effect is evidently seen as *logical* connection of some sort, that was overthrown by Hume, the most influential of all philosophers on this subject in the English-speaking and allied schools. For he made us see that, given any particular cause – or 'total causal situation' for that matter – and its effect, there is not in general any contradiction in supposing the one to occur and the other not to occur. That is to say, we'd know what was being described – what it would be like for it to be true – if it were reported for example that a kettle of water was put, and kept, directly on a hot fire, but the water did not heat up.

Were it not for the preceding philosophers who had made causality out as some species of logical connection, one would wonder at this being called a discovery on Hume's part: for vulgar humanity has always been over-willing to believe in miracles and marvels and *lusus naturae*. Mankind at large saw no contradiction, where Hume worked so hard to show the philosophic world – the Republic of Letters – that there was none.

The discovery was thought to be great. But as touching the equation of causality with necessitation, Hume's thinking did nothing against this but curiously reinforced it. For he himself assumed that NECESSARY CONNECTION is an essential part of the idea of the relation of cause and effect (*A Treatise of Human Nature*, Book I, Part III, Sections II and VI), and he sought for its nature. He thought this could not be found in the situations, objects or events called 'causes' and 'effects', but was to be found in the human mind's being determined, by experience of CONSTANT CONJUNCTION, to pass from the sensible impression or memory of one term of the relation to the convinced idea of the other. Thus to say that an event was caused was to say that its occurrence was an instance of some exceptionless generalization connecting such an event with such antecedents as it occurred in. The twist that Hume gave to the topic thus suggested a connection of the notion of causality with that of deterministic laws – i.e. laws such that always, given initial conditions and the laws, a unique result is determined.

The well-known philosophers who have lived after Hume may have aimed at following him and developing at least some of his ideas, or they may have put up a resistance; but in no case, so far as I know,[1] has the resistance called in question the equation of causality with necessitation.

Kant, roused by learning of Hume's discovery, laboured to establish causality as an *a priori* conception and argued that the objective time order consists 'in that order of the manifold of appearance according to which, IN CONFORMITY WITH A RULE, the apprehension of that which happens follows upon the apprehension of that which precedes. . . . In conformity with such a rule there must be in that which precedes an event the condition of a rule according to which this event INVARIABLY and NECESSARILY follows' (*Critique of Pure Reason*, Book II, Chapter II, Section III, Second Analogy). Thus Kant tried to give back to causality the character of a *justified* concept which Hume's considerations had taken away from it. Once again the connection between causation and necessity was reinforced. And this has been the general characteristic of those who have sought to oppose Hume's conception of causality. They have always tried to establish the necessitation that they saw in causality: either *a priori*, or somehow out of experience.

Since Mill it has been fairly common to explain causation one way or another in terms of 'necessary' and 'sufficient' conditions. Now 'sufficient condition' is a term of art whose users may therefore lay down its meaning as they please. So they are in their rights to rule out the query: 'May not the sufficient conditions of an event be present, and the event yet not take place?' For 'sufficient condition' is so used that if the sufficient conditions for X are there, X occurs. But at the same time, the phrase cozens the understanding into not noticing an assumption. For 'sufficient condition' sounds like: 'enough'. And one certainly *can* ask: 'May there not be *enough* to have made something happen – and yet it not have happened?'

Russell wrote of the notion of cause, or at any rate of the 'law of causation' (and he seemed to feel the same way about 'cause' itself), that, like the British monarchy, it had been allowed to survive because it had been erroneously thought to do no harm. In a destructive essay of great brilliance he cast doubt on the notion of necessity involved, unless it is explained in terms of universality, and he argued that upon examination the concepts of determination and of invariable succession of like objects upon like turn out to be empty: they do not differentiate between any conceivable course of things and any other. Thus Russell too assumes that necessity or universality is what is in question, and it never occurs to him that there may be any other conception of causality ('The Notion of Cause', in *Mysticism and Logic*).[2]

Now it's not difficult to show it prima facie wrong to associate the notion of cause with necessity or universality in this way. For, it being much easier to trace effects back to causes with certainty than to predict effects from causes, we often know a cause without knowing whether there is an exceptionless generalization of the kind envisaged, or whether there is a necessity.

For example, we have found certain diseases to be contagious. If, then, I have had one and only one contact with someone suffering from such a disease, and I get it myself, we suppose I got it from him. But what if, having had the contact, I ask a doctor whether I will get the disease? He will usually only be able to say, 'I don't know – maybe you will, maybe not.'

But, it is said, knowledge of causes here is partial; doctors seldom even know any of the conditions under which one invariably gets a disease, let alone all the sets of conditions. This comment betrays the assumption that there is such a thing to know. Suppose there is: still, the question whether there is does not have to be settled before we can know what we mean by speaking of the contact as cause of my getting the disease.

All the same, might it not be like this: knowledge of causes is possible without any satisfactory grasp of what is involved in causation? Compare the possibility of wanting clarification of 'valency' or 'long-run frequency', which yet have been handled by chemists and statisticians without such clarification; and valencies and long-run frequencies, whatever the right way of explaining them, have been known. Thus one of the familiar philosophic analyses of causality, or a new one in the same line, may be correct, though knowledge of it is not necessary for knowledge of causes.

There is something to observe here, that lies under our noses. It is little attended to, and yet still so obvious as to seem trite. It is this: causality consists in the derivativeness of an effect from its causes. This is the core, the common feature, of causality in its various kinds. Effects derive from, arise out of, come of, their causes. For example, everyone will grant that physical parenthood is a causal relation. Here the derivation is material, by fission. Now analysis in terms of necessity or universality does not tell us of this derivedness of the effect; rather it forgets about that. For the necessity will be that of laws of nature; through it *we* shall be able to derive knowledge of the effect from knowledge of the cause, or vice versa, but that does not show us the cause as source of the effect. Causation, then, is not to be identified with necessitation.

If *A* comes from *B*, this does not imply that every *A*-like thing comes from some *B*-like thing or set-up or that every *B*-like thing or set-up has an *A*-like thing coming from it; or that given *B*, *A* had to come from it, or that given *A*, there had to be *B* for it to come from. Any of these may be true, but if any is, that will be an additional fact, not comprised in *A*'s coming from *B*. If we take 'coming from' in the sense of travel, this is perfectly evident.

'But that's because we can observe travel!' The influential Humeian argument at this point is that we can't similarly observe causality in the individual case (*A Treatise of Human Nature*, Book I, Part III, Section II). So the reason why we connect what we call the cause and what we call the effect as we do must lie elsewhere. It must lie in the fact that the succession of the latter upon the former is of a kind regularly observed.

There are two things for me to say about this. First, as to the statement that we can never observe causality in the individual case. Someone who says this is just not going to count anything as 'observation of causality'. This often happens in philosophy; it is argued that 'all we find' is such-and-such, and it turns out that the arguer has excluded from his idea of 'finding' the sort of thing he says we don't 'find'. And when we consider what we are allowed to say we do 'find', we have the right to turn the tables on Hume, and say that neither do we perceive bodies, such as billiard balls, approaching one another. When we 'consider the matter with the utmost attention', we find only an impression of travel made by the successive positions of a round white patch in our visual fields . . . etc. Now a 'Humeian' account of causality has to be given in terms of constant conjunction of physical things, events, etc., not of experiences of them. If, then, it must be allowed that we 'find' bodies in motion, for example, then what theory of perception can justly disallow the perception of a lot of causality? The truthful – though unhelpful – answer to the question: "How did we come by our primary knowledge of causality?' is that in learning to speak we learned the linguistic representation and application of a host of causal concepts. Very many of them were represented by transitive and other verbs of action used in reporting what is observed. Others – a good example is 'infect' – form, not observation statements, but rather expressions of causal hypotheses. The word 'cause' itself is highly general. How does someone show that he has the concept *cause*? We may wish to say: only by having such a word in his vocabulary. If so, then the manifest possession of the concept presupposes the mastery of much else in language. I mean: the word 'cause' can be *added* to a language in which are already represented many causal concepts. A small selection: *scrape, push, wet, carry, eat, burn, knock over, keep off, squash, make* (e.g. noises, paper boats), *hurt*. But if we care to imagine languages in which no special causal concepts are represented, then no description of the use of a word in such languages will be able to present it as meaning *cause*. Nor will it even contain words for natural kinds of stuff, nor yet words equivalent to 'body', 'wind', or 'fire'. For learning to use special causal verbs is part and parcel of learning to apply the concepts answering to these and many other substantives. As surely as we learned to call people by name or to report from seeing it that the cat was on the table, we also learned to report from having observed it that someone drank up the milk or that the dog made a funny noise or that things were cut or broken by whatever we saw cut or break them.

(I will mention, only to set on one side, one of the roots of Hume's argument, the implicit appeal to Cartesian scepticism. He confidently challenges us to 'produce some instance, wherein the efficacy is plainly discoverable to the mind, and its operations obvious to our consciousness or sensation' (*A Treatise of Human Nature*, Book I, Part III, Section XIV). Nothing easier: is cutting, is drinking, is purring not 'efficacy'? But it is true that the apparent perception of such things may be only apparent: we may be deceived by false appearances. Hume presumably wants us to 'produce an instance' in which *efficacy* is related to sensation as *red* is. It is true that we can't do that; it is not *so* related to sensation. He is also helped, in making his argument that we don't perceive 'efficacy', by his curious belief that 'efficacy' means much the same thing as 'necessary connection'! But as to the Cartesian-sceptical root of the argument, I will not delay upon it, as my present topic is not the philosophy of perception.)

Secondly, as to that instancing of a universal generalization, which was supposed to supply what could not be observed in the individual case, the causal relation, the needed examples are none too common. 'Motion in one body in all past instances that have fallen under our observation, is follow'd upon impulse by motion in another': so Hume (*A Treatise of Human Nature*, Book II, Part III, Section I). But, as is always a danger in making large generalizations, he was thinking only of the cases where we do observe this – billiard balls against free-standing billiard balls in an ordinary situation; not billiard balls against stone walls. Neo-Humeians are more cautious. They realize that if you take a case of cause and effect, and relevantly describe the cause *A* and the effect *B*, and then construct a universal proposition, 'Always, given an *A*, a *B* follows', you usually won't get anything true. You have got to describe the absence of circumstances in which an *A* would not cause a *B*. But the task of excluding all such circumstances can't be carried out. There is, I suppose, a vague association in people's minds between the universal propositions which would be examples of the required type of generalizations, and scientific laws. But there is no similarity.

Suppose we were to call propositions giving the properties of substances 'laws of nature'. Then there will be a law of nature running 'The flash-point of such a substance is . . .', and this will be important in explaining why striking matches usually causes them to light. This law of nature has not the form of a generalization running 'Always, if a sample of such a substance is raised to such a temperature, it ignites'; nor is it equivalent to such a generalization, but rather to: 'If a sample of such a substance is raised to such a temperature and doesn't ignite, there must be a cause of its not doing so.' Leaving aside questions connected with the idea of a pure sample, the point here is that 'normal conditions' is quite properly a vague notion. That fact makes generalizations running 'Always . . .' merely fraudulent in such cases; it will always be necessary for them to be hedged about with clauses referring to normal conditions; and we may not know in advance whether conditions are normal or not, or what to count as an abnormal condition. In exemplar analytical practice, I suspect, it will simply be a relevant condition in which the generalization, 'Always if such and such, such and such happens . . .', supplemented with a few obvious conditions that have occurred to the author, turns out to be untrue. Thus the conditional 'If it doesn't ignite then there must be some cause' is the better gloss upon the original proposition, for it does not pretend to say specifically, or even disjunctively specifically, what *always* happens. It is probably these facts which make one hesitate to call propositions about the action of substances 'laws of nature'. The law of inertia, for example, would hardly be glossed: 'If a body accelerates without any force acting on it, there must be some cause of its doing so.' (Though I wonder what the author of *Principia* himself would have thought of that.) On the other hand just such 'laws' as that about a substance's flash-point are connected with the match's igniting because struck.

Returning to the medical example, medicine is of course not interested in the hopeless task of constructing lists of all the sets of conditions under each of which people always get a certain disease. It is interested in finding what that is special, if anything, is always the case when people get a particular disease; and, given such a cause or condition (or in any case), in finding circumstances in which people don't get the disease, or tend not to. This is connected with medicine's concern first, and last, with things as they happen in the messy and mixed up conditions of life: only between its first and its last concern can it look for what happens unaffected by uncontrolled and inconstant conditions.

II

Yet my argument lies always open to the charge of appealing to ignorance. I must therefore take a different sort of example.

Here is a ball lying on top of some others in a transparent vertical pipe. I know how it got there: it was forcibly ejected with many others out of a certain aperture into the enclosed space above a row of adjacent pipes. The point of the whole construction is to show how a totality of balls so ejected always build up in rough conformity to the same curve. But I am interested in this one ball. Between its ejection and its getting into this pipe, it kept hitting sides, edges, other balls. If I made a film of it I could run it off in slow motion and tell the impact which produced each stage of the journey. Now was the result necessary? We would probably all have said it was in the time when Newton's mechanics was undisputed for truth. It was the impression made on Hume and later philosophers by that mechanics, that gave them so strong a conviction of the iron necessity with which everything happens, the 'absolute fate' by which 'Every object is determin'd to a certain degree and direction of its motion' (*A Treatise of Human Nature*, Book II, Part III, Section I).

Yet no one could have deduced the resting place of the ball – because of the indeterminateness that you get even in the Newtonian mechanics, arising from the finite accuracy of measurements. From exact figures for positions, velocities, directions, spins and masses you might be able to calculate the result as accurately as you chose. But the minutest inexactitudes will multiply up factor by factor, so that in a short time your information is gone. Assuming a given margin of error in your initial figure, you could assign an associated probability to that ball's falling into each of the pipes. If you want the highest probability you assign to be really high, so that you can take it as practical certainty, it will be a problem to reckon how tiny the permitted margins of inaccuracy must be – analogous to the problem: how small a fraction of a grain of millet must I demand is put on the first square of the chess board, if after doubling up at every square I end up having to pay out only a pound of millet? It would be a figure of such smallness as to have no meaning as a figure for a margin of error.

However, so long as you believed the classical mechanics you might also think there could be no such thing as a figure for a difference that had no meaning. Then you would think that though it was not feasible for us to find the necessary path of the ball because our margins of error are too great, yet there *was* a necessary path, which could be assigned a sufficient probability for firm acceptance of it, by anyone (not one of us) capable of reducing his limits of accuracy in measurement to a sufficiently small compass. Admittedly, so small a compass that he'd be down among the submicroscopic particles and no longer concerned with the measurements, say, of the ball. And now we can say: with certain degrees of smallness we get to a region for which Newton's mechanics is no longer believed.

If the classical mechanics can be used to calculate a certain real result, we may give a sense to, and grant, the 'necessity' of the result, given the antecedents. Here, however, you can't use the mechanics to calculate the result, but at most to give yourself a belief in its necessity. For this to be reasonable the system has got to be acknowledged as true. Not, indeed, that that would be enough; but if so much were secured, then it would be worthwhile to discuss the metaphysics of absolute measures of continuous quantities.

The point needs some labouring precisely because 'the system does apply to such bodies' – that is, to moderately massive balls. After all, it's Newton we use to calculate Sputniks! 'The system applies to these bodies' is true only in the sense and to the extent that it yields sufficient results of calculations about these bodies. It does not mean: in respect of these bodies the system is the truth, so that it just doesn't matter that we can't use it to calculate such a result in such a case. I am not saying that a deterministic system involves individual predictability: it evidently does not. But in default of predictability the determinedness declared by the deterministic system has got to be believed because the system itself is believed.

I conclude that we have no ground for calling the path of the ball determined – at least, until it has taken its path – but, it may be objected, is not each stage of its path determined, even though we cannot determine it? My argument has partly relied on loss of information through multiplicity of impacts. But from one impact to the next the path is surely determined, and so the whole path is so after all.

It sounds plausible to say: each stage is determined and so the whole is. But what does 'determined' mean? The word is a curious one (with a curious history);

in this sort of context it is often used as if it *meant* 'caused'. Or perhaps 'caused' is used as if it meant 'determined'. But there is at any rate one important difference – a thing hasn't been caused until it has happened; but it may be determined before it happens.

(It is important here to distinguish between being *determined* and being *determinate*. In indeterministic physics there is an apparent failure of both. I am concerned only with the former.)

When we call a result determined we are implicitly relating it to an antecedent range of possibilities and saying that all but one of these is disallowed. What disallows them is not the result itself but something antecedent to the result. The antecedences may be logical or temporal or in the order of knowledge. Of the many – antecedent – possibilities, *now* only one is – antecedently – possible.

Mathematical formulae and human decisions are limiting cases; the former because of the obscurity of the notion of antecedent possibilities, and the latter because decisions can be retrieved.

In a chess-game, the antecedent possibilities are, say, the powers of the pieces. By the rules, a certain position excludes all but one of the various moves that were in that sense antecedently possible. This is logical antecedence. The next move is determined.

In the zygote, sex and eye-colour are already determined. Here the antecedent possibilities are the possibilities for sex and eye-colour for a child; or more narrowly: for a child of these parents. *Now*, given the combination of this ovum and this spermatozoon, all but one of these antecedent possibilities is excluded.

It might be said that anything was determined once it had happened. There is now no possibility open: it *has* taken place! It was in this sense that Aristotle said that past and present were necessary. But this does not concern us: what interests us is *pre*-determination.

Then 'each stage of the ball's path is determined' must mean 'Upon any impact, there is only one path possible for the ball up to the next impact (and assuming no air currents, etc.).' But what ground could one have for believing this, if one does not believe in some system of which it is a consequence? Consider a steel ball dropping between two pins on a Galton board to hit the pin centred under the gap between them. That it should balance on this pin is not to be expected. It has two possibilities; to go to the right or to the left. If you have a system which forces this on you, you can say: 'There has to be a determining factor; otherwise, like Buridan's ass, the ball must balance.' But if you have not, then you should say that the ball may be undetermined until it does move to the right or the left. Here the ball had only two significant possibilities and was perhaps unpredetermined between them. This was because it cannot be called determined – no reasonable account can be given of insisting that it is so – within a small range of possibility, actualization within which will lead on to its falling either to the right or to the left. With our flying ball there will also be such a small range of possibility. The further consequences of the path it may take are not tied down to just two significant possibilities, as with one step down the Galton board: the range of further possibility gets wider as we consider the paths it may take. Otherwise, the two cases are similar.

We see that to give content to the idea of something's being determined, we have to have a set of possibilities, which something narrows down to one – before the event.

This accords well with our understanding of part of the dissatisfaction of some physicists with the quantum theory. They did not like the undeterminedness of individual quantum phenomena. Such a physicist might express himself by saying 'I believe in causality!' He means: 'I believe that the real physical laws and the initial conditions must entail uniqueness of result.' Of course, within a range of co-ordinate and mutually exclusive identifiable possible results, only one happens: he means that the result that happens ought to be understood as the only one that was possible before it happened.

Must such a physicist be a 'determinist'? That is, must he believe that the whole universe is a system such that, if its total states at t and t' are thus and so, the laws of nature are such as then to allow only one possibility for its total state at any other time? No. He may not think that the idea of a total state of the universe at a time is one he can do anything with. He may even have no views on the uniqueness of possible results for whatever may be going on in any arbitrary volume of space. For 'Our theory should be such that only the actual result was possible for that experiment' doesn't mean 'Our theory should be such that only this result was possible as *the result of the experiment*.' He hates a theory, even if he has to put up with it for the time being, that essentially assigns only probability to a result, essentially allows of a range of possible results, never narrowed down to one until the event itself.

It must be admitted that such dissatisfied physicists very often have been determinists. Witness Schrödinger's account of the 'principle of causality': 'The exact physical situation at *any* point P at a given moment t is unambiguously determined by the exact physical situation within a certain surrounding of P at any previous time, say $t - U$. If U is large, that is, if that previous time lies far back, it may be necessary to know the previous situation for a wide domain around P.'[3] Or Einstein's more modest version of a notorious earlier claim: if you knew all about the contents of a sphere of radius 186,000 miles, and knew the laws, you would be able to know for sure what would happen at the centre for the next second. Schrödinger says: *any* point P; and *a* means *any* sphere of that radius. So their view of causality was not that of my hypothetical physicist, who I said may not have views on the uniqueness of possible results for whatever may be going on in any arbitrary volume of space. My physicist restricts his demand for uniqueness of result to situations in which he has got certain processes going in isolation from inconstant external influences, or where they do not matter, as the weather on a planet does not matter for predicting its course round the sun.

The high success of Newton's astronomy was in one way an intellectual disaster: it produced an illusion from which we tend still to suffer. This illusion was created by the circumstance that Newton's mechanics *had a good model in the solar system*. For this gave the impression that we had here an ideal of scientific explanation; whereas the truth was, it was mere obligingness on the part of the solar system, by having had so peaceful a history in recorded time, to provide such a model. For suppose that some planet had at some time erupted with such violence that its shell was propelled rocket-like out of the solar system. Such an event would not have violated Newton's laws; on the contrary, it would have illustrated them. But also it would not have been calculable as the past and future motions of the planets are presently calculated on the assumption that they can be treated as the simple 'bodies' of his mechanics, with no relevant properties but mass, position and velocity and no forces mattering except gravity.

Let us pretend that Newton's laws were still to be accepted without qualification: no reserve in applying them in electrodynamics; no restriction to bodies travelling a good deal slower than light; and no quantum phenomena. Newton's mechanics is a deterministic system; but this does not mean that believing them commits us to determinism. We could say: of course nothing violates those axioms or the laws of the force of gravity. But animals, for example, run about the world in all sorts of paths and no path is dictated for them by those laws, as it is for planets. Thus in relation to the solar system (apart from questions like whether in the past some planet has blown up), the laws are like the rules of an infantile card game: once the cards are dealt we turn them up in turn, and make two piles each, one red, one black; the winner has the biggest pile of red ones. So once the cards are dealt the game is determined, and from any position in it you can derive all others back to the deal and forward to win or draw. But in relation to what happens on and inside a planet the laws are, rather, like the rules of chess; the play is seldom determined, though nobody breaks the rules.[4]

Why this difference? A natural answer is: the mechanics does not give the special laws of all the forces. Not, for example, for thermal, nuclear, electrical, chemical, muscular forces. And now the Newtonian model suggests the picture: given the laws of all the forces, then there is total coverage of what happens and then the whole game of motion is determined; for, by the first law, any acceleration implies a force of some kind, and must not forces have laws? My hypothetical physicist at least would think so; and would demand that they be deterministic. Nevertheless he still does not have to be a 'determinist'; for many forces, unlike gravity, can be switched on and off, are generated, and also shields can be put up against them. It is one thing to hold that in a clear-cut situation – an astronomical or a well-contrived experimental one designed to discover laws – 'the result' should be determined: and quite another to say that in the hurly-burly of many crossing contingencies whatever happens next must be determined; or to say that the generation of forces (by human experimental procedures, among other things) is always determined in advance of the generating procedure; or to say that there is always a law of composition, of such a kind that the combined effect of a set of forces is determined in every situation.

Someone who is inclined to say those things, or implicitly to assume them, has almost certainly been affected by the impressive relation between Newton's mechanics and the solar system.

We remember how it was in mechanics. By knowing the position and velocity of a particle at one single instant, by knowing the acting forces, the whole future path of the particle could be foreseen. In Maxwell's theory, if we know the field at one instant only, we can deduce from the equations of the theory how the whole field will change in space and time. Maxwell's equations enable us to follow the history of the field, just as the mechanical equations enabled us to follow the history of material particles. . . . With the help of Newton's laws we can deduce the motion of the earth from the force acting between the sun and the earth.[5]

'By knowing the acting forces' – that must of course include the *future* acting forces, not merely the present ones. And similarly for the equations which enable us to follow the history of the field; a change may be produced by an external influence. In reading both Newton and later writers one is often led to ponder that word 'external'. Of course, to be given 'the acting forces' is to be given the external forces too and any new forces that may later be introduced into the situation. Thus those first sentences are true, if true, without the special favour of fate, being general truths of mechanics and physics, but the last one is true by favour, by the brute fact that only the force acting between earth and sun matters for the desired deductions.

The concept of necessity, as it is connected with causation, can be explained as follows: a cause C is a necessitating cause of an effect E *when* (I mean: on the occasions when) if C occurs it is certain to cause E unless something prevents it. C and E are to be understood as general expressions, not singular terms. If 'certainty' should seem too epistemological a notion: a necessitating cause C of a given kind of effect E is such that it *is not* possible (on the occasion) that C should occur and should not cause an E, given that there is nothing that prevents an E from occurring. A non-necessitating cause is then one that can fail of its effect without the intervention of anything to frustrate it. We may discover *types* of necessitating and non-necessitating cause; e.g. rabies is a necessitating cause of death, because it is not possible for one who has rabies to survive without treatment. We don't have to tie it to the occasion. An example of a non-necessitating cause is mentioned by Feynman: a bomb is connected with a Geiger counter, so that it will go off if the Geiger counter registers a certain reading; whether it will or not is not determined, for it is so placed near some radioactive material that it may or may not register that reading.

There would be no doubt of the cause of the reading or of the explosion if the bomb did go off. Max Born is one of the people who has been willing to dissociate causality from determinism: he explicates cause and effect in terms of dependence of the effect on the cause. It is not quite clear what 'dependence' is supposed to be, but at least it seems to imply that you would not get the effect without the cause. The trouble about this is that you might – from some other cause. That this effect was produced by this cause does not at all show that it could not, or would not, have been produced by something else in the absence of this cause.

Indeterminism is not a possibility unconsidered by philosophers. C. D. Broad, in his inaugural lecture, given in 1934, described it as a possibility; but added that whatever happened without being determined was accidental. He did not explain what he meant by being accidental; he must have meant more than not being necessary. He may have meant being uncaused; but, if I am right, not being determined does not imply not being caused. Indeed, I should explain indeterminism as the thesis that not all physical effects are necessitated by their causes. But if we think of Feynman's bomb, we get some idea of what is meant by 'accidental'. It was random: it 'merely happened' that the radioactive material emitted particles in such a way as to activate the Geiger counter enough to set off the bomb. Certainly the motion of the Geiger counter's needle is caused; and the actual emission is caused too; it occurs because there is this mass of radioactive material here. (I have already indicated that, contrary to the opinion of Hume, there are many different sorts of causality.) But all the same the *causation* itself is, one could say, *mere hap*. It is difficult to explain this idea any further.

Broad used the idea to argue that indeterminism, if applied to human action, meant that human actions are 'accidental'. Now he had a picture of choices as being determining causes, analogous to determining physical causes, and of choices in their turn being either determined or accidental. To regard a choice as such – i.e. any case of choice – as a predetermining causal event, now appears as a naive mistake in the philosophy of mind, though that is a story I cannot tell here.

It was natural that when physics went indeterministic, some thinkers should have seized on this indeterminism as being just what was wanted for defending the freedom of the will. They received severe criticism on two counts: one, that this 'mere hap' is the very last thing to be invoked as the physical correlate of 'man's ethical behaviour'; the other, that quantum laws predict statistics of events when situations are repeated; interference with these, by the *will's* determining individual events which the laws of nature leave undetermined, would be as much a violation of natural law as would have been interference which falsified a deterministic mechanical law.

Ever since Kant it has been a familiar claim among philosophers, that one can believe in both physical determinism and 'ethical' freedom. The reconciliations have always seemed to me either to be so much gobbledegook, or to make the alleged freedom of action quite unreal. My actions are mostly physical movements; if these physical movements are physically predetermined by processes which I do not control, then my freedom is perfectly illusory. The truth of physical indeterminism is thus indispensable if we are to make anything of the claim to freedom. But certainly it is insufficient. The physically undetermined is not thereby 'free'. For freedom at least involves the power of acting according to an idea, and no such thing is ascribed to whatever is the subject (what would be the relevant subject?) of unpredetermination in indeterministic physics. Nevertheless, there is nothing unacceptable about the idea that that 'physical haphazard' should be the only physical correlate of human freedom of action; and perhaps also of the voluntariness and intentionalness in the conduct of other animals which we do not call 'free'. The freedom, intentionalness and voluntariness are not to be analysed as the same thing as, or as produced by, the physical haphazard. Different sorts of pattern altogether are being spoken of when we mention them, from those involved in describing elementary processes of physical causality.

The other objection is, I think, more to the point. Certainly if we have a statistical law, but undetermined individual events, and then enough of these are supposed to be pushed by will in one direction to falsify the statistical law, we have again a supposition that puts will into conflict with natural laws. But it is not at all clear that the same train of minute physical events should have to be the regular correlate of the same action; in fact, that suggestion looks immensely implausible. It is, however, required by the objection.

Let me construct an analogy to illustrate this point. Suppose that we have a large glass box full of millions of extremely minute coloured particles, and the box is constantly shaken. Study of the box and particles leads to statistical laws, including laws for the random generation of small unit patches of uniform colour. Now the box is remarkable for also presenting the following phenomenon: the word 'Coca-Cola' formed like a mosaic, can always be read when one looks at one of the sides. It is not always the same shape in the formation of its letters, not always the same size or in the same position, it varies in its colours; but there it always is. It is not at all clear that those statistical laws concerning the random motion of the particles and their formation of small unit patches of colour would have to be supposed violated by the operation of a cause for this phenomenon which did not derive it from the statistical laws.

It has taken the inventions of indeterministic physics to shake the rather common dogmatic conviction that determinism is a presupposition, or perhaps a conclusion, of scientific knowledge. Not that that conviction has been very much shaken even so. Of course, the belief that the laws of nature are deterministic has been shaken. But I believe it has often been supposed that this makes little difference to the assumption of macroscopic determinism: as if undeterminedness were always encapsulated in systems whose internal workings could be described only by statistical laws, but where the total upshot, and in particular the outward effect, was as near as makes no difference always the same. What difference does it make, after all, that the scintillations, whereby my watch dial is luminous, follow only a statistical law – so long as the gross manifest effect is sufficiently guaranteed by the statistical law? Feynman's example of the bomb and Geiger counter smashes this conception; but as far as I can judge it takes time for the lesson to be learned. I find deterministic assumptions more common now among people at large, and among philosophers, than when I was an undergraduate.

The lesson is welcome, but indeterministic physics (if it succeeds in giving the lesson) is only culturally, not logically, required to make the deterministic picture doubtful. For it was always a mere extravagant fancy, encouraged in the 'age of science' by the happy relation of Newtonian mechanics to the solar system. It ought not to have mattered whether the laws of nature were or were not deterministic. For them to be deterministic is for them, together with the description of the situation, to entail unique results in situations defined by certain relevant objects and measures, and where no part is played by inconstant factors external to such definition. If that is right, the laws' being deterministic does not tell us whether 'determinism' is true. It is the total coverage of every motion that happens, that is a fanciful claim. But I do not mean that any motions lie outside the scope of physical laws, or that one cannot say, in any given context, that certain motions would be violations of physical law. Remember the contrast between chess and the infantile card game.

Meanwhile in non-experimental philosophy it is clear enough what are the dogmatic slumbers of the day. It is over and over again assumed that any singular causal proposition implies a universal statement running 'Always when this, then that'; often assumed that true singular causal statements are derived from such 'inductively believed' universalities. Examples indeed are recalcitrant, but that does not seem to disturb. Even a philosopher acute enough to be conscious of this, such as Davidson, will say, without offering any reason at all for saying it, that a singular causal statement implies *that there is* such a true universal proposition[6] – though perhaps we can never have knowledge of it. Such a thesis needs some reason for believing it! 'Regularities in nature': that is not a reason. The most neglected of the key topics in this subject are: interference and prevention.

Notes

1 My colleague Ian Hacking has pointed out C. S. Peirce to me as an exception to this generalization.
2 Bertrand Russell, *Mysticism and Logic* (New York: Longmans, Green, 1918).
3 Erwin Schrödinger, *'Nature and the Greeks' and 'Science and Humanism'* (Cambridge: Cambridge University Press, 1996), pp. 132–3.
4 I should have made acknowledgements to Gilbert Ryle (*Concept of Mind* (London: Hutchinson, 1949) p. 77) for this comparison. But his use of the openness of chess is somewhat ambiguous and is not the same as mine. For the contrast with a closed card game I was indebted to A. J. P. Kenny.
5 Albert Einstein and Leopold Infeld, *The Evolution of Physics* (New York, 1938; paperback edn 1967), p. 146.
6 'Causal Relations', *Journal of Philosophy*, 64 (November 1967).

PART II

WHAT IS OUR PLACE IN THE WORLD?

Introduction

Some readers may have found the air a bit thin while exploring topics like existence, universals, time, space, change, and causation. The subject matter of this section brings metaphysical reflection to bear on questions of more immediate importance to *us*. Where do we fit into reality?

Reflections on one's place in the world are most compellingly presented in the first-person-singular. For the moment, then, we shall follow the example of Descartes in his *Meditations* and use the first-person-singular to ask: What is *my* place in the world?

Metaphysicians want to know how the mental and physical aspects of human beings are interrelated. In the attempt, they have encountered a host of difficulties, which together are sometimes called the "mind-body problem." Section A takes up the two main aspects of the mind–body problem: (i) Am I identical with some physical object, and, if so, what kind of physical object (chs. 35–9)? (ii) What is the relationship between my mental states (for example, the thoughts and sensations I am now experiencing) and the physical states of my body (for example, the firings of neurons that happen in my brain) (chs. 40–2)?

Another perennial set of questions about our place in the natural world concerns the amount of freedom we enjoy. If determinism is true, might we still be free? For that matter, could we be free if determinism is false? Philosophers have disagreed radically in their answers to these questions; this is reflected in the wide spectrum of opinion to be found in section B.

A How Are Mind and Body Related?

Introduction

The so-called "mind–body problem" can be divided into two rather different issues. (i) There is the question that each of us can put to herself or himself by asking: What is the relationship between *me* (the thing that is thinking these thoughts, asking itself these questions, and experiencing certain sensations right now) and the physical body that I see in the mirror every morning? Different answers to this question are defended in chs. 35–39. (ii) Chs. 40–2 pose a slightly different question: What is the relationship between my mental states (the thoughts I'm now thinking, the sensations I'm now experiencing) and the physical states of my body (its shape, its weight, the pattern of neural firings going off in its brain, etc.)?

The two most plausible answers to the first question are: (a) I'm identical with this body or some part of it (say, my brain); and (b) I'm identical with something altogether different. Call the first answer "substance materialism," and the second "substance dualism." Chisholm's argument in ch. 35 (closely related to the themes of Olson's ch. 25) leads him to espouse (or at least to take seriously) a kind of substance materialism. But it is a peculiar materialism (identification of a person with a tiny particle!), and its difficulties explain why Chisholm typically defended dualism or agnosticism about the answer to question (i). Much of the action in chs. 36–9 revolves around the question: What sorts of changes could I survive, and what changes would bring about my destruction? Shoemaker defends the view that, although persons are large-scale material objects (living human bodies), the conditions that determine whether or not someone survives are largely *psychological*. Olson denies this, arguing that the continuance of a person's organic life is sufficient for the continued existence of the person, even if the brain is too damaged to support anything like a psychology. In ch. 38, Derek Parfit calls attention to the behavior of "split brain" patients and the vagueness of ordinary physical objects; and argues from these phenomena to the conclusion that we are radically mistaken about the kinds of changes we can survive – we are not at all as we take ourselves to be. In ch. 39, Richard Swinburne, appealing to some of the same facts as Parfit, argues that a person can survive changes that no mere physical object could survive; so, substance dualism must be true.

Question (ii) admits only two answers: With respect to each type of mental state (say, a certain sort of intense pain), either the state is identical with some physical state or it is not. Call the former "mental state materialism" and the latter "mental state dualism." Clearly, mental state materialism is incompatible with substance dualism. But the other three combinations of these four views seem, on the face of it, to be coherent. Mental state materialism and substance materialism are a natural pairing, as are mental state dualism and substance dualism. But combining mental state dualism and substance materialism would not seem to be out of the question. Indeed, Chisholm and Chalmers seek to draw a sharp line between (at least some of) our mental states and our physical states; but they do not advocate (at least in these selections) a dualism of *substances*.

This way of formulating the alternatives raises several difficult questions. There are deep puzzles about just what it means to call a state "physical." Is it just to say that it can be possessed by a physical object? In that case, no sensible view could count as combining substance materialism and mental state dualism. On the other hand, we might restrict "physical" to mean "something mentioned in the complete, true science of the ultimate constituents of matter" – call this use of the term "physics-physical." The good candidates for physics-physical properties are spatiotemporal relations and simple theoretical properties like mass and charge. But then, if we interpret mental state dualism and materialism using this notion of "physical," *being in pain* would almost certainly not qualify as a physical state of a dog, cat, or human being. After all, not even a table's *having four legs* and *being made of wood* will be physics-physical states – there is no need to talk about legs, wood, or, presumably, pain when doing fundamental physics. So the restriction of physical states to just those that show up in physics threatens to make mental state materialism false, but for trivial reasons.

A more interesting sense of "physical" would be this: If a property or state is physical, then whether a thing has it is completely determined by the physics-physical states of the thing's parts. The table's *having four legs*, for instance, is a physical property in this new sense, because anything made out of similar particles similarly arranged would also have to have four legs. (Contemporary philosophers would introduce this idea by saying that physical states are those that "strongly supervene upon" physics-physical states.)

Interpreting mental state dualism and materialism in this way, where do our authors fall? Armstrong's theory of mental states (ch. 40) is a straightforward (and popular) form of mental state materialism. In "The Puzzle of Conscious Experience," David Chalmers argues that such materialisms inevitably leave something out – namely, the *way it feels* to be in this or that sensory state. Chalmers champions a form of mental state dualism. Russell's "Neutral Monism" is harder to place. Russell takes the nature of sensory states – phenomenal experiences like sensing patches of color at various perceived distances, feeling warmth or coolness, etc. – to be obvious, open to introspection. Like Chalmers, he does not think that the kind of mathematical descriptions of the world that physics affords could ever capture information about what it feels like to be in these phenomenal states. After all, says Russell, everything physics can tell us is highly "abstract"; physics describes the interrelations among various kinds of events involving matter, but not the "intrinsic character of matter." Why not suppose, then, that the phenomenal experiences we have *just are* some of the states of matter, ones that our physical theories characterize in a purely abstract way? Experience shows us what these states are really like, while physics merely describes them "from the outside." Russell's neutral monism is, then, a kind of mental state materialism; but inert matter has turned out to have an intrinsic character somewhat like that of an experiencing mind!

A fascinating argument for mental state dualism may be found at the end of ch. 54 (Saul Kripke's "Identity and Necessity"). And there are numerous connections between chs. 35–9 and those of Part I, section D. In addition, ch. 23 (Lewis's "The Paradoxes of Time Travel") contains a splendid, succinct presentation of a materialist theory of persons and their persistence conditions in the context of the doctrine of temporal parts. Ch. 53 extends his theory in important – but complex – ways.

Suggestions for further reading

Aune, Bruce, *Metaphysics: The Elements* (Minneapolis: University of Minnesota, 1985) ch. 5 ("Changing Things").

Campbell, Keith, *Body and Mind*, 2nd ed. (Notre Dame: University of Notre Dame, 1984).

Carter, William R., *The Elements of Metaphysics* (Philadelphia, Penn.: Temple University Press, 1990) chs. 3, 7 and 8 ("Material Minds," "Personal Identity," and "Responsibility").

Disch, Thomas M., *Echo Round His Bones* (New York: Pocket Books, 1979; first publication, 1969) A science fiction novel supporting a Parfit-like view of personal identity.

Gardner, Martin, *The Whys of a Philosophical Scrivener* (New York: St. Martin's, 1999) chs. 17, 18, and 19 ("Immortality: Why I am Not Resigned," "Immortality: Why I Do Not Think It Strange," and "Immortality: Why I Do Not Think It Impossible").

Hamlyn, D. W., *Metaphysics* (Cambridge, UK: Cambridge University Press, 1984) chs. 8 and 9 ("Minds" and "Persons and Personal Identity").

Hasker, William, *Metaphysics: Constructing a World View* (Downers Grove, Ill., and Leicester, UK: InterVarsity press, 1983) ch. 3 ("Minds and Bodies").

Jubien, Michael, *Contemporary Metaphysics* (Oxford: Blackwell, 1997) ch. 6 ("Color").

Miedaner, Terry, *The Soul of Anna Klane* (New York: Ballantine, 1978) A science fiction novel in which the empirical evidence conclusively favors substance dualism . . . or is it Chisholm's strange materialism? Is there a difference?

Parfit, Derek, "Persons, bodies, and human beings," in Sider, Hawthorne, and Zimmerman (eds.), *Contemporary Debates in Metaphysics* (Malden, Mass.: Blackwell, 2007).

Perry, John, *A Dialogue on Personal Identity and Immortality* (Indianapolis: Hackett, 1978).

—, ed., *Personal Identity* (Berkeley, Cal.: University of California Press, 1975).

Post, John F., *Metaphysics: A Contemporary Introduction* (New York: Paragon House, 1991) ch. 6 ("Metaphysics and Human Being").

Smith, Quentin, and Oaklander, L. Nathan, *Time, Change and Freedom: an Introduction to Metaphysics* (London: Routledge, 1995) Dialogue 7 ("Personal Identity") .

Taylor, Richard, *Metaphysics* (Englewood Cliffs, N.J.: Prentice-Hall, 1992) chs. 2, 3, and 4 ("Persons and Bodies," "Interactionism," and "The Mind as a Function of the Body").

Thomson, Judith Jarvis, "People and their bodies," in Sider, Hawthorne, and Zimmerman (eds.), *Contemporary Debates in Metaphysics* (Malden, Mass.: Blackwell, 2007).

van Inwagen, Peter, *Metaphysics*, 2nd edn (Cambridge, Mass.: Westview Press, 2002) chs. 10 and 11 ("The Nature of Rational Beings: Dualism and Physicalism" and "The Nature of Rational Beings: Dualism and Personal Identity").

35   Which Physical Thing Am I?: an Excerpt from "Is There a Mind–Body Problem?"

Roderick M. Chisholm

. . .The "double aspect theory" tells us this: There are certain things which have physical properties and therefore are physical objects; some of these things also have certain mental or intentional properties; and persons – you and I – are such things as these.

C. A. Strong put this last point clearly. He wrote:

> *I* am to outer appearance physical but to inner perception psychical; there is therefore no contradiction in a thing being at once physical, that is, extended, composed of parts, productive of effects, and psychical, that is of the nature of feeling.[1]

Strong is not here saying that "my mind" is an aspect of a physical thing, much less that *I* am an aspect of a physical thing. What he says is that there *is* a certain physical thing which has inner and outer aspects and that that physical thing is identical with me.

If we were to accept this theory, then we could ask: "*Which* physical thing am I?" I am afraid we could not provide a precise answer to this question.

If I am in fact a physical thing, then, it should be obvious, that physical thing is either this gross physical body now standing before you or it is some proper part of this gross physical body. There are, of course, many philosophical arguments professing to show that the person cannot be identical with his gross macroscopic physical body. Some of these arguments, I think, are sound – in particular those appealing to certain facts about persistence through time.

The body that persists through time – the one I have been carrying with me, so to speak – is an *ens successivum*. That is to say, it is an entity which is made up of different things at different times. The set of things that make it up today is not identical with the set of things that made it up yesterday or with the set of things that made it up the day before. Now one could say that an *ens successivum* has different "stand-ins" at different times and that these stand-ins do duty for the successive entity at the different times. Thus the thing that does duty for my body today is other than the thing that did duty for it yesterday and other than the thing that will do duty for it tomorrow. But what of me?

Am *I* an entity such that different things do duty for *me* at different days? Is it *one* thing that does my feeling depressed for me today and *another* thing that did it yesterday and still another thing that will do it tomorrow? If I happen to be feeling sad, then, surely, there is no *other* thing that is doing my feeling sad for me. We must reject the view that persons are thus *entia successiva*.

Our reasoning can be summarized. Suppose (i) that I am now sad. Now (ii) if there is an *ens successivum* that bears my name and is now sad, then it is sad in virtue of the fact that one of its stand-ins is now sad. But (iii) I am not sad in virtue of the fact that some *other* thing is doing my feeling sad for me. Therefore (iv) I am not an *ens successivum*.

What would be an *ens nonsuccessivum*? If an individual thing were a nonsuccessive entity, what would it be like? If an *ens successivum* is an individual thing that is made up of different things at different times, then an *ens nonsuccessivum* would be an individual thing that is *not* made up of different things at different times. This means that, at any moment of its existence, it has precisely the same parts it has at any other moment of its existence; at no time during which it exists, does it have a part it does not have at any other time during which it exists.

It is tempting to reason, in Leibnizian fashion: "There are *entia successiva*. Therefore there are *entia nonsuccessiva*." I believe this reasoning is sound. I would add, moreover, that every extended period of time, however short, is such that some *ens nonsuccessivum* exists during some part of that time. For I believe it is only by presupposing this thesis that we can make sense of the identity or persistence of *any* individual thing through time.

Might I not be, then, such an *ens nonsuccessivum*? Leibniz mentions – and rejects – a theory which is similar to this. "The soul," he says, "does not dwell in certain atoms appropriated to itself, nor in a little incorruptible bone such as the *Luz* of the Rabbis."[2] Of course, the hypothesis I have suggested, if filled in by reference to such a material thing as the *Luz* bone, would not imply that "the soul" dwells there – if the soul is understood to be something *other* than the person, still another thing that the person "has." We would be saying rather that the person dwells there. And to say that he "dwells" there would be to say that the person *is* the *Luz* bone or some proper part of it.

If we accept this theory, then, of course, we part company with personalism. The doctrine that persons are physical things – even intactly persisting physical things – would not have been taken seriously by Borden Parker Bowne and his followers. Yet, if we view the person in the way I have suggested, we may go on to affirm many of the *other* philosophical theses that the personalists felt to be important. Thus we could say, as Bishop Butler did, that "our gross organized bodies with which we perceive the objects of sense, and with which we act, are no part of ourselves. . . . We see with our eyes in the same way we see with our glasses."[3] The eyes are the *organs* of sight, not the *subject* of sight. We could say, as Butler and the personalists did, that the destruction of the gross physical body does not logically imply the destruction of the person. And we could accept the view that St Thomas attributes to Plato: the person is "in a body in somewhat the same way as a sailor is in a ship."[4]

Some Objections Considered

To understand the view that is being proposed, let us formulate certain objections that readily come to mind and then attempt to reply to them. I will consider five such objections.

(1) "The hypothesis you are considering implies, then, that there is a kind of matter that is incorruptible and that the person is a material thing of that sort? But this is hardly adequate to the facts of physics."

The reply is that the theory does not imply that there is certain matter that is incorruptible. It implies rather that there are certain material things – in all probability, certain material particles or subparticles – that are incorrupted and remain incorrupted as long as the person survives.

The theory would be, then, that I am literally identical with some proper part of this macroscopic body, some intact, nonsuccessive part that has been in this larger body all along. This part is hardly likely to be the *Luz* bone, of course; more likely, it would be something of a microscopic nature, and presumably something that is located within the brain.

(2) "Persons, being thinking things, must have a complex structure. But no microscopic entity that is known to physics has the equipment that is necessary for thinking. After all, you can't think unless you have a brain. And *those* little things don't have brains!"

The hypothesis being criticized is the hypothesis that *I* am such a microscopic entity. But note that I do have a brain. And therefore, according to the hypothesis in question, the microscopic entity has one, too – the same one that I have, the one that is inside my head. It is only a confusion to suppose that the microscopic entity – which may in fact be inside my brain – has *another* brain which is in fact inside of it.[5]

The brain is the *organ* of consciousness, not the *subject* of consciousness – unless I am myself my brain.[6] The nose, similarly, is the organ of smell and not the subject of smell – unless I am myself my nose. But if I am one or the other – the brain or the nose – then, I the subject, will have some organs that are spatially outside me.

The hypothesis in question, then, is that I am a certain proper part of my brain. This would imply that the subject of consciousness is a proper part of the organ of consciousness.

(3) "You say I'm identical with some microscopic particle or some subparticle. But I am 6 feet tall and weigh 175 pounds. Therefore your theory would imply that there is a certain microscopic particle which is 6 feet tall and weighs 175 pounds. But this is absurd and therefore your theory is absurd."

The argument, of course, errs in taking too literally the premise expressed by saying "I am 6 feet tall and weigh 175 pounds." For what the premise actually tells us is that I have a body which is 6 feet tall and weighs 175 pounds.

(4) "Do you mean to suggest seriously, then, that instead of weighing 175 pounds, you may weigh less than a milligram?" The answer has to be yes. We must be ready, therefore, to be ridiculed, for, in this case, even those who know better may be unable to resist the temptation. But those who do know better will realize that a person can truly say, in *one* sense, that he weighs 175 pounds, and in *another* sense, that he weighs less than a milligram. The formulation of the first statement would be more nearly accurate (I say "more nearly *accurate*," not "more nearly *correct*") if it read: "I have a body that weighs 175 pounds."

Speaking in a loose and popular sense, I may attribute to myself certain properties of my gross macroscopic body. (And speaking to a filling station attendant I may attribute certain properties of my automobile to myself: "I'm down there on the corner of Jay Street without any gasoline." The response needn't be: "How, then, can you be standing here?" One might say that the property of being down there is one I have "borrowed" from my automobile.) But if I am a microscopic part of my gross body, then, strictly and philosophically, one cannot attribute to *me* the properties of *it*. The properties of weighing 175 pounds and being 6 feet tall are properties I "borrow" from my body. Strictly and philosophically, *it* has them and I do not.[7]

(5) "You say that you might be a small physical part that uses the mainframe brain as its organ of thought – it thinks by means of the brain. Theoretically,

then, there is the possibility that you might exchange brains with another person – either by transferring brains from one body to another or by transferring persons from one body to another. But what makes you the person you are is your *consciousness*: your present beliefs, desires, memories, and perceptions. Recall what Locke said:

> It being the same consciousness that makes a man be himself to himself, personal identity depends on that only, whether it be annexed to one individual substance, or can be continued in a succession of several substances. (*Essay Concerning Human Understanding*, book II, ch. xxiii, section 10)

But our consciousness is dependent upon our brains. We have the beliefs, memories and perceptions we do have because of the present make-up of our brains. Therefore, if you and I exchange brains, we will also exchange consciousnesses. And this means that you will become me and I will become you. But isn't that absurd?"

That is absurd. But the absurd consequence follows from the assumption that personal identity is a function of the nature of one's consciousness. The objection confuses the *criteria* of personal identity with its *truth-conditions*. The *criteria* of personal identity are simply the *means* by which one *identifies* any given person. We may say, if we choose, that they are the means by which one "determines the identity" of the person. But they do not determine the identity of the person in the sense of *making* that person the person that he is. Compare the criteria by means of which we decide whether a certain event occurred in the past. If we decide that it rained yesterday, we do so by means of certain *traces* which we find today (puddles, testimonies, pictures, recordings). These traces are not truth-conditions of yesterday's rain – it is logically possible that they occur even though it did not rain yesterday. They enable us to determine whether or not it rained – but they do not themselves determine the rain.

Conclusion

What are the possibilities, after all? There *are* persons. Therefore either the person is a physical thing or . . . the person is a nonphysical thing. But does anything we know about persons justify us in assuming that persons are *nonphysical* individual things?

What if we suppose that the concept of an extended thing presupposes the concept of ultimate nonextended things which, somehow, make up the extended thing? Could we then identify the person with such an unextended thing? I believe that this hypothesis would contradict the assumption that persons are *entia per se*. For I would say that the unextended things (boundaries, lines, points, surfaces) that are said to be presupposed by extended things are ontological parasites and not instances of *entia per se*: they depend for their own properties upon the extended things which are said to presuppose them.[8]

What point would there be in the hypothesis that certain individual thing
have the property of being nonphysical? How could that help us in explaining
anything?[9]

If I *am* a physical thing, then the most plausible hypothesis would seem to be
that I am a proper part of this gross macroscopic body, even if there is no way
of telling from the "outside" which proper part I happen to be.

I would suggest that, if this philosophic hypothesis seems implausible to you,
you try to formulate one that is less implausible.

Notes

1 C. A. Strong, "Final Observations," *Journal of Philosophy*, XXXVIII (1941), pp. 233–43;
   the quotation is on page 237.
2 *New Essays Concerning Human Understanding*, book II, ch. XXVIII (La Salle, Ill.,
   Open Court Publishing, 1916), p. 242. Alfred Langley, editor of this edition of
   Leibniz, quotes an ancient discussion of the *Luz* bone: "The old Rabbis of blessed
   memory have not only seen this bone, but have found it actually so strong and hard
   that their hammer and rock flew in pieces before this bone was injured in the least"
   (p. 242n).
3 Joseph Butler, *The Analogy of Religion*, part I, chapter 1 ("Of a Future Life"); see
   The Whole Works of Joseph Butler, LL.D. (London: Thomas Tegg, 1839), p. 7.
4 St Thomas Aquinas, *On Spiritual Creatures*, Article II (Milwaukee: Marquette University Press, 1949), p. 35.
5 I have illustrated this confusion in Richard Taylor's *Action and Purpose* (Englewood
   Cliffs, N.J., Prentice-Hall, 1966), p. 137.
6 Compare Franz Brentano, *Religion und Philosophie* (Bern: A. Francke Verlag).
7 Strawson emphasizes that persons have both psychological and physical properties.
   But, if what I say is true, most of the physical properties that we ordinarily attribute
   to the person are "borrowed" in this sense from the person's body.
8 Compare Brentano, *Religion und Philosophie*, p. 224.
9 For a clear formulation of this point, see Richard Taylor, *Metaphysics*, 2nd edition
   (Englewood Cliffs, N.J., Prentice-Hall, 1974), pp. 34–35.

---

36   Personal Identity: a Materialist Account

Sydney Shoemaker

1   Introduction

From earliest times people have found intelligible, and sometimes believable, the
idea that persons are capable of surviving death, either in disembodied form or
through bodily resurrection or reincarnation. And many a piece of popular fiction

relies on the idea that a person might have different bodies at different times. We are also familiar, both from fiction and from the annals of psychiatric medicine, with the idea of two or more distinct 'personalities' successively manifesting themselves in one and the same body. Yet another such idea is that two distinct minds or consciousnesses might simultaneously inhabit the same body – and recent studies of 'split-brain patients' have suggested to some investigators not only that this is conceivable but that it actually happens.[1] One way of raising the problem of personal identity is by asking whether, or to what extent, such ideas are coherent, and what it is about the nature of personal identity, or our concept of it, which permits, or forbids, such envisioned departures from the normal course of events.

The problem of personal identity can be viewed as an aspect of the 'mind–body problem'. For a variety of reasons we are inclined to resist the view, so strongly suggested by the current scientific world view, that mental states and processes are nothing over and above certain highly complex physical and chemical processes. One reason is the 'special access' we have to our own mental states. One comes to have knowledge of these states without observing, or gathering evidence about, the physical states of one's own body; and possession of the knowledge seems compatible with total ignorance of one's own inner physiological states, and, more generally, the condition of one's body. And if one reflects on what one knows in having this self-knowledge – the existence of intentional states like believing that Argentina's inflation rate is higher than Brazil's, and qualitative states like seeing blue and having an itch – it is difficult at best to see how this could be reducible to any facts about one's behaviour or neurophysiology. Puzzlement about the nature of mental states is bound to give rise to puzzlement about the nature of persons, the pre-eminent subjects of such states. And this in turn manifests itself in puzzlement about personal identity – for a central part of understanding the nature of a kind of things (like persons) is understanding the identity conditions for things of that sort. The considerations that make it seem that mental states cannot be physical states also make it seem that persons cannot simply be physical bodies, and that personal identity must consist in something other than bodily identity.

Among the things to which persons have a 'special access' are facts about their own identity over time; they have this in their memory knowledge of their own past histories. One's memory knowledge of one's own past differs strikingly from one's knowledge, including memory knowledge, of the past histories of other persons. If I claim to remember *you* doing something yesterday, it is at least a theoretical possibility that my claim is in error, not because my memory is mistaken, but because the person I remember doing that thing is not you but someone who looks just like you and whom I have misidentified as you. But if I claim to remember that I did such-and-such yesterday, it is absurd to suppose that I could be mistaken in *that* way. And whatever may be said of my judgements about the identity of others, it is certainly not the case that I ground such judgements about myself on evidence of bodily identity. Here again the nature of self-knowledge raises questions about personal identity, in part by calling into question the natural view that the identity of a person is simply the identity of a living human body.

A rather different source of perplexity about personal identity has to do with the special concern persons have for their own continued existence and their own future welfare. Imagine that a wizard demonstrates to you his ability to reduce any object to a pile of dust by a wave of his wand and then, with another wave, to create an exact duplicate of that thing out of another pile of dust. If one really believes that he can do this, one probably would not be too averse to letting him do it to one's kitchen stove. But only a monster would offer his wife or child as a subject for the wizard's trick, and only a madman (or a suicide) would offer himself. Or so it initially strikes us. Our concern for personal identity, the kind of importance it has for us, seems totally different in kind from the concern we have for the identity of other sorts of things. And this is linked to the special concern each person has for his or her own future welfare. It is this that gives point to many of our moral, social and legal practices, and explains the significance they attach to considerations of personal identity. If a person does an action, it is that same person who can later be held responsible for the action, and whom it is appropriate to punish or reward for doing it. If someone buys something, it is that person who is subsequently entitled to the use of the item purchased. These principles, which are constitutive of the institutions of punishment and property and the concept of moral responsibility, are intelligible only against the background of a conception of human motivation in which a central role is played by the special concern each person has for his own future well-being.

An account of personal identity ought to make intelligible the knowledge we have of personal identity including the special access each of us has, in memory, to his own identity, and it ought to make intelligible the special sort of importance personal identity has for us. It ought also to cohere with the rest of what we know about the world. In my own view, this last requirement means that an account of personal identity ought to be compatible with a naturalistic, or materialistic, account of mind. To a large extent, the mind–body problem, including the problem of personal identity, arises because of considerations that create the appearance that no naturalistic account could be true; and I think that solving the problem has got to consist in large part in dispelling that appearance (while acknowledging and explaining the facts that give rise to it). Finally, our account of personal identity must be compatible with the logical principles that govern the notion of identity itself. It is to these that we now turn.

2   The Concept of Identity

Logicians characterize identity as an 'equivalence relation', meaning by this a relation that is transitive (if a has it to b, and b has it to c, then a has it to c), symmetrical (if a has it to b, b has it to a), and reflexive (everything has it to itself). It is marked off from other equivalence relationships by its conformity to Leibniz's Law (the principle of the indiscernibility of identicals), which says that if *a* is identical to *b*, then whatever is true of *a* is true of *b*, and conversely. Identity is even more briefly characterizable as the relation which everything has, necessarily, to itself, and which nothing has to anything other than itself (but the last clause makes this definition circular, since it means 'and which nothing has to anything not identical to itself').

It is important to distinguish the relation of identity we are here concerned with from another relation that bears the same name. In the baggage claim areas of some airports are signs reading 'Careful: many suitcases are identical'.[2] This is a perfectly correct use of 'identical', but not in the sense of it relevant to the problem of personal identity. In the airport sign, 'identical' means 'exactly alike'; it expresses what is sometimes called 'qualitative identity' (or 'qualitative sameness'). This must be distinguished from the sense of 'identical' in which it means 'one and the same', and expresses 'numerical identity' (or 'numerical sameness'). It is the latter, the sense of 'identical' in which 'identical twins' (and identical suitcases) are not identical, that concerns us here.

Confusion of these two senses of 'identical' (and 'same') is one source of the idea that identity over time is incompatible with change. If something changes, then in some respect it is no longer the same as it was; the thing at the earlier time and the thing at the later time are not 'identical'. Indeed, we may seem to be driven into contradiction here: if I say 'A is not the same as *it* was', I seem to imply identity with the pronoun 'it' while denying it by saying 'not the same'. But the contradiction is only apparent; the identity that is implied is numerical identity, while that which is denied is qualitative identity. Change is incompatible with qualitative identity between the successive states of the changing thing; but it not only allows, but logically requires, that the successive states be states of numerically the same thing.

Another source of the view that identity over time is incompatible with change is a misunderstanding of Leibniz's Law. If a leaf is green in the summer and yellow in the fall, then in a certain sense something is true of it in the summer which is not true of it in the fall, and vice versa. But this is no violation of Leibniz's Law. If A is a leaf in the summer and B is a leaf in the fall, what Leibniz's Law holds to follow from 'A is identical to B' is not that if A is green in the summer then B is green in the fall; it is rather that if A is green in the summer then B is green in the summer (and if B is yellow in the fall, A is yellow in the fall). More generally, it tells us that whatever property A has at a time, B must have at that time, and conversely; and this is entirely compatible with A (=B) having different properties at different times.

More common than the view that identity over time is incompatible with any sort of change is the view that it is incompatible with one particular sort of change – change of composition. This stems in part from the confusions already mentioned, but has another source as well. If over a period of time some of the molecules in a tree are replaced by others, then in one sense we no longer have the same 'substance' as we had before. Now there is a well established philosophical sense of 'substance', going back to Aristotle, in which a tree *is* a substance. And to say in *this* sense that we no longer have the same substance is to say (in the case at hand) that we no longer have the same tree – which is the view Bishop

Butler took of the case in which, over time, all of the matter in a tree is replaced.[3] But surely we should distinguish these senses of 'substance'. When we say that we no longer have the same substance in this case, what counts as a substance is a particular portion or quantity of matter. But it is not in *this* sense that a tree is a substance. The tree is, at a particular time, composed of a particular portion of matter, but that is not to say that it is identical to that portion of matter and that it could not at some later time be composed of some quite different matter. And of course we regularly do take things like trees to survive the gradual (and in the case of things like rivers and waterfalls, not so gradual) replacement of the matter of which they are composed. To argue that such replacement is impossible on the grounds that being the same tree requires being the same substance either equivocates on the word 'substance' or begs the question. I think that we can see from this that it is either false or vacuous to say that the identity of things like trees consists in their being or having the same substance; it is false if 'substance' means 'portion of stuff', and vacuous if 'substance' means 'persisting subject of properties' (for then the claim comes to: being the same tree consists in being the same tree).

Some writers like to speak of the identity over time of a person or a table as consisting in the occurrence of a succession of momentary 'person-stages' or 'table-stages' that are related to one another in certain ways. (Some speak of 'time-slices' rather than of 'stages'). So, for example, if I say 'The table I am sitting at now is the table I was sitting at yesterday', I am asserting a relation to hold between a table-stage occurring now and one occurring yesterday. But it is important to be clear that the relation I assert to hold between the stages is not itself identity; today's table-stage and yesterday's table-stage cannot be the same, since stages are individuated by the time at which they occur. Let us pretend, for the moment, that different table-stages are stages of one and the same table if they belong to a single spatiotemporally continuous succession of table-stages – or, for short, if they are 'table-linked'. Here we can say, following John Perry, that the relation of being table-linked is the *unity relation* for tables.[4] The unity relation is not identity; it is rather the relation that holds between different table-stages when they are stages of one and the same table. Nevertheless, to specify the unity relation for tables is to say what the identity over time of tables consists in. And one way of formulating the problem of personal identity is to ask what the unity relation for persons is, i.e., what is the relation between person-stages occurring at different times, in virtue of which they are stages of one and the same person.

What sort of thing is a 'person-stage' or 'table-stage'? Some philosophers who use this terminology think of persons and other continuants as four-dimensional objects which have temporal as well as spatial parts. For them momentary stages will be either temporally very small parts of continuants or temporally unextended cross-sections of them taken at particular moments of time. But one need not be committed to the four-dimensional view of ordinary continuants in order to use this terminology. Person-stages can be thought of as 'temporal slices', not of persons, but of the histories or careers of persons. One might think of a momentary stage as a set of property instantiations; if C is a continuant existing at time

t, and P is the set of properties possessed by C at t, then C's stage at t will be the set consisting of the instantiations in C at t of the properties in P. Or one can think of a momentary stage as an ordered pair consisting of a thing and a time; C's stage at t will be just the ordered pair <C, t>.

Questions about identity over time can be said to be questions about the *diachronic* unity of continuants of some kind, e.g., persons or tables. Questions can also be raised about the *synchronic* unity of such things. In some cases the latter are questions about 'identity across space'; for example, if we were concerned (with Heraclitus) about the identity of rivers we might ask why it is that the river (or river part) at Minneapolis and that at New Orleans count as (parts of) the same river. In the case of persons, questions about synchronic unity are more likely to be asked about momentary experiences and other mental states than about spatial parts. The question will be: in virtue of what do different experiences or mental states occurring at the same time count as belonging to one and the same person? This is sometimes posed as the problem of the 'unity of consciousness'. A useful term for the unity relation for persons (both diachronic and synchronic) is Bertrand Russell's term 'copersonal'.[5]

There is a tradition, going back to Bishop Butler, of holding that personal identity is indefinable and unanalysable, that no non-trivial account can be given of the identity conditions for persons, and that personal identity does not 'consist' in anything. Butler (and likewise Thomas Reid) seemed to think that this is a consequence of personal identity being identity in a 'strict and philosophical sense' – as contrasted with the 'loose and popular sense' he believed to be invoked in our ascription of identity over time to such things as trees and ships. There are contemporary philosophers who think that Butler was right. But we will begin with the working assumption that an account of personal identity can be given. Indeed, we will begin with the view Butler was primarily attacking, that of John Locke.

3   The Memory Theory

Locke's central thesis was that personal identity consists, not in sameness of substance, but in 'sameness of consciousness'.[6] It is by no means uncontroversial what Locke meant by this. But it is clear enough that 'consciousness' for Locke includes memory, and that it is primarily memory he has in mind when he speaks of consciousness in his discussion of personal identity. Rightly or wrongly, Locke has been taken as the founder of the view that the identity over time of a person consists in facts about memory and the capacity to remember. He seems, in fact, to have held a fairly extreme version of that view: that a person A existing at a time t_2 is the same as a person B existing at an earlier time t_1 if and only if A remembers, or 'can remember', at t_2 actions or experiences of B occurring at t_1.

Before we consider the objections that have been raised against this view we must try to understand its initial appeal. We have already noted (section 1) that the way a person knows of his own past on the basis of memory is different from that in which he knows of the past of any other person. When I claim to remember *your* doing such-and-such yesterday, a question can arise whether the person I remember doing that thing was really you, and not someone else who looked like you (and this is so even if the accuracy of my memory of the incident is conceded); when I claim to remember *my* doing such-and-such a thing yesterday, no such question can arise. There seems to be a way of remembering past experiences and actions – I call it 'remembering from the inside' – such that if someone remembers X (an action or experience) in that way, it follows that X was an experience or action of that person.[7] Already, then, we seem to have an intimate connection between memory and personal identity: the person who remembers from the inside must be identical to the person who earlier had the remembered experience or did the remembered action. What I am calling 'remembering from the inside' is the kind of memory a person has of a past action when he remembers *doing* it, or of an experience when he remembers *having* it. But there also seems to be a more general connection between personal identity and memory which is not restricted to remembering from the inside: if someone remembers any event whatever, he must be identical to one of those who witnessed that event, or otherwise knew of it in a direct way, at the time of its occurrence. I can remember *that* the Battle of Hastings occurred in 1066, but no one now alive can be said to remember the Battle of Hastings.

It is not only from the first-person point of view that the memory theory, and the allied view that personal identity is independent of bodily identity, can seem attractive. Locke remarks that 'should the soul of a prince, carrying with it the consciousness of the prince's past life, enter and inform the body of a cobbler, as soon deserted by his own soul, everyone sees he would be the same person with the prince, accountable only for the prince's actions.'[8] It is easy enough to develop this into a case in which we could have rather compelling evidence, based on considerations having to do with memory, that someone had 'changed bodies'. For those who are sceptical about 'souls', it may help to imagine a case in which what are switched are not souls but brains. Suppose, then, that by a surgical blunder (of rather staggering proportions!) Brown's brain gets into Robinson's head.[9] When the resulting person, call him 'Brownson', regains consciousness, he claims to be Brown, and exhibits detailed knowledge of Brown's past life, always reporting Brown's deeds and experiences in the first person. It is hard to resist the conclusion that we, viewing the case from the outside, ought to accept Brownson's claim to be Brown, precisely on the basis of the evidence that he remembers Brown's life from the inside. This gives prima facie support to the Lockean view that personal identity consists in part in facts having to do with memory.

A variety of objections have been raised against the memory theory, and some of these are clearly telling against the version apparently held by Locke. What I want to do next is to consider how Locke's view might be modified to meet these objections, with a view to seeing whether a modified version of it can provide an acceptable theory of personal identity.

4   Objections and Revisions

The most famous objections to Locke's account are those raised in the eighteenth century by Bishop Butler and Thomas Reid. Butler charged that the account is circular: 'one should really think it self-evident, that consciousness of personal identity presupposes, and therefore cannot constitute, personal identity, any more than knowledge, in any other case, can constitute truth, which it presupposes'.[10] Reid charged that the account is self-contradictory, and sought to show this with his 'brave officer' example.[11] At a certain time a boy is flogged for robbing an orchard. Years later the same person, now a young officer, performs a valiant deed in battle, remembering still his boyhood flogging. Many years later our man is an elderly general, who remembers the valiant deed in battle, but no longer remembers the flogging. Reid charges that on Locke's theory the old general both is and is not the same person as the small boy; he is the same because he is identical to the young officer who is identical to the small boy (and because identity is transitive); he is not the same because he has no memory of the flogging (and, let us suppose, has no memory at all of that period of the boy's life).

Let us begin with Reid's objection. Plainly the objection is decisive if the memory theory makes it a necessary and sufficient condition of someone's being the person who did a past action that he should remember that action. A defender of Locke might try to parry the objection by pointing out that what Locke requires for personal identity is that one *can* remember the action of the earlier person, not that one *does* remember it, and that it is plausible that under some possible circumstances (hypnosis, psychoanalysis) Reid's old general would remember the childhood incident, and so in that sense 'can' remember it. What Reid says, however, is that the old general had 'absolutely lost consciousness of the flogging', and it seems plausible to take the 'absolutely' as implying that the memory was lost without any possibility of recall. The example still seems possible under that interpretation.

Plainly the simple Lockean theory must be revised. The standard revision to meet this difficulty is most conveniently put in the person-stage terminology. Take the simple Lockean theory to hold that two person-stages belong to the same person if and only if the later contains memories (from the inside) of experiences, etc., contained in the earlier one. Here we should allow that one's current person-stage contains a memory of something even if one has temporarily forgotten that thing, as long as one has the potentiality of remembering it. In such a case the stage will retain a 'memory trace' that is the basis of that potentiality. Let us say that two person-stages that are so related are 'memory-connected'. The revised Lockean account says that the unity relation for persons is not the relation of being memory-connected but the 'ancestral' of this relation. This comes to saying that two stages belong to the same person if and only if they are the end-points of a series of stages such that each member of the series is memory-connected with the preceding member. One such series consists of the stage of the boy at the time of his flogging, the stage of the young officer at the time of his valiant deed, and a stage of the old general at a time at which he remembers the valiant deed but not the flogging. What this account makes necessary for identity with a 'past self' is not that one remember the actions and experiences of that past self but that one have 'memory continuity' with that past self – memory continuity consisting in the occurrence of a chain of memory-connected person-stages of the sort just described.[12]

Rather than address myself directly to Butler's objection, which seems to me to attack something Locke never said, I shall consider some circularity objections, perhaps descendants of Butler's, which seem to me more fundamental. It is arguable, first of all, that, far from personal identity being definable in terms of memory, memory must be defined in terms of personal identity. A definition of what it is for a person S to remember a particular event E could be expected to include the provisions (1) that S now has a state (which could be dispositional) which could be called an apparent memory, and (2) that the content of that apparent memory 'matches' in an appropriate way the nature of the past event E. But it is obvious that these conditions are not sufficient; if your first haircut was exactly like mine, I do not automatically remember yours in remembering mine. The obvious remedy is to supplement conditions (1) and (2) with the additional requirement (3) that S was appropriately related to E at the time of its occurrence, i.e., he witnessed it, underwent it (if it was a haircut), performed it (if it was an action), and so on. But if the definition of 'S remembers E' contains condition (3), then we cannot without circularity use the notion of event memory to define personal identity, since (3) implicitly invokes the notion of personal identity – it implies that the person S who now satisfies condition (1) is *the same person* as someone in the past who was involved in a certain way with event E. It may further be argued (and this is perhaps closer to what Butler had in mind) that the particular sort of memory I have called 'remembering from the inside' cannot be characterized without the use of the notion of personal identity. For it may be claimed that to say that someone remembers *doing* an action, or *having* an experience, is elliptical for saying that he remembers *himself* doing the action or having the experience, and that for this reason these locutions (and the notion of 'remembering from the inside' which is explained in terms of them) cannot without circularity be used in an account of personal identity.

The first step towards answering these objections is to see that the addition of condition (3) to conditions (1) and (2) does not give us a sufficient condition for the truth of 'S remembers E'. There can be memory illusions, and it is perfectly possible for an illusory memory to happen to correspond to something that happened to its subject in the past. For example, a hypnotist induces in me an apparent memory of having visited Yellowstone Park as a child, and it just so happens (unbeknownst to the hypnotist) that I did visit Yellowstone Park as a child, but have completely forgotten about it. The case I want is not one in which the hypnotist brings to consciousness a latent memory which was already present, but rather one in which my apparent memory of the visit to Yellowstone is entirely due to the hypnotist's suggestion, and not at all due to my childhood visit to the Park – i.e., it is such that I would have had the very same apparent memory even if I had never visited Yellowstone. In this case I clearly do not remember the visit to Yellowstone, even though conditions (1)–(3) are all satisfied. What this brings out is that the notion of memory is a *causal* notion; it is a necessary condition of a person's remembering a past event that his apparent memory of that event should be caused, in an appropriate way, by that event itself.[13]

What this may seem to call for is the replacement of condition (3) by something like this: (3′) S's apparent memory (mentioned in (1)) was caused, in an appropriate way, by his experiencing (or otherwise being involved in) E at the time of its occurrence. Of course, (3′) implicitly invokes the notion of personal identity in the same way that (3) does, and so does not get us out of the circularity. But it is not obvious that we cannot formulate the causal requirement, and make it do the work done by (3) and (3′), without invoking the notion of personal identity. The requirement might be: (3″) S's apparent memory (mentioned in (1)) was caused, in an appropriate way, by someone's experiencing (or otherwise being involved in) E at the time of its occurrence. Replacing 'his' (or 'S's') with 'someone's' eliminates the circularity – or rather, it does so *if* the notion of 'being caused in an appropriate way' can be spelled out without invoking the notion of personal identity.

That some such phrase as 'in an appropriate way' is needed in the causal condition can be seen from a modification of my Yellowstone Park example. Suppose that at some time in my life a traumatic experience completely obliterated my memory of that incident. Prior to that time, however, I told someone about the visit, on the basis of the accurate memory I then had of it, and that person subsequently told the hypnotist about it. What the hypnotist did was instil in me an apparent memory which corresponded to the account he was given of my visit, an account which originally came from me. But he did not restore or revive my memory – it was irretrievably gone. Rather, he instilled in me a memory illusion which he could just as easily have instilled in someone who had never been to Yellowstone. Yet my apparent memory not only 'matches' the past event but is traceable back to it by a causal chain that goes through the hypnotist and his informant back to my earlier memory of the event, and via that back to the event itself. Here we have a causal connection, but not one of the 'appropriate sort'.

If 'causal connection of the appropriate sort' could only be explained as meaning something like 'connection via a causal chain that does not go outside the states of a single person', obviously (3″) would invoke the notion of personal identity as much as (3) did, and the circularity objection would stand. However, there are reasons for thinking that this is not so.

One thing that seems clear is that we can *know* that there is a causal connection of the appropriate sort, and therefore that a person remembers a past event, without *first* knowing the relevant fact of personal identity (i.e., that the rememberer is identical to someone who experienced the remembered past event). For consider again the brain transfer example described earlier. If Brownson does indeed manifest apparent memories of Brown's past life, the fact that he has Brown's brain would seem to provide sufficient reason for thinking that these memories are 'caused in an appropriate way' by Brown's past actions and experiences, and thus that Brownson really does remember those actions and experiences, which in turn can serve as a basis for saying that Brownson is

Brown. If we had to settle the question of identity prior to discovering whether Brownson's apparent memories really are memories of Brown's life, we could not use an affirmative answer to the latter question as a basis for an affirmative answer to the former. Yet it seems that we can do this.

Moreover, there seem to be conceivable cases in which we can have the appropriate sort of causal connection for memory in the absence of identity between the rememberer and the person who experienced the remembered event. It may seem that if such cases are possible, they get us out of the circularity problem only at the cost of falsifying the memory theory; but we will see that the memory theory can easily be modified so as to accommodate such cases. The possible cases I have in mind are what have been called cases of 'fission' – cases (entirely imaginary, of course) in which a person somehow divides into two persons. The most realistic such case is one described by David Wiggins.[14] He imagines a complex brain-transplant in which the two hemispheres of someone's brain are transplanted, separately, into the skulls of two different bodies. The result of the operation, we will suppose, is that both offshoots have memories from the inside of the life of the original person. It would be difficult to maintain that each offshoot is identical to the original person, since plainly they are not identical to each other (after the operation they go their separate ways, and soon can be distinguished on psychological grounds as well as by spatial location and physical properties).[15] And it would seem arbitrary to suggest that one is identical to the original person and the other not.[16] Yet it would be hard to deny that the apparent memories both have of the original person's life are genuine memories, and are related to events in that past life by causal connections 'of the appropriate sort'.

It is easy to see how the Lockean memory theory can be modified to allow for this case. We will simply say that memory continuity is sufficient for personal identity as long as there is no 'branching' in the chain of person-stages – where the fission case illustrates what is meant by 'branching'. I will have more to say about the fission example later on. Its importance here is that its possibility seems to count against the claim that the 'appropriate sort' of causal connection for memory can only be characterized as one that involves personal identity, and thus helps to defuse the circularity objection.

The fission case also helps with the objection that memory 'from the inside' can only be characterized as the sort of memory a person has of his own past, and thus that any attempt to define personal identity in terms of it will be circular. If the offshoots in the fission case are not identical to the original person, then their memories of that person's actions and experiences will not be memories of their own actions and experiences. Yet, for all that, they will remember those actions and experiences in the way in which normally one can remember only one's own actions and experiences. This is remembering from the inside, and it is something which in principle we can have in the absence of personal identity.

It will be seen that I have abandoned the claims, tentatively made in section 3, that it is necessarily the case that one can remember a past event only if one was a witness to it, and can remember a past experience or action from the inside only if it was an experience or action of one's own. An alternative approach, which differs only verbally from that presented here, is to hold on to these claims and to introduce a technical term, 'quasi-remember', for the notion defined in terms of conditions (1), (2) and (3″). The definition of personal identity will then be in terms of quasi-remembering (quasi-memory) rather than in terms of remembering (memory). Remembering will now be a special case of quasi-remembering; it will be quasi-remembering in which the rememberer is identical to the person who experienced or underwent the quasi-remembered event.[17]

There remains, however, an objection to the memory theory which is simpler and more direct than those considered so far. This is just that it seems conceivable that someone should survive total amnesia, total loss of memory.[18] If that happens, there will be no chain of memory-connected person-stages going from stages prior to the onset of the amnesia to stages subsequent to it. So this possibility counts against the modified Lockean theory as well as against the simple theory.

We must be careful here about what is meant by 'amnesia'. What is ordinarily meant is a total or partial loss of memory which can be recovered from; it is a condition that is treatable by hypnosis and in other ways. The possibility of total amnesia in this sense is no threat to the memory theory, since the amnesia victim can be presumed to retain memories in latent form. What is needed to refute the memory theory is the possibility of what might be called 'philosophical amnesia' i.e., the irreversible loss of all memory of the past.

But in addition to distinguishing different sorts of amnesia we must distinguish different sorts of memory. What we have meant by memory up until now is what is sometimes called 'event memory' – memory of particular events in the past. But there are other sorts of memory that are equally important. There is 'factual memory' – remembering *that* De Soto discovered the Mississippi River, *that* sulphuric acid is H_2SO_4, *that* there will be an eclipse tomorrow. There is remembering how to do something – ride a bicycle, tie a bow tie, etc. There is remembering the meaning of 'soigner', the smell of lilacs, and so on. If the claim that philosophical amnesia is possible means that someone can suffer total and irreversible loss of memories of all past events, so that from a certain time onwards the person has, and can have, no memory of events prior to that time, then I think that we must allow that this is possible. But if 'philosophical amnesia' is taken to mean total and irretrievable loss of all memories of all kinds, then the claim that a person can survive such amnesia is far more questionable. For what we are now imagining is something close to what has been called a 'brain zap' – the total destruction of all of the effects of the person's past experience, learning, reasoning, deliberation, and so on.[19] Whether it is physiologically possible that a human body should survive a brain zap and remain alive and capable of realizing a mental life of a human sort seems questionable, to say the least. But let us suppose this is possible. Suppose that in a terrible accident a person suffers brain damage amounting to a total brain zap, and that somehow the surgeons manage to repair the brain in such a way that its possessor is able to start again, as it were, as if he were an infant. Eventually that body is again the body of someone with the mental life of a mature human being; but it is someone whose conception of the world, along with his personality and character, was formed by the experience of that body since the time of the accident and the reconstitution of the brain. It is anything but obvious that this person would be the person who had the body prior to the accident. So if total amnesia means this sort of brain zap, it is far from uncontroversial – indeed it seems just false – that it is something a person could survive.

But perhaps a total and irreversible loss of all memories need not amount to a brain zap. A person's personality, character, tastes, interests and so on are the product (at least in part) of his past experience, and it is not obvious that the loss of all memories would necessarily involve the loss of all such traits as these. To be sure, to a certain extent personality and character traits do seem inseparable from memories of certain kinds. It is hard to see how someone's pacifism could survive his loss of all of his beliefs about the effects of warfare. However, let us assume that there are some traits of personality that could, at least in principle, survive a total and irreversible loss of all memories. If that is so, such a loss of memory would not necessarily amount to a total brain zap; and then it becomes more plausible to suppose that such a loss of memory is something a person could survive – in which case the memory theory, even as revised, is false.

5 Personal Identity as Psychological Continuity

This requires us to consider something we would have had to consider anyhow, namely the role *vis-à-vis* personal identity of kinds of psychological continuity other than memory continuity – I mean continuity with respect to the sorts of traits just mentioned: interests, tastes, talents, and traits of personality and character. Let us return to the Brown–Brownson case. If Brownson's possession of Brown's brain makes it plausible that he will have memories from the inside of Brown's past life, it makes it equally plausible that he will resemble Brown psychologically in all of the ways one expects a person on one day to resemble himself as he was the day before, and this resemblance would certainly be part of our reason for regarding Brownson as the same person as Brown. Suppose just for the moment that while Brownson's memories-from-the-inside are all of Brown's past, his personality and character traits are those of the old Robinson; I think that in this case (which would be physiologically unintelligible, and perhaps psychologically unintelligible as well) we would be much more hesitant about identifying Brownson with Brown.

We know, of course, that different people can share personality and character traits. And this may seem a reason for saying that Brownson's similarity to Brown with respect to such traits could not be part of what constitutes his identity with Brown, even though it might be evidence for it. This may suggest that, conceptually speaking, memory continuity is much more intimately related to personal identity than is similarity and continuity of personality. But all of this ignores the fact that what we have in the Brown–Brownson case is not merely similarity of personality and character. Brownson does not merely have the same personality traits as Brown did; he has those traits *because* Brown's life was such as to lead him to acquire such traits. The fact that Brownson has Brown's brain gives us reason to suppose that there is a relationship of causal or counterfactual dependence between Brownson's traits subsequent to the brain transfer and Brown's traits prior to it – we have reason to think that if Brown's traits had been different, Brownson's traits would have been different in corresponding ways. It is precisely when the circumstances are such that evidence of similarity is evidence of such a causal or counterfactual dependence that evidence of similarity is evidence of identity. Indeed, it is for the same reason that the nature of Brownson's memories is evidence that he is Brown; we have reason to think that if Brown's life had been different, Brownson's memories would have been correspondingly different, and thus that Brownson's memories are causally and counterfactually dependent on Brown's past life. Thus the status of similarity and continuity of personality traits as evidence of personal identity seems no different than that of memory continuity; both are evidence only in so far as they include, or are evidence for, causal relations between earlier and later states.

Henceforth I shall use the term 'psychological continuity' to cover both of these sorts of causally grounded continuity. The memory continuity account of personal identity thus gives way to a more general psychological continuity account.[20] Memory continuity is now seen as just a special case of psychological continuity, and it is in psychological continuity that personal identity is now held to consist. Reverting to the 'person-stage' terminology, two person-stages will be directly connected, psychologically, if the later of them contains a psychological state (a memory impression, personality trait, etc.) which stands in the appropriate relation of causal dependence to a state contained in the earlier one; and two stages belong to the same person if and only if (1) they are connected by a series of stages such that each member of the series is directly connected, psychologically, to the immediately preceding member, and (2) no such series of stages which connects them 'branches' at any point, i.e., contains a member which is directly connected, psychologically, to two different stages occurring at the same time.

It is not peculiar to persons that their identity over time involves there being relationships of causal or counterfactual dependence between successive stages. The same is true of continuants generally. It is, I think, a point in favour of the psychological continuity account of personal identity that it can be seen as applying to the special case of personal identity an account of identity through time – call it the 'causal continuity account' – which holds of continuants generally.[21] . . .

Notes

1   Thomas Nagel, 'Brain Bisection and the Unity of Consciousness', in Nagel, *Mortal Questions* (Cambridge, 1979).
2   Reported by Saul Kripke, in a lecture.
3   John Perry, *Personal Identity* (Berkeley, 1975), pp. 100–1.
4   See Perry, 'The Problem of Personal Identity', in his *Personal Identity*.

5   Russell, 'The Philosophy of Logical Atomism', in R. C. Marsh (ed.), *Lo͸ Knowledge* (London, 1956), p. 277.
6   Locke's *Essay* was first published in 1690, but the chapter on 'Identity and Diversity' was added in the second edition, which appeared in 1694.
7   See Shoemaker, 'Persons and their Pasts', *American Philosophical Quarterly*, 7 (1970), pp. 269–85; see esp. p. 180.
8   Locke, *Essay Concerning Human Understanding*, ed. P. H. Nidditch, p. 340.
9   See S. Shoemaker, *Self-Knowledge and Self-Identity* (Ithaca, N.Y., 1963), pp. 22–5.
10 Perry, *Personal Identity*, p. 100.
11 Ibid., pp. 114–15.
12 For more precise formulations of such modified Lockean accounts, see H. P. Grice, 'Personal Identity', *Mind*, 50 (1941), pp. 330–50; and Perry, 'The Problem of Personal Identity'.
13 See Max Deutscher and C. B. Martin, 'Remembering', *The Philosophical Review*, 75 (1966), pp. 161–97.
14 David Wiggins, *Identity and Spatio-temporal Continuity* (Oxford, 1967), p. 53.
15 For attempts to circumvent this difficulty, see John Perry, 'Can the Self Divide?', *Journal of Philosophy*, 69 (1972), pp. 463–88; and David Lewis, 'Survival and Identity', in Amélie Rorty (ed.), *The Identities of Persons* (Berkeley, Cal., 1976).
16 It is really only for materialists (or anti-dualists) that this would be arbitrary. A believer in indivisible immaterial souls would of course insist that at most one of the offshoots would inherit the soul of the original person.
17 This was my approach in Shoemaker, 'Persons and their Pasts'.
18 See David Wiggins, *Sameness and Substance* (Oxford, 1980), p. 167 and pp. 176–7.
19 Perry, review of Bernard Williams, *Problems of the Self, Journal of Philosophy*, 73 (1976), pp. 416–18; see esp. p. 421.
20 A psychological continuity account is given in Anthony Quinton, 'The Soul', *Journal of Philosophy*, 59 (1962), pp. 393–403.
21 See Sydney Shoemaker, 'Identity, Properties and Causality', *Midwest Studies in Philosophy*, no, 4 (Minneapolis, 1979), pp. 321–42.

37   An Argument for Animalism

Eric T. Olson

It is a truism that you and I are human beings. It is also a truism that a human being is a kind of animal: roughly a member of the primate species *Homo sapiens*. It would seem to follow that we are animals. Yet that claim is deeply controversial. Plato, Augustine, Descartes, Spinoza, Leibniz, Locke, Berkeley, Hume, Kant, and Hegel all denied it. With the notable exception of Aristotle and his followers, it is hard to find a major figure in the history of Western philosophy who thought that we are animals. The view is no more popular in non-Western traditions. And probably nine out of ten philosophers writing about personal identity today either deny outright that we are animals or say things that are clearly incompatible with it.

This is surprising. Isn't it obvious that we are animals? I will try to show that it isn't obvious, and that Plato and the others have their reasons for thinking otherwise. Before doing that I will explain how I understand the claim that we are animals. My main purpose, though, is to make a case for this unpopular view. I won't rely on the brief argument I began with. My strategy is to ask what it would mean if we weren't animals. Denying that we are animals is harder than you might think.

1.   What Animalism Says

When I say that we are animals, I mean that each of us is numerically identical with an animal. There is a certain human organism, and that organism is you. You and it are one and the same. This view has been called animalism (not a very nice name, but I haven't got a better one). Simple though it may appear, this is easily misunderstood. Many claims that sound like animalism are in fact different.

First, some say that we are animals and yet reject animalism.[1] How is that possible? How can you be an animal, and yet not be one? The idea is that there is a sense of the verb *to be* in which something can "be" an animal without being identical with any animal. Each of us "is" an animal in the sense of being "constituted" by one. That means roughly that you are in the same place and made of the same matter as an animal. But you and that animal could come apart (more on this later). And since a thing can't come apart from itself, you and the animal are not identical.

I wish people wouldn't say things like this. If you are not identical with a certain animal, that animal is something other than you. And I doubt whether there is any interesting sense in which you can be something other than yourself. Even if there is, expressing a view on which no one is identical with an animal by saying that we *are* animals is badly misleading. It discourages us from asking important questions: what we *are* identical with if not animals, for instance. Put plainly and honestly, these philosophers are saying that each of us is a non-animal that relates in some intimate way to an animal. They put it by saying that we *are* animals because that sounds more plausible. This is salesman's hype, and we shouldn't be fooled. In any case, the "constitutionalists" do not say that we are animals in the straightforward sense in which I mean it. They are not animalists.

The existence of the constitution view shows that animalism is not the same as *materialism*. Materialism is the view that we are material things; and we might be material things but not animals. Animalism implies materialism (animals are material things), but not vice versa. It may seem perverse for a materialist to reject animalism. If we are material things of any sort, surely we are animals? Perverse or not, though, the view that we are material non-organisms is widely held.

Animalism says that *we* are animals. That is compatible with the existence of non-animal people (or persons, if you prefer). It is often said that to be a person is to have certain mental qualities: to be rational, intelligent, and self-conscious, say. Perhaps a person must also be morally responsible, and have free will. If something like that is right, then gods or angels might be people but not animals.

Nor does our being animals imply that all animals, or even all human animals, are people. Human beings in a persistent vegetative state are biologically alive, but their mental capacities are permanently destroyed. They are certainly human animals. But we might not want to call them people. The same goes for human embryos.

So the view that we are animals does not imply that to be a person is nothing other than to be an animal of a certain sort – that being an animal is part of what it is to be a person. Inconveniently enough, this view has also been called animalism. It isn't the animalism that I want to defend. In fact it looks rather implausible. I don't know whether there could be inorganic people, as for instance traditional theism asserts. But mere reflection on what it is to be a person doesn't seem to rule it out. Of course, if people are animals by definition, it follows that we are animals, since we are obviously people. But the reverse entailment doesn't hold: we might be animals even if something could be a person without being an animal.

If I don't say that all people are animals, which people do I mean? Is animalism the mere tautology that all animal people are animals? No. I say that you and I and the other people who walk the earth are animals. If you like, all *human* people are animals, where a human person is roughly someone who relates to a human animal in the way that you and I do, whatever way that is. (Even idealists can agree that we are in some sense human, and not, say, feline or angelic.) Many philosophers deny that *any* people are animals. So there is nothing trivial about this claim.

"Animalism" is sometimes stated as the view that we are *essentially or most fundamentally* animals. We are essentially animals if we couldn't possibly exist without being animals. It is less clear what it is for us to be most fundamentally animals, but this is usually taken to imply at least that our identity conditions derive from our being animals, rather than from our being, say, people or philosophers or material objects – even though we *are* people and philosophers and material objects.

Whether our being animals implies that we are essentially or most fundamentally animals depends on whether human animals are essentially or most fundamentally animals. If the animal that you are is essentially an animal, then so are you. If it is only contingently an animal, then you are only contingently an animal. Likewise, you are most fundamentally an animal if and only if the animal that you are is most fundamentally an animal. The claim that each of us is identical with an animal is neutral on these questions. Most philosophers think that every animal is essentially and most fundamentally an animal, and I am inclined to agree. But you could be an animalist in my sense without accepting this.

Is animalism the view that we are identical with our bodies? That depends on what it is for something to be someone's body. If a person's body is by definition a sort of animal, then I suppose being an animal amounts to being one's body.

It is often said, though, that someone could have a partly or wholly inorganic body. One's body might include plastic or metal limbs. Someone might even have an entirely robotic body. I take it that no animal could be partly or wholly inorganic. If you cut off an animal's limb and replace it with an inorganic prosthesis, the animal just gets smaller and has something inorganic attached to it. So perhaps after having some or all of your parts replaced by inorganic gadgets of the right sort you would be identical with your body, but would not be an animal. Animalism may imply that you are your body, but you could be your body without being an animal. Some philosophers even say that being an animal rules out being identical with one's body. If you replaced enough of an animal's parts with new ones, they say, it would end up with a different body from the one it began with.

Whether these claims about bodies are true depends on what it is for something to be someone's body. What does it *mean* to say that your body is an animal, or that someone might have a robotic body? I have never seen a good answer to this question (see van Inwagen 1980 and Olson 2006). So I will talk about people and animals, and leave bodies out of it.

Finally, does animalism say that we are *merely* animals? That we are nothing more than biological organisms? This is a delicate point. The issue is whether being "more than just" or "not merely" an animal is compatible with being an animal – that is, with being identical with an animal.

If someone complains that the committee is more than just the chairman, she means that it is not the chairman: it has other members too. If we are more than just animals in something like this sense, then we are not animals. We have parts that are not parts of any animal: immaterial souls, perhaps.

On the other hand, we say that Descartes was more than just a philosopher: he was also a mathematician, a Frenchman, a Roman Catholic, and many other things. That is of course compatible with his being a philosopher. We can certainly be more than "mere" animals in this sense, and yet still be animals. An animal can have properties other than being an animal, and which don't follow from its being an animal. Our being animals does not rule out our being mathematicians, Frenchmen, or Roman Catholics – or our being people, socialists, mountaineers, and many other things. At least there is no evident reason why it should. Animalism does not imply that we have a fixed, "animal" nature, or that we have only biological or naturalistic properties, or that we are no different, in any important way, from other animals. There may be a vast psychological and moral gulf between human animals and organisms of other species. We may be very special animals. But for all that we may be animals.

2.   Alternatives

One reason why it may seem obvious that we are animals is that it is unclear what else we could be. If we're not animals, what are we? What are the alternatives to animalism? This is a question that philosophers ought to ask more often. Many views about personal identity clearly rule out our being animals, but leave it a mystery what sort of things we might be instead. Locke's account is a notorious example. His detailed account of personal identity doesn't even tell us whether we are material or immaterial.

Well, there is the traditional idea that we are simple immaterial substances, or, alternatively, compound things made up of an immaterial substance and a biological organism.

There is the view, mentioned earlier, that we are material objects "constituted by" human animals. You and a certain animal are physically indistinguishable. Nonetheless you and it are two different things.

Some say that we are temporal parts of animals. Animals and other persisting objects exist at different times by having different temporal parts or "stages" located at those times. You are made up of those stages of a human animal (or, in science fiction, of several animals) that are "psychologically interconnected" (Lewis 1976). Since your animal's embryonic stages have no mental properties at all, they aren't psychologically connected with anything, and so they aren't parts of you. Hence, you began later than the animal did.

Hume famously proposed that each of us is "a bundle or collection of different perceptions, which succeed each other with an inconceivable rapidity, and are in a perpetual flux and movement" (1888: 252). Strictly speaking you are not made of bones and sinews, or of atoms, or of matter. You are literally composed of thoughts. Whether Hume actually believed this is uncertain; but some do (e.g. Quinton 1962).

Every teacher of philosophy has heard it said that we are something like computer programs. You are a certain complex of information "realized" in your brain. (How else could you survive Star-Trek teletransportation?) That would mean that you are not a concrete object at all. You are a universal. There could literally be more than one of you, just as there is more than one concrete instance of the web browser *Netscape 6.2*.

There is even the paradoxical view that we don't really exist at all. There are many thoughts and experiences, but no beings that *have* those thoughts or experiences. The existence of human people is an illusion – though of course no one is deluded about it. Philosophers who have denied or at least doubted their own existence include Parmenides, Spinoza, Hume, Hegel (as I read them, anyway), Russell (1985: 50), and Unger (1979). We also find the view in Indian Buddhism.

There are other views about what we might be, but I take these to be animalism's main rivals. One of these claims, or another one that I haven't mentioned, must be true. There must be *some* sort of thing that we are. If there is anything sitting in your chair and reading these words, it must have some basic properties or other.

For those who enjoy metaphysics, these are all fascinating proposals. Whatever their merits, though, they certainly are strange. No one but a philosopher could have thought of them. And it would take quite a bit of philosophy to get anyone to believe one of them. Compared with these claims, the idea that we are animals looks downright sensible. That makes its enduring unpopularity all the more surprising.

3. Why Animalism is Unpopular

Why is animalism so unpopular? Historically, the main reason (though by no means the only one) is hostility to materialism. Philosophers have always found it hard to believe that a material object, no matter how physically complex, could produce thought or experience. And an animal is a material object (I assume that vitalism is false). Since it is plain enough that *we* can think, it is easy to conclude that we couldn't be animals.

But why do modern-day materialists reject animalism, or at least say things that rule it out? The main reason, I believe, is that when they think about personal identity they don't ask what sort of things we are. They don't ask whether we are animals, or what we might be if we aren't animals, or how we relate to the human animals that are so intimately connected with us. Or at least they don't ask that first. No one who *began* by asking what we are would hit on the idea that we must be computer programs or bundles of thoughts or non-animals made of the same matter as animals.

The traditional problem of personal identity is not what we are, but what it takes for us to persist. It asks what is necessary, and what is sufficient, for a person existing at one time to be identical with something present at another time: what sorts of adventures we could survive, and what would inevitably bring our existence to an end. Many philosophers seem to think that an answer to this question would tell us all there is to know about the metaphysics of personal identity. This is not so. Claims about what it takes for us to persist do not by themselves tell us what other fundamental properties we have: whether we are material or immaterial, simple or composite, abstract or concrete, and so on. At any rate, the single-minded focus on our identity over time has tended to put other metaphysical questions about ourselves out of philosophers' minds.

What is more, the most popular solution to this traditional problem rules out our being animals. It is that we persist by virtue of some sort of psychological continuity. You are, necessarily, that future being that in some sense inherits its mental features – personality, beliefs, memories, values, and so on – from you. And you are that past being whose mental features you have inherited. Philosophers disagree about what sort of inheritance this has to be: whether those mental features must be continuously physically realized, for instance. But most accept the general idea. The persistence of a human animal, on the other hand, does not consist in mental continuity.

The fact that each human animal starts out as an unthinking embryo and may end up as an unthinking vegetable shows that no sort of mental continuity is necessary for a human animal to persist. No human animal is mentally continuous with an embryo or vegetable.

To see that no sort of mental continuity is sufficient for a human animal to persist, imagine that your cerebrum is put into another head. The being who gets that organ, and he alone, will be mentally continuous with you on any account of what mental continuity is. So if mental continuity of any sort suffices for you to persist, you would go along with your transplanted cerebrum. You wouldn't stay behind with an empty head.

What would happen to the human animal associated with you? Would *it* go along with its cerebrum? Would the surgeons pare that animal down to a small chunk of yellowish-pink tissue, move it across the room, and then supply it with a new head, trunk, and other parts? Surely not. A detached cerebrum is no more an organism than a detached liver is an organism. The empty-headed thing left behind, by contrast, *is* an animal. It may even remain alive, if the surgeons are careful to leave the lower brain intact. The empty-headed being into which your cerebrum is implanted is also an animal. It looks for all the world like there are two human animals in the story. One of them loses its cerebrum and gets an empty head. The other has its empty head filled with that organ. No animal moves from one head to another. The surgeons merely move an organ from one animal to another. If this is right, then no sort of psychological continuity suffices for the identity of a human animal over time. One human animal could be mentally continuous with another one (supposing that they can have mental properties at all).

If we tell the right kind of story, it is easy enough to get most people, or at any rate most Western-educated philosophy students, to say that *you* would go along with your transplanted cerebrum. After all, the one who got that organ would act like you and think she was you. Why deny that she would be who she thinks she is? But "your" animal – the one you would be if you were any animal – would stay behind. That means that you and that animal could go your separate ways. And a thing and itself can never go their separate ways.

It follows that you are not that animal, or indeed any other animal. Not only are you not essentially an animal. You are not an animal at all, even contingently. Nothing that is even contingently an animal would move to a different head if its cerebrum were transplanted. The human animals in the story stay where they are and merely lose or gain organs.[2]

So the thought that leads many contemporary philosophers to reject animalism – or that would lead them to reject it if they accepted the consequences of what they believe – is something like this: You would go along with your transplanted cerebrum; but no human animal would go along with its transplanted cerebrum. More generally, some sort of mental continuity suffices for us to persist, yet no sort of mental continuity suffices for an animal to persist. It follows that we are not animals. If we were animals, we should have the identity conditions of animals. Those conditions would have nothing to do with psychological facts. Psychology would be irrelevant to our identity over time. That goes against 300 years of thinking about personal identity.

This also shows that animalism is a substantive metaphysical thesis with important consequences. There is nothing harmless about it.

4. The Thinking-Animal Argument

I turn now to my case for animalism.

It seems evident that there *is* a human animal intimately related to you. It is the one located where you are, the one we point to when we point to you, the one sitting in your chair. It seems equally evident that human animals can think.

They can act. They can be aware of themselves and the world. Those with mature nervous systems in good working order can, anyway. So there is a thinking, acting human animal sitting where you are now. But you think and act. *You* are the thinking being sitting in your chair.

It follows from these apparently trite observations that you are an animal. In a nutshell, the argument is this: (1) There is a human animal sitting in your chair. (2) The human animal sitting in your chair is thinking. (If you like, every human animal sitting there is thinking.) (3) You are the thinking being sitting in your chair. The one and only thinking being sitting in your chair is none other than you. Hence, you are that animal. That animal is you. And there is nothing special about you: we are all animals. If anyone suspects a trick, here is the argument's logical form:

1. $(x)(x$ is a human animal & x is sitting in your chair)
2. $(x)((x$ is a human animal & x is sitting in your chair) $\supset x$ is thinking)
3. $(x)((x$ is thinking & x is sitting in your chair) $\supset x =$ you)
4. $(x)(x$ is a human animal & $x =$ you)

The reader can verify that it is formally valid. (Compare: A man entered the bank vault. The man who entered the vault – any man who did – stole the money. Snodgrass, and no one else, entered the vault and stole the money. Doesn't it follow that Snodgrass is a man?)

Let us be clear about what the thinking-animal argument purports to show. Its conclusion is that we are human animals. That is, one of the things true of you is that you are (identical with) an animal. That of course leaves many metaphysical questions about ourselves unanswered. It doesn't by itself tell us whether we are essentially or most fundamentally animals, for instance, or what our identity conditions are. That depends on the metaphysical nature of human animals: on whether human animals are essentially animals, and what their identity conditions are. These are further questions. I argued in the previous section that no sort of mental continuity is either necessary or sufficient for a human animal to persist. If that is right, then our being animals has important and highly contentious metaphysical implications. But it might be disputed, even by those who agree that we are animals. The claim that we are animals is not the end of the story about personal identity. It is only the beginning. Still, it is important to begin in the right place.

The thinking-animal argument is deceptively simple. I suspect that its very simplicity has prevented many philosophers from seeing its point. But there is nothing sophistical about it. It has no obvious and devastating flaw that we teach our students. It deserves to be better known.[3]

In any case, the argument has three premises, and so there are three ways of resisting it. One could deny that there is any human animal sitting in your chair. One could deny that any such animal thinks. Or one could deny that you are the thinking being sitting there. Anyone who denies that we are animals is committed to accepting one of these claims. They are not very plausible. But let us consider them.

5. Alternative One: There Are No Human Animals

Why suppose that there is no human animal sitting in your chair? Presumably because there are no human animals anywhere. If there are any human animals at all, there is one sitting there. (I assume that you aren't a Martian foundling.) And if there are no human animals, it is hard to see how there could be any organisms of other sorts. So denying the argument's first premise amounts to denying that there are, strictly speaking, any organisms. There appear to be, of course. But that is at best a well-founded illusion.

There are venerable philosophical views that rule out the existence of organisms. Idealism, for instance, denies that there are any material objects at all (so I should describe it, anyway). And there is the view that nothing can have different parts at different times (Chisholm 1976: 145–158). Whenever something appears to lose or gain a part, the truth of the matter is that one object, made of the first set of parts, ceases to exist (or becomes scattered) and is instantly replaced by a numerically different object made of the second set of parts. Organisms, if there were such things, would constantly assimilate new particles and expel others. If nothing can survive a change of any of its parts, organisms are metaphysically impossible. What we think of as an organism is in reality only a succession of different "masses of matter" that each take on organic form for a brief moment – until a single particle is gained or lost – and then pass that form on to a numerically different mass.

But few opponents of animalism deny the existence of animals. They have good reason not to, quite apart from the fact that this is more or less incredible. Anything that would rule out the existence of animals would also rule out most of the things we might be if we are not animals. If there are no animals, there are no beings constituted by animals, and no temporal parts of animals. And whatever rules out animals may tell against Humean bundles of perceptions as well. If there are no animals, it is not easy to see what we *could* be.

6. Alternative Two: Human Animals Can't Think

The second alternative is that there is an animal sitting in your chair, but it isn't thinking. (Let any occurrence of a propositional attitude, such as the belief that it's raining or the hope that it won't, count as "thinking".) *You* think, but the animal doesn't. The reason for this can only be that the animal can't think. If it were able to think, it would be thinking now. And if *that* animal can't think – despite its healthy, mature human brain, lengthy education, surrounding community of thinkers, and appropriate evolutionary history – then no human animal can. And if no human animal can think, no animal of any sort could. (We can't very well say that dogs can think but human animals can't.) Finally, if no animal could ever think – not even a normal adult human animal – it is hard to see how any organism could have any mental property whatever. So if your animal isn't thinking, that is apparently because it is impossible for any organism to have mental properties.

The claim, then, is that animals, including human animals, are no more intelligent or sentient than trees. We could of course say that they are "intelligent" in the sense of being the bodies of intelligent people who are not themselves animals. And we could call organisms like dogs "sentient" in the sense of being the bodies of sentient non-animals that stand to those animals as you and I stand to human animals. But that is loose talk. The strict and sober truth would be that only non-organisms could ever think.

This is rather hard to believe. Anyone who denies that animals can think (or that they can think in the way that we think) needs to explain why they can't. What stops a typical human animal from using its brain to think? Isn't that what that organ is *for*?

Traditionally, those who deny that animals can think deny that any material object could do so. That seems natural enough: if *any* material thing could think, it would be an animal. Thinking things must be immaterial, and so must we. Of course, simply denying that any material thing could think does nothing to explain why it couldn't. But again, few contemporary opponents of animalism believe that we are immaterial.

Someone might argue like this: "The human animal sitting in your chair is just your body. It is absurd to suppose that your body reads or thinks about philosophy. The thinking thing there – you – must therefore be something other than the animal. But that doesn't mean that you are immaterial. You might be a material thing other than your body."

It may be false to say that your body is reading. There is certainly *something* wrong with that statement. What is less clear is whether it is wrong because the phrase 'your body' denotes something that you in some sense have – a certain human organism – that is unable to read. Compare the word 'body' with a closely related one: *mind*. It is just as absurd to say that Alice's mind weighs 120 pounds, or indeed any other amount, as it is to say that Alice's body is reading. (If that seems less than obvious, consider the claim that Alice's mind is sunburned.) Must we conclude that Alice has something – a clever thing, for Alice has a clever mind – that weighs nothing? Does this show that thinking beings have no mass? Surely not. I think we should be equally wary of drawing metaphysical conclusions from the fact that the phrase 'Alice's body' cannot always be substituted for the name 'Alice'. In any case, the "body" argument does nothing to explain why a human animal should be unable to think.

Anyone who claims that some material objects can think but animals cannot has his work cut out for him. Shoemaker (1984: 92–97, 1999) has argued that animals cannot think because they have the wrong identity conditions. Mental properties have characteristic causal roles, and these, he argues, imply that psychological continuity must suffice for the bearers of those properties to persist. Since this is not true of any organism, no organism could have mental properties. But material things with the right identity conditions *can* think, and organisms can "constitute" such things. I have discussed this argument in another place (Olson 2002a). It is a long story, though, and I won't try to repeat it here.

7.   Alternative Three: You Are Not Alone

Suppose, then, that there is a human animal sitting in your chair, and suppose that it thinks. Is there any way to resist the conclusion that you are that thinking animal? We can hardly say that the animal thinks but you don't. (If anything thinks, you do.) Nor can we deny that you exist, when there is a rational animal thinking your thoughts. How, then, could you fail to be that thinking animal? Only if you are not the only thinker there. If you are not *the* thinking thing sitting there, you must be one of at least two such thinkers. You exist. You think. There is also a thinking human animal there. Presumably it has the same psychological qualities as you have. But it isn't you. There are two thinking beings wherever we thought there was just one. There are two philosophers, you and an animal, sitting there and reading this. You are never truly alone: wherever you go, a watchful human animal goes with you.

This is not an attractive picture. Its adherents may try to comfort us by proposing linguistic hypotheses. Whenever two beings are as intimately related as you and your animal are, they will say, we "count them as one" for ordinary purposes (Lewis 1976). When I write on the copyright form that I am the sole author of this essay, I don't mean that every author of this essay is numerically identical with me. I mean only that every author of this essay bears some relation to me that does not imply identity: that every such author is co-located with me, perhaps. My wife is not a bigamist, even though she is, I suppose, married both to me and to the animal. At any rate it would be seriously misleading to describe our relationship as a *ménage à quatre*.

This is supposed to show that the current proposal needn't contradict anything that we say or believe when engaged in the ordinary business of life. Unless we are doing metaphysics, we don't distinguish strict numerical identity from the intimate relation that each of us bears to a certain human animal. Ordinary people have no opinion about how many numerically different thinking beings there are. Why should they? What matters in real life is not how many thinkers there are strictly speaking, but how many *non-overlapping* thinkers.

Perhaps so. Still, it hardly makes the current proposal easy to believe. Is it not strange to suppose that there are two numerically different thinkers wherever we thought there was just one?

In any event, the troubles go beyond mere overcrowding. If there really are two beings, a person and an animal, now thinking your thoughts and performing your actions, you ought to wonder which one you are. You may think you're the person (the one that isn't an animal). But doesn't the animal think that *it* is a person too? It has all the same reasons for thinking so as you have. Yet it is mistaken. If you *were* the animal and not the person, you'd still think you were the person. So for all you know, you're the one making the mistake. Even if you are a person and not an animal, you could never have any reason to believe that you are.[4]

For that matter, if your animal can think, that ought to make *it* a person. It has the same mental features as you have. (Otherwise we should expect an explanation for the difference, just as we should if the animal can't think at all.) It is, in Locke's words, "a thinking intelligent being, that has reason and reflection, and can consider itself as itself, the same thinking thing, in different times and places" (1975: 335). It satisfies every ordinary definition of 'person'. But it would be mad to suppose that the animal sitting in your chair is a *person* numerically different from you – that each human person shares her location and her thoughts with *another* person. If nothing else, this would contradict the claim that people – all people – have psychological identity conditions, thus sweeping away the main reason for denying that we are animals in the first place.

On the other hand, if ordinary human animals are not people, familiar accounts of what it is to be a person are all far too permissive. Having the psychological and moral features that you and I have would not be enough to make something a person. There could be rational, intelligent, self-conscious *non*-people. In fact there would be at least one such rational non-person for every genuine person. That would deprive personhood of any psychological or moral significance.

8.   Hard Choices

That concludes my argument for animalism. We could put the same point in another way. There are about six billion human animals walking the earth. Those animals are just like ourselves. They sit in our chairs and sleep in our beds. They work, and talk, and take holidays. Some of them do philosophy. They have just the mental and physical attributes that we take ourselves to have. So it seems, anyway. This makes it hard to deny that *we* are those animals. The apparent existence of rational human animals is an inconvenient fact for the opponents of animalism. We might call it the *problem of the thinking animal.*

But what of the case against animalism? It seems that you would go along with your cerebrum if that organ were transplanted. More generally, some sort of mental continuity appears to suffice for us to persist.[5] And that is not true of any animal. Generations of philosophers have found this argument compelling. How can they have gone so badly wrong?

One reason, as I have said, is that they haven't asked the right questions. They have thought about what it takes for us to persist through time, but not about what we are.

Here is another. If someone is mentally just like you, that is strong evidence for his being you. Even stronger if there is continuously physically realized mental continuity between him and you. In fact it is conclusive evidence, given that brain transplants belong to science fiction. Moreover, most of us find mental continuity more interesting and important than brute physical continuity. When we hear a story, we don't much care which person at the end of the tale is the same animal as a given person at the beginning. We care far more who is psychologically continuous with that person. If mental and animal continuity often came apart, we might think differently. But they don't.

These facts can easily lead us to suppose that the one who remembers your life in the transplant story is you. Easier still if we don't know how problematic that claim is – if we don't realize that it would rule out our being animals. To those who haven't reflected on the problem of the thinking animal – and that includes most philosophers – it can seem dead obvious that we persist by virtue of mental continuity. But if we are animals, this is a mistake, though an understandable one.

Of course, opponents of animalism can play this game too. They can attempt to explain why it is natural to suppose that there are human animals, or that human animals can think, or that you are the thinking thing sitting in your chair, in a way that does not imply that those claims are true. (That is the point of the linguistic hypotheses I mentioned earlier.) What to do? Well, I invite you to compare the thinking-animal argument with the transplant argument. Which is more likely: That there are no animals? That no animal could ever think? That you are one of at least two intelligent beings sitting in your chair? Or that you would not, after all, go along with your transplanted cerebrum?

9.   What it Would Mean if We Were Animals

What would it mean if we were animals? The literature on personal identity gives the impression that this is a highly counterintuitive, "tough-minded" idea, radically at odds with our deepest convictions. It is certainly at odds with most of that literature. But I doubt whether it conflicts with anything that we all firmly believe.

If animalism conflicts with any popular beliefs, they will have to do with the conditions of our identity over time. As we have seen, the way we react (or imagine ourselves reacting) to certain fantastic stories suggests that we take ourselves to persist by virtue of mental continuity. Our beliefs about *actual* cases, though, suggest no such thing. In every actual case, the number of people we think there are is just the number of human animals. Every actual case in which we take someone to survive or perish is a case where a human animal survives or perishes.

If anything, the way we regard actual cases suggests a conviction that our identity does not consist in mental continuity, or at any rate that mental continuity is unnecessary for us to persist. When someone lapses into a persistent vegetative state, his friends and relatives may conclude that his life no longer has any value. They may even conclude that he has ceased to exist *as a person*. But they don't ordinarily suppose that their loved one no longer exists at all, and that the living organism on the hospital bed is something numerically different from him – even when they come to believe that there is no mental continuity between the vegetable and the person. *That* would be a tough-minded view.

And most of us believe that we were once foetuses. When we see an ultrasound picture of a 12-week-old foetus, it is easy to believe we are seeing something that will, if all goes well, be born, learn to talk, go to school, and eventually become an adult human person. Yet none of us is in any way mentally continuous with a 12-week-old foetus.

Animalism may conflict with religious beliefs: with the belief in reincarnation or resurrection, for instance (though whether there is any real conflict is less obvious than it may seem: see van Inwagen 1978). But few accounts of personal identity are any more compatible with those beliefs. If resurrection and reincarnation rule out our being animals, they probably rule out our being anything except immaterial substances, or perhaps computer programs. On this score animalism is no worse off than its main rivals.

And don't we have a strong conviction that we are animals? We all think that we are human beings. And until the philosophers got hold of us, we took human beings to be animals. Of course that doesn't show that we *are* animals. But it shows that we seem to be. It is the opponents of animalism who insist that this appearance is deceptive: that the animal you see in the mirror is not really you. That we are animals ought to be the default position. If anything is hard to believe, it's the alternatives.[6]

Notes

1   E.g. Shoemaker 1984: 113f. For what it's worth, my opinion of "constitutionalism" can be found in Olson 2001.
2   For more on this crucial point see Olson 1997: 114–119.
3   The argument is not entirely new. As I see it, it only makes explicit what is implicit in Carter 1989, Ayers 1990: 283f., Snowdon 1990, and Olson 1997: 100–109.
4   Some say that revisionary linguistics can solve this problem too (Noonan 1998). The idea is roughly this. First, not just any rational, self-conscious being is a person, but only those that have psychological identity conditions. Human animals, despite their mental properties, are not people because they lack psychological identity conditions. Second, the word 'I' and other personal pronouns refer only to people. Thus, when the animal associated with you says 'I', it doesn't refer to itself. Rather, it refers to you, the person associated with it. When it says, "I am a person," it does not say falsely that *it* is a person, but truly that *you* are. So the animal is not mistaken about which thing it is, and neither are you. You can infer that you are a person from the linguistic facts that you are whatever you refer to when you say 'I', and that 'I' refers only to people. I discuss this ingenious proposal in Olson 2002b.
5   In fact this is not so. Let the surgeons transplant each of your cerebral hemispheres into a different head. Both offshoots will be mentally continuous with you. But they can't both *be* you, for the simple reason that one thing (you) cannot be identical with two things. We cannot say in general that anyone who is mentally continuous with you must be you. Exceptions are possible. So it ought to come as no great surprise if the original cerebrum transplant is another exception.
6   I thank Trenton Merricks and Gonzalo Rodriguez-Pereyra for comments on an earlier version.

References

Ayers, M. 1990. *Locke*, vol. 2. London: Routledge.
Carter, W. R. 1989. How to change your mind. *Canadian Journal of Philosophy* 19: 1–14.
Chisholm, R. 1976. *Person and Object*. La Salle, IL: Open Court.

Hume, D. 1888. *Treatise of Human Nature*, ed. by L. A. Selby-Bigge. Oxford: Clarendon Press. (Original work 1739. Partly reprinted in Perry 1975.)

Lewis, D. 1976. Survival and identity. In A. Rorty, ed., *The Identities of Persons*. Berkeley: California. (Repr. in his *Philosophical Papers* vol. I. New York: Oxford University Press. 1983.)

Locke, J. 1975. *An Essay Concerning Human Understanding*, ed. P. Nidditch. Oxford: Clarendon Press, (Original work, 2nd ed., originally published 1694. Partly reprinted in Perry 1975.)

Noonan, Harold. 1998. Animalism versus Lockeanism: a current controversy. *Philosophical Quarterly* 48: 302–318.

Olson, E. 1997. *The Human Animal: Personal Identity Without Psychology*. New York: Oxford University Press.

—. 2001. Material coincidence and the indiscernibility problem. *Philosophical Ouarterly* 51: 337–355.

—. 2002a. What does functionalism tell us about personal identity? *Noûs* 36: 682–698.

—. 2002b. Thinking animals and the reference of 'I'. *Philosophical Topics* 30: 189–208.

—. 2006. There is no bodily criterion of personal identity. In F. MacBride, ed., *Identity and Modality*. Oxford: Oxford University Press.

Perry, J., ed. 1975. *Personal Identity*. Berkeley: University of California Press.

Quinton, A. 1962. The soul. *Journal of Philosophy* 59: 393–403. (Reprinted in Perry 1975.)

Russell, B. 1985. *The Philosophy of Logical Atomism*. La Salle, IL: Open Court. Original work 1918.

Shoemaker, S. 1984. Personal identity: a materialist's account. In S. Shoemaker and R. Swinburne, *Personal Identity*. Oxford: Blackwell.

—. 1999. Self, body, and coincidence. *Proceedings of the Aristotelian Society, Supplementary Volume* 73: 287–306.

Snowdon, Paul. 1990. Persons, animals, and ourselves. In C. Gill, ed., *The Person and the Human Mind*. Oxford: Clarendon Press.

Unger, P. 1979. I do not exist. In G. F. MacDonald, ed., *Perception and Identity*. London: Macmillan. (Reprinted in M. Rea, ed., *Material Constitution*. Lanham, MD: Rowman and Littlefield. 1997.)

van Inwagen, P. 1978. The possibility of resurrection. *International Journal for the Philosophy of Religion* 9: 114–121. (Reprinted in his "*The Possibility of Resurrection*" and *Other Essays in Christian Apologetics*. Boulder: Westview. 1997.)

—. 1980. Philosophers and the words 'human body'. In van Inwagen, ed., *Time and Cause*. Dordrecht: Reidel.

38 Divided Minds and the Nature of Persons

Derek Parfit

It was the split-brain cases which drew me into philosophy. Our knowledge of these cases depends on the results of various psychological tests, as described by Donald MacKay.[1] These tests made use of two facts. We control each of our arms, and see what is in each half of our visual fields, with only one of our hemispheres. When someone's hemispheres have been disconnected, psychologists can thus present to this person two different written questions in the two halves of his visual field, and can receive two different answers written by this person's two hands.

Here is a simplified imaginary version of the kind of evidence that such tests provide. One of these people looks fixedly at the centre of a wide screen, whose left half is red and right half is blue. On each half in a darker shade are the words, 'How many colours can you see?' With both hands the person writes, 'Only one'. The words are now changed to read, 'Which is the only colour that you can see?' With one of his hands the person writes 'Red', with the other he writes 'Blue'.

If this is how such a person responds, I would conclude that he is having two visual sensations – that he does, as he claims, see both red and blue. But in seeing each colour he is not aware of seeing the other. He has two streams of consciousness, in each of which he can see only one colour. In one stream he sees red, and at the same time, in his other stream, he sees blue. More generally, he could be having at the same time two series of thoughts and sensations, in having each of which he is unaware of having the other.

This conclusion has been questioned. It has been claimed by some that there are not *two* streams of consciousness, on the ground that the subdominant hemisphere is a part of the brain whose functioning involves no consciousness. If this were true, these cases would lose most of their interest. I believe that it is not true, chiefly because, if a person's dominant hemisphere is destroyed, this person is able to react in the way in which, in the split-brain cases, the sub-dominant hemisphere reacts, and we do not believe that such a person is just an automaton, without consciousness. The sub-dominant hemisphere is, of course, much less developed in certain ways, typically having the linguistic abilities of a three-year-old. But three-year-olds are conscious. This supports the view that, in split-brain cases, there *are* two streams of consciousness.

Another view is that, in these cases, there are two persons involved, sharing the same body. Like Professor MacKay, I believe that we should reject this view. My reason for believing this is, however, different. Professor MacKay denies that there are two persons involved because he believes that there is only one person involved. I believe that, in a sense, the number of persons involved is none.

The Ego Theory and the Bundle Theory

To explain this sense I must, for a while, turn away from the split-brain cases. There are two theories about what persons are, and what is involved in a person's continued existence over time. On the *Ego Theory*, a person's continued existence cannot be explained except as the continued existence of a particular *Ego*, or *subject of experiences*. An Ego Theorist claims that, if we ask what unifies someone's consciousness at any time – what makes it true, for example, that I can now both see what I am typing and hear the wind outside my window – the answer is that these are both experiences which are being had by me, this person, at this time. Similarly, what explains the unity of a person's whole life is the fact that all of the experiences in this life are had by the same person, or subject of experiences. In its best-known form, the *Cartesian view*, each person is a persisting purely mental thing – a soul, or spiritual substance.

The rival view is the *Bundle Theory*. Like most styles in art – Gothic, baroque, rococo, etc. – this theory owes its name to its critics. But the name is good enough. According to the Bundle Theory, we can't explain either the unity of consciousness at any time, or the unity of a whole life, by referring to a person. Instead we must claim that there are long series of different mental states and events – thoughts, sensations, and the like – each series being what we call one life. Each series is unified by various kinds of causal relation, such as the relations that hold between experiences and later memories of them. Each series is thus like a bundle tied up with string.

In a sense, a Bundle Theorist denies the existence of persons. An outright denial is of course absurd. As Reid protested in the eighteenth century, 'I am not thought, I am not action, I am not feeling; I am something which thinks and acts and feels.' I am not a series of events, but a person. A Bundle Theorist admits this fact, but claims it to be only a fact about our grammar, or our language. There are persons or subjects in this language-dependent way. If, however, persons are believed to be more than this – to be separately existing things, distinct from our brains and bodies, and the various kinds of mental states and events – the Bundle Theorist denies that there are such things.

The first Bundle Theorist was Buddha, who taught 'anatta', or the *No Self view*. Buddhists concede that selves or persons have 'nominal existence', by which they mean that persons are merely combinations of other elements. Only what exists by itself, as a separate element, has instead what Buddhists call 'actual existence'. Here are some quotations from Buddhist texts:

> At the beginning of their conversation the king politely asks the monk his name, and receives the following reply: 'Sir, I am known as 'Nagasena'; my fellows in the religious life address me as 'Nagasena'. Although my parents gave me the name . . . it is just an appellation, a form of speech, a description, a conventional usage. 'Nagasena' is only a name, for no person is found here.'

> A sentient being does exist, you think, O Mara? You are misled by a false conception. This bundle of elements is void of Self. In it there is no sentient being. Just as a set of wooden parts Receives the name of carriage, So do we give to elements The name of fancied being.

> Buddha has spoken thus: 'O Brethren, actions do exist, and also their consequences, but the person that acts does not. There is no one to cast away this set of elements, and no one to assume a new set of them. There exists no Individual, it is only a conventional name given to a set of elements.'[2]

Buddha's claims are strikingly similar to the claims advanced by several Western writers. Since these writers knew nothing of Buddha, the similarity of these claims suggests that they are not merely part of one cultural tradition, in one period. They may be, as I believe they are, true.

What We Believe Ourselves to Be

Given the advances in psychology and neurophysiology, the Bundle Theory may now seem to be obviously true. It may seem uninteresting to deny that there are separately existing Egos, which are distinct from brains and bodies and the various kinds of mental states and events. But this is not the only issue. We may be convinced that the Ego Theory is false, or even senseless. Most of us, however, even if we are not aware of this, also have certain beliefs about what is involved in our continued existence over time. And these beliefs would only be justified if something like the Ego Theory was true. Most of us therefore have false beliefs about what persons are, and about ourselves.

These beliefs are best revealed when we consider certain imaginary cases, often drawn from science fiction. One such case is *teletransportation*. Suppose that you enter a cubicle in which, when you press a button, a scanner records the states of all of the cells in your brain and body, destroying both while doing so. This information is then transmitted at the speed of light to some other planet, where a replicator produces a perfect organic copy of you. Since the brain of your Replica is exactly like yours, it will seem to remember living your life up to the moment when you pressed the button, its character will be just like yours, and it will be in every other way psychologically continuous with you. This psychological continuity will not have its normal cause, the continued existence of your brain, since the causal chain will run through the transmission by radio of your 'blueprint'.

Several writers claim that if you chose to be teletransported, believing this to be the fastest way of travelling, you would be making a terrible mistake. This would not be a way of travelling, but a way of dying. It may not, they concede, be quite as bad as ordinary death. It might be some consolation to you that, after your death, you will have this Replica, which can finish the book that you are writing, act as parent to your children, and so on. But, they insist, this Replica won't be you. It will merely be someone else, who is exactly like you. This is why this prospect is nearly as bad as ordinary death.

Imagine next a whole range of cases, in each of which, in a single operation, a different proportion of the cells in your brain and body would be replaced with exact duplicates. At the near end of this range, only 1 or 2 per cent would be replaced; in the middle, 40 or 60 per cent; near the far end, 98 or 99 per cent. At the far end of this range is pure teletransportation, the case in which all of your cells would be 'replaced'.

When you imagine that some proportion of your cells will be replaced with exact duplicates, it is natural to have the following beliefs. First, if you ask, 'Will I survive? Will the resulting person be me?', there must be an answer to this question. Either you will survive, or you are about to die. Second, the answer to this question must be either a simple 'Yes' or a simple 'No'. The person who wakes up either will or will not be you. There cannot be a third answer, such as that the person waking up will be half you. You can imagine yourself later being half-conscious. But if the resulting person will be fully conscious, he cannot be half you. To state these beliefs together: to the question, 'Will the resulting person be me?', there must always *be* an answer, which must be all-or-nothing.

There seem good grounds for believing that in the case of teletransportation, your Replica would not be you. In a slight variant of this case, your Replica might be created while you were still alive, so that you could talk to one another. This seems to show that, if 100 per cent of your cells were replaced, the result would merely be a Replica of you. At the other end of my range of cases, where only 1 per cent would be replaced, the resulting person clearly *would* be you. It there-fore seems that, in the cases in between, the resulting person must be either you, or merely a Replica. It seems that one of these must be true, and that it makes a great difference which is true.

How We are Not What We Believe

If these beliefs were correct, there must be some critical percentage, somewhere in this range of cases, up to which the resulting person would be you, and beyond which he would merely be your Replica. Perhaps, for example, it would be you who would wake up if the proportion of cells replaced were 49 per cent, but if just a few more cells were also replaced, this would make all the difference, causing it to be someone else who would wake up.

That there must be some such critical percentage follows from our natural beliefs. But this conclusion is most implausible. How could a few cells make such a difference? Moreover, if there is such a critical percentage, no one could ever discover where it came. Since in all these cases the resulting person would believe that he was you, there could never be any evidence about where, in this range of cases, he would suddenly cease to be you.

On the Bundle Theory, we should reject these natural beliefs. Since you, the person, are not a separately existing entity, we can know exactly what would happen without answering the question of what will happen to you. Moreover, in the cases in the middle of my range, it is an empty question whether the resulting person would be you, or would merely be someone else who is exactly like you. These are not here two different possibilities, one of which must be true. These are merely two different descriptions of the very same course of events. If 50 per cent of your cells were replaced with exact duplicates, we could call the resulting person you, or we could call him merely your Replica. But since these are not here different possibilities, this is a mere choice of words.

As Buddha claimed, the Bundle Theory is hard to believe. It is hard to accept that it could be an empty question whether one is about to die, or will instead live for many years.

What we are being asked to accept may be made clearer with this analogy. Suppose that a certain club exists for some time, holding regular meetings. The meetings then cease. Some years later, several people form a club with the same name, and the same rules. We can ask, 'Did these people revive the very same club? Or did they merely start up another club which is exactly similar?' Given certain further details, this would be another empty question. We could know just what happened without answering this question. Suppose that someone said: 'But there must be an answer. The club meeting later must either be, or not be, the very same club.' This would show that this person didn't understand the nature of clubs.

In the same way, if we have any worries about my imagined cases, we don't understand the nature of persons. In each of my cases, you would know that the resulting person would be both psychologically and physically exactly like you, and that he would have some particular proportion of the cells in your brain and body – 90 per cent, or 10 per cent, or, in the case of teletransportation, 0 per cent. Knowing this, you know everything. How could it be a real question what would happen to you, unless you are a separately existing Ego, distinct from a brain and body, and the various kinds of mental state and event? If there are no such Egos, there is nothing else to ask a real question about.

Accepting the Bundle Theory is not only hard; it may also affect our emotions. As Buddha claimed, it may undermine our concern about our own futures. This effect can be suggested by redescribing this change of view. Suppose that you are about to be destroyed, but will later have a Replica on Mars. You would naturally believe that this prospect is about as bad as ordinary death, since your Replica won't be you. On the Bundle Theory, the fact that your Replica won't be you just consists in the fact that, though it will be fully psychologically continuous with you, this continuity won't have its normal cause. But when you object to teletransportation you are not objecting merely to the abnormality of this cause. You are objecting that this cause won't get *you* to Mars. You fear that the abnormal cause will fail to produce a further and all-important fact, which is different from the fact that your Replica will be psychologically continuous with you. You do not merely want there to be psychological continuity between you and some future person. You want to *be* this future person. On the Bundle Theory, there is no such special further fact. What you fear will not happen, in this imagined case, *never* happens. You want the person on Mars to be you in a specially intimate way in which no future person will ever be you. This means that, judged from the standpoint of your natural beliefs, even ordinary survival is about as bad as teletransportation. *Ordinary survival is about as bad as being destroyed and having a Replica.*

How the Split-Brain Cases Support the Bundle Theory

The truth of the Bundle Theory seems to me, in the widest sense, as much a scientific as a philosophical conclusion. I can imagine kinds of evidence which would have justified believing in the existence of separately existing Egos, and believing that the continued existence of these Egos is what explains the continuity of each mental life. But there is in fact very little evidence in favour of this Ego Theory, and much for the alternative Bundle Theory.

Some of this evidence is provided by the split-brain cases. On the Ego Theory, to explain what unifies our experiences at any one time, we should simply claim that these are all experiences which are being had by the same person. Bundle Theorists reject this explanation. This disagreement is hard to resolve in ordinary cases. But consider the simplified split-brain case that I described. We show to my imagined patient a placard whose left half is blue and right half is red. In one of this person's two streams of consciousness, he is aware of seeing only blue, while at the same time, in his other stream, he is aware of seeing only red. Each of these two visual experiences is combined with other experiences, like that of being aware of moving one of his hands. What unifies the experiences, at any time, in each of this person's two streams of consciousness? What unifies his awareness of seeing only red with his awareness of moving one hand? The answer cannot be that these experiences are being had by the same person. This answer cannot explain the unity of each of this person's two streams of consciousness, since it ignores the disunity between these streams. This person is now having all of the experiences in both of his two streams. If this fact was what unified these experiences, this would make the two streams one.

These cases do not, I have claimed, involve two people sharing a single body. Since there is only one person involved, who has two streams of consciousness, the Ego Theorist's explanation would have to take the following form. He would have to distinguish between persons and subjects of experiences, and claim that, in split-brain cases, there are *two* of the latter. What unifies the experiences in one of the person's two streams would have to be the fact that these experiences are all being had by the same subject of experiences. What unifies the experiences in this person's other stream would have to be the fact that they are being had by another subject of experiences. When this explanation takes this form, it becomes much less plausible. While we could assume that 'subject of experiences', or 'Ego', simply meant 'person', it was easy to believe that there are subjects of experiences. But if there can be subjects of experiences that are not persons, and if in the life of a split-brain patient there are at any time two different subjects of experiences – two different Egos – why should we believe that there really are such things? This does not amount to a refutation. But it seems to me a strong argument against the Ego Theory.

As a Bundle Theorist, I believe that these two Egos are idle cogs. There is another explanation of the unity of consciousness, both in ordinary cases and in split-brain cases. It is simply a fact that ordinary people are, at any time, aware of having several different experiences. This awareness of several different experiences can be helpfully compared with one's awareness, in short-term memory, of several different experiences. Just as there can be a single memory of just having had several experiences, such as hearing a bell strike three times, there can be a single state of awareness both of hearing the fourth striking of this bell, and of seeing, at the same time, ravens flying past the bell-tower.

Unlike the Ego Theorist's explanation, this explanation can easily be extended to cover split-brain cases. In such cases there is, at any time, not one state of awareness of several different experiences, but two such states. In the case I described, there is one state of awareness of both seeing only red and of moving one hand, and there is another state of awareness of both seeing only blue and moving the other hand. In claiming that there are two such states of awareness, we are not postulating the existence of unfamiliar entities, two separately existing Egos which are not the same as the single person whom the case involves. This explanation appeals to a pair of mental states which would have to be described anyway in a full description of this case.

I have suggested how the split-brain cases provide one argument for one view about the nature of persons. I should mention another such argument, provided by an imagined extension of these cases, first discussed at length by David Wiggins.[3]

In this imagined case a person's brain is divided, and the two halves are transplanted into a pair of different bodies. The two resulting people live quite separate lives. This imagined case shows that personal identity is not what matters. If I was about to divide, I should conclude that neither of the resulting people will be me. I will have ceased to exist. But this way of ceasing to exist is about as good – or as bad – as ordinary survival.

Some of the features of Wiggins's imagined case are likely to remain technically impossible. But the case cannot be dismissed, since its most striking feature, the division of one stream of consciousness into separate streams, has already happened. This is a second way in which the actual split-brain cases have great theoretical importance. They challenge some of our deepest assumptions about ourselves.[4]

Notes

1 See Donald MacKay, 'Divided Brains – Divided Minds?', chapter 1 of *Mindwaves*, ed. Colin Blakemore and Susan Greenfield (Oxford: Blackwell, 1987).
2 For the sources of these and similar quotations, see my *Reasons and Persons* (Oxford: Oxford University Press, 1984), pp. 502–3, 532.
3 At the end of his *Identity and Spatio-temporal Continuity* (Oxford: Blackwell, 1967).
4 I discuss these assumptions further in part 3 of my *Reasons and Persons*.

39 Personal Identity: the Dualist Theory

Richard Swinburne

1 Empiricist Theories

There are two philosophical questions about personal identity. The first is: what are the logically necessary and sufficient conditions for a person P_2 at a time, t_2 being the same person as a person P_1 at an earlier time t_1,[1] or, loosely, what does it mean to say that P_2 is the same person as P_1? The second is: what evidence of observation and experience can we have that a person P_2 at t_2 is the same person as a person P_1 at t_1 (and how are different pieces of evidence to be weighed against each other)? Many writers about personal identity have, however, needed to give only one account of personal identity, because their account of the logically necessary and sufficient conditions of personal identity was in terms of the evidence of observation and experience which would establish or oppose claims of personal identity. They have made no sharp distinction between the meaning of such claims and the evidence which supported them. Theories of this kind we may call empiricist theories.

In this section I shall briefly survey the empiricist theories which have been offered and argue that they are ultimately unsatisfactory, and so go on to argue that my two questions have very different answers. What we mean when we say that two persons are the same is one thing; the evidence which we may have to support our claim is something very different.

The most natural theory of personal identity which readily occurs to people, is that personal identity is constituted by bodily identity. P_2 is the same person as P_1 if P_2's body is the same body as P_1's body. The person to whom you are talking now and call 'John' is the same person as the person to whom you were talking last week and then called 'John' if and only if he has the same body. To say that the two bodies – call them B_1 and B_2 – are the same is not to say that they contain exactly the same bits of matter. Bodies are continually taking in new matter (by people eating and drinking and breathing in) and getting rid of matter. But what makes the bodies the same is that the replacement of matter is only gradual. The matter which forms my body is organized in a certain way, into parts – legs, arms, heart, liver, etc. – which are interconnected and exchange matter and energy in regular ways. What makes my body today the same body as my body yesterday is that most of the matter is the same (although I may have lost some and gained some) and its organization has remained roughly the same.

This bodily theory of personal identity gives a somewhat similar account of personal identity to the account which it is natural to give of the identity of any material object or plant, and which is due ultimately to Aristotle (*Metaphysics*, Book 7). Aristotle distinguished between substances and properties. Substances are the individual things, like tables and chairs, cars and plants, which have properties (such as being square or round or red). Properties are 'universals', that is they can be possessed by many different substances; many different substances can be square or red. Substances are the individual substances which they are because of the matter out of which they are made and the form which is given to that matter. By 'the form' is meant those properties (normally of shape and organization) the possession of which is essential if a substance is to be the substance in question, the properties which it cannot lose without ceasing to exist. We thus distinguish between the essential properties of a substance – those which constitute its form – and the accidental properties of a substance. It is among the essential properties of a certain oak tree that it has, under normal conditions, a certain general shape and appearance, a certain life cycle (of producing leaves in spring and acorns in autumn); but its exact height, its position, and the distribution of leaves on its tallest branch are accidental properties. If the matter of the oak tree is reduced to a heap of planks, the oak tree, lacking its essential properties, has ceased to exist. We think of substances as belonging to different kinds, natural – e.g., oak trees or ferns; or artificial – e.g., cars or desks; and the defining properties of a kind constitute the form of a substance which belongs to it. . . .

What makes a substance the same substance as an earlier substance is that its matter is the same, or obtained from the matter of the former substance by gradual replacement, while continuing to possess the essential properties which constitute its form. The table at which I am writing today is the same table at which I was writing yesterday because it consists of the same matter (or at any rate, most of the same matter), organized in the same way – into the form of a table. For inanimate things, however, too much replacement of matter, however gradual, will destroy identity. If I replace the drawer of my desk by another drawer, the desk remains the same desk. But if, albeit gradually, I replace first the drawers and then the sides and then the top, so that there is none of the original matter left, we would say that the resulting desk was no longer the same desk as the original desk. For living things, such as plants, total replacement of matter – so long as it is gradual, and so long as physiology and anatomy also change only gradually if at all – will not destroy identity. The oak tree is the same as the sapling out of which it has grown, because replacement of matter has been gradual, and form (i.e., shape, physiology, and behaviour) has been largely preserved while any changes in it have been gradual. . . .

Persons too are substances. (Men, or human beings, are persons of a certain kind – viz., those with similar anatomy, physiology, and evolutionary origin to ourselves. There may be persons, e.g., on another planet, who are not human beings.) If we apply Aristotle's general account of the identity of substances to persons, it follows that for a person to be the same person as an earlier person, he has to have the same matter (or matter obtained from that earlier person by gradual replacement) organized into the form of a person. The essential properties which make the form of a person would include, for Aristotle, not merely shape and physiological properties, but a kind of way of behaving and a capacity for a mental life of thought and feeling. For P_2 at t_2 to be the same person as P_1 at t_1, both have to be persons (to have a certain kind of body and mental life) and to be made of the same matter (i.e., to be such that P_2's body is obtained from P_1's by gradual replacement of parts). Such is the bodily theory of personal identity. It does not deny that persons have a mental life, but insists that what makes a person the same person as an earlier person is sameness of body.

The difficulty which has been felt by those modern philosophers basically sympathetic to a bodily theory of personal identity is this. One part of the body – viz., the brain – seems to be of crucial importance for determining the characteristic behaviour of the rest. The brain controls not merely the physiology of the body but the way people behave and talk and think. If a man loses an arm or a leg, we do not think that the subsequent person is in any way different from the original person. If a man has a heart transplant or a liver transplant, again we do not think that the replacement makes a different person. On the other hand, if the brain of a person P_1 were removed from his body B_1 and transplanted into the skull of a body B_2 of a person P_2, from which the brain was removed and then transplanted into the empty skull of B_1 (i.e., if brains were interchanged), we would have serious doubt whether P_1 had any more the same body. We would be inclined to say that the person went where his brain went – viz., that P_1 at first had body B_1, and then, after the transplant, body B_2. The reason why we would say this is that (we have very good scientific reason to believe) the person with B_2's body would claim to be P_1, to have done and experienced the things which we know P_1 to have done, and would have the character, beliefs, and attitudes of P_1. What determines my attitude towards a person is not so much the matter out of which his body is made, but who he claims to be, whether he has knowledge of my past life purportedly on the basis of previous acquaintance with me, and more generally what his beliefs about the world are and what are his attitudes towards it. Hence a philosopher seeking a materialist criterion of personal identity, will come to regard the brain, the core of the body, rather than the rest of the body as what matters for personal identity. So this modified bodily theory states: that P_2 is the same person as P_1 if and only if P_2 has the same central organ controlling memory and character, viz., same brain, as P_1. Let us call it the brain theory of personal identity. A theory along these lines (with a crucial qualification, to be discussed shortly) was tentatively suggested by David Wiggins in *Identity and Spatiotemporal Continuity* (Oxford, 1967).[2]

The traditional alternative to a bodily theory of personal identity is the memory-and-character theory. This claims that, given the importance for our attitude towards persons of their memory claims and character, continuity in respect of these would constitute personal identity – whether or not this continuity is caused by continuity of some bodily organ, such as the brain; and the absence of continuity of memory and character in some particular case involves the absence of personal identity, even if there is continuity in respect of that bodily organ which produces such continuity between other persons on other occasions.

The simplest version of this theory was that given by John Locke. According to Locke, memory alone (or 'consciousness', as he often calls it) constitutes personal identity. Loosely – P_2 at t_2 is the same person as P_1 at an earlier time t_1, if and only if P_2 remembers having done and experienced various things, where these things were in fact done and experienced by P_1.

Before expounding Locke's theory further we need to be clear about the kind of memory which is involved. First, it is what is sometimes called personal memory, i.e., memory of one's own past experiences. It is thus to be distinguished from factual memory, which is memory of some fact known previously; as when I remember that the battle of Hastings was fought in 1066. This is not a memory of a past experience. . . . Secondly, it is personal memory in the weak sense. In the normal or strong sense of 'remember', one can only remember doing something if one really did it. I may say that I 'remember' going up the Eiffel Tower, but if I didn't do it, it seems natural to say that I cannot really remember having done it. In this sense, just as you can only know what is true, so you can only remember what you really did. However, there is also a weak sense of 'remember' in which a man remembers whatever he believes that he remembers in the strong sense. One's weak memories are not necessarily true ones. Now if the memory criterion defined personal identity in terms of memory in the strong sense, it would not be very useful; for to say that P_2 remembers having done what P_1 did would already entail their being the same person, and anyone in doubt as to whether P_2 was the same person as P_1, would have equal doubt whether P_2 really did remember doing what P_1 did. What the criterion as stated is concerned with is memory in the weak sense, which (because the strong sense is the more natural one) I shall henceforward call apparent memory.

So Locke's theory can now be rephrased as follows: P_2 at t_2 is the same person as P_1 at an earlier time t_1, if and only if P_2 apparently remembers having done and experienced various things when those things were in fact done and experienced by P_1. A person is who he thinks that he is. . . .

Locke's theory needs tidying up if we are to avoid absurdity. Consider, first, the following objection made by Thomas Reid:

> Suppose a brave officer to have been flogged when a boy at school for robbing an orchard, to have taken a standard from the enemy in his first campaign, and to have been made a general in advanced life; suppose also, which must be admitted to be possible, that, when he took the standard, he was conscious of his having been flogged at school, and that, when made a general, he was conscious of his taking the standard, but had absolutely lost the consciousness of his flogging. These things being supposed, it follows, from Mr Locke's doctrine, that he who was flogged at school is the same person who took the standard, and that he who took the standard is the same person who was made a general. Whence it follows if there be any truth in logic, that the general is the same person with him who was flogged at school. But the general's consciousness does not reach so far back as his flogging; therefore according to Mr Locke's doctrine, he is not the same person who was flogged. Therefore the general is, and at the same time is not, the same person with him who was flogged at school. (Reid, *Essays on the Intellectual Powers of Man*, book III, ch. 6)

The objection illustrates the important point that identity is a transitive relation; if *a* is identical with *b* and *b* is identical with *c*, then necessarily *a* is identical with *c*. We can meet the objection by reformulating Locke's theory as follows: P_2 at t_2 is the same person as P_1 at an earlier time t_1 if and only if *either* P_2 apparently remembers what P_1 did and experienced, or he apparently remembers what some person P' at an intermediate time t' did and experienced, when P' apparently remembers what P_1 did and experienced, *or* they are linked by some longer intermediate chain. (That is, P_2 apparently remembers what P' did and experienced, P' apparently remembers what P'' did and experienced, and so on until we reach a person who apparently remembers what P_1 did and experienced.) If P_1 and P_2 are linked by such a chain, they are, we may say, linked by continuity of memory. Clearly, the apparent memories of the deeds and experiences of the previous person at each stage in the chain need not be completely accurate memories of what was done and experienced. But they do need to be fairly accurate memories of what was done and experienced, if the later person is to be the person who did and experienced those things. . . .

Many advocates of a memory theory have not always been very clear in their exposition about whether the apparent memories which form the links in the chain of memory need to be actual memories, or whether they need only to be hypothetical memories. By 'actual memories' I mean actual recallings of past experiences. The trouble with the suggestion that actual memories are required is that we do not very often recall our past, and it seems natural to suppose that the deeds and experiences of some moments of a person's life never get recalled. Yet the memory theory, as stated so far, rules out that possibility. If I am not connected by a chain of memories with the deeds and experiences done by a person at a certain time, then I am not identical with that person. It is perhaps better if the theory claims that the apparent memories which form the links need only be hypothetical memories – i.e., what a person would apparently remember if he were to try to remember the deeds and experiences in question, e.g., in consequence of being prompted.

There is, however, a major objection to any memory theory of personal identity, arising from the possibility of duplication. The objection was made briefly by Reid and at greater length in an influential article by Bernard Williams. Williams imagines the case of a man whom he calls Charles who turns up in the twentieth century claiming to be Guy Fawkes:

> All the events he claims to have witnessed and all the actions he claims to have done point unanimously to the life-history of some one person in the past – for instance Guy Fawkes. Not only do all Charles' memory-claims that can be checked fit the pattern of Fawkes' life as known to historians, but others that cannot be checked are plausible, provide explanations of unexplained facts, and so on.[3]

The fact that memory claims which 'cannot be checked are plausible, provide explanations of unexplained facts, and so on' is evidence that Charles is not merely claiming to remember what he has in fact read in a book about Guy Fawkes, and so leaves us back with the supposition, natural to make in normal cases, that he is reporting honestly his apparent memories. So, by a memory theory Charles would be Guy Fawkes. But then suppose, Williams imagines, that another man Robert turns up, who satisfies the memory criteria for being Guy Fawkes equally well. We cannot say that they are both identical with Guy Fawkes, for if they were, they would be identical with each other – which they are not since they currently live different lives and have different thoughts and feelings from each other. So apparent memory cannot constitute personal identity, although it may be fallible evidence of it.

The objection from the possibility of duplication, together with other difficulties which will be mentioned in later chapters, have inclined the majority of contemporary writers to favour a theory which makes some sort of bodily continuity central to personal identity. As we have seen, the brain theory takes into account the insight of memory-and-character theory into the importance of these factors for personal identity, by selecting the brain, as the organ causally responsible for the continuity of memory and character, as that part of the body the continuity of which constitutes the continuity of the person.

The trouble is that any brain theory is also open to the duplication objection. The human brain has two very similar hemispheres – a left and a right hemisphere. The left hemisphere plays a major role in the control of limbs of, and processing of sensory information from, the right side of the body (and from the right sides of the two eyes); and the right hemisphere plays a major role in the control of limbs of, and processing of sensory information from, the left side of the body (and from the left sides of the two eyes). The left hemisphere plays a major role in the control of speech. Although the hemispheres have different roles in the adult, they interact with each other; and if parts of a hemisphere are removed, at any rate early in life, the roles of those parts are often taken over by parts of the other hemisphere. Brain operations which remove substantial parts of the brain are not infrequent. It might be possible one day to remove a whole hemisphere, without killing the person. There are no logical difficulties in supposing that we could transplant one of P_1's hemispheres into one skull from which a brain had been removed, and the other hemisphere into another such skull, and that both transplants should take, and it may well be practically possible to do so. It is certainly more likely to occur than the Guy Fawkes story told by Williams! If these transplants took, clearly each of the resulting persons would behave to some extent like P_1, and indeed both would probably have some of the apparent memories of P_1. Each of the resulting persons would then be good candidates for being P_1.

After all, if one of P_1's hemispheres had been destroyed and the other remained intact and untransplanted, and the resulting person continued to behave and make memory claims somewhat like those of P_1, we would have had little hesitation in declaring that person to be P_1. The same applies, whichever hemisphere was preserved – although it may well be that the resulting person would have greater capacities (e.g., speech) if one hemisphere was preserved than if the other one was preserved. We have seen earlier, good reason for supposing that the person goes where his brain goes, and if his brain consists only of one hemisphere, that should make no difference. So if the one remaining hemisphere is then transplanted, we ought to say that the person whose body it now controls is P_1. Whether that person is P_1 can hardly be affected by the fact that instead of being destroyed, the other hemisphere is also transplanted so as to constitute the brain of a person. But if it is, that other person will be just as good a candidate for being P_1. So a Wiggins-type account might lead us to say that both resulting persons are P_1. But, for the reason given earlier in connection with the Guy Fawkes examples, that cannot be – since the two later persons are not identical with each other. Hence, Wiggins adds to his tentative definition a clause stating that P_2 who satisfies his criterion stated earlier is the same person as P_1, only if there is no other later person who also satisfies the criterion.[4]

But the introduction into any theory, whether a memory theory, a brain theory, or whatever, of a clause stating that a person who satisfies the criterion in question for being the same as an earlier person is the same, only so long as there is no other person who satisfies the criterion also or equally well, does have an absurd consequence. Let us illustrate this for the brain theory. Suppose P_1's left hemisphere is transplanted into some skull and the transplant takes. Then, according to the theory, whether the resulting person is P_1, i.e., whether P_1 survives, will depend on whether the other transplant takes. If it does, since both resulting persons will satisfy the memory and brain continuity criteria equally well, neither will be P_1. But if the other transplant does not take, then since there is only one person who satisfies the criterion, that person is P_1. So whether I survive an operation will depend on what happens in a body entirely different from the body which will be mine, if I do survive. But how can who I am depend on what happens to you? A similar absurd consequence follows when a similar clause forbidding duplication is added to a memory theory.

Yet if we abandon the duplication clause, we are back with the original difficulty – that there may be more than one later person who satisfies any memory criterion or brain criterion, or combination thereof, for being the same person as an earlier person. Our discussion brings to our attention also the fact that both these criteria are criteria which may be satisfied to varying degrees. P_2 can have 90 per cent, or 80 per cent, or less than 50 per cent of the brain of P_1; and likewise the similarity of apparent memory and character may vary along a spectrum. Just how well do criteria have to be satisfied for the later person to be the same person as the earlier person? Any line one might draw seems totally artificial. One might think that it was non-arbitrary to insist on more than 50 per cent of the original brain matter – for only one later person could have more than 50 per cent of the original brain matter (whereas if our criterion demands only a smaller proportion, more than one later person could satisfy it). But would we really want to say that P_6 was the same person as P_1 if P_2 was obtained from P_1 by a transplant of 60 per cent (and so more than half) of P_1's brain matter, P_3 was obtained from P_2 by a transplant of 60 per cent of P_2's brain matter, and so on until we came to P_6? By the criterion of 'more than half of the brain matter', P_6 would be the same person as P_5, P_5 as P_4 and so on, and so by the transitivity of identity P_6 would be the same person as P_1 – although he would have very little of P_1's brain matter. Any criterion of the proportion of brain matter transferred, to be plausible, would have to take account of whether there had been similar transplants in the past, and the length of the interval between them. And then the arbitrariness of the criterion would stare us in the face.

This problem pushes the thinker towards one of two solutions. The first solution is to say that personal identity is a matter of degree. P_2 is the same person as P_1 to the extent to which there is sameness of brain matter and continuity of memory. After all, survival for inanimate things is a matter of degree. As we gradually replace bits of a desk with new bits, the resulting desk is only more or less the same as the original desk. And if my car is taken to pieces and some of the bits are used to make one new car, and some of the bits used to make another new car, both cars are partly the same as and partly different from the old car. Why cannot we say the same of people? Normally we are not inclined to talk thus, because brain operations are rare and brain hemisphere transplants never happen. Hence there is normally at most only one candidate for being the same person as an earlier person, and he is normally a very strong candidate indeed – having a more or less identical brain and very great similarities of apparent memory and character. So we tend to think of personal identity as all or nothing.

But it is not thus in its logic, the argument goes. There is the logical possibility, which could become an empirical possibility, of intermediate cases – of persons who are to some extent the same as and to some extent different from original persons.

This view has been advocated by Derek Parfit.[5] When a person divides, as a result of a split brain transplant, he 'survives' in part, Parfit holds, as each of two persons. They constitute his later 'selves', neither of whom, to speak strictly, are identical with the original person.

This theory, which Parfit calls the complex view,[6] does, however, run up against a fundamental difficulty that it commits him to substantial empirical claims which to all appearance could very easily be false. I can bring this out by adopting Bernard Williams's famous mad surgeon story.[7] Suppose that a mad surgeon captures you and announces that he is going to transplant your left cerebral hemisphere into one body, and your right one into another. He is going to torture one of the resulting persons and free the other with a gift of a million pounds. You can choose which person is going to be tortured and which to be rewarded, and the surgeon promises to do as you choose. You believe his promise. But how are you to choose? You wish to choose that you are rewarded, but you do not know which resultant person will be you. Now on the complex theory each person will be you to the extent to which he has your brain and resembles you in his apparent memories and character. It would be in principle empirically ascertainable whether and to what extent persons with right hemisphere transplants resemble their originals in apparent memories and character more or less than persons with left hemisphere transplants. But clearly the difference is not going to be great. So Parfit must say that your choice does not greatly matter. Both subsequent persons will be in part you – although perhaps to slightly different degrees. And so you will – although perhaps to slightly different degrees – in part suffer and in part enjoy what each suffers and enjoys. So you have reason both for joyous expectation and for terrified anticipation. But one problem is: how could you have reason for part joyous expectation and part terrified anticipation, when no one future person is going to suffer a mixed fate?

But even if this notion of partial survival does make sense, the more serious difficulty remains, which is this. We can make sense of the supposition that the victim makes the wrong choice, and has the experience of being tortured and not the experience of being rewarded; or the right choice, and has the experience of being rewarded and not the experience of being tortured. A mere philosophical analysis of the concept of personal identity cannot tell you which experiences will be yours tomorrow. To use Bernard Williams's telling word, any choice would be a 'risk'. But on Parfit's view no risk would be involved – for knowing the extent of continuity of brain, apparent memory, and character, you would know the extent to which a future person would be you and so the extent to which his experiences would be yours. Although it *may* be the case that if my cerebral hemispheres are transplanted into different bodies, I survive partly as the person whose body is controlled by one and partly as the person whose body is controlled by the other, it may not be like that at all. Maybe I go where the left hemisphere goes; and when my right hemisphere is separated from the left hemisphere and comes to control a body by itself, either a new person is formed, or the resulting organism, although behaving to some extent like a person, is really a very complicated non-conscious machine. As we have noted, the fate of some parts of my body, such as my arms and legs, is quite irrelevant to the fate of me. And plausibly the fate of some parts of my brain is irrelevant – can I not survive completely a minor brain operation which removes a very small tumour? But then maybe it is the same with some larger parts of the brain too. We just don't know. If the mad surgeon's victim took the attitude that it didn't matter which way he chose, we must, I suggest, regard him as taking an unjustifiably dogmatic attitude.

The alternative way out of the duplication problem is to say that although apparent memory and brain continuity are, as they obviously are, evidence of personal identity, they are fallible evidence and personal identity is something distinct from them. Just as the presence of blood stains and fingerprints matching those of a given man are evidence of his earlier presence at the scene of the crime, and the discovery of Roman-looking coins and buildings is evidence that the Romans lived in some region, so the similarity of P_2's apparent memory to that of P_1 and his having much the same brain matter, is evidence that P_2 is the same person as P_1. Yet blood stains and fingerprints are one thing and a man's earlier presence at the scene of the crime another. His presence at the scene of the crime is not analysable in terms of the later presence of blood stains and fingerprints. The latter is evidence of the former, because you seldom get blood stains and fingerprints at a place, matching those of a given man, unless he has been there leaving them around. But it might happen. So, the suggestion is, personal identity is distinct from, although evidenced by, similarity of memory and continuity of brain.

This account, which for the moment I will follow Parfit in calling the simple view, can meet all the difficulties which have beset the other theories which we have discussed. The difficulty for the complex view was that it seemed very peculiar to suppose that mere logic could determine which of the experiences had by various persons, each of which was to some extent continuous with me in apparent memory and brain matter, would be mine. There seemed to be a further truth – that I would or would not have those experiences – beyond any truths about the extent of similarity in apparent memory and matter of future persons to myself. The simple view claims explicitly that personal identity is one thing, and the extent of similarity in matter and apparent memory another. There is no contradiction in supposing that the one should occur without the other. Strong similarity of matter and apparent memory is powerful evidence of personal identity. I and the person who had my body and brain last week have virtually the same brain matter and such similar apparent memory, that it is well-nigh certain that we are the same person. But where the brain matter is only in part the same and the memory connection less strong, it is only fairly probable that the persons are the same. Where there are two later persons P_2 and P_2^*, each of whom had some continuity with the earlier person P_1, the evidence supports to some extent each of the two hypotheses – that P_2 is the same person as P_1, and that P_2^* is the same person as P_1. It may give more support to one hypothesis than to the other, but the less well supported hypothesis might be the true one, or maybe neither hypothesis is true. Perhaps P_1 has ceased to exist, and two different persons have come into existence. So the simple view fully accepts that mere logic cannot determine which experiences will be mine, but it allows that continuity of apparent memory and brain provides fallible evidence about this. And of course the duplication objection that they allow for the two subsequent persons being the same person, which we brought against the brain and the memory theories, has no force against the simple theory. For although there can be equally good evidence that each of two later persons is the same person as an earlier person, that evidence is fallible; and since clearly only one person at one time can be strictly the same person as some person at an earlier time, it follows that in one case the evidence is misleading – although we may not know in which case.

.... In the next section I will expound and develop the simple view, and show that it amounts to the same as Cartesian dualism – the view that a person consists of two parts, soul, and body....

2   The Dualist Theory

The brain transplant considerations of the first section leading to the simple view of personal identity showed that significant continuity of brain and memory was not enough to ensure personal identity. They did not show that continuity of brain or memory were totally dispensable; that P_2 at time t_2 could be the same person as P_1 at an earlier time t_1, even though P_2 had none of the brain matter (or other bodily matter) of P_1 and had no apparent memory of P_1's actions and experiences. A number of more extravagant thought-experiments do, however, show that there is no contradiction in this latter supposition.

There seems no contradiction in the supposition that a person might acquire a totally new body (including a completely new brain) – as many religious accounts of life after death claim that men do. To say that this body, sitting at the desk in my room is my body is to say two things. First it is to say that I can move parts of this body (arms, legs, etc.), just like that, without having to do any other intentional action and that I can make a difference to other physical objects only by moving parts of this body. By holding the door handle and turning my hand, I open the door. By bending my leg and stretching it I kick the ball and make it move into the goal. But I do not turn my hand or bend my leg by doing some other intentional action; I just do these things. Secondly, it is to say that my knowledge of states of the world outside this body is derived from their effects on this body – I learn about the positions of physical objects by seeing them, and seeing them involves light rays reflected by them impinging on my eyes and setting up nervous impulses in my optic nerve. My body is the vehicle of my agency in the world and my knowledge of the world. But then is it not coherent to suppose that I might suddenly find that my present body no longer served this function, that I could no longer acquire information through these eyes or move these limbs, but might discover that another body served the same function? I might find myself moving other limbs and acquiring information through other eyes. Then I would have a totally new body. If that body, like my last body, was an occupant of the Earth, then we would have a case of reincarnation, as Eastern religions have understood that. If that body was an occupant of some distant planet, or an environment which did not belong to the same space as our world, then we would have a case of resurrection as, on the whole, Western religions (Christianity, Judaism and Islam) have understood that. . . .

Equally coherent, I suggest, is the supposition that a person might become disembodied. A person has a body if there is one particular chunk of matter through which he has to operate on and learn about the world. But suppose that he finds himself able to operate on and learn about the world within some small finite region, without having to use one particular chunk of matter for this purpose. He might find himself with knowledge of the position of objects in a room (perhaps by having visual sensations, perhaps not), and able to move such objects just like that, in the ways in which we know about the positions of our limbs and can move them. But the room would not be, as it were, the person's body; for we may suppose that simply by choosing to do so he can gradually shift the focus of his knowledge and control, e.g., to the next room. The person would be in no way limited to operating and learning through one particular chunk of matter. Hence we may term him disembodied. The supposition that a person might become disembodied also seems coherent.

I have been arguing so far that it is coherent to suppose that a person could continue to exist with an entirely new body or with no body at all. . . . Could a person continue to exist without any apparent memory of his previous doings? Quite clearly, we do allow not merely the logical possibility, but the frequent actuality of amnesia – a person forgetting all or certain stretches of his past life. Despite Locke, many a person does forget much of what he has done. But, of course, we normally only suppose this to happen in cases where there is the normal bodily and brain continuity. Our grounds for supposing that a person forgets what he has done are that the evidence of bodily and brain continuity suggests that he was the previous person who did certain things which he now cannot remember having done. And in the absence of both of the main kinds of evidence for personal identity, we would not be justified in supposing that personal identity held. . . . For that reason I cannot describe a case where we would have good reason to suppose that P_2 was identical with P_1 even though there was neither brain continuity nor memory continuity between them. However, only given verificationist dogma is there any reason to suppose that the only things which are true are those of whose truth we can have evidence, and I shall suggest in section 3 [not included here] that there is no good reason for believing verificationism to be true. We can make sense of states of affairs being true, of which we can have no evidence that they are true. And among them surely is the supposition that the person who acquires another body loses not merely control of the old one, but memories of what he did with its aid. . . .

Those who hope to survive their death, despite the destruction of their body, will not necessarily be disturbed if they come to believe that they will then have no memory of their past life on Earth; they may just want to survive and have no interest in continuing to recall life on Earth. Again, apparently, there seems to be no contradiction involved in their belief. It seems to be a coherent belief (whether or not true or justified). Admittedly, there may be stories or beliefs which involve a hidden contradiction when initially they do not seem to do so. But the fact that there seems (and to so many people) to be no contradiction hidden in these stories is good reason for supposing that there is no contradiction hidden in them – until a contradiction is revealed. If this were not a good reason for believing there to be no contradiction, we would have no good reason for believing any sentence at all to be free of hidden contradiction. . . .

In section 1, I set out Aristotle's account of the identity of substances: that a substance at one time is the same substance as a substance at an earlier time if and only if the later substance has the same form as, and continuity of matter with, the earlier substance. On this view a person is the same person as an earlier person if he has the same form as the earlier person (i.e., both are persons) and has continuity of matter with him (i.e., has the same body).

Certainly, to be the same person as an earlier person, a later person has to have the same form – i.e., has to be a person. If my arguments for the logical possibility of there being disembodied persons are correct, then the essential characteristics of a person constitute a narrower set than those which Aristotle would have included. My arguments suggest that all that a person needs to be a person are certain mental capacities – for having conscious experiences (i.e., thoughts or sensations) and performing intentional actions. Thought-experiments of the kind described earlier allow that a person might lose his body, but they describe his continuing to have conscious experiences and his performing or being able to perform intentional actions, i.e., to do actions which he means to do, bring about effects for some purpose.

Yet if my arguments are correct, showing that two persons can be the same, even if there is no continuity between their bodily matter, we must say that in the form stated the Aristotelian account of identity applies only to inanimate objects and plants and has no application to personal identity.[8] We are then faced with a choice either of saying that the criteria of personal identity are different from those for other substances, or of trying to give a more general account than Aristotle's of the identity of substances which would cover both persons and other substances. It is possible to widen the Aristotelian account so that we can do the latter. We have only to say that two substances are the same if and only if they have the same form and there is continuity of the stuff of which they are made, and allow that there may be kinds of stuff other than matter. I will call this account of substance identity the wider Aristotelian account. We may say that there is a stuff of another kind, immaterial stuff, and that persons are made of both normal bodily matter and of this immaterial stuff but that it is the continuity of the latter which provides that continuity of stuff which is necessary for the identity of the person over time.

This is in essence the way of expressing the simple theory which is adopted by those who say that a person living on Earth consists of two parts – a material part, the body; and an immaterial part, the soul. The soul is the essential part of a person, and it is its continuing which constitutes the continuing of the person. While on Earth, the soul is linked to a body (by the body being the vehicle of the person's knowledge of and action upon the physical world). But, it is logically possible, the soul can be separated from the body and exist in a disembodied state (in the way described earlier) or linked to a new body. This way of express-ing things has been used in many religious traditions down the centuries, for it is a very natural way of expressing what is involved in being a person once you allow that a person can survive the death of his body. Classical philosophical statements of it are to be found in Plato and, above all, in Descartes. I shall call this view classical dualism.

I wrote that 'in essence' classical dualism is the view that there is more stuff to the person than bodily matter, and that it is the continuing of this stuff which is necessary for the continuing of the person, because a writer such as Descartes did not distinguish between the immaterial stuff, let us call it soul-stuff, and that stuff being organized (with or without a body) as one soul. Descartes and other classical dualists however did not make this distinction, because they assumed (implicitly) that it was not logically possible that persons divide – i.e., that an earlier person could be in part the same person as each of two later persons. Hence they implicitly assumed that soul-stuff comes in essentially indivisible units. That is indeed what one has to say about soul-stuff, if one makes the sup-position (as I was inclined to do, in section 1) that it is not logically possible that persons divide. There is nothing odd about supposing that soul-stuff comes in essentially indivisible units. Of any chunk of matter, however small, it is always logically, if not physically, possible that it be divided into two. Yet it is because matter is extended, that one can always make sense of it being divided. For a chunk of matter necessarily takes up a finite volume of space. A finite volume of space necessarily is composed of two half-volumes. So it always makes sense to suppose that part of the chunk which occupies the left half-volume of space to be separated from that part of the chunk which occupies the right half-volume. But that kind of consideration has no application to immaterial stuff. There is no reason why there should not be a kind of immaterial stuff which necessarily is indivisible; and if the supposition of section 1 is correct, the soul-stuff will have that property. . . .

Given that for any present person who is currently conscious, there is no logical impossibility, whatever else may be true now of that person, that that person continue to exist without his body, it follows that that person must now actually have a part other than a bodily part which can continue, and which we may call his soul – and so that his possession of it is entailed by his being a conscious thing. For there is not even a logical possibility, that if I now consist of nothing but matter and the matter is destroyed, I should nevertheless continue to exist. From the mere logical possibility of my continued existence there follows the actual fact that there is now more to me than my body; and that more is the essential part of myself. A person's being conscious is thus to be analysed as an immaterial core of himself, his soul being conscious.[9]

So Descartes argues, and his argument seems to me correct – given the wider Aristotelian framework. If we are prepared to say that substances can be the same, even though none of the stuff (in a wide sense) of which they are made is the same, the conclusion does not follow. The wider Aristotelian framework provides a partial definition of 'stuff' rather than a factual truth.

To say that a person has an immaterial soul is not to say that if you examine him closely enough under an acute enough microscope you will find some very rarefied constituent which has eluded the power of ordinary microscopes. It is just a way of expressing the point within a traditional framework of thought that persons can – it is logically possible – continue, when their bodies do not. It does, however, seem a very natural way of expressing the point – especially once we allow that persons can become disembodied. Unless we adopt a wider Aristotelian framework, we shall have to say that there can be substances which are not made of anything, and which are the same substances as other substances which are made of matter.

It does not follow from all this that a person's body is no part of him. Given that what we are trying to do is to elucidate the nature of those entities which we normally call 'persons', we must say that arms and legs and all other parts of the living body are parts of the person. My arms and legs are parts of me. . . .

As we have seen, classical dualism is the way of expressing the simple view of personal identity within what I called the wider Aristotelian framework. However, this framework is a wider one than Aristotle himself would have been happy with, allowing a kind of stuff other than Aristotle would have countenanced. There has been in the history of thought a different and very influential way of modifying Aristotle, to take account of the kind of point made by the simple view. This way was due to St Thomas Aquinas (see, e.g., *Summa contra Gentiles*). Aquinas accepted Aristotle's general doctrine that substances are made of matter, organized by a form; the desk is the desk which it is because of the matter of which it is made and the shape which is imposed upon it. The form was normally a system of properties, universals which had no existence except in the particular substances in which they were instantiated. However, Aquinas claimed that for man the form of the body, which he called the soul, was separable from the body and capable of independent existence. The soul of man, unlike the souls of animals or plants, was, in Aquinas's terminology, an 'intellectual substance'.

However, if we are going to modify Aristotle to make his views compatible with the simple theory of personal identity, this seems definitely the less satisfactory way of doing so. Properties seem by their very nature to be universals and so it is hard to give any sense to their existing except when conjoined to some stuff. Above all, it is hard to give sense to their being individual – a universal can be instantiated in many different substances. What makes the substances differ is the different stuff of which they are composed. The form of man can be instantiated in many different men. But Aquinas wants a form which is a particular, and so could only be combined with one body. All of this seems to involve a greater distortion of Aristotle's system than does classical dualism. Aquinas's system does have some advantages over classical dualism – for example, it enables him to bring out the naturalness of a person being embodied and the temporary and transitory character of any disembodiment – but the disadvantages of taking Aristotle's approach and then distorting it to this unrecognizable extent are in my view very great. Hence my preference for what I have called classical dualism. . . .

Notes

1 The logically necessary and sufficient conditions for something being so are those conditions such that if they are present, that thing must be so; and if they are absent, that thing cannot be so – all this because of considerations of logic.

2 Wiggins is even more tentative in the amended version of the book, *Sameness and Substance* (Oxford, 1980).

3 Bernard Williams, 'Personal Identity and Individuation', *Proceedings of the Aristotelian Society*, (1956–57), p. 332.

4 He suggests analysing 'person' in such a way that 'coincidence under the concept person logically required the continuance in one organized parcel of all that was causally sufficient and causally necessary to the continuance of essential and characteristic functioning, no autonomously sufficient part achieving autonomous and functionally separate existence' (Wiggins, *Identity and Spatiotemporal Continuity*, p. 55).

5 'Personal Identity', *Philosophical Review*, 80 (1971), pp. 3–27.

6 He introduces this terminology in his paper, 'On the Importance of Self-Identity', *Journal of Philosophy*, 68 (1971), pp. 683–90.

7 Bernard Williams, 'The Self and the Future', *Philosophical Review*, 79 (1970), pp. 161–80.

8 I do not discuss the difficult issue of whether the Aristotelian account applies to animals other than man, e.g., whether continuity of matter and form is necessary and sufficient for the identity of a dog at a later time with a dog at an earlier time.

9 It may be useful, in case anyone suspects the argument of this paragraph of committing some modal fallacy, to set it out in a more formal logical shape. I use the usual logical symbols – '.' means 'and', '~' means 'not', '◊' means 'it is logically possible'. I then introduce the following definitions:

p = I am a conscious person, and I exist in 1984
q = My body is destroyed at the end of 1984
r = I have a soul in 1984
s = I exist in 1985
x ranges over all consistent propositions compatible with (p.q) and describing 1984 states of affairs
('(x)' is to be read in the normal way as 'for all states x...')

The argument may now be set out as follows:

p	Premise (1)
(x) ◊ (p.q.x.s)	Premise (2)
~◊ (p.q.~r.s)	Premise (3)

∴~r is not within the range of x.

But since ~r describes a state of affairs in 1984, it is not compatible with (p.q). But q can hardly make a difference to whether or not r. So p is incompatible with ~r.

∴r

The argument is designed to show that r follows from p; and so, more generally, that every conscious person has a soul. Premise (3) is justified by the wider Aristotelian principle that if I am to continue, some of the stuff out of which I am made has to continue. As I argued in the text, that stuff must be non-bodily stuff. The soul is defined as that non-bodily part whose continuing is essential for my continuing.

Premise (2) relies on the intuition that whatever else might be the case in 1984, compatible with (p.q), my stream of consciousness could continue thereafter.

If you deny (2) and say that r is a state of affairs not entailed by (p.q), but which has to hold if it is to be possible that s, you run into this difficulty. There may be two people in 1984, Oliver, who has a soul, and Fagin, who does not. Both are embodied and conscious, and to all appearances indistinguishable. God (who can do all things logically possible, compatible with how the world is up to now), having forgotten to give Fagin a soul, has, as he annihilates Fagin's body at the end of 1984, no power to continue his stream of thought. Whereas he has the power to continue Oliver's stream of thought. This seems absurd.

---

40   The Causal Theory of the Mind

David M. Armstrong

The Concept of a Mental State

[. . .] The present state of scientific knowledge makes it probable that we can give a purely physico-chemical account of man's body. It seems increasingly likely that the body and the brain of man are constituted and work according to exactly the same principles as those physical principles that govern other, non-organic, matter. The differences between a stone and a human body appear to lie solely in the extremely complex material set-up that is to be found in the living body and which is absent in the stone. Furthermore, there is rather strong evidence that it is the state of our brain that completely determines the state of our consciousness and our mental state generally.

All this is not beyond the realm of controversy, and it is easy to imagine evidence that would upset the picture. In particular, I think that it is just possible that evidence from psychical research might be forthcoming that a physico-chemical view of man's brain could not accommodate. But suppose that the physico-chemical view of the working of the brain is correct, as I take it to be. It will be very natural to conclude that mental states are not simply *determined* by corresponding states of the brain, but that they are actually *identical* with these brain-states, brain-states that involve nothing but physical properties.

The argument just outlined is quite a simple one. [. . .] But although many contemporary thinkers would accept its conclusion, there are others, including many philosophers, who would not. To a great many thinkers it has seemed obvious *a priori* that mental states could not be physical states of the brain. Nobody would identify a number with a piece of rock: it is sufficiently obvious that the two entities fall under different categories. In the same way, it has been thought, a perception or a feeling of sorrow must be a different category of thing from an electro-chemical discharge in the central nervous system.

Here, it seems to me, is a question to which philosophers can expect to make a useful contribution. It is a question about mental concepts. Is our concept of a mental state such that it is an intelligible hypothesis that mental states are physical states of the brain? If the philosopher can show that it is an *intelligible* proposition (that is, a non-self-contradictory proposition) that mental states are physical states of the brain, then the scientific argument just given above can be taken at its face value as a strong reason for accepting the truth of the proposition.

My view is that the identification of mental states with physical states of the brain is a perfectly intelligible one, and that this becomes clear once we achieve a correct view of the analysis of the mental concepts. I admit that my analysis of the mental concepts was itself adopted because it permitted this identification, but such a procedure is commonplace in the construction of theories, and perfectly legitimate. In any case, whatever the motive for proposing the analysis, it is there to speak for itself, to be measured against competitors, and to be assessed as plausible or implausible independently of the identification it makes possible.

The problem of the identification may be put in a Kantian way: "How is it possible that mental states should be physical states of the brain?" The solution will take the form of proposing an *independently plausible* analysis of the concept of a mental state that will permit this identification. In this way, the philosopher makes the way smooth for a first-order doctrine, which, true or false, is a doctrine of the first importance: a purely physicalist view of man.

The analysis proposed may be called the Causal analysis of the mental concepts. According to this view, the concept of a mental state essentially involves, and is exhausted by, the concept of a state that is *apt to be the cause of certain effects or apt to be the effect of certain causes.*

An example of a causal concept is the concept of poison. The concept of poison is the concept of something that when introduced into an organism causes that organism to sicken and/or die.[1] This is but a rough analysis of the concept the structure of which is in fact somewhat more complex and subtle than this. If *A* pours molten lead down *B*'s throat, then he may cause B to die as a result, but he can hardly be said to have poisoned him. For a thing to be called a poison, it is necessary that it act in a certain *sort* of way: roughly, in a biological as opposed to a purely physical way. Again, a poison can be introduced into the system of an organism and that organism fail to die or even to sicken. This might occur if an antidote were administered promptly. Yet again, the poison may be present in insufficient quantities to do any damage. Other qualifications could be made.

But the essential point about the concept of poison is that it is the concept of *that, whatever it is, which produces certain effects.* This leaves open the possibility of the *scientific identification* of poisons, of discovering that a certain sort of substance, such as cyanide, is a poison, and discovering further what it is about the substance that makes it poisonous.

Poisons are accounted poisons in virtue of their active powers, but many sorts of thing are accounted the sorts of thing they are by virtue of their *passive* powers. Thus brittle objects are accounted brittle because of the disposition they have to break and shatter when sharply struck. This leaves open the possibility of discovering empirically what sorts of thing are brittle and what it is about them that makes them brittle.

Now *if* the concepts of the various sorts of mental state are concepts of that which is, in various sorts of way, apt for causing certain effects and apt for being the effect of certain causes, then it would be a quite unpuzzling thing if mental states should turn out to be physical states of the brain.

The concept of a mental state is the concept of something that is, characteristically, the cause of certain effects and the effect of certain causes. What sort of effects and what sort of causes? The effects caused by the mental state will be certain patterns of behaviour of the person in that state. For instance, the desire for food is a state of a person or animal that characteristically brings about food-seeking and food-consuming behaviour by that person or animal. The causes of mental states will be objects and events in the person's environment. For instance, a sensation of green is the characteristic effect in a person of the action upon his eyes of a nearby green surface.

The general pattern of analysis is at its most obvious and plausible in the case of *purposes*. If a man's purpose is to go to the kitchen to get something to eat, it is completely natural to conceive of this purpose as a cause within him that brings about, or tends to bring about, that particular line of conduct. It is, furthermore, notorious that we are unable to characterize purposes *except* in terms of that which they tend to bring about. How can we distinguish the purpose to go to the kitchen to get something to eat from another purpose to go to the bedroom to lie down? Only by the different outcomes that the two purposes tend to bring about. This fact was an encouragement to Behaviourism. It is still more plausibly explained by saying that the concept of purpose is a causal concept. The further hypothesis that the two purposes are, in their own nature, different physical patterns in, or physical states of, the central nervous system is then a natural (although, of course, not logically inevitable) supplement to the causal analysis.

Simple models have great value in trying to grasp complex conceptions, but they are ladders that may need to be kicked away after we have mounted up by their means. It is vital to realize that the mental concepts have a far more complex logical structure than simple causal notions such as the concept of poison. The fact should occasion no surprise. In the case of poisons, the effect of which they are the cause is a gross and obvious phenomenon and the level of causal explanation involved in simply calling a substance "a poison" is crude and simple. But in the case of mental states, their effects are all those complexities of behaviour that mark off men and higher animals from the rest of the objects in the world. Furthermore, differences in such behaviour are elaborately correlated with differences in the mental causes operating. So it is only to be expected that the causal patterns invoked by the mental concepts should be extremely complex and sophisticated.

In the case of the notion of a purpose, for instance, it is plausible to assert that it is the notion of a cause within which drives, or tends to drive, the man or animal through a series of actions to a certain end-state. But this is not the whole story. A purpose is only a purpose if it works to bring about behavioural effects in *a certain sort of way*. We may sum up this sort of way by saying that purposes are *information-sensitive* causes. By this is meant that purposes direct behaviour by utilizing *perceptions* and *beliefs*, perceptions and beliefs about the agent's current situation and the way it develops, and beliefs about the way the world works. For instance, it is part of what it is to be a purpose to achieve X that this cause will cease to operate, will be "switched off", if the agent perceives or otherwise comes to believe that X has been achieved.

At this point, we observe that an account is being given of that special species of cause that is a purpose in terms of *further* mental items: perceptions and beliefs. This means that if we are to give a purely causal analysis even of the concept of a purpose we also will have to give a purely causal analysis of perceptions and beliefs. We may think of man's behaviour as brought about by the joint operation of two sets of causes: first, his purposes and, second, his perceptions of and/or his beliefs about the world. But since perceptions and beliefs are quite different sorts of thing from purposes, a Causal analysis must assign quite different causal *roles* to these different things in the bringing about of behaviour.

I believe that this can be done by giving an account of perceptions and beliefs as *mappings* of the world. They are structures within us that model the world beyond the structure. This model is created in us by the world. Purposes may then be thought of as driving causes that utilize such mappings.

This is a mere thumb-nail, which requires much further development as well as qualification. One point that becomes clear when that development is given is that just as the concept of purpose cannot be elucidated without appealing to the concepts of perception and belief, so the latter cannot be elucidated without appealing to the concept of purpose. (This comes out, for instance, when we raise Hume's problem: what marks off beliefs from the mere entertaining of the same proposition? It seems that we can only mark off beliefs as those mappings in the light of which we are prepared to *act*, that is, which are potential servants of our purposes.) The logical dependence of purpose on perception and belief, and of perception and belief upon purpose, is not circularity in definition. What it shows is that the corresponding concepts *must be introduced together or not at all*. In itself, there is nothing very surprising in this. Correlative or mutually implicated concepts are common enough: for instance, the concepts of husband and wife or the concepts of soldier and army. No husbands without wives or wives without husbands. No soldiers without an army, no army without soldiers. But if the concepts of purpose, perception and belief are (i) correlative concepts and (ii) different species of purely causal concepts, then it is clear that they are far more complex in structure than a simple causal concept like poison. What falls under the mental concepts will be a complex and interlocking set of causal factors, which together are responsible for the "minded" behaviour of men and the higher animals.

The working out of the Causal theory of the mental concepts thus turns out to be an extremely complex business. Indeed when it is merely baldly stated, the Causal theory is, to use the phrase of Imre Lakatos, a *research programme* in conceptual analysis rather than a developed theory. I have tried to show that it is a hopeful programme by attempting, at least in outline, a Causal analysis of all the main mental concepts in *A Materialist Theory of the Mind* (1968); and I have supplemented the rather thin account given there of the concepts of belief, knowledge and inferring in *Belief, Truth and Knowledge* (1973).

Two examples of mental concepts where an especially complex and sophisticated type of Causal analysis is required are the notions of introspective awareness (one sense of the word "consciousness") and the having of mental imagery. Introspective awareness is analysable as a mental state that is a "perception" of mental states. It is a mapping of the causal factors themselves. The having of mental imagery is a sort of mental state that cannot be elucidated in *directly* causal terms, but only by resemblance to the corresponding perceptions, which *are* explicated in terms of their causal role.

Two advantages of the Causal theory may now be mentioned. First, it has often been remarked by philosophers and others that the realm of mind is a shadowy one, and that the nature of mental states is singularly elusive and hard to grasp. This has given aid and comfort to Dualist or Cartesian theories of mind, according to which minds are quite different sorts of thing from material objects. But if the Causal analysis is correct, the facts admit of another explanation. What Dualist philosophers have grasped in a confused way is that our direct acquaintance with mind, which occurs in introspective awareness, is an acquaintance with something that we are aware of only as something that is causally linked, directly or indirectly, with behaviour. In the case of our purposes and desires, for instance, we are often (though not invariably) introspectively aware of them. What we are aware of is the presence of factors within us that drive in a certain direction. We are not aware of the intrinsic nature of the factors. This emptiness or gap in our awareness is then interpreted by Dualists as immateriality. In fact, however, if the Causal analysis is correct, there is no warrant for this interpretation and, if the Physicalist identification of the nature of the causes is correct, the interpretation is actually false.

Second, the Causal analysis yields a still more spectacular verification. It shows promise of explaining a philosophically notorious feature of all or almost all mental states: their *intentionality*. This was the feature of mental states to which Brentano in particular drew attention, the fact that they may point towards certain objects or states of affairs, but that these objects and states of affairs need not exist. When a man strives, his striving has an objective, but that objective may never be achieved. When he believes, there is something he believes, but what he believes may not be the case. This capacity of mental states to "point" to what does not exist can seem very special. Brentano held that intentionality set the mind completely apart from matter.

Suppose, however, that we consider a concept like the concept of poison. Does it not provide us with a miniature and unsophisticated model for the intentionality of mental states? Poisons are substances apt to make organisms sicken and die when the poison is administered. So it may be said that this is what poisons "point" to. Nevertheless, poisons may fail of their effect. A poison does not fail to be a poison because an antidote neutralizes the customary effect of the poison.

May not the intentionality of mental states, therefore, be in principle a no more mysterious affair, although indefinitely more complex, than the death that lurks in the poison? As an intermediate case between poisons and mental states, consider the mechanisms involved in a homing rocket. Given a certain setting of its mechanism, the rocket may "point" towards a certain target in a way that is a simulacrum of the way in which purposes point towards their objectives. The mechanism will only bring the rocket to the target in "standard" circumstances: many factors can be conceived that would "defeat" the mechanism. For the mechanism to operate successfully, some device will be required by which the developing situation is "mapped" in the mechanism (i.e. what course the rocket is currently on, etc.). This mapping is an elementary analogue of perception, and so the course that is "mapped" in the mechanism may be thought of as a simulacrum of the perceptual intentional object. Through one circumstance or another (e.g. malfunction of the gyroscope) this mapping may be "incorrect".

It is no objection to this analogy that homing rockets are built by men with purposes, who deliberately stamp a crude model of their own purposes into the rocket. Homing rockets might have been natural products, and non-minded objects that operate in a similar but far more complex way are found in nature. The living cell is a case in point.

So the Causal analyses of the mental concepts show promise of explaining both the transparency and the intentionality of mental states. One problem quite frequently raised in connection with these analyses, however, is in what sense they can be called "analyses". The welter of complications in which the so-called analyses are involved make it sufficiently obvious that they do not consist of *synonymous translations* of statements in which mental terms figure. But, it has been objected, if synonymous translations of mental statements are unavailable, what precisely can be meant by speaking of "analyses of concepts"?

I am far from clear what should be said in reply to this objection. Clearly, however, it does depend upon taking all conceptual analyses as claims about the synonymy of sentences, and that seems to be too simple a view. Going back to the case of poison: it is surely not an empirical fact, to be learnt by experience, that poisons kill. It is at the centre of our notion of what poisons are that they have the power to bring about this effect. If they did not do that, they would not be properly called "poisons". But although this seems obvious enough, it is extremely difficult to give exact translations of sentences containing the word "poison" into other sentences that do not contain the word or any synonym. Even in this simple case, it is not at all clear that the task can actually be accomplished.

For this reason, I think that sentence translation (with synonymy) is too strict a demand to make upon a purported conceptual analysis. What more relaxed demand can we make and still have a conceptual analysis? I do not know. One thing that we clearly need further light upon here is the concept of a concept, and how concepts are tied to language. I incline to the view that the connection between concepts and language is much less close than many philosophers have assumed. Concepts are linked primarily with belief and thought, and belief and thought, I think, have a great degree of logical independence of language, however close the empirical connection may be in many cases. If this is so, then an analysis of concepts, although of course conducted *in* words, may not be an investigation *into* words. (A compromise proposal: analysis of concepts might be an investigation into some sort of "deep structure" – to use the currently hallowed phrase – which underlies the use of certain words and sentences.) I wish I were able to take the topic further.

The Problem of the Secondary Qualities

No discussion of the Causal theory of the mental concepts is complete that does not say something about the *secondary qualities.* If we consider such mental states as purposes and intentions, their "transparency" is a rather conspicuous feature. It is notorious that introspection cannot differentiate such states except in terms of their different objects. It is not so immediately obvious, however, that *perception* has this transparent character. Perception involves the experience of colour and of visual extension, touch of the whole obscure range of tactual properties, including tactual extension, hearing, taste and smell the experience of sounds, tastes and smells. These phenomenal qualities, it may be argued, endow different perceptions with different qualities. The lack of transparency is even more obvious in the case of bodily sensations. Pains, itches, tickles and tingles are mental states, even if mental states of no very high-grade sort, and they each seem to involve their own peculiar qualities. Again, associated with different emotions it is quite plausible to claim to discern special emotion qualities. If perception, bodily sensation and emotions involve qualities, then this seems to falsify a purely Causal analysis of these mental states. They are not mere "that whiches" known only by their causal role.

However, it is not at all clear how strong is the line of argument sketched in the previous paragraph. We distinguish between the intention and what is intended, and in just the same way we must distinguish between the perception and what is perceived. The intention is a mental state and so is the perception, but what is intended is not in general something mental and nor is what is perceived. What is intended may not come to pass, it is a merely intentional object, and the same may be said of what is perceived. Now in the case of the phenomenal qualities, it seems plausible to say that they are qualities not of the perception but rather of what is perceived. "Visual extension" is the shape, size, etc. that some object of visual perception is perceived to have (an object that need not exist). Colour seems to be a quality of that object. And similarly for the other phenomenal qualities. Even in the case of the bodily sensations, the qualities associated with the sensations do not *appear* to be qualities of mental states but instead to be qualities of portions of our bodies: more or less fleeting qualities that qualify the place where the sensation is located. Only in the case of the emotions does it seem natural to place the quality on the mental rather than the object side: but then it is not so clear whether there really *are* peculiar qualities associated with the emotions. The different patterns of bodily sensations associated with the different emotions may be sufficient to do phenomenological justice to the emotions.

For these reasons, it is not certain whether the phenomenal qualities pose any threat to the Causal analysis of the mental concepts. But what a subset of these qualities quite certainly does pose a threat to, is the doctrine that the Causal analysis of the mental concepts is a step towards: Materialism or Physicalism.

The qualities of colour, sound, heat and cold, taste and smell together with the qualities that appear to be involved in bodily sensations and those that may be involved in the case of the emotions, are an embarrassment to the modern Materialist. He seeks to give an account of the world and of man purely in terms of *physical* properties, that is to say in terms of the properties that the physicist appeals to in his explanations of phenomena. The Materialist is not committed to the *current set* of properties to which the physicist appeals, but he is committed to whatever set of properties the physicist in the end will appeal to. It is clear that such properties as colour, sound, taste and smell – the so-called "secondary qualities" – will never be properties to which the physicist will appeal.

It is, however, a plausible thesis that associated with different secondary qualities are properties that are respectable from a physicist's point of view. Physical surfaces *appear* to have colour. They not merely appear to, but undoubtedly do, emit light-waves, and the different mixtures of lengths of wave emitted are linked with differences in colour. In the same way, different sorts of sound are linked with different sorts of sound-wave and differences in heat with differences in the mean kinetic energy of the molecules composing the hot things. The Materialist's problem therefore would be very simply solved if the secondary qualities could be identified with these physically respectable properties. (The qualities associated with bodily sensations would be identified with different sorts of stimulation of bodily receptors. If there are unique qualities associated with the emotions, they would presumably be identified with some of the physical states of the brain linked with particular emotions.)

But now the Materialist philosopher faces a problem. Previously he asked: "How is it possible that mental states could be physical states of the brain?" This question was answered by the Causal theory of the mental concepts. Now he must ask: "How is it possible that secondary qualities could be purely physical properties of the objects they are qualities of?" A Causal analysis does not seem to be of any avail. To try to give an analysis of, say, the quality of being red in Causal terms would lead us to produce such analyses as "those properties of a physical surface, whatever they are, that characteristically produce *red sensations* in us." But this analysis simply shifts the problem unhelpfully from property of surface to property of sensation. Either the red sensations involve nothing but physically respectable properties or they involve something more. If they involve something more, Materialism fails. But if they are simply physical states of the brain, having nothing but physical properties, then the Materialist faces the problem: "How is it possible that red sensations should be physical states of the brain?" This question is no easier to answer than the original question about the redness of physical surfaces. (To give a Causal analysis of red sensations as the characteristic effects of the action of red surfaces is, of course, to move round in a circle.)

The great problem presented by the secondary qualities, such as redness, is that they are *unanalysable*. They have certain relations of resemblance and so on to each other, so they cannot be said to be completely simple. But they are simple in the sense that they resist any analysis. You cannot give any complete account of the concept of redness without involving the notion of redness itself. This has seemed to be, and still seems to many philosophers to be, an absolute bar to identifying redness with, say, certain patterns of emission of light-waves.

But I am not so sure. I think it can be maintained that although the second-ary qualities *appear* to be simple, they are not in fact simple. Perhaps their sim-plicity is *epistemological* only, not ontological, a matter of our awareness of them rather than the way they are. The best model I can given for the situation is the sort of phenomena made familiar to us by the *Gestalt* psychologists. It is possible to grasp that certain things or situations have a certain special property, but be unable to analyse that property. For instance, it may be possible to perceive that certain people are all alike in some way without being able to make it clear to oneself what the likeness is. We are aware that all these people have a certain likeness to each other, but are unable to define or specify that likeness. Later psychological research may achieve a specification of the likeness, a specification that may come as a complete surprise to us. Perhaps, therefore, the secondary qualities are in fact complex, and perhaps they are complex characteristics of a sort demanded by Materialism, but we are unable to grasp their complexity in perception.

There are two divergences between the model just suggested and the case of the secondary qualities. First, in the case of grasping the indefinable likeness of people, we are under no temptation to think that the likeness is a likeness in some simple quality. The likeness is indefinable, but we are vaguely aware that it is complex. Second, once research has determined the concrete nature of the likeness, our attention can be drawn to, and we can observe individually, the features that determine the likeness.

But although the model suggested and the case of the secondary qualities undoubtedly exhibit these differences, I do not think that they show that the secondary qualities cannot be identified with respectable physical characteristics of objects. Why should not a complex property appear to be simple? There would seem to be no contradiction in adding such a condition to the model. It has the consequence that perception of the secondary qualities involves an element of illusion, but the consequence involves no contradiction. It is true also that in the case of the secondary qualities the illusion cannot be overcome within perception: it is impossible to see a coloured surface as a surface emitting certain light-waves. (Though one sometimes seems to *hear* a sound as a vibration of the air.) But while this means that the identification of colour and light-waves is a purely *theo-retical* one, it still seems to be a possible one. And if the identification is a possible one, we have general scientific reasons to think it a *plausible* one.

The doctrine of mental states and of the secondary qualities briefly presented in this paper seems to me to show promise of meeting many of the traditional philosophical objections to a Materialist or Physicalist account of the world. As I have emphasized, the philosopher is not professionally competent to argue the positive case for Materialism. There he must rely upon the evidence presented by the scientist, particularly the physicist. But at least he may neutralize the objections to Materialism advanced by his fellow philosophers.

Note

1   "Any substance which, when introduced into or absorbed by a living organism, destroys life or injures health." (*Shorter Oxford Dictionary*, 3rd edn., rev., 1978.)

---

41   The Puzzle of Conscious Experience

David J. Chalmers

Conscious experience is at once the most familiar thing in the world and the most mysterious. There is nothing we know about more directly than consciousness, but it is extraordinarily hard to reconcile it with everything else we know. Why does it exist? What does it do? How could it possibly arise from neural processes in the brain? These questions are among the most intriguing in all of science.

From an objective viewpoint, the brain is relatively comprehensible. When you look at this page, there is a whir of processing: photons strike your retina, electrical signals are passed up your optic nerve and between different areas of your brain, and eventually you might respond with a smile, a perplexed frown or a remark. But there is also a subjective aspect. When you look at the page, you are conscious of it, directly experiencing the images and words as part of your private, mental life. You have vivid impressions of colored flowers and vibrant sky. At the same time, you may be feeling some emotions and forming some thoughts. Together such experiences make up consciousness: the subjective, inner life of the mind.

For many years consciousness was shunned by researchers studying the brain and the mind. The prevailing view was that science, which depends on objectivity, could not accommodate something as subjective as consciousness. The behaviorist movement in psychology, dominant earlier in this century, concentrated on external behavior and disallowed any talk of internal mental processes. Later, the rise of cognitive science focused attention on processes inside the head. Still, consciousness remained off-limits, fit only for late-night discussion over drinks.

Over the past several years, however, an increasing number of neuroscientists, psychologists and philosophers have been rejecting the idea that consciousness cannot be studied and are attempting to delve into its secrets. As might be expected of a field so new, there is tangle of diverse and conflicting theories, often using basic concepts in incompatible ways. To help unsnarl the tangle, philosophical reasoning is vital.

The myriad views within the field range from reductionist theories, according to which consciousness can be explained by the standard methods of neuroscience and psychology, to the position of the so-called mysterians, who say we will never understand consciousness at all. I believe that on close analysis both of these views can be seen to be mistaken and that the truth lies somewhere in the middle.

Against reductionism I will argue that the tools of neuroscience cannot provide a full account of conscious experience, although they have much to offer. Against mysterianism I will hold that consciousness might be explained by a new kind of theory. The full details of such a theory are still out of reach, but careful reasoning and some educated inferences can reveal something of its general nature. For example, it will probably involve new fundamental laws, and the concept of information may play a central role. These faint glimmerings suggest that a theory of consciousness may have startling consequences for our view of the universe and of ourselves.

The Hard Problem

Researchers use the word "consciousness" in many different ways. To clarify the issues, we first have to separate the problems that are often clustered together under the name. For this purpose, I find it useful to distinguish between the "easy problems" and the "hard problem" of consciousness. The easy problems are by no means trivial – they are actually as challenging as most in psychology and biology – but it is with the hard problem that the central mystery lies.

The easy problems of consciousness include the following: How can a human subject discriminate sensory stimuli and react to them appropriately? How does the brain integrate information from many different sources and use this information to control behavior? How is it that subjects can verbalize their internal states? Although all these questions are associated with consciousness, they all concern the objective mechanisms of the cognitive system. Consequently, we have every reason to expect that continued work in cognitive psychology and neuroscience will answer them.

The hard problem, in contrast, is the question of how physical processes in the brain give rise to subjective experience. This puzzle involves the inner aspect of thought and perception: the way things feel for the subject. When we see, for example, we experience visual sensations, such as that of vivid blue. Or think of the ineffable sound of a distant oboe, the agony of an intense pain, the sparkle of happiness or the meditative quality of a moment lost in thought. All are part of what I am calling consciousness. It is these phenomena that pose the real mystery of the mind.

To illustrate the distinction, consider a thought experiment devised by the Australian philosopher Frank Jackson. Suppose that Mary, a neuroscientist in the twenty-third century, is the world's leading expert on the brain processes responsible for color vision. But Mary has lived her whole life in a black-and-white room and has never seen any other colors. She knows everything there is to know about physical processes in the brain – its biology, structure and function. This understanding enables her to grasp everything there is to know about the easy problems: how the brain discriminates stimuli, integrates information and produces verbal reports. From her knowledge of color vision, she knows the way color names correspond with wavelengths on the light spectrum. But there is still something crucial about color vision that Mary does not know: what it is like to experience a color such as red. It follows that there are facts about conscious experience that cannot be deduced from physical facts about the functioning of the brain.

Indeed, nobody knows why these physical processes are accompanied by conscious experience at all. Why is it that when our brains process light of a certain wavelength, we have an experience of deep purple? Why do we have any experience at all? Could not an unconscious automaton have performed the same tasks just as well? These are questions that we would like a theory of consciousness to answer.

I am not denying that consciousness arises from the brain. We know, for example, that the subjective experience of vision is closely linked to processes in the visual cortex. It is the link itself that perplexes, however. Remarkably, subjective experience seems to emerge from a physical process. But we have no idea how or why this is.

Is Neuroscience Enough?

Given the flurry of recent work on consciousness in neuroscience and psychology, one might think this mystery is starting to be cleared up. On closer examination, however, it turns out that almost all the current work addresses only the easy problems of consciousness. The confidence of the reductionist view comes from the progress on the easy problems, but none of this makes any difference where the hard problem is concerned.

Consider the hypothesis put forward by neurobiologists Francis Crick of the Salk Institute for Biological Studies in San Diego and Christof Koch of the California Institute of Technology. They suggest that consciousness may arise from certain oscillations in the cerebral cortex, which become synchronized as neurons fire 40 times per second. Crick and Koch believe the phenomenon might explain how different attributes of a single perceived object (its color and shape, for example), which are processed in different parts of the brain, are merged into a coherent whole. In this theory, two pieces of information become bound together precisely when they are represented by synchronized neural firings.

The hypothesis could conceivably elucidate one of the easy problems about how information is integrated in the brain. But why should synchronized oscillations give rise to a visual experience, no matter how much integration is taking place? This question involves the hard problem, about which the theory has nothing to offer. Indeed, Crick and Koch are agnostic about whether the hard problem can be solved by science at all.

The same kind of critique could be applied to almost all the recent work on consciousness. In his 1991 book *Consciousness Explained*, philosopher Daniel C. Dennett laid out a sophisticated theory of how numerous independent processes in the brain combine to produce a coherent response to a perceived event. The theory might do much to explain how we produce verbal reports on our internal states, but it tells us very little about why there should be a subjective experience behind these reports. Like other reductionist theories, Dennett's is a theory of the easy problems.

The critical common trait among these easy problems is that they all concern how a cognitive or behavioral function is performed. All are ultimately questions about how the brain carries out some task – how it discriminates stimuli, integrates information, produces reports and so on. Once neurobiology specifies appropriate neural mechanisms, showing how the functions are performed, the easy problems are solved. The hard problem of consciousness, in contrast, goes beyond problems about how functions are performed. Even if every behavioral and cognitive function related to consciousness were explained, there would still remain a further mystery: Why is the performance of these functions accompanied by conscious experience? It is this additional conundrum that makes the hard problem hard.

The Explanatory Gap

Some have suggested that to solve the hard problem, we need to bring in new tools of physical explanation: nonlinear dynamics, say, or new discoveries in neuroscience, or quantum mechanics. But these ideas suffer from exactly the same difficulty. Consider a proposal from Stuart R. Hameroff of the University of Arizona and Roger Penrose of the University of Oxford. They hold that consciousness arises from quantum-physical processes taking place in microtubules, which are protein structures inside neurons. It is possible (if not likely) that such a hypothesis will lead to an explanation of how the brain makes decisions or even how it proves mathematical theorems, as Hameroff and Penrose suggest. But even if it does, the theory is silent about how these processes might give rise to conscious experience. Indeed, the same problem arises with any theory of consciousness based only on physical processing.

The trouble is that physical theories are best suited to explaining why systems have a certain physical structure and how they perform various functions. Most problems in science have this form; to explain life, for example, we need to describe how a physical system can reproduce, adapt and metabolize. But consciousness is a different sort of problem entirely, as it goes beyond the explanation of structure and function.

Of course, neuroscience is not irrelevant to the study of consciousness. For one thing, it may be able to reveal the nature of the neural correlate of consciousness – the brain processes most directly associated with conscious experience. It may even give a detailed correspondence between specific processes in the brain and related components of experience. But until we know why these processes give rise to conscious experience at all, we will not have crossed what philosopher Joseph Levine has called the explanatory gap between physical processes and consciousness. Making that leap will demand a new kind of theory.

A True Theory of Everything

In searching for an alternative, a key observation is that not all entities in science are explained in terms of more basic entities. In physics, for example, space-time, mass and charge (among other things) are regarded as fundamental features of the world, as they are not reducible to anything simpler. Despite this irreducibility, detailed and useful theories relate these entities to one another in terms of fundamental laws. Together these features and laws explain a great variety of complex and subtle phenomena.

It is widely believed that physics provides a complete catalogue of the universe's fundamental features and laws. As physicist Steven Weinberg puts it in his 1992 book *Dreams of a Final Theory,* the goal of physics is a "theory of everything" from which all there is to know about the universe can be derived. But Weinberg concedes that there is a problem with consciousness. Despite the power of physical theory, the existence of consciousness does not seem to be derivable from physical laws. He defends physics by arguing that it might eventually explain what he calls the objective correlates of consciousness (that is, the neural correlates), but of course to do this is not to explain consciousness itself. If the existence of consciousness cannot be derived from physical laws, a theory of physics is not a true theory of everything. So a final theory must contain an additional fundamental component.

Toward this end, I propose that conscious experience be considered a fundamental feature, irreducible to anything more basic. The idea may seem strange at first, but consistency seems to demand it. In the nineteenth century it turned out that electromagnetic phenomena could not be explained in terms of previously known principles. As a consequence, scientists introduced electromagnetic charge as a new fundamental entity and studied the associated fundamental laws. Similar reasoning should apply to consciousness. If existing fundamental theories cannot encompass it, then something new is required.

Where there is a fundamental property, there are fundamental laws. In this case, the laws must relate experience to elements of physical theory. These laws will almost certainly not interfere with those of the physical world; it seems that the latter form a closed system in their own right. Rather the laws will serve as a bridge, specifying how experience depends on underlying physical processes. It is this bridge that will cross the explanatory gap.

Thus, a complete theory will have two components: physical laws, telling us about the behavior of physical systems from the infinitesimal to the cosmological, and what we might call psychophysical laws, telling us how some of those systems are associated with conscious experience. These two components will constitute a true theory of everything.

Searching for a Theory

Supposing for the moment that they exist, how might we uncover such psycho-physical laws? The great hindrance in this pursuit will be a lack of data. As I have described it, consciousness is subjective, so there is no direct way to monitor it in others. But this difficulty is an obstacle, not a dead end. For a start, each one of us has access to our own experiences, a rich trove that can be used to formulate theories. We can also plausibly rely on indirect information, such as subjects' descriptions of their experiences. Philosophical arguments and thought experiments also have a role to play. Such methods have limitations, but they give us more than enough to get started.

These theories will not be conclusively testable, so they will inevitably be more speculative than those of more conventional scientific disciplines. Nevertheless, there is no reason why they should not be strongly constrained to account accurately for our own first-person experiences, as well as the evidence from subjects' reports. If we find a theory that fits the data better than any other theory of equal simplicity, we will have good reason to accept it. Right now we do not have even a single theory that fits the data, so worries about testability are premature.

We might start by looking for high-level bridging laws, connecting physical processes to experience at an everyday level. The basic contour of such a law might be gleaned from the observation that when we are conscious of something, we are generally able to act on it and speak about it – which are objective, physical functions. Conversely, when some information is directly available for action and speech, it is generally conscious. Thus, consciousness correlates well with what we might call "awareness": the process by which information in the brain is made globally available to motor processes such as speech and bodily action.

The notion may seem trivial. But as defined here, awareness is objective and physical, whereas consciousness is not. Some refinements to the definition of awareness are needed, in order to extend the concept to animals and infants, which cannot speak. But at least in familiar cases, it is possible to see the rough outlines of a psychophysical law: where there is awareness, there is consciousness, and vice versa.

To take this line of reasoning a step further, consider the structure present in the conscious experience. The experience of a field of vision, for example, is a constantly changing mosaic of colors, shapes and patterns and as such has a detailed geometric structure. The fact that we can describe this structure, reach out in the direction of many of its components and perform other actions that depend on it suggests that the structure corresponds directly to that of the information made available in the brain through the neural processes of awareness.

Similarly, our experiences of color have an intrinsic three-dimensional structure that is mirrored in the structure of information processes in the brain's visual cortex. This structure is illustrated in the color wheels and charts used by artists. Colors are arranged in a systematic pattern – red to green on one axis, blue to yellow on another, and black to white on a third. Colors that are close to one another on a color wheel are experienced as similar. It is extremely likely that they also correspond to similar perceptual representations in the brain, as part of a system of complex three-dimensional coding among neurons that is not yet fully understood. We can recast the underlying concept as a principle of structural coherence: the structure of conscious experience is mirrored by the structure of information in awareness, and vice versa.

Another candidate for a psychophysical law is a principle of organizational invariance. It holds that physical systems with the same abstract organization will give rise to the same kind of conscious experience, no matter what they are made of. For example, if the precise interactions between our neurons could be duplicated with silicon chips, the same conscious experience would arise. The idea is somewhat controversial, but I believe it is strongly supported by thought experiments describing the gradual replacement of neurons by silicon. The remarkable implication is that consciousness might someday be achieved in machines.

Information: Physical and Experiential

The ultimate goal of a theory of consciousness is a simple and elegant set of fundamental laws, analogous to the fundamental laws of physics. The principles described above are unlikely to be fundamental, however. Rather they seem to be high-level psychophysical laws, analogous to macroscopic principles in physics such as those of thermodynamics or kinematics. What might the underlying fundamental laws be? No one knows, but I don't mind speculating.

I suggest that the primary psychophysical laws may centrally involve the concept of information. The abstract notion of information, as put forward in the 1940s by Claude E. Shannon of the Massachusetts Institute of Technology, is that of a set of separate states with a basic structure of similarities and differences between them. We can think of a 10-bit binary code as an information state, for example. Such information states can be embodied in the physical world. This happens whenever they correspond to physical states (voltages, say); the differences between them can be transmitted along some pathway, such as a telephone line.

We can also find information embodied in conscious experience. The pattern of color patches in a visual field, for example, can be seen as analogous to that of the pixels covering a display screen. Intriguingly, it turns out that we find the same information states embedded in conscious experience and in underlying physical processes in the brain. The three-dimensional encoding of color spaces, for example, suggests that the information state in a color experience corresponds directly to an information state in the brain. We might even regard the two states as distinct aspects of a single information state, which is simultaneously embodied in both physical processing and conscious experience.

A natural hypothesis ensues. Perhaps information, or at least some information, has two basic aspects: a physical one and an experiential one. This hypothesis has the status of a fundamental principle that might underlie the relation between physical processes and experience. Wherever we find conscious experience, it exists as one aspect of an information state, the other aspect of which is embedded in a physical process in the brain. This proposal needs to be fleshed out to make a satisfying theory. But it fits nicely with the principles mentioned earlier – systems with the same organization will embody the same information, for example – and it could explain numerous features of our conscious experience.

The idea is at least compatible with several others, such as physicist John A. Wheeler's suggestion that information is fundamental to the physics of the universe. The laws of physics might ultimately be cast in informational terms, in which case we would have a satisfying congruence between the constructs in both physical and psychophysical laws. It may even be that a theory of physics and a theory of consciousness could eventually be consolidated into a single grander theory of information.

A potential problem is posed by the ubiquity of information. Even a thermostat embodies some information, for example, but is it conscious? There are at least two possible responses. First, we could constrain the fundamental laws so that only some information has an experiential aspect, perhaps depending on how it is physically processed. Secondly, we might bite the bullet and allow that all information has an experiential aspect – where there is complex information processing, there is complex experience, and where there is simple information processing, there is simple experience. If this is so, then even a thermostat might have experiences, although they would be much simpler than even a basic color experience, and there would certainly be no accompanying emotions or thoughts. This seems odd at first, but if experience is truly fundamental, we might expect it to be widespread. In any case, the choice between these alternatives should depend on which can be integrated into the most powerful theory.

Of course, such ideas may be all wrong. On the other hand, they might evolve into a more powerful proposal that predicts the precise structure of our conscious experience from physical processes in our brains. If this project succeeds, we will have good reason to accept the theory. If it fails, other avenues will be pursued, and alternative fundamental theories may be developed. In this way, we may one day resolve the greatest mystery of the mind.

Appendix: Dancing Qualia in a Synthetic Brain

Whether consciousness could arise in a complex, synthetic system is a question many people find intrinsically fascinating. Although it may be decades or even centuries before such a system is built, a simple thought experiment offers strong evidence that an artificial brain, if organized appropriately, would indeed have precisely the same kind of conscious experiences as a human being.

Consider a silicon-based system in which the chips are organized and function in the same way as the neurons in your brain. That is, each chip in the silicon system does exactly what its natural analogue does and is interconnected to surrounding elements in precisely the same way. Thus, the behavior exhibited by the artificial system will be exactly the same as yours. The crucial question is: Will it be conscious in the same way that you are?

Let us assume, for the purpose of argument, that it would not be. (Here we use a reasoning technique known as reductio ad absurdum, in which the opposite hypothesis is assumed and then shown to lead to an untenable conclusion.) That is, it either has different experiences – an experience of blue, say, when you are seeing red – or no experience at all. We will consider the first case; the reasoning proceeds similarly in both cases.

Because chips and neurons have the same function, they are interchangeable, with the proper interfacing. Chips therefore can replace neurons, producing a continuum of cases in which a successively larger proportion of neurons are replaced by chips. Along this continuum, the conscious experience of the system will also change. For example, we might replace all the neurons in your visual cortex with an identically organized version made of silicon. The resulting brain, with an artificial visual cortex, will have a different conscious experience from the original: where you had previously seen red, you may now experience purple (or perhaps a faded pink, in the case where the wholly silicon system has no experience at all).

Both visual cortices are then attached to your brain, through a two-position switch. With the switch in one mode, you use the natural visual cortex; in the other, the artificial cortex is activated. When the switch is flipped, your experience changes from red to purple, or vice versa. When the switch is flipped repeatedly, your experiences "dance" between the two different conscious states (red and purple), known as qualia.

Because your brain's organization has not changed, however, there can be no behavioral change when the switch is thrown. Therefore, when asked about what you are seeing, you will say that nothing has changed. You will hold that you are seeing red and have seen nothing but red – even though the two colors are dancing before your eyes. This conclusion is so unreasonable that it is best taken as a reductio ad absurdum of the original assumption – that an artificial system with identical organization and functioning has a different conscious experience from that of a neural brain. Retraction of the assumption establishes the opposite: that systems with the same organization have the same conscious experience.

---

42   Neutral Monism: an Excerpt from *Philosophy*

Bertrand Russell

Physical and Perceptual Space

Perhaps there is nothing so difficult for the imagination as to teach it to feel about space as modern science compels us to think. This is the task which must be attempted in the present chapter.

We said in Chapter XII that we know about what is happening in the brain exactly what naive realism thinks it knows about what is happening in the world. This remark may have seemed cryptic; it must now be expanded and expounded.

The gist of the matter is that percepts, which we spoke about at the end of the last chapter, are in our heads; that percepts are what we can know with most certainty; and that percepts contain what naive realism thinks it knows about the world.

But when I say that my percepts are in my head, I am saying something which is ambiguous until the different kinds of space have been explained, for the statement is only true in connection with *physical* space. There is also a space in our percepts, and of this space the statement would not be true. When I say that there is space in our percepts, I mean nothing at all difficult to understand. I mean – to take the sense of sight, which is the most important in this connection – that in what we see at one time there is up and down, right and left, inside and outside. If we see, say, a circle on a blackboard, all these relations exist within what we see. The circle has a top half and a bottom half, a right-hand half and a left-hand half, an inside and an outside. Those relations alone are enough to make up a space of sorts. But the space of every-day life is filled out with what we derive from touch and movement – how a thing feels when we touch it, and what movements are necessary in order to grasp it. Other elements also come into the genesis of the space in which everybody believes who has not been troubled by philosophy; but it is unnecessary for our purposes to go into this question any more deeply. The point that concerns us is that a man's percepts are private to himself: what I see, no one else sees; what I hear, no one else hears; what I touch, no one else touches; and so on. True, others hear and see something very like what I hear and see, if they are suitably placed; but there are always differences. Sounds are less loud at a distance; objects change their visual appearance according to the laws of perspective. Therefore it is impossible for two persons at the same time to have exactly identical percepts. It follows that the space of percepts, like the percepts, must be private; there are as many perceptual spaces as there are percipients. My percept of a table is outside my percept of my head, in my perceptual space; but it does not follow that it is outside my head as a physical object in physical space. Physical space is neutral and public: in this space, all my percepts are in my head, even the most distant star *as I see it*. Physical and perceptual space have relations, but they are not identical, and failure to grasp the difference between them is a potent source of confusion.

To say that you see a star when you see the light that has come from it is no more correct than to say that you see New Zealand when you see a New Zealander in London. Your perception when (as we say) you see a star is causally connected, in the first instance, with what happens in the brain, the optic nerve, and the eye, then with a light-wave which, according to physics, can be traced back to the star as its source. Your sensations will be closely similar if the light comes from a lamp at the top of a mast. The physical space in which you believe the "real" star to be is an elaborate inference; what is given is the private space in which the speck of light you see is situated. It is still an open question whether the space of sight has depth, or is merely a surface, as Berkeley contended. This does not matter for our purposes. Even if we admit that sight alone shows a difference between an object a few inches from the eyes and an object several feet distant, yet you certainly cannot, by sight alone, see that a cloud is less distant than a fixed star, though you may *infer* that it is, because it can hide the star. The world of astronomy, from the point of view of sight, is a surface. If you were put in a dark room with little holes cut in the ceiling in the pattern of the stars letting light come through, there would be nothing in your immediate visual data to show that you were not "seeing the stars". This illustrates what I mean by saying that what you see is *not* "out there" in the sense of physics.

We learn in infancy that we can sometimes touch objects we see, and sometimes not. When we cannot touch them at once, we can sometimes do so by walking to them. That is to say, we learn to correlate sensations of sight with sensations of touch, and sometimes with sensations of movement followed by sensations of touch. In this way we locate our sensations in a three-dimensional world. Those which involve sight alone we think of as "external", but there is no justification for this view. What you see when you see a star is just as internal as what you feel when you feel a headache. That is to say, it is internal from the standpoint of *physical* space. It is distant in your private space, because it is not associated with sensations of touch, and cannot be associated with them by means of any journey you can perform.

Your own body, as known to you through direct experience, is quite different from your own body as considered in physics. You know more about your own body than about any other through direct experience, because your own body can give you a number of sensations that no other body can, for instance all kinds of bodily pains. But you still know it only through sensations; apart from inference, it *is* a bundle of sensations, and therefore quite different, *prima facie*, from what physics calls a body.

Most of the things you see are outside what you see when (as one says) you see your own body. That is to say: you see certain other patches of colour, differently situated in visual space, and say you are seeing things outside your body. But from the point of view of physics, all that you see must count as inside your body; what goes on elsewhere can only be inferred. Thus the whole space of your sensible world with all its percepts counts as one tiny region from the point of view of physics.

There is no direct spatial relation between what one person sees and what another sees, because no two ever see exactly the same object. Each person carries about a private space of his own, which can be located in physical space by indirect methods, but which contains no place in common with another person's private space. This shows how entirely physical space is a matter of inference and construction.

To make the matter definite, let us suppose that a physiologist is observing a living brain – no longer an impossible supposition, as it would have been formerly. It is natural to suppose that what the physiologist sees is in the brain he is observing. But if we are speaking of physical space, what the physiologist sees is in his own brain. It is in no sense in the brain that he is observing, though it is in the percept of that brain, which occupies part of the physiologist's perceptual space. Causal continuity makes the matter perfectly evident: light-waves travel from the brain that is being observed to the eye of the physiologist, at which they only arrive after an interval of time, which is finite though short. The physiologist sees what he is observing only after the light-waves have reached his eye; therefore the event which constitutes his seeing comes at the end of a series of events which travel from the observed brain into the brain of the physiologist. We cannot, without a preposterous kind of discontinuity, suppose that the physiologist's percept, which comes at the end of this series, is anywhere else but in the physiologist's head.

This question is very important, and must be understood if metaphysics is ever to be got straight. The traditional dualism of mind and matter, which I regard as mistaken, is intimately connected with confusions on this point. So long as we adhere to the conventional notions of mind and matter, we are condemned to a view of perception which is miraculous. We suppose that a physical process starts from a visible object, travels to the eye, there changes into another physical process, causes yet another physical process in the optic nerve, finally produces some effect in the brain, simultaneously with which we see the object from which the process started, the seeing being something "mental", totally different in character from the physical processes which precede and accompany it. This view is so queer that metaphysicians have invented all sorts of theories designed to substitute something less incredible. But nobody noticed an elementary confusion.

To return to the physiologist observing another man's brain: what the physiologist sees is by no means identical with what happens in the brain he is observing, but is a somewhat remote effect. From what he sees, therefore, he cannot judge whether what is happening in the brain he is observing is, or is not, the sort of event that he would call "mental". When he says that certain physical events in the brain are accompanied by mental events, he is thinking of physical events as if they were what he sees. He does not see a mental event in the brain he is observing, and therefore supposes there is in that brain a physical process which he can observe and a mental process which he cannot. This is a complete mistake. In the strict sense, he cannot observe anything in the other brain, but only the percepts which he himself has when he is suitably related to that brain (eye to microscope, etc.). We first identify physical processes with our percepts, and then, since our percepts are not other people's thoughts, we argue that the physical processes in their brains are something quite different from their thoughts. In fact, everything that we can directly observe of the physical world happens inside our heads, and consists of "mental" events in at least one sense of the word "mental". It also consists of events which form part of the physical world. The development of this point of view will lead us to the conclusion that the distinction between mind and matter is illusory. The stuff of the world may be called physical or mental or both or neither, as we please; in fact, the words serve no purpose. There is only one definition of the words that is unobjectionable:

"physical" is what is dealt with by physics, and "mental" is what is dealt with by psychology. When, accordingly, I speak of "physical" space, I mean the space that occurs in physics.

It is extraordinarily difficult to divest ourselves of the belief that the physical world is the world we perceive by sight and touch; even if, in our philosophic moments, we are aware that this is an error, we nevertheless fall into it again as soon as we are off our guard. The notion that what we see is "out there" in physical space is one which cannot survive while we are grasping the difference between what physics supposes to be really happening, and what our senses show us as happening; but it is sure to return and plague us when we begin to forget the argument. Only long reflection can make a radically new point of view familiar and easy.

Our illustrations hitherto have been taken from the sense of sight; let us now take one from the sense of touch. Suppose that, with your eyes shut, you let your finger-tip press against a hard table. What is really happening? The physicist says that your finger-tip and the table consist, roughly speaking, of vast numbers of electrons and protons; more correctly, each electron and proton is to be thought of as a collection of processes of radiation, but we can ignore this for our present purposes. Although you think you are touching the table, no electron or proton in your finger ever really touches an electron or proton in the table, because this would develop an infinite force. When you press, repulsions are set up between parts of your finger and parts of the table. If you try to press upon a liquid or a gas, there is room in it for the parts that are repelled to get away. But if you press a hard solid, the electrons and protons that try to get away, because electrical forces from your finger repel them, are unable to do so, because they are crowded close to others which elbow them back to more or less their original position, like people in a dense crowd. Therefore the more you press the more they repel your finger. The repulsion consists of electrical forces, which set up in the nerves a current whose nature is not very definitely known. This current runs into the brain, and there has effects which, so far as the physiologist is concerned, are almost wholly conjectural. But there is one effect which is not conjectural, and that is the sensation of touch. This effect, owing to physiological inference or perhaps to a reflex, is associated by us with the finger-tip. But the sensation is the same if, by artificial means, the parts of the nerve nearer the brain are suitably stimulated – *e.g.* if your hand has been amputated and the right nerves are skilfully manipulated. Thus our confidence that touch affords evidence of the existence of bodies at the place which we think is being touched is quite misplaced. As a rule we are right, but we can be wrong; there is nothing of the nature of an infallible revelation about the matter. And even in the most favorable case, the perception of touch is something very different from the mad dance of electrons and protons trying to jazz out of each other's way, which is what physics maintains is really taking place at your finger-tip. Or, at least, it *seems* very different. But as we shall see, the knowledge we derive from physics is so abstract that we are not warranted in saying that what goes on in the physical world is, or is not, intrinsically very different from the events that we know through our own experiences.

Perception and Physical Causal Laws

In an earlier chapter we saw the inadequacy of the traditional notion of cause, without adequately explaining the causal laws which are a substitute in the practice of science. The time has now come when it is possible to remedy this defect, and, in so doing, to fit perception into its place in the chain of physical causation and recapitulate the main points of previous arguments.

The old view was that an event A will always be followed by a certain event B, and that the problem of discovering causal laws is the problem, given an event B, of finding that event A which is its invariable antecedent or *vice versa*. At an early stage of a science this point of view is useful; it gives laws which are true usually, though probably not always, and it affords the basis for more exact laws. But it has no philosophical validity, and is superseded in science as soon as we arrive at genuine laws. Genuine laws, in advanced sciences, are practically always quantitative laws of *tendency*. I will try to illustrate by taking the simplest possible case in physics.

Imagine a hydrogen atom, in which the electron is revolving not in the minimum orbit, but in the next, which has four times the minimum radius. So long as this state continues, the atom has no external effects, apart from its infinitesimal gravitational action; we cannot, therefore, obtain any evidence of its existence except when it changes its state. In fact, our knowledge of atoms is like that which a ticket collector has of the population of his town: he knows nothing of those who stay quietly at home. Now at some moment, according to laws of which we have only statistical knowledge, the electron in our atom jumps to a smaller orbit, and the energy lost to the atom travels outward in a light-wave. We know no causal law as to when the electron will jump, though we know how far it will jump and exactly what will happen in the neighbourhood when it does. At least, when I say we know exactly what will happen, I ought to say that we know exactly the mathematical laws of what will happen. A series of events, having quantitative characteristics which obey certain equations, will travel outward in all directions from the electron, and will proceed quite regularly, like ripples on a pool, until other matter is encountered. We have here one important and apparently fundamental kind of causal law, the kind regulating the propagation of light *in vacuo*. This is summed up in Maxwell's equations, which enable us to calculate the diffusion of an electro-magnetic disturbance starting from a source. So long as two such disturbances do not meet, the matter is exceedingly simple; but the equations also tell us what happens when they do meet. We then have, as always in traditional physics, two separate tendencies, which have a resultant compounded according to mathematical laws, of which the parallelogram law is the oldest and simplest. That is to say, each previous circumstance in the space-time neighbourhood contributes a tendency, and the resulting event is obtained by compounding these tendencies according to a mathematical law.

So far, we have been considering only electro-magnetic phenomena in empty space. We have another set of facts about empty space, namely those upon which gravitation depends. These have to do with the structure of space-time, and show that this structure has singularities in the regions where there is matter, which spread with diminishing intensity as we get away from these regions. You may conceive the structure of space-time on the analogy of a pond with a fountain playing in it, so that wherever a spray falls from the fountain there is a little hill of water which flattens quickly as you get away from the spot where the spray falls. Here again the same sort of thing applies: to infer the structure in a small region of space-time from that in the neighbourhood, it will be necessary to superpose a number of tendencies according to mathematical rules. Thus philosophically this introduces no novelty.

But now consider what happens when the wave of light which started from our hydrogen atom comes in contact with matter. Various things may happen. The matter may absorb all or some of the energy of the light-ray; this is the interesting case from our point of view. The absorption may take the form of causing the electrons to move in larger orbits, in which case, later, when they return to their previous orbits, we get the phenomenon of fluorescence. Or the body may become heated; or it may visibly move, like a radiometer. The effects upon bodies depend upon the bodies as well as the light. Some of them can be individually predicted, others can only be calculated in statistical averages; this depends upon whether quantum considerations come in or not. Where they do, we can enumerate possibilities, and state the relative frequencies with which they will be realised, but we cannot tell which will be realised in any given case.

So far, we have considered the radiation of energy from matter into empty space, its propagation in empty space and its impact on matter from empty space. We have not considered the history of a given piece of matter, or the distinction between matter and empty space.

The essence of matter appears to be this: We can distinguish series of events in space-time which have a certain kind of close resemblance to each other, such that common sense regards them as manifestations of one "thing". But when we look closely at the question, it turns out that what physics offers is something more abstract than this. Take, *e.g.* the continued existence of a certain electron. This means to say that events in a certain neighbourhood will be such as can be calculated on the assumption that there is an electric charge of a certain standard magnitude in the middle of that neighbourhood; and that the neighbourhoods of which this is true form a tube in space-time.

So long as we stick to the standpoint of pure physics there is a certain air of taking in each other's washing about the whole business. Events in empty space are only known as regards their abstract mathematical characteristics; matter is only an abstract mathematical characteristic of events in empty space. This seems rather a cold world. But as a matter of fact we know some things that are a little more concrete. We know, *e.g.* what it feels like when we see things. From the point of view of physics, when our light-wave starts out through empty space, if it presently reaches our eye we know one link in the causal chain, namely the visual sensation, otherwise than as a term in an abstract mathematical formula. And it is this one term which forms the basis for our belief in all the rest. Seeing is believing.

At this point I propose to make a brief digression on the subject of our evidence for causal laws. The laws for which we first get evidence are such as do not hold always, but only as a general rule. As a rule, when you decide to move your arm, it moves: but sometimes it is paralysed and remains motionless. As a rule, when you say how-do-you-do to an old friend, he says the same to you; but he may have grown blind and deaf since you last saw him, and not notice your words or gesture. As a rule, if you put a match to gunpowder, it explodes; but it may have got damp. It is such common but not invariable rules of sequence that we notice first. But science is always seeking to replace them by laws that may have no exceptions. We notice first that heavy bodies fall, then that some bodies do not fall. Then we generalise both sets of facts into the law of gravitation and the laws of resistance of the air. These more general laws do not state that anything will actually happen: they state a tendency, and lead to the conclusion that what actually happens is the resultant of a number of tendencies. We cannot know what the resultant will be unless we know a great deal about the neighbourhood concerned. For example, I might, within the next few seconds be hit on the head by a meteorite; to know whether this is going to happen, I must know what matter is to be found in the neighbourhood of the earth. This illustrates that actual predictions based upon laws which are perfectly valid may always be falsified by some unknown fact of what we may call geography. Moreover, we can never be *sure* that our scientific laws are quite right; of this the Einsteinian modification of the law of gravitation has afforded a notable instance.

Let us now return to the relation between perception and the causal laws of physics.

Having realised the abstractness of what physics has to say, we no longer have any difficulty in fitting the visual sensation into the causal series. It used to be thought "mysterious" that purely physical phenomena should end in something mental. That was because people thought they knew a lot about physical phenomena, and were sure they differed in quality from mental phenomena. We now realise that we know nothing of the intrinsic quality of physical phenomena except when they happen to be sensations, and that therefore there is no reason to be surprised that some are sensations, or to suppose that the others are totally unlike sensations. The gap between mind and matter has been filled in, partly by new views of mind, but much more by the realisation that physics tells us nothing as to the intrinsic character of matter.

I conceive what happens when we see an object more or less on the following lines. For the sake of simplicity, let us take a small self-luminous object. In this object, a certain number of atoms are losing energy and radiating it according to the quantum principle. The resulting light-waves become superposed according to the usual mathematical principles; each part of each light-wave consists of events in a certain region of space-time. On coming in contact with the human body, the energy in the light-wave takes new forms, but there is still causal continuity. At last it reaches the brain, and there one of its constituent events is what we call a visual sensation. This visual sensation is popularly called seeing the object from which the light-waves started – or from which they were reflected if the object was not self-luminous.

Thus what is called a perception is only connected with its object through the laws of physics. Its relation to the object is causal and mathematical; we cannot say whether or not it resembles the object in any intrinsic respect, except that both it and the object are brief events in space-time.

I think we may lay down the following universal characteristics of causal laws in an advanced science. Given any event, there are other events at neighbouring places in space-time which will occur slightly later if no other factors intervene; but in practice other factors almost always do intervene, and, in that case, the event which actually occurs at any point of space-time is a mathematical resultant of those which would have followed the various neighbouring events if they had been alone concerned. The equations of physics give the rules according to which events are connected, but all are of the above sort.

Formerly it was thought that the equations of physics sufficed, theoretically, to determine the course of affairs in the physical world, given all the facts about some finite stretch of time, however short. Now it appears that this is not the case, so far as the known equations are concerned. The known equations suffice to determine what happens in empty space, and statistical averages as to what happens to matter; but they do not tell us when an individual atom will absorb or radiate energy. Whether there are laws, other than those of statistics, governing the behaviour of an individual atom in this respect, we do not know.

It should be observed that there are causal laws of a different sort from those of pure physics; such are the laws that light-waves "cause" visual sensations and sound-waves "cause" auditory sensations. All the empirical evidence for physics rests upon such laws, therefore nothing in physics can have a higher degree of certainty than such laws have. Let us stop a moment to ask what we mean by "cause" in this connection.

The connection of light-waves and visual sensations looks a little different according as we start with physics or with psychology, though, of course, ultimately the result must be the same. Let us first start with physics. I say, then, that when a light-wave travels outwards from a body there are successive events at successive places, and that the corresponding event in a brain behind a normal eye is a visual sensation. This is the only event in the whole series about which I can say anything not purely abstract and mathematical.

Now let us start from the sensation. I say, then, that this sensation is one of a vast series of connected events, travelling out from a centre according to certain mathematical laws, in virtue of which the sensation enables me to know a good deal about events elsewhere. That is why the sensation is a source of physical knowledge.

It will be seen that, according to the view I have been advocating, there is no difficulty about interaction between mind and body. A sensation is merely one link in a chain of physical causation; when we regard the sensation as the end of such a chain, we have what would be regarded as an effect of matter on mind; when as the beginning, an effect of mind on matter. But mind is merely a cross-section in a stream of physical causation, and there is nothing odd about its being both an effect and a cause in the physical world. Thus physical causal laws are those that are fundamental.

B Is it Possible for Us to Act Freely?

Introduction

Questions about freedom and determinism are not difficult to motivate, and little need be said by way of introduction to these readings. Ch. 43 contains Baron d'Holbach's infamous avowal of "hard determinism": the world is a deterministic system, and so we never act freely. In contrast, Hobart (Dickinson S. Miller under a pseudonym) defends "compatibilism" – the thesis that free will is compatible with determinism. John Wisdom's chapter culminates in a little known argument from compatibilism and determinism to the *preexistence of the soul*! Chisholm defends "incompatibilism," the denial of compatibilism. He claims that, when we act freely, we must be able to cause certain things to happen – and not just by virtue of our having mental states (beliefs and desires) that cause our behavior in an appropriate way, but which may themselves have been caused deterministically. Chisholm gives the name "immanent causation" to the causal relation supposed to hold between an agent and the events she causes but that aren't caused by any other events. (Note that Chisholm's distinction between "immanent" and "transeunt" causation is quite different from the distinction Susan Stebbing makes using these terms in Ch. 33. Stebbing's use corresponds much more closely to that of the medieval philosophers who introduced the terms.) Van Inwagen, in an essay written especially for this edition, sets forth "the Consequence Argument" for incompatibilism. In "The Mystery of Metaphysical Freedom," van Inwagen emphasizes the difficulties in supposing that freedom is compatible with either determinism or *in*determinism. He denies that Chisholm's appeal to a special sort of causal relation between agent and event can overcome this difficulty. O'Connor's paper includes a response to van Inwagen's criticism of Chisholm.

The first of the two essays by Harry Frankfurt attacks the idea that freedom requires the ability to do otherwise, which was crucial to the arguments of Holbach, Chisholm, and van Inwagen. "Freedom of the Will and the Concept of a Person" contains Frankfurt's famous defense of a theory of freedom consistent with determinism, according to which to act freely is to act in accord with "higher order desires."

There is an obvious similarity between the "immanent" or "agent" causation posited by Chisholm and O'Connor, and Reid's notion of "Active Power" (see Ch. 31). In Ch. 16, A. N. Prior affirms a connection between freedom of action and theories of time. In Ch. 23, David Lewis offers an analysis of "could have done otherwise" that is compatible with determinism.

Suggestions for further reading

Aune, Bruce, *Metaphysics: The Elements* (Minneapolis: University of Minnesota, 1985) ch. 9 ("Metaphysical Freedom").

Borges, Jorge Luis, "The Garden of Forking Paths," included in *Labyrinths, Selected Stories and Other Writings* (New York: New Directions, 1964).

Carter, William R., *The Elements of Metaphysics* (Philadelphia, Penn.: Temple University Press, 1990) chs. 9 and 10 ("Causal Determinism" and "Fate").

Gardner, Martin, *The Whys of a Philosophical Scrivener* (New York: St. Martin's, 1999) ch. 6 ("Free Will: Why I Am Not a Determinist or Haphazardist").

Hasker, William, *Metaphysics: Constructing a World View* (Downers Grove, Ill., and Leicester, UK: InterVarsity press, 1983) ch. 2 ("Freedom and Necessity").

Jubien, Michael, *Contemporary Metaphysics* (Oxford: Blackwell, 1997) ch. 7 ("Determinism, Freedom, and Fatalism").

Kane, Robert, "Incompatibilism," in Sider, Hawthorne, and Zimmerman (eds.), *Contemporary Debates in Metaphysics* (Malden, Mass.: Blackwell, 2007).

Post, John F., *Metaphysics: A Contemporary Introduction* (New York: Paragon House, 1991) ch. 1 ("Is Metaphysics Possible?").

Smith, Quentin, and Oaklander, L. Nathan, *Time, Change and Freedom: an Introduction to Metaphysics* (London: Routledge, 1995) Dialogues 9, 10, and 11 ("Fatalism and Tenseless Time," "God, Time and Freedom," and "Freedom, Determinism and Responsibility").

Taylor, Richard, *Metaphysics* (Englewood Cliffs, N.J.: Prentice-Hall, 1992) chs. 5 and 6 ("Freedom and Determinism" and "Fate").

van Inwagen, Peter, *Metaphysics*, 2nd edn (Cambridge, Mass.: Westview Press, 2002) ch. 12 ("The Powers of Rational Beings: Freedom of the Will").

Vihvelin, Kadri, "Compatibilism, Incompatibilism, and Impossibilism," in Sider, Hawthorne, and Zimmerman (eds.), *Contemporary Debates in Metaphysics* (Malden, Mass.: Blackwell, 2007).

Watson, Gary (ed.), *Free Will* (Oxford: Oxford University Press, 1982).

43   We Are Never Free: an Excerpt from *The System of Nature*

Paul-Henri Dietrich, Baron d'Holbach

Those who have pretended that the *soul* is distinguished from the body, is immaterial, draws its ideas from its own peculiar source, acts by its own energies, without the aid of any exterior object, have, by a consequence of their own system, enfranchised it from those physical laws according to which all beings of which we have a knowledge are obliged to act. They have believed that the soul is mistress of its own conduct, is able to regulate its own peculiar operations, has the faculty to determine its will by its own natural energy; in a word, they have pretended that man is *a free agent*.

It has been already sufficiently proved that the soul is nothing more than the body considered relatively to some of its functions more concealed than others: it has been shown that this soul, even when it shall be supposed immaterial, is continually modified conjointly with the body, is submitted to all its motion, and that without this it would remain inert and dead: that, consequently, it is subjected to the influence of those material and physical causes which give impulse to the body; of which the mode of existence, whether habitual or transitory, depends upon the material elements by which it is surrounded, that form its texture, constitute its temperament, enter into it by means of the elements, and penetrate it by their subtility. The faculties which are called *intellectual*, and those qualities which are styled *moral*, have been explained in a manner purely physical and natural. In the last place it has been demonstrated that all the ideas, all the systems, all the affections, all the opinions, whether true or false, which man forms to himself, are to be attributed to his physical and material senses. Thus man is a being purely physical; in whatever manner he is considered, he is connected to universal nature, and submitted to the necessary and immutable laws that she imposes on all the beings she contains, according to their peculiar essences or to the respective properties with which, without consulting them, she endows each particular species. Man's life is a line that nature commands him to describe upon the surface of the earth, without his ever being able to swerve from it, even for an instant. He is born without his own consent; his organization does in nowise depend upon himself; his ideas come to him involuntarily; his habits are in the power of those who cause him to contract them; he is unceasingly modified by causes, whether visible or concealed, over which he has no control, which necessarily regulate his mode of existence, give the hue to his way of thinking, and determine his manner of acting. He is good or bad, happy or miserable, wise or foolish, reasonable or irrational, without his will being for any thing in these various states. Nevertheless, in despite of the shackles by which he is bound, it is pretended he is a free agent, or that independent of the causes by which he is moved, he determines his own will, and regulates his own condition. However slender the foundation of this opinion, of which every thing ought to point out to him the error, it is current at this day and passes for an incontestable truth with a great number of people, otherwise extremely enlightened; it is the basis of religion, which, supposing relations between man and the unknown being she has placed above nature, has been incapable of imagining how man could either merit reward or deserve punishment from this being, if he was not a free agent. Society has been believed interested in this system; because an idea has gone abroad, that if all the actions of man were to be contemplated as necessary, the right of punishing those who injure their associates would no longer exist. At length human vanity accommodated itself to a hypothesis which, unquestionably, appears to distinguish man from all other physical beings, by assigning to him the special privilege of a total independence of all other causes, but of which a very little reflection would have shown him the impossibility.

. . .

The will, as we have elsewhere said, is a modification of the brain, by which it is disposed to action, or prepared to give play to the organs. This will is necessarily determined by the qualities, good or bad, agreeable or painful, of the object or the motive that acts upon his senses, or of which the idea remains with him, and is resuscitated by his memory. In consequence, he acts necessarily, his action is the result of the impulse he receives either from the motive, from the object, or from the idea which has modified his brain, or disposed his will. When he does not act according to this impulse, it is because there comes some new cause, some new motive, some new idea, which modifies his brain in a different manner, gives him a new impulse, determines his will in another way, by which the action of the former impulse is suspended: thus, the sight of an agreeable object, or its idea, determines his will to set him in action to procure it; but if a new object or a new idea more powerfully attracts him, it gives a new direction to his will, annihilates the effect of the former, and prevents the action by which it was to be procured. This is the mode in which reflection, experience, reason, necessarily arrests or suspends the action of man's will: without this he would of necessity have followed the anterior impulse which carried him towards a then desirable object. In all this he always acts according to necessary laws, from which he has no means of emancipating himself.

If when tormented with violent thirst, he figures to himself an idea, or really perceives a fountain, whose limpid streams might cool his feverish want, is he sufficient master of himself to desire or not to desire the object competent to satisfy so lively a want? It will no doubt be conceded, that it is impossible he should not be desirous to satisfy it; but it will be said – if at this moment it is announced to him that the water he so ardently desires is poisoned, he will, notwithstanding his vehement thirst, abstain from drinking it: and it has, therefore, been falsely concluded that he is a free agent. The fact, however, is, that the motive in either case is exactly the same: his own conservation. The same necessity that determined him to drink before he knew the water was deleterious, upon this new discovery equally determines him not to drink; the desire of conserving himself either annihilates or suspends the former impulse; the second motive becomes stronger than the preceding, that is, the fear of death, or the desire of preserving himself, necessarily prevails over the painful sensation caused by his eagerness to drink: but, it will be said, if the thirst is very parching, an inconsiderate man without regarding the danger will risk swallowing the water. Nothing is gained by this remark: in this case, the anterior impulse only regains the ascendancy; he is persuaded that life may possibly be longer preserved, or that he shall derive a greater good by drinking the poisoned water than by enduring the torment, which, to his mind, threatens instant dissolution: thus the first becomes the strongest and necessarily urges him on to action. Nevertheless, in either case, whether he partakes of the water, or whether he does not, the two actions will be equally necessary; they will be the effect of that motive which finds itself most puissant; which consequently acts in the most coercive manner upon his will. This example will serve to explain the whole phenomena of the human will. This will, or rather the brain, finds itself in the same situation as a bowl [i.e., a ball], which, although it has received an impulse that drives it forward in a straight line, is deranged in its course whenever a force superior to the first obliges it to change its direction. . . .

Choice by no means proves the free agency of man: he only deliberates when he does not yet know which to choose of the many objects that move him, he is then in an embarrassment, which does not terminate until his will is decided by the greater advantage he believes he shall find in the object he chooses, or the action he undertakes. From whence it may be seen, that choice is necessary, because he would not determine for an object, or for an action, if he did not believe that he should find in it some direct advantage. That man should have free agency it were needful that he should be able to will or choose without motive, or that he could prevent motives coercing his will. Action always being the effect of his will once determined, and as his will cannot be determined but by a motive which is not in his own power, it follows that he is never the master of the determination of his own peculiar will; that consequently he never acts as a free agent. It has been believed that man was a free agent because he had a will with the power of choosing; but attention has not been paid to the fact that even his will is moved by causes independent of himself; is owing to that which is inherent in his own organization, or which belongs to the nature of the beings acting on him. . . .

The errors of philosophers on the free agency of man, have arisen from their regarding his will as the *primum mobile*, the original motive of his actions; for want of recurring back, they have not perceived the multiplied, the complicated causes which, independently of him, give motion to the will itself; or which dispose and modify his brain, whilst he himself is purely passive in the motion he receives. Is he the master of desiring or not desiring an object that appears desirable to him? Without doubt it will be answered, no: but he is the master of resisting his desire, if he reflects on the consequences. But, I ask, is he capable of reflecting on these consequences, when his soul is hurried along by a very lively passion, which entirely depends upon his natural organization, and the causes by which he is modified? Is it in his power to add to these consequences all the weight necessary to counterbalance his desire? Is he the master of preventing the qualities which render an object desirable from residing in it? I shall be told: he ought to have learned to resist his passions; to contract a habit of putting a curb on his desires. I agree to it without any difficulty. But in reply, I again ask, is his nature susceptible of this modification? Does his boiling blood, his unruly imagination, the igneous fluid that circulates in his veins, permit him to make, enable him to apply true experience in the moment when it is wanted? And even when his temperament has capacitated him, has his education, the examples set before him, the ideas with which he has been inspired in early life, been suitable to make him contract this habit of repressing his desires? Have not all these things rather contributed to induce him to seek with avidity, to make him actually desire those objects which you say he ought to resist?
. . .

In despite of these proofs of the want of free agency in man, so clear to unprejudiced minds, it will, perhaps, be insisted upon with no small feeling of triumph, that if it be proposed to any one, to move or not to move his hand, an action in the number of those called *indifferent*, he evidently appears to be the master of choosing; from which it is concluded that evidence has been offered of his free agency. The reply is, this example is perfectly simple; man in performing some action which he is resolved on doing, does not by any means prove his free agency: the very desire of displaying this quality, excited by the dispute, becomes a necessary motive, which decides his will either for the one or the other of these actions: what deludes him in this instance, or that which persuades him he is a free agent at this moment, is, that he does not discern the true motive which sets him in action, namely, the desire of convincing his opponent: if in the heat of the dispute he insists and asks, "Am I not the master of throwing myself out of the window?" I shall answer him, no; that whilst he preserves his reason there is no probability that the desire of proving his free agency, will become a motive sufficiently powerful to make him sacrifice his life to the attempt: if, not-withstanding this, to prove he is a free agent, he should actually precipitate himself from the window, it would not be a sufficient warranty to conclude he acted freely, but rather that it was the violence of his temperament which spurred him on to this folly. Madness is a state, that depends upon the heat of the blood, not upon the will. A fanatic or a hero, braves death as necessarily as a more phlegmatic man or a coward flies from it.

It *is* said that free agency is the absence of those obstacles competent to oppose themselves to the actions of *man*, or to the exercise of his faculties: it is pretended that he is a free agent whenever, making use of these faculties, he produces the effect he has proposed to himself. In reply to this reasoning, it is sufficient to consider that it in nowise depends upon himself to place or remove the obstacles that either determine or resist him; the motive that causes his action is no more in his own power than the obstacle that impedes him, whether this obstacle or motive be within his own machine or exterior of his person: he is not master of the thought presented to his mind, which determines his will; this thought is excited by some cause independent of himself. To be undeceived on the system of his free agency, man has simply to recur to the motive by which his will is determined; he will always find this motive is out of his own controul. It is said: that in consequence of an idea to which the mind gives birth, man acts freely if he encounters no obstacle. But the question is, what gives birth to this idea in his brain? Was he the master either to prevent it from presenting itself, or from renewing itself in his brain? Does not this idea depend either upon objects that strike him exteriorly and in despite of himself, or upon causes, that without his knowledge, act within himself and modify his brain? Can he prevent his eyes, cast without design upon any object whatever, from giving him an idea of this object, and from moving his brain? He is not more master of the obstacles; they are the necessary effects of either interior or exterior causes, which always act according to their given properties. . . .

The partisans of the system of free agency appear ever to have confounded constraint with necessity. Man believes he acts as a free agent, every time he does not see any thing that places obstacles to his actions; he does not perceive that the motive which causes him to will, is always necessary and independent of himself. A prisoner loaded with chains is compelled to remain in prison; but he is not a free agent in the desire to emancipate himself; his chains prevent him from acting, but they do not prevent him from willing; he would save himself if they would loose his fetters; but he would not save himself as a free agent; fear or the idea of punishment would be sufficient motives for his action.

Man may, therefore, cease to be restrained, without, for that reason, becoming a free agent: in whatever manner he acts, he will act necessarily, according to motives by which he shall be determined. He may be compared to a heavy body that finds itself arrested in its descent by any obstacle whatever: take away this obstacle, it will gravitate or continue to fall; but who shall say this dense body is free to fall or not? Is not its descent the necessary effect of its own specific gravity? The virtuous Socrates submitted to the laws of his country, although they were unjust; and though the doors of his jail were left open to him, he would not save himself; but in this he did not act as a free agent: the invisible chains of opinion, the secret love of decorum, the inward respect for the laws, even when they were iniquitous, the fear of tarnishing his glory, kept him in his prison; they were motives sufficiently powerful with this enthusiast for virtue, to induce him to wait death with tranquility; it was not in his power to save himself, because he could find no potential motive to bring him to depart, even for an instant, from those principles to which his mind was accustomed.

Man, it is said, frequently acts against his inclination, from whence it is falsely concluded he is a free agent; but when he appears to act contrary to his inclination, he is always determined to it by some motive sufficiently efficacious to vanquish this inclination. . . .

When it is said, that man is not a free agent, it is not pretended to compare him to a body moved by a simple impulsive cause: he contains within himself causes inherent to his existence; he is moved by an interior organ, which has its own peculiar laws, and is itself necessarily determined in consequence of ideas formed from perceptions resulting from sensations which it receives from exterior objects. As the mechanism of these sensations, of these perceptions, and the manner they engrave ideas on the brain of man, are not known to him; because he is unable to unravel all these motions; because he cannot perceive the chain of operations in his soul, or the motive principle that acts within him, he supposes himself a free agent; which, literally translated, signifies, that he moves himself by himself; that he determines himself without cause: when he rather ought to say, that he is ignorant how or for why he acts in the manner he does. . . .

It is, then, for want of recurring to the causes that move him; for want of being able to analyze, from not being competent to decompose the complicated motion of his machine, that man believes himself a free agent: it is only upon his own ignorance that he founds the profound yet deceitful notion he has of his free agency; that he builds those opinions which he brings forward as a striking proof of his pretended freedom of action. . . .

From all that has been advanced in this chapter, it results, that in no one moment of his existence is man a free agent. He is not the architect of his own conformation, which he holds from nature; he has no controul over his own ideas, or over the modification of his brain; these are due to causes, that, in despite of him, and without his own knowledge, unceasingly act upon him; he is not the master of not loving or coveting that which he finds amiable or desirable; he is not capable of refusing to deliberate, when he is uncertain of the effects certain objects will produce upon him; he cannot avoid choosing that which he believes will be most advantageous to him; in the moment when his will is determined by his choice he is not competent to act otherwise than he does. In what instance, then, is he the master of his own actions? In what moment is he a free agent?

That which a man is about to do, is always a consequence of that which he has been – of that which he is – of that which he has done up to the moment of the action: his total and actual existence, considered under all its possible circumstances, contains the sum of all the motives to the action he is about to commit; this is a principle the truth of which no thinking being will be able to refuse accrediting: his life is a series of necessary moments; his conduct, whether good or bad, virtuous or vicious, useful or prejudicial, either to himself or to others, is a concatenation of action, as necessary as all the moments of his existence. . . .

If he understood the play of his organs, if he was able to recall to himself all the impulsions they have received, all the modifications they have undergone, all the effects they have produced, he would perceive that all his actions are submitted to that *fatality*, which regulates his own particular system, as it does the entire system of the universe: no one effect in him, any more than in nature, produces itself by *chance*; this, as has been before proved, is a word void of sense. All that passes in him; all that is done by him; as well as all that happens in nature, or that is attributed to her, is derived from necessary causes, which act according to necessary laws, and which produce necessary effects from whence necessarily flow others. *Fatality*, is the eternal, the immutable, the necessary order, established in nature; or the indispensable connexion of causes that act, with the effects they operate. Conforming to this order, heavy bodies fall; light bodies rise; that which is analogous in matter reciprocally attracts; that which is heterogeneous mutually repels; man congregates himself in society, modifies each his fellow; becomes either virtuous or wicked; either contributes to his mutual happiness, or reciprocates his misery; either loves his neighbour, or hates his companion necessarily, according to the manner in which the one acts upon the other. From whence it may be seen, that the same necessity which regulates the physical, also regulates the moral world, in which every thing is in consequence submitted to fatality. Man, in running over, frequently without his own knowledge, often in despite of himself, the route which nature has marked out for him, resembles a swimmer who is obliged to follow the current that carries him along: he believes himself a free agent, because he sometimes consents, sometimes does not consent, to glide with the stream, which, notwithstanding, always hurries him forward; he believes himself the master of his condition, because he is obliged to use his arms under the fear of sinking.

> *Volentem ducunt fata, nolentem trahunt.*[1]
> Seneca

The false ideas he has formed to himself upon free agency, are in general thus founded: there are certain events which he judges *necessary*; either because he sees that they are effects constantly and invariably linked to certain causes, which nothing seems to prevent; or because he believes he has discovered the chain of causes and effects that is put in play to produce those events: whilst he contemplates as *contingent* other events of whose causes he is ignorant, and with whose mode of acting he is unacquainted: but in nature, where every thing is connected by one common bond, there exists no effect without a cause. In the moral as well as in the physical world, every thing that happens is a necessary consequence of causes, either visible or concealed, which are of necessity obliged to act after their peculiar essences. *In man, free agency is nothing more than necessity contained within himself.*

Note

1   [Editors: "The Fates guide the willing; the unwilling, they drag."]

44   Free Will as Involving Determination and Inconceivable without It

R. E. Hobart

The thesis of this article is that there has never been any ground for the controversy between the doctrine of free will and determinism, that it is based upon a misapprehension, that the two assertions are entirely consistent, that one of them strictly implies the other, that they have been opposed only because of our natural want of the analytical imagination. In so saying I do not tamper with the meaning of either phrase. That would be unpardonable. I mean free will in the natural and usual sense, in the fullest, the most absolute sense in which for the purposes of the personal and moral life the term is ever employed. I mean it as implying responsibility, merit and demerit, guilt and desert. I mean it as implying, after an act has been performed, that one 'could have done otherwise' than one did, I mean it as conveying these things also, not in any subtly modified sense but in exactly the sense in which we conceive them in life and in law and in ethics. These two doctrines have been opposed because we have not realised that free will can be analysed without being destroyed, and that determinism is merely a feature of the analysis of it. And if we are tempted to take refuge in the thought of an 'ultimate', an 'innermost' liberty that eludes the analysis, then we have implied a deterministic basis and constitution for this liberty as well. For such a basis and constitution lie in the idea of liberty. . . .

I am not maintaining that determinism is true; only that it is true in so far as we have free will. That we are free in willing is, broadly speaking, a fact of experience. That broad fact is more assured than any philosophical analysis. It is therefore surer than the deterministic analysis of it, entirely adequate as that in the end appears to be. But it is not here affirmed that there are no small exceptions, no slight undetermined swervings, no ingredient of absolute chance. All that is here said is that such absence of determination, if and so far as it exists, is no gain to freedom, but sheer loss of it; no advantage to the moral life, but blank subtraction from it. – When I speak below of 'the indeterminist' I mean the libertarian indeterminist, that is, him who believes in free will and holds that it involves indetermination.

By the analytical imagination is meant, of course, the power we have, not by nature but by training, of realising that the component parts of a thing or process, taken together, each in its place, with their relations, are identical with the thing or process itself. If it is 'more than its parts', then this 'more' will appear in the analysis. It is not true, of course, that all facts are susceptible of analysis, but so far as they are, there is occasion for the analytical imagination. We have been accustomed to think of a thing or a person as a whole, not as a combination of parts. We have been accustomed to think of its activities as the way in which, as a whole, it naturally and obviously behaves. It is a new, an unfamiliar and an awkward act on the mind's part to consider it, not as one thing acting in its natural manner, but as a system of parts that work together in a complicated process. Analysis often seems at first to have taken away the individuality of the thing, its unity, the impression of the familiar identity. For a simple mind this is strikingly true of the analysis of a complicated machine. The reader may recall Paulsen's ever significant story about the introduction of a railway into Germany. When it reached the village of a certain enlightened pastor, he took his people to where a locomotive engine was standing, and in the clearest words explained of what parts it consisted and how it worked. He was much pleased by their eager nods of intelligence as he proceeded. But on his finishing they said: 'Yes, yes, Herr Pastor, but there's a horse inside, isn't there?' They could not *realise* the analysis. They were wanting in the analytical imagination. Why not? They had never been trained to it. It is in the first instance a great effort to think of all the parts working together to produce the simple result that the engine glides down the track. It is easy to think of a horse inside doing all the work. A horse is a familiar totality that does familiar things. They could no better have grasped the physiological analysis of a horse's movements had it been set forth to them.

The reason for thinking that there is no occasion for the controversy lies exclusively in the analysis of the terms employed in it. But the several analyses must all be taken together, realised jointly, before the position can be fully understood.

Self and Character

We are not concerned with the total nature of the self, but only with the aspect of it strictly involved in our question . . . It is the concrete, active self, existing through time and differing from others. The whole stress of morality arises because moral selves are not alike, because there is need of influencing some moral selves to make them refrain from certain acts or neglects, that is, in order to make them better moral selves. How do we express the difference? We call it a difference of moral qualities, traits, or character. We are having regard to the question what acts will come from these selves. By character we mean, do we not? the sum of a man's tendencies to action, considered in their relative strength; or that sum in so far as it bears upon morals.

Now the position of the indeterminist is that a free act of will is the act of the self. The self becomes through it the author of the physical act that ensues. This volition of the self causes the physical act but it is not in its turn caused, it is 'spontaneous'. To regard it as caused would be determinism. The causing self to which the indeterminist here refers is to be conceived as distinct from character; distinct from temperament, wishes, habits, impulses. He emphasises two things equally: the physical act springs from the self through its volition, and it does not spring merely from character, it is not simply the result of character and circumstances. If we ask, 'Was there anything that induced the self thus to act?' we are answered in effect, 'Not definitively. The self feels motives but its act is not determined by them. It can choose between them.'

The next thing to notice is that this position of the indeterminist is taken in defence of moral conceptions. There would be no fitness, he says, in our reproaching ourselves, in our feeling remorse, in our holding ourselves or anyone guilty, if the act in question were not the act of the self instead of a product of the machinery of motives.

We have here one of the most remarkable and instructive examples of something in which the history of philosophy abounds – of a persistent, an age-long deadlock due solely to the indisposition of the human mind to look closely into the meaning of its terms.

How do we reproach ourselves? We say to ourselves, 'How negligent of me!' 'How thoughtless!' 'How selfish!' 'How hasty and unrestrained!' 'That I should have been capable even for a moment of taking such a petty, irritated view!' etc. In other words, we are attributing to ourselves at the time of the act, in some respect and measure, a bad character, and regretting it. And that is the entire point of our self-reproach. . . . All the most intimate terms of the moral life imply that the act has proceeded from *me*, the distinctive me, from the manner of man I am or was. And this is the very thing on which the libertarian lays stress. What the indeterminist prizes with all his heart, what he stoutly affirms and insists upon, is precisely what he denies, namely, that I, the concrete and specific moral being, am the author, the source of my acts. For, of course, that is determinism. To say that they come from the self is to say that they are determined by the self – the moral self, the self with a moral quality. He gives our preferrings the bad name of the machinery of motives, but they are just what we feel in ourselves when we decide. When he maintains that the self at the moment of decision may act to some extent independently of motives, *and is good or bad according as it acts in this direction or that*, he is simply setting up one character within another, he is separating the self from what he understands by the person's character as at first mentioned, only thereupon to attribute to it a character of its own, *in that he judges it good or bad*. . . .

If in conceiving the self you detach it from all motives or tendencies, what you have is not a morally admirable or condemnable, not a morally characterisable self at all. Hence it is not subject to reproach. You cannot call a self good because of its courageous free action, and then deny that its action was determined by its character. In calling it good because of that action you have implied that the action came from its goodness (which means its good character) and was a sign thereof. By their fruits ye shall know them. The indeterminist appears to imagine that he can distinguish the moral 'I' from all its propensities, regard its act as arising in the moment undetermined by them, and yet can then (for the first time, in his opinion, with propriety!) ascribe to this 'I' an admirable quality. At the very root of his doctrine he contradicts himself. . . .

We are told, however, that it is under determinism that we should have no right any more to praise or to blame. At least we could not do so in the old sense of the terms. We might throw words of praise to a man, or throw words of blame at him, because we know from observation that they will affect his action; but the old light of meaning in the terms has gone out. Well, all we have to do is to keep asking what this old meaning was. We praise a man by saying that he is a good friend, or a hard worker, or a competent man of business, or a trusty assistant, or a judicious minister, or a gifted poet, or one of the noblest of men – one of the noblest of characters! In other words, he is a being with such and such qualities. If it is moral praise, he is a being with such and such tendencies to bring forth good acts. If we describe a single act, saying, for instance: 'Well done!' we mean to praise the person for the act as being the author of it. It is he who has done well and proved himself capable of doing so. If the happy act is accidental we say that no praise is deserved for it. If a person is gratified by praise it is because of the estimate of him, in some respect or in general, that is conveyed. Praise . . . means description, with expressed or implied admiration. If any instance of it can be found which does not consist in these elements our analysis fails. 'Praise the Lord, O my soul, *and forget not all His benefits*,' – and the Psalm goes on to tell His loving and guarding acts toward human-kind. To praise the Lord is to tell His perfections, especially the perfections of His character. This is the old light that has always been in words of praise and there appears no reason for its going out.

Indeterminism maintains that we need not be impelled to action by our wishes, that our active will need not be determined by them. Motives 'incline without necessitating'. We choose amongst the ideas of action before us, but need not choose solely according to the attraction of desire, in however wide a sense that word is used. Our inmost self may rise up in its autonomy and moral dignity, independently of motives, and register its sovereign decree.

Now, *in so far* as this 'interposition of the self' is undetermined, the act is not *its* act, it does not issue from any concrete continuing self; it is born at the moment, of nothing, hence it expresses no quality; it bursts into being from no source. The self does not register *its* decree, for the decree is not the product of just that '*it*'. The self does not rise up in *its* moral dignity, for dignity is the quality of an enduring being, influencing its actions, and therefore expressed by them, and that would be determination. *In proportion* as an act of volition starts of itself without cause it is exactly, so far as the freedom of the individual is concerned, as if it had been thrown into his mind from without – 'suggested' to him – by a freakish demon. It is exactly like it in this respect, that in neither case does the volition arise from what the man is, cares for or feels allegiance to; it does not come out of him. *In proportion* as it is undetermined, it is just as if his legs should suddenly spring up and carry him off where he did not prefer to go. Far from constituting freedom, that would mean, in the exact measure in which it took place, the loss of freedom. It would be an interference, and an utterly uncontrollable interference, with his power of acting as he prefers. In fine, then, *just so far* as the volition is undetermined, the self can neither be praised nor blamed for it, since it is not the act of the self.

The principle of free will says: '*I* produce my volitions.' Determinism says: 'My volitions are produced by *me*.' Determinism is free will expressed in the passive voice.

After all, it is plain what the indeterminists have done. It has not occurred to them that our free will may be resolved into its component elements. (Thus far a portion only of this resolution has been considered.) When it is thus resolved they do not recognise it. The analytical imagination is considerably taxed to perceive the identity of the free power that we feel with the component parts that analysis shows us. We are gratified by their nods of intelligence and their bright, eager faces as the analysis proceeds, but at the close are a little disheartened to find them falling back on the innocent supposition of a horse inside that does all the essential work. They forget that they may be called upon to analyse the horse. They solve the problem by forgetting analysis. The solution they offer is merely: 'There is a self inside which does the deciding.' Or, let us say, it is as if the *Pfarrer* were explaining the physiology of a horse's motion. They take the whole thing to be analysed, imagine a duplicate of it reduced in size, so to speak, and place this duplicate-self inside as an explanation – making it the elusive source of the 'free decisions'. They do not see that they are merely pushing the question a little further back, since the process of deciding, with its constituent factors, must have taken place within that inner self. Either it decided in a particular way because, on the whole, it preferred to decide in that way, or the decision was an underived event, a rootless and sourceless event. It is the same story over again. In neither case is there any gain in imagining a second self inside, however wonderful and elusive. Of course, it is the first alternative that the indeterminist is really imagining. If you tacitly and obscurely conceive the self as deciding *its own way*, i.e., according to its preference, but never admit or recognise this, then you can happily remain a libertarian indeterminist; but upon no other terms. In your theory there is a heart of darkness.

Freedom

In accordance with the genius of language, free will means freedom of persons in willing, just as 'free trade' means freedom of persons (in a certain respect) in trading. The freedom of anyone surely always implies his possession of a power, and means the absence of any interference (whether taking the form of restraint or constraint) with his exercise of that power. Let us consider this in relation to freedom in willing.

'Can'

We say, 'I can will this or I can will that, whichever I choose.' Two courses of action present themselves to my mind. I think of their consequences, I look on this picture and on that, one of them commends itself more than the other, and I will an act that brings it about. I knew that I could choose either. That means that I had the power to choose either.

What is the meaning of 'power'? A person has a power if it is a fact that when he sets himself in the appropriate manner to produce a certain event that event will actually follow. I have the power to lift the lamp; that is, if I grasp it and exert an upward pressure with my arm, *it will rise*. I have the power to will so and so; that is, if I want, that act of will will take place. That and none other is the meaning of power, is it not? A man's being in the proper active posture of body or of mind is the cause, and the sequel in question will be the effect. (Of course, it may be held that the sequel not only does but must follow, in a sense opposed to Hume's doctrine of cause. Very well; the question does not here concern us.)

Thus power depends upon, or rather consists in, a law. The law in question takes the familiar form that if something happens a certain something else will ensue. If A happens then B will happen. The law in this case is that if the man definitively so desires then volition will come to pass. There is a series, wish – will – act. The act follows according to the will (that is a law – I do not mean an underived law) and the will follows according to the wish (that is another law). A man has the power (sometimes) to act as he wishes. He has the power (whenever he is not physically bound or held) to act as he wills. He has the power always (except in certain morbid states) to will as he wishes. All this depends upon the laws of his being. Wherever there is a power there is a law. In it the power wholly consists. A man's power to will as he wishes is simply the law that his will follows his wish.

What, again, does freedom mean? It means the absence of any interference with all this. Nothing steps in to prevent my exercising my power.[1]

All turns on the meaning of 'can'. 'I can will either this or that' means, I am so constituted that if I definitively incline to this, the appropriate act of will will take place, and if I definitively incline to that, the appropriate act of will will take place. The law connecting preference and will exists, and there is nothing to interfere with it. My free power, then, is not an exemption from law but in its inmost essence an embodiment of law.

Thus it is true, after the act of will, that I could have willed otherwise. It is most natural to add, 'if I had wanted to'; but the addition is not required. The point is the meaning of 'could'. I could have willed whichever way I pleased. I had the power to will otherwise, there was nothing to prevent my doing so, and I should have done so if I had wanted. If someone says that the wish I actually had prevented my willing otherwise, so that I could not have done it, he is merely making a slip in the use of the word 'could'. He means, that wish could not have produced anything but this volition. But 'could' is asserted not of the wish (a transient fact to which power in this sense is not and should not be ascribed) but of the person. And the person *could* have produced something else than that volition. He could have produced any volition he wanted; he had the power to do so.

But the objector will say, 'The person as he was at the moment – the person as animated by that wish – could not have produced any other volition.' Oh, yes, he could. 'Could' has meaning as applied not to a momentary actual phase of a person's life, but to the person himself of whose life that is but a phase; and it means that (even at that moment) he had the power to will just as he preferred. *The idea of power, because it is the idea of a law, is hypothetical, carries in itself hypothesis as part of its very intent and meaning – 'if he should prefer this, if he should prefer that', – and therefore can be truly applied to a person irrespective of what at the moment he does prefer. It remains hypothetical even when applied.*[2] This very peculiarity of its meaning is the whole point of the idea of power. It is just because determinism is true, because a law obtains, that one 'could have done otherwise'.

Sidgwick set over against 'the formidable array of cumulative evidence' offered for determinism the 'affirmation of consciousness' 'that I can now choose to do' what is right and reasonable, 'however strong may be my inclination to act unreasonably'.[3] But it is not against determinism. It is a true affirmation (surely not of immediate consciousness but of experience), the affirmation of my power to will what I deem right, however intense and insistent my desire for the wrong. I can will anything, and can will effectively anything that my body will enact. I can will it despite an inclination to the contrary of any strength you please – strength as felt by me before decision. We all know cases where we have resisted impulses of great strength in this sense and we can imagine them still stronger. I have the power to do it, and shall do it, shall exercise that power, if I prefer. Obviously in that case (be it psychologically remarked) my solicitude to do what is right will have proved itself even stronger (as measured by ultimate tendency to prevail, though not of necessity by sensible vividness or intensity) than the inclination to the contrary, for that is what is meant by my preferring to do it. I am conscious that the field for willing is open; 'I can will' anything that I elect to will. Sidgwick did not analyse the meaning of 'can', that is all. He did not precisely catch the outlook of consciousness when it says, 'I can.' He did not distinguish the function of the word, which is to express the availability of the alternatives I see when, before I have willed, and perhaps before my preference is decided, I look out on the field of conceivable volition. He did not recognise that I must have a word to express my power to will as I please, quite irrespective of what I shall please, and that 'can' is that word. It is no proof that I cannot do something to point out that I shall not do it if I do not prefer. A man, let us say, can turn on the electric light; but he will not turn it on if he walks away from it; though it is still true that he can turn it on. When we attribute power to a man we do not mean that something will accomplish itself without his wanting it to. That would never suggest the idea of power. We mean that if he makes the requisite move the thing will be accomplished. It is part of the idea that the initiative shall rest with him. The initiative for an act of will is a precedent phase of consciousness that we call the definitive inclination, or, in case of conflict, the definitive preference for it. If someone in the throes of struggle with temptation says to himself, 'I can put this behind me,' he is saying truth and precisely the pertinent truth. He is bringing before his mind the act of will, unprevented, quite open to him, that would deliver him from what he deems noxious. It may still happen that the noxiousness of the temptation does not affect him so powerfully as its allurement, and that he succumbs. It is no whit less true, according to determinism, that he could have willed otherwise. To analyse the fact expressed by 'could' is not to destroy it.

But it may be asked, 'Can I will in opposition to my strongest desire at the moment when it is strongest?' If the words 'at the moment when it is strongest' qualify 'can', the answer has already been given. If they qualify 'will', the suggestion is a contradiction in terms. Can I turn-on-the-electric-light-at-a-moment-when-I-am-not-trying-to-do-so? This means, if I try to turn on the light at a moment when I am not trying to, will it be turned on? A possible willing as I do not prefer to will is not a power on my part, hence not to be expressed by 'I can.'

Everybody knows that we often will what we do not want to will, what we do not prefer. But when we say this we are using words in another sense than that in which I have just used them. In *one* sense of the words, whenever we act we are doing what we prefer, on the whole, in view of all the circumstances. We are acting for the greatest good or the least evil or a mixture of these. In the *other* and more usual sense of the words, we are very often doing what we do not wish to do, i.e., doing some particular thing we do not wish because we are afraid of the consequences or disapprove of the moral complexion of the particular thing we do wish. We do the thing that we do not like because the other thing has aspects that we dislike yet more. We are still doing what we like best on the whole. It is again a question of the meaning of words.

If the initiative for volition is not a wish, what is it? Indeterminism says that a moral agent sometimes decides against the more tempting course. He does so, let us say, because it is wrong, the other course is the right one. In other words, the desire to do right is at the critical moment stronger within him than the temptation. No, no, replies indeterminism, it is not that; he sometimes decides against the stronger desire. Very well; 'can' meaning what it does, tell us what is the leaning or favourable disposition on the part of the ego, in a case of undetermined willing, toward the volition it adopts; what is that which constitutes the ego's initiative in that direction, – since it is not a wish? Shall we say it is an approval or conscientious acceptance? Does this approval or acceptance arise from the agent's distinctive moral being? That is determinism, quite as much as if you called the initiative a wish. But the indeterminist has already answered in effect that there is no such initiative, or no effectual initiative. The act of will causes the physical act but is not itself caused. This is to deny the presence of power, according to its definition. How has it a meaning to say in advance that 'I can' will this way or that? The self, considering the alternatives beforehand, is not in a position to say, 'If I feel thus about it, this volition will take place, or if I feel otherwise the contrary will take place; I know very well how I shall feel, so I know how I shall will.' The self now existing has not control over the future 'free' volition, since that may be undetermined, nor will the self's future feelings, whatever they may be, control it. Hence the sense expressed by 'I can', the sense of power inhering in one's continuous self to sway the volition as it feels disposed, is denied to it. All it is in a position to mean by 'I can' is, 'I do not know which will happen', which is not 'I can' at all. Nay, even looking backward, it is unable to say: 'I could have willed otherwise', for that clearly implies, 'Had I been so disposed the other volition would have taken place', which is just what cannot, according to indeterminism, be said. Surely, to paraphrase a historic remark, our 'liberty' does not seem to be of very much use to us. The indeterminist is in a peculiarly hapless position. The two things that he is most deeply moved to aver, that the free volition is the act of the self, and that the self can will one way or the other – these two things on his own theory fall utterly to pieces, and can only be maintained on the view that he opposes.

Compulsion

The indeterminist conceives that according to determinism the self is carried along by wishes to acts which it is thus necessitated to perform. This mode of speaking distinguishes the self from the wishes and represents it as under their dominion. This is the initial error. This is what leads the indeterminist wrong on all the topics of his problem. And the error persists in the most recent writings. In fact, the moral self is the wishing self. The wishes are its own. It cannot be described as under their dominion, for it has no separate predilections to be overborne by them; they themselves are its predilections. To fancy that because the person acts according to them he is compelled, a slave, the victim of a power from whose clutches he cannot extricate himself, is a confusion of ideas, a mere slip of the mind. The answer that has ordinarily been given is surely correct; all compulsion is causation, but not all causation is compulsion. Seize a man and violently force him to do something, and he is compelled – also caused – to do it. But induce him to do it by giving him reasons and his doing it is caused but not compelled.

Passivity

We have to be on our guard even against conceiving the inducement as a cause acting like the impact of a billiard ball, by which the self is precipitated into action like a second billiard ball, as an effect. The case is not so simple. Your reasons have shown him that his own preferences require the action. He does it of his own choice; he acts from his own motives in the light of your reasons. The sequence of cause and effect goes on within the self, with contributory information from without.

It is not clarifying to ask, 'Is a volition free or determined?' It is the person who is free, and his particular volition that is determined. Freedom is something that we can attribute only to a continuing being, and he can have it only so far as the particular transient volitions within him are determined. (According to the strict proprieties of language, it is surely events that are caused, not things or persons; a person or thing can be caused or determined only in the sense that its beginning to be, or changes in it, are caused or determined.)

It is fancied that, owing to the 'necessity' with which an effect follows upon its cause, if my acts of will are caused I am not free in thus acting. Consider an analogous matter. When I move I use ligaments. 'Ligament' means that which binds, and a ligament does bind bones together. But *I* am not bound. *I* (so far as my organism is concerned) am rendered possible by the fact that my bones are bound one to another; that is part of the secret of my being able to act, to move about and work my will. If my bones ceased to be bound one to another I should be undone indeed. The human organism is detached, but it is distinctly important that its component parts shall not be detached. Just so my free power of willing is built up of tight cause-and-effect connections.

The point is that when I employ the power thus constituted nothing determines the particular employment of it but *me*. Each particular act of mine is determined from outside itself, i.e., by a cause, a prior event. But not from outside me. I, the possessor of the power, am not in my acts passively played upon by causes outside me, but am enacting my own wishes in virtue of a chain of causation within me. What is needed is to distinguish broadly between a particular effect, on the one hand, and, on the other, the detached, continuous life of a mental individual and his organism; a life reactive, but reacting according to its own nature. . . .

Prediction

If we knew a man's character thoroughly and the circumstances that he would encounter, determinism (which we are not here completely asserting) says that we could foretell his conduct. This is a thought that repels many libertarians. Yet to predict a person's conduct need not be repellent. If you are to be alone in a room with £1000 belonging to another on the table and can pocket it without anyone knowing the fact, and if I predict that you will surely *not* pocket it, that is not an insult. I say, I know you, I know your character; you will not do it. But if I say that you are 'a free being' and that I really do not know whether you will pocket it or not, that is rather an insult. On the other hand, there are cases where prediction is really disparaging. If I say when you make a remark, 'I knew you were going to say that', the impression is not agreeable. My exclamation seems to say that your mind is so small and simple that one can predict its ideas. That is the real reason why people resent in such cases our predicting their conduct; that if present human knowledge, which is known to be so limited, can foresee their conduct, it must be more naive and stereotyped than they like to think it. It is no reflection upon the human mind or its freedom to say that one who knew it through and through (a human impossibility) could foreknow its preferences and its spontaneous choice. It is of the very best of men that even we human beings say, 'I am sure of him.' It has perhaps in this controversy hardly been observed how much at this point is involved, how far the question of prediction reaches. The word 'reliable' or 'trustworthy' is a prediction of behaviour. Indeed, all judgement of persons whatever, in the measure of its definitude, is such a prediction.

Material Fate

The philosopher in the old story, gazing at the stars, falls into a pit. We have to notice the pitfall in our subject to which, similarly occupied, Professor Eddington has succumbed.

> What significance is there in my mental struggle to-night whether I shall or shall not give up smoking, if the laws which govern the matter of the physical universe

already pre-ordain for the morrow a configuration of matter consisting of pipe, tobacco, and smoke connected with my lips?[4]

No laws, according to determinism, pre-ordain such a configuration, unless I give up the struggle. Let us put matter aside for the moment, to return to it. Fatalism says that my morrow is determined no matter how I struggle. This is of course a superstition. Determinism says that my morrow is determined through my struggle. There is this significance in my mental effort, that it is deciding the event. The stream of causation runs through my deliberations and decision, and, if it did not run as it does run, the event would be different. The past cannot determine the event except through the present. And no past moment determined it any more truly than does the present moment. In other words, each of the links in the causal chain must be in its place. Determinism (which, the reader will remember, we have not here taken for necessarily true in all detail) says that the coming result is 'pre-ordained' (literally, caused) at each stage, and therefore the whole following series for to-morrow may be described as already determined; so that did we know all about the struggler, how strong of purpose he was and how he was influenced (which is humanly impossible), we could tell what he would do. But for the struggler this fact (supposing it to be such) is not pertinent. If, believing it, he ceases to struggle, he is merely revealing that the forces within him have brought about that cessation. If on the other hand he struggles manfully he will reveal the fact that they have brought about his success. Since the causation of the outcome works through his struggle in either case equally, it cannot become for him a moving consideration in the struggle. In it the question is, 'Shall I do this or that?' It must be answered in the light of what there is to recommend to me this or that. To this question the scientific truth (according to determinism) that the deliberation itself is a play of causation is completely irrelevant; it merely draws the mind delusively away from the only considerations that concern it.

As regards the rôle of matter in the affair, if, as Professor Eddington on behalf of the determinists is here supposing, the behaviour of all matter, including the human organism, takes place according to a deterministic scheme of physical law, then we must conceive, according to the familiar formula, that the mental process is paralleled in the brain by a physical process. The whole psycho-physical occurrence would then be the cause of what followed, and the psychic side of it, the mental struggle proper, a concause or side of the cause. To-morrow's configuration of matter will have been brought about by a material process with which the mental process was inseparably conjoined. I make this supposition merely to show that supposing the existence of a physically complete mechanism through which all human action is caused and carried out has no tendency to turn determinism into fatalism. For the mental struggle must in that case be paralleled by a physical struggle which, so to speak, represents it and is in a manner its agent in the physical world; and upon this struggle the physical outcome will depend. (The determinist need not, but may of course, hold this doctrine of automatism, of a physically complete mechanism in human action.) . . .

Responsibility

Again, it is said that determinism takes from man all responsibility. As regards the origin of the term, a man is responsible when he is the person to respond to the question why the act was performed, how it is to be explained or justified. That is what he must answer; he is answerable for the act. It is the subject of which he must give an account; he is accountable for the act. The act proceeded from him. He is to say whether it proceeded consciously. He is to give evidence that he did or did not know the moral nature of the act and that he did or did not intend the result. He is to say how he justifies it or if he can justify it. If the act proceeded from him by pure accident, if he can show that he did the damage (if damage it was) by brushing against something by inadvertence, for example, then he has not to respond to the question what he did it for – he is not consciously responsible – nor how it is justified – he is not morally responsible, though of course he may have been responsible in these respects for a habit of carelessness.

But why does the peculiar moral stain of guilt or ennoblement of merit belong to responsibility? If an act proceeds from a man and not merely from his accidental motion but from his mind and moral nature, we judge at once that like acts may be expected from him in the future. The colour of the act for good or bad is reflected on the man. We see him now as a living source of possible acts of the same kind. If we must be on our guard against such acts we must be on our guard against such men. If we must take steps to defend ourselves against such acts we must take steps to defend ourselves against such men. If we detest such acts, we must detest that tendency in such men which produced them. He is guilty in that he knowingly did evil, in that the intentional authorship of evil is in him. Because the act proceeded in every sense from him, for that reason he is (so far) to be accounted bad or good according as the act is bad or good, and he is the one to be punished if punishment is required. And that is moral responsibility.

But how, it is asked, can I be responsible for what I will if a long train of past causes has made me will it. . . . Is it not these causes that are 'responsible' for my act – to use the word in the only sense, says the objector, that seems to remain for it?

The parent past produced the man, none the less the man is responsible for his acts. We can truly say that the earth bears apples, but quite as truly that trees bear apples. The earth bears the apples by bearing trees. It does not resent the claim of the trees to bear the apples, or to take the business out of the trees' hands. Nor need the trees feel their claim nullified by the earth's part in the matter. There is no rivalry between them. A man is a being with free will and responsibility; where this being came from, I repeat, is another story. The past finished its functions in the business when it generated him as he is. So far from interfering with him and coercing him the past does not even exist. If we could imagine it as lingering on into the present, standing over against him and stretching out a ghostly hand to stay his arm, then indeed the past would be interfering

ıs liberty and responsibility. But so long as it and he are never on the scene
ıer they cannot wrestle; the past cannot overpower him. The whole alarm
evil dream, a nightmare due to the indigestion of words. The past has
ᴄ.~ .ed, and left extant, a free-willed being.

Notes

1   A word as to the relation of power and freedom. Strictly power cannot exist without freedom, since the result does not follow without it. Freedom on the other hand is a negative term, meaning the absence of something, and implies a power only because that whose absence it signifies is interference, which implies something to be interfered with. Apart from this peculiarity of the term itself, there might be freedom without any power. Absence of interference (of what would be interference if there were a power) might exist in the absence of a power; a man might be free to do something because there was nothing to interfere with his doing it, but might have no power to do it. Similarly and conveniently we may speak of a power as existing though interfered with; that is, the law may exist that would constitute a power if the interference were away.
2   I am encouraged by finding in effect the same remark in Prof. G. E. Moore's *Ethics* (Oxford: Oxford University Press, 1912), ch. vi, at least as regards what he terms one sense of the word 'could'. I should hazard saying, the only sense in this context.
3   Sidgwick, *Methods of Ethics*, 7th edn (London: Macmillan, 1907), p. 65.
4   *Philosophy*, Jan. 1933, p. 41.

---

45   Freedom, Causation, and Preexistence: an Excerpt from *Problems of Mind and Matter*

John Wisdom

1.   **Freewill and Causation.** The problem of the freedom of the will arises, like so many philosophical problems, from an apparent contradiction between two beliefs which both seem well justified. We believe that everything which happens is due to something else which caused it to happen. This is the belief in the Law of Causation. We also believe that, when we decide to do one thing rather than another, then we are free to do otherwise. For example, you were free to get up five minutes earlier this morning. This is the belief in Freewill. Now by the Law of Causation your decision to act as you did was due to something which happened before, that is, it was caused and determined by what had gone before. But, if that is so, how can we say that you were free to have acted otherwise?

. . .Suppose we find *a* sense of Freewill compatible with the Law of Causation – would that be enough? Certainly not. We want to be sure with regard to *every* sense, in which it can be plausibly claimed that we have Freewill, that it is compatible with the Law of Causation. Now there is one sense of Freewill which it is very hard to reconcile with the Law of Causation. This is why even serious philosophers, who have tried to reconcile the two, have been reluctantly compelled to give up the attempt and quell the disturbance by slaughtering one of the combatants. This sense of Freewill is really the only one which need give any trouble. It is the sense of Freewill which is implied by Blame.

2. **Blame entails Freewill.** If anyone has ever done something for which he is to blame, then he has been free to do differently. Suppose that a man is on trial for not having prevented the murder of his cook. It is suggested that he is to blame for not having thrown out the murderer. Directly it is shown that he was physically incapable of doing so, the suggestion is withdrawn; though of course it would still be held that he ought to have thrown out the murderer *if* he could. It is next suggested that he is to blame for not telephoning to the police. But directly it is shown that he did not know how to use a telephone it is no longer held that he is to blame for not telephoning. It may, indeed, be thought that "he ought to have known at his age"; but that is to accuse him of a different crime; for it is to accuse him of carelessness in the past, not callousness in the present. In general then: You cannot be to blame for not doing what you were not able or free to do, and you cannot be to blame for doing what you could not avoid. This has been expressed briefly by saying that *Ought* implies *Can*; and we will express it by saying that *Blame* entails *Freewill*. But in what sense?

3. **In what sense?**

3.1.   BLAME ENTAILS FREEDOM OF SELF-DETERMINATION. Unless our behaviour is partly determined by our nature, we are never to blame. Unless it is true that with a different nature I should have behaved differently, I cannot be to blame for anything I have done. But this is not enough.

3.2.   BLAME ENTAILS MORE THAN FREEDOM OF SELF-DETERMINATION. For watches and motor-cars have freedom of self-determination. A good watch keeps good time in spite of vibration, but a bad one does not; the behaviour of your car on steep hills would be different if its gear ratios were different. And we do not blame ourselves for reflex acts, such as uncontrollable coughing. Yet these are due to our nature. We blame ourselves only for willed acts, i.e. actions which are due to decision or desire. The more deliberate a wrong act, the more to blame is the agent.

3.3.   BLAME ENTAILS FREEDOM OF SELF-DIRECTION. We are not to blame for an act unless we could have done differently if we had wanted to. We are not to blame for failing to do an act unless we could have done it, i.e. we are not to blame unless it was open to us to do it, in the sense that we should have done it if we had decided to do it. Watches cannot make decisions. Therefore they lack free*will* or freedom of self-direction.

Freedom of self-direction is necessary for blame. It has been claimed that it is sufficient. It has been suggested that to blame a man for an act is to say that he did it from an evil motive; that to blame a man for speaking so as to hurt someone's feelings is just to say that his decision to speak so was due to evil intentions.[1] This suggestion is extremely plausible. It explains why we can blame only conscious things and why we can blame these only when the harm they do is intentional. But it has also been claimed that this freedom of self-direction is not enough. Let us examine this claim.

3.4.   BLAME ENTAILS MORE THAN FREEDOM OF SELF-DIRECTION. Suppose that all your acts are determined by your decisions, and your decisions by your knowledge (no doubt imperfect) of the consequences of your acts together with your desires for these consequences. But suppose that on the occasion of each decision the strength of your various desires is fixed by the Devil. Suppose that you float a bogus company and ruin thousands. Are you to blame? I believe that you are not. It is a question for inspection. I have confirmed what I seem to see from inspection by asking others to inspect the same problem. I have carefully asked this question of more than one person who was highly intelligent but sufficiently ignorant of philosophy to have no axe to grind, and have received the reply that in such a case you would not be to blame. And I have asked at least two, and I think three, groups of about eighty students this same question, and a large majority favour the answer that in such a case you would not be to blame.[2]

Yet in this case your act was due to your nature – you had freedom of self-determination. Further your act was due to that part of your nature which is called your will – you had freedom of self-direction.

Before deciding this question take one more case. Suppose again that your acts are determined by your decisions, and your decisions by your wishes, and your wishes by the possibilities which your environment presents to you together with your disposition on which that environment acts. Suppose that your disposition is determined by the nature of your parents, and the nature of your parents by the natures of Adam and Eve. Suppose that the natures of Adam and Eve were determined by God. In such a case are you rightly blamed for your acts? You are responsible for them but is it not God who is *ultimately* responsible for them?[3]

I think that here again, in this example, which does not differ in principle from the first, we must agree with those who say that you are not to blame.

And that this is the right answer is now confirmed by our being able to see *why* you are not to blame. You are not to blame because, although responsible for your acts, you are not *ultimately* responsible for them.

3.5.   BLAME ENTAILS NOT ONLY SELF-DIRECTION BUT ULTIMATE SELF-DIREC-TION. You can, then, be blamed for an act only in so far as that act is caused by your nature, and, in particular, by your will; further, your will must be at least part of the *ultimate* cause of your act. To say that your will is part of the ultimate cause of your act is to say that while your will determines your act that will is not in its turn completely determined by something which is not your will. What blame requires is that, however far back we go in setting out the causes of your act, we shall never come to a time at which a set of purely external circumstances, i.e. not involving you and your will, formed a complete cause of your act.[4] Therefore, if you are to blame for an act *A*, then either (*α*) at some time the series of causes of your decision to do *A* becomes incomplete or ceases altogether, or (*β*) the series is an infinite series of determinations of your will by your will.

4.   Compatibility of ultimate Self-direction with the Law of Causation. Let

us consider a typical decision and act: you decide to take cocaine and take it. You realize the danger you run of ill-health for yourself, and thus of injury to your friends. You are to blame for this act. Hence as we have seen that act must be ultimately due to your will.

It looks as if alternative (*α*) above, according to which you are ultimately responsible in that your decision or one of its direct or indirect causes is wholly or partially undetermined, is incompatible with the Law of Causation. There are, however, two ways in which it might be suggested that even Indeterminism can be reconciled with the Law of Causation.

4.1.   DETERMINATION BY DISPOSITION. (i) Your act in taking cocaine was due in part to your disposition. For your act was due to your decision, and your decision to your desires, and your desires were due in part to your environment (your packet of cocaine) and in part to your disposition which that environment acted upon. (ii) Your disposition is an undetermined fact. (iii) This is not incompatible with the Law of Causation. For the Law of Causation states that every *event* has a cause. Now your disposition is not an event, and it is not even a complete particular fact equivalent to an event. For your disposition is made up, not of *actual* thoughts and feelings, but of *tendencies* to feel in such and such a way whenever you are stimulated in such and such a way. For example, to say that you are irritable is to say that *if* anyone thwarts you at all *then* you will strongly desire to injure him.

It must be admitted that these 'if-then' facts, which make up one's disposition, are not events nor equivalent to events. They do not state that anything *is* occurring. They state what event *would* occur if such and such another event took place. And these 'if-then' facts about individuals may well be ultimate, just as the most general physical properties of particles are ultimate. No one explains the fact that particles react to stimuli in accordance with the laws of motion.

Now it must be admitted that we do in some sense 'explain' the fact that *you* accepted cocaine while *I* refused it, by saying that you are of a rash disposition while I am cautious, that is, by a difference in our properties.

But is this explanation in the sense of *giving the cause of* the difference in our reactions? Is it not merely to bring the particular case of the reaction to cocaine and neglect of its dangers under a general heading – *another* instance of your neglecting danger?

When I explain the fact that *my* watch stops when I ride a motor-cycle while *your* watch keeps going, by saying that my watch stops from vibration, then I explain only in the sense of bringing the motor-cycle case under a general heading. But the cause of the difference in reaction is not given until there is found that difference of structure (actual condition) between the two watches which caused the difference in reaction. This explanation will again involve properties, but the final explanation will involve only properties which apply to *all* material things, and there will then remain no cases of different reaction to the same stimulus. Thus in physics and chemistry it is assumed that for every difference of property there is a difference in structure, and that the only causes of difference in reaction are differences in structure, i.e. the actual state, i.e. the qualities and relations of the particles involved, as opposed to 'if-then' facts about them.

Perhaps persons are different. Perhaps differences in the properties or dispositions of persons are not reducible to differences in actual state. It may be that there are differences, at least in degree or strength, between the *ultimate* dispositions or properties of one person and those of another. If so, these differences in degree between your dispositions and mine will be part of the cause of the differences in our reactions. If this is possible, we may welcome this suggestion as supplementary to the suggestion of the long series of determinations of decision and desires by preceding decisions and desires which we shall have to consider later.

But *is* it sense to say that part of the cause of your strong desire for cocaine now is the fact that, if and when you are offered cocaine, then you strongly desire it? Again, *is* it sense to say that part of the cause of your disregard for this danger is the fact that you always disregard any danger? This question is enough to show that the disposition theory is, on the face of it, unsatisfactory.

It may be answered that, even if differences in property are not ultimate, their ultimacy can be avoided only by supposing corresponding 'structural' differences – differences in the actual state of people with different properties. That is so. But then must the 'structural' differences be differences in *mental* condition, for example, prevailing mood? May they not be quite literally structural differences in the nervous system, etc.? Perhaps the irritable man is irritable wholly because of his digestion.

It is impossible to carry this discussion further here. In any case the suggestion of Determination by Disposition would, I think, supplement rather than supplant the possibilities of reconciliation which we shall next consider.

4.2.   THE FINITE SERIES OF INTERNAL DETERMINATIONS. There is another way in which alternative (α) (p. 435), according to which one of the causes direct or indirect of your decision was partially or wholly undetermined, is reconcilable with the Law of Causation in a mild form.

The Law of Causation in a mild form is not incompatible with a First Cause. The Law of Causation in a mild form is not the law that *every* event has a cause but is the law that all events, *except those which occurred first in order of time*, have causes. So that we might suppose that, if we trace back the causes of your decision, we shall find, not indeed an endless series of determinations of your will by your will, but a world-long series which ended not at your birth but at the beginning of time amongst the events which were the first causes.

It must, however, be clearly understood that the series shall not end or become incomplete[5] until the first causes are reached. Anything else is incompatible with even the mild form of the Law of Causation. There cannot be decisions now which are incompletely determined in that their direct causes are incomplete.

4.3. THE INFINITE SERIES OF INTERNAL DETERMINATIONS. If one set of events, namely the first, is not determined, it is difficult to see how we know that all the rest are. This suggests that we know the stronger form of the Law of Causation according to which *every* event is completely determined.

This form of the Law of Causation is not reconcilable with the finite, though world-long, series of internal determinations. It requires alternative (β) according to which every decision is determined by an infinite series of internal determinations. This alternative, of course, is compatible with the strict form of the Law of Causation; and, since the determinations which it contemplates are all of the will by the will, it is compatible with ultimate self-direction and blame.

4.4. THE SERIES OF INTERNAL DETERMINATIONS MUST BE EITHER INFINITE OR WORLD-LONG. It appears then that if (i) either form of the Law of Causation is true, and (ii) we are to blame for our acts, then each decision is due to an either infinite or world-long series of determinations of the will by the will. We shall find that this consequence, so far from being incredible, is merely surprising to the western world. For there is no good reason against it, and we shall see in a moment that it is what we might have expected on independent grounds.

4.5. INDEPENDENT SUPPORT OF THIS CONCLUSION. When you decide to take cocaine, your decision is caused by the ratio of your strong desire for its taste to your feeble desire to avoid its dangers; and your desires are caused partly by something in your environment – you see your packet of cocaine – but also partly by your past decisions to take cocaine. For your present strong desire is acquired and thus due to past decisions to take cocaine. Of course, when you were first offered cocaine, your decision to take it cannot have been determined by past decisions to take cocaine. Nevertheless, it was probably in part determined by past decisions. For it was in part due, as we say, to your character at the time that the cocaine was first offered to you. And is not your character at any given time, in part at least, determined by what you have done in the past?

"But", you will say, "what about the first decision I made after I was born? That cannot have been in part determined by other decisions of mine."

But was it your first decision? We are too ignorant of what happens at birth to have any good reason from experience for asserting that the first decision which you made after birth was your first decision. Nor is there any good philosophical reason for this assertion.

On the contrary, we have a reason independent of the argument from responsibility in favour of supposing that it was not your first decision, or at least that it was preceded by the manifestation of will in desire. Let us suppose, for the sake of simplicity, that the first mental event at birth was a decision. By the principle of continuity we know that a mental event and therefore a decision is not completely explained by purely material circumstances. The decision therefore was partly caused by and therefore preceded by a non-material event.

We know of no non-material events which are not mental. Further, by the principle of the resemblance of the cause this non-material event must at least contain a mental event.

Now I submit that the most probable hypothesis as to the nature of that mental event which contributed to your decision is that (*a*) it was a mental event in *your* mind, and (*b*) involved your *will*. For without (*a*) we have to suppose the *direct* action of one mind on another – a thing which rarely if ever happens. And, as for (*b*), if a decision has a mental explanation at all, it is always in terms of desires; and, if desires have a mental explanation at all, it is always in terms of other desires.[6]

So far then from its being incredible that your decision at birth should be not the first manifestation of your will but determined by previous manifestations, this is what we might have expected quite apart from any argument from ultimate responsibility.

What the argument from blame and ultimate self-direction does, is to confirm the conclusion that a decision (i) cannot have purely material causes, (ii) has a cause which (*a*) is mental, (*b*) is an event in the history of the mind which makes the decision, and (*c*) is concerned with that mind's will, that is, its desires or decision.

From the Law of Causation it follows that this second voluntary event has in its turn a cause. This cause by another application of the argument from the principles of continuity and ultimate responsibility must again be a voluntary event in the history of the same mind.

This process continues indefinitely or until the first causes are reached.

The argument from responsibility is particularly important for the following reason. It proves that the mental event, which by the principle of the resemblance of the cause must precede any mental event in the mind of X, must be a mental event *in the mind of X* and not in the mind of God or some 'general consciousness'.

5.   **Freedom of Indeterminism.** You will have noticed that we have refused to accept freedom of indeterminism, that is, the doctrine that our decisions are not completely determined by our desires or else our desires are not completely determined by our environment, character and preceding mental state. We refused to accept this view because it conflicts with the Law of Causation. Most of those who have accepted indeterminism have done so, I think, because they mistakenly supposed that blame requires it. But other reasons have been advanced and we

must consider them, especially as freedom of indeterminism would save us from pre-existence.

(i) *Inspection.* It has been urged, in the first place, that in the case of some of our decisions we can see by inspection that they are not completely determined.

This is a surprising contention. We must admit, at once, that there are a great many facts about the causation of our decisions which we can learn by inspection. But all these facts are *positive* like the fact *I decided to go because I hated him.* How can I know by inspection the *negative* fact that my decision is not completely determined?

I believe that people have maintained that they do know that their decisions are not completely determined because of one of two confusions. First they confuse this freedom of indeterminism with freedom of self-direction. I *can* tell by inspection (roughly speaking) that I could have done otherwise *if I would.* But this is merely to say that different causes, namely different desires, would have caused a different result, namely different decision and action. This is quite consistent with the Law of Causation. But then it is not indeterminism.

Secondly, people have confused the claim that they know directly that their decisions are not completely determined, with the claim that this can be *proved* by the argument from Action in the Line of Greatest Resistance. Let us consider this argument.

(ii) *Action in the Line of Greatest Resistance.* It is asserted that we sometimes do an act *A* instead of an act *A'* even when our discoverable motives for *A* are weaker than our discoverable motives for *A'* . . . [W]e sometimes treat people unkindly when we are very fond of them; and we sometimes do this continually, even when we are not suffering from liver or some other temporary disturbance. And we sometimes make great efforts to see someone who is 'nothing to us'. From this again it is concluded that our decisions and acts are not completely determined by our desires and are therefore not completely determined.

. . . One does not admire oneself for making great efforts to see *X*, nor does one expect others to admire one for making these efforts. Much less does one admire oneself for being unkind to a friend. Indeed we must admit that in such cases we can sometimes be sure that the observable motives were not the complete cause of the decision. But how do we know that there is not some other motive which is unobservable and which yet affects one's decision and one's acts? We cannot know this unless we assume that every desire affecting decision can be detected by introspection. And no one will maintain this; especially in view of the evidence which the psycho-analysts provide for motives undiscoverable by introspection.

6. **Summary.** We found that the fact that a person is to blame for an act entails, not merely self-determination and not merely self-direction, but ultimate self-direction. In other words, however far back we trace the causes of a culprit's conduct, we must never reach a set of causes which were the complete cause of his conduct but were none of them concerned with him and his will. Therefore

either (α) at some time the series of causes of his act ceases or becomes incomplete, or (β) for ever the complete cause of his conduct will concern in some degree him and his will.

The indeterminist accepts (α) and tries to support his position by an argument from action in the line of greatest resistance. But this argument is unsound. And we reject (α) unless it is admitted that the series of complete causes, each involving the culprit's will, does not cease until the beginning of time among the first causes. With so much admitted, this alternative is not incompatible with the mild form of the Law of Causation, according to which all events are completely determined except those which occurred first in order of time. It is, however, incompatible with the more plausible form of the Law of Causation, according to which *every* event is determined. In this form the Law of Causation can be reconciled with ultimate responsibility[7] only by supposing that the series of determinations of the will by the will is endless.

Therefore, in any case, the series of determinations of X's will by X's will must be at least world-long.

This conclusion is independently supported by the principles of continuity and resemblance.

Pre-existence then follows from our considerations in this Part of the book.[8] This pre-existence must have been world-long.[9] It may or may not have been of a very feeble kind.[10]

Notes

1   McTaggart, *Some Dogmas of Religion*, Chap. V, Sect. 127.
2   I propose to obtain exact figures later.
3   "Thou wilt not with Predestination round enmesh me, and impute my Fall to Sin." Omar Khayyam, *Rubaiyat*.
4   The expression "the complete cause of X" is ambiguous. It may mean "all the events *of a given period* which made up a complete cause of X" and it may mean "all the sets of events in the chain of sets of events which caused X". A complete cause of an act is a set of events *of a given period* which sufficed completely to determine the occurrence of the act.
5   The series cannot become incomplete, as opposed to ending. For let E be an event which is incompletely but partially determined. Then since it is partially determined, it must have been preceded by an event which partially determined it. But if it is preceded by an event, it cannot be among the first causes. Therefore it must be completely determined.
6   The principle of the resemblance of the cause is probably at work here. For though we have said that *is wishing* and *is cognizing* are species of *is conscious*, it may well be that they are both in a sense supreme variables related to *is conscious* as *has an extensive quality* and *has a spatial character* are related to *is material*. Extensive quality and spatial character are aspects of materiality, each of which implies the other though neither is explainable by the other.
7   The considerations in this chapter suggest that the usual judgments of blame are considerably exaggerated.

8   It is hardly necessary to warn the reader that this sort of conclusion is unfashionable.

9   If every event is determined then there is no finite period such that the totality of determinations did not occupy a longer period. This does not follow from the fact that the number of determinations is infinite, but from the fact that any set of events, the earlier of which determine the later, is itself an event.

10 Compare Dr Broad's theory of a psychical factor. The psychical factor would not serve unless it were at least feeble consciousness. *The Mind and Its Place in Nature*, p. 535.

---

46   Human Freedom and the Self

Roderick M. Chisholm

A staff moves a stone, and is moved by a hand, which is moved by a man.
Aristotle, *Physics*, 256a

1.   The metaphysical problem of human freedom might be summarized in the following way: Human beings are responsible agents; but this fact appears to conflict with a deterministic view of human action (the view that every event that is involved in an act is caused by some other event); and it *also* appears to conflict with an indeterministic view of human action (the view that the act, or some event that is essential to the act, is not caused at all). To solve the problem, I believe, we must make somewhat far-reaching assumptions about the self or the agent – about the man who performs the act.

Perhaps it is needless to remark that, in all likelihood, it is impossible to say anything significant about this ancient problem that has not been said before.[1]

2.   Let us consider some deed, or misdeed, that may be attributed to a responsible agent: one man, say, shot another. If the man *was* responsible for what he did, then, I would urge, what was to happen at the time of the shooting was something that was entirely up to the man himself. There was a moment at which it was true, both that he could have fired the shot and also that he could have refrained from firing it. And if this is so, then, even though he did fire it, he could have done something else instead. (He didn't find himself firing the shot "against his will," as we say.) I think we can say, more generally, then, that if a man is responsible for a certain event or a certain state of affairs (in our example, the shooting of another man), then that event or state of affairs was brought about by some act of his, and the act was something that was in his power either to perform or not to perform.

But now if the act which he *did* perform was an act that was also in his power *not* to perform, then it could not have been caused or determined by any event that was not itself within his power either to bring about or not to bring about. For example, if what we say he did was really something that was brought about by a second man, one who forced his hand upon the trigger, say, or who, by means of hypnosis, compelled him to perform the act, then since the act was caused by the *second* man it was nothing that was within the power of the *first* man to prevent. And precisely the same thing is true, I think, if instead of referring to a second man who compelled the first one, we speak instead of the *desires* and *beliefs* which the first man happens to have had. For if what we say he did was really something that was brought about by his own beliefs and desires, if these beliefs and desires in the particular situation in which he happened to have found himself caused him to do just what it was that we say he did do, then since *they* caused it, *he* was unable to do anything other than just what it was that he did do. It makes no difference whether the cause of the deed was internal or external; if the cause was some state or event for which the man himself was not responsible, then he was not responsible for what we have been mistakenly calling his act. If a flood caused the poorly constructed dam to break, then, given the flood and the constitution of the dam, the break, we may say, *had* to occur and nothing could have happened in its place. And if the flood of desire caused the weak-willed man to give in, then he, too, had to do just what it was that he did do and he was no more responsible than was the dam for the results that followed. (It is true, of course, that if the man is responsible for the beliefs and desires that he happens to have, then he may also be responsible for the things they lead him to do. But the question now becomes: *is* he responsible for the beliefs and desires he happens to have? If he is, then there was a time when they were within his power either to acquire or not to acquire, and we are left, therefore, with our general point.)

One may object: But surely if there were such a thing as a man who is really *good*, then he would be responsible for things that he would do; yet, he would be unable to do anything other than just what it is that he does do, since, being good, he will always choose to do what is best. The answer, I think, is suggested by a comment that Thomas Reid makes on an ancient author. The author had said of Cato, "He was good because he could not be otherwise," and Reid observes: "But this saying, if understood literally and strictly, is not the praise of Cato, but of his constitution, which was no more the work of Cato, than his existence."[2] If Cato was himself responsible for the good things that he did, then Cato, as Reid suggests, was such that, although he had the power to do what was not good, he exercised his power only for that which was good.

All of this, if it is true, may give a certain amount of comfort to those who are tender-minded. But we should remind them that it also conflicts with a familiar view about the nature of God – with the view that St Thomas Aquinas expresses by saying that "every movement both of the will and of nature proceeds from God as the Prime Mover."[3] If the act of the sinner *did* proceed from God as the Prime Mover, then God was in the position of the second agent we just discussed – the man who forced the trigger finger, or the hypnotist – and the

sinner, so-called, was *not* responsible for what he did. (This may be a bold assertion, in view of the history of western theology, but I must say that I have never
encountered a single good reason for denying it.)

There is one standard objection to all of this and we should consider it briefly.

3.   The objection takes the form of a stratagem – one designed to show that
determinism (and divine providence) is consistent with human responsibility. The
stratagem is one that was used by Jonathan Edwards and by many philosophers
in the present century, most notably, G. E. Moore.[4]
   One proceeds as follows: The expression

(a)   He could have done otherwise,

it is argued, means no more nor less than

(b)   If he had chosen to do otherwise, then he would have done otherwise.

(In place of "chosen," one might say "tried," "set out," "decided," "under-
taken," or "willed.") The truth of statement (b), it is then pointed out, is consistent with determinism (and with divine providence); for even if all of the man's
actions were causally determined, the man could still be such that, *if* he had
chosen otherwise, then he would have done otherwise. What the murderer saw,
let us suppose, along with his beliefs and desires, *caused* him to fire the shot; yet
he was such that *if*, just then, he had chosen or decided *not* to fire the shot, then
he would not have fired it. All of this is certainly possible. Similarly, we could
say, of the dam, that the flood caused it to break and also that the dam was such
that, *if* there had been no flood or any similar pressure, then the dam would have
remained intact. And therefore, the argument proceeds, if (b) is consistent with
determinism and if (a) and (b) say the same thing, then (a) is also consistent with
determinism; hence we can say that the agent *could* have done otherwise even
though he was caused to do what he did do; and therefore determinism and
moral responsibility are compatible.
   Is the argument sound? The conclusion follows from the premises, but the
catch, I think, lies in the first premise – the one saying that statement (a) tells
us no more nor less than what statement (b) tells us. For (b), it would seem,
could be true while (a) is false. That is to say, our man might be such that, if
he had chosen to do otherwise, then he would have done otherwise, and yet
also such that he could not have done otherwise. Suppose, after all, that our
murderer could not have *chosen,* or could not have *decided,* to do otherwise.
Then the fact that he happens also to be a man such that, if he had chosen not
to shoot he would not have shot, would make no difference. For if he could
not have chosen *not* to shoot, then he could not have done anything other than
just what it was that he did do. In a word: from our statement (b) above ("If
he had chosen to do otherwise, then he would have done otherwise"), we cannot

make an inference to (a) above ("He could have done otherwise") unless we can *also* assert:

(c)   He could have chosen to do otherwise.

And therefore, if we must reject this third statement (c), then, even though we may be justified in asserting (b), we are not justified in asserting (a). If the man could not have chosen to do otherwise, then he would not have done otherwise – *even if* he was such that, if he *had* chosen to do otherwise, then he would have done otherwise.

The stratagem in question, then, seems to me not to work, and I would say, therefore, that the ascription of responsibility conflicts with a deterministic view of action.

4.   Perhaps there is less need to argue that the ascription of responsibility also conflicts with an indeterministic view of action – with the view that the act, or some event that is essential to the act, is not caused at all. If the act – the firing of the shot – was not caused at all, if it was fortuitous or capricious, happening so to speak out of the blue, then, presumably, no one – and nothing – was responsible for the act. Our conception of action, therefore, should be neither deterministic nor indeterministic. Is there any other possibility?

5.   We must not say that every event involved in the act is caused by some other event; and we must not say that the act is something that is not caused at all. The possibility that remains, therefore, is this: We should say that at least one of the events that are involved in the act is caused, not by any other events, but by something else instead. And this something else can only be the agent – the man. If there is an event that is caused, not by other events, but by the man, then there are some events involved in the act that are not caused by other events. But if the event in question is caused by the man then it *is* caused and we are not committed to saying that there is something involved in the act that is not caused at all.

But this, of course, is a large consequence, implying something of considerable importance about the nature of the agent or the man.

6.   If we consider only inanimate natural objects, we may say that causation, if it occurs, is a relation between *events* or *states of affairs*. The dam's breaking was an event that was caused by a set of other events – the dam being weak, the flood being strong, and so on. But if a man is responsible for a particular deed, then, if what I have said is true, there is some event, or set of events, that is caused, *not* by other events or states of affairs, but by the agent, whatever he may be.

I shall borrow a pair of medieval terms, using them, perhaps, in a way that is slightly different from that for which they were originally intended. I shall say that when one event or state of affairs (or set of events or states of affairs) causes some other event or state of affairs, then we have an instance of *transeunt* causation. And I shall say that when an *agent,* as distinguished from an event, causes an event or state of affairs, then we have an instance of *immanent* causation.

The nature of what is intended by the expression "immanent causation" may be illustrated by this sentence from Aristotle's *Physics*. "Thus, a staff moves a stone, and is moved by a hand, which is moved by a man" (Book VII, Chap. 5, 256a, 6–8). If the man was responsible, then we have in this illustration a number of instances of causation – most of them transeunt but at least one of them immanent. What the staff did to the stone was an instance of transeunt causation, and thus we may describe it as a relation between events: "the motion of the staff caused the motion of the stone." And similarly for what the hand did to the staff: "the motion of the hand caused the motion of the staff." And, as we know from physiology, there are still other events which caused the motion of the hand. Hence we need not introduce the agent at this particular point, as Aristotle does – we *need* not, though we *may*. We *may* say that the hand was moved by the man, but we may *also* say that the motion of the hand was caused by the motion of certain muscles; and we may say that the motion of the muscles was caused by certain events that took place within the brain. But some event, and presumably one of those that took place within the brain, was caused by the agent and not by any other events.

There are, of course, objections to this way of putting the matter; I shall consider the two that seem to me to be most important.

7.   One may object, firstly: "If the *man* does anything, then, as Aristotle's remark suggests, what he does is to move the *hand*. But he certainly does not *do* anything to his brain – he may not even know that he *has* a brain. And if he doesn't do anything to the brain, and if the motion of the hand was caused by something that happened within the brain, then there is no point in appealing to 'immanent causation' as being something incompatible with 'transeunt causation' – for the whole thing, after all, is a matter of causal relations among events or states of affairs."

The answer to this objection, I think, is this: It is true that the agent does not *do* anything with his brain, or to his brain, in the sense in which he *does* something with his hand and does something to the staff. But from this it does not follow that the agent was not the immanent cause of something that happened within his brain.

We should note a useful distinction that has been proposed by Professor A. I. Melden – namely, the distinction between "making something A happen" and "doing A."[5] If I reach for the staff and pick it up, then one of the things that I *do* is just that – reach for the staff and pick it up. And if it is something that I do, then there is a very clear sense in which it may be said to be something that I know that I do. If you ask me, "Are you doing something, or trying to do something, with the staff?", I will have no difficulty in finding an answer. But in doing something with the staff, I also make various things happen which are not in this same sense things that I do: I will make various air-particles move; I will free a number of blades of grass from the pressure that had been upon them; and I may cause a shadow to move from one place to another. If these are merely

446 RODERICK M. CHISHOLM

things that I make happen, as distinguished from things that I do, then I may know nothing whatever about them; I may not have the slightest idea that, in moving the staff, I am bringing about any such thing as the motion of air-particles, shadows, and blades of grass.

We may say, in answer to the first objection, therefore, that it is true that our agent does nothing to his brain or with his brain; but from this it does not follow that the agent is not the immanent cause of some event within his brain; for the brain event may be something which, like the motion of the air-particles, he made happen in picking up the staff. The only difference between the two cases is this: in each case, he made something happen when he picked up the staff; but in the one case – the motion of the air-particles or of the shadows – it was the motion of the staff that caused the event to happen; and in the other case – the event that took place in the brain – it was this event that caused the motion of the staff.

The point is, in a word, that whenever a man does something A, then (by "immanent causation") he makes a certain cerebral event happen, and this cerebral event (by "transeunt causation") makes A happen.

8.   The second objection is more difficult and concerns the very concept of "immanent causation," or causation by an agent, as this concept is to be interpreted here. The concept is subject to a difficulty which has long been associated with that of the prime mover unmoved. We have said that there must be some event A, presumably some cerebral event, which is caused not by any other event, but by the agent. Since A was not caused by any other event, then the agent himself cannot be said to have undergone any change or produced any other event (such as "an act of will" or the like) which brought A about. But if, when the agent made A happen, there was no event involved other than A itself, no event which could be described as *making* A happen, what did the agent's causation consist of? What, for example, is the difference between A's just happening, and the agent's *causing* A to happen? We cannot attribute the difference to any event that took place within the agent. And so far as the event A itself is concerned, there would seem to be no discernible difference. Thus Aristotle said that the activity of the prime mover is nothing in addition to the motion that it produces, and Suarez said that "the action is in reality nothing but the effect as it flows from the agent."[6] Must we conclude, then, that there is no more to the man's action in causing event A than there is to the event A's happening by itself? Here we would seem to have a distinction without a difference – in which case we have failed to find a *via media* between a deterministic and an indeterministic view of action.

The only answer, I think, can be this: that the difference between the man's causing A, on the one hand, and the event A just happening, on the other, lies in the fact that, in the first case but not the second, the event A *was* caused and was caused by the man. There was a brain event A; the agent did, in fact, cause the brain event; but there was nothing that he did to cause it.

This answer may not entirely satisfy and it will be likely to provoke the following question: "But what are you really *adding* to the assertion that A happened when you utter the words 'The agent *caused* A to happen'?" As soon as we have put the question this way, we see, I think, that whatever difficulty we may have encountered is one that may be traced to the concept of causation generally – whether "immanent" or "transeunt." The problem, in other words, is not a problem that is peculiar to our conception of human action. It is a problem that must be faced by anyone who makes use of the concept of causation at all; and therefore, I would say, it is a problem for everyone but the complete indeterminist.

For the problem, as we put it, referring just to "immanent causation," or causation by an agent, was this: "What is the difference between saying, of an event A, that A just happened and saying that someone caused A to happen?" The analogous problem, which holds for "transeunt causation," or causation by an event, is this: "What is the difference between saying, of two events A and B, that B happened and then A happened, and saying that B's happening was the *cause* of A's happening?" And the only answer that one can give is this – that in the one case the agent was the cause of A's happening and in the other case event B was the cause of A's happening. The nature of transeunt causation is no more clear than is that of immanent causation.

9.   But we may plausibly say – and there is a respectable philosophical tradition to which we may appeal – that the notion of immanent causation, or causation by an agent, is in fact more clear than that of transeunt causation, or causation by an event; and that it is only by understanding our own causal efficacy, as agents, that we can grasp the concept of *cause* at all. Hume may be said to have shown that we do not derive the concept of *cause* from what we perceive of external things. How, then, do we derive it? The most plausible suggestion, it seems to me, is that of Reid, once again: namely that "the conception of an efficient cause may very probably be derived from the experience we have had . . . of our own power to produce certain effects."[7] If we did not understand the concept of immanent causation, we would not understand that of transeunt causation.

10.   It may have been noted that I have avoided the term "free will" in all of this. For even if there is such a faculty as "the will," which somehow sets our acts agoing, the question of freedom, as John Locke said, is not the question "*whether the will be free*"; it is the question "*whether a man be free*."[8] For if there is a "will," as a moving faculty, the question is whether the man is free to will to do these things that he does will to do – and also whether he is free *not* to will any of those things that he does will to do, and, again, whether he is free to will any of those things that he does not will to do. Jonathan Edwards tried to restrict himself to the question – "Is the man free to do what it is that he wills?" – but the answer to the question will not tell us whether the man is responsible for what it is that he *does* will to do. Using still another pair of medieval terms, we may say that the metaphysical problem of freedom does not concern the *actus imperatus*; it does not concern the question whether we are free to accomplish

whatever it is that we will or set out to do; it concerns the *actus elicitus,* the question whether we are free to will or to set out to do those things that we do will or set out to do.

11.   If we are responsible, and if what I have been trying to say is true, then we have a prerogative which some would attribute only to God: each of us, when we act, is a prime mover unmoved. In doing what we do, we cause certain events to happen, and nothing – or no one – causes us to cause those events to happen.

12.   If we are thus prime movers unmoved and if our actions, or those for which we are responsible, are not causally determined, then they are not causally determined by our *desires.* And this means that the relation between what we want or what we desire, on the one hand, and what it is that we do, on the other, is not as simple as most philosophers would have it.

We may distinguish between what we might call the "Hobbist approach" and what we might call the "Kantian approach" to this question. The Hobbist approach is the one that is generally accepted at the present time, but the Kantian approach, I believe, is the one that is true. According to Hobbism, if we *know,* of some man, what his beliefs and desires happen to be and how strong they are, if we know what he feels certain of, what he desires more than anything else, and if we know the state of his body and what stimuli he is being subjected to, then we may *deduce,* logically, just what it is that he will do – or, more accurately, just what it is that he will try, set out, or undertake to do. Thus Professor Melden has said that "the connection between wanting and doing is logical."[9] But according to the Kantian approach to our problem, and this is the one that I would take, there is no such logical connection between wanting and doing, nor need there even be a causal connection. No set of statements about a man's desires, beliefs, and stimulus situation at any time implies any statement telling us what the man will try, set out, or undertake to do at that time. As Reid put it, though we may "reason from men's motives to their actions and, in many cases, with great probability," we can never do so "with absolute certainty."[10]

This means that, in one very strict sense of the terms, there can be no science of man. If we think of science as a matter of finding out what laws happen to hold, and if the statement of a law tells us what kinds of events are caused by what other kinds of events, then there will be human actions which we cannot explain by subsuming them under any laws. We cannot say, "It is causally necessary that, given such and such desires and beliefs, and being subject to such and such stimuli, the agent will do so and so." For at times the agent, if he chooses, may rise above his desires and do something else instead.

But all of this is consistent with saying that, perhaps more often than not, our desires do exist under conditions such that those conditions necessitate us to act. And we may also say, with Leibniz, that at other times our desires may "incline without necessitating."

13.   Leibniz's phrase presents us with our final philosophical problem. What does it mean to say that a desire, or a motive, might "incline without necessitat-

ing"? There is a temptation, certainly, to say that "to incline" means to cause and that "not to necessitate" means not to cause, but obviously we cannot have it both ways. . . .

Let us consider a public official who has some moral scruples but who also, as one says, could be had. Because of the scruples that he does have, he would never take any positive steps to receive a bribe – he would not actively solicit one. But his morality has its limits and he is also such that, if we were to confront him with a *fait accompli* or to let him see what is about to happen ($10,000 in cash is being deposited behind the garage), then he would succumb and be unable to resist. The general situation is a familiar one and this is one reason that people pray to be delivered from temptation. (It also justifies Kant's remark: "And how many there are who may have led a long blameless life, who are only *fortunate* in having escaped so many temptations."[11]) Our relation to the misdeed that we contemplate may not be a matter simply of being able to bring it about or not to bring it about. As St Anselm noted, there are at least four possibilities. We may illustrate them by reference to our public official and the event which is his receiving the bribe, in the following way: (i) he may be able to bring the event about himself (*facere esse*), in which case he would actively cause himself to receive the bribe; (ii) he may be able to refrain from bringing it about himself (*non facere esse*), in which case he would not himself do anything to insure that he receive the bribe; (iii) he may be able to do something to prevent the event from occurring (*facere non esse*), in which case he would make sure that the $10,000 was *not* left behind the garage; or (iv) he may be unable to do anything to prevent the event from occurring (*non facere non esse*), in which case, though he may not solicit the bribe, he would allow himself to keep it.[12] We have envisaged our official as a man who can resist the temptation to (i) but cannot resist the temptation to (iv): he can refrain from bringing the event about himself, but he cannot bring himself to do anything to prevent it.

Let us think of "inclination without necessitation," then, in such terms as these. First we may contrast the two propositions:

(1)   He can resist the temptation to do something in order to make A happen;
(2)   He can resist the temptation to allow A to happen (i.e. to do nothing to prevent A from happening).

We may suppose that the man has some desire to have A happen and thus has a motive for making A happen. His motive for making A happen, I suggest, is one that *necessitates* provided that, because of the motive, (1) is false; he cannot resist the temptation to do something in order to make A happen. His motive for making A happen is one that *inclines* provided that, because of the motive, (2) is false; like our public official, he cannot bring himself to do anything to prevent A from happening. And therefore we can say that this motive for making A happen is one that *inclines but does not necessitate* provided that, because of the motive, (1) is true and (2) is false; he can resist the temptation to make it happen but he cannot resist the temptation to allow it to happen.

Notes

1   The general position to be presented here is suggested in the following writings, among others: Aristotle, *Eudemian Ethics,* book II, ch. 6; *Nicomachean Ethics,* book III, chs 1–5; Thomas Reid, *Essays on the Active Powers of Man;* C. A. Campbell, "Is 'Free Will' a Pseudo-Problem?" *Mind,* n.s. 60 (1951), pp. 441–65; Roderick M. Chisholm, "Responsibility and Avoidability," and Richard Taylor "Determination and the Theory of Agency," in Sidney Hook, ed., *Determinism and Freedom in the Age of Modern Science* (New York: New York University Press, 1958).
2   Thomas Reid, *Essays on the Active Powers of the Human Mind* (Cambridge, Mass.: MIT Press, 1969; first published 1788), p. 261.
3   *Summa Theologia,* First Part of the Second Part, Question VI: "On the Voluntary and Involuntary."
4   Jonathan Edwards, *Freedom of the Will* (New Haven, Conn.: Yale University Press, 1957); G. E. Moore, *Ethics* (Home University Library, 1912), ch. 6.
5   A. I. Melden, *Free Action* (Oxford: Blackwell, 1961), especially ch. 3. Mr Melden's own views, however, are quite the contrary of those proposed here.
6   Aristotle, *Physics,* book III, ch, 3; Suarez, *Disputationes Metaphysicae,* Disputation 18, Section 10.
7   Reid, *Essays on the Active Powers,* p. 39.
8   John Locke, *Essay Concerning Human Understanding,* book II, ch. 21.
9   Melden, *Free Action,* p. 166.
10 Reid, *Essays on the Active Powers,* p. 291.
11 In the preface to the *Metaphysical Elements of Ethics,* in T. K. Abbot, ed., *Kant's Critique of Practical Reason and Other Works on the Theory of Ethics* (London: Longman's Green, 1959), p. 303.
12 Cf. D. P. Henry, "Saint Anselm's 'De Grammatico'," *Philosophical Quarterly,* 10 (1960); pp. 115–26. . . .

47   The Consequence Argument

Peter van Inwagen

In a book I once wrote about free will, I contended that the best and most important argument for the incompatibility of free will and determinism was "the Consequence Argument." I gave the following brief sketch of the Consequence Argument as a prelude to several more careful and detailed statements of the argument:

> If determinism is true, then our acts are the consequences of the laws of nature and events in the remote past. But it is not up to us what went on before we were born, and neither is it up to us what the laws of nature are. Therefore, the consequences of these things (including our present acts) are not up to us.[1]

The reading that follows this one, Reading 48, "The Mystery of Metaphysical Freedom," contains a statement of the Consequence Argument. The argument is contained in the paragraph (p. 460–1) that starts, "As Carl Ginet has said. . . ." But, as you will see if you compare the "brief sketch" with that paragraph, "The Mystery of Metaphysical Freedom" presents the Consequence Argument in a disguise that is not easy to penetrate. Some teachers of philosophy who have used the first edition of *Metaphysics: The Big Questions* as a textbook have asked for a more straightforward statement of the Consequence Argument (since much of the recent discussion of the question of the compatibility of free will and determinism in the philosophical literature has taken the form of criticisms of the Consequence Argument that are rather hard to apply to the argument in the form in which it is presented in Reading 48). This essay is an attempt to meet this request.

Some truths, some true propositions, have this important feature (well, it's important to *me*): their truth, the fact that they are true, is something that is or once was *up to me*. For example, the proposition that the title of this essay is "The Consequence Argument" is true, and it was once up to me whether it would be true. Or, at any rate, almost everyone would suppose that it was once up to me whether it would be true. If we believe that the truth of this proposition is something that is up to me, we believe this because we believe that (in this matter, at any rate) I have free will: that it is, or once was, up to me what title the essay would have, that I was *able* to give it any of various other appropriate titles. If I have free will, in short, then some things are up to me. (Even the outcome of a process that is not under my control can be up to me, provided it was up to me whether the process occurred at all. I cannot control the way a fair die falls, but the truth of the true proposition "The die fell 'four'" was up to me if it was up to me whether the die was thrown at all.) Some things are up to me – but not, of course, all things, for free will does not imply omnipotence. I was, for example, born in 1942, and whether I was born in that year is not, and never was, up to me. If, however, my parents had free will, the truth of this proposition is something that was up to them: if they had chosen not to marry or never to have children or to wait to have children till my father was released from military service (which happened in 1944), then the proposition that I was born in 1942 would have been false.

Some truths, however, are not up to *anyone* (to any human being). For example: that human beings exist, that the earth has a large moon, that the presence of mass changes the local curvature of spacetime, that there is no largest prime number. Let us call a true proposition whose truth is up to no one (to no human being, past, present, or future) an *untouchable* proposition. (We shall sometimes find it convenient to say that it is *an untouchable fact that* or *an untouchable truth that*, e.g., the earth has a large moon.)

An untouchable proposition has the following feature: it is true and nothing that anyone is or ever has been able to do (no possible combination or series of actions that any human being has been able to perform individually or that any human beings have been able to perform collectively) would have had the consequence that it was false. It might even be supposed that this would be another way of saying that an untouchable proposition is a true proposition whose truth is up to no one. And perhaps this supposition would be consistent with the meaning of "true proposition whose truth is up to no one." However that may be, I mean something stronger than this by "untouchable proposition" or "true proposition whose truth is up to no one." I mean this:

> An untouchable proposition is a true proposition that is such that nothing that anyone is or ever has been able to do *might* have had the consequence that it was false.

To see the difference between the (weaker) "would have had" and the (stronger) "might have had" understanding of 'untouchable', consider this case. Suppose that no human being is ever invisible. And suppose I once had a single vial of magical potion (which I was able to drink but in fact did not drink – in fact I chose to pour it down the drain) with this property: if I had drunk it I *might have* become invisible – and I might *not* have. Let us say, in fact, that if I had drunk the potion in the vial, there was a *fifty-fifty chance* that my ingesting it would have resulted in my becoming invisible. And let us say that drinking the potion is the *only* thing I have (or anyone has) ever been able to do that might have had the consequence that I (or anyone else) became invisible. If all this is true, then the true proposition "No human being is ever invisible" is not, as I have defined the term, an untouchable proposition. Although nothing I have ever been able to do *would have had* the consequence that this proposition was false, something I was once able to do *might have had* the consequence that this proposition was false; and that is sufficient for this proposition's not being untouchable.

Untouchability seems to have a certain logic to it. One part of this logic is this: any necessary truth (any proposition that *has to* be true, that would be true *no matter what*, like "2 + 2 = 4" or "An airplane can't be made entirely out of gaseous hydrogen") is untouchable. Let us call the following rule of logical inference:

> It is a necessary truth that p
>
> *hence*, it is an untouchable truth that p

the *Necessity Rule*. Another part of the logic of untouchability is captured in a rule about conditional (if-then) statements:

> It is an untouchable truth that p
> It is an untouchable truth that (if p, then q)
>
> *hence*, it is an untouchable truth that q.

Let us call this the *Conditional Rule*. Examination of a few examples will, I think, convince the reader that it is at least very plausible to suppose that the Conditional Rule is valid. Consider, for instance, the result of replacing '*p*' in the Conditional Rule with 'The sun explodes in the year 2027' and '*q*' with 'All life on the earth ends in the year 2027':

It is an untouchable truth that the sun explodes in the year 2027

It is an untouchable truth that (if the sun explodes in the year 2027, then all life on the earth ends in the year 2027)

hence, it is an untouchable truth that all life on the earth ends in the year 2027.

If in fact the sun does explode in 2027, then the first premise is no doubt true. (If the sun is going to explode in 2027, then nothing human beings can do would – or *might* – prevent that catastrophic event.) And the second premise seems very plausible, too: If the sun explodes, then nothing human beings can do would – or might – prevent the immediate extinction of all terrestrial life. Whether the two premises of this argument are true or not, however, it seems evident beyond all possibility of dispute that the conclusion of the argument follows from them: if we can't prevent the explosion of the sun, and if we can't do anything about the fact that such an explosion would have the end of life on the earth as a consequence, then we can't prevent the end of all life on the earth. The reader is invited to try to construct a counterexample to the Conditional Rule. That is, to imagine a possible case in which, for some argument that comes from the rule by substitution of any sentences for '*p*' and '*q*', the premises of the argument are both true and its conclusion false. It is at least very hard to find a counterexample to the Conditional Rule. But the rule is invalid only if there is some possible counterexample to it.

Having set out these two rules governing the notion of untouchability, let us turn to the idea of determinism. Let P_0 be a proposition that gives a complete and correct description of the state of the whole universe at some time in the remote past (a million years ago, say). And let L be the conjunction into a single proposition of all the laws of nature (or the laws of physics). (By the laws of nature we do not mean what physicists or other scientists now happen to *think* the laws of nature are. We mean the *real* laws of nature, the laws as God sees them, or as a complete and perfect science at the end of all enquiry would see them.) Determinism implies that the following conditional (if-then) proposition is a *necessary* truth:

(1) If P_0 and L are both true, van Inwagen writes an essay called "The Consequence Argument."

For suppose that determinism is true. Determinism says that the past (the past at any given instant, a complete specification of the universe at any given instant in the past) and the laws of nature together determine *everything*, that they leave no open possibilities whatever. And since van Inwagen *did* write an essay called "The Consequence Argument," the fact that he wrote this essay is one aspect of the "everything" that is determined by the past and the laws.

The laws of elementary logic tell us that (1) is logically equivalent to

> (2)   If P_0 is true, then, if L is true, van Inwagen writes an essay called "The Consequence Argument."

If (1) is a necessary truth (as we have seen that it is), then (2), being logically equivalent to (1), must also be a necessary truth. And if (2) is a necessary truth, it is, by the Necessity Rule, an untouchable truth.

Now consider P_0. P_0 is obviously an untouchable truth. P_0 is an untouchable truth for the same reason that "Dinosaurs once walked the earth" is an untouchable truth: both are truths about the past, and, indeed, truths about the prehuman past.

Let us now examine the following argument:

> It is an untouchable truth that P_0 is true
> It is an untouchable truth that (if P_0 is true, then, if L is true, van Inwagen writes an essay called "The Consequence Argument")
>
> *hence*, it is an untouchable truth that if L is true, van Inwagen writes an essay called "The Consequence Argument."

Examination shows that this argument is valid if the Conditional Rule is valid. (It comes from the Conditional Rule by substitution of 'P_0 is true' for 'p' and 'if L is true, van Inwagen writes an essay called "The Consequence Argument"' for 'q'.) And the two premises of the argument are, as we have seen, true. (Note that what follows 'it is an untouchable truth that' in the second premise is just statement (2).) The conclusion of the argument is therefore true (given that the Conditional Rule is valid).

Now examine a second argument:

> It is an untouchable truth that L is true
> It is an untouchable truth that (if L is true, van Inwagen writes an essay called "The Consequence Argument")
>
> *hence*, it is an untouchable truth that van Inwagen writes an essay called "The Consequence Argument."

This argument, too, comes from the Conditional Rule by substitution: of 'L is true' for 'p' and of 'Van Inwagen writes an essay called "The Consequence Argument"' for 'q'. The first premise of this second argument is true, for L is the conjunction into a single proposition of all the laws of nature. And the laws of nature are untouchable truths. As far as human beings (at any rate) are concerned, the laws of nature are just *there*, one of the givens of our existence. Nothing anyone is able to do is such that it would, or even might, result in the falsity of a proposition that is a law of nature. (If there is an experiment that physicists are able to perform – even if they never do – that might result in a violation of the principle of the conservation of angular momentum, it follows that the principle of the conservation of angular momentum is not a law of nature.) And the second premise is the conclusion of the first argument. The conclusion of the argument is therefore true (if, again, the Conditional Rule is valid).

What does the conclusion say? Well it certainly implies that I do not have, and never had, any free will in the matter of whether I should write an essay called "The Consequence Argument." It implies that I was never able *not* to write an essay of that title: for if I did have that ability, then there is something I was able to do such that, if I had done it, the proposition "Van Inwagen writes an essay called 'The Consequence Argument'" would have been false. If I did have that ability, then that proposition would not have been an untouchable proposition.

This is, of course, a rather limited conclusion. It says nothing about anyone's free will but mine, and it leaves plenty of room for free will for me in matters unrelated to the above essay and its title. But it is obvious that the argument we have gone through is easily generalized to show that no one has any free will in any matter whatever. For, if there is no error in the above argument, then there will be no error in any argument that is obtained from it by replacing each occurrence of 'Van Inwagen writes an essay called "The Consequence Argument"' with any sentence that expresses a truth. Appropriate substitution, for example, will yield arguments whose conclusions are:

It is an untouchable truth that James Earl Ray assassinated Martin Luther King, Jr.

It is an untouchable truth that the World Trade Center was destroyed by terrorists on September 11th, 2001.

It is an untouchable truth that six million Jews were murdered in the Holocaust.

And this implies that if determinism is true (if the past and the laws of nature determine a unique future), *every* true proposition is an untouchable truth. And if every true proposition is an untouchable truth, then free will simply does not exist: no one is ever able to do anything other than just exactly those things that he or she does.

This conclusion, which is called incompatibilism, is a very strong thesis indeed. Is there any way to avoid it? Anyone who wishes to avoid it – anyone who wishes to be a *compatibilist*, anyone who wishes to believe that free will and determinism can co-exist – must deny at least one of the following propositions, each of which the argument depends on in one way or another:

The Necessity Rule is valid

The Conditional Rule is valid

P_0 is an untouchable truth

L is an untouchable truth.

Or, at any rate, this is the case if the meanings of all four propositions (or the meanings of the sentences that express them) are perfectly clear. The philosopher David Lewis has contended (this is a translation of what he has contended into the terms used in this essay) that our technical term 'untouchable' is ambiguous, and that if the word is understood in one of its possible senses, the Conditional Rule is invalid, and, if it is understood in the other of its possible senses, L is not an untouchable truth.[2] I will count this as a special case of denying that all four propositions are true.

Most critics of the argument agree that its weak point is the validity of the Conditional Rule. Most of its defenders would concede that if the argument *has* a weak point, that weak point is the validity of the Conditional Rule. It would seem, therefore, that the lesson of the Consequence Argument is that the question of the compatibility of free will and determinism, in the last analysis, comes down to the question whether the Conditional Rule is valid.

Notes

1   Peter van Inwagen, *An Essay on Free Will* (Oxford: at the Clarendon Press, 1983), p. 16 and p. 56.
2   David Lewis, "Are We Free to Break the Laws?", *Theoria* 47 (1981), pp. 113–21. Reprinted in David Lewis, *Philosophical Papers, Vol. II* (New York and Oxford: Oxford University Press, 1986), pp. 291–98. See also Peter van Inwagen, "Freedom to Break the Laws," *Midwest Studies in Philosophy Vol. XXVIII* (2004), pp. 334–50.

48   The Mystery of Metaphysical Freedom

Peter van Inwagen

There are many kinds of freedom – or, as I prefer to say, the word "freedom" has many senses. In one sense of the word, an agent is "free" to the extent that his actions are not subject to control by the state. It is, however, obvious that an agent may be free in this sense but unfree in other senses. However little the state may interfere with my actions, I may be unfree because I am paralyzed from the waist down or because I am subject to a neurotic fear of open spaces that makes it impossible for me to venture out of doors or because I am so poor that I am unable to afford the necessary means to do what I want to do. These examples suggest that freedom is a merely negative concept – that freedom is freedom from constraint, that freedom consists in the mere absence of constraint. If freedom is in this sense a negative concept, this explains why there are many kinds of freedom: there are many kinds of freedom because there are many kinds of constraint. Because there are political constraints, there is political freedom, which exists in their absence; because there are internal psychological constraints (such as neurosis), there is psychological freedom, which exists in their absence; because there are economic constraints, there is economic freedom, which exists in their absence – and so on.

When we turn from politics and psychology and economics to metaphysics, however, we encounter discussions of freedom – discussions involving words like "freedom," "free," and "freely" – that it is hard to account for if freedom is no more than a negative concept. Consider, for example, the following words of Holbach:

> Man's life is a line that nature commands him to describe upon the surface of the earth, without his ever being able to swerve from it, even for an instant. . . . Nevertheless, in spite of the shackles by which he is bound, it is pretended he is a free agent. . . .

Or consider the ancient problem of future contingents, which would seem to depend on considerations different from those adduced by Holbach, for it has only to do with whether statements about future events must be either true or false, and has nothing to do with causation and physical law. Consider, again, the problem of divine knowledge of future human action. Consider, finally, the problem of evil and the attempts to solve that problem that appeal to the freedom of creatures and the alleged impossibility of a free creature that is certain to do no evil.

I think it is fairly evident that the concept of freedom that figures in the discussions raised by these metaphysical problems is the same concept. I think it is not easy to see how this concept could be understood as a merely negative concept, as a concept that applies to any agent just in the case that that agent's acts are not subject to some sort of constraint.

Consider, for example, the problem of free will and determinism, the problem that is raised by the above quotation from Holbach. Although my present actions may be determined by the laws of nature and the state of the world before my birth (indeed, millions of years ago), it does not follow that this state of affairs places me under any sort of constraint. A constraint on one's behavior is an impediment to the exercise of one's will. If the state places me in chains, then my will to be elsewhere, if I attempt to exercise it, will soon come into conflict with the length and solidity of my chain. If I am an extreme agoraphobe, then my will to go about the ordinary business of life will come into conflict with sensations of panic and dislocation the moment I step out of doors. If I am very poor, my will to own a warm overcoat will come into conflict with my lack of the price of the coat. It is things of these sorts that are meant by "constraint." And it is evident that determinism places me under no constraints. It is true that in a deterministic world, *what my will is on a given occasion* will be a consequence of the way the world was millions of years ago and the laws of nature. It is true that in a deterministic world, *whether my will happens to encounter an obstacle on a given occasion* will be a consequence of the way the world was millions of years ago and the laws of nature. But it is certainly not inevitable that my will encounter an obstacle on any given occasion in a deterministic world, and even in an inde-terministic world, my will must encounter obstacles on many occasions. Indeed, there is no reason to suppose that my will will encounter obstacles more fre-quently in a deterministic world than in an indeterministic world. Anyone who believes that freedom is a negative concept will therefore conclude that the so-called problem of free will and determinism is founded on confusion. (So Hobbes, Hume, Mill, and many other philosophers have concluded.)

The situation is similar with the problem of divine knowledge of future human actions. We are often told that there really is no problem about this, since the fact that God knows that one is going to tell a lie (for example) in no way forces one to lie. Since God's knowledge does not interfere with the exercise of one's will, since the false words that issue from one's mouth are the words that it was one's will to speak, God's knowledge that one was going to lie is consistent with the lie's being a free act.

All this can sound very sensible. And yet one is left with the feeling that the freedom this leaves us with is, in Kant's words, a "wretched subterfuge." This feeling can be embodied in an argument. The argument is, to my mind, a rather powerful one. If the argument is correct, then freedom is not a merely negative concept. Or, at any rate, there is *a* concept of freedom that is not a merely nega-tive concept, and this concept is a very important one. It is this concept, I believe, that figures in the metaphysical problems I have cited. I will call it metaphysical freedom. In calling it metaphysical freedom, however, I do not mean to imply that it is of interest only to the metaphysician. I believe that this concept is also of importance in everyday life, and that the concept that metaphysicians employ is just this everyday concept, or perhaps a refinement of it. (I should be willing to argue that all concepts that we employ in philosophy or science or any other area of inquiry are either everyday concepts or explicable in terms of everyday concepts.)

In ordinary English, the concept of metaphysical freedom finds its primary expression in simple, common words and phrases, and not in the grand, abstract terms of philosophical art that one is apt to associate with metaphysics. (The situ-ation is similar in French, German, and Latin. I should be surprised to learn of a language in which the concept I am calling "metaphysical freedom" could not be expressed in simple, common words and phrases.) It is true that philosophical analysis is needed to distinguish those uses of these simple words and phrases on which they express this concept from other uses on which they express other concepts. Nevertheless, in particular concrete contexts, these simple words express that very concept of freedom (not, as we shall see, a negative concept) that figures in metaphysical problems like the problem of freedom and determinism. But perhaps the meaning of these abstract remarks will not be clear without an example.

One of the simple words that expresses the concept of metaphysical freedom in English is "can." What are we asking when we ask whether I am free to tell the truth tomorrow if it has been determined by events in the remote past and the laws of nature that when, tomorrow, I confront a choice between lying and telling the truth, I shall lie? Only this: "I am free to tell the truth" means "I *can* tell the truth," and "I am not free to tell the truth" means "I *cannot* tell the truth." Metaphysical freedom, therefore, is simply what is expressed by "can." If we accept this thesis, however, we must take care to understand it properly. We must take care to avoid two possible sources of confusion: the ambiguity of the word "can" and false philosophical theories about what is expressed by certain sentences in which it occurs.

As to the first point, the word "can" is extremely versatile, and can be used to express many ideas other than the idea of metaphysical freedom (a fact illustrated by this sentence). One example must suffice. In negative constructions, "can" sometimes expresses an idea that might be called "moral impossibility." One might say to a hard-hearted son, "You can't refuse to take your own mother into your house" – even though one knows perfectly well that in the sense of "can" we have been discussing he certainly *can* refuse to take his own mother into his house because he has already done so. We must take care that if we propose to use the simple word "can" as our means to an understanding of metaphysical freedom, we do not allow our understanding of metaphysical freedom to be influenced by any of the many other concepts this simple word can be used to express. The best way to avoid such influence is not to rely on the word "can" alone in our attempt to understand metaphysical freedom, but to examine also as many as possible of the other simple, ordinary words and phrases that can be used to express the concept of metaphysical freedom (or unfreedom). To illustrate what I mean, here are three sentences in which idioms of ordinary speech that do not involve "can" are used to express the concepts of metaphysical freedom and unfreedom:

- He will *be able* to be there in time for the meeting.
- You must not blame her for missing the meeting; she *had no choice* about that.
- It was simply *not within my power* to attend the meeting.

(Oddly enough, the phrase "of his own free will" does not express the concept of metaphysical freedom, despite the fact that "free will," as a philosophical term of art, means just exactly what I mean by "metaphysical freedom." To say that someone attended a meeting of his own free will is simply to say that no one forced him to attend the meeting. The phrase "of his own free will" thus expresses a merely negative concept, the concept of the absence of coercion.)

False theories about the meanings of philosophically important words and phrases abound, and the philosophically important word "can" is no exception to this generalization. There are those who, recognizing the importance of idioms like "I can do X" for the metaphysical problems of freedom, have simply insisted that this word means something that supports their favorite philosophical theories. An example of such a theory would be: "I can do X" means "There exists no impediment, obstacle, or barrier to my doing X; nothing prevents my doing X." I will not argue specifically for the conclusion that this theory is false; the argument I will later present for the incompatibility of metaphysical freedom and determinism, however, will have the consequence that this theory about the meaning of "I can" is false – since, if the theory were true, metaphysical freedom would be compatible with determinism. At this point, I wish merely to call attention to the fact that there do exist tendentious theories about the meaning of "I can do X."

If we consider carefully the meaning of "I can do X" ("I am able to do X"; "It is within my power to do X") do we find that the idea expressed by this form of words is a merely negative one, the idea of the absence of some constraint or barrier or obstacle to action? It would seem not. It is true that the presence of an obstacle to the performance of an action can be sufficient for one's being unable to perform that action. But it does not follow that the absence of all obstacles to the performance of an action is sufficient for one's being *able* to perform that action. And the idea that ability could consist in the absence of obstacles does seem, on consideration, to be a very puzzling idea indeed. To see this, let us examine carefully the relation between the concept of ability and the concept of an obstacle. We should note that not just any obstacle to one's performance of an action is such that its presence renders one unable to perform that action – for some obstacles can be surmounted or eliminated or bypassed (in short: some obstacles can be overcome). Let us ask a simple question: *which* obstacles to the performance of an action are such that their presence renders one unable to perform that action? Why, just those obstacles that one is *unable* to overcome, of course. And it seems fairly obvious that the concept of an obstacle that one is unable to overcome cannot be analyzed or explained in terms of the concept of an obstacle *simpliciter*. (Is the concept of an obstacle that one cannot overcome the concept of an obstacle such that there is some "decisive" obstacle to one's overcoming it? – No, not unless a "decisive" obstacle is understood as an obstacle that one is unable to overcome. . . .) These reflections suggest very strongly that the concept expressed by the words "I can do X" or "I am able to do X" cannot be a merely negative concept, the concept of the absence of some sort of obstacle or barrier or impediment to action. But let us turn now to the question of the compatibility of determinism and metaphysical freedom. I shall present an argument for the conclusion that determinism is incompatible with metaphysical freedom. Since, as we have seen, determinism and metaphysical freedom are compatible if metaphysical freedom (the concept expressed by "I can do X") is a merely negative concept, this argument will be in effect an argument for the conclusion that metaphysical freedom is not a merely negative concept.

As Carl Ginet has said, our freedom can only be the freedom to add to the actual past – for the past is unalterable; it is what we *find ourselves with* in any situation in which we are contemplating some course of action. (Or to put this point in the terms I have been recommending, all we *can* do, all we are *able to do*, is add to the actual past.) And, unless we are bona fide miracle workers, we can make only such additions to the actual past as conform to the laws of nature. But the only additions to the actual past that conform to a deterministic set of laws are the additions that are actually made, the additions that collectively make up the actual present and the actual future. This is simply a statement of what is meant by determinism, which is the thesis that the laws of nature and the past together determine a unique future. Therefore, if the laws of nature are deterministic, we are free to do only what we in fact do – that is, we are unable to act otherwise than we do and are ipso facto not free in the sense in which the term "free" is properly used in metaphysics.

This little argument has great persuasive power, and it is probably no more than an articulation of the reasons that lead, almost without exception, the undergraduates to whom I lecture to join Kant in regarding the merely negative freedom of Hobbes and Hume as a wretched subterfuge. If the argument is correct, as I have said, it refutes the idea that metaphysical freedom is a merely negative concept, for the past and the laws of nature are not impediments to the exercise of one's will. But, more generally, we may well ask what we are to say of this argument and its consequences, for these consequences go far beyond establishing that metaphysical freedom is not a negative concept. One possible reaction to the argument would be to say, with Holbach, that, because determinism is true, we therefore do not possess metaphysical freedom. (An epistemologically more modest reaction would be to say that, because we do not know whether determinism is true, we do not know whether we possess metaphysical freedom.) I shall return to the possibility that we lack freedom (or that we do not know whether we have freedom). For the moment, let us see where the argument leaves those of us who would like to say that we are free and that we know this. Many philosophers have regarded it as evident that we are free, and have accepted something like our argument for the incompatibility of determinism and metaphysical freedom. These philosophers, therefore, have denied that the world is deterministic, have denied that the laws of nature and the past together determine a unique future.

These philosophers (among whom I count myself) face a difficult problem. They assert or postulate that the laws of nature are indeterministic. One might ask how they know this, or what gives them the right to this postulate. These are good questions, but I will not consider them. I want to consider instead another question that these philosophers must answer: does postulating or asserting that the laws of nature are indeterministic provide any comfort to those who would like to believe in metaphysical freedom? If the laws are indeterministic, then more than one future is indeed consistent with those laws and the actual past and present – but how can anyone have any choice about which of these futures becomes actual? Isn't it just a matter of chance which becomes actual? If God were to "return" an indeterministic world to precisely its state at some time in the past, and then let the world go forward again, things might indeed happen differently the "second" time. But then, if the world is indeterministic, isn't it just a matter of chance how things *did* happen in the one, actual course of events?

And if what we do is just a matter of chance – well, who would want to call that freedom?

It seems, therefore, that, in addition to our argument for the incompatibility of metaphysical freedom and determinism, we have an argument for the incompatibility of metaphysical freedom and *in*determinism. But the world must be either deterministic or indeterministic. It follows that, unless one of the two arguments contains some logical error or proceeds from a false premise, metaphysical freedom must be a contradiction in terms, as much an impossibility as a round square or a liquid wine bottle. We may in fact *define* the problem of metaphysical freedom as the problem of discovering whether either of the two arguments is defective, and (if so) of locating the defect or defects.

The problem of metaphysical freedom, so conceived, is a very *abstract* problem. Although, for historical reasons, it is natural to think of the problem as essentially involving reference to the physical world and its supposedly intransigent laws ("man's life is a line that nature commands him to describe on the surface of the earth . . ."), it does not. For suppose that man's life is in fact *not* a line that nature commands him to describe on the surface of the earth. Suppose that nature presents us with two or seventeen or ten thousand lines inscribed on the surface of the earth, and says to us (in effect), "Choose whichever one of them you like." How could it be that we really had any choice about which "line" we followed, when any deliberations we might undertake would themselves have to be segments of the lines that nature has offered us? Imagine that two of the lines that nature offers me diverge at some point – that is, imagine that the lines present the aspect of a fork in a road or a river. The common part of the two lines, the segment that immediately precedes their divergence, represents the course of my deliberations; their divergence from a common origin represents diagrammatically the fact that *either* of two futures is a possible outcome of my deliberations. My deliberations, therefore, do not determine which future I shall choose. But then what *does* determine which future I shall choose? Only chance, it would seem, and if only chance determines which of two paths into the future I follow, then how can it be that I have a choice about which of them I follow?

The problem of metaphysical freedom is so abstract, so very nearly independent of the features of the world in which agents happen to find themselves, that it could – it would; it must – arise in essentially the same form in a world inhabited only by immaterial intelligences, a world whose only inhabitants were, let us say, angels.

Let us consider such a world. It is true that if there were only angels, there would be no physical laws – or at any rate there would be nothing for the laws to apply to, so we might as well say there would be none. But if we assume the angels make choices, we have to assume that time (somehow) exists in this non-physical world, and that the angels are in different "states" at different times. And what is responsible for the way an angel changes its states with the passage of time? One possibility is that it is something structurally analogous to the laws of physics – something that stands to angels as our laws of physics stand to electrons and quarks. (I'm assuming, by the way, that these angels are metaphysical simples, that they are not composed of smaller immaterial things. If they were, we could conduct the argument in terms of the smallest immaterial things, the "elementary particles" of this imaginary immaterial world.) This "something" takes the properties of the angels at any time (and the relations they bear to one another at that time: the analogue, whatever it may be, of spatial relations in a material world) as "input," and delivers as output a sheaf of possible futures and histories of the world. In other words, given the "state of the world" at any time, it tells you what temporal sequences of states could have preceded the world's being in that state at that time, and it tells you what temporal sequences of states could follow the world's being in that state at that time. Maybe it couldn't be written as a set of differential equations (since nothing I have said implies that the properties of and relations among angels are quantifiable) as the laws of our physical world presumably can, but I don't think that affects the point. And the point is: either "the sheaf of possible futures" relative to each moment has only one member or it has more than one. If it has only one, the world of angels is deterministic. And then where is their free will? (Their freedom is the freedom to add to the actual past. And they can only add to the actual past in accordance with the laws that govern the way angels change their properties and their relations to one another with time.) If it has more than one, then the fact that one possible future rather than another, equally possible, future becomes actual seems to be simply a matter of chance. And then where is their free will?

I said above that this way of looking at a postulated "world of angels" was one possibility. But are there really any others? We have to think of the angels as being temporal and as changing their properties with the passage of time if we are to think of them as making choices. And we have to think of them as bearing various relations to one another if we are to think of them as belonging to the same world. And we have to think of them as having natures if we are to think of them as being real things. Every real thing that is in time must have a nature that puts some kinds of constraints on how it can change its states with the passage of time. Or so, at any rate, it seems to me. But if we grant this much, it seems that, insofar as we can imagine a world of non-physical things (angels or any others) we must imagine the inhabitants of this world as being subject to something analogous to the laws of physics. If this "something" is deterministic, then (it seems) we can't think of the inhabitants of our imaginary world as having free will. And if this "something" is *in*deterministic, then (it seems) we can't think of the inhabitants of our imaginary world as having free will. Thus, the "problem of metaphysical freedom" is a problem so abstract and general that it arises in any imaginable world in which there are beings who make choices. The problem, in fact, arises in exactly the same way in relation to God. God, the theologians tell us, although He did in fact create a world, was free not to. (That is, He was *able* not to create a world.) But God has His own nature, which even He cannot violate and cannot change. (He cannot, for example, make Himself less than omnipotent; He cannot break a promise He has made; He cannot command immoral behavior.) And either this nature determines that He shall create a world or it does not. If it does, He was not free not to create. If it does not, then, it would seem, the fact that He *did* create a world was merely a matter of chance. For what, other than chance, could be responsible for the fact that

He created a world? His choice or His will? But what determined that he should make *that* choice when the choice not to make a world was also consistent with His nature? What determined that His will should be set on making a world, when a will set on *not* making a world was also consistent with His nature? We should not be surprised that our dilemma concerning metaphysical freedom applies even to God, for the dilemma does not depend on the nature of the agent to whom the concept of metaphysical freedom is applied. The dilemma arises from the concept of metaphysical freedom itself, and its conclusion is that metaphysical freedom is a contradictory concept. And a contradictory concept can no more apply to God than it can apply to anything else.

The concept of metaphysical freedom seems, then, to be contradictory. One way to react to the seeming contradiction in this concept would be to conclude that it was real: metaphysical freedom seems contradictory because it *is* contradictory. (This was the conclusion reached by C. D. Broad.)

But none of us really believes this. A philosopher may argue that consciousness does not exist or that knowledge is impossible or that there is no right or wrong. But no one really believes that he himself is not conscious or that no one knows whether there is such a city as Warsaw; and only interested parties believe that there is nothing morally objectionable about child brothels or slavery or the employment of poison gas against civilians. And everyone really believes in metaphysical freedom, whether or not he would call it by that name. Dr Johnson famously said, "Sir, we know our will's free, and there's an end on't." Perhaps he was wrong, but he was saying something we all believe. Whether or not we are all, as the existentialists said, condemned to freedom, we are certainly all condemned to *believe in* freedom – and, in fact, condemned to believe that we *know* that we are free. (I am not disputing the sincerity of those philosophers who, like Holbach, have denied in their writings the reality of metaphysical freedom. I am saying rather that their beliefs are contradictory. Perhaps, as they say, they believe that there is no freedom – but, being human beings, they also believe that there is. In my book on freedom, I compared them to the Japanese astronomer who was said to have believed, in the 1930s, that the sun was an astronomically distant ball of hot gas vastly larger than the earth, and also to have believed that the sun was the ancestress of the Japanese imperial dynasty.)

I would ask you to try a simple experiment. Consider some important choice that confronts you. You must, perhaps, decide whether to marry a certain person, or whether to undergo a dangerous but promising course of medical treatment, or whether to report to a superior a colleague you suspect of embezzling money. (Tailor the example to your own life.) Consider the two courses of action that confront you; since I don't know what you have chosen, I'll call them simply A and B. Do you really not believe that you are *able* to do A and *able* to do B? If you do not, then how can it be that you are trying to decide which of them to do? It seems clear to me that when *I* am trying to decide which of two things to do, I commit myself, by the very act of attempting to decide between the two, to the thesis that I am able to do each of them. If I am trying to decide whether to report my colleague, then, by the very act of trying to reach a decision about this matter, I commit myself both to the thesis that I am able to report him and to the thesis that I am able to refrain from reporting him: although I obviously cannot do *both* these things, I can (I believe) do *either*. In sum: whether we are free or not, we believe that we are – and I think we believe, too, that we *know* this. We believe that we know this even if, like Holbach, we *also* believe that we are not free, and, therefore, that we do not know that we are free.

But if we know that we are free – indeed, if we are free and do not know it – there is some defect in one or both of our two arguments. Either there is something wrong with our argument for the conclusion that metaphysical freedom is incompatible with determinism or there is something wrong with our argument for the conclusion that metaphysical freedom is incompatible with *in*determinism – or there is something wrong with both arguments. But which argument is wrong, and why? (Or are they both wrong?) I do not know. I think no one knows. That is why my title is, "The *Mystery* of Metaphysical Freedom." I believe I know, as surely as I know anything, that at least one of the two arguments contains a mistake. And yet, having thought very hard about the two arguments for almost thirty years, I confess myself unable to identify even a possible candidate for such a mistake. My *opinion* is that the first argument (the argument for the incompatibility of freedom and determinism) is essentially sound, and that there is, therefore, something wrong with the second argument (the argument for the incompatibility of freedom and indeterminism). But if you ask me *what* it is, I have to say that I am, as current American slang has it, absolutely clueless. Indeed the problem seems to me to be so evidently impossible of solution that I find very attractive a suggestion that has been made by Noam Chomsky (and which was developed by Colin McGinn in his recent book *The Problems of Philosophy*) that there is something about our biology, something about the ways of thinking that are "hardwired" into our brains, that renders it impossible for us human beings to dispel the mystery of metaphysical freedom. However this may be, I am certain that I cannot dispel the mystery, and I am certain that no one else has in fact done so.

---

49 The Agent as Cause

Timothy O'Connor

In the previous essay, Peter van Inwagen argues that "metaphysical freedom" is incompatible with a certain abstract picture of the world (commonly dubbed "determinism"), on which it evolves in strict accordance with physical laws, laws such that the state of the world at any given time ensures a unique outcome at any subsequent moment. I agree that the two are incompatible. But what, in positive terms, does the ordinary understanding of ourselves as intelligent beings who "freely" decide how we shall act require? Where do the "springs of action" lie for beings that truly enjoy "free will"? This is surprisingly difficult to answer with any confidence. A useful way of approaching this question is to consider the various ways we might modify determinism in order to accommodate free will.

The most economical change in the determinist's basic picture is to introduce a causal "loose fit" between those factors influencing my choice (such as my beliefs and desires) and the choice itself. We might suppose, that is, that such factors *cause* my choice in an *in*deterministic way. To say that the causation involved is "indeterministic" is perhaps to say that the laws governing the evolution of the world through time (including that bit of the world which is me) are fundamentally statistical: they allow that (at least at various junctures) a range of alternatives are possible, though they will specify that certain of them are far more likely than others, in accordance with some measure of probability. Applying this general idea to the case of human choices, one might suppose that a free choice requires the following features: I have reasons to act in accordance with each of a range of options. In each case, my having those reasons gives me an objective (probabilistic) tendency to act accordingly. But whatever the relative probabilities of the alternatives, each of them is possible. And whichever of them occurs, the agent's having had a specific reason so to act will have been among the factors that caused it. Let us call this modification of the deterministic picture "causal indeterminism."

Would this be freedom? In my judgment, it would not. It is not enough that any of a range of possible actions are *open* to me to perform. I must have the right sort of *control* over the way the decision goes in a given case. And we may ask of the causal indeterminist, how is it up to me that, on this occasion, this one among two or more causally possible choices was made? I find myself with competing motivations – in my present case, a desire to watch a basketball game, a desire to play a game with my children, and a desire to finish this article – each of a particular "strength." On this occasion, we may suppose, the least probable outcome occurs. On other occasions, more probable outcomes occur. If I am truly acting freely, then presumably I in some way directly control or determine which outcome occurs on a given occasion. But in what does that control consist? The causal indeterminist does not have resources, it seems, to satisfactorily answer this question. Given a sufficiently large number of choices of a large number of people, the pattern of outcomes is likely to conform, more or less, to the statistical character of the underlying laws. There seems nothing more that one can say – in particular, nothing more one can say about the outcome of any particular choice. The indeterministic tendencies arising from my reasons confer a *kind* of control that is too "chancy" to ground significant responsibility. Indeed, it does not differ at all in *kind* from the control that would be had in a deterministic world; it merely introduces an element of "looseness" into its exercise. Given this added looseness, the future *is* open to alternative possibilities. But it remains unclear how I myself could be responsible (in part) for which of those alternatives is realized.

A dilemma is forming. Responsibility for our actions is inconsistent with the deterministic picture of the world. But it is also inconsistent with at least one straightforward kind of indeterministic picture, the kind that most directly carries into the sphere of human action the sort of indeterminism that many theorists believe operates at the level of fundamental physics. Indeed, a good many philosophers suppose that these two pictures (which we have labeled "causal determinism" and "causal indeterminism") exhaust the plausible alternatives. If all this is right, then the conclusion to be drawn is that free will is simply an inconsistent notion. It's not that we just don't happen to have free will; rather, we don't have it because it simply can't be had.

One alternative to this unpalatable conclusion is that entertained by Peter van Inwagen, in his contribution to this volume. Perhaps, van Inwagen writes, "there is something about our biology, something about the ways of thinking that are 'hardwired' into our brains, that renders it impossible for us human beings to dispel the mystery of metaphysical freedom" (see p. 465). That is, though the notion of free will isn't truly inconsistent, its nature is "cognitively closed" to us. (After all, we have no reason to be confident that we are able, even "in principle," to grasp *every* difficult notion that, say, God grasps. And the history of philosophical reflection on the idea of freedom of will suggests that it has its subtleties.)

Well, there is certainly no *arguing* against this suggestion, absent the emergence of a stable consensus of opinion on the matter – rather unlikely at this stage of the game. But one may well distrust it on the general grounds that it counsels complacency. (And why stop at the notion of free will? Philosophers disagree over the correct understanding of most significant philosophical concepts.) Furthermore, once a philosopher takes this suggestion seriously, he may well be drawn into a deeper measure of skepticism about the notion of freedom of will than initially intended. Van Inwagen, for example, tells us that he is of the opinion that free will is *in*compatible with determinism. So he supposes that it must be *compatible* with *indeterminism*, even though he fails to see *which* sort of indeterminism will clearly do the trick. But if he and the rest of us are "hardwired" in some manner that precludes our coming to understand adequately the nature of free will, is it likely that we understand it sufficiently to know even *some* of its features? At any rate, the hypothesis ought to automatically undercut one's confidence in any highly *disputed* claims, such as van Inwagen's relative confidence in the thesis that free will is incompatible with determinism. (I note that Colin McGinn, whom van Inwagen cites in this connection, supposes that free will *can* be had under determinism, even though he "can't see how".)

Rather than embrace the despair and skepticism of the "cognitive closure" hypothesis, then, let us pick up the argument where we last left it, and see whether a "positive" solution to our problem is in the offing. I argued that, if my decisions to act are simply the indeterministic effects of my beliefs and desires, then they are not up to me. What more do we *want* to say about our decisions, that causal indeterminism leaves out?

Just this, it seems: that I myself freely and directly control the outcome, where "control" here (as everywhere) is evidently a *causal* notion. And the unsatisfactoriness of causal indeterminism suggests that we have to be rather literal about the referent of "I," in this context. If I do something freely, I cannot be thought of as simply an arena in which internal and external factors work together to bring about my action (whether or not these factors are thought to operate in a strictly deterministic fashion). Instead, we want to say with Roderick Chisholm that I am the "end-of-the-line" initiator of the resulting action. What we are after, that is, is a notion of a distinctively personal form of causality (in the parlance of philosophers, "agent causation"), as against the broadly mechanistic form of causality ("event causation") that both the deterministic and causal indeterministic pictures represent as governing *all* forms of activity in nature without exception.

Many philosophers find this notion of "personal" or "agent" causation to be utterly mysterious, or downright incoherent. (Some of those philosophers will agree that it is natural to talk of "agent causation" when trying to articulate an understanding of free will, even though it is an incoherent idea. On their view, the term encapsulates the inconsistent strands in that notion.) Here is a simple reflection that fosters the sense of mystery. We often talk loosely of inanimate objects as causing certain things to happen. An example is the statement that Zimmerman's car knocked down the telephone pole. But it's clear that this does not perspicuously capture the metaphysics of the situation. It is instead simply shorthand for the assertion that the *movement* of Zimmerman's car (a car with a certain mass) caused the pole's falling down. It is, then, this *event* involving Zimmerman's car that brought about the effect, and not simply the car, *qua* enduring object. (No such effects emanate from his car when Zimmerman wisely decides to keep it parked in his garage.) The problem that many see with agent causation is that it rejects any expansion of "loose" talk of agents' causing things to happen into statements asserting that particular events *involving* those agents cause the effects in question. And that can seem mysterious: how can agents cause things to happen without its being true that they do so in virtue of certain features of themselves at the time? The agent is, after all, always an agent; yet he is not always causing some particular effect, such as deciding to complete an article on agent causation. Doesn't this force us to acknowledge that if the agent has decided to complete that article at one particular time, there must have been something *about him* at that time in virtue of which that effect was realized? And isn't that just to say that the *event* of the agent's having those distinguishing features, whatever they were, is what caused the decision?

This simple reflection is perhaps the deepest basis for philosophical suspicion about the notion of agent causation. However, I have come to suspect the suspicion and its various bases. In order to have a clear view of this matter, we need to reflect further on what is involved in our ordinary understanding of causation. Unfortunately, there is precious little agreement among philosophers about these matters. But the brief remarks I will make on this score at least have the advantage of representing a fairly commonsensical view of causation.

On the theory of causation I favor, objects are inherently active or dynamic. That is, they have causal capacities, and these are not "free-floating", but rather are linked to their intrinsic properties – those basic properties whose exact character it is the business of science to investigate.

In the more generally applicable case of *event* (or broadly mechanistic) causation, the *exercise* of such a capacity or tendency proceeds "as a matter of course": a thing's having, in the right circumstances, the capacity-grounding cluster of properties directly generates one of the effects within its range. (For indeterministic capacities, that effect will be but one of a range of *possible* effects; whereas in the deterministic case, there is only one possible outcome.)

The way that agent or personal causation differs from this mechanistic paradigm is in the way the relevant causal capacities are *exercised*. An agent's capacity to freely and directly control the outcome of his deliberation also requires underlying intrinsic properties which ground that capacity. (What sort of properties these might be is an interesting and in certain respects puzzling question, but it is at least partly empirical and not conceptual in nature. In any case, I shall not consider it here.) And no doubt the range of its operation is sharply circumscribed. For what is it, after all, that I directly act on, according to the agency theory? Myself – a complex system regulated by a host of stratified dynamic processes. I don't introduce events *ex nihilo*; (at best) I influence the direction of what is already going on within me. What is going on is a structured, dynamic situation open to some possibilities and not others. So the capacity is also circumscribed by physical and psychological factors at work within the agent while he deliberates. But (and here is the difference from the mechanistic paradigm) having the properties that subserve an *agent*-causal capacity does not suffice to bring about a particular effect (or even the occurrence of some effect or other within a range of possible effects); rather, it *enables* the agent to determine an effect (within the corresponding range). Whether, when, and how such a capacity will be exercised is freely determined by the agent.

That is the core metaphysical difference between the two causal paradigms. But we have yet to discuss how prior desires, intentions, and beliefs (more simply, "reasons") may explain such agent-causal activity. I suggest that we think of the agent's immediate effect as an action-triggering state of *intention* (which endures throughout the action and guides its completion). The content of that intention, in part, is that I act here and now in a particular sort of way. But another aspect of that intention, in my view, is that an action of a specific sort be performed *for certain reasons* the agent had at the time. (After a brief deliberation, I formed the intention to continue to type these words *in order to get the editors of this volume off my back*.) And the basis of the explanatory link lies precisely in this fact that the intention refers to the guiding reason. That is, the caused intention bears its explanation on its sleeve, so to speak. Had the agent generated a different intention, it would have been done (in most cases) for a different reason, to which reason the content of the intention itself would have referred. And if the agent had *several* reasons for performing a particular action, the reason(s) that *actually* moved the agent to act, again, would be reflected in the content of the intention. (None of this is to suggest that determining this content, in retrospect, is always easy. Clearly, I can be mistaken about my own reasons for acting.)

Some say that this account of the explanatory nature of reasons cannot be right: we can simply see that any undetermined instance of agent causation would be random, since by hypothesis nothing causes it. (Even some proponents of agent causation have been worried about this, and have been led to posit infinite hierarchies of agent-causings.) But it is hard to credit this objection. Consider what is being demanded. Agent causation is a form of direct control over one's behavior *par excellence*. But this is held to be insufficient. What is needed, it is argued, is some mechanism by virtue of which the agent controls this controlling. Put thus (though understandably it is not generally put in this way), its absurdity is evident. We needn't control our exercises of control. (For if we did, then wouldn't we also need yet another exercise of control, and so on?) On any coherent conception of human action, there is going to be a *basic* form of activity on which rests all control over less immediate effects. On the agent-causal picture, this basic activity is that of an agent's directly generating an intention to act in accordance with certain reasons.

Others have argued that the suggested account of explanations of free actions by reasons cannot be right, since the reasons to which one points in a given case won't explain why the agent acted as he did *rather than* in one of the other ways that were open to him (alternatives that by hypothesis remained open up to the very moment of choice). But while the issues involved here are subtler, this objection also fails. The objection assumes that adequately explaining an occurrence *ipso facto* involves explaining why that event occurred rather than any imaginable alternative. And this seems too strong a requirement. At bottom, explaining an occurrence involves uncovering the causal factor that generated it. In deterministic cases, where only one outcome is possible, such an explanation will also show why that event occurred rather than any other. But this should not blind us to the fact that the two targets of explanation are distinct: the simple *occurrence* itself and the *contrastive fact* that the outcome occurred rather than any other alternative. We need this distinction not just to understand human free agency, but to understand any indeterministic causal activity, including the apparently indeterministic mechanisms described by physical science. Whether (and in what circumstances) there can *also* be contrastive explanations of such indeterministic outcomes is a difficult question. But whatever we say here, there is little to recommend the claim that an occurrence that has been caused, though not uniquely determined, by some factor is thereby wholly inexplicable.

More might be said about the "nature of reasons" explanation on the picture just sketched, but I want to turn instead to the complaint that we've swung too far in the direction of freedom. In place of the diminished, freedom-less conception of human action entailed by the deterministic picture, we've substituted a rather god-like one: the agent selects from among reasons that are merely passively present before the agent as he deliberates, reasons that do not *move* the agent to act. Though rather implausible on the face of it, such a consequence is embraced by some advocates of agent causation. Chisholm, for example, compares agent causation with divine action:

> If we are responsible, and if what I have been trying to say is true, then we have a prerogative which some would attribute only to God: each of us, when we act, is a prime mover unmoved. In doing what we do, we cause certain events to happen, and nothing – or no one – causes us to cause those events to happen.[1]

But perhaps this is unnecessarily heroic. Though defenders of agent causation have generally insisted on a sharp divide between it and mechanistic causation, we may be able to move tentatively toward greater integration of the two. The goal is not to *reduce* agent causation, in the end, to an all-encompassing mechanistic paradigm, but rather to see how event-causal factors such as the possession of reasons to act may *shape* the distinctively agent-causal capacity. Two things, in particular, seem needed here – if not for all conceivable agents (including God and angels), then at least for human beings as we know them. First, our account should capture the way reasons (in some sense) *move* us to act as we do – and not as external pressures, but as *our* reasons, as our own internal tendencies to act to satisfy certain desires or aims. Secondly, the account should acknowledge that those reasons typically do not have "equal weight," so to speak. It is a truism that, given the structure of my preferences, stable intentions, and so forth, and the situation with which I am faced, I am often far more likely to act in one way rather than in any other. But how might we account for this, if not in terms of a relative tendency, on the part of reasons, to *produce* our actions?

In my view, this is the biggest obstacle to a clear understanding of what free will requires. What we need is a way to modify the traditional notion of a distinctively personal kind of causal capacity and to see it, not as utterly unfettered, but as one that comes "structured", in the sense of having built-in propensities to act (though ones that shift over time in accordance with the agent's changing preferences). But we must do so in such a way that it remains up to me to act on these tendencies or not, so that what I do is not simply the consequence of the vagaries of "chance-like" indeterministic activity, as may be true of microphysical quantum phenomena.

So, the task of harmonizing free and responsible human agency with a world that is fundamentally mechanistic in character remains unfinished. But perhaps we've seen enough to dispel much of the air of profound mystery that some profess to find on considering the very idea of metaphysical freedom.

Note

1   "Human Freedom and the Self," p. 448, this volume.

---

50   Alternate Possibilities and Moral Responsibility

Harry G. Frankfurt

A dominant role in nearly all recent inquiries into the free-will problem has been played by a principle which I shall call "the principle of alternate possibilities." This principle states that a person is morally responsible for what he has done only if he could have done otherwise. Its exact meaning is a subject of controversy, particularly concerning whether someone who accepts it is thereby committed to believing that moral responsibility and determinism are incompatible.

Practically no one, however, seems inclined to deny or even to question that the principle of alternate possibilities (construed in some way or other) is true. It has generally seemed so overwhelmingly plausible that some philosophers have even characterized it as an *a priori* truth. People whose accounts of free will or of moral responsibility are radically at odds evidently find in it a firm and convenient common ground upon which they can profitably take their opposing stands.

But the principle of alternate possibilities is false. A person may well be morally responsible for what he has done even though he could not have done otherwise. The principle's plausibility is an illusion, which can be made to vanish by bringing the relevant moral phenomena into sharper focus.

I

In seeking illustrations of the principle of alternate possibilities, it is most natural to think of situations in which the same circumstances both bring it about that a person does something and make it impossible for him to avoid doing it. These include, for example, situations in which a person is coerced into doing something, or in which he is impelled to act by a hypnotic suggestion, or in which some inner compulsion drives him to do what he does. In situations of these kinds there are circumstances that make it impossible for the person to do otherwise, and these very circumstances also serve to bring it about that he does whatever it is that he does.

However, there may be circumstances that constitute sufficient conditions for a certain action to be performed by someone and that therefore make it impossible for the person to do otherwise, but that do not actually impel the person to act or in any way produce his action. A person may do something in circumstances that leave him no alternative to doing it, without these circumstances actually moving him or leading him to do it – without them playing any role, indeed, in bringing it about that he does what he does.

An examination of situations characterized by circumstances of this sort casts doubt, I believe, on the relevance to questions of moral responsibility of the fact that a person who has done something could not have done otherwise. I propose to develop some examples of this kind in the context of a discussion of coercion and to suggest that our moral intuitions concerning these examples tend to disconfirm the principle of alternate possibilities. Then I will discuss the principle in more general terms, explain what I think is wrong with it, and describe briefly and without argument how it might appropriately be revised.

II

It is generally agreed that a person who has been coerced to do something did not do it freely and is not morally responsible for having done it. Now the doctrine that coercion and moral responsibility are mutually exclusive may appear to be no more than a somewhat particularized version of the principle of alternate possibilities. It is natural enough to say of a person who has been coerced to do something that he could not have done otherwise. And it may easily seem that being coerced deprives a person of freedom and of moral responsibility simply because it is a special case of being unable to do otherwise. The principle of alternate possibilities may in this way derive some credibility from its association with the very plausible proposition that moral responsibility is excluded by coercion.

It is not right, however, that it should do so. The fact that a person was coerced to act as he did may entail both that he could not have done otherwise and that he bears no moral responsibility for his action. But his lack of moral responsibility is not entailed by his having been unable to do otherwise. The doctrine that coercion excludes moral responsibility is not correctly understood, in other words, as a particularized version of the principle of alternate possibilities.

Let us suppose that someone is threatened convincingly with a penalty he finds unacceptable and that he then does what is required of him by the issuer of the threat. We can imagine details that would make it reasonable for us to think that the person was coerced to perform the action in question, that he could not have done otherwise, and that he bears no moral responsibility for having done what he did. But just what is it about situations of this kind that warrants the judgment that the threatened person is not morally responsible for his act?

This question may be approached by considering situations of the following kind. Jones decides for reasons of his own to do something, then someone threatens him with a very harsh penalty (so harsh that any reasonable person would submit to the threat) unless he does precisely that, and Jones does it. Will we hold Jones morally responsible for what he has done? I think this will depend on the roles we think were played, in leading him to act, by his original decision and by the threat.

One possibility is that Jones₁ is not a reasonable man: he is, rather, a man who does what he has once decided to do no matter what happens next and no matter what the cost. In that case, the threat actually exerted no effective force upon him. He acted without any regard to it, very much as if he were not aware that it had been made. If this is indeed the way it was, the situation did not involve coercion at all. The threat did not lead Jones₁ to do what he did. Nor was it in fact sufficient to have prevented him from doing otherwise: if his earlier decision had been to do something else, the threat would not have deterred him in the slightest. It seems evident that in these circumstances the fact that Jones₁ was threatened in no way reduces the moral responsibility he would otherwise bear for his act. This example, however, is not a counterexample either to the doctrine that coercion excuses or to the principle of alternate possibilities. For we have supposed that Jones₁ is a man upon whom the threat had no coercive effect and, hence, that it did not actually deprive him of alternatives to doing what he did.

Another possibility is that Jones₂ was stampeded by the threat. Given that threat, he would have performed that action regardless of what decision he had already made. The threat upset him so profoundly, moreover, that he completely forgot his own earlier decision and did what was demanded of him entirely because he was terrified of the penalty with which he was threatened. In this case, it is not relevant to his having performed the action that he had already decided on his own to perform it. When the chips were down he thought of nothing but the threat, and fear alone led him to act. The fact that at an earlier time Jones$_2$ had decided for his own reasons to act in just that way may be relevant to an evaluation of his character; he may bear full moral responsibility for having made *that* decision. But he can hardly be said to be morally responsible for his action. For he performed the action simply as a result of the coercion to which he was subjected. His earlier decision played no role in bringing it about that he did what he did, and it would therefore be gratuitous to assign it a role in the moral evaluation of his action.

Now consider a third possibility. Jones$_3$ was neither stampeded by the threat nor indifferent to it. The threat impressed him, as it would impress any reasonable man, and he would have submitted to it wholeheartedly if he had not already made a decision that coincided with the one demanded of him. In fact, however, he performed the action in question on the basis of the decision he had made before the threat was issued. When he acted, he was not actually motivated by the threat but solely by the considerations that had originally commended the action to him. It was not the threat that led him to act, though it would have done so if he had not already provided himself with a sufficient motive for performing the action in question.

No doubt it will be very difficult for anyone to know, in a case like this one, exactly what happened. Did Jones$_3$ perform the action because of the threat, or were his reasons for acting simply those which had already persuaded him to do so? Or did he act on the basis of two motives, each of which was sufficient for his action? It is not impossible, however, that the situation should be clearer than situations of this kind usually are. And suppose it is apparent to us that Jones$_3$ acted on the basis of his own decision and not because of the threat. Then I think we would be justified in regarding his moral responsibility for what he did as unaffected by the threat even though, since he would in any case have submitted to the threat, he could not have avoided doing what he did. It would be entirely reasonable for us to make the same judgment concerning his moral responsibility that we would have made if we had not known of the threat. For the threat did not in fact influence his performance of the action. He did what he did just as if the threat had not been made at all.

III

The case of Jones$_3$ may appear at first glance to combine coercion and moral responsibility, and thus to provide a counterexample to the doctrine that coercion excuses. It is not really so certain that it does so, however, because it is unclear whether the example constitutes a genuine instance of coercion. Can we say of Jones$_3$ that he was coerced to do something, when he had already decided on his own to do it and when he did it entirely on the basis of that decision? Or would it be more correct to say that Jones$_3$ was not coerced to do what he did, even though he himself recognized that there was an irresistible force at work in virtue of which he had to do it? My own linguistic intuitions lead me toward the second alternative, but they are somewhat equivocal. Perhaps we can say either of these things, or perhaps we must add a qualifying explanation to whichever of them we say.

This murkiness, however, does not interfere with our drawing an important moral from an examination of the example. Suppose we decide to say that Jones$_3$ was *not* coerced. Our basis for saying this will clearly be that it is incorrect to regard a man as being coerced to do something unless he does it *because of* the coercive force exerted against him. The fact that an irresistible threat is made will not, then, entail that the person who receives it is coerced to do what he does. It will also be necessary that the threat is what actually accounts for his doing it. On the other hand, suppose we decide to say that Jones$_3$ *was* coerced. Then we will be bound to admit that being coerced does not exclude being morally responsible. And we will also surely be led to the view that coercion affects the judgment of a person's moral responsibility only when the person acts as he does because he is coerced to do so – i.e., when the fact that he is coerced is what accounts for his action.

Whichever we decide to say, then, we will recognize that the doctrine that coercion excludes moral responsibility is not a particularized version of the principle of alternate possibilities. Situations in which a person who does something cannot do otherwise because he is subject to coercive power are either not instances of coercion at all, or they are situations in which the person may still be morally responsible for what he does if it is not because of the coercion that he does it. When we excuse a person who has been coerced, we do not excuse him because he was unable to do otherwise. Even though a person is subject to a coercive force that precludes his performing any action but one, he may nonetheless bear full moral responsibility for performing that action.

IV

To the extent that the principle of alternate possibilities derives its plausibility from association with the doctrine that coercion excludes moral responsibility, a clear understanding of the latter diminishes the appeal of the former. Indeed the case of Jones$_3$ may appear to do more than illuminate the relationship between the two doctrines. It may well seem to provide a decisive counterexample to the principle of alternate possibilities and thus to show that this principle is false. For the irresistibility of the threat to which Jones$_3$ is subjected might well be taken to mean that he cannot but perform the action he performs. And yet the threat, since Jones$_3$ performs the action without regard to it, does not reduce his moral responsibility for what he does.

The following objection will doubtless be raised against the suggestion that the case of Jones$_3$ is a counterexample to the principle of alternate possibilities. There is perhaps a sense in which Jones$_3$ cannot do otherwise than perform the action he performs, since he is a reasonable man and the threat he encounters is sufficient to move any reasonable man. But it is not this sense that is germane to the principle of alternate possibilities. His knowledge that he stands to suffer an intolerably harsh penalty does not mean that Jones₃, strictly speaking, *cannot* perform any action but the one he does perform. After all it is still open to him, and this is crucial, to defy the threat if he wishes to do so and to accept the penalty his action would bring down upon him. In the sense in which the principle of alternate possibilities employs the concept of "could have done otherwise," Jones₃'s inability to resist the threat does not mean that he cannot do otherwise than perform the action he performs. Hence the case of Jones₃ does not constitute an instance contrary to the principle.

I do not propose to consider in what sense the concept of "could have done otherwise" figures in the principle of alternate possibilities, nor will I attempt to measure the force of the objection I have just described.[1] For I believe that whatever force this objection may be thought to have can be deflected by altering the example in the following way.[2] Suppose someone – Black, let us say – wants Jones₄ to perform a certain action. Black is prepared to go to considerable lengths to get his way, but he prefers to avoid showing his hand unnecessarily. So he waits until Jones₄ is about to make up his mind what to do, and he does nothing unless it is clear to him (Black is an excellent judge of such things) that Jones₄ is going to decide to do something *other* than what he wants him to do. If it does become clear that Jones₄ is going to decide to do something else, Black takes effective steps to ensure that Jones₄ decides to do, and that he does do, what he wants him to do.[3] Whatever Jones₄'s initial preferences and inclinations, then, Black will have his way.

What steps will Black take, if he believes he must take steps, in order to ensure that Jones₄ decides and acts as he wishes? Anyone with a theory concerning what "could have done otherwise" means may answer this question for himself by describing whatever measures he would regard as sufficient to guarantee that, in the relevant sense, Jones₄ cannot do otherwise. Let Black pronounce a terrible threat, and in this way both force Jones₄ to perform the desired action and prevent him from performing a forbidden one. Let Black give Jones₄ a potion, or put him under hypnosis, and in some such way as these generate in Jones₄ an irresistible inner compulsion to perform the act Black wants performed and to avoid others. Or let Black manipulate the minute processes of Jones₄'s brain and nervous system in some more direct way, so that causal forces running in and out of his synapses and along the poor man's nerves determine that he chooses to act and that he does act in the one way and not in any other. Given any conditions under which it will be maintained that Jones₄ cannot do otherwise, in other words, let Black bring it about that those conditions prevail. The structure of the example is flexible enough, I think, to find a way around any charge of irrelevance by accommodating the doctrine on which the charge is based.[4]

Now suppose that Black never has to show his hand because Jones₄, for reasons of his own, decides to perform and does perform the very action Black wants him to perform. In that case, it seems clear, Jones₄ will bear precisely the same moral responsibility for what he does as he would have borne if Black had not been ready to take steps to ensure that he do it. It would be quite unreasonable to excuse Jones₄ for his action, or to withhold the praise to which it would normally entitle him, on the basis of the fact that he could not have done otherwise. This fact played no role at all in leading him to act as he did. He would have acted the same even if it had not been a fact. Indeed, everything happened just as it would have happened without Black's presence in the situation and without his readiness to intrude into it.

In this example there are sufficient conditions for Jones₄'s performing the action in question. What action he performs is not up to him. Of course it is in a way up to him whether he acts on his own or as a result of Black's intervention. That depends upon what action he himself is inclined to perform. But whether he finally acts on his own or as a result of Black's intervention, he performs the same action. He has no alternative but to do what Black wants him to do. If he does it on his own, however, his moral responsibility for doing it is not affected by the fact that Black was lurking in the background with sinister intent, since this intent never comes into play.

V

The fact that a person could not have avoided doing something is a sufficient condition of his having done it. But, as some of my examples show, this fact may play no role whatever in the explanation of why he did it. It may not figure at all among the circumstances that actually brought it about that he did what he did, so that his action is to be accounted for on another basis entirely. Even though the person was unable to do otherwise, that is to say, it may not be the case that he acted as he did *because* he could not have done otherwise. Now if someone had no alternative to performing a certain action but did not perform it because he was unable to do otherwise, then he would have performed exactly the same action even if he *could* have done otherwise. The circumstances that made it impossible for him to do otherwise could have been subtracted from the situation without affecting what happened or why it happened in any way. Whatever it was that actually led the person to do what he did, or that made him do it, would have led him to do it or made him do it even if it had been possible for him to do something else instead.

Thus it would have made no difference, so far as concerns his action or how he came to perform it, if the circumstances that made it impossible for him to avoid performing it had not prevailed. The fact that he could not have done otherwise clearly provides no basis for supposing that he *might* have done otherwise if he had been able to do so. When a fact is in this way irrelevant to the problem of accounting for a person's action it seems quite gratuitous to assign it any weight in the assessment of his moral responsibility. Why should the fact be considered in reaching a moral judgment concerning the person when it does not help in any way to understand either what made him act as he did or what, in other circumstances, he might have done?

This, then, is why the principle of alternate possibilities is mistaken. It asserts that a person bears no moral responsibility – that is, he is to be excused – for having performed an action if there were circumstances that made it impossible for him to avoid performing it. But there may be circumstances that make it impossible for a person to avoid performing some action without those circumstances in any way bringing it about that he performs that action. It would surely be no good for the person to refer to circumstances of this sort in an effort to absolve himself of moral responsibility for performing the action in question. For those circumstances, by hypothesis, actually had nothing to do with his having done what he did. He would have done precisely the same thing, and he would have been led or made in precisely the same way to do it, even if they had not prevailed.

We often do, to be sure, excuse people for what they have done when they tell us (and we believe them) that they could not have done otherwise. But this is because we assume that what they tell us serves to explain why they did what they did. We take it for granted that they are not being disingenuous, as a person would be who cited as an excuse the fact that he could not have avoided doing what he did but who knew full well that it was not at all because of this that he did it.

What I have said may suggest that the principle of alternate possibilities should be revised so as to assert that a person is not morally responsible for what he has done if he did it because he could not have done otherwise. It may be noted that this revision of the principle does not seriously affect the arguments of those who have relied on the original principle in their efforts to maintain that moral responsibility and determinism are incompatible. For if it was causally determined that a person perform a certain action, then it will be true that the person performed it because of those causal determinants. And if the fact that it was causally determined that a person perform a certain action means that the person could not have done otherwise, as philosophers who argue for the incompatibility thesis characteristically suppose, then the fact that it was causally determined that a person perform a certain action will mean that the person performed it because he could not have done otherwise. The revised principle of alternate possibilities will entail, on this assumption concerning the meaning of 'could have done otherwise', that a person is not morally responsible for what he has done if it was causally determined that he do it. I do not believe, however, that this revision of the principle is acceptable.

Suppose a person tells us that he did what he did because he was unable to do otherwise; or suppose he makes the similar statement that he did what he did because he had to do it. We do often accept statements like these (if we believe them) as valid excuses, and such statements may well seem at first glance to invoke the revised principle of alternate possibilities. But I think that when we accept such statements as valid excuses it is because we assume that we are being told more than the statements strictly and literally convey. We understand the person who offers the excuse to mean that he did what he did *only because* he was unable to do otherwise, or *only because* he had to do it. And we understand him to mean, more particularly, that when he did what he did it was not because that was what he really wanted to do. The principle of alternate possibilities should thus be replaced, in my opinion, by the following principle: a person is not morally responsible for what he has done if he did it only because he could not have done otherwise. This principle does not appear to conflict with the view that moral responsibility is compatible with determinism.

The following may all be true: there were circumstances that made it impossible for a person to avoid doing something; these circumstances actually played a role in bringing it about that he did it, so that it is correct to say that he did it because he could not have done otherwise; the person really wanted to do what he did; he did it because it was what he really wanted to do, so that it is not correct to say that he did what he did only because he could not have done otherwise. Under these conditions, the person may well be morally responsible for what he has done. On the other hand, he will not be morally responsible for what he has done if he did it only because he could not have done otherwise, even if what he did was something he really wanted to do.

Notes

1 The two main concepts employed in the principle of alternate possibilities are "morally responsible" and "could have done otherwise." To discuss the principle without analyzing either of these concepts may well seem like an attempt at piracy. The reader should take notice that my Jolly Roger is now unfurled.

2 After thinking up the example that I am about to develop I learned that Robert Nozick, in lectures given several years ago, had formulated an example of the same general type and had proposed it as a counterexample to the principle of alternate possibilities.

3 The assumption that Black can predict what Jones$_4$ will decide to do does not beg the question of determinism. We can imagine that Jones$_4$ has often confronted the alternatives – A and B – that he now confronts, and that his face has invariably twitched when he was about to decide to do A and never when he was about to decide to do B. Knowing this, and observing the twitch, Black would have a basis for prediction. This does, to be sure, suppose that there is some sort of causal relation between Jones$_4$'s state at the time of the twitch and his subsequent states. But any plausible view of decision or of action will allow that reaching a decision and performing an action both involve earlier and later phases, with causal relations between them, and such that the earlier phases are not themselves part of the decision or of the action. The example does not require that these earlier phases be deterministically related to still earlier events.

4 The example is also flexible enough to allow for the elimination of Black altogether. Anyone who thinks that the effectiveness of the example is undermined by its reliance on a human manipulator, who imposes his will on Jones$_4$, can substitute for Black a machine programmed to do what Black does. If this is still not good enough, forget both Black and the machine and suppose that their role is played by natural forces involving no will or design at all.

51   Freedom of the Will and the Concept of a Person

Harry G. Frankfurt

What philosophers have lately come to accept as analysis of the concept of a person is not actually analysis of *that* concept at all. Strawson, whose usage represents the current standard, identifies the concept of a person as "the concept of a type of entity such that *both* predicates ascribing states of consciousness *and* predicates ascribing corporeal characteristics ... are equally applicable to a single individual of that single type."[1] But there are many entities besides persons that have both mental and physical properties. As it happens – though it seems extraordinary that this should be so – there is no common English word for the type of entity Strawson has in mind, a type that includes not only human beings but animals of various lesser species as well. Still, this hardly justifies the mis-appropriation of a valuable philosophical term.

Whether the members of some animal species are persons is surely not to be settled merely by determining whether it is correct to apply to them, in addition to predicates ascribing corporeal characteristics, predicates that ascribe states of consciousness. It does violence to our language to endorse the application of the term 'person' to those numerous creatures which do have both psychological and material properties but which are manifestly not persons in any normal sense of the word. This misuse of language is doubtless innocent of any theoretical error. But although the offense is "merely verbal," it does significant harm. For it gra-tuitously diminishes our philosophical vocabulary, and it increases the likelihood that we will overlook the important area of inquiry with which the term 'person' is most naturally associated. It might have been expected that no problem would be of more central and persistent concern to philosophers than that of under-standing what we ourselves essentially are. Yet this problem is so generally neglected that it has been possible to make off with its very name almost without being noticed and, evidently, without evoking any widespread feeling of loss.

There is a sense in which the word 'person' is merely the singular form of 'people' and in which both terms connote no more than membership in a certain biological species. In those senses of the word which are of greater philosophical interest, however, the criteria for being a person do not serve primarily to dis-tinguish the members of our own species from the members of other species. Rather, they are designed to capture those attributes which are the subject of our most humane concern with ourselves and the source of what we regard as most important and most problematical in our lives. Now these attributes would be of equal significance to us even if they were not in fact peculiar and common to the members of our own species. What interests us most in the human condition would not interest us less if it were also a feature of the condition of other crea-tures as well.

Our concept of ourselves as persons is not to be understood, therefore, as a concept of attributes that are necessarily species-specific. It is conceptually possible that members of novel or even of familiar nonhuman species should be persons; and it is also conceptually possible that some members of the human species are not persons. We do in fact assume, on the other hand, that no member of another species is a person. Accordingly, there is a presumption that what is essential to persons is a set of characteristics that we generally suppose – whether rightly or wrongly – to be uniquely human.

It is my view that one essential difference between persons and other creatures is to be found in the structure of a person's will. Human beings are not alone in having desires and motives, or in making choices. They share these things with the members of certain other species, some of whom even appear to engage in deliberation and to make decisions based upon prior thought. It seems to be peculiarly characteristic of humans, however, that they are able to form what I shall call "second-order desires" or "desires of the second order."

Besides wanting and choosing and being moved *to do* this or that, men may also want to have (or not to have) certain desires and motives. They are capable of wanting to be different, in their preferences and purposes, from what they are. Many animals appear to have the capacity for what I shall call "first-order desires" or "desires of the first order," which are simply desires to do or not to do one thing or another. No animal other than man, however, appears to have the capacity for reflective self-evaluation that is manifested in the formation of second-order desires.[2]

I

The concept designated by the verb 'to want' is extraordinarily elusive. A statement of the form "A wants to X" – taken by itself, apart from a context that serves to amplify or to specify its meaning – conveys remarkably little information. Such a statement may be consistent, for example, with each of the following statements: (a) the prospect of doing X elicits no sensation or introspectible emotional response in A; (b) A is unaware that he wants to X; (c) A believes that he does not want to X; (d) A wants to refrain from X-ing; (e) A wants to Y and believes that it is impossible for him both to Y and to X; (f) A does not "really" want to X; (g) A would rather die than X; and so on. It is therefore hardly sufficient to formulate the distinction between first-order and second-order desires, as I have done, by suggesting merely that someone has a first-order desire when he wants to do or not to do such-and-such, and that he has a second-order desire when he wants to have or not to have a certain desire of the first order.

As I shall understand them, statements of the form "A wants to X" cover a rather broad range of possibilities.[3] They may be true even when statements like (a) through (g) are true: when A is unaware of any feelings concerning X-ing, when he is unaware that he wants to X, when he deceives himself about what he wants and believes falsely that he does not want to X, when he also has other desires that conflict with his desire to X, or when he is ambivalent. The desires in question may be conscious or unconscious, they need not be univocal, and A may be mistaken about them. There is a further source of uncertainty with regard to statements that identify someone's desires, however, and here it is important for my purposes to be less permissive.

Consider first those statements of the form "A wants to X" which identify first-order desires – that is, statements in which the term 'to X' refers to an action. A statement of this kind does not, by itself, indicate the relative strength of A's desire to X. It does not make it clear whether this desire is at all likely to play a decisive role in what A actually does or tries to do. For it may correctly be said that A wants to X even when his desire to X is only one among his desires and when it is far from being paramount among them. Thus, it may be true that A wants to X when he strongly prefers to do something else instead; and it may be true that he wants to X despite the fact that, when he acts, it is not the desire to X that motivates him to do what he does. On the other hand, someone who states that A wants to X may mean to convey that it is this desire that is motivating or moving A to do what he is actually doing or that A will in fact be moved by this desire (unless he changes his mind) when he acts.

It is only when it is used in the second of these ways that, given the special usage of 'will' that I propose to adopt, the statement identifies A's will. To identify an agent's will is either to identify the desire (or desires) by which he is motivated in some action he performs or to identify the desire (or desires) by which he will or would be motivated when or if he acts. An agent's will, then, is identical with one or more of his first-order desires. But the notion of the will, as I am employing it, is not coextensive with the notion of first-order desires. It is not the notion of something that merely inclines an agent in some degree to act in a certain way. Rather, it is the notion of an *effective* desire – one that moves (or will or would move) a person all the way to action. Thus the notion of the will is not coextensive with the notion of what an agent intends to do. For even though someone may have a settled intention to do X, he may nonetheless do something else instead of doing X because, despite his intention, his desire to do X proves to be weaker or less effective than some conflicting desire.

Now consider those statements of the form "A wants to X" which identify second-order desires – that is, statements in which the term 'to X' refers to a desire of the first order. There are also two kinds of situation in which it may be true that A wants to want to X. In the first place, it might be true of A that he wants to have a desire to X despite the fact that he has a univocal desire, altogether free of conflict and ambivalence, to refrain from X-ing. Someone might want to have a certain desire, in other words, but univocally want that desire to be unsatisfied.

Suppose that a physician engaged in psychotherapy with narcotics addicts believes that his ability to help his patients would be enhanced if he understood better what it is like for them to desire the drug to which they are addicted. Suppose that he is led in this way to want to have a desire for the drug. If it is a genuine desire that he wants, then what he wants is not merely to feel the sensations that addicts characteristically feel when they are gripped by their desires for the drug. What the physician wants, insofar as he wants to have a desire, is to be inclined or moved to some extent to take the drug.

It is entirely possible, however, that, although he wants to be moved by a desire to take the drug, he does not want this desire to be effective. He may not want it to move him all the way to action. He need not be interested in finding out what it is like to take the drug. And insofar as he now wants only to *want* to take it, and not to *take* it, there is nothing in what he now wants that would be satisfied by the drug itself. He may now have, in fact, an altogether univocal desire *not* to take the drug; and he may prudently arrange to make it impossible for him to satisfy the desire he would have if his desire to want the drug should in time be satisfied.

It would thus be incorrect to infer, from the fact that the physician now wants to desire to take the drug, that he already does desire to take it. His second-order desire to be moved to take the drug does not entail that he has a first-order desire to take it. If the drug were now to be administered to him, this might satisfy no desire that is implicit in his desire to want to take it. While he wants to want to take the drug, he may have *no* desire to take it; it may be that *all* he wants is to taste the desire for it. That is, his desire to have a certain desire that he does not have may not be a desire that his will should be at all different than it is.

Someone who wants only in this truncated way to want to X stands at the margin of preciosity, and the fact that he wants to want to X is not pertinent to the identification of his will. There is, however, a second kind of situation that may be described by '*A* wants to want to X'; and when the statement is used to describe a situation of this second kind, then it does pertain to what *A* wants his will to be. In such cases the statement means that *A* wants the desire to X to be the desire that moves him effectively to act. It is not merely that he wants the desire to X to be among the desires by which, to one degree or another, he is moved or inclined to act. He wants this desire to be effective – that is, to provide the motive in what he actually does. Now when the statement that *A* wants to want to X is used in this way, it does entail that *A* already has a desire to X. It could not be true both that *A* wants the desire to X to move him into action and that he does not want to X. It is only if he does want to X that he can coherently want the desire to X not merely to be one of his desires but, more decisively, to be his will.[4]

Suppose a man wants to be motivated in what he does by the desire to concentrate on his work. It is necessarily true, if this supposition is correct, that he already wants to concentrate on his work. This desire is now among his desires. But the question of whether or not his second-order desire is fulfilled does not turn merely on whether the desire he wants is one of his desires. It turns on whether this desire is, as he wants it to be, his effective desire or will. If, when the chips are down, it is his desire to concentrate on his work that moves him to do what he does, then what he wants at that time is indeed (in the relevant sense) what he wants to want. If it is some other desire that actually moves him when he acts, on the other hand, then what he wants at that time is not (in the relevant sense) what he wants to want. This will be so despite the fact that the desire to concentrate on his work continues to be among his desires.

II

Someone has a desire of the second order either when he wants simply to have a certain desire or when he wants a certain desire to be his will. In situations of the latter kind, I shall call his second-order desires "second-order volitions" or "volitions of the second order." Now it is having second-order volitions, and not having second-order desires generally, that I regard as essential to being a person. It is logically possible, however unlikely, that there should be an agent with second-order desires but with no volitions of the second order. Such a creature, in my view, would not be a person. I shall use the term 'wanton' to refer to agents who have first-order desires but who are not persons because, whether or not they have desires of the second order, they have no second-order volitions.[5]

The essential characteristic of a wanton is that he does not care about his will. His desires move him to do certain things, without its being true of him either that he wants to be moved by those desires or that he prefers to be moved by other desires. The class of wantons includes all nonhuman animals that have desires and all very young children. Perhaps it also includes some adult human beings as well. In any case, adult humans may be more or less wanton; they may act wantonly, in response to first-order desires concerning which they have no volitions of the second order, more or less frequently.

The fact that a wanton has no second-order volitions does not mean that each of his first-order desires is translated heedlessly and at once into action. He may have no opportunity to act in accordance with some of his desires. Moreover, the translation of his desires into action may be delayed or precluded either by conflicting desires of the first order or by the intervention of deliberation. For a wanton may possess and employ rational faculties of a high order. Nothing in the concept of a wanton implies that he cannot reason or that he cannot deliberate concerning how to do what he wants to do. What distinguishes the rational wanton from other rational agents is that he is not concerned with the desirability of his desires themselves. He ignores the question of what his will is to be. Not only does he pursue whatever course of action he is most strongly inclined to pursue, but he does not care which of his inclinations is the strongest.

Thus a rational creature, who reflects upon the suitability to his desires of one course of action or another, may nonetheless be a wanton. In maintaining that the essence of being a person lies not in reason but in will, I am far from suggesting that a creature without reason may be a person. For it is only in virtue of his rational capacities that a person is capable of becoming critically aware of his own will and of forming volitions of the second order. The structure of a person's will presupposes, accordingly, that he is a rational being.

The distinction between a person and a wanton may be illustrated by the difference between two narcotics addicts. Let us suppose that the physiological condition accounting for the addiction is the same in both men, and that both succumb inevitably to their periodic desires for the drug to which they are addicted. One of the addicts hates his addiction and always struggles desperately, although to no avail, against its thrust. He tries everything that he thinks might enable him to overcome his desires for the drug. But these desires are too powerful for him to withstand, and invariably, in the end, they conquer him. He is an unwilling addict, helplessly violated by his own desires.

The unwilling addict has conflicting first-order desires: he wants to take the drug, and he also wants to refrain from taking it. In addition to these first-order desires, however, he has a volition of the second order. He is not a neutral with regard to the conflict between his desire to take the drug and his desire to refrain from taking it. It is the latter desire, and not the former, that he wants to constitute his will; it is the latter desire, rather than the former, that he wants to be effective and to provide the purpose that he will seek to realize in what he actually does.

The other addict is a wanton. His actions reflect the economy of his first-order desires, without his being concerned whether the desires that move him to act are desires by which he wants to be moved to act. If he encounters problems in obtaining the drug or in administering it to himself, his responses to his urges to take it may involve deliberation. But it never occurs to him to consider whether he wants the relations among his desires to result in his having the will he has. The wanton addict may be an animal, and thus incapable of being concerned about his will. In any event he is, in respect of his wanton lack of concern, no different from an animal.

The second of these addicts may suffer a first-order conflict similar to the first-order conflict suffered by the first. Whether he is human or not, the wanton may (perhaps due to conditioning) both want to take the drug and want to refrain from taking it. Unlike the unwilling addict, however, he does not prefer that one of his conflicting desires should be paramount over the other; he does not prefer that one first-order desire rather than the other should constitute his will. It would be misleading to say that he is neutral as to the conflict between his desires, since this would suggest that he regards them as equally acceptable. Since he has no identity apart from his first-order desires, it is true neither that he prefers one to the other nor that he prefers not to take sides.

It makes a difference to the unwilling addict, who is a person, which of his conflicting first-order desires wins out. Both desires are his, to be sure; and whether he finally takes the drug or finally succeeds in refraining from taking it, he acts to satisfy what is in a literal sense his own desire. In either case he does something he himself wants to do, and he does it not because of some external influence whose aim happens to coincide with his own but because of his desire to do it. The unwilling addict identifies himself, however, through the formation of a second-order volition, with one rather than with the other of his conflicting first-order desires. He makes one of them more truly his own and, in so doing, he withdraws himself from the other. It is in virtue of this identification and withdrawal, accomplished through the formation of a second-order volition, that the unwilling addict may meaningfully make the analytically puzzling statements that the force moving him to take the drug is a force other than his own, and that it is not of his own free will but rather against his will that this force moves him to take it.

The wanton addict cannot or does not care which of his conflicting first-order desires wins out. His lack of concern is not due to his inability to find a convincing basis for preference. It is due either to his lack of the capacity for reflection or to his mindless indifference to the enterprise of evaluating his own desires and motives.[6] There is only one issue in the struggle to which his first-order conflict may lead: whether the one or the other of his conflicting desires is the stronger. Since he is moved by both desires, he will not be altogether satisfied by what he does no matter which of them is effective. But it makes no difference *to him* whether his craving or his aversion gets the upper hand. He has no stake in the conflict between them and so, unlike the unwilling addict, he can neither win nor lose the struggle in which he is engaged. When a *person* acts, the desire by which he is moved is either the will he wants or a will he wants to be without. When a *wanton* acts, it is neither.

III

There is a very close relationship between the capacity for forming second-order volitions and another capacity that is essential to persons – one that has often been considered a distinguishing mark of the human condition. It is only because a person has volitions of the second order that he is capable both of enjoying and of lacking freedom of the will. The concept of a person is not only, then, the concept of a type of entity that has both first-order desires and volitions of the second order. It can also be construed as the concept of a type of entity for whom the freedom of its will may be a problem. This concept excludes all wantons, both infrahuman and human, since they fail to satisfy an essential condition for the enjoyment of freedom of the will. And it excludes those suprahuman beings, if any, whose wills are necessarily free.

Just what kind of freedom is the freedom of the will? This question calls for an identification of the special area of human experience to which the concept of freedom of the will, as distinct from the concepts of other sorts of freedom, is particularly germane. In dealing with it, my aim will be primarily to locate the problem with which a person is most immediately concerned when he is concerned with the freedom of his will.

According to one familiar philosophical tradition, being free is fundamentally a matter of doing what one wants to do. Now the notion of an agent who does what he wants to do is by no means an altogether clear one: both the doing and the wanting, and the appropriate relation between them as well, require elucidation. But although its focus needs to be sharpened and its formulation refined, I believe that this notion does capture at least part of what is implicit in the idea of an agent who *acts* freely. It misses entirely, however, the peculiar content of the quite different idea of an agent whose *will* is free.

We do not suppose that animals enjoy freedom of the will, although we recognize that an animal may be free to run in whatever direction it wants. Thus, having the freedom to do what one wants to do is not a sufficient condition of having a free will. It is not a necessary condition either. For to deprive someone of his freedom of action is not necessarily to undermine the freedom of his will. When an agent is aware that there are certain things he is not free to do, this doubtless affects his desires and limits the range of choices he can make. But suppose that someone, without being aware of it, has in fact lost or been deprived of his freedom of action. Even though he is no longer free to do what he wants to do, his will may remain as free as it was before. Despite the fact that he is not free to translate his desires into actions or to act according to the determinations of his will, he may still form those desires and make those determinations as freely as if his freedom of action had not been impaired.

When we ask whether a person's will is free we are not asking whether he is in a position to translate his first-order desires into actions. That is the question of whether he is free to do as he pleases. The question of the freedom of his will does not concern the relation between what he does and what he wants to do. Rather, it concerns his desires themselves. But what question about them is it?

It seems to me both natural and useful to construe the question of whether a person's will is free in close analogy to the question of whether an agent enjoys freedom of action. Now freedom of action is (roughly, at least) the freedom to do what one wants to do. Analogously, then, the statement that a person enjoys freedom of the will means (also roughly) that he is free to want what he wants to want. More precisely, it means that he is free to will what he wants to will, or to have the will he wants. Just as the question about the freedom of an agent's action has to do with whether it is the action he wants to perform, so the question about the freedom of his will has to do with whether it is the will he wants to have.

It is in securing the conformity of his will to his second-order volitions, then, that a person exercises freedom of the will. And it is in the discrepancy between his will and his second-order volitions, or in his awareness that their coincidence is not his own doing but only a happy chance, that a person who does not have this freedom feels its lack. The unwilling addict's will is not free. This is shown by the fact that it is not the will he wants. It is also true, though in a different way, that the will of the wanton addict is not free. The wanton addict neither has the will he wants nor has a will that differs from the will he wants. Since he has no volitions of the second order, the freedom of his will cannot be a problem for him. He lacks it, so to speak, by default.

People are generally far more complicated than my sketchy account of the structure of a person's will may suggest. There is as much opportunity for ambivalence, conflict, and self-deception with regard to desires of the second order, for example, as there is with regard to first-order desires. If there is an unresolved conflict among someone's second-order desires, then he is in danger of having no second-order volition; for unless this conflict is resolved, he has no preference concerning which of his first-order desires is to be his will. This condition, if it is so severe that it prevents him from identifying himself in a sufficiently decisive way with *any* of his conflicting first-order desires, destroys him as a person. For it either tends to paralyze his will and to keep him from acting at all, or it tends to remove him from his will so that his will operates without his participation.

In both cases he becomes, like the unwilling addict though in a different way, a helpless bystander to the forces that move him.

Another complexity is that a person may have, especially if his second-order desires are in conflict, desires and volitions of a higher order than the second. There is no theoretical limit to the length of the series of desires of higher and higher orders; nothing except common sense and, perhaps, a saving fatigue prevents an individual from obsessively refusing to identify himself with any of his desires until he forms a desire of the next higher order. The tendency to generate such a series of acts of forming desires, which would be a case of humanization run wild, also leads toward the destruction of a person.

It is possible, however, to terminate such a series of acts without cutting it off arbitrarily. When a person identifies himself *decisively* with one of his first-order desires, this commitment "resounds" throughout the potentially endless array of higher orders. Consider a person who, without reservation or conflict, wants to be motivated by the desire to concentrate on his work. The fact that his second-order volition to be moved by this desire is a decisive one means that there is no room for questions concerning the pertinence of desires or volitions of higher orders. Suppose the person is asked whether he wants to concentrate on his work. He can properly insist that this question concerning a third-order desire does not arise. It would be a mistake to claim that, because he has not considered whether he wants the second-order volition he has formed, he is indifferent to the question of whether it is with this volition or with some other that he wants his will to accord. The decisiveness of the commitment he has made means that he has decided that no further question about his second-order volition, at any higher order, remains to be asked. It is relatively unimportant whether we explain this by saying that this commitment implicitly generates an endless series of confirming desires of higher orders, or by saying that the commitment is tantamount to a dissolution of the pointedness of all questions concerning higher orders of desire.

Examples such as the one concerning the unwilling addict may suggest that volitions of the second order, or of higher orders, must be formed deliberately and that a person characteristically struggles to ensure that they are satisfied. But the conformity of a person's will to his higher-order volitions may be far more thoughtless and spontaneous than this. Some people are naturally moved by kindness when they want to be kind, and by nastiness when they want to be nasty, without any explicit forethought and without any need for energetic self-control. Others are moved by nastiness when they want to be kind and by kindness when they intend to be nasty, equally without forethought and without active resistance to these violations of their higher-order desires. The enjoyment of freedom comes easily to some. Others must struggle to achieve it.

IV

My theory concerning the freedom of the will accounts easily for our disinclination to allow that this freedom is enjoyed by the members of any species inferior to our own. It also satisfies another condition that must be met by any such theory, by making it apparent why the freedom of the will should be regarded as desirable. The enjoyment of a free will means the satisfaction of certain desires – desires of the second or of higher orders – whereas its absence means their frustration. The satisfactions at stake are those which accrue to a person of whom it may be said that his will is his own. The corresponding frustrations are those suffered by a person of whom it may be said that he is estranged from himself, or that he finds himself a helpless or a passive bystander to the forces that move him.

A person who is free to do what he wants to do may yet not be in a position to have the will he wants. Suppose, however, that he enjoys both freedom of action and freedom of the will. Then he is not only free to do what he wants to do; he is also free to want what he wants to want. It seems to me that he has, in that case, all the freedom it is possible to desire or to conceive. There are other good things in life, and he may not possess some of them. But there is nothing in the way of freedom that he lacks.

It is far from clear that certain other theories of the freedom of the will meet these elementary but essential conditions: that it be understandable why we desire this freedom and why we refuse to ascribe it to animals. Consider, for example, Roderick Chisholm's quaint version of the doctrine that human freedom entails an absence of causal determination.[7] Whenever a person performs a free action, according to Chisholm, it's a miracle. The motion of a person's hand, when the person moves it, is the outcome of a series of physical causes; but some event in this series, "and presumably one of those that took place within the brain, was caused by the agent and not by any other events" (18). A free agent has, therefore, "a prerogative which some would attribute only to God: each of us, when we act, is a prime mover unmoved" (23).

This account fails to provide any basis for doubting that animals of subhuman species enjoy the freedom it defines. Chisholm says nothing that makes it seem less likely that a rabbit performs a miracle when it moves its leg than that a man does so when he moves his hand. But why, in any case, should anyone *care* whether he can interrupt the natural order of causes in the way Chisholm describes? Chisholm offers no reason for believing that there is a discernible difference between the experience of a man who miraculously initiates a series of causes when he moves his hand and a man who moves his hand without any such breach of the normal causal sequence. There appears to be no concrete basis for preferring to be involved in the one state of affairs rather than in the other.[8]

It is generally supposed that, in addition to satisfying the two conditions I have mentioned, a satisfactory theory of the freedom of the will necessarily provides an analysis of one of the conditions of moral responsibility. The most common recent approach to the problem of understanding the freedom of the will has been, indeed, to inquire what is entailed by the assumption that someone is morally responsible for what he has done. In my view, however, the relation between moral responsibility and the freedom of the will has been very widely misunderstood. It is not true that a person is morally responsible for what he has done only if his will was free when he did it. He may be morally responsible for having done it even though his will was not free at all.

A person's will is free only if he is free to have the will he wants. This means that, with regard to any of his first-order desires, he is free either to make that desire his will or to make some other first-order desire his will instead. Whatever his will, then, the will of the person whose will is free could have been otherwise; he could have done otherwise than to constitute his will as he did. It is a vexed question just how 'he could have done otherwise' is to be understood in contexts such as this one. But although this question is important to the theory of freedom, it has no bearing on the theory of moral responsibility. For the assumption that a person is morally responsible for what he has done does not entail that the person was in a position to have whatever will he wanted.

This assumption *does* entail that the person did what he did freely, or that he did it of his own free will. It is a mistake, however, to believe that someone acts freely only when he is free to do whatever he wants or that he acts of his own free will only if his will is free. Suppose that a person has done what he wanted to do, that he did it because he wanted to do it, and that the will by which he was moved when he did it was his will because it was the will he wanted. Then he did it freely and of his own free will. Even supposing that he could have done otherwise, he would not have done otherwise; and even supposing that he could have had a different will, he would not have wanted his will to differ from what it was. Moreover, since the will that moved him when he acted was his will because he wanted it to be, he cannot claim that his will was forced upon him or that he was a passive bystander to its constitution. Under these conditions, it is quite irrelevant to the evaluation of his moral responsibility to inquire whether the alternatives that he opted against were actually available to him.[9]

In illustration, consider a third kind of addict. Suppose that his addiction has the same physiological basis and the same irresistible thrust as the addictions of the unwilling and wanton addicts, but that he is altogether delighted with his condition. He is a willing addict, who would not have things any other way. If the grip of his addiction should somehow weaken, he would do whatever he could to reinstate it; if his desire for the drug should begin to fade, he would take steps to renew its intensity.

The willing addict's will is not free, for his desire to take the drug will be effective regardless of whether or not he wants this desire to constitute his will. But when he takes the drug, he takes it freely and of his own free will. I am inclined to understand his situation as involving the overdetermination of his first-order desire to take the drug. This desire is his effective desire because he is physiologically addicted. But it is his effective desire also because he wants it to be. His will is outside his control, but, by his second-order desire that his desire for the drug should be effective, he has made this will his own. Given that it is therefore not only because of his addiction that his desire for the drug is effective, he may be morally responsible for taking the drug.

My conception of the freedom of the will appears to be neutral with regard to the problem of determinism. It seems conceivable that it should be causally determined that a person is free to want what he wants to want. If this is conceivable, then it might be causally determined that a person enjoys a free will. There is no more than an innocuous appearance of paradox in the proposition that it is determined, ineluctably and by forces beyond their control, that certain people have free wills and that others do not. There is no incoherence in the proposition that some agency other than a person's own is responsible (even *morally* responsible) for the fact that he enjoys or fails to enjoy freedom of the will. It is possible that a person should be morally responsible for what he does of his own free will and that some other person should also be morally responsible for his having done it.[10]

On the other hand, it seems conceivable that it should come about by chance that a person is free to have the will he wants. If this is conceivable, then it might be a matter of chance that certain people enjoy freedom of the will and that certain others do not. Perhaps it is also conceivable, as a number of philosophers believe, for states of affairs to come about in a way other than by chance or as the outcome of a sequence of natural causes. If it is indeed conceivable for the relevant states of affairs to come about in some third way, then it is also possible that a person should in that third way come to enjoy the freedom of the will.

Notes

1   P. F. Strawson, *Individuals* (London: Methuen, 1959), pp. 101–102. Ayer's usage of 'person' is similar: "it is characteristic of persons in this sense that besides having various physical properties … they are also credited with various forms of consciousness" [A. J. Ayer, *The Concept of a Person* (New York: St. Martin's, 1963), p. 82]. What concerns Strawson and Ayer is the problem of understanding the relation between mind and body, rather than the quite different problem of understanding what it is to be a creature that not only has a mind and a body but is also a person.

2   For the sake of simplicity, I shall deal only with what someone wants or desires, neglecting related phenomena such as choices and decisions. I propose to use the verbs 'to want' and 'to desire' interchangeably, although they are by no means perfect synonyms. My motive in forsaking the established nuances of these words arises from the fact that the verb 'to want', which suits my purposes better so far as its meaning is concerned, does not lend itself so readily to the formation of nouns as does the verb 'to desire'. It is perhaps acceptable, albeit graceless, to speak in the plural of someone's "wants." But to speak in the singular of someone's "want" would be an abomination.

3   What I say in this paragraph applies not only to cases in which 'to X' refers to a possible action or inaction. It also applies to cases in which 'to X' refers to a first-order desire and in which the statement that 'A wants to X' is therefore a shortened version of a statement – "A wants to want to X" – that identifies a desire of the second order.

4   It is not so clear that the entailment relation described here holds in certain kinds of cases, which I think may fairly be regarded as nonstandard, where the essential difference between the standard and the nonstandard cases lies in the kind of description by which the first-order desire in question is identified. Thus, suppose that A admires B so fulsomely that, even though he does not know what B wants to do, he wants to be effectively moved by whatever desire effectively moves B; without knowing what B's will is, in other words, A wants his own will to be the same. It

certainly does not follow that *A* already has, among his desires, a desire like the one that constitutes *B*'s will. I shall not pursue here the questions of whether there are genuine counterexamples to the claim made in the text or of how, if there are, that claim should be altered.

5   Creatures with second-order desires but no second-order volitions differ significantly from brute animals, and, for some purposes, it would be desirable to regard them as persons. My usage, which withholds the designation 'person' from them, is thus somewhat arbitrary. I adopt it largely because it facilitates the formulation of some of the points I wish to make. Hereafter, whenever I consider statements of the form "*A* wants to want to *X*," I shall have in mind statements identifying second-order volitions and not statements identifying second-order desires that are not second-order volitions.

6   In speaking of the evaluation of his own desires and motives as being characteristic of a person, I do not mean to suggest that a person's second-order volitions necessarily manifest a *moral* stance on his part toward his first-order desires. It may not be from the point of view of morality that the person evaluates his first-order desires. Moreover, a person may be capricious and irresponsible in forming his second-order volitions and give no serious consideration to what is at stake. Second-order volitions express evaluations only in the sense that they are preferences. There is no essential restriction on the kind of basis, if any, upon which they are formed.

7   "Freedom and Action," in K. Lehrer, ed., *Freedom and Determinism* (New York: Random House, 1966), pp. 11–44.

8   I am not suggesting that the alleged difference between these two states of affairs is unverifiable. On the contrary, physiologists might well be able to show that Chisholm's conditions for a free action are not satisfied, by establishing that there is no relevant brain event for which a sufficient physical cause cannot be found.

9   For another discussion of the considerations that cast doubt on the principle that a person is morally responsible for what he has done only if he could have done otherwise, see my "Alternate Possibilities and Moral Responsibility," *The Journal of Philosophy*, LXVI, 23 (Dec. 4, 1969): 829–839.

10 There is a difference between being *fully* responsible and being *solely* responsible. Suppose that the willing addict has been made an addict by the deliberate and calculated work of another. Then it may be that both the addict and this other person are fully responsible for the addict's taking the drug, while neither of them is solely responsible for it. That there is a distinction between full moral responsibility and sole moral responsibility is apparent in the following example. A certain light can be turned on or off by flicking either of two switches, and each of these switches is simultaneously flicked to the "on" position by a different person, neither of whom is aware of the other. Neither person is solely responsible for the light's going on, nor do they share the responsibility in the sense that each is partially responsible; rather, each of them is fully responsible.

PART III

ARE THERE
MANY WORLDS?

Introduction

The word "world" can be used to mean several different kinds of thing. In one sense, the planets are worlds – the earth, our world, only one among many. But sometimes we speak of the entire space-time universe, not just planet earth, as "our world." One way to make this usage precise is to stipulate that, by a "world," we mean the complete contents of a region of space-time that is "maximal" – that is, a region with no further regions of space or time earlier or later than, or at spatial distances from, any of its parts. A world, in this sense, is a complete space-time universe; and "our world" seems to be one that began with the Big Bang and that will continue to exist forever (though it will eventually become homogeneous and boring). If there is a God, or any other sort of thing, that exists "outside of space and time" (like Russell's universals – see Ch. 4), it would not be part of our world, but outside of it, in this sense of "world." If there are other universes, not temporally or spatially connected to this one – so that "you can't get there from here" by traveling in any direction, including backwards and forwards in time – then they, too, are not part of "our world" (this use of "world" is very close to, perhaps identical with, what Derek Parfit means by "local world" in Ch. 60). But "world" can be used in yet another way to mean something even more inclusive: *Everything that there is*, whether in our space-time universe, or some other, or outside space and time altogether.

Philosophers have been led to appeal to worlds in a slightly more abstract sense: A world is a complete "way things could have been." Such worlds can be merely possible, and have been of much use in philosophers' attempts to shed light on the nature of possibility and necessity. The arguments of section A include Lewis's defense, and Kripke's criticism, of the idea that possible worlds can be identified with concrete, spatiotemporally disconnected universes (Parfit's "local worlds"). But there is much more in these essays, including opposing views about the essential properties of things.

Another context in which "worlds" are pressed into philosophical service is in debates about "ontological relativity," the topic of section B. When asking what the world contains, in the "absolutely-everything-there-is" sense of the term, should we expect a single right answer, a catalogue of everything that exists? Or might there be answers that disagree, despite the fact that each is just as truly a complete inventory of what the actual world contains? We describe this set of issues as the question whether there is just one actual world.

A Are There Worlds Other than the Actual World?

Introduction

This is a question about the status of "possible worlds." In formalizing ordinary reasoning about what is possible and what is necessary – what *could* have been, and what *had* to be – philosophers have found it immensely useful to think in terms of possible worlds. As most philosophers use the term, "possible world" does not mean just a complete spatio-temporal universe, or the sum-total of everything that exists. A possible world is a complete "way that things could have been." It is not too hard to grasp the idea of a complete possible world. Possible worlds are just very large – in fact, maximally large – possible situations. Take a "smaller" possibility – for example, the possible situation in which I (Dean Zimmerman) am an English professor. Surely that *is* a possibility (I was, after all, an English major before I was a philosophy major). Furthermore, I could have been an English professor whether or not van Inwagen had pursued a career in philosophy or in something else instead, like the law. So there are some larger possible situations in which I am an English professor and van Inwagen is, say, a judge; and others in which I am an English professor and van Inwagen is a philosophy professor. To arrive at a *complete* "way things could have been" – a maximal possibility, or possible world – one would just go on filling in all the other details of how things are with respect to everybody and everything else – van Inwagen is a judge, Clarence Thomas is a philosopher, the Falklands war never occurred, Gore became president, etc. – being careful to fill in the details in such a way that the result remains possible. (For instance, don't include both van Inwagen's being a judge and also his parents' never meeting and his never being born!) If one were able to fill in *all* the details in this way, answering every question of the form "Would such-and-such have been the case, in this envisaged possible situation?", then one would arrive at a complete possible world. Of course finite minds cannot grasp a possible world in all its specifics; but we can get the hang of the *idea* of a possible world; and we can see that, had things been different, they would have been different in some precise, complete way – so, another possible world would have been actual instead of this one.

Few philosophers, if any, doubt the heuristic usefulness of possible worlds as a guide to our thinking about possibility and necessity (the fundamental "modal" concepts, the subject matter of "modality"). Philosophers do disagree about just how seriously to take this talk of possible worlds. Are possible worlds abstract objects of some kind – gigantic "propositions" or Platonic universals, say? Are they mere fictions that provide a useful way of thinking about modality, but that must, in the end, be discarded as not really being what possibility and necessity are about? Or are they, as David Lewis would have it, worlds in the second sense stipulated above: local worlds, complete space-time universes? Shocking as the hypothesis may be, Lewis makes a case for a plurality of disconnected spatiotemporal worlds in Ch. 52, showing how much work they could do in a metaphysical theory about modality. In "Counterparts of Persons and Their Bodies," he spells out the details of the "counterpart theory" sketched in Ch. 52 – a theory about what it means to say, of a particular individual, that it has such-and-such properties essentially or contingently. Kripke, on the other hand, thinks it is a great mistake to take possible worlds as seriously as Lewis does. And he rejects counterpart theory, seeing it as the unhappy result of Lewis's implausible theory about the nature of possible worlds.

A glance at these papers will reveal that they are considerably more difficult than the rest of the readings in this anthology. Necessity and possibility are complicated, and contemporary discussions of these modal notions are closely intertwined with the program of developing logics for modality. As a consequence, much of this section will remain opaque to those who have not had at least an introductory logic course.

Lewis's materialist metaphysics of persons (developed in Chs. 23 and 27) faces an objection based upon ostensible differences between the essences of persons and mere sums of temporal parts (an objection pressed by Eric Olson in section 11 of Ch. 25). The counterpart theory Lewis develops in Chs. 52 and 53 includes his answer to this objection.

Suggestions for further reading

Bricker, Phillip, "Concrete possible worlds," in Sider, Hawthorne, and Zimmerman (eds.), *Contemporary Debates in Metaphysics* (Malden, Mass.: Blackwell, 2007).

Jubien, Michael, *Contemporary Metaphysics* (Oxford: Blackwell, 1997) ch. 8 ("Modality").

Kripke, Saul, *Naming and Necessity* (Cambridge, Mass.: Harvard University Press, 1980).

Laurence, Stephen, and Macdonald, Cynthia (eds.), *Contemporary Readings in the Foundations of Metaphysics* (Oxford: Basil Blackwell, 1998) Part II ("Possible Worlds and Possibilia").

Loux, Michael J., *Metaphysics: A Contemporary Introduction*, 2nd edn (London: Routledge, 2002) ch. 5 ("The Necessary and the Possible").

Loux, Michael J. (ed.), *The Possible and the Actual* (Ithaca: Cornell University Press, 1979), chs. 1, 7, 10, and 12 (Loux, "Introduction: Modality and Metaphysics"; Alvin Plantinga, "Transworld Identity or Worldbound Individuals?"; Robert M. Adams, "Theories of Actuality"; and Robert Stalnaker, "Possible Worlds").

Melia, Joseph, "Ersatz possible worlds," in Sider, Hawthorne, and Zimmerman (eds.), *Contemporary Debates in Metaphysics* (Malden, Mass.: Blackwell, 2007).

Plantinga, Alvin, *The Nature of Necessity* (Oxford: Clarendon Press, 1974), chs. 1 and 2.

52   Modal Realism at Work: an Excerpt from *On The Plurality of Worlds*

David Lewis

1.1   The Thesis of Plurality of Worlds

The world we live in is a very inclusive thing. Every stick and every stone you have ever seen is part of it. And so are you and I. And so are the planet Earth, the solar system, the entire Milky Way, the remote galaxies we see through telescopes, and (if there are such things) all the bits of empty space between the stars and galaxies. There is nothing so far away from us as not to be part of our world. Anything at any distance at all is to be included. Likewise the world is inclusive in time. No long-gone ancient Romans, no long-gone pterodactyls, no long-gone primordial clouds of plasma are too far in the past, nor are the dead dark stars too far in the future, to be part of this same world. Maybe, as I myself think, the world is a big physical object; or maybe some parts of it are entelechies or spirits or auras or deities or other things unknown to physics. But nothing is so alien in kind as not to be part of our world, provided only that it does exist at some distance and direction from here, or at some time before or after or simultaneous with now.

The way things are, at its most inclusive, means the way this entire world is. But things might have been different, in ever so many ways. This book of mine might have been finished on schedule. Or, had I not been such a commonsensical chap, I might be defending not only a plurality of possible worlds, but also a plurality of impossible worlds, whereof you speak truly by contradicting yourself. Or I might not have existed at all – neither I myself, nor any counterpart of me. Or there might never have been any people. Or the physical constants might have had somewhat different values, incompatible with the emergence of life. Or there might have been altogether different laws of nature; and instead of electrons and quarks, there might have been alien particles, without charge or mass or spin but with alien physical properties that nothing in this world shares. There are ever so many ways that a world might be; and one of these many ways is the way that this world is.

Are there other worlds that are other ways? I say there are. I advocate a thesis of plurality of worlds, or *modal realism*,[1] which holds that our world is but one world among many. There are countless other worlds, other very inclusive things. Our world consists of us and all our surroundings, however remote in time and space; just as it is one big thing having lesser things as parts, so likewise do other worlds have lesser other-worldly things as parts. The worlds are something like remote planets; except that most of them are much bigger than mere planets, and they are not remote. Neither are they nearby. They are not at any spatial distance whatever from here. They are not far in the past or future, nor for that matter near; they are not at any temporal distance whatever from now. They are isolated: there are no spatiotemporal relations at all between things that belong to different worlds. Nor does anything that happens at one world cause anything to happen at another. Nor do they overlap; they have no parts in common, with the exception, perhaps, of immanent universals exercising their characteristic privilege of repeated occurrence.

The worlds are many and varied. There are enough of them to afford worlds where (roughly speaking) I finish on schedule, or I write on behalf of *impossibilia*, or I do not exist, or there are no people at all, or the physical constants do not permit life, or totally different laws govern the doings of alien particles with alien properties. There are so many other worlds, in fact, that absolutely *every* way that a world could possibly be is a way that some world *is*. And as with worlds, so it is with parts of worlds. There are ever so many ways that a part of a world could be; and so many and so varied are the other worlds that absolutely every way that a part of a world could possibly be is a way that some part of some world is.

The other worlds are of a kind with this world of ours. To be sure, there are differences of kind between things that are parts of different worlds – one world has electrons and another has none, one has spirits and another has none – but these differences of kind are no more than sometimes arise between things that are parts of one single world, for instance in a world where electrons coexist with spirits. The difference between this and the other worlds is not a categorial difference.

Nor does this world differ from the others in its manner of existing. I do not have the slightest idea what a difference in manner of existing is supposed to be. Some things exist here on earth, other things exist extraterrestrially, perhaps some exist no place in particular; but that is no difference in manner of existing, merely a difference in location or lack of it between things that exist. Likewise some things exist here at our world, others exist at other worlds; again, I take this to be a difference between things that exist, not a difference in their existing. You might say that strictly speaking, only this-worldly things *really* exist; and I am ready enough to agree; but on my view this 'strict' speaking is *restricted* speaking, on a par with saying that all the beer is in the fridge and ignoring most of all the beer there is. When we quantify over less than all there is, we leave out things that (unrestrictedly speaking) exist *simpliciter*. If I am right, other-worldly things exist *simpliciter*, though often it is very sensible to ignore them and quantify restrictedly over our worldmates. And if I am wrong, other-worldly things fail *simpliciter* to exist. They exist, as the Russell set does, only according to a false theory. That is not to exist in some inferior manner – what exists only according to some false theory just does not exist at all.

The worlds are not of our own making. It may happen that one part of a world makes other parts, as we do; and as other-worldly gods and demiurges do on a grander scale. But if worlds are causally isolated, nothing outside a world ever makes a world; and nothing inside makes the whole of a world, for that would be an impossible kind of self-causation. We make languages and concepts and descriptions and imaginary representations that apply to worlds. We make stipulations that select some worlds rather than others for our attention. Some of us even make assertions to the effect that other worlds exist. But none of these things we make are the worlds themselves.

Why believe in a plurality of worlds? – Because the hypothesis is serviceable, and that is a reason to think that it is true. The familiar analysis of necessity as truth at all possible worlds was only the beginning. In the last two decades, philosophers have offered a great many more analyses that make reference to possible worlds, or to possible individuals that inhabit possible worlds. I find that record most impressive. I think it is clear that talk of *possibilia* has clarified questions in many parts of the philosophy of logic, of mind, of language, and of science – not to mention metaphysics itself. Even those who officially scoff often cannot resist the temptation to help themselves abashedly to this useful way of speaking.

Hilbert called the set-theoretical universe a paradise for mathematicians. And he was right (though perhaps it was not he who should have said it). We have only to believe in the vast hierarchy of sets, and there we find entities suited to meet the needs of all the branches of mathematics;[2] and we find that the very meagre primitive vocabulary of set theory, definitionally extended, suffices to meet our needs for mathematical predicates; and we find that the meagre axioms of set theory are first principles enough to yield the theorems that are the content of the subject. Set theory offers the mathematician great economy of primitives and premises, in return for accepting rather a lot of entities unknown to *Homo javanensis*. It offers an improvement in what Quine calls ideology, paid for in the coin of ontology. It's an offer you can't refuse. The price is right; the benefits in theoretical unity and economy are well worth the entities. Philosophers might like to see the subject reconstructed or reconstrued; but working mathematicians insist on pursuing their subject in paradise, and will not be driven out. Their thesis of plurality of sets is fruitful; that gives them good reason to believe that it is true.

Good reason; I do not say it is conclusive. Maybe the price is higher than it seems because set theory has unacceptable hidden implications – maybe the next round of set-theoretical paradoxes will soon be upon us. Maybe the very idea of accepting controversial ontology for the sake of theoretical benefits is misguided – so a sceptical epistemologist might say, to which I reply that mathematics is better known than any premise of sceptical epistemology. Or perhaps some better paradise might be found. Some say that mathematics might be pursued in a paradise of *possibilia*, full of unactualised idealisations of things around us, or of things we do – if so, the parallel with mathematics serves my purpose better than ever! Conceivably we might find some way to accept set theory, just as is and just as nice a home for mathematics, without any ontological commitment to sets. But even if such hopes come true, my point remains. It has been the judgement of mathematicians, which modest philosophers ought to respect, that *if* that is indeed the choice before us, then it is worth believing in vast realms of controversial entities for the sake of enough benefit in unity and economy of theory.

As the realm of sets is for mathematicians, so logical space is a paradise for philosophers. We have only to believe in the vast realm of *possibilia*, and there we find what we need to advance our endeavours. We find the wherewithal to reduce the diversity of notions we must accept as primitive, and thereby to improve the unity and economy of the theory that is our professional concern – total theory, the whole of what we take to be true. What price paradise? If we want the theoretical benefits that talk of *possibilia* brings, the most straightforward way to gain honest title to them is to accept such talk as the literal truth. It is my view that the price is right, if less spectacularly so than in the mathematical parallel. The benefits are worth their ontological cost. Modal realism is fruitful; that gives us good reason to believe that it is true.

Good reason; I do not say it is conclusive. Maybe the theoretical benefits to be gained are illusory, because the analyses that use *possibilia* do not succeed on their own terms. Maybe the price is higher than it seems, because modal realism has unacceptable hidden implications. Maybe the price is *not* right; even if I am right about what theoretical benefits can be had for what ontological cost, maybe those benefits just are not worth those costs. Maybe the very idea of accepting controversial ontology for the sake of theoretical benefits is misguided. Maybe – and this is the doubt that most interests me – the benefits are not worth the cost, because they can be had more cheaply elsewhere. Some of these doubts are too complicated to address here, or too simple to address at all; others will come in for discussion in the course of this book.

1.2   Modal Realism at Work: Modality

In the next four sections, I consider what possible worlds and individuals are good for. Even a long discussion might be too short to convince all readers that the applications I have in mind are workable at all, still less that approaches employing *possibilia* are superior to all conceivable rivals. (Still less that *possibilia* are absolutely indispensable, something I don't believe myself.) Each application could have a book of its own. Here I shall settle for less.

The best known application is to modality. Presumably, whatever it may mean to call a world actual (see section 1.9), it had better turn out that the world we are part of is the actual world. What actually is the case, as we say, is what goes on here. That is one possible way for a world to be. Other worlds are other, that is *un*actualised, possibilities. If there are many worlds, and every way that a world could possibly be is a way that some world is, then whenever such-and-such might be the case, there is some world where such-and-such is the case. Conversely, since it is safe to say that no world is any way that a world could not possibly be, whenever there is some world at which such-and-such is the case, then it might be that such-and-such is the case. So modality turns into quantification: possibly there are blue swans iff, for some world W, at W there are blue swans.

But not just quantification: there is also the phrase 'at W' which appears within the scope of the quantifier, and which needs explaining. It works mainly by restricting the domains of quantifiers in its scope, in much the same way that the restricting modifier 'in Australia' does. In Australia, all swans are black – all swans are indeed black, if we ignore everything not in Australia; quantifying only over things in Australia, all swans are black. At some strange world W, all swans are blue – all swans are indeed blue, if we ignore everything not part of the world W; quantifying only over things that are part of W, all swans are blue.

Such modifiers have various other effects. For one thing, they influence the interpretation of expressions that are not explicitly quantificational, but that reveal implicit quantification under analysis: definite descriptions and singular terms definable by them, class abstracts and plurals, superlatives, etc. An example: it is the case at world W that nine numbers the solar planets iff nine numbers those solar planets that are part of W. Another example: words like 'invent' and 'discover' are implicitly superlative, hence implicitly quantificational; they imply doing something *first*, before *anyone* else did. So the inventor of bifocals at W is the one who is part of W and thought of bifocals before anyone else who is part of W did. For another thing, besides restricting explicit or implicit quantifiers, our modifiers can restrict proper names. In Australia, and likewise at a possible world where the counterparts of British cities are strangely rearranged, Cardiff is a suburb of Newcastle – there are various places of those names, and we banish ambiguity by restricting our attention to the proper domain. Here I am supposing that the way we bestow names attaches them not only to this-worldly things, but also to other-worldly counterparts thereof. That is how the other-worldly Cardiffs and Newcastles bear those names in our this-worldly language. In the same way, the solar planets at W are those that orbit the star Sol of the world W, a counterpart of the Sol of this world. Natural language being complex, doubtless I have not listed all the effects of our modifiers. But I believe the principle will always stay the same: whatever they do, they do it by instructing us, within limits, to take account only of things that are part of a limited domain – the domain of things in Australia, or the domain of parts of a certain world.

Two qualifications concerning our restrictive modifiers. (1) I do not suppose that they must restrict all quantifiers in their scope, without exception. 'In Australia, there is a yacht faster than any other' would mean less than it does if the modifier restricted both quantifiers rather than just the first. 'Nowadays there are rulers more dangerous than any ancient Roman' would be trivialised if we ignored those ancient Romans who are not alive nowadays. 'At some small worlds, there is a natural number too big to measure any class of individuals' can be true even if the large number that makes it true is no part of the small world. (2) Of course there will usually be other restrictions as well; doubtless we are already ignoring various immigrant swans and their descendants, and also whatever freak or painted swans there may be in Australia or among the parts of world W, so our modifier 'in Australia' or 'at W' adds more restrictions to the ones already in force. In short, while our modifiers tend to impose restrictions on quantifiers, names, etc., a lot is left up to the pragmatic rule that what is said should be interpreted so as to be sensible. If that means adding extra tacit restrictions, or waiving some of the restrictions imposed by our modifiers, then – within limits – so be it.[3]

As possibility amounts to existential quantification over the worlds, with restricting modifiers inside the quantifiers, so necessity amounts to universal quantification. Necessarily all swans are birds iff, for any world W, quantifying only over parts of W, all swans are birds. More simply: iff all swans, no matter what world they are part of, are birds. The other modalities follow suit. What is impossible is the case at no worlds; what is contingent is the case at some but not at others.

More often than not, modality is *restricted* quantification; and restricted from the standpoint of a given world, perhaps ours, by means of so-called 'accessibility' relations. Thus it is nomologically necessary, though not unrestrictedly necessary, that friction produces heat: at every world that obeys the laws of our world, friction produces heat. It is contingent which world is ours; hence what are the laws of our world; hence which worlds are nomologically 'accessible' from ours; hence what is true throughout these worlds, i.e. what is nomologically necessary.

Likewise it is historically necessary, now as I write these words, that my book is at least partly written: at every world that perfectly matches ours up to now, and diverges only later if ever, the book is at least partly written.

Putting together nomological and historical accessibility restrictions, we get the proper treatment of predetermination – a definition free of red herrings about what can in principle be known and computed, or about the analysis of causation. It was predetermined at his creation that Adam would sin iff he does so at every world that both obeys the laws of our world and perfectly matches the history of our world up through the moment of Adam's creation.

As other worlds are alternative possibilities for an entire world, so the parts of other worlds are alternative possibilities for lesser individuals. Modality *de re*, the potentiality and essence of things, is quantification over possible individuals. As quantification over possible worlds is commonly restricted by accessibility relations, so quantification over possible individuals is commonly restricted by counterpart relations. In both cases, the restrictive relations usually involve similarity. A nomologically or historically accessible world is similar to our world in the laws it obeys, or in its history up to some time. Likewise a counterpart of Oxford is similar to Oxford in its origins, or in its location *vis-à-vis* (counterparts of) other places, or in the arrangement and nature of its parts, or in the role it plays in the life of a nation or a discipline. Thus Oxford might be noted more for the manufacture of locomotives than of motor cars, or might have been a famous centre for the study of paraconsistent hermeneutics, iff some other-worldly counterpart of our Oxford, under some suitable counterpart relation, enjoys these distinctions.

Sometimes one hears a short list of the restricted modalities: nomological, historical, epistemic, deontic, maybe one or two more. And sometimes one is expected to take a position, once and for all, about what is or isn't possible *de re* for an individual. I would suggest instead that the restricting of modalities by accessibility or counterpart relations, like the restricting of quantifiers generally, is a very fluid sort of affair: inconstant, somewhat indeterminate, and subject to instant change in response to contextual pressures. Not anything goes, but a great deal does. And to a substantial extent, saying so makes it so: if you say what would only be true under certain restrictions, and your conversational partners acquiesce, straightway those restrictions came into force.[4]

The standard language of modal logic provides just two modal expressions: the diamond, read as 'possibly', and the box, read as 'necessarily'. Both are sentential operators: they attach to sentences to make sentences, or to open formulas to make open formulas. So a modal logician will write

◇ for some x, x is a swan and x is blue

to mean that possibly some swan is blue, i.e. that there might be a blue swan; or

□ for all x, if x is a swan then x is a bird

to mean that necessarily all swans are birds. Likewise

◇ x is blue

is a formula satisfied by anything that could possibly be blue, and

□ x is a bird

is a formula satisfied by anything that must necessarily be a bird. When they attach to sentences we can take the diamond and the box as quantifiers, often restricted, over possible worlds. How to take them when they attach to open formulas – sentential expressions with unbound variables – is more questionable.

A simple account would be that in that case also they are just quantifiers over worlds. But that raises a question. Start with something that is part of this world:

Hubert Humphrey, say. He might have won the presidency but didn't, so he satisfies the modal formula 'possibly x wins' but not the formula 'x wins'. Taking the diamond 'possibly' as a quantifier over worlds, (perhaps restricted, but let me ignore that), that means that there is some world W such that, at W, he satisfies 'x wins'. But how does he do that if he isn't even part of W?

You might reply that he *is* part of W as well as part of this world. If this means that the whole of him is part of W, I reject that for reasons to be given in section 4.2; if it means that part of him is part of W, I reject that for reasons to be given in section 4.3. Then to save the simple account, we have to say that Humphrey needn't be part of a world to satisfy formulas there; there is a world where somehow he satisfies 'x wins' *in absentia*.

We might prefer a more complex account of how modal operators work.[5] We might say that when 'possibly' is attached to open formulas, it is a quantifier not just over worlds but also over other-worldly counterparts of this-worldly individuals; so that Humphrey satisfies 'possibly x wins' iff, for some world W, for some counterpart of Humphrey in W, that counterpart satisfies 'x wins' at W. The satisfaction of 'x wins' by the counterpart is unproblematic. Now we need no satisfaction *in absentia*.

The simple and complex accounts are not in competition. Both do equally well, because there is a counterpart-theoretic account of satisfaction *in absentia* that makes them come out equivalent. Satisfaction *in absentia* is vicarious satisfaction: Humphrey satisfies 'x wins' vicariously at any world where he has a winning counterpart. Then according to both accounts alike, he satisfies 'possibly x wins' iff at some world he has a counterpart who wins.

The box and diamond are interdefinable: 'necessarily' means 'not possibly not'. So what I have said for one carries over to the other. According to the simple account, Humphrey satisfies the modal formula 'necessarily x is human' iff it is not the case that there is some world W such that, at W, he satisfies 'x is not human'; that is, iff at no world does he satisfy – *in absentia* or otherwise – 'x is not human'. According to the complex account, Humphrey satisfies 'necessarily x is human' iff it is not the case that for some world W, for some counterpart of Humphrey in W, that counterpart satisfies 'x is not human' at W; that is, iff there is no counterpart in any world of Humphrey who satisfies 'x is not human'. Taking satisfaction *in absentia* to be vicarious satisfaction through a counterpart, the simple and complex accounts again agree: Humphrey satisfies 'necessarily x is human' iff he has no non-human counterpart at any world.

(It is plausible enough that Humphrey has no non-human counterpart. Or, if I am right to say that counterpart relations are an inconstant and indeterminate affair, at any rate it is plausible enough that there is *some* reasonable counterpart relation under which Humphrey has no non-human counterpart – so let's fix on such a counterpart relation for the sake of the example.)

The alert or informed reader will know that if what I've said about how Humphrey satisfies modal formulas sounds right, that is only because I took care to pick the right examples. A famous problem arises if instead we consider whether Humphrey satisfies modal formulas having to do with the contingency of his existence. According to what I've said, be it in the simple or the complex formulation, Humphrey satisfies 'necessarily x exists' and fails to satisfy 'possibly x does not exist' iff he has no counterpart at any world W who does not exist at W. But what can it mean to say that the counterpart is 'at W' if not that, at W, the counterpart exists?[6] So it seems that Humphrey *does* satisfy 'necessarily x exists' and *doesn't* satisfy 'possibly x does not exist'. That is wrong. For all his virtues, still it really will not do to elevate Humphrey to the ranks of the Necessary Beings.

What I want to say, of course, is that Humphrey exists necessarily iff at every world he has some counterpart, which he doesn't; he has the possibility of not existing iff at some world he lacks a counterpart, which he does. It's all very well to say this; but the problem is to square it with my general account of the satisfaction of modal formulas.

So shall we give a revised account of the satisfaction of modal formulas? Should we say that Humphrey satisfies 'necessarily ϕx' iff at every world he has some counterpart who satisfies 'ϕx'? Then, by the interdefinability of box and diamond, Humphrey satisfies 'possibly x is a cat' iff it is not the case that at every world he has some counterpart who satisfies 'not x is a cat'; and indeed that is not the case, since at some worlds he has no counterparts at all; so it seems that he *does* satisfy 'possibly x is a cat' even if he has not a single cat among his counterparts! This is no improvement. What next?

Shall we dump the method of counterparts? – That wouldn't help, because we can recreate the problem in a far more neutral framework. Let us suppose only this much. (1) We want to treat the modal operators simply as quantifiers over worlds. (2) We want to grant that Humphrey somehow satisfies various formulas at various other worlds, never mind how he does it. (3) We want it to come out that he satisfies the modal formula 'necessarily x is human', since that seems to be the way to say something true, namely that he is essentially human. (4) We want it to come out that he satisfies the modal formula 'possibly x does not exist', since that seems to be the way to say something else true, namely that he might not have existed. (5) We want it to come out that he does *not* satisfy the model formula 'possibly x is human and x does not exist' since that seems to be the way to say something false, namely that he might have been human without even existing. So he satisfies 'x is human' at all worlds and 'x does not exist' at some worlds; so he satisfies both of them at some worlds; yet though he satisfies both conjuncts he doesn't satisfy their conjunction! How can that be?

There might be a fallacy of equivocation. Maybe what it means for Humphrey to satisfy a formula *in absentia* is different in the case of different kinds of formulas, or in the case of different kinds of worlds. Maybe, for instance, he can satisfy 'x does not exist' at a world by not having a counterpart there; but to satisfy 'x is human' at a world he has to have a counterpart there who is human, and to satisfy 'x is human and x does not exist' he would have to have one who was human and yet did not exist. Or maybe the language is uniformly ambiguous, and different cases invite different disambiguations. Either way, that would disappoint anyone who hopes that the language of quantified modal logic will be a well-behaved formal language, free of ambiguity and free of devious semantic rules that work different ways in different cases.

Or maybe the satisfying of modal formulas does not always mean what we would intuitively take it to mean after we learn how to pronounce the box and diamond. Maybe, for instance, saying that Humphrey satisfies 'necessarily x is human' is *not* the right way to say that he is essentially human. That would disappoint anyone who hopes that the language of boxes and diamonds affords a good regimentation of our ordinary modal thought.

Whichever it is, the friend of boxes and diamonds is in for a disappointment. He can pick his disappointment to suit himself. He can lay down uniform and unambiguous semantic rules for a regimented formal language – and re-educate his intuitions about how to translate between that language and ordinary modal talk. He can discipline himself, for instance, never to say 'necessarily human' when he means 'essentially human'; but instead, always to say 'necessarily such that it is human if it exists'. Alternatively, he can build his language more on the pattern of what we ordinarily say – and equip it either with outright ambiguities, or else with devious rules that look at what a formula says before they know what it means to satisfy it.[7]

What is the correct counterpart-theoretic interpretation of the modal formulas of the standard language of quantified modal logic? – Who cares? We can make them mean whatever we like. We are their master. We needn't be faithful to the meanings we learned at mother's knee – because we didn't. If this language of boxes and diamonds proves to be a clumsy instrument for talking about matters of essence and potentiality, let it go hang. Use the resources of modal realism *directly* to say what it would mean for Humphrey to be essentially human, or to exist contingently.

. . .

1.9 Actuality

I say that ours is one of many worlds. Ours is the actual world; the rest are not actual. Why so? – I take it to be a trivial matter of meaning. I use the word 'actual' to mean the same as 'this-worldly'. When I use it, it applies to my world and my worldmates; to this world we are part of, and to all parts of this world. And if someone else uses it, whether he be a worldmate of ours or whether he be unactualised, then (provided he means by it what we do) it applies likewise to his world and his worldmates. Elsewhere I have called this the 'indexical analysis' of actuality and stated it as follows.

> I suggest that 'actual' and its cognates should be analyzed as *indexical* terms: terms whose reference varies, depending on relevant features of the context of utterance. The relevant feature of context, for the term 'actual', is the world at which a given utterance occurs. According to the indexical analysis I propose, 'actual' (in its primary sense) refers at any world w to the world w. 'Actual' is analogous to 'present', an indexical term whose reference varies depending on a different feature of context: 'present' refers at any time t to the time t. 'Actual' is analogous also to 'here', 'I', 'you', and 'aforementioned' – indexical terms depending for their refer-

ence respectively on the place, the speaker, the intended audience, the speaker's acts of pointing, and the foregoing discourse. ('Anselm and Actuality', *Noûs*, 4 (1970), pages 184–5.)

This makes actuality a relative matter: every world is *actual at* itself, and thereby all worlds are on a par. This is *not* to say that all worlds are actual – there's no world at which that is true, any more than there's ever a time when all times are present. The 'actual at' relation between worlds is simply identity.

Given my acceptance of the plurality of worlds, the relativity is unavoidable. I have no tenable alternative. For suppose instead that one world alone is *absolutely* actual. There is some special distinction which that one world alone possesses, not relative to its inhabitants or to anything else but *simpliciter*. I have no idea how this supposed absolute distinction might be understood, but let us go on as if we did understand it. I raise two objections.

The first objection concerns our knowledge that we are actual. Note that the supposed absolute distinction, even if it exists, doesn't make the relative distinction go away. It is still true that one world alone is ours, is this one, is the one we are part of. What a remarkable bit of luck for us if the very world we are part of is the one that is absolutely actual! Out of all the people there are in all the worlds, the great majority are doomed to live in worlds that lack absolute actuality, but we are the select few. What reason could we ever have to think it was so? How could we ever know? Unactualised dollars buy no less unactualised bread, and so forth. And yet we *do* know for certain that the world we are part of is the actual world – just as certainly as we know that the world we are part of is the very world we are part of. How could this be knowledge that we are the select few?

D. C. Williams asks the same question. Not about 'actuality' but about 'existence'; but it comes to the same thing, since he is discussing various doctrines on which so-called 'existence' turns out to be a special status that distinguishes some of the things there are from others. He complains that Leibniz 'never intimates, for example, how he can tell that *he* is a member of the existent world and not a mere possible monad on the shelf of essence' ('Dispensing with Existence', *Journal of Philosophy*, 59 (1962) page 752).

Robert M. Adams, in 'Theories of Actuality' (*Noûs*, 8 (1974), pp. 211–31), dismisses this objection. He says that a simple-property theory of absolute actuality can account for the certainty of our knowledge of our own actuality by maintaining that we are as immediately acquainted with our own absolute actuality as we are with our thoughts, feelings, and sensations. But I reply that if Adams and I and all the other actual people really have this immediate acquaintance with absolute actuality, wouldn't my elder sister have had it too, if only I'd had an elder sister? So there she is, unactualised, off in some other world getting fooled by the very same evidence that is supposed to be giving me my knowledge.

This second objection concerns contingency. (It is due to Adams, and this time he and I agree.) Surely it is a contingent matter which world is actual. A contingent matter is one that varies from world to world. At one world, the contingent matter goes one way; at another, another. So at one world, one world is actual; and at another, another. How can this be *absolute* actuality? – The relativity is manifest!

. . .

Notes

1   Or 'extreme' modal realism, as Stalnaker calls it – but in what dimension does its extremity lie?
2   With the alleged exception of category theory – but here I wonder if the unmet needs have more to do with the motivational talk than with the real mathematics.
3   This discussion of restricting modifiers enables me to say why I have no use for impossible worlds, on a par with the possible worlds. For comparison, suppose travellers told of a place in this world – a marvellous mountain, far away in the bush – where contradictions are true. Allegedly we have truths of the form 'On the mountain both P and not P'. But if 'on the mountain' is a restricting modifier, which works by limiting domains of implicit and explicit quantification to a certain part of all that there is, then it has no effect on the truth-functional connectives. Then the order of modifier and connectives makes no difference. So 'On the mountain both P and Q' is equivalent to 'On the mountain P, and on the mountain Q'; likewise 'On the mountain not P' is equivalent to 'Not: on the mountain P'; putting these together, the alleged truth 'On the mountain both P and not P' is equivalent to the overt contradiction 'On the mountain P, and not: on the mountain P'. That is, there is no difference between a contradiction within the scope of the modifier and a plain contradiction that has the modifier within it. So to tell the alleged truth about the marvellously contradictory things that happen on the mountain is no different from contradicting yourself. But there is no subject matter, however marvellous, about which you can tell the truth by contradicting yourself. Therefore there is no mountain where contradictions are true. An impossible world where contradictions are true would be no better. The alleged truth about its contradictory goings-on would itself be contradictory. At least, that is so if I am right that 'at so-and-so world' is a restricting modifier. Other modifiers are another story. 'According to the Bible' or 'Fred says that' are *not* restricting modifiers; they do not pass through the truth-functional connectives. 'Fred says that not P' and 'Not: Fred says that P' are independent: both, either, or neither might be true. If worlds were like stories or story-tellers, there would indeed be room for worlds according to which contradictions are true. The sad truth about the prevarications of these worlds would not itself be contradictory. But worlds, as I understand them, are *not* like stories or story-tellers. They are like this world; and this world is no story, not even a true story. Nor should worlds be replaced by their stories, for reasons discussed in section 3.2.
4   See section 4.5; Angelika Kratzer, 'What "Must" and "Can" Must and Can Mean', *Linguistics and Philosophy*, (1977), pp. 337–55; and my 'Scorekeeping in a Language Game', *Journal of Philosophical Logic*, 8 (1979), pp. 339–59.
5   This is essentially the account I gave in 'Counterpart Theory and Quantified Modal Logic', *Journal of Philosophy*, 65 (1968), pp. 113–26.
6   We might just *say* it, and not mean anything by it. That is Forbes's solution to our present difficulty, in his so-called 'canonical counterpart theory' – my own version is hereby named 'official standard counterpart theory' – in which, if Humphrey has no ordinary counterpart among the things which exist at W, he does nevertheless have a counterpart at W. This extraordinary counterpart is none other than Humphrey

himself – he then gets in as a sort of associate member of W's population, belonging to its 'outer domain' but not to the 'inner domain' of things that exist there fair and square. This isn't explained, but really it needn't be. It amounts to a stipulation that there are two different ways that Humphrey – he himself, safe at home in this world – can satisfy formulas *in absentia*. Where he has proper counterparts, he does it one way, namely the ordinary vicarious way. Where he doesn't, he does it another way – just by not being there he satisfies 'x does not exist'.

7 If he likes, he can give himself more than one of these disappointments. As I noted, Forbes's talk of non-existent counterparts in outer domains amounts to a stipulation that satisfaction *in absentia* works different ways in different cases; so I find it strange that he offers it in rejoinder to a proposal of Hunter and Seager that modal formulas of parallel form needn't always be given parallel counterpart-theoretic translations. But this divided treatment does not pay off by making the modal formulas mean what we would offhand expect them to – it is exactly the non-existent counterparts in the outer domains that keep Humphrey from satisfying 'necessarily x is human' even if he is essentially human.

---

53 Counterparts of Persons and Their Bodies

David Lewis

Materialists like myself hold that persons and their bodies are identical. But there is a simple argument to show that this identity thesis is refuted by the mere possibility that a person might switch bodies. To defeat the argument it seems necessary to revise my counterpart theory by providing for a multiplicity of counterpart relations. This revision has an odd result. Modal predications may be *de re*, yet not referentially transparent.

The thesis I wish to defend here may be stated more precisely, as follows:

(T) Necessarily, a person occupies a body at a time if and only if that person is identical with that body at that time.

Note that the thesis (T) is formulated not in terms of identity itself, a two-place relation, but in terms of a derivative three-place relation of identity at a time. I wish to regard enduring things such as persons and bodies as aggregates – sets, mereological sums, or something similar – of momentary stages. Enduring things X and Y are *identical at* a time t if and only if they both have stages at t – that is, *exist at* t – and their stages at t are identical. Therefore X and Y are identical *simpliciter* if and only if they are identical whenever either one exists. Note that (T) does not say that persons and bodies must be identical *simpliciter*. It does imply that *if* a certain person occupies a certain body whenever either the person or the body exists, *then* the person and the body are identical. In such a case, all and only those stages which are stages of the person are stages of the body he occupies. But (T) also permits other cases: for instance, a body consisting of the stages of a certain person together with some final dead stages that are not stages of any person (and some initial prenatal stages that perhaps are not stages of any person); or a person consisting of stages of a certain body together with some initial or final ghostly stages that are not stages of any body; or even a body-switching person consisting partly of stages of one body and partly of stages of another body. A person consists of stages related pairwise by a certain relation we may call the relation of *personal unity*; a body consists of stages related pairwise by another relation we may call the relation of *bodily unity*.[1] Since for the most part persons occupy bodies and bodies are occupied by persons, it follows according to (T) that the two relations of unity are relations on almost the same set of stages. The exceptions are dead stages, perhaps prenatal stages, and perhaps ghostly stages. Moreover, if we leave out the dead or ghostly or perhaps prenatal stages, then at least for the most part the two relations of unity are coextensive. The exceptions would be body-switchers and perhaps split personalities. Nevertheless, the two relations of unity are different relations-in-intension; so they are coextensive only contingently if at all.

Now I shall present an argument against (T). I regard it as a simplified descendant of an argument put forth by Jerome Shaffer,[2] but I have changed it so much that he might not wish to acknowledge it as his own.

Body-switching is logically possible. Because I might have switched out of my present body yesterday, though in fact I did not, I and my actual present body are such that the former might not have occupied the latter today. Whether or not persons are identical with bodies they occupy, certainly persons are never identical with bodies they do not occupy. So we have:

(1)   I and my body are such that they might not have been identical today.

Suppose that, as is surely at least possible, I occupy the same body from the time when it and I began until the time when it and I will end. Then, by (T), it and I are identical whenever it or I exist. Hence my body and I, enduring things, are identical *simpliciter*. By this identity and Leibniz's law, (1) yields (2):

(2)   My body and my body are such that they might not have been identical today.

Since (2) is self-contradictory, (T) has apparently been refuted.

To rescue (T) without denying the possibility of body-switching and without denying that I might occupy the same body throughout the time that it or I exist, I plan to show that the step from (1) to (2) by Leibniz's law is illegitimate – in other words, that (1) is not referentially transparent with respect to the term 'I'.

I have used the familiar "are such that" construction to indicate that (1) and (2) are to be taken as *de re* rather than *de dicto* modal predications. That is, we are to consider what happens in other possible worlds to the things denoted *here* in our actual world by the terms 'I' and 'my body,' not what happens in other worlds to the things denoted *there* by those terms. Suppose (1) were taken *de dicto*, as if it were this:

It might have been the case that I and my body were not identical today.

There is no problem explaining why this is not referentially transparent. Its truth conditions involve the denotations in other worlds of the terms 'I' and 'my body'; even if these denote the same thing here in our world, they denote different things in some other worlds, for instance in a world in which I switched bodies yesterday. Hence they are not interchangeable. But it would be wrong to take (1) as *de dicto*, for the argument leading up to (1) would then be incoherent and question-begging. As we understand (1) in the argument, it seems true even given (T) because of the fact that I might have switched bodies yesterday. But (1) taken *de dicto* is a straightforward denial of an instance of (T), and the possibility of body-switching is irrelevant to its truth or falsity. For (1) taken *de dicto* is true today if and only if there is some world such that the things denoted in that world today by 'I' and 'my body' are not identical today. But in any world, 'my body' today denotes whichever body is today occupied by the person who is today denoted by 'I', regardless of whether that person occupied that body yesterday. If (T) is true, then in any world the person today denoted there by 'I' and the body today denoted there by 'my body' are identical today; so (1) taken *de dicto* is false. (It should be understood that when I speak of the denotation in another world of 'I' and 'my body,' I am not concerned with any utterance of these terms by some inhabitant of the other world, but rather with the denotation of these terms in the other world on the occasion of their utterance by me here in our world.)

I have suggested elsewhere[3] that *de re* modal predications may best be understood by the method of counterparts. To say that something here in our actual world is such that it might have done so-and-so is not to say that there is a possible world in which that thing *itself* does so-and-so, but that there is a world in which a *counterpart* of that thing does so-and-so. To say that I am such that I might have been a Republican, but I am not such that I might have been a cockatrice, is to say that in some world I have a counterpart who is a Republican, but in no world do I have a counterpart who is a cockatrice. That is plausible enough, for the counterpart relation is a relation of similarity. X's counterparts in other worlds are all and only those things which resemble X closely enough in important respects, and more closely than do the other things in their worlds. It is easier for a Republican than for a cockatrice to resemble me enough to be my counterpart.

The counterpart relation serves as a substitute for identity between things in different worlds. The principal advantage of the method of counterparts over the method of interworld identities is that if we adopted the latter in its most plausible form, we would say that things were identical with all and only those things which we would otherwise call their counterparts. But that could not be correct: first, because the counterpart relation is not transitive or symmetric, as identity is; and second, because the counterpart relation depends on the relative importances we attach to various different respects of similarity and dissimilarity, as identity does not.

To recapitulate: in each possible world there is a set of momentary stages and a set of enduring things composed of stages related pairwise by various relations of unity. An enduring thing and its stages exist only in one world, but may have counterparts in other worlds. We shall be concerned here only with counterparts of enduring things, though we can allow that stages also have their counterparts.

Applying the method of counterparts to the problem at hand, we immediately encounter a bothersome distraction. The translation of (2), which seemed self-contradictory, is this:

> There are a world W, a counterpart X in W of my body, and a counterpart Y in W of my body, such that X and Y are not identical today.

Unfortunately, this translation comes out true, but for an irrelevant reason. I, and also my body whether or not I am identical with it, might have been twins. My body therefore does have two different counterparts in certain worlds. Not only is the translation true; it seems to me to show that (2) itself is true. But the argument against (T) can easily be repaired. Replace (1) and (2) by:

(1′)   I and my body are such that (without any duplication of either) they might not have been identical today.

(2′)   My body and my body are such that (without any duplication of either) they might not have been identical today.

The argument works as well with (1′) and (2′) as it did with (1) and (2). Indeed, (1′) and (2′) correspond to (1) and (2) as we would have understood them if we had forgotten that I might have been twins.[4]

Applying counterpart theory to the repaired argument, we obtain these translations of (1′) and (2′):

(1*)   There are a world W, a unique counterpart X in W of me, and a unique counterpart Y in W of my body, such that X and Y are not identical today.

(2*)   There are a world W, a unique counterpart X in W of my body, and a unique counterpart Y in W of my body, such that X and Y are not identical today.

The argument against (T) seems to go through, using (1*) and (2*): (1*) seems true because I might have switched bodies yesterday; (2*) is self-contradictory; yet (1*) implies (2*) by Leibniz's law, given (T) and the supposition that I occupy the same body whenever I or it exist.

In defense of (T), however, I claim that (1*) *is false*, despite the fact that I might have switched bodies yesterday. What is true because I might have switched bodies is not (1*) but rather (1**):

(1**)   There are a world *W*, a unique *personal counterpart X* in *W* of me, and a unique *bodily counterpart Y* in *W* of my body, such that *X* and *Y* are not identical today.

I now propose a revision of counterpart theory to the effect that, at least in the context, (1**) rather than (1*) is the correct translation of (1′). What follows from (1**) by Leibniz's law, given (T) and the supposition that I occupy the same body whenever I exist, is not the self-contradiction (2*) but rather the truth:

There are a world *W*, a unique personal counterpart *X* in *W* of my body, and a unique bodily counterpart *Y* in *W* of my body, such that *X* and *Y* are not identical today.

Two other truths follow from (1**) in the same way:

There are a world *W*, a unique personal counterpart *X* in *W* of me, and a unique bodily counterpart *Y* in *W* of me, such that *X* and *Y* are not identical today.

There are a world *W*, a unique personal counterpart *X* in *W* of my body, and a unique bodily counterpart *Y* in *W* of me, such that *X* and *Y* are not identical today.

However, the translation of (2′) is none of these. If the translation of (1′) is (1**), the translation of (2′) should be (2**):

(2**)   There are a world *W*, a unique bodily counterpart *X* in *W* of my body, and a unique bodily counterpart *Y* in *W* of my body, such that *X* and *Y* are not identical today.

Though (2**) is not (2*), it is still a self-contradiction.

As we already noted, counterpart relations are a matter of over-all resemblance in a variety of respects. If we vary the relative importances of different respects of similarity and dissimilarity, we will get different counterpart relations. Two respects of similarity or dissimilarity among enduring things are, first, personhood and personal traits, and, second, bodyhood and bodily traits. If we assign great weight to the former, we get the *personal counterpart* relation. Only a person, or something very like a person, can resemble a person in respect of personhood and personal traits enough to be his personal counterpart. But if we assign great weight to the latter, we get the *bodily counterpart* relation. Only a body, or something very like a body, can resemble a body in respect to bodyhood and bodily traits enough to be its bodily counterpart.

If I am my body, then in many worlds there are things that are both personal and bodily counterparts of me and *ipso facto* of my body. These things, like me, are both persons and bodies. But in other worlds I (and my body) have neither personal counterparts nor bodily counterparts; or personal counterparts that are not bodily counterparts; or bodily counterparts that are not personal counterparts; or personal and bodily counterparts that are not identical. A world in which I switched out of my body – that is, my personal counterpart switched out of my bodily counterpart – yesterday is of this last sort. I and my body have there a personal counterpart that is a person but not a body and also a bodily counterpart that is a body but not a person. These are not identical today, and not identical *simpliciter*, though they were identical at times before yesterday since they shared their earlier stages. However, my personal counterpart is identical today with a different body. My bodily counterpart is identical today with a different person (if the body-switching was a trade) or with none.

We may draw an analogy between the relations of personal and bodily unity among stages of persons and bodies and the personal and bodily counterpart relations among enduring persons and bodies. If I ask of something that is both a stage of a body and a stage of a body-switching person "Was this ever in Borneo?" you should ask whether I mean this person or this body. If the former, I am asking whether the given stage is linked by personal unity to an earlier stage located in Borneo. If the latter, I am asking whether it is linked by bodily unity to an earlier stage located in Borneo. Similarly, if I ask of something that is both an enduring person and an enduring body "Might this have been an orangutan?" you should again ask whether I mean this person or this body. If the former, I am asking whether it has an orangutan for a personal counterpart; if the latter, whether it has an orangutan for a bodily counterpart.

But the analogy is imperfect. The two relations of unity are equivalence relations, at least for the most part and as a matter of contingent fact. Therefore it is easy and natural to form the concept of an enduring person or body, consisting of stages linked together pairwise by a relation of personal or bodily unity. It is tempting to do the same with the counterpart relations, forming the concept of a superperson or superbody consisting of persons or bodies in different worlds, linked together by a personal or bodily counterpart relation. But this cannot be done in any straightforward way because counterpart relations are not equivalence relations. Like all similarity relations on a sufficiently variegated domain, they fail to be transitive because chains of little differences add up to big differences.

Why should I think it plausible to employ multiple counterpart relations to translate (1') as (1**) rather than (1*)? Precisely because by doing so I escape the refutation of (T), and I am convinced of (T). I am offered a trade: instead of a multiplicity of kinds of thing I can have a multiplicity of counterpart relations. A *reductio* refutes the whole combination of assumptions that led to contradiction; if all but one of those assumptions are highly plausible, whichever remains is the refuted one. And in addition, if I contemplate the propositions I express by means of (1') and (1**), it seems to me that they are the same.

I would like to present the translation of (1') by (1**) and (2') by (2**) as instances of a general scheme for translating English modal predications into sentences of counterpart theory with multiple counterpart relations. I do not know how to do this. Roughly, the idea is that the sense of a term somehow selects the counterpart relation that is to be used to find the counterparts of the thing denoted by that term. The terms 'I', 'you,' 'that person,' 'the lady I saw you with last night,' 'George,' all select the personal counterpart relation. 'This thing' (pointing at myself), 'this body,' 'my body,' 'that which will be my corpse after I die,' all select the bodily counterpart relation. Similarly for indefinite terms (phrases of restricted quantification): 'everybody' selects the personal counterpart relation, whereas 'every body' selects the bodily counterpart relation. Even if everybody is his body, and conversely, "Everybody is such that he might have been a disembodied spirit" is true, whereas "Every body is such that it might have been a disembodied spirit" is false. The former means that each of those things which are both persons and bodies has a disembodied spirit as personal counterpart, whereas the latter means that each of those same things has a disembodied spirit as bodily counterpart.

In certain modal predications, the appropriate counterpart relation is selected not by the subject term but by a special clause. To say that something, regarded as a such-and-such, is such that it might have done so-and-so is to say that in some world it has a such-and-such-counterpart that does so-and-so. With these "regarded as" clauses in mind, I might say that I translate (1') as (1**) because I take it to be synonymous with (1"):

(1")   I, regarded as a person, and my body, regarded as a body, are such that (without any duplication of either) they might not have been identical today.

Likewise I translated (2') as if it had contained two "regarded as a body" clauses.

If we are to have multiple counterpart relations, we may well wonder how many to have. One for every sortal? One for every natural kind? One for any common noun phrase whatever that can grammatically be inserted into 'regarded as a ——,' even the phrase 'yellow pig or prime number'? One for any kind of entity, even kinds that cannot be specified in our language?[5] I do not know. Nor do I know whether one of the counterpart relations, corresponding perhaps to the clause 'regarded as an entity,' can be identified with the single counterpart relation of my original counterpart theory.

It is customary to distinguish real essences of things from their nominal essences under descriptions. Now, however, we have a third, intermediate, kind of essence. My real essence consists of the properties common to all my counterparts. (Here I use the original single counterpart relation.) My nominal essence under the description 'person' consists of the properties common to all possible persons. My intermediate essence under the description 'person' consists of the properties common to all my personal counterparts. I have no reason to think that any two of these sets of properties are the same. It may even be that none of the three is properly included in any other, if my personal counterparts include some entities (robots, say) which are almost persons but not quite. Counterpart relations are vague, being dependent on the relative weights assigned to respects of similarity or dissimilarity. Hence real essences are vague in a way nominal essences are not. Intermediate essences under descriptions share this vagueness, for the new multiple counterpart relations are no less vague than the original counterpart relation.

In my original counterpart theory, any *de re* modal predication is referentially transparent. Something has the same counterparts however we may choose to refer to it. Given a *de re* modal predication, we find the thing denoted by the subject term in the actual world; then we consider what befalls that thing – or rather, its counterparts – in other worlds. Only the denotation of the subject term matters. We can substitute another subject term with the same denotation but different sense, and the truth value of the modal predication will not change.

But in the present revision of counterpart theory, *de re* modal predications are not in general transparent. Not only the denotation of the subject term matters, but also the counterpart relation it selects. If we substitute another subject term with the same denotation but different sense, it may change the truth value of the modal predication by selecting a different counterpart relation. Then even though the denoted thing here in our world remains the same, we have a different way of following the fortunes of that thing in other worlds.

Nevertheless, these modal predications are still *de re*, not *de dicto*. We still find the denoted thing in our actual world and then find counterparts of that thing eleswhere. We do not at all consider the things denoted by the subject term in other worlds, as we would in the case of a *de dicto* modal predication.

Transparency of modal predications can fail whenever the sense of the subject term is used to do anything beyond determining the actual denotation of the subject term. One further thing it might do is determine the denotation of the subject term in other worlds; that is the *de dicto* case. Another, and altogether different, further thing it might do is select a counterpart relation. (These two are not the only alternatives.) It is the latter, I suggest, that happens in the argument we are considering. Therefore we can accept (1') as a consequence of the possibility that I might have switched bodies, reject (2') as self-contradictory, and yet accept (T) and its consequence that if I occupy the same body whenever I or it exist then I am my body.

Notes

1 The so-called "problem of personal identity" is the problem of explicating the relation of personal unity between stages. This view is expounded more fully by John Perry in "Can the Self Divide?" *Journal of Philosophy* 69 (1972): 463–88.
2 "Persons and Their Bodies," *Philosophical Review* 75, no. 1 (January 1966): 59–77.
3 "Counterpart Theory and Quantified Modal Logic," *Journal of Philosophy*, 65 (1968): 113–26.
4 I do not know how or whether (1') and (2') can be expressed in the language of quantified modal logic. That does not bother me. I know how to express them in English and in counterpart theory.
5 We could also put this question another way: given a three-place relation "—— is a —— al counterpart of ——," which kinds are appropriate middle arguments?

54 Identity and Necessity

Saul Kripke

A problem which has arisen frequently in contemporary philosophy is: "How are *contingent* identity statements possible?" This question is phrased by analogy with the way Kant phrased his question "How are synthetic a priori judgments possible?" In both cases, it has usually been taken for granted in the one case by Kant that synthetic a priori judgments were possible, and in the other case in contemporary philosophical literature that contingent statements of identity are possible. I do not intend to deal with the Kantian question except to mention this analogy: After a rather thick book was written trying to answer the question how synthetic a priori judgments were possible, others came along later who claimed that the solution to the problem was that synthetic a priori judgments were, of course, impossible and that a book trying to show otherwise was written in vain. I will not discuss who was right on the possibility of synthetic a priori judgments. But in the case of contingent statements of identity, most philosophers have felt that the notion of a contingent identity statement ran into something like the following paradox. An argument like the following can be given against the possibility of contingent identity statements:[1]

First, the law of the substitutivity of identity says that, for any objects x and y, if x is identical to y, then if x has a certain property F, so does y:

(1) $(x)(y)[(x = y) \supset (Fx \supset Fy)]$

On the other hand, every object surely is necessarily self-identical:

(2) $(x) \Box (x = x)$

But

(3) $(x)(y) (x = y) \supset [\Box (x = x) \supset \Box (x = y)]$

is a substitution instance of (1), the substitutivity law. From (2) and (3), we can conclude that, for every x and y, if x equals y, then, it is necessary that x equals y:

(4) $(x)(y) ((x = y) \supset \Box (x = y))$

This is because the clause $\Box (x = x)$ of the conditional drops out because it is known to be true.

This is an argument which has been stated many times in recent philosophy. Its conclusion, however, has often been regarded as highly paradoxical. For example, David Wiggins, in his paper, "Identity-Statements," says,

> Now there undoubtedly exist contingent identity-statements. Let $a = b$ be one of them. From its simple truth and (5) [= (4) above] we can derive '$\Box(a = b)$'. But how then can there be any contingent identity statements?[2]

He then says that five various reactions to this argument are possible, and rejects all of these reactions, and reacts himself. I do not want to discuss all the possible reactions to this statement, except to mention the second of those Wiggins rejects. This says,

> We might accept the result and plead that provided 'a' and 'b' are proper names nothing is amiss. The consequence of this is that no contingent identity-statements can be made by means of proper names.

And then he says that he is discontented with this solution and many other philosophers have been discontented with this solution, too, while still others have advocated it.

What makes the statement (4) seem surprising? It says, for any objects x and y, if x is y, then it is necessary that x is y. I have already mentioned that someone might object to this argument on the grounds that premise (2) is already false, that it is not the case that everything is necessarily self-identical. Well, for example, am I myself necessarily self-identical? Someone might argue that in some situations which we can imagine I would not even have existed and therefore the statement "Saul Kripke is Saul Kripke" would have been false or it would not be the case that I was self-identical. Perhaps, it would have been neither true nor false, in such a world, to say that Saul Kripke is self-identical. Well, that may be so, but really it depends on one's philosophical view of a topic that I will not discuss, that is, what is to be said about truth values of statements mentioning objects that do not exist in the actual world or any given possible world or counterfactual situation. Let us interpret necessity here weakly. We can count statements as necessary if whenever the objects mentioned therein exist, the statement would be true. If we wished to be very careful about this, we would have to go into the question of existence as a predicate and ask if the statement can be reformulated in the form: For every x it is necessary that, if x exists, then x is self-identical. I will not go into this particular form of subtlety here because it is not going to be relevant to my main theme. Nor am I really going to consider formula (4). Anyone who believes formula (2) is, in my opinion, committed to formula (4). If x and y are the same things and we can talk about modal properties of an object at all, that is, in the usual parlance, we can speak of modality *de re* and an object *necessarily* having certain properties as such, then formula (1), I think, has to hold. Where x is any property at all, including a property involving modal operators, and if x and y are the same object and x had a certain property F, then y has to have the same property F. And this is so even if the property F

is itself of the form of necessarily having some other property G, in particular that of necessarily being identical to a certain object. Well, I will not discuss the formula (4) itself because by itself it does not assert, of any particular true statement of identity, that it is necessary. It does not say anything about *statements* at all. It says for every *object x* and *object y*, if x and y are the same object, then it is necessary that x and y are the same object. And this, I think, if we think about it (anyway, if someone does not think so, I will not argue for it here), really amounts to something very little different from the statement (2). Since x, by definition of identity, is the only object identical with x, "$(y)(y = x \supset Fy)$" seems to me to be little more than a garrulous way of saying 'Fx', and thus (x) $(y)(y = x \supset Fx)$ says the same as $(x)Fx$ no matter what 'F' is – in particular, even if 'F' stands for the property of necessary identity with x. So if x has this property (of necessary identity with x), trivially everything identical with x has it, as (4) asserts. But, from statement (4) one may apparently be able to deduce that various particular statements of identity must be necessary and this is then supposed to be a very paradoxical consequence.

Wiggins says, "Now there undoubtedly exist contingent identity statements." One example of a contingent identity statement is the statement that the first Postmaster General of the United States is identical with the inventor of bifocals, or that both of these are identical with the man claimed by the *Saturday Evening Post* as its founder (*falsely* claimed, I gather, by the way). Now some such statements are plainly contingent. It plainly is a contingent fact that one and the same man both invented bifocals and took on the job of Postmaster General of the United States. How can we reconcile this with the truth of statement (4)? Well, that, too, is an issue I do not want to go into in detail except to be very dogmatic about it. It was I think settled quite well by Bertrand Russell in his notion of the scope of a description. According to Russell, one can, for example, say with propriety that the author of Hamlet might not have written "Hamlet," or even that the author of Hamlet might not have been the author of "Hamlet." Now here, of course, we do not deny the necessity of the identity of an object with itself; but we say it is true concerning a certain man that he in fact was the unique person to have written "Hamlet" and secondly that the man, who in fact was the man who wrote "Hamlet," might not have written "Hamlet." In other words, if Shakespeare had decided not to write tragedies, he might not have written "Hamlet." Under these circumstances, the man who in fact wrote "Hamlet" would not have written "Hamlet." Russell brings this out by saying that in such a statement, the first occurrence of the description "the author of 'Hamlet'" has large scope.[3] That is, we say "The author of 'Hamlet' has the following property: that he might not have written 'Hamlet.'" We *do not* assert that the following statement might have been the case, namely that the author of "Hamlet" did not write "Hamlet," for that is not true. That would be to say that it might have been the case that someone wrote "Hamlet" and yet did not write "Hamlet," which would be a contradiction. Now, aside from the details of Russell's particular formulation of it, which depends on his theory of descriptions, this seems to be the distinction that any theory of descriptions has to make. For example, if someone were to meet the

President of Harvard and take him to be a Teaching Fellow, he might say: "I took the President of Harvard for a Teaching Fellow." By this he does not mean that he took the proposition "The President of Harvard is a Teaching Fellow" to be true. He could have meant this, for example, had he believed that some sort of democratic system had gone so far at Harvard that the President of it decided to take on the task of being a Teaching Fellow. But that probably is not what he means. What he means instead, as Russell points out, is "Someone is President of Harvard and I took him to be a Teaching Fellow." In one of Russell's examples someone says, "I thought your yacht is much larger than it is." And the other man replies, "No, my yacht is not much larger than it is."

Provided that the notion of modality *de re,* and thus of quantifying into modal contexts, makes any sense at all, we have quite an adequate solution to the problem of avoiding paradoxes if we substitute descriptions for the universal quantifiers in (4) because the only consequence we will draw,[4] for example, in the bifocals case, is that there is a man who both happened to have invented bifocals and happened to have been the first Postmaster General of the United States, and is necessarily self-identical. There is an object x such that x invented bifocals, and as a matter of contingent fact an object y, such that y is the first Postmaster General of the United States, and finally, it is necessary, that x is y. What are x and y here? Here, x and y are both Benjamin Franklin, and it can certainly be necessary that Benjamin Franklin is identical with himself. So, there is no problem in the case of descriptions if we accept Russell's notion of scope.[5] And I just dogmatically want to drop that question here and go on to the question about names which Wiggins raises. And Wiggins says he might accept the result and plead that, provided a and b are proper names, nothing is amiss. And then he rejects this.

Now what is the special problem about proper names? At least if one is not familiar with the philosophical literature about this matter, one naively feels something like the following about proper names. First, if someone says "Cicero was an orator," then he uses the name 'Cicero' in that statement simply to pick out a certain object and then to ascribe a certain property to the object, namely, in this case, he ascribes to a certain man the property of having been an orator. If someone else uses another name, such as say 'Tully', he is still speaking about the same man. One ascribes the same property, if one says "Tully is an orator," to the same man. So to speak, the fact, or state of affairs, represented by the statement is the same whether one says "Cicero is an orator" or one says "Tully is an orator." It would, therefore, seem that the function of names is *simply* to refer, and not to describe the objects so named by such properties as "being the inventor of bifocals" or "being the first Postmaster General." It would seem that Leibniz' law and the law (1) should not only hold in the universally quantified form, but also in the form "if $a = b$ and Fa, then Fb," wherever 'a' and 'b' stand in place of names and 'F' stands in place of a predicate expressing a genuine property of the object:

$$(a = b \cdot Fa) \supset Fb$$

We can run the same argument through again to obtain the conclusion where '*a*' and '*b*' replace any names, "if *a* = *b*, then necessarily *a* = *b*." And so, we could venture this conclusion: that whenever '*a*' and '*b*' are proper names, if *a* is *b*, it is necessary that *a* is *b*. Identity statements between proper names have to be necessary if they are going to be true at all. This view in fact has been advocated, for example, by Ruth Barcan Marcus in a paper of hers on the philosophical interpretation of modal logic.[6] According to this view, whenever, for example, someone makes a correct statement of identity between two names, such as, for example, that Cicero is Tully, his statement has to be necessary if it is true. But such a conclusion *seems* plainly to be false. (I, like other philosophers, have a habit of understatement in which "it seems plainly false" means "it is plainly false." Actually, I think the view is true, though not quite in the form defended by Mrs. Marcus.) At any rate, it seems plainly false. One example was given by Professor Quine in his reply to Professor Marcus at the symposium: "I think I see trouble anyway in the contrast between proper names and descriptions as Professor Marcus draws it. The paradigm of the assigning of proper names is tagging. We may tag the planet Venus some fine evening with the proper name 'Hesperus'. We may tag the same planet again someday before sun rise with the proper name 'Phosphorus'." (Quine thinks that something like that actually was done once.) "When, at last, we discover that we have tagged the same planet twice, our discovery is empirical, and not because the proper names were descriptions." According to what we are told, the planet Venus seen in the morning was originally thought to be a star and was called "the Morning Star," or (to get rid of any question of using a description) was called 'Phosphorus'. One and the same planet, when seen in the evening, was thought to be another star, the Evening Star, and was called "Hesperus." Later on, astronomers discovered that Phosphorus and Hesperus were one and the same. Surely no amount of a priori ratiocination on their part could conceivably have made it possible for them to deduce that Phosphorus is Hesperus. In fact, given the information they had, it might have turned out the other way. Therefore, it is argued, the statement 'Hesperus is Phosphorus' has to be an ordinary contingent, empirical truth, one which might have come out otherwise, and so the view that true identity statements between names are necessary has to be false. Another example which Quine gives in *Word and Object* is taken from Professor Schrödinger, the famous pioneer of quantum mechanics: A certain mountain can be seen from both Tibet and Nepal. When seen from one direction it was called 'Gaurisanker'; when seen from another direction, it was called 'Everest'; and then, later on, the empirical discovery was made that Gaurisanker *is* Everest. (Quine further says that he gathers the example is actually geographically incorrect. I guess one should not rely on physicists for geographical information.)

Of course, one possible reaction to this argument is to deny that names like 'Cicero', 'Tully', 'Gaurisanker', and 'Everest' really are proper names. "Look," someone might say (someone has said it: his name was 'Bertrand Russell'), just because statements like "Hesperus is Phosphorus" and "Gaurisanker is Everest" are contingent, we can see that the names in question are not really purely referential. You are not, in Mrs. Marcus' phrase, just 'tagging' an object; you are actually describing it. What does the contingent fact that Hesperus is Phosphorus amount to? Well, it amounts to the fact that *the* star in a certain portion of the sky in the evening is *the* star in a certain portion of the sky in the morning. Similarly, the contingent fact that Gaurisanker is Everest amounts to the fact that the mountain viewed from such and such an angle in Nepal is the mountain viewed from such and such another angle in Tibet. Therefore, such names as 'Hesperus' and 'Phosphorus' can only be abbreviations for descriptions. The term 'Phosphorus' *has* to mean "the star seen . . . ," or (let us be cautious because it actually turned out not to be a star), "the *heavenly body* seen from such and such a position at such and such a time in the morning," and the name 'Hesperus' has to mean "the heavenly body seen in such and such a position at such and such a time in the evening." So, Russell concludes, if we want to reserve the term "name" for things which really just name an object without describing it, the only real proper names we can have are names of our own immediate sense data, objects of our own 'immediate acquaintance'. The only such names which occur in language are demonstratives like "this" and "that." And it is easy to see that this requirement of necessity of identity, understood as exempting identities between names from all imaginable doubt, can indeed be guaranteed only for demonstrative names of immediate sense data; for only in such cases can an identity statement between two different names have a general immunity from Cartesian doubt. There are some other things Russell has sometimes allowed as objects of acquaintance, such as one's self; we need not go into details here. Other philosophers (for example, Mrs. Marcus in her reply, at least in the verbal discussion as I remember it – I do not know if this got into print, so perhaps this should not be 'tagged' on her[7]) have said, "If names are really just tags, genuine tags, then a good dictionary should be able to tell us that they are names of the same object." You have an object *a* and an object *b* with names 'John' and 'Joe'. Then, according to Mrs. Marcus, a dictionary should be able to tell you whether or not 'John' and 'Joe' are names of the same object. Of course, I do not know what ideal dictionaries should do, but ordinary proper names do not seem to satisfy this requirement. You certainly *can,* in the case of ordinary proper names, make quite empirical discoveries that, let's say, Hesperus is Phosphorus, though we thought otherwise. We can be in doubt as to whether Gaurisanker is Everest or Cicero is in fact Tully. Even now, we could conceivably discover that we were wrong in supposing that Hesperus was Phosphorus. Maybe the astronomers made an error. So it seems that this view is wrong and that if by a name we do not mean some artificial notion of names such as Russell's, but a proper name in the ordinary sense, then there can be contingent identity statements using proper names, and the view to the contrary seems plainly wrong.

In recent philosophy a large number of other identity statements have been emphasized as examples of contingent identity statements, different, perhaps, from either of the types I have mentioned before. One of them is, for example, the statement "Heat is the motion of molecules." First, science is supposed to have discovered this. Empirical scientists in their investigations have been supposed to discover (and, I suppose, they did) that the external phenomenon which we call "heat" is, in fact, molecular agitation. Another example of such a discovery is that water is H_2O, and yet other examples are that gold is the element with such and such an atomic number, that light is a stream of photons, and so on. These are all in some sense of "identity statement" identity statements. Second, it is thought, they are plainly contingent identity statements, just because they were scientific discoveries. After all, heat might have turned out not to have been the motion of molecules. There were other alternative theories of heat proposed, for example, the caloric theory of heat. If these theories of heat had been correct, then heat would not have been the motion of molecules, but instead, some substance suffusing the hot object, called "caloric." And it was a matter of course of science and not of any logical necessity that the one theory turned out to be correct and the other theory turned out to be incorrect.

So, here again, we have, apparently, another plain example of a contingent identity statement. This has been supposed to be a very important example because of its connection with the mind-body problem. There have been many philosophers who have wanted to be materialists, and to be materialists in a particular form, which is known today as "the identity theory." According to this theory, a certain mental state, such as a person's being in pain, is identical with a certain state of his brain (or, perhaps, of his entire body, according to some theorists), at any rate, a certain material or neural state of his brain or body. And so, according to this theory, my being in pain at this instant, if I were, would be identical with my body's being or my brain's being in a certain state. Others have objected that this cannot be because, after all, we can imagine my pain existing even if the state of the body did not. We can perhaps imagine my not being embodied at all and still being in pain, or, conversely, we could imagine my body existing and being in the very same state even if there were no pain. In fact, conceivably, it could be in this state even though there were no mind 'back of it', so to speak, at all. The usual reply has been to concede that all of these things might have been the case, but to argue that these are irrelevant to the question of the identity of the mental state and the physical state. This identity, it is said, is just another contingent scientific identification, similar to the identification of heat with molecular motion, or water with H_2O. Just as we can imagine heat without any molecular motion, so we can imagine a mental state without any corresponding brain state. But, just as the first fact is not damaging to the identification of heat and the motion of molecules, so the second fact is not at all damaging to the identification of a mental state with the corresponding brain state. And so, many recent philosophers have held it to be very important for our theoretical understanding of the mind-body problem that there can be contingent identity statements of this form.

To state finally what *I* think, as opposed to what seems to be the case, or what others think, I think that in both cases, the case of names and the case of the theoretical identifications, the identity statements are necessary and not contingent. That is to say, they are necessary if *true*; of course, false identity statements are not necessary. How can one possibly defend such a view? Perhaps I lack a complete answer to this question, even though I am convinced that the view is true. But to begin an answer, let me make some distinctions that I want to use. The first is between a *rigid* and a *nonrigid designator*. What do these terms mean?

As an example of a nonrigid designator, I can give an expression such as 'the inventor of bifocals'. Let us suppose it was Benjamin Franklin who invented bifocals, and so the expression, 'the inventor of bifocals', designates or refers to a certain man, namely, Benjamin Franklin. However, we can easily imagine that the world could have been different, that under different circumstances someone else would have come upon this invention before Benjamin Franklin did, and in that case, *he* would have been the inventor of bifocals. So, in this sense, the expression 'the inventor of bifocals' is nonrigid: Under certain circumstances one man would have been the inventor of bifocals; under other circumstances, another man would have. In contrast, consider the expression 'the square root of 25'. Independently of the empirical facts, we can give an arithmetical proof that the square root of 25 is in fact the number 5, and because we have proved this mathematically, what we have proved is necessary. If we think of numbers as entities at all, and let us suppose, at least for the purpose of this lecture, that we do, then the expression 'the square root of 25' necessarily designates a certain number, namely 5. Such an expression I call 'a *rigid* designator'. Some philosophers think that anyone who even uses the notions of rigid or nonrigid designator has already shown that he has fallen into a certain confusion or has not paid attention to certain facts. What do I mean by 'rigid designator'? I mean a term that designates the same object in all possible worlds. To get rid of one confusion which certainly is not mine, I do not use "might have designated a different object" to refer to the fact that language might have been used differently. For example, the expression 'the inventor of bifocals' might have been used by inhabitants of this planet always to refer to the man who corrupted Hadleyburg. This would have been the case, if, first, the people on this planet had not spoken English, but some other language, which phonetically overlapped with English; and if, second, in that language the expression 'the inventor of bifocals' meant the 'man who corrupted Hadleyburg'. Then it would refer, of course, in their language, to whoever in fact corrupted Hadleyburg in this counterfactual situation. That is not what I mean. What I mean by saying that a description might have referred to something different, I mean that in *our* language as *we* use it in describing a counterfactual situation, there might have been a different object satisfying the descriptive conditions *we* give for reference. So, for example, we use the phrase 'the inventor of bifocals', when we are talking about another possible world or a counterfactual situation, to refer to whoever in that counterfactual situation would have invented bifocals, not to the person whom people *in* that counterfactual situation would have called 'the inventor of bifocals'. *They* might have spoken a different language which phonetically overlapped with English in which 'the inventor of bifocals' is used in some other way. I am *not* concerned with that question here. For that matter, they might have been deaf and dumb, or there might have been no people at all. (There still could have been an inventor of bifocals even if there were no people – God, or Satan, will do.)

Second, in talking about the notion of a rigid designator, I do not mean to imply that the object referred to has to exist in all possible worlds, that is, that it has to necessarily exist. Some things, perhaps mathematical entities such as the positive integers, if they exist at all, necessarily exist. Some people have held that

God both exists and necessarily exists; others, that He contingently exists; others, that He contingently fails to exist; and others, that he necessarily fails to exist:[8] all four options have been tried. But at any rate, when I use the notion of rigid designator, I do not imply that the object referred to necessarily exists. All I mean is that in any possible world where the object in question *does* exist, in any situation where the object *would* exist, we use the designator in question to designate that object. In a situation where the object does not exist, then we should say that the designator has no referent and that the object in question so designated does not exist.

As I said, many philosophers would find the very notion of rigid designator objectionable per se. And the objection that people make may be stated as follows: Look, you're talking about situations which are counterfactual, that is to say, you're talking about other possible worlds. Now these worlds are completely disjoint, after all, from the actual world which is not just another possible world; it is the actual world. So, before you talk about, let us say, such an object as Richard Nixon in another possible world at all, you have to say which object in this other possible world would *be* Richard Nixon. Let us talk about a situation in which, as *you* would say, Richard Nixon would have been a member of SDS. Certainly the member of SDS you are talking about is someone very different in many of his properties from Nixon. Before we even can say whether this man would have been Richard Nixon or not, we have to set up criteria of identity across possible worlds. Here are these other possible worlds. There are all kinds of objects in them with different properties from those of any actual object. Some of them resemble Nixon in some ways, some of them resemble Nixon in other ways. Well, which of these objects is Nixon? One has to give a criterion of identity. And this shows how the very notion of rigid designator runs in a circle. Suppose we designate a certain number as the number of planets. Then, if that is our favorite way, so to speak, of designating this number, then in any other possible worlds we will have to identify whatever number is the number of planets with the number 9, which in the actual world is the number of planets. So, it is argued by various philosophers, for example, implicitly by Quine, and explicitly by many others in his wake, we cannot really ask whether a designator is rigid or nonrigid because we first need a criterion of identity across possible worlds. An extreme view has even been held that, since possible worlds are so disjoint from our own, we cannot really say that any object in them is the *same* as an object existing now but only that there are some objects which resemble things in the actual world, more or less. We, therefore, should not really speak of what would have been true of Nixon in another possible world but, only of what 'counterparts' (the term which David Lewis uses[9]) of Nixon there would have been. Some people in other possible worlds have dogs whom they call 'Checkers'. Others favor the ABM but do not have any dog called Checkers. There are various people who resemble Nixon more or less, but none of them can really be said to be Nixon; they are only *counterparts* of Nixon, and you choose which one is the best counterpart by noting which resembles Nixon the most closely, according to your favorite criteria. Such views are widespread, both among the defenders of quantified modal logic and among its detractors.

All of this talk seems to me to have taken the metaphor of possible worlds much too seriously in some way. It is as if a 'possible world' were like a foreign country, or distant planet way out there. It is as if we see dimly through a telescope various actors on this distant planet. Actually David Lewis' view seems the most reasonable if one takes this picture literally. No one far away on another planet can be strictly identical with someone here. But, even if we have some marvelous methods of transportation to take one and the same person from planet to planet, we really need some epistemological criteria of identity to be able to say whether someone on this distant planet is the same person as someone here.

All of this seems to me to be a totally misguided way of looking at things. What it amounts to is the view that counterfactual situations have to be described purely qualitatively. So, we cannot say, for example, "If Nixon had only given a sufficient bribe to Senator X, he would have gotten Carswell through" because that refers to certain people, Nixon and Carswell, and talks about what things would be true of them in a counterfactual situation. We must say instead "If a man who has a hairline like such and such, and holds such and such political opinions had given a bribe to a man who was a senator and had such and such other qualities, then a man who was a judge in the South and had many other qualities resembling Carswell would have been confirmed." In other words, we must describe counterfactual situations purely qualitatively and then ask the question, "Given that the situation contains people or things with such and such qualities, which of these people is (or is a counterpart of) Nixon, which is Carswell, and so on?" This seems to me to be wrong. Who is to prevent us from saying "Nixon might have gotten Carswell through had he done certain things"? We are speaking of *Nixon* and asking what, in certain counterfactual situations, would have been true of *him*. We can say that if Nixon had done such and such, he would have lost the election to Humphrey. Those I am opposing would argue, "Yes, but how do you find out if the man you are talking about is in fact Nixon?" It would indeed be very hard to find out, if you were looking at the whole situation through a telescope, but that is not what we are doing here. Possible worlds are not something to which an epistemological question like this applies. And if the phrase 'possible worlds' is what makes anyone think some such question applies, he should just *drop* this phrase and use some other expression, say "counterfactual situation," which might be less misleading. If we say "If Nixon had bribed such and such a Senator, Nixon would have gotten Carswell through," what is *given* in the very description of that situation is that it is a situation in which we are speaking of Nixon, and of Carswell, and of such and such a Senator. And there seems to be no less objection to *stipulating* that we are speaking of certain *people* than there can be objection to stipulating that we are speaking of certain *qualities*. Advocates of the other view take speaking of certain qualities as unobjectionable. They do not say, "How do we know that this quality (in another possible world) is that of redness?" But they do find speaking of certain *people* objectionable. But I see no more reason to object in the one case than in the other. I think it really comes from the idea of possible worlds as existing out there, but very far off, viewable only through a special telescope. Even more objectionable is the view of David Lewis. According to Lewis, when we say "Under certain circumstances Nixon would have gotten Carswell through," we really mean "Some man, other than Nixon but closely resembling him, would have gotten some judge, other than Carswell but closely resembling him, through." Maybe that is so, that some man closely resembling Nixon could have gotten some man closely resembling Carswell through. But *that* would not comfort either Nixon or Carswell, nor would it make Nixon kick himself and say "*I* should have done such and such to get Carswell through." The question is whether under certain circumstances Nixon *himself* could have gotten *Carswell* through. And I think the objection is simply based on a misguided picture.

Instead, we can perfectly well talk about rigid and nonrigid designators. Moreover, we have a simple, intuitive test for them. We can say, for example, that the number of planets might have been a different number from the number it in fact is. For example, there might have been only seven planets. We can say that the inventor of bifocals might have been someone other than the man who *in fact* invented bifocals.[10] We cannot say, though, that the square root of 81 might have been a different number from the number it in fact is, for that number just has to be 9. If we apply this intuitive test to proper names, such as for example 'Richard Nixon', they would seem intuitively to come out to be rigid designators. First, when we talk even about the counterfactual situation in which we suppose Nixon to have done different things, we assume we are still talking about Nixon himself. We say, "If Nixon had bribed a certain Senator, he would have gotten Carswell through," and we assume that by 'Nixon' and 'Carswell' we are still referring to the very same people as in the actual world. And it seems that we cannot say "Nixon might have been a different man from the man he in fact was," unless, of course, we mean it metaphorically: He might have been a different *sort* of person (if you believe in free will and that people are not inherently corrupt). You might think the statement true in that sense, but Nixon could not have been in the other literal sense a different person from the person he, in fact, is, even though the thirty-seventh President of the United States might have been Humphrey. So the phrase "the thirty-seventh President" is nonrigid, but 'Nixon', it would seem, is rigid.

Let me make another distinction before I go back to the question of identity statements. This distinction is very fundamental and also hard to see through. In recent discussion, many philosophers who have debated the meaningfulness of various categories of truths, have regarded them as identical. Some of those who identify them are vociferous defenders of them, and others, such as Quine, say they are all identically meaningless. But usually they're not distinguished. These are categories such as 'analytic', 'necessary, 'a priori', and sometimes even 'certain'. I will not talk about all of these but only about the notions of a prioricity and necessity. Very often these are held to be synonyms. (Many philosophers probably should not be described as holding them to be synonyms; they simply *use* them interchangeably.) I wish to distinguish them. What do we mean by calling a statement *necessary?* We simply mean that the statement in question, first, is true, and, second, that it could not have been otherwise. When we say that something is *contingently* true, we mean that, though it is in fact the case, it could have been the case that things would have been otherwise. If we wish to assign this distinction to a branch of philosophy, we should assign it to metaphysics. To the contrary, there is the notion of an *a priori truth*. An a priori truth is supposed to be one which can be *known* to be true independently of all experience. Notice that this does not in and of itself say anything about all possible worlds, unless this is put into the definition. All that it says is that it can be known to be true of the actual world, independently of all experience. It may, by some philosophical argument, follow from our knowing, independently of experience, that something is true of the actual world, that it has to be known to be true also of all possible worlds. But if this is to be established, it requires some philosophical argument to establish it. Now, *this* notion, if we were to assign it to a branch of philosophy, belongs, not to metaphysics, but to epistemology. It has to do with the way we can know certain things to be in fact true. Now, it may be the case, of course, that anything which is necessary is something which *can* be known a priori. (Notice, by the way, the notion a priori truth as thus defined has in it *another* modality: it *can* be known independently of all experience. It is a little complicated because there is a double modality here.) I will not have time to explore these notions in full detail here, but one thing we can see from the outset is that these two notions are by no means trivially the same. If they are coextensive, it takes some philosophical argument to establish it. As stated, they belong to different domains of philosophy. One of them has something to do with *knowledge*, of what can be known in certain ways about the *actual* world. The other one has to do with *metaphysics*, how the world *could* have been; given that it is the way it is, could it have been otherwise, in certain ways? Now I hold, as a matter of fact, that neither class of statements is contained in the other. But, all we need to talk about here is this: Is everything that is necessary knowable a priori or known a priori? Consider the following example: the Goldbach conjecture. This says that every even number is the sum of two primes. It is a mathematical statement and if it is true at all, it has to be necessary. Certainly, one could not say that though in fact every even number is the sum of two primes, there could have been some extra number which was even and not the sum of two primes. What would that mean? On the other hand, the answer to the question whether every even number *is* in fact the sum of two primes is unknown, and we have no method at present for deciding. So we certainly do not know, a priori or even a posteriori, that every even number is the sum of two primes. (Well, perhaps we have some evidence in that no counterexample has been found.) But we certainly do not know a priori anyway, that every even number is, in fact, the sum of two primes. But, of course, the definition just says "*can* be known independently of experience," and someone might say that if it is true, we *could* know it independently of experience. It is hard to see exactly what this claim means. It might be so. One thing it might mean is that if it were true we could *prove* it. This claim is certainly wrong if it is generally applied to mathematical statements and we have to work within some fixed system. This is what Gödel proved. And even if we mean an 'intuitive proof in general' it might just be the case (at least, this view is as clear and as probable as the contrary) that though the statement is true, there is just no way the human mind could ever prove it.

Of course, one way an *infinite* mind might be able to prove it is by looking through each natural number one by one and checking. In this sense, of course, it can, perhaps, be known a priori, but only by an infinite mind, and then this gets into other complicated questions. I do not want to discuss questions about the conceivability of performing an infinite number of acts like looking through each number one by one. A vast philosophical literature has been written on this: Some have declared it is logically impossible; others that it is logically possible; and some do not know. The main point is that it is not trivial that just because such a statement is necessary it can be known a priori. Some considerable clarification is required before we decide that it can be so known. And so this shows that even if everything necessary is a priori in some sense, it should not be taken as a trivial matter of definition. It is a substantive philosophical thesis which requires some work.

Another example that one might give relates to the problem of essentialism. Here is a lectern. A question which has often been raised in philosophy is: What are its essential properties? What properties, aside from trivial ones like self-identity, are such that this object has to have them if it exists at all,[11] are such that if an object did not have it, it would not be this object?[12] For example, being made of wood, and not of ice, might be an essential property of this lectern. Let us just take the weaker statement that it is not made of ice. That will establish it as strongly as we need it, perhaps as dramatically. Supposing this lectern is in fact made of wood, could this very lectern have been made from the very beginning of its existence from ice, say frozen from water in the Thames? One has a considerable feeling that it could *not*, though in fact one certainly could have made a lectern of water from the Thames, frozen it into ice by some process, and put it right there in place of this thing. If one had done so, one would have made, of course, a *different* object. It would not have been *this very lectern*, and so one would not have a case in which this very lectern here was made of ice, or was made from water from the Thames. The question of whether it could afterward, say in a minute from now, turn into ice is something else. So, it would seem, if an example like this is correct – and this is what advocates of essentialism have held – that this lectern could not have been made of ice, that is in any counterfactual situation of which we would say that this lectern existed at all, we would have to say also that it was not made from water from the Thames frozen into ice. Some have rejected, of course, any such notion of essential property as meaningless. Usually, it is because (and I think this is what Quine, for example, would say) they have held that it depends on the notion of identity across possible worlds, and that this is itself meaningless. Since I have rejected this view already, I will not deal with it again. We can talk about *this very object*, and whether it could have had certain properties which it does not in fact have. For example, it could have been in another room from the room it in fact is in, even at this very time, but it could not have been made from the very beginning from water frozen into ice.

If the essentialist view is correct, it can only be correct if we sharply distinguish between the notions of a posteriori and a priori truth on the one hand, and contingent and necessary truth on the other hand, for although the statement that this table, if it exists at all, was not made of ice, is necessary, it certainly is not something that we know a priori. What we know is that first, lecterns usually are not made of ice, they are usually made of wood. This looks like wood. It does not feel cold and it probably would if it were made of ice. Therefore, I conclude, probably this is not made of ice. Here my entire judgment is a posteriori. I could find out that an ingenious trick has been played upon me and that, in fact, this lectern is made of ice; but what I am saying is, given that it is in fact not made of ice, in fact is made of wood, one cannot imagine that under certain circumstances it could have been made of ice. So we have to say that though we cannot know a priori whether this table was made of ice or not, given that it is not made of ice, it is *necessarily* not made of ice. In other words, if P is the statement that the lectern is not made of ice, one knows by a priori philosophical analysis, some conditional of the form "if P, then necessarily P." If the table is not made of ice, it is necessarily not made of ice. On the other hand, then, we know by empirical investigation that P, the antecedent of the conditional, is true – that this table is not made of ice. We can conclude by *modus ponens:*

$$P \supset \Box P$$
$$\underline{P}$$
$$\Box P$$

The conclusion – '$\Box P$' – is that it is necessary that the table not be made of ice, and this conclusion is known a posteriori, since one of the premises on which it is based is a posteriori. So, the notion of essential properties can be maintained only by distinguishing between the notions of a priori and necessary truth, and I do maintain it.

Let us return to the question of identities. Concerning the statement 'Hesperus is Phosphorus' or the statement 'Cicero is Tully', one can find all of these out by empirical investigation, and we might turn out to be wrong in our empirical beliefs. So, it is usually argued, such statements must therefore be contingent. Some have embraced the other side of the coin and have held "Because of this argument about necessity, identity statements between names have to be knowable a priori, so, only a very special category of names, possibly, really works as names; the other things are bogus names, disguised descriptions, or something of the sort. However, a certain very narrow class of statements of identity are known a priori, and these are the ones which contain the genuine names." If one accepts the distinctions that I have made, one need not jump to either conclusion. One can hold that certain statements of identity between names, though often known a posteriori, and maybe not knowable a priori, are in fact necessary, if true. So, we have some room to hold this. But, of course, to have some room to hold it does not mean that we should hold it. So let us see what the evidence is. First, recall the remark that I made that proper names seem to be rigid designators, as when we use the name 'Nixon' to talk about a certain man, even in counterfactual situations. If we say, "If Nixon had not written the letter to Saxbe, maybe he would have gotten Carswell through," we are in this statement talking about Nixon, Saxbe, and Carswell, the very same men as in the actual world, and what would have happened to them under certain counterfactual circumstances. If names are rigid designators, then there can be no question about identities being necessary, because '*a*' and '*b*' will be rigid designators of a certain man or thing *x*. Then even in every possible world, *a* and *b* will both refer to this same object *x*, and to no other, and so there will be no situation in which *a* might not have been *b*. That would have to be a situation in which the object which we are also now calling '*x*' would not have been identical with itself. Then one could not possibly have a situation in which Cicero would not have been Tully or Hesperus would not have been Phosphorus.[13]

Aside from the identification of necessity with a prioricity, what has made people feel the other way? There are two things which have made people feel the other way.[14] Some people tend to regard identity statements as metalinguistic statements, to identify the statement "Hesperus is Phosphorus" with the metalinguistic statement, " 'Hesperus' and 'Phosphorus' are names of the same heavenly body." And that, of course, might have been false. We might have used the terms 'Hesperus' and 'Phosphorus' as names of *two* different heavenly bodies. But, of course, this has nothing to do with the necessity of identity. In the same sense "2 + 2 = 4" might have been false. The phrases "2 + 2" and "4" might have been used to refer to two different numbers. One can imagine a language, for example, in which "+", "2", and "=" were used in the standard way, but "4" was used as the name of, say, the square root of minus 1, as we should call it, "*i*." Then "2 + 2 = 4" would be false, for 2 plus 2 is not equal to the square root of minus 1. But this is not what we want. We do not want just to say that a certain statement which we in fact use to express something true could have expressed something false. We want to use the statement in *our* way and see if it could have been false. Let us do this. What is the idea people have? They say, "Look, Hesperus might not have been Phosphorus. Here a certain planet was seen in the morning, and it was seen in the evening; and it just turned out later on as a matter of empirical fact that they were one and the same planet. If things had turned out otherwise, they would have been two different planets, or two different heavenly bodies, so how can you say that such a statement is necessary?"

Now there are two things that such people can mean. First, they can mean that we do not know a priori whether Hesperus is Phosphorus. This I have already conceded. Second, they may mean that they can actually imagine circumstances that they would call circumstances in which Hesperus would not have been Phosphorus. Let us think what would be such a circumstance, using these terms here as *names* of a planet. For example, it could have been the case that Venus did indeed rise in the morning in exactly the position in which we saw it, but that on the other hand, in the position which is in fact occupied by Venus in the evening, Venus was not there, and Mars took its place. This is all counterfactual because in fact Venus is there. Now one can also imagine that in this counterfactual other possible world, the earth would have been inhabited by people and that they should have used the names 'Phosphorus' for Venus in the morning and 'Hesperus' for Mars in the evening. Now, this is all very good, but would it be a situation in which Hesperus was not Phosphorus? Of course, it is a situation in which people would have been able to *say*, truly, "Hesperus is not Phosphorus"; but we are supposed to describe things in our language, not in theirs. So let us describe it in our language. Well, how could it actually happen that Venus would not be in that position in the evening? For example, let us say that there is some comet that comes around every evening and yanks things over a little bit. (That would be a very simple scientific way of imagining it: not really too simple – that is very hard to imagine actually.) It just happens to come around every evening, and things get yanked over a little bit. Mars gets yanked over to the very position where Venus is, then the comet yanks things back to their normal position in the morning. Thinking of this planet which we now call 'Phosphorus', what should we say? Well, we can say that the comet passes it and yanks Phosphorus over so that it is not in the position normally occupied by Phosphorus in the evening. If we do say this, and really use 'Phosphorus' as the name of a planet, then we have to say that, under such circumstances, Phosphorus in the evening would not be in the position where we, in fact, saw it; or alternatively, Hesperus in the evening would not be in the position in which we, in fact, saw it. We might say that under such circumstances, we would not have called Hesperus 'Hesperus' because Hesperus would have been in a different position. But that still would not make Phosphorus different from Hesperus; but what would then be the case instead is that Hesperus would have been in a different position from the position it in fact is and, perhaps, not in such a position that people would have called it 'Hesperus'. But that would not be a situation in which Phosphorus would not have been Hesperus.

Let us take another example which may be clearer. Suppose someone uses 'Tully' to refer to the Roman orator who denounced Catiline and uses the name 'Cicero' to refer to the man whose works he had to study in third-year Latin in high school. Of course, he may not know in advance that the very same man who denounced Catiline wrote these works, and that is a contingent statement. But the fact that this statement is contingent should not make us think that the statement that Cicero is Tully, if it is true, and it is in fact true, is contingent. Suppose, for example, that Cicero actually did denounce Catiline, but thought that this political achievement was so great that he should not bother writing any literary works. Would we say that these would be circumstances under which he would not have been Cicero? It seems to me that the answer is no, that instead we would say that, under such circumstances, Cicero would not have written any literary works. It is not a necessary property of Cicero – the way the shadow follows the man – that he should have written certain works; we can easily imagine a situation in which Shakespeare would not have written the works of Shakespeare, or one in which Cicero would not have written the works of Cicero. What may be the case is that we *fix the reference* of the term 'Cicero' by use of some descriptive phrase, such as 'the author of these works'. But once we have this reference fixed, we then use the name 'Cicero' *rigidly* to designate the man whom in fact we have identified by his authorship of these works. We do not use it to designate whoever would have written these works in place of Cicero, if someone else wrote them. It might have been the case that the man who wrote these works was not the man who denounced Catiline. Cassius might have written these works. But we would not then say that Cicero would have been Cassius, unless we were speaking in a very loose and metaphorical way. We would say that Cicero, whom we may have identified and come to know by his works, would not have written them, and that someone else, say Cassius, would have written them in his place.

Such examples are not grounds for thinking that identity statements are contingent. To take them as such grounds is to misconstrue the relation between a *name* and a *description used to fix its reference*, to take them to be *synonyms*. Even if we fix the reference of such a name as 'Cicero' as the man who wrote such and such works, in speaking of counterfactual situations, when we speak of Cicero, we do not then speak of whoever in such counterfactual situations *would* have written such and such works, but rather of Cicero, whom we have identified by the contingent property that he is the man who in fact, that is, in the actual world, wrote certain works.[15]

I hope this is reasonably clear in a brief compass. Now, actually I have been presupposing something I do not really believe to be, in general, true. Let us suppose that we do fix the reference of a name by a description. Even if we do so, we do not then make the name *synonymous* with the description, but instead we use the name *rigidly* to refer to the object so named, even in talking about counterfactual situations where the thing named would not satisfy the description in question. Now, this is what I think in fact is true for those cases of naming where the reference is fixed by description. But, in fact, I also think, contrary to most recent theorists, that the reference of names is rarely or almost never fixed by means of description. And by this I do not just mean what Searle says: "It's not a single description, but rather a cluster, a family of properties which fixes the reference." I mean that properties in this sense are not used *at all*. But I do not have the time to go into this here. So, let us suppose that at least one half of prevailing views about naming is true, that the reference is fixed by descriptions. Even were that true, the name would not be synonymous with the description, but would be used to *name* an object which we pick out by the contingent fact that it satisfies a certain description. And so, even though we can imagine a case where the man who wrote these works would not have been the man who denounced Catiline, we should not say that that would be a case in which Cicero would not have been Tully. We should say that it is a case in which Cicero did not write these works, but rather that Cassius did. And the identity of Cicero and Tully still holds.

Let me turn to the case of heat and the motion of molecules. Here surely is a case that is contingent identity! Recent philosophy has emphasized this again and again. So, if it is a case of contingent identity, then let us imagine under what circumstances it would be false. Now, concerning this statement I hold that the circumstances philosophers apparently have in mind as circumstances under which it would have been false are not in fact such circumstances. First, of course, it is argued that "Heat is the motion of molecules" is an a posteriori judgment; scientific investigation might have turned out otherwise. As I said before, this shows nothing against the view that it is necessary – at least if I am right. But here, surely, people had very specific circumstances in mind under which, so they thought, the judgment that heat is the motion of molecules would have been false. What were these circumstances? One can distill them out of the fact that we found out empirically that heat is the motion of molecules. How was this? What did we find out first when we found out that heat is the motion of molecules? There is a certain external phenomenon which we can sense by the sense of touch, and it produces a sensation which we call "the sensation of heat." We then discover that the external phenomenon which produces this sensation, which we sense, by means of our sense of touch, is in fact that of molecular agitation in the thing that we touch, a very high degree of molecular agitation. So, it might be thought, to imagine a situation in which heat would not have been the motion of molecules, we need only imagine a situation in which we would have had the very same sensation and it would have been produced by something other than the motion of molecules. Similarly, if we wanted to imagine a situation in which light was not a stream of photons, we could imagine a situation in which we were sensitive to something else in exactly the same way, producing what we call visual experiences, though not through a stream of photons. To make the case stronger, or to look at another side of the coin, we could also consider a situation in which we *are* concerned with the motion of molecules but in which such motion does not give us the sensation of heat. And it might also have happened that we, or, at least, the creatures inhabiting this planet, might have been so constituted that, let us say, an increase in the motion of molecules did not give us this sensation but that, on the contrary, a slowing down of the molecules did give us the very same sensation. This would be a situation, so it might be thought, in which heat would not be the motion of molecules, or, more precisely, in which temperature would not be mean molecular kinetic energy.

But I think it would not be so. Let us think about the situation again. First, let us think about it in the actual world. Imagine right now the world invaded by a number of Martians, who do indeed get the very sensation that we call "the sensation of heat" when they feel some ice which has slow molecular motion, and who do not get a sensation of heat – in fact, maybe just the reverse – when they put their hand near a fire which causes a lot of molecular agitation. Would we say, "Ah, this casts some doubt on heat being the motion of molecules, because there are these other people who don't get the same sensation"? Obviously not, and no one would think so. We would say instead that the Martians somehow feel the very sensation we get when we feel heat when they feel cold and that they do not get a sensation of heat when they feel heat. But now let us think of a counterfactual situation.[16] Suppose the earth had from the very beginning been inhabited by such creatures. First, imagine it inhabited by no creatures at all: then there is no one to feel any sensations of heat. But we would not say that under such circumstances it would necessarily be the case that heat did not exist; we would say that heat might have existed, for example, if there were fires that heated up the air.

Let us suppose the laws of physics were not very different: Fires do heat up the air. Then there would have been heat even though there were no creatures around to feel it. Now let us suppose evolution takes place, and life is created, and there are some creatures around. But they are not like us, they are more like the Martians. Now would we say that heat has suddenly turned to cold, because of the way the creatures of this planet sense it? No, I think we should describe this situation as a situation in which, though the creatures on this planet got our sensation of heat, they did not get it when they were exposed to heat. They got it when they were exposed to cold. And that is something we can surely well imagine. We can imagine it just as we can imagine our planet being invaded by creatures of this sort. Think of it in two steps. First there is a stage where there are no creatures at all, and one can certainly imagine the planet still having both heat and cold, though no one is around to sense it. Then the planet comes through an evolutionary process to be peopled with beings of different neural structure from ourselves. Then these creatures could be such that they were insensitive to heat; they did not feel it in the way we do; but on the other hand, they felt cold in much the same way that we feel heat. But still, heat would be heat, and cold would be cold. And particularly, then, this goes in no way against saying that in this counterfactual situation heat would still *be* the molecular motion, *be* that which is produced by fires, and so on, just as it would have been if there had been no creatures on the planet at all. Similarly, we could imagine that the planet was inhabited by creatures who got visual sensations when there were sound waves in the air. We should not therefore say, "Under such circumstances, sound would have been light." Instead we should say, "The planet was inhabited by creatures who were in some sense visually sensitive to sound, and maybe even visually sensitive to light." If this is correct, it can still be and will still be a necessary truth that heat is the motion of molecules and that light is a stream of photons.

To state the view succinctly: we use both the terms 'heat' and 'the motion of molecules' as rigid designators for a certain external phenomenon. Since heat is in fact the motion of molecules, and the designators are rigid, by the argument I have given here, it is going to be *necessary* that heat is the motion of molecules. What gives us the illusion of contingency is the fact we have identified the heat by the contingent fact that there happen to be creatures on this planet – (namely, ourselves) who are sensitive to it in a certain way, that is, who are sensitive to the motion of molecules or to heat – these are one and the same thing. And this is contingent. So we use the description, 'that which causes such and such sensations, or that which we sense in such and such a way', to identify heat. But in using this fact we use a contingent property of heat, just as we use the contingent property of Cicero as having written such and such works to identify him. We then use the terms 'heat' in the one case and 'Cicero' in the other *rigidly* to designate the objects for which they stand. And of course the term 'the motion of molecules' is rigid; it always stands for the motion of molecules, never for any other phenomenon. So, as Bishop Butler said, "everything is what it is and not another thing." Therefore, "Heat is the motion of molecules" will be necessary, not contingent, and one only has the *illusion* of contingency in the way one could have the illusion of contingency in thinking that this table might have been made of ice. We might think one could imagine it, but if we try, we can see on reflection that what we are really imagining is just there being another lectern in this very position here which was in fact made of ice. The fact that we may identify this lectern by being the object we see and touch in such and such a position is something else.

Now how does this relate to the problem of mind and body? It is usually held that this is a contingent identity statement just like "Heat is the motion of molecules." That cannot be. It cannot be a contingent identity statement just like "Heat is the motion of molecules" because, if I am right, "Heat is the motion of molecules" is not a contingent identity statement. Let us look at this statement. For example, "My being in pain at such and such a time is my being in such and such a brain state at such and such a time," or, "Pain in general is such and such a neural (brain) state."

This is held to be contingent on the following grounds. First, we can imagine the brain state existing though there is no pain at all. It is only a scientific fact that whenever we are in a certain brain state we have a pain. Second, one might imagine a creature being in pain, but not being in any specified brain state at all, maybe not having a brain at all. People even think, at least prima facie, though they may be wrong, that they can imagine totally disembodied creatures, at any rate certainly not creatures with bodies anything like our own. So it seems that we can imagine definite circumstances under which this relationship would have been false. Now, if these circumstances are circumstances, notice that we cannot deal with them simply by saying that this is just an illusion, something we can apparently imagine, but in fact cannot in the way we thought erroneously that we could imagine a situation in which heat was not the motion of molecules. Because although we can say that we pick out heat contingently by the contingent property that it affects us in such and such a way, we cannot similarly say that we pick out pain contingently by the fact that it affects us in such and such a way. On such a picture there would be the brain state, and we pick it out by the contingent fact that it affects us as pain. Now that might be true of the brain state, but it cannot be true of the pain. The experience itself has to be *this experience*, and I cannot say that it is contingent property of the pain I now have that it is a pain.[17] In fact, it would seem that both the terms, 'my pain' and 'my being in such and such a brain state' are, first of all, both rigid designators. That is, whenever anything is such and such a pain, it is essentially that very object, namely, such and such a pain, and wherever anything is such and such a brain state, it is essentially that very object, namely, such and such a brain state. So both of these are rigid designators. One cannot say this pain might have been something else, some other state. These are both rigid designators.

Second, the way we would think of picking them out – namely, the pain by its being an experience of a certain sort, and the brain state by its being the state of a certain material object, being of such and such molecular configuration – both of these pick out their objects essentially and not accidentally, that is, they pick them out by essential properties. Whenever the molecules *are* in this configuration, we *do* have such and such a brain state. Whenever you feel *this*, you do have a pain. So it seems that the identity theorist is in some trouble, for, since we have two rigid designators, the identity statement in question is necessary. Because they pick out their objects essentially, we cannot say the case where you seem to imagine the identity statement false is really an illusion like the illusion one gets in the case of heat and molecular motion, because that illusion depended on the fact that we pick out heat by a certain contingent property. So there is very little room to maneuver; perhaps none.[18] The identity theorist, who holds that pain is the brain state, also has to hold that it necessarily is the brain state. He therefore cannot concede, but has to deny, that there would have been situations under which one would have had pain but not the corresponding brain state. Now usually in arguments on the identity theory, this is very far from being denied. In fact, it is conceded from the outset by the materialist as well as by his opponent. He says, "Of course, it *could* have been the case that we had pains without the brain states. It is a contingent identity." But that cannot be. He has to hold that we are under some illusion in thinking that we can imagine that there could have been pains without brain states. And the only model I can think of for what the illusion might be, or at least the model given by the analogy the materialists themselves suggest, namely, heat and molecular motion, simply does not work in this case. So the materialist is up against a very stiff challenge. He has to show that these things we think we can see to be possible are in fact not possible. He has to show that these things which we can imagine are not in fact things we can imagine. And that requires some very different philosophical argument from the sort which has been given in the case of heat and molecular motion. And it would have to be a deeper and subtler argument than I can fathom and subtler than has ever appeared in any materialist literature that I have read. So the conclusion of this investigation would be that the analytical tools we are using go against the identity thesis and so go against the general thesis that mental states are just physical states.[19]

The next topic would be my own solution to the mind-body problem, but that I do not have.

Notes

1   This paper was presented orally, without a written text, to the New York University lecture series on identity which makes up this volume. The lecture was taped, and the present paper represents a transcription of these tapes, edited only slightly with no attempt to change the style of the original. If the reader imagines the sentences of this paper as being delivered, extemporaneously, with proper pauses and emphases, this may facilitate his comprehension. Nevertheless, there may still be passages which are hard to follow, and the time allotted necessitated a condensed presentation of the argument. (A longer version of some of these views, still rather compressed and still representing a transcript of oral remarks, will appear elsewhere.) Occasionally, reservations, amplifications, and gratifications of my remarks had to be repressed, especially in the discussion of theoretical identification and the mind-body problem. The footnotes, which were added to the original, would have become even more unwieldy if this had not been done.

2   R. J. Butler. ed., *Analytical Philosophy, Second Series*, Basil Blackwell, Oxford, 1965, p. 41.

3   The second occurrence of the description has small scope.

4 In Russell's theory, $F(\imath x G x)$ follows from $(x)Fx$ and $(\exists! x)Gx$, provided that the description in $F(\imath x G x)$ has the entire context for its scope (in Russell's 1905 terminology, has a 'primary occurrence'). Only then is $F(\imath x G x)$ 'about' the denotation of '$\imath x G x$'. Applying this rule to (14), we get the results indicated in the text. Notice that, in the ambiguous form $\Box(\imath x G x = \imath x H x)$, if one or both of the descriptions have 'primary occurrences' the formula does not assert the necessity of $\imath x G x = \imath x H x$; if both have secondary occurrences, it does. Thus in a language without explicit scope indicators, descriptions must be construed with the smallest possible scope – only then will $\sim A$ be the negation of A, $\Box A$ the necessitation of A, and the like.

5 An earlier distinction with the same purpose was, of course, the medieval one of *de dicto–de re*. That Russell's distinction of scope eliminates modal paradoxes has been pointed out by many logicians, especially Smullyan.

So as to avoid misunderstanding, let me emphasize that I am of course not asserting that Russell's notion of scope solves Quine's problem of 'essentialism'; what it does show, especially in conjunction with modern model-theoretic approaches to modal logic, is that quantified modal logic need not deny the truth of all instances of $(x)(y)(x = y \cdot \supset \cdot Fx \supset Fy)$, nor of all instances of '$(x)(Gx \supset Ga)$' (where 'a' is to be replaced by a nonvacuous definite description whose scope is all of 'Ga'), in order to avoid making it a necessary truth that one and the same man invented bifocals and headed the original Postal Department. Russell's contextual definition of descriptions need not be adopted in order to ensure these results; but other logical theories, Fregean or other, which take descriptions as primitive must somehow express the same logical facts. Frege showed that a simple, non-iterated context containing a definite description with small scope, which cannot be interpreted as being 'about' the denotation of the description, can be interpreted as about its 'sense'. Some logicians have been interested in the question of the conditions under which, in an intensional context, a description with small scope is equivalent to the same one with large scope. One of the virtues of a Russellian treatment of descriptions in modal logic is that the answer (roughly that the description be a 'rigid designator' in the sense of this lecture) then often follows from the other postulates for quantified modal logic; no special postulates are needed, as in Hintikka's treatment. Even if descriptions are taken as primitive, special postulation of when scope is irrelevant can often be deduced from more basic axioms.

6 "Modalities and Intensional Languages," *Boston Studies in the Philosophy of Science*, Vol. 1, Humanities Press, New York, 1963, pp. 71ff. See also the "Comments" by Quine and the ensuing discussion.

7 It should. See her remark on p. 115, *op. cit.*, in the discussion following the papers.

8 If there is no deity, and especially if the nonexistence of a deity is *necessary*, it is dubious that we can use "He" to refer to a deity. The use in the text must be taken to be non-literal.

9 David K. Lewis, "Counterpart Theory and Quantified Modal Logic," *Journal of Philosophy* 65 (1968), pp. 113ff.

10 Some philosophers think that definite descriptions, in English, are ambiguous, that sometimes 'the inventor of bifocals' rigidly designates the man who in fact invented bifocals. I am tentatively inclined to reject this view, construed as a thesis about English (as opposed to a possible hypothetical language), but I will not argue the question here.

What I do wish to note is that, contrary to some opinions, this alleged ambiguity cannot replace the Russellian notion of the scope of a description. Consider the sentence, "The number of planets might have been necessarily even." This sentence plainly can be read so as to express a truth; had there been eight planets, the number of planets would have been necessarily even. Yet without scope distinctions, both a referential' (rigid) and a non-rigid reading of the description will make the statement false. (Since the number of planets is nine, the rigid reading amounts to the falsity that nine might have been necessarily even.)

The 'rigid' reading is equivalent to the Russellian primary occurrence; the non-rigid, to innermost scope – some, following Donnellan, perhaps loosely, have called this reading the 'attributive' use. The possibility of intermediate scopes is then ignored. In the present instance, the intended reading of $\Diamond\Box$ (the number of planets is even) makes the scope of the description $\Box$ (the number of planets is even), neither the largest nor the smallest possible.

11   This definition is the usual formulation of the notion of essential property, but an exception must be made for existence itself; on the definition given, existence would be trivially essential. We should regard existence as essential to an object only if the object necessarily exists. Perhaps there are other recherché properties, involving existence, for which the definition is similarly objectionable. (I thank Michael Slote for this observation.)

12   The two clauses of the sentence footnoted give equivalent definitions of the notion of essential property, since $\Box((\exists x)\ (x = a) \supset Fa)$ is equivalent to $\Box(x)\ (\sim Fx \supset x \neq a)$. The second formulation, however, has served as a powerful seducer in favor of theories of 'identification across possible worlds'. For it suggests that we consider 'an object b in another possible world' and test whether it is identifiable with a by asking whether it lacks any of the essential properties of a. Let me therefore emphasize that, although an essential property is (trivially) a property without which an object cannot be a, it by no means follows that the essential, purely qualitative properties of a jointly form a sufficient condition for being a, nor that any purely qualitative conditions are sufficient for an object to be a. Further, even if necessary and sufficient qualitative conditions for an object to be Nixon may exist, there would still be little justification for the demand for a purely qualitative description of all counterfactual situations. We can ask whether Nixon might have been a Democrat without engaging in these subtleties.

13   I thus agree with Quine, that "Hesperus is Phosphorus" is (or can be) an empirical discovery; with Marcus, that it is necessary. Both Quine and Marcus, according to the present standpoint, err in identifying the epistemological and the metaphysical issues.

14   The two confusions alleged, especially the second, are both related to the confusion of the metaphysical question of the necessity of "Hesperus is Phosphorus" with the epistemological question of its a prioricity. For if Hesperus is identified by its position in the sky in the evening, and Phosphorus by its position in the morning, an investigator may well know, in advance of empirical research, that Hesperus is Phosphorus if and only if one and the same body occupies position x in the evening and position y in the morning. The a priori material equivalence of the two statements, however, does not imply their strict (necessary) equivalence. (The same remarks apply to the case of heat and molecular motion below.) Similar remarks apply to some extent to the relationship between "Hesperus is Phosphorus" and "'Hesperus' and 'Phosphorus' name the same thing." A confusion that also operates is, of course, the confusion between what we would say of a counterfactual situation and how people in that situation would have described it; this confusion, too, is probably related to the confusion between a prioricity and necessity.

15   If someone protests, regarding the lectern, that it *could* after all have *turned out* to have been made of ice, and therefore could have been made of ice, I would reply that what he really means is that *a lectern* could have looked just like this one, and have been placed in the same position as this one, and yet have been made of ice. In short, I could have been in the *same epistemological situation* in relation to *a lectern made of ice* as I actually am in relation to *this* lectern. In the main text, I have argued that the same reply should be given to protests that Hesperus could have turned out to be other than Phosphorus, or Cicero other than Tully. Here, then, the notion of 'counterpart' comes into its own. For it is not this table, but an epistemic 'counterpart', which was hewn from ice; not Hesperus-Phosphorus-Venus, but two distinct counterparts thereof, in two of the roles Venus actually plays (that of Evening Star and Morning Star), which are different. Precisely because of this fact, it is not *this table* which could have been made of ice. Statements about the modal properties of *this table* never refer to counterparts. However, if someone confuses the epistemological and the metaphysical problems, he will be well on the way to the counterpart theory Lewis and others have advocated.

16   Isn't the situation I just described also counterfactual? At least it may well be, if such Martians never in fact invade. Strictly speaking, the distinction I wish to draw compares how we *would* speak *in* a (possibly counterfactual) situation, *if* it obtained, and how we *do* speak *of* a counterfactual situation, knowing that it does not obtain – i.e., the distinction between the language we would have used in a situation and the language we *do* use to describe it. (Consider the description: "Suppose we all spoke German." This description is in English.) The former case can be made vivid by imagining the counterfactual situation to be actual.

17   The most popular identity theories advocated today explicitly fail to satisfy this simple requirement. For these theories usually hold that a mental state is a brain state, and that what makes the brain state into a mental state is its 'causal role', the fact that it tends to produce certain behavior (as intentions produce actions, or pain, pain behavior) and to be produced by certain stimuli (e.g. pain, by pinpricks). If the relations between the brain state and its causes and effects are regarded as contingent, then *being such-and-such-a-mental state* is a contingent property of the brain state. Let X be a pain. The causal-role identity theorist holds (1) that X is a brain state, (2) that the fact that X is a pain is to be analyzed (roughly) as the fact that X is produced by certain stimuli and produces certain behavior. The fact mentioned in (2) is, of course, regarded as contingent; the brain state X might well exist and not tend to produce the appropriate behavior in the absence of other conditions. Thus (1) and (2) assert that a certain pain X might have existed, yet not have been a pain. This seems to me self-evidently absurd. Imagine any pain: is it possible that *it itself* could have existed, yet not have been a pain?

If $X = Y$, then X and Y share all properties, including modal properties. If X is a pain and Y the corresponding brain state, then *being a pain* is an essential property of X, and *being a brain state* is an essential property of Y. If the correspondence relation is, in fact, identity, then it must be *necessary* of Y that it corresponds to a pain, and *necessary* of X that it correspond to a brain state, indeed to this particular brain state, Y. Both assertions seem false; it *seems* clearly possible that X should have existed without the corresponding brain state; or that the brain state should have existed without being felt as pain. Identity theorists cannot, contrary to their almost universal present practice, accept these intuitions; they must deny them, and explain them away. This is none too easy a thing to do.

18 A brief restatement of the argument may be helpful here. If "pain" and "C-fiber stimulation" are rigid designators of phenomena, one who identifies them must regard the identity as necessary. How can this necessity be reconciled with the apparent fact that C-fiber stimulation might have turned out not to be correlated with pain at all? We might try to reply by analogy to the case of heat and molecular motion; the latter identity, too, is necessary, yet someone may believe that, before scientific investigation showed otherwise, molecular motion might have turned out not to be heat. The reply is, of course, that what really is possible is that people (or some rational sentient beings) could have been in the *same epistemic situation* as we actually are, and identify *a phenomenon* in the same way we identify heat, namely, by feeling it by the sensation we call "the sensation of heat," without the phenomenon being molecular motion. Further, the beings might not have been sensitive to molecular motion (i.e., to heat) by any neural mechanism whatsoever. It is impossible to explain the apparent possibility of C-fiber stimulations not having been pain in the same way. Here, too, we would have to suppose that we could have been in the same epistemological situation, and identify something in the same way we identify pain, without its corresponding to C-fiber stimulation. But the way we identify pain is by feeling it, and if a C-fiber stimulation could have occurred without our feeling any pain, then the C-fiber stimulation would have occurred without there *being* any pain, contrary to the necessity of the identity. The trouble is that although 'heat' is a rigid designator, heat is picked out by the contingent property of its being felt in a certain way; pain, on the other hand, is picked out by an essential (indeed necessary and sufficient) property. For a sensation to be *felt* as pain is for it to *be* pain.

19 All arguments against the identity theory which rely on the necessity of identity, or on the notion of essential property, are, of course, inspired by Descartes' argument for his dualism. The earlier arguments which superficially were rebutted by the analogies of heat and molecular motion, and the bifocals inventor who was also Postmaster General, had such an inspiration; and so does my argument here. R. Albritton and M. Slote have informed me that they independently have attempted to give essentialist arguments against the identity theory, and probably others have done so as well.

The simplest Cartesian argument can perhaps be restated as follows: Let 'A' be a *name* (rigid designator) of Descartes' body. Then Descartes argues that since he could exist even if A did not, $\Diamond$ (Descartes $\neq$ A), hence Descartes $\neq$ A. Those who have accused him of a modal fallacy have forgotten that 'A' is rigid. His argument is valid, and his conclusion is correct, provided its (perhaps dubitable) premise is accepted. On the other hand, provided that Descartes is regarded as having ceased to exist upon his death, "Descartes $\neq$ A" can be established without the use of a modal argument; for if so, no doubt A survived Descartes when A was a corpse. Thus A had a property (existing at a certain time) which Descartes did not. The same argument can establish that a statue is not the hunk of stone, or the congery of molecules, of which it is composed. Mere non-identity, then, may be a weak conclusion. (See D. Wiggins, *Philosophical Review*, Vol. 77 (1968), pp. 90 ff.) The Cartesian modal argument, however, surely can be deployed to maintain relevant stronger conclusions as well.

B Is There More than One Actual World?

Introduction

As noted in the introduction to Part III, "world" can mean something besides "complete space-time universe" (Parfit's "local universe"); it can also mean "the sum total of *everything that exists*, period." In this sense of the word "world," there could be no more than one world, even if Lewis's "plurality of worlds" existed.

Or so one might have thought. But some philosophers have questioned whether there is just one true answer to the question, "What is the sum total of everything that exists?" They have argued that there is more than one meaning for the expression "everything that exists" – even when it comes from the mouths of metaphysicians, with all restrictions of intended reference removed (see van Inwagen's general introduction).

Hilary Putnam and Ernest Sosa both suggest that there is no such thing as a *unique* "complete inventory of the universe" (to use C. D. Broad's phrase). Instead there is only what exists-according-to-X, and what exists-according-to-Y, and so on – where each list generated by one of these relations may be complete, including everything there is, while nonetheless leaving out items on other lists.

It is not entirely clear what "X" and "Y" should stand for, however. Putnam's candidate is different languages. And the idea has a certain plausibility. It is natural to say things like: Relative to a certain Eskimo language, there are ever so many distinct kinds of snow; but relative to English there are fewer. Sosa rejects Putnam's linguistic turn; if there is to be real "ontological relativity," it cannot be mere "linguistic relativity." He develops an alternative, more robust notion of "nonabsolute existence."

Putnam claims that ontological relativity signals the death of metaphysics. But if Sosa is right about the emptiness or implausibility of linguistic relativism, then Putnam's eulogy is premature. Substantive, nonlinguistic varieties of relativity end up being "just more metaphysics" – for the thesis that existence is not absolute, as Sosa understands it, is surely a substantive metaphysical thesis if ever there was one. (This is in keeping with our general claim about what happens when philosophers try to show that metaphysics is impossible; see section two of the introductory essay, "What Is Metaphysics?")

By our lights, the relativity of what there is to a language or (in Sosa's version) "conceptual scheme" remains a rather unattractive hypothesis. Sosa himself puts his finger on some of the most serious objections to the view: How can someone who makes existence relative to the conceptual scheme of human beings (or some extension thereof) allow for the existence of things "at present unrecognized" by that scheme, things that surpass "our present acuity and acumen"? Is it not simple hubris to suppose that the concepts we puny humans can grasp provide the measure of everything there is? – to insist that there can be no "God's eye view" of the world (with or without a God to view things from there), no view according to which the world contains things we can never comprehend?

The relativistic views of Putnam and Sosa should be contrasted with those of van Inwagen's introduction, and Quine's "On What There Is" (Ch. 2). In Ch. 6, Price seems to be going in for a certain amount of ontological relativity, at least where universals are concerned.

Suggestions for further reading

Aune, Bruce, *Metaphysics: The Elements* (Minneapolis: University of Minnesota, 1985) pp. 126–130.

Benardete, José, *Metaphysics: The Logical Approach* (Oxford: Oxford University Press, 1989) Parts 1 and 2, and ch. 23 ("Anti-Realism").

Carter, William R., *The Elements of Metaphysics* (Philadelphia, Penn.: Temple University Press, 1990) ch. 12 ("Being Realistic").

Eklund, Matti, "The Picture of Reality as an Amorphous Lump," in Sider, Hawthorne, and Zimmerman (eds.), *Contemporary Debates in Metaphysics* (Malden, Mass.: Blackwell, 2007).

Gardner, Martin, *The Whys of a Philosophical Scrivener* (New York: St. Martin's, 1999) chs. 1 and 2 ("The World: Why I Am Not a Solipsist" and "Truth: Why I Am Not a Pragmatist").

Goodman, Nelson, *Ways of Worldmaking* (Indianapolis, Ind.: Hackett, 1978).

Hales, Stephen, *Metaphysics: Contemporary Readings* (Belmont, Cal.: Wadsworth, 1998) Section 3 ("Realism/Anti-Realism").

Hamlyn, D. W., *Metaphysics* (Cambridge, UK: Cambridge University Press, 1984) ch. 3 ("Ontology").

Hasker, William, *Metaphysics: Constructing a World View* (Downers Grove, Ill., and Leicester, UK: InterVarsity Press, 1983) ch. 1 ("Introducing Metaphysics").

Hirsch, Eli, "Ontological arguments: interpretive charity and quantifier variance," in Sider, Hawthorne, and Zimmerman (eds.), *Contemporary Debates in Metaphysics* (Malden, Mass.: Blackwell, 2007).

Jubien, Michael, *Contemporary Metaphysics* (Oxford: Blackwell, 1997) ch. 5 ("Is Truth Relative?").

Loux, Michael, *Metaphysics: A Contemporary Introduction*, 2nd edn (London: Routledge, 2002) Introduction.

Plantinga, Alvin, "How to Be an Anti-Realist," *Proceedings and Addresses of the American Philosophical Association*, 56 (1982), pp. 47–70.

Post, John F., *Metaphysics: A Contemporary Introduction* (New York: Paragon House, 1991) chs. 2 and 3 ("Language and Reality" and "Piercing the Veil of Language").

Putnam, Hilary, *The Many Faces of Realism* (LaSalle, Ill.: Open Court, 1987).

Quine, W. V. O., *Ontological Relativity and Other Essays* (New York: Columbia University Press, 1969).

Searle, John, *The Construction of Social Reality* (New York: The Free Press, 1995), chs. 7–9 ("Does the Real World Exist? Part I: Attacks on Realism," "Does the Real World Exist? Part II: Could There Be a Proof of External Realism?," and "Truth and Correspondence").

van Inwagen, Peter, *Metaphysics*, 2nd edn (Cambridge, Mass.: Westview Press, 2002) ch. 5 ("Objectivity").

55 After Metaphysics, What?

Hilary Putnam

The death of metaphysics is a theme that entered philosophy with Kant. In our own century, a towering figure – Ludwig Wittgenstein – sounded that note both powerfully and in a uniquely personal way; and he did not hesitate to lump epistemology together with metaphysics. (According to some of Wittgenstein's interpreters, what is today called "analytic philosophy" was, for Wittgenstein, the most confused form of metaphysics!) At the same time, even the man on the street could see that metaphysical discussion did not abate. A simple induction from the history of thought suggests that metaphysical discussion is not going to disappear as long as reflective people remain in the world. As Gilson said at the end of a famous book, "Philosophy always buries its undertakers."

The purpose of this lecture is not to engage in a further debate about the question "Is (or: 'In what sense is') metaphysics dead?" I take it as a fact of life that there is a sense in which the task of philosophy is to overcome metaphysics and a sense in which its task is to continue metaphysical discussion. In every philosopher there is a part that cries, "This enterprise is vain, frivolous, crazy – we must say, 'Stop!'," and a part that cries, "This enterprise is simply reflection at the most general and most abstract level; to put a stop to it would be a crime against reason." *Of course*, philosophical problems are unsolvable; but as Stanley Cavell once remarked, "There are better and worse ways of thinking about them."

What I just said could have been said at virtually any time since the beginning of modernity. I also take it – and this too is something I am not going to argue, but take as another fact of life, although I know that there are still those who would disagree – that the enterprises of providing a *foundation* for Being and Knowledge – a successful description of the Furniture of the World or a successful description of the Canons of Justification – are enterprises that have disastrously failed, and this could not have been seen until these enterprises had been given time to prove their futility (although Kant did say something like this about the former enterprise long ago). There is a sense in which the futility of something that was called metaphysics and the futility of something that was called epistemology is a sharper, more painful, problem for *our* period – a period that hankers to be called "Post-Modern" rather than modern.

What I want to do is lay out some principles that we *should not* abandon in our despair at the failure of something that was called metaphysics and something that was called epistemology. It will soon be evident that I have been inspired to do this, in large part, by a very fruitful ongoing exchange with my friend Richard Rorty, and this paper may be viewed as yet another contribution to that exchange. For Rorty, as for the French thinkers that he admires, two ideas seem gripping: (1) the failure of our philosophical "foundations" is a failure of the whole culture, and accepting that we were wrong in wanting or thinking we could have a "foundation" requires us to be *philosophical revisionists*. By this I mean that, for Rorty or Foucault or Derrida, the failure of foundationalism makes a difference to how we are allowed to talk in ordinary life – a difference as to whether and when we are allowed to use words like "know," and "objective," and "fact," and "reason." The picture is that philosophy was not a reflection *on* the culture, a reflection some of whose ambitious projects failed, but a *basis*, a sort of pedestal, on which the culture rested, and which has been abruptly yanked out. Under the pretense that philosophy is no longer "serious" there lies hidden a gigantic seriousness. If I am right, Rorty hopes to be a doctor to the modern soul. (2) At the same time, Rorty's analytic past shows up in this: when he rejects a philosophical controversy, as, for example, he rejects the "realism anti-realism" controversy, or the "emotive cognitive" controversy, his rejection is expressed in a Carnapian tone of voice – he *scorns* the controversy.

I am often asked, "Just where do you disagree with Rorty?" Apart from technical issues – of course, any two philosophers have a host of technical disagreements – I think our disagreement concerns, at bottom, these two broad attitudes. I hope that philosophical reflection may be of some real cultural value; but I do not think it has been the pedestal on which the culture rested, and I do not think our reaction to the failure of a philosophical project – even a project as central as "metaphysics" – should be to abandon ways of talking and thinking which have practical and spiritual weight. I am not, in that sense, a philosophical revisionist. And I think that what is important in philosophy is not just to say, "I reject the realist anti-realist controversy," but to show that (and *how*) both sides *misrepresent* the lives we live with our concepts. That a controversy is "futile" does not mean the rival pictures are unimportant. Indeed, to reject a controversy without examining the pictures involved is almost always just a way of *defending* one of those pictures (usually the one that claims to be "anti-metaphysical"). In short, I think philosophy is both more important and less important than Rorty does. It is not a pedestal on which we rest (or have rested until Rorty). The illusions that philosophy spins are illusions that belong to the nature of human life itself, and that need to be illuminated. Just saying, "That's a pseudo-issue," is not of itself therapeutic; it is an aggressive form of the metaphysical disease itself.

These remarks are, of course, much too general to serve as answers to the question which titles this lecture. But no one philosopher can answer that question. "After metaphysics" there can only be *philosophers* – that is, there can only be the search for those "better and worse ways of thinking" that Cavell called for. . . .

Realism with a Small "r" and with an "R"

. . . If saying what we say and doing what we do is being a "realist," then we had better be realists – realists with a small "r." But metaphysical versions of "realism" go beyond realism with a small "r" into certain characteristic kinds of philosophical fantasy. Here I agree with Rorty.

Here is one feature of our intellectual practice that these versions have enormous difficulty in accommodating. On the one hand, trees and chairs – the "thises and thats we can point to" – are paradigms of what we call "real," as Wittgenstein remarked.[1] But consider now a question about which Quine, Lewis, Kripke all disagree: what is the relation between the tree or the chair and the space-time region it occupies? According to Quine the chair and the electromagnetic, etc., fields that make it up and the space-time region that contains these fields are one and the same: so the chair *is* a space-time region. According to Kripke, Quine is just wrong: the chair and the space-time region are two numerically distinct objects. (They have the same mass, however!) The proof is that the chair *could have occupied a different space-time region.* According to Quine, modal predicates are hopelessly vague, so this "proof" is worthless. According to Lewis, Quine is right about the chair but wrong about the modal predicates: the correct answer [according] to Lewis is that if the chair could have been in a different place, as we say, what that means is that a *counterpart* of this chair could have been in that place; not that *this very chair* (in the sense of the logical notion of identity [=]) could have been in that place.

Well, who is right? Are chairs really *identical* with their matter or does a chair somehow coexist in the same space-time region with its matter while remaining numerically distinct from it? And is their matter really identical with the fields? And are the fields really identical with the space-time regions? To me it seems clear that at least the first, and probably all three, of these questions is nonsensical. We can formalize our language in the way Kripke would and we can formalize our language in the way Lewis would, and (thank God!) we can leave it unformalized and not pretend the ordinary language "is" obeys the same rules as the sign "=" in systems of formal logic. Not even God could tell us if the chair is "identical" with its matter (or with the space-time region); and not because there is something He doesn't know.

So it looks as if even something as paradigmatically "real" as a chair *has aspects that are conventional. That the chair is blue is paradigmatically a "reality," and yet that the chair [is/is not/don't have to decide] a space-time region is a matter of convention.*

And what of the space-time region itself? Some philosophers think of points as location *predicates,* not objects. So a space-time region is just a set of properties (if these philosophers are right) and not an object (in the sense of concrete object) at all, if this view is right. Again, it doesn't so much seem that there is a "view" here at all, as yet *another* way we could reconstruct our language. But how can the existence of a concrete object (the space-time region) be a matter of *convention*? And how can the identity of A (the chair) and B (the space-time region) be a matter of *convention*? The realist with a small "r" needn't have an answer to these questions. It is just a fact of life, he may feel, that certain alternatives are equally good while others are visibly forced. But metaphysical realism is not just the view that there are, after all, chairs, and some of them are, after all, blue, and we didn't just *make all that up*. Metaphysical realism presents itself as a powerful transcendental picture: a picture in which there is a fixed set of "language independent" objects (and some of them are abstract and others are concrete) and a fixed "relation" between terms and their extensions. What I am saying is that the picture only partly agrees with the common sense view it purports to interpret; it has consequences which, from a common sense view, are quite absurd. There is nothing wrong at all with holding on to our realism with a small "r" and jettisoning the Big "R" Realism of the philosophers.

Although he was far from being a Big "R" realist, Hans Reichenbach had a conception of the task of philosophy[2] which, if it had succeeded, might well have saved Realism from the objection just raised: the task of philosophy, he wrote, is to *distinguish what is fact and what is convention ("definition") in our system of knowledge.* The trouble, as Quine pointed out, is that the philosophical distinction between "fact" and "definition" on which Reichenbach depended has collapsed. As another example, not dissimilar to the one I just used, consider the conventional character of any possible answer to the question, "Is a point identical with a series of spheres that converge to it?" We know that we can take extended regions as the primitive objects, and "identify" points with sets of concentric spheres, and all geometric facts are perfectly well represented. We know that we can also take points as primitives and take spheres to be sets of points.

But the very statement "we can do either" assumes a diffuse background of empirical facts. Fundamental changes in the way we do physics could change the whole picture. So "convention" does not mean *absolute convention* – truth by stipulation, free of every element of "fact." And, on the other hand, even when we see such a "reality" as a tree, the possibility of that perception is dependent on a whole conceptual scheme, on a language in place. What is factual and what is conventional is a matter of degree; we cannot say, "these and these elements of the world are the raw facts; the rest is convention, or a mixture of these raw facts with convention."

What I am saying, then, is that elements of what we call "language" or "mind" *penetrate so deeply into what we call "reality" that the very project of representing ourselves as being "mappers" of something "language independent" is fatally compromised from the very start.* Like Relativism, but in a different way, Realism is an impossible attempt to view the world from Nowhere.

In this situation it is a temptation to say, "So we make the world," or "our language makes up the world," or "our culture makes up the world"; but this is just another form of the same mistake. If we succumb, once again we view the world – the only world we know – as a *product.* One kind of philosopher views it as a product from a raw material: Unconceptualized Reality. The other views it as a creation *ex nihilo. But the world isn't a product. It's just the world.*

Where are we then? On the one hand – this is where I hope Rorty will sympathize with what I am saying – our image of the world cannot be "justified" by anything but its success as judged by the interests and values which evolve and get modified at the same time and in interaction with our evolving image of the world itself. Just as the absolute "convention/fact" dichotomy had to be abandoned, so (as Morton White[3] long ago urged) the absolute "fact/value" dichotomy has to be abandoned, and for similar reasons. On the other hand, it is part of that image itself that the world is not the product of our will – or our dispositions to talk in certain ways, either.

Notes

1 Lecture xxv, *Wittgenstein's Lectures on Mathematics,* ed. Cora Diamond. "Thises and thats we can point to" is from this lecture.
2 Hans Reichenbach's *Philosophy of Space and Time* (New York: Dover, 1957).
3 Morton White, *Toward Reunion in Philosophy* (Cambridge, Mass.: Harvard University Press, 1956).

56   Truth and Convention

Hilary Putnam

The 'internal realism' I have defended[1] has both a positive and a negative side. Internal realism denies that there is a fact of the matter as to which of the conceptual schemes that serve us so well – the conceptual scheme of commonsense objects, with their vague identity conditions and their dispositional and counterfactual properties, or the scientific-philosophical scheme of fundamental particles and their 'aggregations' (i.e., their mereological sums), is 'really true'. Each of these schemes contains, in its present form, bits that will turn out to be 'wrong' in one way or another – bits that are right and wrong *by the standards appropriate to the scheme itself* – but the question 'which kind of "true" is really Truth' – is one that internal realism rejects.

A simple example[2] will illustrate what I mean. Consider 'a world with three individuals' (Carnap often used examples like this when we were doing inductive logic together in the early nineteen fifties), x_1, x_2, x_3. How many *objects* are there in this world?

Well, I *said* 'consider a world with just three individuals' didn't I? So mustn't there be three objects? Can there be non-abstract entities which are not 'individuals'?

One possible answer is 'no'. We can identify 'individual', 'object', 'particular', etc., and find no absurdity in a world with just three objects which are independent, unrelated, 'logical atoms'. But there are perfectly good logical doctrines which lead to different results.

Suppose, for example, like some Polish logicians, I believe that for every two particulars there is an object which is their sum. (This is the basic assumption of 'mereology', the calculus of parts and wholes invented by Lesniewski.) If I ignore, for the moment, the so-called 'null object', then I will find that the world of 'three individuals' (as Carnap might have had it, at least when he was doing inductive logic) actually contains *seven* objects (as shown in table 2).

Some logicians (though not Lesniewski) would also say that there is a 'null object' which they count as a part of every object. If we accepted this suggestion, and added this individual (call it **O**), then we would say that Carnap's world contains *eight* objects.

Table 2

World 1	World 2
x_1, x_2, x_3	x_1, x_2, x_3, $x_1 + x_2$, $x_1 + x_3$, $x_2 + x_3$, $x_1 + x_2 + x_3$
(A world à la Carnap)	('Same' world à la Polish logician)

Now, the classic metaphysical realist way of dealing with such problems is well known. It is to say that there is a single world (think of this as a piece of dough) which we can slice into pieces in different ways. But this 'cookie cutter' metaphor founders on the question, 'What are the "parts" of this dough?' If the answer is that x_1, x_2, x_3, $x_1 + x_2$, $x_1 + x_3$, $x_2 + x_3$, $x_1 + x_2 + x_3$ are all the different 'pieces', then we have not a *neutral* description, but rather a *partisan* description – just the description of the Warsaw logician! And it is no accident that metaphysical realism cannot really recognize the phenomenon of conceptual relativity – for that phenomenon turns on the fact that *the logical primitives themselves, and in particular the notions of object and existence, have a multitude of different uses rather than one absolute 'meaning'.*

An example which is historically important, if more complex than the one just given, is the ancient dispute about the ontological status of the Euclidean plane. Imagine a Euclidean plane. Think of the points in the plane. Are these *parts* of the plane, as Leibniz thought? Or are they 'mere limits', as Kant said?

If you say, in *this* case, that these are 'two ways of slicing the same dough', then you must admit that what is a *part* of space, in one version of the facts, is an abstract entity (say, a set of convergent spheres – although there is not, of course, a *unique* way of construing points as limits) in the other version. But then you will have conceded that which entities are 'abstract entities' and which are 'concrete objects', at least, is version-relative. Metaphysical realists to this day continue to argue about whether points (spacetime points, nowadays, rather than points in the plane or in three-dimensional space) are individuals or properties, particulars or mere limits, etc. My view is that God himself, if he consented to answer the question 'Do points really exist or are they mere limits?', would say 'I don't know'; not because His omniscience is limited, but because there is a limit to how far questions make sense.

One last point before I leave these examples: *given* a version, the question 'How many objects are there?' has an answer, namely 'three' in the case of the first version ('Carnap's World') and 'seven' in the case of the second version ('The Polish Logician's World'). Once we make clear how we are using 'object' (or 'exist'), the question 'How many objects exist?' has an answer that is not at all a matter of 'convention'. That is why I say that this sort of example does not support cultural relativism. Of course, our concepts are culturally relative; but it does not follow that the truth or falsity of what we say using those concepts is simply 'determined' by the culture. But the idea that there is an Archimedean point (or a use of 'exist' inherent in the world itself) from which the question 'How many objects *really* exist?' makes sense, is an illusion.

Nor does it help, in general, to talk about 'meanings' or 'truth conditions'. Consider again the two sentences (I am referring to the same example as before):

(1)   There is an object which is partly red and partly black.
(2)   There is an object which is red and an object which is black.

Observe that (2) is a sentence which is true in both the Carnapian and the Polish logician's version if, say, x_1 is red and x_2 is black. (1) is a sentence which is true in the Polish logician's version. What is its status in the Carnapian version?

Let me introduce an imaginary philosopher whom I will call 'Professor Antipode'. Professor Antipode is violently opposed to Polish mereology. He talks like this, 'I know what you're talking about if by an object you mean a car, or a bee, or a human being, or a book, or the Eiffel Tower. I even understand it if you refer to my nose or the hood of my car as "an object". But when philosophers say that there is an "object" consisting of *the Eiffel Tower and my nose*, that's just plain crazy. There simply is no such object. Carnap was talking just fine when he said to you "consider a world with just three objects" – I ignore Carnap's regrettable tendency to what he called "tolerance" – and it's crazy to suppose that every finite universe contains all the objects those Poles would invent, or, if you please, "postulate". You can't create objects by "postulation" any more than you can bake a cake by "postulation".'

Now, the language Carnap had in mind (we were working together on inductive logic at the time, and most often the languages we considered had only one-place predicates) probably did not contain a two-place predicate for the relation 'part of'; but even if it did, we can imagine Professor Antipode denying that there is any object of which x_1 and x_2 are both 'parts'. 'If there were such an object, it would have to be different from both of them,' he would say (and here the Polish logician would agree), 'and the only object different from both of them in the world you showed us is x_3. But x_3 does not overlap with either x_1 or x_2. Only in the overheated imagination of the Polish logician is there such an additional object as $x_1 + x_2$.' If we add 'Part of' to Carnap's little language, so that sentence (1) can be expressed in it, thus:

(3)   (Ex)(Ey)(Ez) (y is Part Of x & z is Part Of x & Red(y) & Black (z)).

then, true to his anti-Polish form, Professor Antipode will say that this sentence is false. 'Whether you say it in plain English or in fancy symbols' he growls, 'if you have a world of three non-overlapping individuals, which is what Carnap described, and each is wholly red or wholly black, which is what Carnap said, then there cannot be such a thing in that world as an "object which is partly red and partly black". Talking about the "mereological sum of x_1 and x_2" makes no more sense than talking about "the mereological sum of my nose and the Eiffel Tower".'

Professor Antipode, it will be seen, is a staunch metaphysical realist. He *knows* that only some objects are parts of other objects, and that to say that for *every* pair of objects there is an object of which they both are parts (which is an axiom of mereology) is just 'rubbish'. In the world Carnap imagined (1) is false and (2) is true, and there's the whole story.

Carnap himself would have taken a very different attitude. Carnap was a conceptual relativist (that is, in part, what his famous Principle of Tolerance is all about), and he would have said that we can choose to make (1) false (that is, we can choose to talk the way Professor Antipode talks) *or* we can choose to make

(1) true – to talk as the Polish logician talks. There is even – and this is very important – there is even a way in which we can have the best of both worlds. We keep Carnap's version as our official version (our 'unabbreviated language'); we refrain from adding Part Of as a new primitive, as we did before, but we introduce Part Of as a *defined* expression (as 'abbreviated language', or, as Quine often puts it, as a *façon de parler*). This can be done, not by giving an *explicit* definition of Part Of, but by giving a scheme which translates the Polish logician's language into Carnap's language (and such a scheme can easily be given in a recursive way, in the case of the kind of first order language with finitely many individuals that Carnap had in mind). Under such a scheme, (1) turns out to say no more and no less than (2).

(To verify this, assuming that 'red' and 'black' are predicates of Carnap's language, observe that the only way a Polish logician's object – a mereological sum – can be partly red is by containing a red atom, and the only way it can be partly black is by containing a black atom. So if (1) is true in the Polish logician's language, then there is at least one red atom and at least one black atom – which is what (2) says in Carnap's language. Conversely, if there is at least one black atom and at least one red atom, then their mereological sum is an 'object' (in the Polish logician's sense) which is partly red and partly black.)

While the formal possibility of doing this – of 'interpreting' the Polish logician's version in Carnap's version – is easy to establish, as a result in mathematical logic, the philosophical significance of this fact, of the interpretability of the second language in the first, is more controversial. An objection – an objection to the idea that this kind of interpretability supports conceptual relativity in any way – might come from a philosopher who pursues what is called 'meaning theory'. Such a philosopher might ask, 'What is the point of treating (1) as an abbreviation of (2), if it doesn't, in fact, have the same *meaning* as (2)?' Meaning theorists who follow Donald Davidson might argue that, while (1) and (2) are 'mathematically equivalent' (if, like the Polish logician, and unlike Professor Antipode, we are willing to count the axioms of mereology as having the status of logical or mathematical truths), still, sentence (2) is not a sentence one would ordinarily offer as an explanation of the truth conditions of sentence (1); or at least, doing so would hardly be in accordance with what is called 'translation practice'. And a 'meaning theory', it is said, must not correlate just *any* extensionally or even mathematically correct truth conditions with the sentences of the language the theory describes; the sentence used to state a truth condition for a sentence must be one that might be correlated with that sentence by 'translation practice'. Whatever one is doing when one invents reductive definitions that enable one to explain away talk about 'suspicious' entities as a mere *façon de parler*, it obviously isn't just 'radical translation'.

One suggestion as to what one *is* doing comes from a classic article by Quine. In 'On What There Is' he suggested that the stance to take in a case such as the one I have been describing – in a case in which one language seems more useful than another, because it countenances entities which (although philosophically 'suspicious') enable us to say various things in fewer words, and in which the, at first blush, 'richer' language is formally interpretable in the, at first blush, 'poorer' language – might be to say – this is a stance Professor Antipode might adopt –

'Sentence (1), asserting as it does the existence of mereological sums, is literally false. But if one wants to go on talking like the Polish logician while rejecting his undesirable ontological commitments, one can do that. One can responsibly take the view that the Polish logician's story is only a useful make-believe, and yet employ its idioms, on the ground that each of the sentences in that idiom, whatever its "meaning", *can* be regarded – by fiat, if you like – as merely a convenient abbreviation of whatever sentence in the "unabbreviated language" it is correlated with by the interpretation scheme.'

To give another example, one long familiar to students of mathematical philosophy, Frege and Russell showed that number theory is interpretable in set theory. This means that, if one wants to avoid ontological commitments to 'unreduced numbers' (to numbers as objects over and above sets) – and if one does not mind commitment to *sets*! – one can treat every sentence of number theory, and, indeed, every sentence in the language which uses a number word, as a mere abbreviation for another sentence, one which quantifies over sets, but not over any such entities as 'numbers'. One need not claim that the sentence of number theory and its translation in set theory have the same 'meaning'. If they don't, so much the worse for our intuitive notion of a 'number'! What this kind of interpretation – call it *reductive interpretation* – provides is evidence against the real existence of the unreduced entities, as anything over and above the entities countenanced by the language to which we are doing the reducing. The moral we should draw from the work of Frege and Russell is not that there is a conceptual *choice* to be made between using a language which countenances only sets and one which countenances sets *and* numbers, but that – unless the numbers are in fact identical with the set with which we identified them – there is no reason to believe in the existence of numbers. Talk of numbers is best treated as a mere *façon de parler*. Or so Quine maintains.

It is easy to see why Professor Antipode should like this line. In the case of the two versions we have been discussing, the reductive interpretation is syncategorematic; that is, it interprets sentence (1) (and likewise any other sentence of Carnap's language) as a whole, but does not identify the individual words in (1) with individual words and phrases in (2); nor does it identify 'mereological sums' with any objects in the language to which the reducing is being done. (1) as a whole is 'translated' by (2) as a whole; but the noun-phrase 'object which is partly red and partly black' has no translation by itself. In this case the moral of the translation – the moral if Professor Antipode imitates Quine's rhetoric – is slightly different. We cannot say *either mereological sums are identical with the entities with which we identified them or they don't really exist* (because the 'translation', or relative interpretation of the Polish logician's language in Carnap's language, didn't identify 'mereological sums' with *anything*, it just showed how to translate sentences about them syncategorematically). The moral is rather, *mereological sums don't really exist, but it is sometimes useful to talk as if they existed.* Of course Professor Antipode would be delighted with *this* moral!

I don't mean to give the impression that the possibility of reducing entities away by a formal translation scheme is always decisive evidence that they don't really exist, according to Quine. Sometimes we have the choice of either doing without one batch of entities, call them the **A** entities, or doing without another batch, call them the **B** entities – the reduction may be possible in either direction. In such a case, Occam's Razor doesn't know who to shave! Or the reducing language may itself seem suspicious (some people think *sets* are very suspicious entities). But, when the reducing language (the prima facie 'poorer' language) is one we are happy with, and the reduction does not go both ways, it is clear that Quine regards this as very strong evidence for denying the real existence of the unreduced entities.

Carnap, on the other hand, rejected the idea that there is 'evidence' against the 'existence' of numbers (or against the existence of numbers as objects distinct from sets). He would, I am sure, have similarly rejected the idea that there is evidence against the 'existence' of mereological sums. I know what he would have said about this question: he would have said that the question is one of a choice of a language. On some days it may be convenient to use what I have been calling 'Carnap's language' (although he would not have *objected* to the other language); on other days it may be convenient to use the Polish logician's language. For some purposes it may be convenient to regard the Polish logician's language of mereological sums as 'primitive notation'; in other contexts it may be better to take Carnap's language as the primitive notation and to regard the Polish logician's language as 'abbreviations', or defined notation. And I agree with him.

It will be seen that there are a number of different stances one could take to the question of the *relation* between (1) and (2). One could say:

(a)   The two sentences are mathematically equivalent.
(b)   The two sentences are logically equivalent.
(c)   The two sentences are neither logically nor mathematically equivalent.
(d)   The first sentence is false and the second true (Professor Antipode's position).
(e)   The two sentences are alike in truth value and meaning.
(f)   The two sentences are alike in truth value and unlike in meaning.
(g)   The second sentence can be used as an abbreviation of the first, but this is really just a useful 'make-believe'.

My own position – and my own internal realism – is that there is no fact of the matter as to which of *these* positions is correct. Taking the original dispute up into the 'metalevel' and reformulating it as a dispute about the properties – mathematical or logical equivalence, synonymy, or whatever – of linguistic forms doesn't help. None of these notions is well defined enough to be a useful tool in such cases. . . .

Notes

1   Cf. my *Reason, Truth and History* (Cambridge: Cambridge University Press, 1981).
2   This example comes from my *The Many Faces of Realism* (LaSalle, Ill.: Open Court, 1987).

57 Nonabsolute Existence and Conceptual Relativity: an Excerpt from "Putnam's Pragmatic Realism"

Ernest Sosa

Suppose a world with just three individuals $x1$, $x2$, $x3$. Such a world is held by some "mereologists" to have in it a total of seven things or entities or objects, namely, $x1$, $x2$, $x3$, $x1 + x2$, $x1 + x3$, $x2 + x3$, $x1 + x2 + x3$. Antimereologists by contrast prefer the more austere ontology that recognizes only the three individuals as objects that *really* exist in that world. Talk of the existence of $x1 + x2$ and its ilk is just convenient abbreviation of a more complex discourse that refers to nothing but the three individuals. Thus, suppose $x1$ is wholly red and $x2$ is wholly black. And consider

(1)   There is an object that is partly red and partly black.
(2)   There is an object that is red and an object that is black.

For the antimereologist, statement 1 is not true, if we assume that $x3$ is also wholly red or wholly black. It is at best a convenient way of abbreviating the likes of 2.

Putnam has now joined Rudolf Carnap in viewing our controversy as follows:

> ... the question is one of the choice of language. On some days it may be convenient to use [antimereological language]; ... on other days it may be convenient to use [mereological] language.[1]

Take the question

> How many objects with a volume of at least 6 cubic centimeters are there in this container?

This question can have no absolute answer on the Carnap–Putnam view, even in a case where the container contains a vacuum except for three marbles each with a volume of 6 cubic centimeters. The antimereologist may say

(3)   There are three objects in the box.

But the mereologist will reply:

(4)   There are at least seven objects in the box.

The Carnap–Putnam line is now this: *which statement we accept – 3 or 4 – is a matter of linguistic convenience.* The language of mereology has criteria of existence and identity according to which sums of individuals are objects. The language of antimereology rejects such criteria, and may even claim that by its criteria only individuals are objects.

There is a valuable insight here, I believe, but I am puzzled by the linguistic wrapping in which it is offered. After all, none of 1–4 mentions any language or any piece of language, nor does any of them say that we shall or shall not or should or should not use any language or bit of language. So I do not see how our decision actually to use or not to use any or all of the sentences 1–4 can settle the question of whether what these sentences *say* is true or false. And if the point is that these sentences do not really *say* anything, then how can they be incompatible in the first place so that a conflict or problem can arise that requires resolution? Also, it is not clear how we gain by replacing questions about atoms (or the like) with questions about *sentences* and *our* relations to some specific ones of these sentences. This is all very puzzling, and we should pause to peer more closely.

What does the proposed linguistic relativity amount to? Can it be spelled out more fully and prosaically? Here, for a start, is a possibility:

LR1 In order to say *anything* you must adopt a language. So you must "adopt a meaning" even for so basic a term as "object". And you might have adopted another. Thus you might adopt Carnap-language (CL) or you might adopt Polish-logician-language (PL). What you say, i.e., the utterances you make, the sentences you affirm, are not true or false absolutely, but are true or false only relative to a given language. Thus, if you say "There are three objects in this box" your utterance or sentence may be true understood as a statement of CL while it is false understood as a statement in PL.

But under this interpretation linguistic relativity seems trivially true. Who could deny that inscriptions of shapes and emissions of sounds are not true or false independently of their meaning, independently of all relativization to language or idiolect? Of course, you must "adopt a language" in order to speak (though such "adoption" need not be a conscious and voluntary act), and indeed you might have adopted another. And it seems quite uncontroversial that an utterance of yours might be true relative to one language while it is false relative to another.

Perhaps then the point is rather this:

LR2 When we say "There are 3 objects here, not 8" we are really saying: "The following is assertible as true in our CL: 'There are 3 objects here, not 8'."

This is indeed in the spirit of Carnap's philosophy, whose *Logical Syntax of Language*,[2] published in English in 1937, defends the following theses:

(i) Philosophy, when cognitive at all, amounts to the logical syntax of scientific language.

(ii) But there can be alternative such languages and we are to choose between them on grounds of convenience.

(iii) A language is completely characterized by its formation and transformation rules.

In that book Carnap also distinguishes between:

(s1) Object sentences: e.g., "Five is a prime number," "Babylon was a big town."

(s2) Pseudo-object sentences: e.g., "Five is not a thing but a number," "Babylon was treated of in yesterday's lecture."

(s3) Syntactical sentences: e.g., "'Five' is not a thing-word but a number-word," "'Babylon' occurred in yesterday's lecture."

And he defends the thesis that *s2* sentences seem deceptively like *s1* sentences but are really *s3* sentences in "material mode" disguise.

It was W. V. Quine who in 1934 suggested "material mode" to Carnap (as Quine himself reports in the section on "Semantic Ascent" in *Word and Object*[3]). Quine agrees that a kind of "semantic ascent" is possible, as when we shift from talk of miles to talk of "mile", but he thinks this kind of semantic ascent is *always* trivially available, not just in philosophy but in science generally and even beyond. Thus, we can paraphrase "There are wombats in Tasmania" as " 'Wombat' is true of some creatures in Tasmania." Quine does grant that semantic ascent tends to be especially useful in philosophy. But he explains why as follows:

> The strategy of semantic ascent is that it carries the discussion into a domain where both parties are better agreed on the objects (viz., words) and on the main terms concerning them. Words, or their inscriptions, unlike points, miles, classes, and the rest, are tangible objects of the size so popular in the marketplace, where men of unlike conceptual schemes communicate at their best. . . . No wonder it helps in philosophy.[4]

The use of this strategy, however, is clearly limited to discourse about recondite entities of controversial status. No relevant gain is to be expected from semantic ascent when the subject matter is the inventory of the marketplace itself. Tables and chairs are no more controversial than words: in fact, they seem less so, by a good margin. No general internal realism, with its conceptual or linguistic relativity, can be plausibly supported by the semantic ascent strategy offered by Quine.

In addition, questions of coherence arise concerning LR2. When we say something of the form "The following is assertible in our CL: . . ." can we rest with a literal interpretation that does not require ascent and relativization? If not, where does ascent stop? Are we then *really* saying "The following is assertible in our CL: 'The following is assertible in our CL: . . .' " This way lies vicious regress. But if we *can* stop the regress with our metalinguistic reference to our sentences of CL (and to ourselves), why can we not stop it with our references to tables and chairs and other medium-sized dry goods? . . .

There is hence reason to doubt the linguistic turn taken by Carnap and now Putnam. We have found no very plausible way to conceive of the turn so that it discloses an attractive new direction in metaphysics. The only direction that seems certainly right and clearly defensible is that provided by our first interpretation above (interpretation LR1), but that also seemed trivially right, and not something anyone would deny, not even the most hard-line metaphysical realist. Nevertheless, it still seems to me that there is a valuable insight in Putnam's now repeated appeal to the contrast between the Carnapian conceptual scheme and that of the Polish logician. But, given our recent reflections, I would like to put the insight without appeal to language or to any linguistic relativity.

The artifacts and even the natural objects that we recognize as existing at a time are normally composed of stuff or of parts in certain ways, and those which we see as enduring for an interval are normally not only thus composed of stuff or of parts at each instant of their enduring; but also the stuff or parts thus composing them right up to t, must be related in certain restricted ways to the stuff or parts that compose them right after t, for any time t within the history of such an enduring object.

Thus, the existence of a snowball at a time t and location l requires that there be a round quantity of snow at l and t sufficiently separate from other snow, etc.; and for that snowball to endure through an interval I, it is required that for every division of I into a sequence of subintervals $I1$, $I2$, . . . , there must be a corresponding sequence of quantities of snow $Q1$, $Q2$, . . . , related in certain restricted ways. By all this I mean to point to our "criteria of existence and perdurance for snowballs."

I spoke of a snowball, its existence and perdurance, and what that requires of its sequence of constituent quantities of snow. In place of these, I might have talked of chains and constituent links, of boxes and constituent sides, or of a great variety of artifacts or natural entities such as hills or trees; or even – especially – of persons and their constituent bodies. In every case, there are criteria of existence and of perdurance for an entity of the sort in question such that necessarily an entity of the sort exists at t (perdures through I) if and only if its criteria of existence are satisfied at t (its criteria of perdurance are satisfied relative to I). Thus, necessarily a snowball exists at t if and only if at t a quantity of snow is round and separate from other snow; and a snowball perdures through I if and only if for any subdivision of I into a sequence of subintervals $I1$, $I2$, . . . , there must be a corresponding sequence of round, etc., quantities of snow $Q1$, $Q2$, . . . , such that, for all i, Qi satisfies the conditions for being successor of $Qi-1$ in the constitution of the "life" of a snowball. And similarly for chains, boxes, hills, trees, and persons.

I am supposing a snowball to be constituted by a certain piece of snow as constituent matter and the shape of (approximate) roundness as constituent form. That particular snowball exists at that time because of the roundness of that piece of snow. More, if at that time that piece of snow were to lose its roundness, then at that time that snowball would go out of existence.

Compare now with our ordinary concept of a snowball, the concept of a snowdiscall, defined as an entity constituted by a piece of snow as matter and as form any shape between being round and being disc-shaped. At any given time, therefore, any piece of snow that constitutes a snowball constitutes a snowdiscall, but a piece of snow might at a time constitute a snowdiscall without then constituting a snowball. For every round piece of snow is also in shape between disc-shaped and round (inclusive), but a disc-shaped piece of snow is of course not round.

Any snowball SB must hence be constituted by a piece of snow PS which also then constitutes a snowdiscall SD. Now, SB is distinct (a different entity) from PS, since PS would survive squashing and SB would not. By similar reasoning, SD also is distinct from PS. And, again by similar reasoning, SB must also be distinct from SD, since enough partial flattening of PS will destroy SB but not SD. Now, there are infinitely many shapes $S1, S2, \ldots$, between roundness and flatness of a piece of snow, and, for each i, having a shape between flatness and Si would give the form of a distinctive kind of entity to be compared with snowballs and snowdiscalls. Whenever a piece of snow constitutes a snowball, therefore, it constitutes infinitely many entities all sharing its place with it.

Under a broadly Aristotelian conception, therefore, the barest flutter of the smallest leaf hence creates and destroys infinitely many things, and ordinary reality suffers a sort of "explosion."

We might perhaps resist this "explosion" of our ordinary world by embracing conceptual relativism. Constituted, supervenient entities do not just objectively supervene on their requisite, constitutive matters and forms, outside all conceptual schemes, with absolute independence from the categories recognized by any person or group. Perhaps snowballs do exist relative to all actual conceptual schemes ever, but not relative to all conceivable conceptual schemes. Just as we are not willing to countenance the existence of snowdiscalls, just so another culture might have been unwilling to countenance snowballs. We do not countenance snowdiscalls, because our conceptual scheme does not give to the snowdiscall form (being in shape between round and disc-shaped) the status required for it to be a proper constitutive form of a separate sort of entity – at least not with snow as underlying stuff.

That would block the explosion of reality, but the price is conceptual relativity. Supervenient, constituted entities do not just exist or not in themselves, free of any dependence on or relativity to a conceptual scheme. What thus exists relative to one conceptual scheme may not do so relative to another. In order for such a sort of entity to exist relative to a conceptual scheme, that conceptual scheme must recognize its constituent form as an appropriate way for a separate sort of entity to be constituted.

Must we now conceive of the existence even of the conceptual scheme itself and of its framers and users as also relative to that conceptual scheme? And are we not then caught in a vicious circle? The framers exist only relative to the scheme and this they do in virtue of the scheme's giving their constituent form-cum-matter the required status. But to say that the scheme gives to this form-cum-matter the required status – is that not just to say that the *framers* of that scheme do so? Yet are not the framers themselves dependent on the scheme for their existence relative to it?

Answer: existence *relative* to a conceptual scheme is *not* equivalent to existence *in virtue* of that conceptual scheme. Relative to scheme *C* the framers of *C* exist *in virtue* of their constitutive matter and form, and in virtue of how these satisfy certain criteria for existence and perdurance of such subjects (among whom happen to be the framers themselves). This existence of theirs is in that way relative to *C* but not in virtue of *C*. There is hence no vicious circularity.

The picture then is roughly this. Each of us acquires and develops a view of things that includes criteria of existence and perdurance for categories of objects. When we consider whether an object of a certain sort exists, the specification of the sort will entail the relevant criteria of existence and perdurance. And when we correctly recognize that an object of that sort does exist, our claim is elliptical for "... exists relative to *this* our conceptual scheme."

Again, this is *not* the only conceivable view of the matter. We could try to live with the explosion. And that does seem almost inevitable if we view it this way: a sort of object *O* – a constituted, supervenient sort – comes with a sort of constituent matter *M,* or sorts of constituent matters $M1, M2, \ldots$, and a sort of constituent form *F.* These – *M* (or $M1, M2, \ldots$), and *F* – we may take to be given independently of any acceptance by anyone of any criteria of existence or perdurance. For the sake of argument, then, we are accepting as given the sorts of items – $M1, M2, \ldots$ – that will play the role of constituent matters, and also the property or relation – *F* – that will play the role of constituent form. And presumably whether or not any particular sequence of matters $[m1, m2, \ldots]$ of sorts $M1, M2, \ldots$, respectively, does or does not satisfy form *F* is also generally independent of whether or not we accept any criteria of existence or perdurance, and indeed independent of whether *anyone* does so.

Suppose there is a time *t* when our conceptual scheme *C* first recognizes the appropriate criteria of existence and perdurance. According to our conceptual relativism, prior to that time *t* there were, relative to *C*, no objects of sort *O*, and in particular object *o* did not exist. But if there were no objects of sort *O*, such as *o*, relative to our scheme *C*, then why complicate our own scheme by supplementing it with criteria of existence and perdurance which do give standing to objects of sort *O*? After all, it is not as though we would fail to recognize the existence of something already in existence. By hypothesis *there are no objects of sort O*, not right up to that time *t*, anyhow.

On the other side, there is the threat of exploding reality, however. If we allow the satisfaction by any sequence *S* of any form *F* of the appropriate polyadicity and logical form to count as a criterion of existence for a corresponding sort of object, then reality right in us, before us, and all around us is unimaginably richer and more bizarre than we have ever imagined. And anyway we shall still face the problem of giving some explanation for why we focus so narrowly on the objects we do attend to, whose criteria of existence and perdurance we do recognize, to the exclusion of the plethora of other objects all around and even in the very same place.

A third option is a disappearance or elimination theory that refuses to countenance supervenient, constituted objects. But then most if not all of ordinary reality will be lost. Perhaps we shall allow ourselves to continue to use its forms of speech "... but only as a convenience or abbreviation." But in using those forms of speech, in speaking of snowballs, chains, boxes, trees, hills, or even people, we shall *not* believe ourselves to be seriously representing reality and its contents. "As a convenience": to *whom* and for what *ends?* "As an abbreviation": of *what?*

With alternatives so grim, we are encouraged to return to our relativistic reflections. Our conceptual scheme encompasses criteria of existence and of perdurance for the sorts of objects that it recognizes. Shall we say now that a sort of object O exists (has existed, exists now, or will exist) relative to a scheme C at t if and only if, at t, C recognizes sort O by allowing the corresponding criteria? But surely there are sorts of objects that our present conceptual scheme does not recognize, such as artifacts yet uninvented and particles yet undiscovered, to take only two obvious examples. Of course, we allow there might be and probably are many such things. Not that there could be any such entities relative to our *present* conceptual scheme, however, for by hypothesis it does not recognize them. So are there sorts of objects – constituted sorts among them, as are the artifacts at least – such that they exist but not relative to our present scheme C? In that case we are back to our problem. What is it for there to be such objects? Is it just the in-itself satisfaction of constitutive forms by constitutive matters? That yields the explosion of reality.

Shall we say then that a constituted, supervenient sort of object O exists relative to our present scheme C if and only if O is recognized by C directly or recognized by it indirectly through being recognized by some predecessor or successor scheme? That, I fear, cannot suffice, since there might be sorts of particles that always go undiscovered by us, and sorts of artifacts in long disappeared cultures unknown to us, whose conceptual schemes are not predecessors of ours.

Shall we then say that what exists relative to our present scheme C is what it recognizes directly, what it recognizes indirectly through its predecessors or successors, and what it *would* recognize if we had developed appropriately or were to do so now, and had been or were to be appropriately situated? This seems the sort of answer required, but it obviously will not be easy to say what appropriateness amounts to in our formula, in its various guises.

Regardless of whatever success may await any further specification of our formula, there is the following further objection. Take a sort of object O recognized by our scheme C, with actual instances o1, o2, ... ; for example, the sort Planet, with various particular planets as instances: Mercury, Venus, etc. Its instances, say we, exist, which amounts to saying that they exist relative to our scheme. But if we had not existed there would have been no scheme of ours for anything to exist relative to; nor would there have been our actual scheme C either. For one thing, we may just assume the contingent existence of our actual scheme to depend on people's actually granting a certain status to certain constitutive forms. If we had not existed, therefore, the constitutive form for the sort Planet would not have had, relative to our conceptual scheme, the status required for it to be possible that there be instances of that sort, particular planets. And from this it apparently follows that if we had not existed there would have been no planets: no Mercury, no Venus, etc.

This objection conceptual relativism can rebut as follows. While existing in the actual world *x* we now have a conceptual scheme *Cx* relative to which we assert existence, when we assert it at all. Now, we suppose a possible world *w* in which we are not to be found, in which indeed no life of any sort is to be found. Still we may, in *x*: (a) consider alternative world *w* and recognize that our absence there would have no effect on the existence or course of a single planet or star, that Mercury, Venus, and the rest, would all still make their appointed rounds just as they do in *x*; while yet (b) this recognition, which after all takes place in *x*, is still relativized to *Cx*, so that the existence in *w* of whatever exists in *w* relative to *Cx* need not be affected at all by the absence from *w* of *Cx*, and indeed of every conceptual scheme and of every being who could have a conceptual scheme. For when we suppose existence in *w*, or allow the possibility of existence in *w*, *we* do so *in x*, and we do so there still relative to *Cx*, to our present conceptual scheme, and what it recognizes directly or indirectly, or ideally.

If I am right we have three choices:

Eliminativism:	a disappearance view for which our ordinary talk is so much convenient abbreviation. Problem: we still need to hear: "abbreviation" of what, and "convenient" for what ends and whose ends? Most puzzling of all is how we are to take this "abbreviation" – not literally, surely.
Absolutism:	snowballs, hills, trees, planets, etc., are all constituted by the in-itself satisfaction of certain conditions by certain chunks of matter, and the like, and all this goes on independently of any thought or conceptualization on the part of anyone. Problem: this leads to the "explosion of reality."
Conceptual relativism:	we recognize potential constituted objects only relative to our implicit conceptual scheme with its criteria of existence and of perdurance. Problem: is there not much that is very small, or far away, or long ago, or yet to come, which surpasses our present acuity and acumen? How can we allow the existence of such sorts at present unrecognized by our conceptual scheme?

Right now I cannot decide which of these is least disastrous. But is there any other option?

Notes

1   Hilary Putnam, "Truth and Convention: On Davidson's Refutation of Conceptual Relativism," *Dialectica*, XLI (1987), pp. 69–77; p. 75 [reprinted in this volume].

2 Rudolf Carnap, *Logical Syntax of Language* (New York: Harcourt Brace, 1937).
3 W. V. Quine, *Word and Object* (Cambridge, Mass.: MIT, 1960).
4 Ibid., p. 272.

58 Addendum to "Nonabsolute Existence and Conceptual Relativity": Objections and Replies

Ernest Sosa

Objection 1

What does it matter whether we "recognize" the snowdiscall form (being in shape between round and disc-shaped, inclusive)? We are anyhow "committed" to there being such a property in any case, to there being the property or condition of being shaped in that inclusive way. If a piece of snow is in shape anywhere between disc-shaped and round then it just is a snowdiscall. So there must be lots of snowdiscalls in existence and that must be nothing new. What's the problem? Can't we even just define a "glug" as anything that is a cat or a dog, and are there not as many glugs in existence as are in the union of the set of cats and the set of dogs? Why should anyone worry about this "explosion?" Why not just admit the obvious: that, yes, there are snowdiscalls, and glugs, even if heretofore they had not been so-called?

Not only is that obvious. If anyone is misguided enough to want to avoid admitting the obvious, it does not really help to introduce some conceptually relative notion of existence according to which the entities that so exist are only those that we are committed to through the properties and kinds that we admit in our ideology and ontology. For if we admit being a dog as an ordinary, harmless enough property, and the kind dog as well, along with being a cat, etc., then we are implicitly committed to admitting anything that is either a dog or a cat, as being "either a dog or a cat," and that is tantamount to admitting that there are glugs – not under this description, of course, but what does that matter?

Reply

That is all quite true, of course, but not in conflict with conceptual relativism, not with the ontological conceptual relativism CR at issue here. Conceptual relativism is a thesis about ontological constitution. It presupposes that there are levels of individuals, and thus individuals on a higher level, constituted out of individuals on a lower level. The question now arises: How are the constituted entities constitutable out of the constituting entities? A partial (Aristotelian) answer is that a constituted entity must derive from the satisfaction by the constituting entity (or entities) of a condition (a property or relation, a "form"). *Any* condition whatever? That is absolutism, and leads to the "explosion." Only conditions from a restricted set? *How*, in what way, restricted? Somehow by reference to the conceptual scheme of the speaker or thinker who attributes existence? This is conceptual relativism (of the sort at issue here).

Returning to the examples of the objection: First, yes, of course there are snowdiscalls if all one means by this is that there are pieces of snow with a shape somewhere between disc-shaped and round. And when something is so shaped and, also, more specifically, round, then it is not only such a snowdiscall but also a round piece of snow, a "snowround" let's say. But it is just one and numerically the same thing which is then both the snowdiscall and the snowround. And this is no more puzzling than is the fact that something can be both a mother and a daughter, or both red and round, or both an apple and a piece of fruit, etc., etc. When *I* introduced the term "snowdiscall" this is not what I had in mind. In my sense, a "snowdiscall" is not just any piece of snow with a shape between round and disc-shaped. Nor is a snowball just a round piece of snow. For a round piece of snow can survive squashing, unlike the snowball that it constitutes, which is destroyed, not just changed, when it is squashed. The question is: what is special about the form of being round combined with an individual piece of snow, what is special about the ordered pair, let's say, that makes it a suitable form/matter pair for the constitution of a constituted individual, a particular snowball? Would any other shape, between roundness and flatness, also serve as such a form, along with that individual piece of snow? Could they together yield a form/matter pair that might also serve, in its own way, for the formation, the constitution of its own individual: not a snowball, presumably, but its own different kind of individual? It is to *this* question that the absolutist would answer in the affirmative, while the conceptual relativist might well answer in the negative.

According to conceptual relativism in ontology, what then is required for a form/matter pair to serve as the form and matter for the constitution of an individual, a constituted individual? Answer: that the sort of form/matter combination in question be countenanced by the relevant conceptual scheme, a conceptual scheme determined by the context of thought and/or utterance.

Objection 2

If it is granted that things can exist prior to the development of any conceptual scheme whatever, prior to the evolution of any thinkers who could have a conceptual scheme, is that not a concession to absolutism? Is it not being conceded that things exist "out there, in themselves," independently of conceptual schemes altogether, so that things do not exist in virtue of our conceptual choices after all? Rather things exist "in themselves." Reality itself manages somehow to cut the cookies unaided by humans. Isn't this just absolutism after all? What can be left of conceptual relativism after this has been granted?

Reply

Compare this. If I say "The Empire State Building is 180 miles southwest of here" my utterance is true, but the sentence I utter is true only relative to my present position. If I had uttered that sentence elsewhere then I might well have said something false. So my sentence is true relative to my spatial position, but it is not true or false just on its own, independently of such context. And, in a sense, that the Empire State Building is 180 miles southwest is something that is true relative to my present position but is false relative to many other positions. However, it is not so that the Empire State Building is 180 miles southwest of here *in virtue of* my present position. The Empire State Building would have been 180 miles southwest of here even if I had been located elsewhere. Whether I am here or not does not determine the distance and direction of the Empire State Building relative to this place here.

Conceptual relativism can be viewed as a doctrine rather like the relativism involved in the evaluation of the truth of indexical sentences or thoughts. In effect, "existence claims" can be viewed as implicitly indexical, and that is what my conceptual relativist in ontology is suggesting. So when someone says or thinks that Os exist, this is to be evaluated relative to the position of the speaker or thinker in "conceptual space" (in a special sense). Relative to the thus distinguished conceptual scheme, it might be that Os do exist, although relative to many other conceptual schemes it might rather be true to say that "Os do *not* exist."

But what is it about a "conceptual scheme" that determines whether or not it is true to say that "Os exist"? Answer: what determines whether "there are" constituted entities of a certain sort relative to a certain conceptual scheme would be that scheme's Criteria of Existence (or Individuation). And what are these? They are specifications of the appropriate pairings of kinds of individuals with properties or relations. Appropriate for what? For the constitution of constituted entities, *in the dispensation of that conceptual scheme.*

When one says or thinks "Os exist," then, according to conceptual relativism this is not true or false absolutely. Its truth value must be determined relative to one's conceptual scheme, to one's "conceptual position," including its criteria of existence. However, even if one's claim that "Os exist" must be determined relative to one's conceptual position, so that it can be very naturally said that "Os exist" relative to one's conceptual position (in that sense), it does not follow that "Os exist" only *in virtue* of one's conceptual position, in the sense that if one had not existed with some such conceptual scheme, or at least if no-one had existed with some such conceptual scheme, then there would have been "no Os in existence." This no more follows than it follows from the relativity of the truth of my statement "The Empire State Building is 180 miles southwest of here" that the Empire State Building has the distance and direction that it has from here as a result of *my* being here (even if I am the speaker or thinker). Despite the relativity of the truth of my statement, the Empire State Building *would have been* exactly where it is, 180 miles from here, even if I had not been here. Similarly, Os might have existed relative to this my (our) conceptual position, even if no-one had existed to occupy this position.

PART IV

WHY IS THERE A WORLD?

Introduction

Returning to our original understanding of "world," according to which it means absolutely everything there is (see the Preface), we can restate the question of Part IV using the traditional philosophical formula: "Why is there something rather than nothing?" Philosophers have disagreed about whether the question even makes sense, and about whether it could possibly have an answer. The authors represented here mostly agree that there could be an answer. But some are skeptical whether there *is* an answer. And they differ in the varieties of answer they are willing to countenance as potential explanations of the existence of the world.

William James and Derek Parfit agree that the question makes sense. Parfit explores a range of forms an answer might take; Richard Swinburne, in his reply, argues that none of the alternatives Parfit suggests is as plausible or explanatorily complete as the traditional answer: God explains the existence of everything besides Himself, His own existence being taken for a "brute fact."

Not content to let the existence of God remain a brute fact, many have held that the deity is a necessary being – something that could not possibly have failed to exist, and so either explains itself or needs no explanation (take your pick). The cosmological and ontological arguments are supposed to show that there must be a necessary being. William Rowe finds Samuel Clarke's version of the cosmological argument to be valid, but of little use for the purposes of convincing a modern-day atheist. Norman Malcolm detects two arguments for a necessary being in Anselm's *Proslogion*. Malcolm argues that, although the first is fallacious, the second is valid and sound, and may even be of use in convincing skeptics that God exists.

Suggestions for further reading

Adams, Robert M., *The Virtue of Faith* (New York and Oxford: Oxford University Press, 1987), chs. 13 and 14 ("Has It Been Proved That All Real Existence Is Contingent?" and "Divine Necessity").

Carter, William R., *The Elements of Metaphysics* (Philadelphia, Penn.: Temple University Press, 1990) ch. 11 ("God").

Edwards, Paul, "Why," in Edwards (ed.) *Encyclopedia of Philosophy* (New York: Macmillan, 1967).

Gardner, Martin, *The Whys of a Philosophical Scrivener* (New York: St. Martin's 1999) chs. 10, 11, 12, 13, and 20 ("The Gods: Why I Am Not a Polytheist," "The All: Why I Am Not a Pantheist," "The Proofs: Why I Do Not Believe God's Existence Can Be Demonstrated," "Faith: Why I Am Not an Atheist," and "Surprise: Why I Cannot Take the World for Granted").

Hasker, William, *Metaphysics: Constructing a World View* (Downers Grove, Ill., and Leicester, UK: InterVarsity Press, 1983) ch. 5 ("God and the World").

Jubien, Michael, *Contemporary Metaphysics* (Oxford: Blackwell, 1997) ch. 11 ("Cosmology").

Munitz, Milton K., *The Mystery of Existence* (New York: New York University Press, 1974).

Plantinga, Alvin, *God, Freedom, and Evil* (Grand Rapids, Mich.: Eerdmans, 1977), Part 2 ("Natural Theology").

Post, John F., *Metaphysics: A Contemporary Introduction* (New York: Paragon House, 1991) chs. 4 and 7 ("Why Does Anything at All Exist?" and "God").

Smith, Quentin, and Oaklander, L. Nathan, *Time, Change and Freedom: an Introduction to Metaphysics* (London: Routledge, 1995) Dialogues 4 and 10 ("Eternity" and "God, time and freedom").

Taylor, Richard, *Metaphysics*, 4th edn (Englewood Cliffs, N.J.: Prentice-Hall, 1992) ch. 11 ("God").

van Inwagen, Peter, *Metaphysics*, 2nd edn (Cambridge, Mass.: Westview Press, 2002) Part 2 ("Why the World Is").

59 The Problem of Being: Chapter 3 of *Some Problems of Philosophy*

William James

Schopenhauer on the Origin of the Problem

How comes the world to be here at all instead of the nonentity which might be imagined in its place? Schopenhauer's remarks on this question may be considered classical. "Apart from man," he says, "no being wonders at its own existence. When man first becomes conscious, he takes himself for granted, as something needing no explanation. But not for long; for, with the rise of the first reflection, that wonder begins which is the mother of metaphysics, and which made Aristotle say that men now and always seek to philosophise because of wonder – The lower a man stands in intellectual respects the less of a riddle does existence seem to him . . . but, the clearer his consciousness becomes the more the problem grasps him in its greatness. In fact the unrest which keeps the never stopping clock of metaphysics going is the thought that the non-existence of this world is just as possible as its existence. Nay more, we soon conceive the world as something the non-existence of which not only is conceivable but would indeed be preferable to its existence; so that our wonder passes easily into a brooding over that fatality which nevertheless could call such a world into being, and mislead the immense force that could produce and preserve it into an activity so hostile to its own interests. The philosophic wonder thus becomes a sad astonishment, and like the overture to Don Giovanni, philosophy begins with a minor chord."[1]

One need only shut oneself in a closet and begin to think of the fact of one's being there, of one's queer bodily shape in the darkness (a thing to make children scream at, as Stevenson says), of one's fantastic character and all, to have the wonder steal over the detail as much as over the general fact of being, and to see that it is only familiarity that blunts it. Not only that *anything* should be, but that *this* very thing should be, is mysterious! Philosophy stares, but brings no reasoned solution, for from nothing to being there is no logical bridge.

Various Treatments of the Problem

Attempts are sometimes made to banish the question rather than to give it an answer. Those who ask it, we are told, extend illegitimately to the whole of being the contrast to a supposed alternative non-being which only particular beings possess. These, indeed, were not, and now are. But being in general, or in some shape, always was, and you cannot rightly bring the whole of it into relation with a primordial nonentity. Whether as God or as material atoms, it is itself primal and eternal. But if you call any being whatever eternal, some philosophers have always been ready to taunt you with the paradox inherent in the assumption. Is past eternity completed? they ask: If so, they go on, it must have had a beginning; for whether your imagination traverses it forwards or backwards, it offers an identical content or stuff to be measured; and if the amount comes to an end in one way, it ought to come to an end in the other. In other words, since we now witness its end, some past moment must have witnessed its beginning. If, however, it had a beginning, when was that, and why?

You are up against the previous nothing, and do not see how it ever passed into being. This dilemma, of having to choose between a regress which, although called infinite, has nevertheless come to a termination, and an absolute first, has played a great part in philosophy's history.

Other attempts still are made at exorcising the question. Non-being is not, said Parmenides and Zeno; only being is. Hence what is, is necessarily being – being, in short, is necessary. Others, calling the idea of nonentity no real idea, have said that on the absence of an idea can no genuine problem be founded. More curtly still, the whole ontological wonder has been called diseased, a case of *Grübelsucht* like asking, "Why am I myself?" or "Why is a triangle a triangle?"

Rationalist and Empiricist Treatments

Rationalistic minds here and there have sought to reduce the mystery. Some forms of being have been deemed more natural, so to say, or more inevitable and necessary than others. Empiricists of the evolutionary type – Herbert Spencer seems a good example – have assumed that whatever had the least of reality, was weakest, faintest, most imperceptible, most nascent, might come easiest first, and be the earliest successor to nonentity. Little by little the fuller grades of being might have added themselves in the same gradual way until the whole universe grew up.

To others not the minimum, but the maximum of being has seemed the earliest First for the intellect to accept. "The perfection of a thing does not keep it from existing," Spinoza said, "on the contrary, it founds its existence."[2] It is mere prejudice to assume that it is harder for the great than for the little to be, and that easiest of all it is to be nothing. What makes things difficult in any line is the alien obstructions that are met with, and the smaller and weaker the thing the more powerful over it these become. Some things are so great and inclusive that to be is implied in their very nature. The anselmian or ontological proof of God's existence, sometimes called the cartesian proof, criticised by Saint Thomas, rejected by Kant, re-defended by Hegel, follows this line of thought. What is conceived as imperfect may lack being among its other lacks, but if God, who is expressly defined as *Ens perfectissimum*, lacked anything whatever, he would contradict his own definition. He cannot lack being therefore: He is *Ens necessarium, Ens realissimum*, as well as *Ens perfectissimum*.[3]

Hegel in his lordly way says: "It would be strange if God were not rich enough to embrace so poor a category as Being, the poorest and most abstract of all." This is somewhat in line with Kant's saying that a real dollar does not contain one cent more than an imaginary dollar. At the beginning of his logic Hegel seeks in another way to mediate nonentity with being. Since "being" in the abstract, mere being, means nothing in particular, it is indistinguishable from "nothing"; and he seems dimly to think that this constitutes an identity between the two notions, of which some use may be made in getting from one to the other. Other still queerer attempts show well the rationalist temper. Mathematically you can deduce 1 from 0 by the following process:

$$\frac{0}{0} = \frac{1-1}{1-1} = 1$$

Or physically if all being has (as it seems to have) a "polar" construction, so that every positive part of it has its negative, we get the simple equation: $+1 - 1 = 0$, *plus* and *minus* being the signs of polarity in physics.

The Same Amount of Existence Must be Begged by All

It is not probable that the reader will be satisfied with any of these solutions, and contemporary philosophers, even rationalistically minded ones, have on the whole agreed that no one has intelligibly banished the mystery of *fact*. Whether the original nothing burst into God and vanished, as night vanishes in day, while God thereupon became the creative principle of all lesser beings; or whether all things have foisted or shaped themselves imperceptibly into existence, the same amount of existence has in the end to be assumed and begged by the philosopher. To comminute the difficulty is not to quench it. If you are a rationalist you beg a kilogram of being at once, we will say; if you are an empiricist you beg a thousand successive grams; but you beg the same amount in each case, and you are the same beggar whatever you may pretend. You leave the logical riddle untouched, of how the coming of whatever is, came it all at once, or came it piecemeal, can be intellectually understood.[4]

Conservation vs. Creation

If being gradually *grew*, its quantity was of course not always the same, and may not be the same hereafter. To most philosophers this view has seemed absurd, neither God, nor primordial matter, nor energy being supposed to admit of increase or decrease. The orthodox opinion is that the quantity of reality must at all costs be conserved, and the waxing and waning of our phenomenal experiences must be treated as surface appearances which leave the deeps untouched.

Nevertheless, within experience, phenomena come and go. There are novelties; there are losses. The world seems, on the concrete and proximate level at least, really to grow. So the question recurs: How do our finite experiences come into being from moment to moment? By inertia? By perpetual creation? Do the new ones come at the call of the old ones? Why do not they all go out like a candle?

Who can tell off-hand? The question of being is the darkest in all philosophy. All of us are beggars here, and no school can speak disdainfully of another or give itself superior airs. For all of us alike, Fact forms a datum, gift, or *Vorgefundenes*, which we cannot burrow under, explain or get behind. It makes itself somehow, and our business is far more with its What than with its Whence or Why.

Notes

1   Schopenhauer, *The World as Will and Representation*: Appendix 17, "On the metaphysical need of man," abridged.
2   Spinoza, *Ethics*, part i, prop. xi, scholium.
3   St Anselm, *Proslogion*, in *Anselm's Basic Writings*, trs. S. N. Deane, with an introduction by Charles Hartshorne, 2nd edn (LaSalle, Ill.: Open Court, 1962); Descartes, *Meditations on First Philosophy*, in *The Philosophical Writings of Descartes*, vol. II, trs. John Cottingham, Robert Stoothoff, and Dugald Murdoch (Cambridge: Cambridge University Press, 1984), Third and Fifth Meditations; Immanuel Kant, *The Critique of Pure Reason*, trs. Norman Kemp Smith (New York: St Martin's Press, 1929), pp. 500–7.
4   In more technical language, one may say that fact or being is "contingent," or matter of "chance," so far as our intellect is concerned. The conditions of its appearance are uncertain, unforeseeable, when future, and when past, elusive.

---

60   Why Anything? Why This?

Derek Parfit

Why does the Universe exist? There are two questions here. First, why is there a Universe at all? It might have been true that nothing ever existed: no living beings, no stars, no atoms, not even space or time. When we think about this possibility, it can seem astonishing that anything exists. Second, why does *this* Universe exist? Things might have been, in countless ways, different. So why is the Universe as it is?

These questions, some believe, may have causal answers. Suppose first that the Universe has always existed. Some believe that, if all events were caused by earlier events, everything would be explained. That, however, is not so. Even an infinite series of events cannot explain itself. We could ask why this series occurred, rather than some other series, or no series. Of the supporters of the Steady State Theory, some welcomed what they took to be this theory's atheistic implications. They assumed that, if the Universe had no beginning, there would be nothing for a Creator to explain. But there would still be an eternal Universe to explain.

Suppose next that the Universe is not eternal, since nothing preceded the Big Bang. That first event, some physicists suggest, may have obeyed the laws of quantum mechanics, by being a random fluctuation in a vacuum. This would causally explain, they say, how the Universe came into existence out of nothing. But what physicists call a vacuum isn't really nothing. We can ask why it exists, and has the potentialities it does. In Hawking's phrase, 'What breathes fire into the equations?'

Similar remarks apply to all suggestions of these kinds. There could not be a causal explanation of why the Universe exists, why there are any laws of nature, or why these laws are as they are. Nor would it make a difference if there is a God, who caused the rest of the Universe to exist. There could not be a causal explanation of why God exists.

Many people have assumed that, since these questions cannot have causal answers, they cannot have any answers. Some therefore dismiss these questions, thinking them not worth considering. Others conclude that they do not make sense. They assume that, as Wittgenstein wrote, 'doubt can exist only where there is a question; and a question only where there is an answer'.

These assumptions are all, I believe, mistaken. Even if these questions could not have answers, they would still make sense, and they would still be worth considering. I am reminded here of the aesthetic category of the *sublime*, as applied to the highest mountains, raging oceans, the night sky, the interiors of some cathedrals, and other things that are superhuman, awesome, limitless. No question is more sublime than why there is a Universe: why there is anything rather than nothing. Nor should we assume that answers to this question must be causal. And, even if reality cannot be fully explained, we may still make progress, since what is inexplicable may become less baffling than it now seems.

1

One apparent fact about reality has recently been much discussed. Many physicists believe that, for life to be possible, various features of the Universe must be almost precisely as they are. As one example of such a feature, we can take the initial conditions in the Big Bang. If these conditions had been more than very slightly different, these physicists claim, the Universe would not have had the complexity that allows living beings to exist. Why were these conditions so precisely right?[1]

Some say: 'If they had not been right, we couldn't even ask this question.' But that is no answer. It could be baffling how we survived some crash even though, if we hadn't, we could not be baffled.

Others say: 'There had to be some initial conditions, and the conditions that make life possible were as likely as any others. So there is nothing to be explained.' To see what is wrong with this reply, we must distinguish two kinds of case. Suppose first that, when some radio telescope is aimed at most points in space, it records a random sequence of incoming waves. There might be nothing here that needed to be explained. Suppose next that, when the telescope is aimed in one direction, it records a sequence of waves whose pulses match the number π, in binary notation, to the first ten thousand digits. That particular number is, in one sense, just as likely as any other. But there *would* be something here that needed to be explained. Though each long number is unique, only a very few are, like π, mathematically special. What would need to be explained is why this sequence of waves exactly matched such a special number. Though this matching might be a coincidence, which had been randomly produced, that would be most unlikely. We could be almost certain that these waves had been produced by some kind of intelligence.

On the view that we are now considering, since any sequence of waves is as likely as any other, there would be nothing to be explained. If we accepted this view, intelligent beings elsewhere in space would not be able to communicate with us, since we would ignore their messages. Nor could God reveal himself. Suppose that, with some optical telescope, we saw a distant pattern of stars which spelled out in Hebrew script the first chapter of Genesis. This pattern of stars, according to this view, would not need to be explained. That is clearly false.

Here is another analogy. Suppose first that, of a thousand people facing death, only one can be rescued. If there is a lottery to pick this one survivor, and I win, I would be very lucky. But there might be nothing here that needed to be explained. Someone had to win, and why not me? Consider next another lottery. Unless my gaoler picks the longest of a thousand straws, I shall be shot. If my gaoler picks that longest straw, there would be something to be explained. It would not be enough to say, 'This result was as likely as any other.' In the first lottery, nothing special happened: whatever the result, someone's life would be saved. In this second lottery, the result *was* special, since, of the thousand possible results, only one would save a life. Why was this special result *also* what happened? Though this might be a coincidence, the chance of that is only one in a thousand. I could be almost certain that, like Dostoyevsky's mock execution, this lottery was rigged.

The Big Bang, it seems, was like this second lottery. For life to be possible, the initial conditions had to be selected with great accuracy. This *appearance of fine-tuning*, as some call it, also needs to be explained.

It may be objected that, in regarding conditions as special if they allow for life, we unjustifiably assume our own importance. But life *is* special, if only because of its complexity. An earthworm's brain is more complicated than a lifeless galaxy. Nor is it only life that requires this fine-tuning. If the Big Bang's initial conditions had not been almost precisely as they were, the Universe would have either almost instantly recollapsed, or expanded so fast, and with particles so thinly spread, that not even stars or heavy elements could have formed. That is enough to make these conditions very special.

It may next be objected that these conditions cannot be claimed to be improbable, since such a claim requires a statistical basis, and there is only one Universe. If we were considering all conceivable Universes, it would indeed be implausible to make judgments of statistical probability. But our question is much narrower.

We are asking what would have happened if, with the same laws of nature, the initial conditions had been different. That provides the basis for a statistical judgment. There is a range of values that these conditions might have had, and physicists can work out in what proportion of this range the resulting Universe could have contained stars, heavy elements, and life.

This proportion, it is claimed, is extremely small. Of the range of possible initial conditions, fewer than one in a billion billion would have produced a Universe with the complexity that allows for life. If this claim is true, as I shall here assume, there is something that cries out to be explained. Why was one of this tiny set *also* the one that actually obtained?

On one view, this was a mere coincidence. That is conceivable, since coincidences happen. But this view is hard to believe since, if it were true, the chance of this coincidence occurring would be below one in a billion billion. Others say: 'The Big Bang *was* fine-tuned. In creating the Universe, God chose to make life possible.' Atheists may reject this answer, thinking it improbable that God exists. But this is not as improbable as the view that would require so great a coincidence. So even atheists should admit that, of these two answers to our question, the answer that invokes God is more likely to be true.

This reasoning revives one of the traditional arguments for belief in God. In its strongest form, this argument appealed to the many features of animals, such as eyes or wings, that look as if they have been designed. Paley's appeal to such features much impressed Darwin when he was young. Darwin later undermined this form of the argument, since evolution can explain this appearance of design. But evolution cannot explain the appearance of fine-tuning in the Big Bang.

This argument's appeal to probabilities can be challenged in a different way. In claiming it to be most improbable that this fine-tuning was a coincidence, the argument assumes that, of the possible initial conditions in the Big Bang, each was equally likely to obtain. That assumption may be mistaken. The conditions that allow for complexity and life may have been, compared with all the others, much more likely to obtain. Perhaps they were even certain to obtain.

To answer this objection, we must broaden this argument's conclusion. If these life-allowing conditions were either very likely or certain to obtain, then – as the argument claims – it would be no coincidence that the Universe allows for complexity and life. But this fine-tuning might have been the work, not of some existing being, but of some impersonal force, or fundamental law. That is what some theists believe God to be.

A stronger challenge to this argument comes from a different way to explain the appearance of fine-tuning. Consider first a similar question. For life to be possible on the Earth, many of the Earth's features have to be close to being as they are. The Earth's having such features, it might be claimed, is unlikely to be a coincidence, and should therefore be regarded as God's work. But such an argument would be weak. The Universe, we can reasonably believe, contains many planets, with varying conditions. We should expect that, on a few of these planets, conditions would be just right for life. Nor is it surprising that we live on one of these few.

Things are different, we may assume, with the appearance of fine-tuning in the Big Bang. While there are likely to be many other planets, there is only one Universe. But this difference may be less than it seems. Some physicists suggest that the observable Universe is only one out of many different worlds, which are all equally parts of reality. According to one such view, the other worlds are related to ours in a way that solves some of the mysteries of quantum physics. On the different and simpler view that is relevant here, the other worlds have the same laws of nature as our world, and they are produced by Big Bangs that are broadly similar, except in having different initial conditions.

On this *Many Worlds Hypothesis*, there is no need for fine-tuning. If there were enough Big Bangs, we should expect that, in a few of these, conditions would be just right to allow for complexity and life; and it would be no surprise that our Big Bang was one of these few. To illustrate this point, we can revise my second lottery. Suppose my gaoler picks a straw, not once, but very many times. That would explain his managing, once, to pick the longest straw, without that's being an extreme coincidence, or this lottery's being rigged.

On most versions of the Many Worlds Hypothesis, these many worlds are not, except through their origins, causally related. Some object that, since our world could not be causally affected by such other worlds, we can have no evidence for their existence, and can therefore have no reason to believe in them. But we do have such a reason, since their existence would explain an otherwise puzzling feature of our world: the appearance of fine-tuning.

Of these two ways to explain this appearance, which is better? Compared with belief in God, the Many Worlds Hypothesis is more cautious, since its claim is merely that there is more of the kind of reality that we can observe around us. But God's existence has been claimed to be intrinsically more probable. According to most theists, God is a being who is omnipotent, omniscient, and wholly good. The uncaused existence of such a being has been claimed to be simpler, and less arbitrary, than the uncaused existence of many highly complicated worlds. And simpler hypotheses, many scientists assume, are more likely to be true.

If such a God exists, however, other features of our world become hard to explain. It may not be surprising that God chose to make life possible. But the laws of nature could have been different, so there are many possible worlds that would have contained life. It is hard to understand why, out of all these possibilities, God chose to create our world. What is most baffling is the problem of evil. There appears to be suffering which any good person, knowing the truth, would have prevented if he could. If there is such suffering, there cannot be a God who is omnipotent, omniscient, and wholly good.

To this problem, theists have proposed several solutions. Some suggest that God is not omnipotent, or not wholly good. Others suggest that undeserved suffering is not, as it seems, bad, or that God could not prevent such suffering without making the Universe, as a whole, less good.

We must ignore these suggestions here, since we have larger questions to consider. I began by asking why things are as they are. Before returning to that question, we should ask *how* things are. There is much about our world that we have not discovered. And, just as there may be other worlds that are like ours, there may be worlds that are very different.

2

It will help to distinguish two kinds of possibilities. *Cosmic* possibilities cover everything that ever exists, and are the different ways that the whole of reality might be. Only one such possibility can be actual, or be the one that *obtains*. *Local* possibilities are the different ways that some part of reality, or *local world*, might be. If some local world exists, that leaves it open whether other worlds exist.

One cosmic possibility is, roughly, that *every* possible local world exists. This we can call the *All Worlds Hypothesis*. Another possibility, which might have obtained, is that nothing ever exists. This we can call the *Null Possibility*. In each of the remaining possibilities, the number of local worlds that exist is between none and all. There are countless of these possibilities, since there are countless combinations of possible local worlds.

Of these different cosmic possibilities, one must obtain, and only one can obtain. So we have two questions: Which obtains, and Why?

These questions are connected. If some possibility would be easier to explain, we may have more reason to believe that this possibility obtains. This is how, rather than believing in only one Big Bang, we have more reason to believe in many. Whether we believe in one or many, we have the question why any Big Bang has occurred. Though this question is hard, the occurrence of many Big Bangs is not more puzzling than the occurrence of only one. Most kinds of thing, or event, have many instances. We also have the question why, in the Big Bang that produced our world, the initial conditions allowed for complexity and life. If there has been only one Big Bang, this fact is also hard to explain, since it is most unlikely that these conditions merely happened to be right. If instead there have been many Big Bangs, this fact is easy to explain, since it is like the fact that, among countless planets, there are some whose conditions allow for life. Since belief in many Big Bangs leaves less that is unexplained, it is the better view.

If some cosmic possibilities would be less puzzling than others, because their obtaining would leave less to be explained, is there some possibility whose obtaining would be in no way puzzling?

Consider first the Null Possibility, in which nothing ever exists. To imagine this possibility, it may help to suppose first that all that ever existed was a single atom. We then imagine that even this atom never existed.

Some have claimed that, if there had never been anything, there wouldn't have been anything to be explained. But that is not so. When we imagine how things would have been if nothing had ever existed, what we should imagine away are such things as living beings, stars, and atoms. There would still have been various truths, such as the truth that there were no stars or atoms, or that 9 is divisible by 3. We can ask why these things would have been true. And such questions may have answers. Thus we can explain why, even if nothing had ever existed, 9 would still have been divisible by 3. There is no conceivable alternative. And we can explain why there would have been no such things as immaterial matter, or spherical cubes. Such things are logically impossible. But why would *nothing* have existed? Why would there have been no stars or atoms, no philosophers or blue-bell woods?

We should not claim that, if nothing had ever existed, there would have been nothing to be explained. But we can claim something less. Of all the cosmic possibilities, the Null Possibility would have needed the least explanation. As Leibniz pointed out, it is much the simplest, and the least arbitrary. And it is the easiest to understand. It can seem mysterious, for example, how things could exist without their existence having some cause, but there cannot be a causal explanation of why the whole Universe, or God, exists. The Null Possibility raises no such problem. If nothing had ever existed, that state of affairs would not have needed to be caused.

Reality, however, does not take its least puzzling form. In some way or other, a Universe has managed to exist. That is what can take one's breath away. As Wittgenstein wrote, 'not how the world is, is the mystical, but *that* it is.' Or, in the words of a thinker as unmystical as Jack Smart: 'That anything should exist at all does seem to me a matter for the deepest awe.'

Consider next the All Worlds Hypothesis, on which every possible local world exists. Unlike the Null Possibility, this may be how things are. And it may be the next least puzzling possibility. This hypothesis is not the same as – though it includes – the Many Worlds Hypothesis. On that more cautious view, the many other worlds have the same elements as our world, and the same fundamental laws, and differ only in such features as their constants and initial conditions. The All Worlds Hypothesis covers every conceivable kind of world, and most of these other worlds would have very different elements and laws.

If all these worlds exist, we can ask why they do. But, compared with most other cosmic possibilities, the All Worlds Hypothesis may leave less that is unex-plained. For example, whatever the number of possible worlds that exist, we have the question, 'Why *that* number?' That question would have been least puzzling if the number that existed were *none*, and the next least arbitrary possibility seems to be that *all* these worlds exist. With every other cosmic possibility, we have a further question. If ours is the only world, we can ask: 'Out of all the possible local worlds, why is *this* the one that exists?' On any version of the Many Worlds Hypothesis, we have a similar question: 'Why do just *these* worlds exist, with *these* elements and laws?' But, if *all* these worlds exist, there is no such further question.

It may be objected that, even if all possible local worlds exist, that does not explain why our world is as it is. But that is a mistake. If all these worlds exist, each world is as it is in the way in which each number is as it is. We cannot sen-sibly ask why 9 is 9. Nor should we ask why our world is the one it is: why it is *this* world. That would be like asking, 'Why are *we* who we are?', or 'Why is it *now* the time that it is?' Those, on reflection, are not good questions.

Though the All Worlds Hypothesis avoids certain questions, it is not as simple, or unarbitrary, as the Null Possibility. There may be no sharp distinction between worlds that are and are not possible. It is unclear what counts as a kind of world. And, if there are infinitely many kinds, there is a choice between different kinds of infinity.

Whichever cosmic possibility obtains, we can ask why it obtains. All that I have claimed so far is that, with some possibilities, this question would be less puzzling. Let us now ask: Could this question have an answer? Might there be a theory that leaves nothing unexplained?

3

It is sometimes claimed that God, or the Universe, make themselves exist. But this cannot be true, since these entities cannot do anything unless they exist.

On a more intelligible view, it is logically necessary that God, or the Universe, exist, since the claim that they might not have existed leads to a contradiction. On such a view, though it may seem conceivable that there might never have been anything, that is not really logically possible. Some people even claim that there may be only one coherent cosmic possibility. Thus Einstein suggested that, if God created our world, he might have had no choice about which world to create. If such a view were true, everything might be explained. Reality might be the way it is because there was no conceivable alternative. But, for reasons that have been often given, we can reject such views.

Consider next a quite different view. According to Plato, Plotinus and others, the Universe exists because its existence is good. Even if we are confident that we should reject this view, it is worth asking whether it makes sense. If it does, that may suggest other possibilities.

This *Axiarchic View* can take a theistic form. It can claim that God exists because his existence is good, and that the rest of the Universe exists because God caused it to exist. But in that explanation God, *qua* Creator, is redundant. If God can exist because his existence is good, so can the whole Universe. This may be why some theists reject the Axiarchic View, and insist that God's existence is a brute fact, with no explanation.

In its simplest form, this view makes three claims:

(1) It would be best if reality were a certain way.
(2) Reality is that way.
(3) (1) explains (2).

(1) is an ordinary evaluative claim, like the claim that it would be better if there was less suffering. The Axiarchic View assumes, I believe rightly, that such claims can be in a strong sense true. (2) is an ordinary empirical or scientific claim, though of a sweeping kind. What is distinctive in this view is claim (3), according to which (1) explains (2).

Can we understand this third claim? To focus on this question, we should briefly ignore the world's evils, and suspend our other doubts about claims (1) and (2). We should suppose that, as Leibniz claimed, the best possible Universe exists. Would it then make sense to claim that this Universe exists *because* it is the best?

That use of 'because', Axiarchists should admit, cannot be easily explained. But even ordinary causation is mysterious. At the most fundamental level, we have no idea why some events cause others; and it is hard to explain what causation is. There are, moreover, non-causal senses of 'because' and 'why', as in the claim that God exists because his existence is logically necessary. We can understand that claim, even if we think it false. The Axiarchic View is harder to understand. But that is not surprising. If there is some explanation of the whole of reality, we should not expect this explanation to fit neatly into some familiar category. This extra-ordinary question may have an extra-ordinary answer. We should reject suggested answers which make no sense; but we should also try to see what might make sense.

Axiarchy might be expressed as follows. We are now supposing that, of all the countless ways that the whole of reality might be, one is both the very best, and is the way that reality is. On the Axiarchic View, *that is no coincidence*. This claim, I believe, makes sense. And, if it were no coincidence that the best way for reality to be is *also* the way that reality is, that might support the further claim that this was *why* reality was this way.

This view has one advantage over the more familiar theistic view. An appeal to God cannot explain why the Universe exists, since God would himself be part of the Universe, or one of the things that exist. Some theists argue that, since nothing can exist without some cause, God, who is the First Cause, must exist. As Schopenhauer objected, this argument's premise is not like some cab-driver whom theists are free to dismiss once they have reached their destination. The Axiarchic View appeals, not to an existing entity, but to an explanatory law. Since such a law would not itself be part of the Universe, it might explain why the Universe exists, and is as good as it could be. If such a law governed reality, we could still ask why it did, or why the Axiarchic View was true. But, in discovering this law, we would have made some progress.

It is hard, however, to believe the Axiarchic View. If, as it seems, there is much pointless suffering, our world cannot be part of the best possible Universe.

4

Some Axiarchists claim that, if we reject their view, we must regard our world's existence as a brute fact, since no other explanation could make sense. But that, I believe, is not so. If we abstract from the optimism of the Axiarchic View, its claims are these:

> Of the countless cosmic possibilities, one both has some very special feature, and is the possibility that obtains. That is no coincidence. This possibility obtains because it has this feature.

Other views can make such claims. This special feature need not be that of being best. Thus, on the All Worlds Hypothesis, reality is *maximal*, or as full as it could be. Similarly, if nothing had ever existed, reality would have been *minimal*, or as empty as it could be. If the possibility that obtained were either maximal, or minimal, that fact, we might claim, would be most unlikely to be a coincidence. And that might support the further claim that this possibility's having this feature would be *why* it obtained.

Let us now look more closely at that last step. When it is no coincidence that two things are both true, there is something that explains why, given the truth of one, the other is also true. The truth of either might make the other true. Or both might be explained by some third truth, as when two facts are the joint effects of a common cause.

Suppose next that, of the cosmic possibilities, one is both very special and is the one that obtains. If that is no coincidence, what might explain why these things are both true? On the reasoning that we are now considering, the first truth explains the second, since this possibility obtains because it has this special feature. Given the kind of truths these are, such an explanation could not go the other way. This possibility could not have this feature because it obtains. If some possibility has some feature, it could not fail to have this feature, so it would have this feature whether or not it obtains. The All Worlds Hypothesis, for example, could not fail to describe the fullest way for reality to be.

While it is necessary that our imagined possibility has its special feature, it is not necessary that this possibility obtains. This difference, I believe, justifies the reasoning that we are now considering. Since this possibility must have this feature, but might not have obtained, it cannot have this feature because it obtains, nor could some third truth explain why it both has this feature and obtains. So, if these facts are no coincidence, this possibility must obtain *because* it has this feature.

When some possibility obtains because it has some feature, its having this feature may be why some agent, or some process of natural selection, made it obtain. These we can call the *intentional* and *evolutionary* ways in which some feature of some possibility may explain why it obtains.

Our world, theists claim, can be explained in the first of these ways. If reality were as good as it could be, it would indeed make sense to claim that this was partly God's work. But, since God's own existence could not be God's work, there could be no intentional explanation of why the whole of reality was as good as it could be. So we could reasonably conclude that this way's being the best explained *directly* why reality was this way. Even if God exists, the intentional explanation could not compete with the different and bolder explanation offered by the Axiarchic View.

Return now to other explanations of this kind. Consider first the Null Possibility. This, we know, does not obtain; but, since we are asking what makes sense, that does not matter. If there had never been anything, would that have had to be a brute fact, which had no explanation? The answer, I suggest, is No. It might have been no coincidence that, of all the countless cosmic possibilities, what obtained was the simplest, and least arbitrary, and the only possibility in which nothing ever exists. And, if these facts had been no coincidence, this possibility would have obtained because – or partly because – it had one or more of these special features. This explanation, moreover, could not have taken an intentional or evolutionary form. If nothing had ever existed, there could not have been some agent, or process of selection, who or which made this possibility obtain. Its being the simplest or least arbitrary possibility would have been, directly, why it obtained.

Consider next the All Worlds Hypothesis, which may obtain. If reality is as full as it could be, is that a coincidence? Does it merely happen to be true that, of all the cosmic possibilities, the one that obtains is at this extreme? As before, that is conceivable, but this coincidence would be too great to be credible. We can reasonably assume that, if this possibility obtains, that is because it is maximal, or at this extreme. On this *Maximalist View*, it is a fundamental truth that being possible, and part of the fullest way that reality could be, is sufficient for being actual. That is the highest law governing reality. As before, if such a law governed reality, we could still ask *why* it did. But, in discovering this law, we would have made some progress.

Here is another special feature. Perhaps reality is the way it is because its fundamental laws are, on some criterion, as mathematically beautiful as they could be. That is what some physicists are inclined to believe.

As these remarks suggest, there is no clear boundary here between philosophy and science. If there is such a highest law governing reality, this law is of the same kind as those that physicists are trying to discover. When we appeal to natural laws to explain some features of reality, such as the relations between light, gravity, space, and time, we are not giving causal explanations, since we are not claiming that one part of reality caused another part to be some way. What such laws explain, or partly explain, are the deeper facts about reality that causal explanations take for granted.

There would be a highest law, of the kind that I have sketched, if some cosmic possibility obtained because it had some special feature. This feature we can call the *Selector*. If there is more than one such feature, they are all partial Selectors. Just as there are various cosmic possibilities, there are various *explanatory* possibilities. For each of these special features, there is the explanatory possibility that this feature is the Selector, or is one of the Selectors. Reality would then be the way it is because, or partly because, this way had this feature.

There is one other explanatory possibility: that there is *no* Selector. If that is true, it is random that reality is as it is. Events may be in one sense random, even though they are causally inevitable. That is how it is random whether a meteorite strikes the land or the sea. Events are random in a stronger sense if they have no cause. That is what most physicists believe about some features of events involving sub-atomic particles. If it is random what reality is like, the Universe not only has no cause. It has no explanation of any kind. This claim we can call the *Brute Fact View*.

Few features can be plausibly regarded as possible Selectors. Though plausibility is a matter of degree, there is a natural threshold to which we can appeal. If we suppose that reality has some special feature, we can ask which of two beliefs would be more credible: that reality merely happens to have this feature, or that reality is the way it is because this way has this feature. If the second would be more credible, this feature can be called a *credible Selector*. Return for example to the question of how many possible local worlds exist. Of the different answers to this question, *all* and *none* give us, I have claimed, credible Selectors. If either all or no worlds existed, that would be unlikely to be a coincidence. But suppose that 58 worlds existed. This number has some special features, such as being the smallest number that is the sum of seven different primes. It may be just conceivable that this would be why 58 worlds existed; but it would be more reasonable to believe that the number that existed merely happened to be 58.

There are, I have claimed, some credible Selectors. Reality might be some way because that way is the best, or the simplest, or the least arbitrary, or because its obtaining makes reality as full and varied as it could be, or because its fundamental laws are, in some way, as elegant as they could be. Presumably there are other such features, which I have overlooked.

In claiming that there are credible Selectors, I am assuming that some cosmic and explanatory possibilities are more probable than others. That assumption may be questioned. Judgments of probability, it may again be claimed, must be grounded on facts about our world, so such judgments cannot be applied either to how the whole of reality might be, or to how reality might be explained.

This objection is, I believe, unsound. When we choose between scientific theories, our judgments of their probability cannot rest only on predictions based on established facts and laws. We need such judgments in trying to decide what these facts and laws are. And we can justifiably make such judgments when considering different ways in which the whole of reality may be, or might have have been. Compare two such cosmic possibilities. In the first, there is a lifeless Universe consisting only of some spherical iron stars, whose relative motion is as it would be in our world. In the second, things are the same, except that the stars move together in the patterns of a minuet, and they are shaped like either Queen Victoria or Cary Grant. We would be right to claim that, of these two possibilities, the first is more likely to obtain.

In making that claim, we would not mean that it is more likely *that* the first possibility obtains. Since this possibility is the existence of a lifeless Universe, we know that it does not obtain. We would be claiming that this possibility is intrinsically more likely, or that, to put it roughly, it had a greater chance of being how reality is. If some possibility is more likely to obtain, that will often make it more likely that it obtains; but though one kind of likelihood supports the other, they are quite different.

Another objection may again seem relevant here. Of the countless cosmic possibilities, a few have special features, which I have called credible Selectors. If such a possibility obtains, we have, I have claimed, a choice of two conclusions. Either reality, by an extreme coincidence, merely happens to have this feature, or – more plausibly – this feature is one of the Selectors. It may be objected that, when I talk of an extreme coincidence, I must be assuming that these cosmic possibilities are all equally likely to obtain. But I have now rejected that assumption. And, if these possibilities are *not* equally likely, my reasoning may seem to be undermined.

As before, that is not so. Suppose that, of the cosmic possibilities, those that have these special features are much more likely to obtain. As this objection rightly claims, it would not then be amazing if such a possibility merely happened to obtain. But that does not undermine my reasoning, since it is another way of stating my conclusion. It is another way of saying that these features are Selectors.

These remarks do show, however, that we should distinguish two ways in which some feature may be a Selector. *Probabilistic* Selectors make some cosmic possibility more likely to obtain, but leave it open whether it does obtain. On any plausible view, there are some Selectors of this kind, since some ways for reality to be are intrinsically more likely than some others. Thus of our two imagined Universes, the one consisting of spherical stars is intrinsically more likely than the one with stars that are shaped like Queen Victoria or Cary Grant. Besides Probabilistic Selectors, there may also be one or more *Effective* Selectors. If some possibility has a certain feature, this may make this possibility, not merely intrinsically more likely, but the one that obtains. Thus, if simplicity had been the Effective Selector, that would have made it true that nothing ever existed. And, if maximality is the Effective Selector, as it may be, that is what makes reality as full as it could be. When I talk of Selectors, these are the kind I mean.

5

There are, then, various cosmic and explanatory possibilities. In trying to decide which of these obtain, we can in part appeal to facts about our world. Thus, from the mere fact that our world exists, we can deduce that the Null Possibility does not obtain. And, since our world seems to contain pointless evils, we have reason to reject the Axiarchic View.

Consider next the Brute Fact View, on which reality merely happens to be as it is. No facts about our world could refute this view. But some facts would make it less likely that this view is true. If reality is randomly selected, what we should expect to exist are many varied worlds, none of which had features that, in the range of possibilities, were at one extreme. That is what we should expect because, in much the largest set of cosmic possibilities, that would be what exists. If our world has very special features, that would count against the Brute Fact View.

Return now to the question whether God exists. Compared with the uncaused existence of one or many complicated worlds, the hypothesis that God exists has been claimed to be simpler, and less arbitrary, and thus more likely to be true. But this hypothesis is not simpler than the Brute Fact View. And, if it is random which cosmic possibility obtains, we should not expect the one that obtains to be as simple, and unarbitrary, as God's existence is claimed to be. Rather, as I have just said, we should expect there to be many worlds, none of which had very special features. Ours may be the kind of world that, on the Brute Fact View, we should expect to observe.

Similar remarks apply to the All Worlds Hypothesis. Few facts about our world could refute this view; but, if all possible local worlds exist, the likely character of our world is much the same as on the Brute Fact View. That claim may seem surprising, given the difference between these two views. One view is about *which* cosmic possibility obtains, the other is about *why* the one that obtains obtains. And these views conflict, since, if we knew that either view was true, we would have strong reason not to believe the other. If all possible worlds exist, that is unlikely to be a brute fact. But, in their different ways, these views are both *non-selective*. On neither view do certain worlds exist *because* they have certain special features. So, if either view is true, we should not expect our world to have such features.

To that last claim, there is one exception. This is the feature with which we began: that our world allows for life. Though this feature is, in some ways, special, it is one that we cannot help observing. That restricts what we can infer from the fact that our world has this feature. Rather than claiming that being life-allowing is one of the Selectors, we can appeal to some version of the Many Worlds Hypothesis. If there are very many worlds, we would expect a few worlds to be life-allowing, and our world is bound to be one of these few.

Consider next other kinds of special feature: ones that we are not bound to observe. Suppose we discover that our world has such a feature, and we ask whether that is no coincidence. It may again be said that, if there are many worlds, we would expect a few worlds to have this special feature. But that would not explain why that is true of *our* world. We could not claim – as with the feature of being life-allowing – that our world is bound to have this feature. So the appeal to many worlds could not explain away the coincidence. Suppose, for example, that our world were very good, or were wholly law-governed, or had very simple natural laws. Those facts would count against both of the unselective views: both the All Worlds Hypothesis and the Brute Fact View. It is true that, if all worlds exist, or there are very many randomly selected worlds, we should expect a few worlds to be very good, or wholly law-governed, or to have very simple laws. But that would not explain why our world had those features. So we would have some reason to believe that our world is the way it is because this way has those features.

Does our world have such features: ones that count against the unselective views? Our world's moral character seems not to count against these views, since it seems the mixture of good and bad that, on the unselective views, we should expect. But our world may have the other two features: being wholly law-governed, and having very simple laws. Neither feature seems to be required in order for life to be possible. And, among possible life-containing worlds, a far greater range would not have these features. Thus, for each law-governed world, there are countless variants that would fail in different ways to be wholly law-governed. And, compared with simple laws, there is a far greater range of complicated laws. So, on both the unselective views, we should not expect our world to have these features. If it has them, as physicists might discover, that would give us reasons to reject both the All Worlds Hypothesis and the Brute Fact View.

We would have some reason to believe that there are at least two partial Selectors: being law-governed and having simple laws.

There may be other features of our world from which we can try to infer what reality is like, and why. But observation can take us only part of the way. If we can get further, that will have to be by pure reasoning.

6

Of those who accept the Brute Fact View, many assume that it must be true. According to these people, though reality merely happens to be some way, *that* it merely happens to be some way does not merely happen to be true. There could not be an explanation of why reality is the way it is, since there could not be a causal explanation, and no other explanation would make sense.

This assumption, I have argued, is mistaken. Reality might be the way it is because this way is the fullest, or the most varied, or obeys the simplest or most elegant laws, or has some other special feature. Since the Brute Fact View is not the only explanatory possibility, we should not assume that it must be true. When supporters of this view recognize these other possibilities, they may switch to the other extreme, claiming that their view's truth is another brute fact. If that were so, not only would there be no explanation of reality's being as it is, there would also be no explanation of there being no such explanation. As before, though this might be true, we should not assume that it must be true. If some explanatory possibility merely happens to obtain, the one that obtains may not be the Brute Fact View. If it is randomly selected *whether* reality is randomly selected, and there are other possibilities, random selection may not be selected.

There is, moreover, another way in which some explanatory possibility may obtain. Rather than merely happening to obtain, this possibility may have some feature, or set of features, which explains why it obtains. Such a feature would be a Selector at a higher level, since it would apply not to factual but to explanatory possibilities. It would determine, not that reality be a certain way, but that it be determined in a certain way how reality is to be.

If the Brute Fact View is true, it may have been selected in this way. Of the explanatory possibilities, this view seems to describe the simplest, since its claim is only that reality has no explanation. This possibility's being the simplest might make it the one that obtains. Simplicity may be the higher Selector, determining that there is no Selector between the ways that reality might be. Once again however, though this may be true, we cannot assume its truth. There may be some other higher Selector. Some explanatory possibility may obtain, for example, because it is the least arbitrary, or is the one that explains most. The Brute Fact View has neither of those features. Or there may be no higher Selector, since some explanatory possibility may merely happen to obtain.

These alternatives are the different possibilities at yet another, higher explanatory level. So we have the same two questions: Which obtains, and Why?

We may now become discouraged. Every answer, it may seem, raises a further question. But that may not be so. There may be some answer that is a necessary truth. With that necessity, our search would end.

Some truth is logically necessary when its denial leads to a contradiction. It cannot be in this sense necessary either that reality is a brute fact, or that there is some Selector. Both these claims can be denied without contradiction.

There are also non-logical necessities. The most familiar, causal necessity, cannot give us the truth we need. It could not be causally necessary that reality is, or isn't, a brute fact. Causal necessities come lower down. Similar remarks apply to the necessities involved in the essential properties of particular things, or natural kinds. Consider next the metaphysical necessity that some writers claim for God's existence. That claim means, they say, that God's existence does not depend on anything else, and that nothing else could cause God to cease to exist. But these claims do not imply that God must exist, and that makes such necessity too weak to end our questions.

There are, however, some kinds of necessity that would be strong enough. Consider the truths that undeserved suffering is bad, and that, if we believe the premises of a sound argument, we ought rationally to believe this argument's conclusion. These truths are not logically necessary, since their denials would not lead to contradictions. But they could not have failed to be true. Undeserved suffering does not merely happen to be bad.

When Leslie defends the Axiarchic View, he appeals to this kind of non-logical necessity. Not only does value rule reality, Leslie suggests, it could not have failed to rule. But this suggestion is hard to believe. While it is inconceivable that undeserved suffering might have failed to be in itself bad, it is clearly conceivable that value might have failed to rule, if only because it seems so clear that value does *not* rule.

Return now to the Brute Fact View, which is more likely to be true. If this view is true, could its truth be non-logically necessary? Is it inconceivable that there might have been some Selector, or highest law, making reality be some way? The answer, I have claimed, is No. Even if reality is a brute fact, it might not have been. Thus, if nothing had ever existed, that might have been no coincidence. Reality might have been that way because, of the cosmic possibilities, it is the simplest and least arbitrary. And, as I have also claimed, just as it is not necessary that the Brute Fact View is true, it is not necessary that this view's truth be another brute fact. This view might be true because it is the simplest of the explanatory possibilities.

We have not yet found the necessity we need. Reality may happen to be as it is, or there may be some Selector. Whichever of these is true, it may happen to be true, or there may be some higher Selector. These are the different possibilities at the next explanatory level, so we are back with our two questions: Which obtains, and Why?

Could these questions continue forever? Might there be, at every level, another higher Selector? Consider another version of the Axiarchic View. Reality might be as good as it could be, and that might be true because its being true is best, and that in turn might be true because its being true is best, and so on for ever. In this way, it may seem, everything might be explained. But that is not so. Like an infinite series of events, such a series of explanatory truths could not explain itself. Even if each truth were made true by the next, we could still ask why the whole series was true, rather than some other series, or no series.

The point can be made more simply. Though there might be some highest Selector, this might not be goodness but some other feature, such as non-arbitrariness. What could select between these possibilities? Might goodness be the highest Selector because that is best, or non-arbitrariness be this Selector because that is the least arbitrary possibility? Neither suggestion, I believe, makes sense. Just as God could not make himself exist, no Selector could make itself the one that, at the highest level, rules. No Selector could settle *whether* it rules, since it cannot settle anything unless it does rule.

If there is some highest Selector, this cannot, I have claimed, be a necessary truth. Nor could this Selector make itself the highest. And, since this Selector would be the highest, nothing else could make that true. So we may have found the necessity we need. If there is some highest Selector, that, I suggest, must merely happen to be true.

Supporters of the Brute Fact View may now feel vindicated. Have we not, in the end, accepted their view?

We have not. According to the Brute Fact View, reality merely happens to be as it is. That, I have argued, may not be true, since there may be some Selector which explains, or partly explains, reality's being as it is. There may also be some higher Selector which explains there being this Selector. My suggestion is only that, at the end of any such explanatory chain, some highest Selector must merely happen to be the one that rules. That is a different view.

This difference may seem small. No Selector could *explain* reality, we may believe, if it merely happened to rule. But this thought, though natural, is a mistake. If some explanation appeals to a brute fact, it does not explain that fact; but it may explain others.

Suppose, for example, that reality is as full as it could be. On the Brute Fact View, this fact would have no explanation. On the Maximalist View, reality would be this way because the highest law is that what is possible is actual. If reality were as full as it could be, this Maximalist View would be better than the Brute Fact View, since it would explain reality's being this way. And this view would provide that explanation even if it merely happened to be true. It makes a difference where the brute fact comes.

Part of the difference here is that, while there are countless cosmic possibilities, there are few plausible explanatory possibilities. If reality is as full as it could be, that's being a brute fact would be very puzzling. Since there are countless cosmic possibilities, it would be amazing if the one that obtained merely happened to be at the maximal extreme. On the Maximalist View, this fact would be no coincidence. And, since there are few explanatory possibilities, it would not be amazing if the Maximalist highest law merely happened to be the one that rules.

We should not claim that, if some explanation rests on a brute fact, it is not an explanation. Most scientific explanations take this form. The most that might be true is that such an explanation is, in a way, merely a better description.

If that were true, there would be a different defence of the kind of reasoning that we have been considering. Even to discover *how* things are, we need explanations. And we may need explanations on the grandest scale. Our world may seem to have some feature that would be unlikely to be a coincidence. We may reasonably suspect that this feature is the Selector, or one of the Selectors. That hypothesis might lead us to confirm that, as it seemed, our world does have this feature. And that might give us reason to conclude either that ours is the only world, or that there are other worlds, with the same or related features. We might thus reach truths about the whole Universe.

Even if all explanations must end with a brute fact, we should go on trying to explain why the Universe exists, and is as it is. The brute fact may not enter at the lowest level. If reality is the way it is because this way has some feature, to know *what* reality is like, we must ask *why*.

7

We may never be able to answer these questions, either because our world is only a small part of reality, or because, though our world is the whole of reality, we could never know that to be true, or because of our own limitations. But, as I have tried to show, we may come to see more clearly what the possible answers are. Some of the fog that shrouds these questions may then disappear.

It can seem astonishing, for example, how reality could be made to be as it is. If God made the rest of reality be as it is, what could have made God exist? And, if God does not exist, what else could have made reality be as it is? When we think about these questions, even the Brute Fact View may seem unintelligible. It may be baffling how reality could be even randomly selected. What kind of *process* could select whether, for example, time had no beginning, or whether anything ever exists? When, and how, could any selection be made?

This is not a real problem. Of all the possible ways that reality might be, there must be one that is the way reality actually is. Since it is logically necessary that reality be some way or other, it is necessary that one way be picked to be the way that reality is. Logic ensures that, without any kind of process, a selection is made. There is no need for hidden machinery.

Suppose next that, as many people assume, the Brute Fact View must be true. If our world has no very special features, there would then be nothing that was deeply puzzling. If it were necessary that some cosmic possibility be randomly selected, while there would be no explanation of why the selection went as it did, there would be no mystery in reality's being as it is. Reality's features would be inexplicable, but only in the way in which it is inexplicable how some particle randomly moves. If a particle can merely happen to move as it does, reality could merely happen to be as it is. Randomness may even be *less* puzzling at the level of the whole Universe, since we know that facts at this level could not have been caused.

The Brute Fact View, I have argued, is not necessary, and may not be true. There may be one or more Selectors between the ways that reality might be, and one or more Selectors between such Selectors. But, as I have also claimed, it may be a necessary truth that it be a brute fact whether there are such Selectors, and, if so, which the highest Selector is.

If that is a necessary truth, similar remarks apply. On these assumptions, there would again be nothing that was deeply puzzling. If it is necessary that, of these explanatory possibilities, one merely happens to obtain, there would be no explanation of why the one that obtains obtains. But, as before, that would be no more mysterious than the random movement of some particle.

The existence of the Universe can seem, in another way, astonishing. Even if it is not baffling that reality was made to be some way, since there is no conceivable alternative, it can seem baffling that the selection went as it did. Why is there a Universe at all? Why doesn't reality take its simplest and least arbitrary form: that in which nothing ever exists?

If we find this astonishing, we are assuming that these features should be the Selectors: that reality should be as simple and unarbitrary as it could be. That assumption has, I believe, great plausibility. But, just as the simplest cosmic possibility is that nothing ever exists, the simplest explanatory possibility is that there is no Selector. So we should not expect simplicity at both the factual and explanatory levels. If there is no Selector, we should not expect that there would also be no Universe. That would be an extreme coincidence.[2]

Notes

1 In my remarks about this question, I am merely summarizing, and oversimplifying, what others have claimed. See, for example, John Leslie, *Universes* (Routledge, 1989).
2 Of several discussions of these questions, I owe most to John Leslie's *Value and Existence* (Blackwell, 1979) and to Robert Nozick's *Philosophical Explanations* (Oxford, 1981); then to Richard Swinburne's *The Existence of God* (Oxford, 1979), John Mackie's *The Miracle of Theism* (Oxford, 1982), Peter Unger's article in *Midwest Studies in Philosophy*, Volume 9 (1989), and some unpublished work by Stephen Grover.

61 Response to Derek Parfit

Richard Swinburne

Derek Parfit is right to suppose that, on (what I take to be) his understanding of 'causal explanation' and of 'the Universe', there cannot be a causal explanation of the existence of the Universe. He apparently understands by 'the Universe' all the substances there are (that is, all the material things – stars and atoms and whatever these are made of – and all the immaterial things, such as souls or God – if these exist). He apparently understands by 'causal explanation', the causing of some event (including the coming-into-existence and continuing-in-existence of substances) by some substance. Since nothing can cause itself to exist, no substance could cause all-the-substances (including the former) to exist.

What, however, is possible is that one substance causes all the others to come into existence and continue in existence. I believe that the basic principles of inductive inference, which we use in science, historical inquiry, detective work and all other rational inquiry, have the consequence that on the evidence of observed events E, it is probable that C (where C is some substance or law or anything else) in so far as: (1) C (if it existed) would make E likely to occur; (2) if C did not exist, E would be less likely to occur; and (3) C is a simple entity (or law). I believe, and have argued at length elsewhere,[1] that where E is the observed universe (including its life-producing features, to which Parfit draws attention) and C is God, postulated as the cause of the Universe (one substance, with zero limits to his power, knowledge and freedom), E makes the existence of C probable. (As Parfit emphasizes, someone who gives this answer needs to explain why God allows suffering to occur.) To postulate one God as cause is immensely simpler than to postulate infinitely many worlds (most of which are not life-producing) in order to explain the occurrence of our life-producing universe. A simple explanation postulates no more entities than are needed to explain the phenomena. Of course postulating God as the cause of the Universe does not explain why God exists; but then, as Parfit acknowledges, in the end there must be some ultimate brute fact (whether law or substance), and I would argue that the existence of God is the existence of the simplest substance there could be.

Parfit has, however, floated the interesting suggestion that there might be an explanation of the existence of the Universe which is not a causal explanation – some ultimate principle or law which might somehow produce a Universe, without the action of a substance. The trouble is that there are no plausible cases of real-life principles which produce effects within the universe without doing so by operating via substances. If some law of nature, say Newton's law of gravity, produces some effect (say that a stone falls to Earth), it always does so by determining how some substance will cause that effect – say, determining that the Earth will attract the stone in a certain way. Indeed, I suggest that all talk about laws of nature is reducible to talk about the powers which substances have, and the liabilities which they have to exercise them.[2]

... Parfit suggests that there might be axiomatic principles, which produce events because it is good to do so. But there are no plausible examples of such principles at work in the world. When food appears on the tables of the hungry, it does not appear there because it is good that it should, but because some person (i.e. a substance) caused it to be there because he thought that it was good that it should. Nor is there operative any principle of simplicity which makes things occur because they are in some way simple – e.g. makes the laws of nature what they are because they are the simplest laws there could be. For it is easy enough to conceive of laws of nature a lot simpler than our actual laws, which are perhaps the laws of Grand Unified Field Theory, or some laws even more complicated. Certainly, as mentioned earlier, we judge that the simplest theory *compatible with observed events* is more probably the true theory than is any other one. But that is a criterion for assessing the force of evidence, not for producing what exists. If simplicity dictated what was to exist, there would be nothing, or at any rate a lot fewer things behaving in a lot simpler ways than there are. So Parfit's suggestion that there might be some non-causal explanation of the existence of the Universe involves his claiming that there is some kind of principle at work in producing the Universe, which is never operative in producing more limited effects within the Universe. But then we have absolutely no reason for supposing that that kind of principle is ever at work, or that such a principle explains anything at all.[3] By contrast, the theist who postulates God as the cause of (the rest of) the Universe postulates a substance who acts intentionally – i.e. brings about some effect because he believes it good to do so. And the universe is full of many other substances including humans who bring about many different effects intentionally. In this respect explanation by God's intentional actions is like explanations by the intentional actions of humans. Of course God is supposed to be very different indeed in the extent of his power, knowledge and freedom from other substances with which we are familiar. But they are also different from each other in these respects. And God is not supposed to be *totally* different from humans. (In the traditional view, humans are made in God's 'image'.) But to postulate axiomatic or similar principles bringing something out of nothing is to postulate a totally different kind of explanation which we have no reason at all to suppose ever to operate.

Notes

1   See my *The Existence of God* (Oxford: Clarendon Press, revised edition, 1990); or the simpler *Is There a God?* (Oxford: Oxford University Press, 1996).
2   See my "Relations between universals or divine laws?", *Australasian Journal of Philosophy*, 84(2), 2006, pp. 179–89.
3   In the terms used earlier our observed E adds no probability to the claim that there is a C of this kind at work, because if such a principle operated in producing E and so such principles were among the explanations of things, one might expect E (which includes things producing other things) to include things produced by the operation of more limited such principles.

62 The Cosmological Argument: an Excerpt from *A Demonstration of the Being and Attributes of God*

Samuel Clarke

I

First, then, it is absolutely and undeniably certain that *something has existed from all eternity*. This is so evident and undeniable a proposition, that no atheist in any age has ever presumed to assert the contrary, and therefore there is little need of being particular in the proof of it. For, since something now is, it is evident that something always was, otherwise the things that now are must have been produced out of nothing, absolutely and without a cause, which is a plain contradiction in terms. For, to say a thing is produced and yet that there is no cause at all for that production, is to say that something is effected when it is effected by nothing, that is, at the same time when it is not effected at all. Whatever exists has a cause, a reason, a ground of its existence, a foundation on which its existence relies, a ground or reason why it does exist rather than not exist, either in the necessity of its own nature (and then it must have been of itself eternal), or in the will of some other being (and then that other being must, at least in the order of nature and causality, have existed before it).

That something, therefore, has really existed from eternity, is one of the most certain and evident truths in the world, acknowledged by all men and disputed by no one. Yet, as to the manner how it can be, there is nothing in nature more difficult for the mind of men to conceive than this very first plain and self-evident truth. For how anything can have existed eternally, that is, how an eternal duration can be now actually past, is a thing utterly as impossible for our narrow understandings to comprehend, as anything that is not an express contradiction can be imagined to be. And yet, to deny the truth of the proposition, that an eternal duration is now actually past, would be to assert something still far more unintelligible, even a real and express contradiction.

The use I would make of this observation is this: that since in all questions concerning the nature and perfections of God (or concerning anything to which the idea of eternity or infinity is joined), though we can indeed demonstrate certain propositions to be true, yet it is impossible for us to comprehend or frame any adequate or complete ideas of the manner how the things so demonstrated can be. Therefore, when once any proposition is clearly demonstrated to be true, it ought not to disturb us that there be perhaps perplexing difficulties on the other side which, merely for want of adequate ideas of the manner of the existence of the things demonstrated, are not easy to be cleared. Indeed, were it possible there should be any proposition which could equally be demonstrated on both sides of the question, or which could on both sides be reduced to imply a contradiction (as some have very inconsiderately asserted), this, it must be confessed, would alter the case. Upon this absurd supposition, all difference of true and false, all thinking and reasoning, and the use of all our faculties, would be entirely at an end. But when to demonstration on the one side there are proposed on the other only difficulties raised from our want of having adequate ideas of the things themselves, this ought not to be esteemed an objection of any real weight.

It is directly and clearly demonstrable, and acknowledged to be so even by all atheists who ever lived, that something has been from eternity. All the objections, therefore, raised against the eternity of anything, grounded merely on our want of having an adequate idea of eternity, ought to be looked upon as of no real solidity. Thus in other like instances. It is demonstrable, for example, that something must be actually infinite. All the metaphysical difficulties, therefore, which arise usually from applying the measures and relations of things finite to what is infinite and from supposing finites to be *aliquot* parts of infinite, when indeed they are not properly so but only as mathematical points to quantity, which have no proportion at all (and from imagining of infinites to be equal, when in things disparate they manifestly are not so, an infinite line being not only not equal to, but infinitely less than, an infinite surface, and an infinite surface than space infinite in all dimensions) – all metaphysical difficulties, I say, arising from false suppositions of this kind, ought to be esteemed vain and of no force. Again, it is in like manner demonstrable that quantity is infinitely divisible. All the objections, therefore, raised by supposing the sum total of all infinites to be equal when in disparate parts they manifestly are not so, and by comparing the imaginary equality or inequality of the number of the parts of unequal quantities whose parts have really no number at all (they all having parts without number), ought to be looked upon as weak and altogether inconclusive; to ask whether the parts of unequal quantities be equal in number or not, when they have no number at all, being the same thing as to ask whether two lines drawn from differently distant points, and each of them continued infinitely, be equal in length or not, that is, whether they end together, when neither of them have any end at all.

II

There has existed from eternity some one unchangeable and independent being.[1] For, since something must needs have been from eternity, as has been already proved and is granted on all hands, either there has always existed some one unchangeable and independent being from which all other beings that are or ever were in the universe have received their original, or else there has been an infinite succession of changeable and dependent beings produced one from another in an endless progression without any original cause at all. Now this latter supposition is so very absurd that, though all atheism must in its accounts of most things (as shall be shown hereafter) terminate in it, yet I think very few atheists ever were so weak as openly and directly to defend it. For it is plainly impossible and contradictory to itself. I shall not argue against it from the supposed impossibility of infinite succession, barely and absolutely considered in itself, for a reason which shall be mentioned hereafter. But, if we consider such an infinite progression as one entire endless series of dependent beings, it is plain this whole series of beings can have no cause from without of its existence because in it are supposed to be included all things that are, or ever were, in the universe. And it is plain it can have no reason within itself for its existence because no one being in this infinite succession is supposed to be self-existent or necessary (which is the only ground or reason of existence of anything that can be imagined within the thing itself, as will presently more fully appear), but every one dependent on the foregoing. And, where no part is necessary, it is manifest the whole cannot be necessary – absolute necessity of existence not being an extrinsic, relative, and accidental denomination but an inward and essential property of the nature of the thing which so exists.

An infinite succession, therefore, of merely dependent beings without any original independent cause is a series of beings that has neither necessity, nor cause, nor any reason or ground at all of its existence either within itself or from without. That is, it is an express contradiction and impossibility. It is a supposing something to be caused (because it is granted in every one of its stages of succession not to be necessarily and of itself), and yet that, in the whole, it is caused absolutely by nothing, which every man knows is a contradiction to imagine done in time; and because duration in this case makes no difference, it is equally a contradiction to suppose it done from eternity. And consequently there must, on the contrary, of necessity have existed from eternity some one immutable and independent being.

To suppose an infinite succession of changeable and dependent beings produced one from another in an endless progression without any original cause at all is only a driving back from one step to another and, as it were, removing out of sight the question concerning the ground or reason of the existence of things. It is, in reality and in point of argument, the very same supposition as it would be to suppose one continued being of beginningless and endless duration neither self-existent and necessary in itself, nor having its existence founded in any self-existent cause, which is directly absurd and contradictory.

Otherwise, thus: either there has always existed some unchangeable and independent being from which all other beings have received their original, or else there has been an infinite succession of changeable and dependent beings, produced one from another in an endless progression without any original cause at all. According to this latter supposition, there is nothing in the universe self-existent or necessarily existing. And if so, then it was originally equally possible that from eternity there should never have existed anything at all, as that there should from eternity have existed a succession of changeable and dependent beings. Which being supposed, then, what is it that has from eternity determined such a succession of beings to exist, rather than that from eternity there should never have existed anything at all? Necessity it was not because it was equally possible, in this supposition, that they should not have existed at all. Chance is nothing but a mere word, without any signification. And other being it is supposed there was none, to determine the existence of these. Their existence, therefore, was determined by nothing; neither by any necessity in the nature of the things themselves, because it is supposed that none of them are self-existent, nor by any other being, because no other is supposed to exist. That is to say, of two equally possible things, viz., whether anything or nothing should from eternity have existed, the one is determined rather than the other absolutely by nothing, which is an express contradiction. And consequently, as before, there must on the contrary of necessity have existed from eternity some one immutable and independent being. Which, what it is, remains in the next place to be inquired.

III

That unchangeable and independent being which has existed from eternity, without any external cause of its existence, must be self-existent, that is, necessarily existing. For whatever exists must either have come into being out of nothing, absolutely without cause, or it must have been produced by some external cause, or it must be self-existent. Now to arise out of nothing absolutely without any cause has been already shown to be a plain contradiction. To have been produced by some external cause cannot possibly be true of every thing, but something must have existed eternally and independently, as has likewise been shown already. Which remains, therefore, that that being which has existed independently from eternity must of necessity be self-existent. Now to be self-existent is not to be produced by itself, for that is an express contradiction, but it is (which is the only idea we can frame of self-existence, and without which the word seems to have no signification at all) – it is, I say, to exist by an absolute necessity originally in the nature of the thing itself. And this necessity must be antecedent, not indeed in time, to the existence of the being itself (because that is eternal), but it must be antecedent in the natural order of our ideas to our supposition of its being. That is, this necessity must not barely be consequent upon our supposition of the existence of such a being (for then it would not be a necessity absolutely such in itself, nor be the ground or foundation of the existence of anything, being on the contrary only a consequent of it), but it must antecedently force itself upon us whether we will or no, even when we are endeavoring to suppose that no such being exists. For example, when we are endeavoring to suppose that there is no being in the universe that exists necessarily, we always find in our minds (besides the foregoing demonstration of something being self-existent from the impossibility of every thing's being dependent) – we always find in our minds, I say, some ideas, as of infinity and eternity, which to remove (that is, to suppose that there is no being, no substance in the universe to which these attributes or modes of existence are necessarily inherent) is a contradiction in the very terms. For modes and attributes exist only by the existence of the substance to which they belong. Now he that can suppose eternity and immensity, and consequently the substance by whose existence these modes or attributes exist, removed out of the universe, may, if he please, as easily remove the relation of equality between twice two and four.

That to suppose immensity removed out of the universe, or not necessarily eternal, is an express contradiction is intuitively evident to every one who attends to his own ideas and considers the essential nature of things. To suppose any part of space removed is to suppose it removed from and out of itself; and to suppose the whole to be taken away is supposing it to be taken away from itself, that is, to be taken away while it still remains, which is a contradiction in terms. There is no obscurity in the argument but what arises to those who think immense space to be absolutely nothing, which notion is itself likewise an express contradiction. For nothing is that which has no properties or modes whatsoever, that is to say, it is that of which nothing can truly be affirmed and of which every thing can truly be denied, which is not the case of immensity or space.

From this third proposition it follows, first, that the only true idea of a self-existent or necessarily existing being is the idea of a being the supposition of whose not-existing is an express contradiction. For, since it is absolutely impossible but there must be somewhat self-existing, that is, which exists by the necessity of its own nature, it is plain that that necessity cannot be a necessity consequent upon any foregoing supposition (because nothing can be antecedent to that which is self-existent, no not its own will, so as to be the cause or ground of its own existence), but it must be a necessity absolutely such in its own nature. Now a necessity not relatively or consequentially, but absolutely such in its own nature, is nothing else but its being a plain impossibility or implying a contradiction to suppose the contrary. For instance, the relation of equality between twice two and four is an absolute necessity only because it is an immediate contradiction in terms to suppose them unequal. This is the only idea we can frame of an absolute necessity, and to use the word in any other sense seems to be using it without any signification at all.

If any one now asks, what sort of idea the idea of that being is, the supposition of whose not-existing is thus an express contradiction, I answer: it is that first and simplest idea we can possibly frame; an idea necessarily and essentially included or presupposed as a *sine qua non* in every other idea whatsoever; an idea which (unless we forbear thinking at all) we cannot possibly extirpate or remove out of our minds of a most simple being, absolutely eternal and infinite, original and independent. For, that he who supposes there is no original independent being in the universe supposes a contradiction, has been shown already. And that he who supposes there may possibly be no eternal and infinite being in the universe, supposes likewise a contradiction, is evident from hence (beside that these two attributes do necessarily follow from self-originate independent existence, as shall be shown hereafter), that when he has done his utmost in endeavoring to imagine that no such being exists, he cannot avoid imagining an eternal and infinite nothing. That is, he will imagine eternity and immensity removed out of the universe, and yet that at the same time they still continue there, as has been above distinctly explained. . . .

Note

1 The meaning of this proposition, and all the argument here requires, is that there must needs have always been some independent being, some one at least. To show that there can be no more than one is not the design of this proposition but of the seventh.

63 The Cosmological Argument and the Principle of Sufficient Reason

William L. Rowe

The Cosmological Argument began with Plato, flourished in the writings of Aquinas, Leibniz, and Samuel Clarke, and was laid to rest by Hume and Kant. Although I think its death premature, if not unjustified, I shall not here attempt its resurrection. What I have in mind is more in the nature of an autopsy. I wish to uncover, clarify, and examine some of the philosophical concepts and theses essential to the reasoning exhibited in the Cosmological Argument. . . .

The Cosmological Argument is an argument for the existence of *God*. As such, the argument has two distinct parts. The first part is an argument to establish the existence of a necessary being, a being that carries the reason of its existence within itself. The second part is an argument to establish that this necessary being is God. A good deal of philosophical criticism has been directed against the first part of the argument. Much less has been directed against the second part. Indeed, some philosophers seem not to have realized that the argument has a second part. For example, in Part IX of his *Dialogues Concerning Natural Religion* Hume has Demea present a summary of only the first part of the Cosmological Argument. Demea appears to *assume* that a necessary being would be God. Thus, after concluding that there exists a necessary being, he simply remarks, "There is consequently such a Being, that is, there is a Deity." But, of course, it is not at all obvious that the necessary being is a Deity. Indeed, Cleanthes quickly asks, "Why may not the material universe be the necessarily existent Being?" Hence, as an argument for the existence of God, the Cosmological Argument not only does but must contain a second part in which it is argued that the necessary being possesses the properties – omnipotence, infinite goodness, infinite wisdom, etc. – that God, and only God, possesses.

Using the expression "dependent being" to mean "a being that has the reason of its existence in the causal efficacy of some other being," and the expression "independent being" to mean "a being that has the reason of its existence within its own nature," we may state the argument for the existence of a necessary being (i.e., the first part of the Cosmological Argument) as follows:

1. Whatever exists is either a dependent being or an independent being; therefore,
2. Either there exists an independent being or every being is dependent;
3. It is false that every being is dependent; therefore,
4. There exists an independent being; therefore,
5. There exists a necessary being.[1]

This argument consists of two premises – propositions (1) and (3) – and three inferences. The first inference is from (1) to (2), the second from (2) and (3) to (4), and the third inference is from (4) to (5). Of the premises neither is obviously true, and of the inferences only the first and second are above suspicion. Before discussing the main subject of this paper – namely, proposition (1) and its connection with the Principle of Sufficient Reason – I want to describe the argument in support of premise (3) and the main criticisms of that argument.

Why is it false that every being is dependent? Well, if every being that exists (or ever existed) is dependent then the whole of existing things, it would seem, consists of a collection of dependent beings, that is, a collection of beings each member of which exists by reason of the causal efficacy of some other being. Now this collection would have to contain an infinite number of members. For suppose it contained a *finite* number, let us say three, a, b, and c. Now if in Scotus's phrase "a circle of causes is inadmissible" then if c is caused by b and b by a, a would exist without a cause, there being no other member of the collection that could be its cause. But in that case a would not be what by supposition it is, namely a *dependent* being. Hence, if we grant that a circle of causes is inadmissible it is impossible that the whole of existing things should consist of a collection of dependent beings *finite* in number.

Let us suppose, then, that the dependent beings making up the collection are *infinite* in number. Why is it impossible that the whole of existing things should consist of such a collection? The proponent of the Cosmological Argument answers as follows.[2] The infinite collection *itself*, he argues, requires an explanation for its existence. For since it is true of each member of the collection that it might not have existed, it is true of the whole infinite collection that it might not have existed. But if the entire infinite collection might not have existed there must be some explanation for why it exists rather than not. The explanation cannot lie in the causal efficacy of some being outside of the collection since by supposition the collection includes every being that is or ever was. Nor can the explanation for why there is an infinite collection be found within the collection itself, for since no member of the collection is independent, has the reason of its existence within itself, the collection as a whole cannot have the reason of its existence within itself. Thus the conception of an infinite collection of dependent beings is the conception of something whose existence has no explanation whatever. But since premise (1) tells us that whatever exists has an explanation for its existence, either within itself or in the causal efficacy of some other being, it cannot be that the whole of existing things consists of an infinite collection of dependent beings.

Two major criticisms have been advanced against this line of reasoning, criticisms which have achieved some degree of acceptance. According to the first criticism it *makes no sense* to apply the notion of cause or explanation to the totality of things, and the arguments used to show that the whole of existing things must have a cause or explanation are fallacious. Thus in his B.B.C. debate with Father Copleston, Bertrand Russell took the view that the concept of cause is inapplicable to the universe conceived as the total collection of things. When pressed by Copleston as to how he could rule out "the legitimacy of asking the question how the total, or anything at all comes to be there," Russell responded: "I can illustrate what seems to me your fallacy. Every man who exists has a mother, and it seems to me your argument is that therefore the human race must have a mother, but obviously the human race hasn't a mother – that's a different logical sphere."[3] According to the second major criticism it is intelligible to ask for an explanation of the existence of the infinite collection of dependent beings. But the answer to this question, so the criticism goes, is provided once we learn that each member of the infinite collection has an explanation of its existence. Thus Hume remarks: "Did I show you the particular causes of each individual in a collection of twenty particles of matter, I should think it very unreasonable, should you afterwards ask me, what was the cause of the whole twenty. This is sufficiently explained in explaining the cause of the parts."[4]

Although neither criticism is, I think, decisive against the argument given in support of proposition (3), they do draw attention to two crucial steps in the Cosmological Argument. First, it seems that the infinite collection is itself viewed as an existing thing. For only if it is so viewed will it follow from premise (1) that it (the infinite collection) must have a cause or explanation of its existence. Second, the question why each member of the infinite collection exists is felt to be different from the question why the infinite collection exists. For the proponent of the argument admits that each member of the collection has an explanation of its existence – namely, in the causal efficacy of some other member – and yet denies that this explains the existence of the entire infinite collection.

Perhaps neither of these steps in the argument for proposition (3) is correct. But even if both steps are correct – that is, even if the infinite collection itself may be viewed as an object or thing, and even if to explain each member is not sufficient to explain the collection – it is important to note that it is premise (1) from which it is then inferred that there must be an explanation for the existence of the infinite collection. Thus proposition (1) plays a crucial role not only as a premise in the main argument but also as a premise in the argument for proposition (3). Having seen the crucial role that proposition (1) plays in the Cosmological Argument, we may now examine that proposition in some detail.

Proposition (1) tells us that *whatever exists* must have an explanation for its existence. The explanation may lie either within the nature of the thing itself or in the causal efficacy of some other being. The claim that whatever exists must have an explanation of its existence I shall call the *strong form* of the Principle of Sufficient Reason. This is to be distinguished from the claim that *whatever comes into existence* must have an explanation of its existence. The latter claim I shall call the *weak form* of the Principle of Sufficient Reason. If we imagine a star that has existed from eternity, a star that never came into existence but has always existed, the strong form of the Principle of Sufficient Reason requires, whereas the weak form does not, that there be an explanation for the existence of that star. The Cosmological Argument, as we have seen, employs the strong form of the Principle of Sufficient Reason.

Can the Principle of Sufficient Reason be proved or otherwise known to be true? Some philosophers, it seems, thought that the Principle could be proved. Hume attributes the following argument to Locke.

(1) If something exists without a cause, it is caused by nothing;
(2) Nothing cannot be the cause of something; therefore,
(3) Whatever exists must have a cause.

About this "proof" Hume remarks:

> It is sufficient only to observe that when we exclude all causes we really do exclude them, and neither suppose nothing nor the object itself to be the causes of the existence, and consequently can draw no argument from the absurdity of that exclusion. If everything must have a cause, it follows that upon the exclusion of other causes we must accept of the object itself or of nothing as causes. But it is the very point in question, whether everything must have a cause or not, and therefore, according to all just reasoning, it ought never to be taken for granted.[5]

It is clear from Hume's comment that he rejects premise (1). For he takes the proponent of the argument to mean by premise (1) that if something exists without a cause it, nevertheless, has a cause – although in this case its cause will not be some other thing, it will be *nothing*. But there is a subtlety in this argument that Hume overlooks. In the natural sense of the expression "caused by nothing" it is *true* that if something exists without a cause it is caused by nothing – to be caused by nothing is simply not to be caused by any thing whatever. Taken in this way, premise (1) is true. Moreover, premise (2) is true as well. For to say that nothing cannot be the cause of something is simply to say that if something has a cause then there must be some *thing* which is its cause. But so interpreted, the premises, although true, do not yield the conclusion that everything has a cause. For from (1) if something exists without a cause then there is no thing which caused it, and (2) if something has a cause then there is a thing which caused it, it in no way follows that everything has a cause. Therefore, if the premises are interpreted so as to be clearly true, the argument is invalid; whereas, if the argument is to appear valid its first premise, as Hume points out, is false or, at the very least, begs the question at issue. In either case the argument fails as a demonstration of the Principle of Sufficient Reason.

Of course, if, as seems likely, the Principle of Sufficient Reason cannot be – at least, has not been – demonstrated, it does not follow that it cannot be *known* to be true. Clearly, if we know any propositions to be true there must be some propositions which we can know to be true without having to *prove* them, without having to derive them from other propositions we know to be true. If this were not so, we would have to know an infinite number of propositions in order to know any proposition whatever. Hence, the fact, if it is a fact, that the Principle of Sufficient Reason cannot be demonstrated does not invalidate the view other philosophers seem to take; namely, that the Principle is a necessary truth, known *a priori*.[6]

If the Principle in its strong form is analytically true then the view of these philosophers – namely, that the Principle is a necessary truth, known *a priori*, is probably correct. For every analytically true proposition is necessary and, if known at all, presumably can be known by simply reflecting on it, without relying on empirical evidence. But is the Principle of Sufficient Reason analytically true? Clearly the Principle is not logically true. Nor, it would seem, does the mere notion of the existence of a thing *definitionally* contain the notion of a thing being caused. Kant argued – correctly, I think – that although the proposition "Every effect has a cause" is analytically true, "Every event has a cause" is not. The idea of an event, of something happening – a leaf falling, a chair collapsing, etc. – does not seem to contain the idea of something *causing* that event. If this is so then the Principle of Sufficient Reason is certainly not analytically true.

But if the Principle is not analytically true how can it be necessary? Indeed, can any proposition be necessary if it is not analytically true? Many philosophers have held that only analytically true propositions are necessary. But it is, I think, reasonable to argue, as some philosophers have, that, for example, the proposition "Whatever is red is colored" is necessary but not analytically true.[7] For (i) we do not seem to have a *definition* of "red" or "colored" in terms of which the sentence "Whatever is red is colored" can be reduced to a sentence expressing a logical truth, and yet (ii) it certainly is *impossible* that something be red and not colored. Thus the proposition "Whatever is red is colored" may well be a synthetic, necessary proposition. Moreover, as Chisholm has argued, there seem to be reasons for the view that the proposition "Necessarily, whatever is red is colored" is known *a priori*. But even if this is correct, as I am inclined to think it is, it is far from clear that the Principle of Sufficient Reason is a synthetic, necessary proposition known *a priori*.

The difficulty with the view that the Principle, in either its strong or weak form, is *necessary* is that we do seem able to conceive of things existing, or even of things coming into existence, without having to conceive of those things as having an explanation or cause. Unlike the proposition "Some red things are not colored," it does seem conceptually possible that something should exist and yet have no cause or explanation of its existence. As Hume remarks, "The separation, therefore, of the idea of a cause from that of a beginning of existence is plainly possible for the imagination, and consequently the actual separation of those objects is so far possible that it implies no contradiction nor absurdity . . ."[8] Indeed, not only does the denial of the Principle seem to be possible, philosophers have held that the denial of the Principle is *true*.

> . . . many philosophers have maintained that it is not true that everything that exists, or even that everything that has a beginning, has a cause, that is to say, is an effect. The world, they say, contains "spontaneous", free, or uncaused and unoriginated events. In any case they assert very positively that there is no way of proving that such uncaused events do not occur.[9]

In view of this and other difficulties, some contemporary defenders of the Cosmological Argument have retreated from the view that the Principle of Sufficient Reason is a synthetic, necessary proposition known *a priori*. Instead, they have adopted the somewhat more modest view that the Principle is a *metaphysical assumption*, a presupposition we are forced to make in order to make sense of our world. Thus, for example, Father Copleston, in his B.B.C. debate with

Russell, argued that something like the Principle of Sufficient Reason is presupposed by science. "I cannot see how science could be conducted on any other assumption than that of order and intelligibility in nature."[10] Another contemporary philosopher, Richard Taylor, has expressed this view as follows:

> The principle of sufficient reason can be illustrated in various ways, as we have done, and if one thinks about it, he is apt to find that he presupposes it in his thinking about reality, but it cannot be proved. It does not appear to be itself a necessary truth, and at the same time it would be most odd to say it is contingent. If one were to try proving it, he would sooner or later have to appeal to considerations that are less plausible than the principle itself. Indeed, it is hard to see how one could even make an argument for it, without already assuming it. For this reason it might properly be called a presupposition of reason itself. One can deny that it is true, without embarrassment or fear of refutation, but one is apt to find that what he is denying is not really what the principle asserts. We shall, then, treat it here as a datum – not something that is provably true, but as something which all men, whether they ever reflect upon it or not, seem more or less to presuppose.[11]

What are we to make of this view? It must be admitted, I think, that this view is a good deal more plausible than the view that the Principle is a necessary truth, known *a priori*. For the proponent of this more modest view is not contending – or, at least, need not contend – that the Principle states a necessary truth about reality. All he contends is that the Principle is presupposed by us in our dealings with the world. To this he may add that without this presupposition we cannot make any sense of the world. However, there are several critical points pertinent to this view that need discussion.

First, does the scientist in his work really assume that everything that happens has a cause? In the debate between Russell and Copleston, Russell took the view that Physicists need not and do not assume that every event has a cause. "As for things not having a cause, the physicists assure us that individual quantum transitions in atoms have no cause."[12] Again, he remarks:

> . . . a physicist looks for causes; that does not necessarily imply that there are causes everywhere. A man may look for gold without assuming that there is gold everywhere; if he finds gold, well and good, if he doesn't he's had bad luck. The same is true when the physicist looks for causes.[13]

How are we to settle this matter? Philosophers who hold that the causal principle is a fundamental assumption reply that the Heisenberg uncertainty principle "tells us something about the success (or the lack of it) of the present atomic theory in correlating observations, but not about nature in itself. . . ."[14] Moreover, it is observed that the failure to find causes does not lead anyone to abandon the causal principle. Indeed, it is sometimes argued that it is *impossible* to obtain empirical evidence against the principle.[15] If we don't find gold in a hill after a careful search, we conclude that there's no gold there to be found. But if we don't find the cause of a certain event, we don't conclude that the event has no cause, only that is is extremely difficult to discover. Perhaps, then, there is some reason to think that we do assume that whatever happens has an explanation or cause.

But even if it is granted that in our dealings with the world we presuppose that whatever happens has a cause, there seems to be a serious difficulty confronting the recent defenders of the Cosmological Argument. For what the Cosmological Argument requires – or, more exactly, what the versions argued by Samuel Clarke, Copleston, and Taylor require – is what I have called the strong form of the Principle of Sufficient Reason. That is, their arguments require as a premise the principle that whatever exists – even an eternal being – has a cause or explanation of its existence. But what we have just granted to be presupposed by us in our dealing with the world is the principle that whatever *happens* has a cause. This latter principle implies that whatever begins to exist has a cause, since the coming into existence of a thing is an event, a happening. Thus the principle we have granted to be presupposed in science and commonsense implies what I have called the weak form of the Principle of Sufficient Reason. But it does not imply the strong form of the Principle; it does not imply that whatever exists has a cause. If something comes into existence, its coming into existence is something that happens. But if something exists from eternity, its eternal existence is not one of the things that happen. Hence, even if it be granted that we presuppose a cause for whatever happens, it does not follow that we presuppose a cause or explanation for whatever exists.

Can it reasonably be argued that the strong form of the Principle of Sufficient Reason is, as Taylor suggests, a presupposition that all men make, a presupposition of reason itself? We have granted as a presupposition of reason that there must be a cause or explanation for any thing that comes into existence.[16] Thus if we imagine a star to have come into existence, say, a thousand years ago, it is presupposed that there must be an explanation for its having come into existence. That is, it is assumed by us that there must be a set of prior events that was sufficient to cause the birth of that star. To say, "Nothing caused the birth of the star, it just popped into existence and there is no reason why it came into existence" is, we have granted, to deny a fundamental presupposition of reason itself. But imagine that there is a star in the heavens that never came into existence, a star that has always existed, that has existed from eternity. Do we presuppose that there must be an explanation for the eternal existence of this star? I am doubtful that we do. But short of a metaphysical investigation of mind and its relation to nature, it seems quite impossible to answer this question. Perhaps, then, our most fruitful course here is simply to note the consequences for the Cosmological Argument *if* the Principle of Sufficient Reason in its strong form is, as Copleston and Taylor maintain, a presupposition all men make.

However, before considering this last question it is, I think, important to clarify the nature of the question concerning a thing's existence to which the Principle of Sufficient Reason demands there be an answer. Of the star that came into existence a thousand years ago, we may ask "Where did it come from?," "What brought it into existence?," or "Why did it come into existence?" Clearly none of these questions can be asked properly of a star that has existed from eternity. Once we learn that it has always existed we realize that it never came into existence. But there is a simpler question that can be asked both about the eternally existing star and about the star that came into existence a thousand years ago; namely, "Why does this thing exist?" Although we may answer – or, at least, show to be improper – the question "Why did this thing come into existence?" by pointing out that it has always existed, the question "Why does this thing exist rather than not?" cannot be answered or even turned aside by pointing out that it has always existed. As Taylor has noted:

> . . . it is no answer to the question, why a thing exists, to state *how long* it has existed. A geologist does not suppose that he has explained why there should be rivers and mountains merely by pointing out that they are old. Similarly, if one were to ask, concerning the ball of which we have spoken, for some sufficient reason for its being, he would not receive any answer upon being told that it had been there since yesterday. Nor would it be any better answer to say that it had existed since before anyone could remember, or even that it had always existed; for the question was not one concerning its age but its existence.[17]

The question, then, to which the Principle of Sufficient Reason requires that there be an answer is: "Why does this thing exist?" This question, I am claiming, may be sensibly asked about a star that has existed from eternity, or one that has existed for only a thousand years.

It should be clear that it is one thing to argue, as I have done, that the question "Why does this thing exist?" makes sense when asked of something that has always existed, and another thing to argue, as I have not done, that all men presuppose that there must be an adequate answer to that question, even when it is asked about something that has existed from eternity. We have granted as a presupposition of reason that there must be an adequate answer to the question when the being of which it is asked has come into existence. But, as I have indicated, it seems at least doubtful that the strong form of the Principle of Sufficient Reason is a presupposition of reason itself.

Suppose, as Taylor, Copleston, and others have claimed, that the Principle of Sufficient Reason in its strong form is a metaphysical assumption that all men make, whether or not they reflect sufficiently to become aware of the assumption. What bearing would this have on the Cosmological Argument? It would not, of course, show that it is a good argument. For (1) the argument could be invalid, (2) some premise other than the premise expressing the Principle could be false, and (3) even the premise expressing the Principle could be false. The fact, if it is a fact, that all of us presuppose that whatever exists has an explanation of its existence does not imply that nothing exists without a reason for its existence. Nature is not bound to satisfy our presuppositions. As James has remarked in another connection, "In the great boarding-house of nature, the cakes and the butter and the syrup seldom come out so even and leave the plates so clean." However, if we do make such a presupposition we could not *consistently* reject the Cosmological Argument solely because it contains as a premise the Principle of Sufficient Reason. That is, if we reject the argument it must be for some reason other than its appeal to the Principle of Sufficient Reason.

If, as seems likely, the strong form of the Principle is not a presupposition of reason itself, and if, as I have argued, the Principle is neither analytically true nor a synthetic, necessary truth, known *a priori*, the Cosmological Argument – in so far as it requires the strong form of the Principle as a premise – cannot, I think, reasonably be maintained to be a *proof* of the existence of God. For unless there is a way of knowing the Principle to be true other than those we have explored, it follows that we do not know the Principle to be true. But if we do not know that one of the essential premises of an argument is true then we do not know that it is a good argument for its conclusion. It may, of course, be a perfectly good argument. But if to claim of an argument that it is a *proof* of its conclusion is to imply that its premises are *known* to be true, then we are not entitled to claim that the Cosmological Argument is a proof of the existence of God.

Notes

1 This argument is an adaptation of Samuel Clarke's discussion in his Boyle lectures of 1704, published under the title *A Demonstration of the Being and Attributes of God*. This work consists of twelve propositions, and arguments in support of these propositions. The first three propositions and their arguments constitute the first part of the Cosmological Argument. That is, the arguments for the first three propositions are designed to establish the existence of a necessary being. The substance of these arguments, I believe, is contained in the argument I have presented. There is also some resemblance between the argument I have presented and the argument Demea states in Part IX of the *Dialogues*. This is to be expected since Demea's argument is a brief restatement by Hume of the argument formulated by Clarke.

2 See, for example, Samuel Clarke's discussion of Propositions II and III in his *Demonstration*.

3 "The Existence of God: a Debate between Bertrand Russell and Father F.C. Copleston," John Hick (ed.), *The Existence of God* (New York: Macmillan, 1964), p. 175. The debate was originally broadcast by the British Broadcasting Corporation in 1948. References are to the debate as reprinted in *The Existence of God*.

4 Hume, *Dialogues*, Part IX.

5 *A Treatise of Human Nature*, book I, part III, section III.

6 Samuel Clarke, for example, makes the following remark in correspondence with a critic:

Nothing can be more absurd, than to suppose that anything (or any circumstance of any thing) is; and yet that there be absolutely no reason why it is, rather than not. Tis easy to conceive, that we may indeed be utterly ignorant of the reasons, or grounds, or causes of many things. But, that anything is; and that there is a real reason in nature why it is, rather than not; these two are as necessarily and essentially connected, as any two correlates whatever, as height and depth, etc.

The letter from which this passage comes is included in the 9th edition of the work from which our quotations from the *Demonstration* have been taken, p. 490.

7 See R. M. Chisholm, *Theory of Knowledge*, pp. 87–90.

8 *Treatise*, book I, part III, section III.

9 John Laird, *Theism and Cosmology* (New York: Philosophical Library, 1942), p. 95. . . .

10 "A Debate," p. 176.

11 Richard Taylor, *Metaphysics* (Englewood Cliffs, N.J.: Prentice-Hall, 1963), pp. 86–7.

12 "A Debate," p. 176.

13 Ibid., p. 177.

14 Father Copleston, "A Debate," p. 176.

15 G. J. Warnock has argued this in "Every Event Has a Cause," *Logic and Language*, II, edited by Antony Flew (London: Blackwell, 1953). . . .

16 Clarke, perhaps for reasons of simplicity, usually speaks of requiring a cause only for the existence of a thing. But, of course, the Principle of Sufficient Reason is not meant to require an explanation only for the existence of a thing. Thus if a table is made by a carpenter and subsequently painted red, sawed in half, or even destroyed, Clarke's view – and the view of others who have appealed to the Principle of Sufficient Reason – is that there *must be* an explanation not only for the fact that the table came into existence but also for any change that occurs to it. Thus Clarke remarks (in a passage quoted earlier), "Nothing can be more absurd, than to suppose that any thing (or any circumstance of any thing) is; and yet that there be absolutely *no reason why* it *is* rather than *not*."

17 Taylor, *Metaphysics*, p. 88.

64 The Ontological Argument: Chapters II–IV of the *Proslogion*

St Anselm

Chapter II

Truly there is a God, although the fool hath said in his heart, There is no God.

And so, Lord, do thou, who dost give understanding to faith, give me, so far as thou knowest it to be profitable, to understand that thou art as we believe; and that thou art that which we believe. And, indeed, we believe that thou art a being than which nothing greater can be conceived. Or is there no such nature, since the fool hath said in his heart, there is no God? (Psalm xiv. 1). But, at any rate, this very fool, when he hears of this being of which I speak – a being than which nothing greater can be conceived – understands what he hears, and what he understands is in his understanding; although he does not understand it to exist.

For, it is one thing for an object to be in the understanding, and another to understand that the object exists. When a painter first conceives of what he will afterwards perform, he has it in his understanding, but he does not yet understand it to be, because he has not yet performed it. But after he has made the painting, he both has it in his understanding, and he understands that it exists, because he has made it.

Hence, even the fool is convinced that something exists in the understanding, at least, than which nothing greater can be conceived. For, when he hears of this, he understands it. And whatever is understood, exists in the understanding. And assuredly that, than which nothing greater can be conceived, cannot exist in the understanding alone. For, suppose it exists in the understanding alone: then it can be conceived to exist in reality; which is greater.

Therefore, if that, than which nothing greater can be conceived, exists in the understanding alone, the very being, than which nothing greater can be conceived, is one, than which a greater can be conceived. But obviously this is impossible. Hence, there is no doubt that there exists a being, than which nothing greater can be conceived, and it exists both in the understanding and in reality.

Chapter III

God cannot be conceived not to exist. – God is that, than which nothing greater can be conceived. – That which can be conceived not to exist is not God.

And it assuredly exists so truly, that it cannot be conceived not to exist. For, it is possible to conceive of a being which cannot be conceived not to exist; and this is greater than one which can be conceived not to exist. Hence, if that, than which nothing greater can be conceived, can be conceived not to exist, it is not that, than which nothing greater can be conceived. But this is an irreconcilable contradiction. There is, then, so truly a being than which nothing greater can be conceived to exist, that it cannot even be conceived not to exist; and this being thou art, O Lord, our God.

So truly, therefore, dost thou exist, O Lord, my God, that thou canst not be conceived not to exist; and rightly. For, if a mind could conceive of a being better than thee, the creature would rise above the Creator; and this is most absurd. And, indeed, whatever else there is, except thee alone, can be conceived not to exist. To thee alone, therefore, it belongs to exist more truly than all other beings, and hence in a higher degree than all others. For, whatever else exists does not exist so truly, and hence in a less degree it belongs to it to exist. Why, then, has the fool said in his heart, there is no God (Psalm xiv. 1), since it is so evident, to a rational mind, that thou dost exist in the highest degree of all? Why, except that he is dull and a fool?

Chapter IV

How the fool has said in his heart what cannot be conceived. – A thing may be conceived in two ways: (1) when the word signifying it is conceived; (2) when the thing itself is understood. As far as the word goes, God can be conceived not to exist; in reality he cannot.

But how has the fool said in his heart what he could not conceive; or how is it that he could not conceive what he said in his heart? since it is the same to say in the heart, and to conceive.

But, if really, nay, since really, he both conceived, because he said in his heart; and did not say in his heart, because he could not conceive; there is more than one way in which a thing is said in the heart or conceived. For, in one sense, an object is conceived, when the word signifying it is conceived; and in another, when the very entity, which the object is, is understood.

In the former sense, then, God can be conceived not to exist; but in the latter, not at all. For no one who understands what fire and water are can conceive fire to be water, in accordance with the nature of the facts themselves, although this is possible according to the words. So, then, no one who understands what God is can conceive that God does not exist, although he says these words in his heart, either without any, or with some foreign, signification. For, God is that than which a greater cannot be conceived. And he who thoroughly understands this, assuredly understands that this being so truly exists, that not even in concept can it be non-existent. Therefore, he who understands that God so exists, cannot conceive that he does not exist.

I thank thee, gracious Lord, I thank thee; because what I formerly believed by thy bounty, I now so understand by thine illumination, that if I were unwilling to believe that thou dost exist, I should not be able not to understand this to be true.

---

65   Anselm's Ontological Arguments

Norman Malcolm

I

I believe that in Anselm's *Proslogion* and *Responsio editoris* there are two different pieces of reasoning which he did not distinguish from one another, and that a good deal of light may be shed on the philosophical problem of "the ontological argument" if we do distinguish them. In Chapter 2 of the *Proslogion*[1] Anselm says that we believe that God is *something a greater than which cannot be conceived.* (The Latin is *aliquid quo nihil maius cogitari possit.* Anselm sometimes uses the alternative expressions *aliquid quo maius nihil cogitari potest, id quo maius cogitari nequit, aliquid quo maius cogitari non valet.*) Even the fool of the

Psalm who says in his heart there is no God, when he hears this very thing that Anselm says, namely, "something a greater than which cannot be conceived," understands what he hears, and what he understands is in his understanding though he does not understand that it exists.

Apparently Anselm regards it as tautological to say that whatever is understood is in the understanding (*quidquid intelligitur in intellectu est*): he uses *intelligitur* and *in intellectu est* as interchangeable locutions. The same holds for another formula of his: whatever is thought is in thought (*quidquid cogitatur in cogitatione est*).[2]

Of course many things may exist in the understanding that do not exist in reality; for example, elves. Now, says Anselm, something a greater than which cannot be conceived exists in the understanding. But it cannot exist *only* in the understanding, for to exist in reality is greater. Therefore that thing a greater than which cannot be conceived cannot exist only in the understanding, for then a greater thing could be conceived: namely, one that exists both in the understanding and in reality.[3]

Here I have a question. It is not clear to me whether Anselm means that (a) existence in reality by itself is greater than existence in the understanding, or that (b) existence in reality and existence in the understanding together are greater than existence in the understanding alone. Certainly he accepts (b). But he might also accept (a), as Descartes apparently does in *Meditation III* when he suggests that the mode of being by which a thing is "objectively in the understanding" is *imperfect*.[4] Of course Anselm might accept both (a) and (b). He might hold that in general something is greater if it has both of these "modes of existence" than if it has either one alone, but also that existence in reality is a more perfect mode of existence than existence in the understanding.

In any case, Anselm holds that something is greater if it exists both in the understanding and in reality than if it exists merely in the understanding. An equivalent way of putting this interesting proposition, in a more current terminology, is: something is greater if it is both conceived of and exists than if it is merely conceived of. Anselm's reasoning can be expressed as follows: *id quo maius cogitari nequit* cannot be merely conceived of and not exist, for then it would not be *id quo maius cogitari nequit*. The doctrine that something is greater if it exists in addition to being conceived of, than if it is only conceived of, could be called the doctrine that *existence is a perfection*. Descartes maintained, in so many words, that existence is a perfection,[5] and presumably he was holding Anselm's doctrine, although he does not, in *Meditation V* or elsewhere, argue in the way that Anselm does in *Proslogion 2*.

When Anselm says "And certainly, that than which nothing greater can be conceived cannot exist merely in the understanding. For suppose it exists merely in the understanding, then it can be conceived to exist in reality, which is greater,"[6] he is claiming that if I conceived of a being of great excellence, that being would be *greater* (more excellent, more perfect) if it existed than if it did not exist. His supposition that "it exists merely in the understanding" is the supposition that it is conceived of but does not exist. Anselm repeated this claim in his reply to the criticism of the monk Gaunilo. Speaking of the being a greater than which cannot be conceived, he says:

> I have said that if it exists merely in the understanding it can be conceived to exist in reality, which is greater. Therefore, if it exists merely in the understanding obviously the very being a greater than which cannot be conceived, is one a greater than which can be conceived. What, I ask, can follow better than that? For if it exists merely in the understanding, can it not be conceived to exist in reality? And if it can be so conceived does not he who conceives of this conceive of a thing greater than it, if it does exist merely in the understanding? Can anything follow better than this: that if a being a greater than which cannot be conceived exists merely in the understanding, it is something a greater than which can be conceived? What could be plainer?[7]

He is implying, in the first sentence, that if I conceive of something which does not exist then it is possible for it to exist, and *it will be greater if it exists than if it does not exist.*

The doctrine that existence is a perfection is remarkably queer. It makes sense and is true to say that my future house will be a better one if it is insulated than if it is not insulated; but what could it mean to say that it will be a better house if it exists than if it does not? My future child will be a better man if he is honest than if he is not; but who would understand the saying that he will be a better man if he exists than if he does not? Or who understands the saying that if God exists He is more perfect than if He does not exist? One might say, with some intelligibility, that it would be better (for oneself or for mankind) if God exists than if He does not – but that is a different matter.

A king might desire that his next chancellor should have knowledge, wit, and resolution; but it is ludicrous to add that the king's desire is to have a chancellor who exists. Suppose that two royal councillors, A and B, were asked to draw up separately descriptions of the most perfect chancellor they could conceive, and that the descriptions they produced were identical except that A included existence in his list of attributes of a perfect chancellor and B did not. (I do not mean that B put nonexistence in his list.) One and the same person could satisfy both descriptions. More to the point, any person who satisfied A's description would *necessarily* satisfy B's description and *vice versa*! This is to say that A and B did not produce descriptions that differed in any way but rather one and the same description of necessary and desirable qualities in a chancellor. A only made a show of putting down a desirable quality that B had failed to include.

I believe I am merely restating an observation that Kant made in attacking the notion that "existence" or "being" is a "real predicate." He says:

> By whatever and by however many predicates we may think a thing – even if we completely determine it – we do not make the least addition to the thing when we further declare that this thing *is*. Otherwise, it would not be exactly the same thing that exists, but something more than we had thought in the concept; and we could not, therefore, say that the exact object of my concept exists.[8]

Anselm's ontological proof of *Proslogion* 2 is fallacious because it rests on the false doctrine that existence is a perfection (and therefore that "existence" is a "real predicate"). It would be desirable to have a rigorous refutation of the doctrine but I have not been able to provide one. I am compelled to leave the matter at the more or less intuitive level of Kant's observation. In any case, I believe that the doctrine does not belong to Anselm's other formulation of the ontological argument. It is worth noting that Gassendi anticipated Kant's criticism when he said, against Descartes:

> Existence is a perfection neither in God nor in anything else; it is rather that in the absence of which there is no perfection. . . . Hence neither is existence held to exist in a thing in the way that perfections do, nor if the thing lacks existence is it said to be imperfect (or deprived of a perfection), so much as to be nothing.[9]

II

I take up now the consideration of the second ontological proof, which Anselm presents in the very next chapter of the *Proslogion*. (There is no evidence that he thought of himself as offering two different proofs.) Speaking of the being a greater than which cannot be conceived, he says:

> And it so truly exists that it cannot be conceived not to exist. For it is possible to conceive of a being which cannot be conceived not to exist; and this is greater than one which can be conceived not to exist. Hence, if that, than which nothing greater can be conceived, can be conceived not to exist, it is not that than which nothing greater can be conceived. But this is a contradiction. So truly, therefore, is there something than which nothing greater can be conceived, that it cannot even be conceived not to exist.
>
> And this being thou art, O Lord, our God.[10]

Anselm is saying two things: first, that a being whose nonexistence is logically impossible is "greater" than a being whose nonexistence is logically possible (and therefore that a being a greater than which cannot be conceived must be one whose nonexistence is logically impossible); second, that *God* is a being than which a greater cannot be conceived.

In regard to the second of these assertions, there certainly is *a* use of the word "God," and I think far the more common use, in accordance with which the statements "God is the greatest of all beings," "God is the most perfect being," "God is the supreme being," are *logically* necessary truths, in the same sense that the statement "A square has four sides" is a logically necessary truth. If there is a man named "Jones" who is the tallest man in the world, the statement "Jones is the tallest man in the world" is merely true and is not a logically necessary truth. It is a virtue of Anselm's unusual phrase, "a being a greater than which cannot be conceived,"[11] to make it explicit that the sentence "God is the greatest of all beings" expresses a logically necessary truth and not a mere matter of fact such as the one we imagined about Jones.

With regard to Anselm's first assertion (namely, that a being whose nonexistence is logically impossible is greater than a being whose nonexistence is logically possible) perhaps the most puzzling thing about it is the use of the word "greater." It appears to mean exactly the same as "superior," "more excellent," "more perfect." This equivalence by itself is of no help to us, however, since the latter expressions would be equally puzzling here. What is required is some explanation of their use.

We do think of *knowledge*, say, as an excellence, a good thing. If A has more knowledge of algebra than B we express this in common language by saying that A has a *better* knowledge of algebra than B, or that A's knowledge of algebra is *superior* to B's, whereas we should not say that B has a better or superior *ignorance* of algebra than A. We do say "greater ignorance," but here the word "greater" is used purely quantitatively.

Previously I rejected *existence* as a perfection. Anselm is maintaining in the remarks last quoted, not that existence is a perfection, but that *the logical impossibility of nonexistence is a perfection*. In other words, *necessary existence is a perfection*. His first ontological proof uses the principle that a thing is greater if it exists than if it does not exist. His second proof employs the different principle that a thing is greater if it necessarily exists than if it does not necessarily exist.

Some remarks about the notion of *dependence* may help to make this latter principle intelligible. Many things depend for their existence on other things and events. My house was built by a carpenter: its coming into existence was dependent on a certain creative activity. Its continued existence is dependent on many things: that a tree does not crush it, that it is not consumed by fire, and so on. If we reflect on the common meaning of the word "God" (no matter how vague and confused this is), we realize that it is incompatible with this meaning that God's existence should *depend* on anything. Whether we believe in Him or not we must admit that the "almighty and everlasting God" (as several ancient prayers begin), the "Maker of heaven and earth, and of all things visible and invisible" (as is said in the Nicene Creed), cannot be thought of as being brought into existence by anything or as depending for His continued existence on anything. To conceive of anything as dependent upon something else for its existence is to conceive of it as a lesser being than God.

If a housewife has a set of extremely fragile dishes, then as dishes they are *inferior* to those of another set like them in all respects except that they are *not* fragile. Those of the first set are *dependent* for their continued existence on gentle handling; those of the second set are not. There is a definite connection in common language between the notions of dependency and inferiority, and independence and superiority. To say that something which was dependent on nothing whatever was superior to ("greater than") anything that was dependent in any way upon anything is quite in keeping with the everyday use of the terms "superior" and "greater." Correlative with the notions of dependence and independence are the notions of *limited* and *unlimited*. An engine requires fuel and this is a limitation. It is the same thing to say that an engine's operation is *dependent* on as that it is *limited* by its fuel supply. An engine that could accomplish the same work in the same time and was in other respects satisfactory, but did not require fuel, would be a *superior* engine.

God is usually conceived of as an *unlimited* being. He is conceived of as a being who *could not* be limited, that is, as an absolutely unlimited being. This is no less than to conceive of Him as *something a greater than which cannot be conceived*. If God is conceived to be an absolutely unlimited being He must be conceived to be unlimited in regard to His existence as well as His operation. In this conception it will not make sense to say that He depends on anything for coming into or continuing in existence. Nor, as Spinoza observed, will it make sense to say that something could *prevent* Him from existing.[12] Lack of moisture can prevent trees from existing in a certain region of the earth. But it would be contrary to the concept of God as an unlimited being to suppose that anything other than God Himself could prevent Him from existing, and it would be self-contradictory to suppose that He Himself could do it.

Some may be inclined to object that although nothing could prevent God's existence, still it might just *happen* that He did not exist. And if He did exist that too would be by chance. I think, however, that from the supposition that it could happen that God did not exist it would follow that, if He existed, He would have mere duration and not eternity. It would make sense to ask, "How long has He existed?," "Will He still exist next week?," "He was in existence yesterday but how about today?," and so on. It seems absurd to make God the subject of such questions. According to our ordinary conception of Him, He is an eternal being. And eternity does not mean endless duration, as Spinoza noted. To ascribe eternity to something is to exclude as senseless all sentences that imply that it has duration. If a thing has duration then it would be merely a *contingent* fact, if it was a fact, that its duration was endless. The moon could have endless duration but not eternity. If something has endless duration it will *make sense* (although it will be false) to say that it will cease to exist, and it will make sense (although it will be false) to say that something will *cause* it to cease to exist. A being with endless duration is not, therefore, an absolutely unlimited being. That God is conceived to be eternal follows from the fact that He is conceived to be an absolutely unlimited being.

I have been trying to expand the argument of *Proslogion* 3. In *Responsio* 1 Anselm adds the following acute point: if you can conceive of a certain thing and this thing does not exist then if it *were* to exist its nonexistence would be *possible*. It follows, I believe, that if the thing were to exist it would depend on other things both for coming into and continuing in existence, and also that it would have duration and not eternity. Therefore it would not be, either in reality or in conception, an unlimited being, *aliquid quo nihil maius cogitari possit*.

Anselm states his argument as follows:

> If it [the thing a greater than which cannot be conceived] can be conceived at all it must exist. For no one who denies or doubts the existence of a being a greater than which is inconceivable, denies or doubts that if it did exist its non-existence, either in reality or in the understanding, would be impossible. For otherwise it would not be a being a greater than which cannot be conceived. But as to whatever can be conceived but does not exist: if it were to exist its non-existence either in reality or in the understanding would be possible. Therefore, if a being a greater than which cannot be conceived, can even be conceived, it must exist.[13]

What Anselm has proved is that the notion of contingent existence or of contingent nonexistence cannot have any application to God. His existence must either be logically necessary or logically impossible. The only intelligible way of rejecting Anselm's claim that God's existence is necessary is to maintain that the concept of God, as a being a greater than which cannot be conceived, is self-contradictory or nonsensical.[14] Supposing that this is false, Anselm is right to deduce God's necessary existence from his characterization of Him as a being a greater than which cannot be conceived.

Let me summarize the proof. If God, a being a greater than which cannot be conceived, does not exist then He cannot *come* into existence. For if He did He would either have been *caused* to come into existence or have *happened* to come into existence, and in either case He would be a limited being, which by our conception of Him He is not. Since He cannot come into existence, if He does not exist His existence is impossible. If He does exist He cannot have come into existence (for the reasons given), nor can He cease to exist, for nothing could cause Him to cease to exist nor could it just happen that He ceased to exist. So if God exists His existence is necessary. Thus God's existence is either impossible or necessary. It can be the former only if the concept of such a being is self-contradictory or in some way logically absurd. Assuming that this is not so, it follows that He necessarily exists.[15]

It may be helpful to express ourselves in the following way: to say, not that *omnipotence* is a property of God, but rather that *necessary omnipotence* is; and to say, not that omniscience is a property of God, but rather that *necessary omniscience* is. We have criteria for determining that a man knows this and that and can do this and that, and for determining that one man has greater knowledge and abilities in a certain subject than another. We could think of various tests to give them. But there is nothing we should wish to describe, seriously and literally, as "testing" God's knowledge and powers. That God is omniscient and omnipotent has not been determined by the application of criteria: rather these are requirements of our conception of Him. They are internal properties of the concept, although they are also rightly said to be properties of God. *Necessary existence* is a property of God in the *same sense* that *necessary omnipotence* and *necessary omniscience* are His properties. And we are not to think that "God necessarily exists" means that it follows necessarily from something that God exists *contingently*. The a priori proposition "God necessarily exists" entails the proposition "God exists," if and only if the latter also is understood as an a priori proposition: in which case the two propositions are equivalent. In this sense Anselm's proof is a proof of God's existence.

Descartes was somewhat hazy on the question of whether existence is a property of things that exist, but at the same time he saw clearly enough that *necessary existence* is a property of God. Both points are illustrated in his reply to Gassendi's remark, which I quoted above:

> I do not see to what class of reality you wish to assign existence, nor do I see why it may not be said to be a property as well as omnipotence, taking the word property as equivalent to any attribute or anything which can be predicated of a thing, as in

the present case it should be by all means regarded. Nay, necessary existence in the case of God is also a true property in the strictest sense of the word, because it belongs to Him and forms part of His essence alone.[16]

Elsewhere he speaks of "the necessity of existence" as being "that crown of perfections without which we cannot comprehend God."[17] He is emphatic on the point that necessary existence applies solely to "an absolutely perfect Being."[18] . . .

IV

I turn to the question of whether the idea of a being a greater than which cannot be conceived is self-contradictory. Here Leibniz made a contribution to the discussion of the ontological argument. He remarked that the argument of Anselm and Descartes

> is not a paralogism, but it is an imperfect demonstration, which assumes something that must still be proved in order to render it mathematically evident; that is, it is tacitly assumed that this idea of the all-great or all-perfect being is possible, and implies no contradiction. And it is already something that by this remark it is proved that, assuming that God is possible, he exists, which is the privilege of divinity alone.[19]

Leibniz undertook to give a proof that God is possible. He defined a *perfection* as a simple, positive quality in the highest degree.[20] He argued that since perfections are *simple* qualities they must be compatible with one another. Therefore the concept of a being possessing all perfections is consistent.

I will not review his argument because I do not find his definition of a perfection intelligible. For one thing, it assumes that certain qualities or attributes are "positive" in their intrinsic nature, and others "negative" or "privative," and I have not been able to clearly understand that. For another thing, it assumes that some qualities are intrinsically simple. I believe that Wittgenstein has shown in the *Investigations* that nothing is *intrinsically* simple, but that whatever has the status of a simple, an indefinable, in one system of concepts, may have the status of a complex thing, a definable thing, in another system of concepts.

I do not know how to demonstrate that the concept of God – that is, of a being a greater than which cannot be conceived – is not self-contradictory. But I do not think that it is legitimate to demand such a demonstration. I also do not know how to demonstrate that either the concept of a material thing or the concept of *seeing* a material thing is not self-contradictory, and philosophers have argued that both of them are. With respect to any particular reasoning that is offered for holding that the concept of seeing a material thing, for example, is self-contradictory, one may try to show the invalidity of the reasoning and thus free the concept from the charge of being self-contradictory *on that ground.* But I do not understand what it would mean to demonstrate *in general*, and not in respect to any particular reasoning, that the concept is not self-contradictory. So it is with the concept of God. I should think there is no more of a presumption that it is self-contradictory than is the concept of seeing a material thing. Both concepts have a place in the thinking and the lives of human beings.

But even if one allows that Anselm's phrase may be free of self-contradiction, one wants to know how it can have any *meaning* for anyone. Why is it that human beings have even *formed* the concept of an infinite being, a being a greater than which cannot be conceived? This is a legitimate and important question. I am sure there cannot be a deep understanding of that concept without an understanding of the phenomena of human life that give rise to it. To give an account of the latter is beyond my ability. I wish, however, to make one suggestion (which should not be understood as autobiographical).

There is the phenomenon of feeling guilt for something that one has done or thought or felt or for a disposition that one has. One wants to be free of this guilt. But sometimes the guilt is felt to be so great that one is sure that nothing one could do oneself, nor any forgiveness by another human being, would remove it. One feels a guilt that is beyond all measure, a guilt "a greater than which cannot be conceived." Paradoxically, it would seem, one nevertheless has an intense desire to have this incomparable guilt removed. One requires a forgiveness that is beyond all measure, a forgiveness "a greater than which cannot be conceived." Out of such a storm in the soul, I am suggesting, there arises the conception of a forgiving mercy that is limitless, beyond all measure.[21] This is one important feature of the Jewish and Christian conception of God.

I wish to relate this thought to a remark made by Kierkegaard, who was speaking about belief in Christianity but whose remark may have a wider application. He says:

> There is only one proof of the truth of Christianity and that, quite rightly, is from the emotions, when the dread of sin and a heavy conscience torture a man into crossing the narrow line between despair bordering upon madness – and Christendom.[22]

One may think it absurd for a human being to feel a guilt of such magnitude, and even more absurd that, if he feels it, he should *desire* its removal. I have nothing to say about that. It may also be absurd for people to fall in love, but they do it. I wish only to say that there *is* that human phenomenon of an unbearably heavy conscience and that it is importantly connected with the genesis of the concept of God, that is, with the formation of the "grammar" of the word "God." I am sure that this concept is related to human experience in other ways. If one had the acuteness and depth to perceive these connections one could grasp the *sense* of the concept. When we encounter this concept as a problem in philosophy, we do not consider the human phenomena that lie behind it. It is not surprising that many philosophers believe that the idea of a necessary being is an arbitrary and absurd construction.

What is the relation of Anselm's ontological argument to religious belief? This is a difficult question. I can imagine an atheist going through the argument, becoming convinced of its validity, acutely defending it against objections, yet remaining an atheist. The only effect it could have on the fool of the Psalm would be that he stopped saying in his heart "There is no God," because he would now realize that this is something he cannot meaningfully say or think. It is hardly to be expected that a demonstrative argument should, in addition, produce in him a living faith. Surely there is a level at which one can view the argument as a piece of logic, following the deductive moves but not being touched religiously? I think so. But even at this level the argument may not be without religious value, for it may help to remove some philosophical scruples that stand in the way of faith. At a deeper level, I suspect that the argument can be thoroughly understood only by one who has a view of that human "form of life" that gives rise to the idea of an infinitely great being, who views it from the *inside* not just from the outside and who has, therefore, at least some inclination to *partake* in that religious form of life. This inclination, in Kierkegaard's words, is "from the emotions." This inclination can hardly be an *effect* of Anselm's argument, but is rather presupposed in the fullest understanding of it. It would be unreasonable to require that the recognition of Anselm's demonstration as valid must produce a conversion.[23]

Notes

1   I have consulted the Latin text of the *Proslogion*, of *Gaunilonis Pro Insipiente*, and of the *Responsio editoris*, in S. Anselmi, *Opera Omnia*, ed. F. C. Schmitt (Secovii, 1938), vol. I. With numerous modifications, I have used the English translation by S. N. Deane: *St Anselm* (La Salle, Ill.: Open Court, 1948).

2   See *Proslogion* 1 and *Responsio* 2.

3   Anselm's actual words are: "Et certe id quo maius cogitari nequit, non potest esse in solo intellectu. Si enim vel in solo intellectu est, potest cogitari esse et in re, quod maius est. Si ergo id quo maius cogitari non potest, est in solo intellectu: id ipsum quo maius cogitari non potest, est quo maius cogitari potest. Sed certe hoc esse non potest." *Proslogion* 2.

4   Haldane and Ross, *The Philosophical Works of Descartes*, vol. I (New York: Macmillan, 1931), p. 163.

5   *Op. cit.*, p. 182.

6   *Proslogion* 2, Deane, *St Anselm*, p. 8.

7   *Responsio* 2; Deane, *St Anselm*, pp. 157–8.

8   *The Critique of Pure Reason*, tr. by Norman Kemp Smith (New York: Macmillan, 1929), p. 505.

9   Haldane and Ross, *The Philosophical Works of Descartes*, vol. II, p. 186.

10   *Proslogion* 3; Deane, *St Anselm*, pp. 8–9.

11   Professor Robert Calhoun has pointed out to me that a similar locution had been used by Augustine. In *De moribus Manichaeorum* (bk II, ch. 11, sec. 24), he says that God is a being *quo esse aut cogitari melius nihil possit* (*Patrologiae Patrum Latinorum*, J. P. Migne, ed. [Paris, 1841–5], vol. 32; *Augustinus*, vol. 1).

12 *Ethics*, Part I, prop. 11.
13 *Responsio* 1; Deane, *St Anselm*, pp. 154–5.
14 Gaunilo attacked Anselm's argument on this very point. He would not concede that a being a greater than which cannot be conceived existed in his understanding (*Gaunilonis Pro Insipiente*, secs. 4 and 5; Deane, *St Anselm*, pp. 148–50). Anselm's reply is: "I call on your faith and conscience to attest that this is most false" (*Responsio* 1; Deane, *St Anselm*, p. 154). Gaunilo's faith and conscience will attest that it is false that "God is not a being a greater than which is inconceivable," and false that "He is not understood (*intelligitur*) or conceived (*cogitatur*)" (ibid). Descartes remarks that one would go to "strange extremes" who denied that we understand the words "*that thing which is the most perfect that we can conceive*; for that is what all men call God" (Haldane and Ross, *The Philosophical Works of Descartes*, vol. II, p. 129).
15 [The following elegant argument occurs in *Responsio* 1: "That than which a greater cannot be conceived cannot be conceived to begin to exist. Whatever can be conceived to exist and does not exist, can be conceived to begin to exist. Therefore, that than which a greater cannot be conceived, cannot be conceived to exist and yet not exist. So if it can be conceived to exist it exists from necessity." (*Nam quo maius cogitari nequit non potest cogitari esse nisi sine initio. Quidquid autem potest cogitari esse et non est, per initium potest cogitari esse. Non ergo quo maius cogitari nequit cogitari potest esse et non est. Si ergo cogitari potest esse, ex necessitate est.*) (Schmitt, *Opera Omnia*, p. 131; Deane, *St Anselm*, p. 154.)]
16 Haldane and Ross, *The Philosophical Works of Descartes*, vol. II, p. 228.
17 Ibid., vol. I, p. 445.
18 E.g., ibid., Principle 15, p. 225.
19 *New Essays Concerning the Human Understanding*, Book IV, ch. 10; A. G. Langley, ed. (La Salle, Ill.: Open Court Publishing, 1949), p. 504.
20 See Ibid., Appendix X, p. 714.
21 [Psalm 116: "The sorrows of death compassed me, and the pains of hell gat hold upon me: I found trouble and sorrow. Then called I upon the name of the Lord; O Lord, I beseech thee, deliver my soul." Psalm 130: "Out of the depths have I cried unto thee, O Lord."]
22 *The Journals*, tr. by A. Dru (New York: Oxford University Press, 1938), sec. 926.
23 [Since the appearance of this essay many acute criticisms of it have been published or communicated to me in private correspondence. In *The Philosophical Review*, LXX, No. 1 (January 1961), there are the following articles: Raziel Abelson, "Not Necessarily"; R. E. Allen, "The Ontological Argument"; Paul Henle, "Uses of the Ontological Argument"; Gareth B. Matthews, "On Conceivability in Anselm and Malcolm"; Alvin Plantinga, "A Valid Ontological Argument?"; Terence Penelhum, "On the Second Ontological Argument." Some other published articles are: Jan Berg, "An Examination of the Ontological Proof," *Theoria*, XXVII, No. 3 (1961); T. P. Brown, "Professor Malcolm on 'Anselm's Ontological Arguments,'" *Analysis*, October 1961; W. J. Huggett, "The Nonexistence of Ontological Arguments," *The Philosophical Review*, LXXI, No. 3 (July 1962); Jerome Shaffer, "Existence, Prediction, and the Ontological Argument," *Mind*, LXXI, No. 283 (July 1962). It would be a major undertaking to attempt to reply to all of the criticisms, and I hope that my not doing so will not be construed as a failure to appreciate them. I do not know that it is possible to meet all of the objections; on the other hand, I do not know that it is impossible.]

INDEX